Early Islamic Law in Basra in the 2nd/8th Century

Islamic History and Civilization

STUDIES AND TEXTS

VOLUME 142

The titles published in this series are listed at *brill.com/ihc*

Early Islamic Law in Basra in the 2nd/8th Century

Aqwāl Qatāda b. Di'āma al-Sadūsī

By

Abdulrahman al-Salimi

BRILL

LEIDEN | BOSTON

Cover illustration: Image from the Aqwal Qatada manuscript from the al-Baruni library on the island of Djerba, Tunisia. Reproduced with kind permission of the al-Baruni library.

The Library of Congress Cataloging-in-Publication Data is available online at http://catalog.loc.gov

Typeface for the Latin, Greek, and Cyrillic scripts: "Brill". See and download: brill.com/brill-typeface.

ISSN 0929-2403
ISBN 978-90-04-33947-7 (hardback)
ISBN 978-90-04-33953-8 (e-book)

This book is printed on acid-free paper and produced in a sustainable manner.

To my Shaykh
Wilferd Madelung

Contents

Introduction 1

Arabic Texts

1 Part One الجزء الأول 25

2 Part Two الجزء الثاني 121

3 Part Three الجزء الثالث 185

4 Part Four الجزء الرابع 257

5 Part Five الجزء الخامس 339

6 Part Six الجزء السادس 387

7 Part Seven الجزء السابع 467

Index of Quranic Verses فهرس الآيات 495
Index of Prophetic Tradition فهرس الأحاديث والآثار 498
Index of Personal Names فهرس الأعلام 511
Index of Places and Locations فهرس الأماكن والبلدان 518
Index of Tribes and Sects فهرس القبائل والفرق والكتب المنزلة 519

Introduction

I

The Ibāḍī movement owes its name to ʿAbd Allāh b. Ibāḍ al-Murrī at-Tamīmī, an almost unknown early Muḥakkima figure who participated in the siege to Mecca under the leadership of Nāfiʿ b. al-Azraq in 64/683, but later broke away from the Khārijī extremists and looked for an understanding with the Umayyad rulers. According to the Ibāḍī biographies he belonged to the second generation (*ṭabaqah*) of scholars and died probably during the reign of the caliph ʿAbd al-Malik b. Marwān (65–86/685–705). With the latter ʿAbd Allāh b. Ibāḍ succeeded in entering into correspondence and he is credited with two letters to him whose authenticity is almost controversial.[1]

The real founding father of the school was ʿAbd Allāh b. Ibāḍ's successor, Abū l-Shaʿthāʾ Jābir b. Zayd al-Azdī (born in 18 or 21/639 or 641 and died around 100/718), who came from Nazwā in Oman and was one of the best friends and a disciple of the celebrated companion of the Prophet ʿAbd Allāh b. ʿAbbās.

At Baṣra he enjoyed enormous prestige as a man of learning, and even Sunni Muslims acknowledge his importance as a transmitter. His teaching was crucial in the formation of the Ibāḍī school: not only did he train the first scholars of the movement, Abū Nūḥ Ṣāliḥ al-Dahhān, Ḥayyān al-Aʿraj, Ḍumām b. al-Sāʾib, Jaʿfar b. al-Sammāk, and Abū ʿUbaydah al-Tamīmī, but also several Sunni traditionists, such as Qatāda b. Diʿāma, ʿAmr b. Harim, ʿAmr b. Dīnār, Tamīm b. Khuwayṣ and ʿUmārah b. Ḥayyān, were among his friends and disciples.

He carried on ʿAbd Allāh b. Ibāḍ's policy of maintaining friendly relations with the Umayyads and kept on good terms with the powerful governor, al-Hajjāj, through whom he even succeeded in obtaining regular payments from the state coffers. But their relationship soon deteriorated mainly due to Jābir's close connections with the family of the former governor of Khurāsān, Yazīd b. al-Muhallab, who had been deposed and arrested in 86/705 by al-Hajjāj. Jābir corresponded with Yazīd's brother, ʿAbd al-Malik b. al-Muhallab (d. 102/721), who was first governor of Khurāsān, then of Iraq (see Jawābāt Jābir

1 R. Rubinacci, "Il califfo ʿAbd al-Malik b. Marwān e gli Ibāḍiti," in *Annali dell'Istituto Universitario Orientale, N. S.* 5 (1954): 99-121; Michael Cook, *Early Muslim Dogma* (Cambridge: Cambridge University Press, 1981), 53; see also Abdulrahman al-Salimi and Wilferd Madelung (eds.), *Ibāḍī Texts from the 2nd/8th Century* (Brill, 2017).

b. Zayd ed. Farhat Jabiri). Moreover, according to the Ibāḍī sources, two women of the Muhallabid family, ʿĀtiqah, the sister of Yazīd b. al-Muhallab, who lived in Baṣra, and Halbiyyah, who lived in Mecca, also converted to Ibadism.

By the end of the first century of Hijra, there was an increasing radicalism in the Baṣran Ibāḍī community; revolutionary elements took control, seeking to move from the position of quietism (*quʿūd*) to that of open revolt (*shurāt*). Their activity, along with Jābir's relations with the Muhallabid family, which al-Hajjāj detested, led to ferocious persecution of the early community's members. Jabir was exiled and other members were imprisoned and released only after the death of al-Hajjāj (95/714), who was succeeded by Yazīd b. al-Muhallab. Among them there was Abū ʿUbaydah Muslim b. Abī Karimah al-Tamīmī who succeeded Jābir as leader of the Ibāḍī Baṣran community.

Abū ʿUbaydah, a *mawlā* of the Tamīm tribe, was the second Ibāḍī imām in Baṣra. He died probably after 150/760,[2] but the exact date of his death is unknown as Ibāḍī historical sources only record that he died during the al-Manṣūr caliphate (136/754–158/775).

Ibāḍī authors describe him as a skillful political leader and a great scholar. He studied under Jābir b. Zayd, Ḍumām b. al-Sāʾib, and other teachers, such as Jaʿfar b. al-Sammāk, Suḥār al-ʿAbdī, and also ʿUrwah b. ʿUdayyah, the first to reject arbitration and fight against ʿAlī.[3] Abū ʿUbaydah was the true organiser of the Ibāḍī movement. He provided the basis for the diaspora that has allowed the survival of Ibadism until today, creating teams of missionaries (*ḥamalat al-ʿilm*) who left Baṣra for the outer regions of the Islamic Empire with a proselytizing intent to create Ibāḍī centres. The activities of the movement in Baṣra took place within meetings (*majālis*) which were held in secret in members' houses. The sources describe three types of *majālis*: the first open to all members in which doctrinal and legal questions were discussed; a second reserved for the elders to organise propaganda (*daʿwa*), and a third intended for the training of missionaries. Thanks to this propaganda activity Ibāḍī revolts broke out in several regions. At the end of the Umayyad period, a short-lived imamate was established in South-Western Arabia under the guidance of Ṭālib al-Ḥaqq (ʿAbd Allāh b. Yaḥyā) who succeeded in taking possession of the Holy Cities in 129/747. An imamate survived for a short time in Ḥaḍramawt, while further imamates were created in both North Africa and Oman, which held out under alternate circumstances for quite a long time.

---

2 Abū ʿUbayda seems to have died after 150/760, as that year he ordered the killing in Sistan of Maʿn b. Zāʾida al-Shaybānī who was guilty of the murder of Zājir al-Ḥaḍramī. A. al-Salimi, "Identifying the (Ibāḍī/Omani) Siyar," *Journal of Semitic Studies* 55.1 (2010): 127 n. 59.

3 ʿAmr Kh. Ennami, *Studies in Ibāḍism* (PhD thesis, Cambridge University, 1971), 57-78.

After Abū 'Ubaydah's death, his pupil al-Rabīʿ b. Ḥabīb (died between 180/796 and 190/806) became the key figure of the movement: he was both a jurist and an activist involved in the organization of the missionary activity in North Africa and in Oman.[4]

Under the leadership of al-Rabīʿ b. Ḥabīb, the Baṣran community was in close contact with the Maghribi Ibāḍī imamate of Tāhirt (761–909). According to the sources, 'Abd al-Wahhāb b. 'Abd al-Raḥmān b. Rustum (208–258 circa/823–72), the second Ibāḍī imām of Tāhirt, bought books from Baṣra for his celebrated library. The Baṣran Ibāḍī leaders were arbitrators in the schism of Nukkār which split the imamate of Tāhirt towards the second half of the 3rd/9th century and succeeded in organizing their own imamate. Among their most outstanding doctors was Hārūn b. al-Yamanī.

But soon after the Nukkār schism, having handed over the leadership of the movement in Baṣra to Abū Ayyūb Wā'il al-Ḥaḍramī, al-Rabīʿ b. Ḥabīb moved to Oman, where he died at his home at Ghaḍfān, near Ṣuḥār.[5] Abū Ayyūb was the last Baṣran imam; after him Ibāḍī leaders moved definitively to Oman.

II

Abū al-Khaṭṭāb Qatāda b. Diʿāma b. Qatāda b. 'Azīz b. 'Amr b. Rabīʿah b. 'Imrān b. al-Ḥārith al-Sadūsī (60–117/680–735) was a blind scholar of Bedouin origin who came to Baṣra from the desert when he was a child and lived there for the rest of his life. He was born in around 60/680 and died of the plague in the Iraqi city of Wāṣiṭ in 117/735. From his earliest days he was famed for his prodigious memory. It is reported that, despite being blind, he came to Baṣra without a guide. It would appear that Baṣra was a magnet for the Bedouin and those who lived in the surrounding regions.[6] Ibn Saʿd lists a number of mem-

4 J. Wilkinson, *Ibādism: Origins and Early Development in Oman* (Oxford: Oxford University Press, 2010), 177.

5 J. Wilkinson, "The Ibāḍī Movement in Baṣra," in *Studies in the First Century of Islamic Society*, ed. G.H.A Juynboll (Carbondale: Southern Illinois University Press, 1982), 142.

6 Ch. Pellat, "Ḳatāda b. Diʿāma," *EI2*,vol: 4: 748. Muḥmmad Ibn Saʿd, *Ṭabaqāt al-Kubrā* (Beirut: Dār Ṣādir, 1977), vol. 7: 171; Aḥmad b. 'Alī Ibn Ḥajar, *Tahdhīb al-Tahdhīb*, ed. Ibrāhīm al-Zaybaq and 'Ādil Murshid (Beirut: Mū'assasat al-Risālah, 1984), vol. 3: 328-30; Al-Dhahabī, *Siyar al-'Ālām al-Nubalā*, ed. Suʿayb al-Ārnāwūṭ (Beirut: Mū'assasat al-Risālah, 1981), vol. 5: 269-83; Abū Ḥātim Muḥammad Ibn Ḥabbān al-Bustī, *al-'Ilal wa maʿrifat al-Rijāl* (Hyderabad: Dā'irat al-Maʿārif al-'Uthmāniyya, 1979), 1st ed., vol. 3: 262; also Abū Ḥātim Muḥammad Ibn Ḥabbān al-Bustī, *Kitāb al-Thiqāt*, (Hyderabad: Dā'irat al-Maʿārif al-'Uthmāniyya, 1973),1 st ed., vol. 5: 322; Abū Ḥātim Muḥammad Ibn Ḥabbān al-Bustī,

bers of the Sadūsī tribe known as *tābiʿīn* or *tābiʿī ʾl-tābiʿīn* who came from the desert and settled in Baṣra.[7] Another leading Bedouin Ibāḍī figure who was well-known in Baṣra was Abū ʾl-Mūʾarrij ʿAmr al-Sadūsī, who was a student of Abū ʿUbaydah Muslim b. Abī Karīmah (d.c. 150/767).[8]

Qatāda enjoyed a reputation as a scholar of *tafsīr* (exegesis), *ḥadīth*, language, genealogy, and literature. He studied in Baṣra as a pupil of Anas b. Mālik (d. 93/712), al-Ḥasan b. Abī ʾl-Ḥasan al-Baṣrī (d. 110/728), and Jābīr b. Zayd al-Azdī (d. 93/712), and in the Hejaz as a pupil of Saʿīd b. al-Musayīb (d. 94/715), Abū ʾl-ʿĀliyah al-Riyāḥī and ʿAṭāʾ b. Abī Rabāḥ. Some *ḥadīth* copyists preferred him to other pupils of al-Ḥasan al-Baṣrī because of his reliability and excellent memory.[9]

It appears that Qatāda set up his own school in Baṣra, where he attracted numerous students who studied under him. Since he was blind, his opinions were written down by his pupils.[10] Qatāda is reported to have collated the following books:

1. *Kitāb al-Nāsikh wa ʾl-Mansūkh fī Kitāb Allāh*, dictated by Qatāda to Hammām b. Yaḥyā[11]
2. *ʿAwāshir al-Qurʾān*[12]
3. *Kitāb al-Manāsik*[13]

Although there are no surviving books by Qatāda on *tafsīr*, his opinions are available to us today from two sources:

Mashāhīr ʿUlamā al-Amṣār, ed. M. Fleischhammer, Cairo, 1379/1959; Shams al-Dīn Aḥmad b. Muḥammad b. Abī Bakir Ibn Khallikān, *Wafiyāt al-Aʿiyān*, ed. Iḥsān ʿAbbās (Beirut: Dār Ṣādr, 1972), vol. 4: 85; Yāqūt al-Ḥamawī, *Muʿjam al-Udabāʾ* (*Irshād al-ʿārīb ilā maʿrifat al-ādīb*) (Beirut: 1993), vol. 17: 9; Abū al-Ḥasan ʿAlī b. Abī al-Karam al-Shaybānī, *al-Kāmil fī al-Tārīkh* (Beirut: Dār al-Kitāb al-ʿArabī, 1967), vol. 4: 224.

7 Ibn Saʿd, *Ṭabaqāt*, vol. 9: 42, 46, 140, 188, 215, 222, 228, 270, 277, 306.

8 Wilkinson, *Ibāḍism*, 227-8.

9 Al-Dhahabī, *Siyar al-ʿĀlām al-Nubalā*, vol. 5: 269-83.

10 Ibn Ḥajar, *Tahdhīb al-Tahdhīb*, vol. 2: 401.

11 Qatāda b. Diʿama al-Sadūsī, *Al-Nāsikh wa al-Mansūkh fī kitāb Allāh*, ed. Aḥmad b. Ṣāliḥ al-Ḍāmin (Beirut: Mūʾassasat al-Risālah, 1984).

12 Ibn Saʿd, *Ṭabaqāt al-Kubrā*, vol. 7: 273.

13 Fuat Sezgin, *Geschichte des Arabischen Schrifttums* (Leiden: Brill, 1967),tr. *Tārīkh al-ādab al-ʿArabī,* trans. ʿArafa Muṣtafā (Riyadh: 1988), vol. 1: 75-6.

1. ʿAbdal-Razzāq b. Hammām al-Ḥimyarī al-Ṣanʿānī (d. 221/836) from the narration of Abū ʿUrwah Maʿmar b. Rāshid (d. 154/771)[14]
2. Al-Ṭabarī (224–310 / 893–923), with four methods of *isnād* (reporting the chains of transmission):
   a. "*Ḥaddathanā Bishr b. Muʿādh ḥaddathanā Yazīd b. Zurayʾ* (d.182/798–9) *ḥaddathanā Saʿīd b. Abī ʿUrūbah ʿan Qatāda*" ("Bishr b. Muʿādh reported to us, Yazīd b. Zarī reported to us, Saʿīd b. Abī ʿUrūbah reported to us from Qatāda").
   b. "*Ḥaddathanā al-Ḥasan b. Yaḥyā qāla ākhbaranā ʿAbd al-Razzāq qāla ākhbaranā Muʿammar ʿan Qatāda*" ("Al-Ḥasan b. Yaḥyā reported to us, he said ʿAbd al-Razzāq informed us, he said Muʿammar informed us from Qatāda").
   c. "*Haddathanā Muḥammad b. ʿAbd al-Āʿlā qāla ḥaddathanā Muḥammad b. Thawr ʿan Muʿammar ʿan Qatāda*" (Muḥammad b. ʿAbd al-Āʿlā reported to us, he said Muḥammad b. Thawr reported to us from Muʿammar from Qatāda").
   d. "*Ḥaddathanā al-Walīd ʿan Saʿīd b. Bashīr ʿan Qatāda*" ("Al-Walīd reported to us from Saʿīd b. Bashīr from Qatāda").[15]

An examination of the Qur'anic verses that were subjected to *tafsīr* suggests that they were not arranged or collated under a uniform or integrated system. Instead, his pupils recorded his opinions on certain verses at the time when he gave them. Qatāda is also said to have given opinions on aspects of *ʿUlūm al-Qurʾān* (Qur'anic sciences) such as *qirāʾāt* (readings) and *āsbāb al-nuzūl* (reasons for revelation).[16]

There is still debate over Qatāda's *ḥadīth* narrations – i.e. over whether they are to be classified as being in the *thiqah* (reliable) or *tadlis* (fraudulent) category.[17] This is because there have been doubts about him since the time of Aḥmad b. Ḥanbal (d. 241/855) and al-Ḥākim al-Nishāpūrī (d. 405/1014), who did not believe that he had met any of the Prophet's Companions apart from

---

14 ʿAbdal-Razzāq b. Hammām al-Ṣanʿānī, *Tafsīr al-Qurʾān*, ed. Muṣṭafā Muslim Muḥammad (Riyadh: Maktabat al-Rashīd, 1410/1980), 1st ed., vol. 2: 182.

15 Muḥammad b. Jarīr al-Ṭabarī, *Jāmiʿ al-Biyān ʿan Tāʾwīl ayī al-Qurʾān*(Beirut: Dār al-Fikr, 1985), vol.1: 42, 62, 68.

16 Ignaz Goldziher, *Die Richtungen der Islamischen Koranauslegung*, tr. *Madhāhib al-Tafsīr al-Islāmi*, trans. ʿAbd al-Ḥalīm al-Najār (Cairo: al-Markaz al-Qawmī li al-Tarjama, 2013), 10, 11, 56, 76.

17 G. Vitestam, "Qatāda b. Diāma as-Sadūsī et la Science du Ḥadīth," in *Actes du Ve Congrès International d'Arabisants et d'Islamisants* (Bruxelles: 1970), 489-98.

Anas b. Mālik, who lived in Baṣra.[18] This was also the view of the *ḥadīth* scholars al-Nasā'ī, Ibn Ḥayyān, al-Dāraquṭnī, al-Sam'ānī, Ibn al-Āthīr al-Jazarī, and Ibn Ḥajar.[19] Indeed, Ibn Ḥajar went even further and regarded him as being one of the prolific *ḥadīth* fabricators, though he excepted the ones that Qatāda declared he had heard directly. Some scholars doubted his narrations from the *Tābi'īn* (the Prophet's Companions' Followers), since Qatāda did not narrate from Mujāhid b. Jabr (d. 104/722), so they were in the category of *mursal* – i.e. a chain of transmission beginning with a "Follower," not a "Companion." Similarly, there were doubts about his narrations from Sa'īd b. Jubayr (d. 95/714) on the grounds that he did not meet him face to face but wrote to him.[20] Thus, Yaḥyā b. Sa'īd al-Qaṭṭān (d. 259/873) considers that, where Qatāda's narration is concerned, there is no difference between *tadlīs* and *mursal* and they are one and the same thing.[21]

On the other hand, some *ḥadīth* scholars have tried to class the *ḥadīth*s attributed by Qatāda to the Prophet as legitimate, whether the chain of transmission was direct or – alternatively – indirect via a Companion or a Follower. Described as *mursal khafī* (hidden *mursal*), the significance of this type of narration is that it points to the birth of *ḥadīth* terminology at the end of the 1st/7th century.[22] Even if Qatāda's narrations were mainly from *muḥaddithūn* (*ḥadīth* transmitters) in Baṣra and to a lesser extent in Kufa, he also recorded narrations in the Hejaz from Sa'īd b. al-Musayb, 'Amr b. Dīnār, and 'Aṭā' b. Abī Rabāḥ.[23] His pupil Abū Ayyūb Yaḥyā b. Mālik al-Āzdī notes that Qatāda did not make precise distinctions between the different terms used in narrations, saying: "If he received something he had heard, he said *Ḥaddathanā Anas b. Mālik* ("Anas b. Mālik reported to us") and so on. And if he received something he had not heard, he said: *Qāla Sa'īd b. Jubayr wa Abū Qalāba etc.*" ("Sa'id bin Jubayr and Abu Qalaba said etc."). Moreover, his pupil Shu'bah b. al-Ḥajjāj (d. 160/777) mentions that Qatāda used to order his pupils to write down what they

18 Ibn Ḥajar, *Tahdhīb al-Tahḍhīb*, vol.3: 328-30.

19 Abū Muḥammad 'Abd al-Raḥmān b. Abī Ḥatīm Muḥammad b. Idrīs al-Tamīmī al-Rāzī, *al-Jarḥ wa al-Ta'dīl* (Hyderabad: Maṭba'at Majlis Dā'rat al-Ma'ārif al-'Uthmāniyya, 1952-3), vol.1: 166, 246; vol. 3/2: 132-5.

20 Ibn Ḥajar, *Tahdhīb al-Tahdhīb*, vol. 3: 428-430.

21 Al-Rāzī, *al-Jarḥ wa al-Ta'dīl*, vol. 1: 166-167; vol. 1: 246.

22 Aḥmad b. 'Alī Ibn Ḥajar al-'Asqalānī, *Nuzhat al-naẓar bi-sharḥ Nukhbat al-fikar fī muṣṭalaḥ Ḥadīth ahl al-athar*, ed. 'Abd Allāh b. Ḍayf Allāh 'Alī (Riyadh: 2001) 99-101.

23 Ṣalāḥ al-Dīn Abū Sa'īd b. Khalīl b. Kīkaldī b. 'Abd Allāh al-'Ālā'ī, *Jāmi' al-Taḥṣīl fī Āḥkām al-Marāsīl*, ed. Ḥamdī b. 'Abd al-Majīd b. Ismā'īl (Beirut: 'Ālam al-Kutub, 1986), 212-16.

heard from him and what came from his memory, and that he would become angry if he was asked about the chain of transmission.[24]

Nevertheless, it seems that the terminology used in the narrating of *ḥadīth*s did not make precise distinctions about methods of transmission until the beginning of the 2nd /8th century.[25] This is according to Ḥammād b. Salama (d. 167/ 784) – another pupil – who states: "We used to come to Qatāda and he would say: '*Balaghanā* ('It has reached us') from the Prophet' and '*Balaghanā* from 'Umar (b. al-Kaṭṭāb)." He hardly ever gave any chain of transmission and when Ḥammād b. Abī Sulaymān (d. 121 /738) came to Baṣra (at the time he was the master of the Murji'ites and also Abū Ḥanīfa's Sheikh), he used to say '*Ḥaddathanā Ibrāhīm al-Nakhaʿī wa Fulān wa Fulān*' ('Ibrāhīm al-Nakhaʿī and so-and so and so-and-so reported to us'). Qatāda learnt of this and he began to make distinctions, so he would say: 'I asked (*sa'altu*) Muṭraf and I asked Saʿīd b. Musayib, and '*Ḥaddathanā Anas b. Mālik fa ākhbara bi'l isnād*' 'Anas b. Mālik reported to us and gave information about the chain of transmission'). So Qatāda reported to us and informed us about the chain of transmission."[26]

The above reports show that *ḥadīth* terminology was not originally in common use in Baṣra or Kufa, nor even in the Hejaz in a way that was recognized as conventional practice among narrators. Even if we raise the question of whether this terminology originated in Isfahan where Ḥammād b. Abī Sulaymān grew up, or in Kufa where he lived, or in the Hejaz (the main centre of *ḥadīth* narration), there is still debate and controversy over how the narrations were transmitted.[27]

Another issue concerns Qatāda's beliefs – specifically, his position on *qadar* (predestination and free will) and the *Qadariyyah* movement. Certainly, this is one of the "problematic areas" where *ḥadīth* narrators are concerned. Qatāda is mentioned in a series of books entitled *Ṭabaqat al-Muʿtazilah*– "Muʿtazilite biographies" (or "Classes of the Muʿtazilites") – as a leading Qadariyyah scholar. It also mentions how he acquired his belief in *qadar* from Abū 'l-Āswad al-Dīyalī/Dūw'alī. According to these books, several leading scholars under whom Qatāda studied as a pupil were notable proponents of the

24 Al-Rāzī, *al-Jarḥ wa al-Taʿdīl*, vol. 1: 166-7; Ibn Saʿd, *Ṭabaqāt*, vol. 7: 230; al-Dhahabī, *Siyar Āʿlām*, vol. 5: 274-5.

25 Josef Schacht, *The Origin of Muhammadan Jurisprudence* (Oxford: Clarendon Press, 1950), 39-40.

26 Ibn Saʿd, *Ṭabaqāt*, vol. 7: 229-231; al-Mazzī, *Tahdhīb al-Kamāl*, vol. 23: 498-517.

27 Schacht, *Origins*, 70; Wael Hallaq, "The Authenticity of Prophetic Ḥadīth: A Pseudo-Problem," *Studia Islamica* 89 (1999): 75-90.

Qadariyyah movement.[28] They included ʿAmr b. Dīnār, ʿĀsim al-Āḥwal, ʿAbd Allāh b. Abī Nājīḥ, Sulaymān b. Abī Muslim, ʿAbd Allāh al-Makkī al-Āḥwal, al-Ḥasan b. Abī ʾl-Ḥasan al-Baṣrī, Muḥammad b. Sīrīn, Saʿīd b. al-Musayīb, Abū al-Āswad al-Dīyalī, and Ṭāwūs. Pupils of Qatāda who believed in *qadar* also included Hishām al-Dastwānī, Saʿīd b. Abī ʿUrūbah, Hamām b. Yaḥyā, Khulayd b. Daʿlaj, ʿImrān al-Qaṣīr, ʿUthmān b. Muqsim al-Barrī, ʿAbdAllāh b. Yazīd al-Salamī, and Abū Shihāb al-Ḥaffāḍ.[29] The above names are mentioned in the texts, all of which clearly indicates that the cultural community in Baṣra during the 2nd/8th century was dominated by revolutionary elements such as the Qadariyyah, Ibāḍīs, and Murjiʾites. Moreover, D. Gimaret suggests the founders of Muʿtazilah gradually left the assembly of Qadariyyah on the discussions of sin while Qatada succeeded his master Ḥasan al-Baṣrī. This split showed the division between Qadariyyah and Muʿtazilite.[30] Remarkably, this work reveals the fact that the narrators mentioned in the text – those from whom Qatāda narrated as well as those who narrated from him – included a fair number of believers in *qadar*, as well as some Muḥakkimah, particularly supporters of the Ibāḍī position, and Murjiʾites. Although they were originally theologians, they also seem to have been *fiqh* scholars, so it is probable that the community of *ḥadīth isnād* specialists represented a variety of positions that were not all specifically Sunni. The revision of J. van Ess has expanded the view of trends within early Muslim society beyond the narrow categorization of a specialized Sunni narrative tradition. Indeed, the *K. Muwaṭṭāʾ* by Mālik b. Anas (d. 179/795), and later al-Shāfiʿī (d. 204/820), addressed issues ranging from *ḥadīth* narration to *fiqh*.[31]

Another thing that emerges from the transmissions is the fact that Ikrimah, Jābīr b. Zayd, and ʿAmr b. Dīnār were all pupils of ʿAbd Allāh b. al-ʿAbbās, and that Qatāda was their pupil. In particular, ʿAbd Allāh b. ʿAbbās enjoyed a special status among Ibāḍīs, as did his *ḥadīth* narrations. Nevertheless, Wilferd Madelung states that early Ibāḍī scholars such as ʿAbd Allāh b. Ibāḍ and Jābir b. Zayd believed in *qadar*.[32] Moreover, van Ess believes that the Ibāḍī exchange

28 Abū al-Qāsim al-Balkhī, al-Qāḍī ʿAbdal-Jabbār and al-Ḥākim al-Jushamī, *Faḍil al-ʾItizāl wa Ṭabaqāt al-Muʿtazila*, ed. Fūʾād Sayid (Tunis: Dār al-Tunisiyya li al-Nashr, 1974),79, 88.

29 Ibid., 94-96, 100-102, 214, 341-2.

30 D. Gimaret, "Muʿtazila," *EI2*, vol. 7: 783.

31 Van Ess, *Theologie und Gesellschaft im 2. und 3. Jahrhundert Hidschra. Eine Geschichte des religiösen Denkens im frühen Islam* (Berlin/New York: De Gruyter, 1991-97), vol. 1: 50-88.

32 Wilferd Madelung, "ʿAbd Allāh Ibn Ibāḍ and the origins of the Ibāḍiyya," in *Authority, Privacy and Public Order in Islam*, ed. Barbara Michalak-Pikulska and Andrzej Pikulski (Leuven: Orientalia Lovaniensia Analecta, 2006),51-7; Crone and Zimmermann, *The Epistle of Sālim ibn Dhakwān* (Oxford: Oxford University Press, 2002), 202-3; Wilkinson, *Ibāḍism*, 152, 163; Wilferd Madelung: "ʿAbd Allâh Ibn Ibâḍ's 'Second Letter to ʿAbd al-

of views on free will and predestination took place during the time of Abū ʿUbaydah Muslim b. Abī Karīmah and that the notion of a balance between predestination and free will was the predominant Ibāḍī position in the middle of the 2nd/8th century.[33] In fact, Muʿtazilite biographical works contain no references to any of the leading Ibāḍī scholars. However, if Madelung's and Van Ess's suggestions about the early Ibāḍī masters' beliefs are taken into consideration, then a belief in *qadar* would mean that it is possible to reconcile doctrinal positions with juridical opinions and *ḥadīth* narrations. Interestingly, in a significant chapter of *Tabaqāt al Muʿtazilah* by the Zaydī scholar Aḥmad b. Yaḥyā al-Murtaḍā, there is quite a long list of scholars who believed in *qadar* and/or were Muʿtazilites in the early Islamic community. This shows that the narration of traditions and *ḥadīth*s was not a characteristic of the Sunni schools alone[34] and again indicates the need for a critical review of the doctrine on the early transmission of *ḥadīth*, which does not necessarily need to be associated with the Sunni schools.

According to Ibāḍī theology, it would appear that Abū ʿUbaydah Muslim b. Abī Karīmah did not strongly oppose those who believed in *qadar*.[35] However, it looks as though Abū ʿUbaydah's pupils who came after him – al-Rabīʿ b. Ḥabīb, ʿAbd Allāh b. Yazīd al-Fazārī, and Abū Ayyūb Wāʾil – were considerably more hostile in their debate on *qadar*.[36] It may well be that the disputes between the different groups began to manifest themselves more clearly in their respective doctrine positions from the middle of the 2nd/8th century.[37]

The *Aqwāl Qatāda* (The Sayings/Teachings of Qatāda) is a collection of writings on *fiqh* (jurisprudence) and *ḥadīth*s (traditions) narrated by Qatāda

---

Malik,'" in *Community, State, History and Change: Festschrift for Prof. Ridwan al-Sayyid on his 60th Birthday* (Beirut: Al-Shabaka al-ʿArabiya li-l-Abḥāth wa al-Nashr, 2011), 7-17.

33 Van Ess, *Theologie und Gesellschaft im 2. und 3. Jahrhundert Hidschra*, vol. 2: 204.

34 Aḥmad b. Yaḥyā Ibn al-Murtaḍā, *Ṭabaqāt al-Muʿtazilah*, ed. Susanna Diwald-Wilzer (Beirut: German Oriental Institute 2009), 133-140.

35 Abū al-ʿAbbās Aḥmad b. Saʿīd al-Darjīnī, *Kitāb Ṭabaqāt al-Mashāʾikh bi-l-Maghrib*, ed. Ibrāhīm Ṭallāy, 2 vols. (Constantine, Algeria: 1394/1974), vol. 2: 258; Josef van Ess, *Anfänge Muslimischer Theologie* (Beirut: 1977), 230.

36 Fazārī, *Early Ibāḍī Theology*, Introduction; Abdulrahman al-Salimi, "Early Ibāḍī Creed in the 2nd/8th Century: a Study of Wāʾil b. Ayyūb's 'Nasab al Islam' (The Lineage of Islam)," *The Muslim World* 105/2 (2015): 194-209.

37 Aḥmad b. Saʿīd Al-Shammākhī, *Kitab al-Siyar*, ed. Aḥmad al-Siyābī (Muscat: Ministry of Heritage and Culture, 1987), vol. 2: 233; Josef van Ess, *Anfänge muslimischer Theologie - Zwei antiqadaritische Traktate aus dem ersten Jahrhundert der Hiǧra* (Wiesbaden-Beirut: 1977), 38; Michael Cook, *Early Muslim Dogma*,142. Abdulrahman al-Salimi, "Themes of the Ibāḍī/Omani Siyar," *Journal of Semitic Studies* 54 (2009): 475-514.

that has frequently attracted the interest of present-day scholars.[38] In addition to these writings, the discovery of a number of previously unknown texts on Ibāḍī jurisprudence and early legal opinions in the Maghrib region by a non-Ibāḍī scholar from Baṣra is now raising questions about early Ibāḍī history and the methods of recording information during Islam's formative period during the first half of the 2nd /8th century. Although these texts have not yet been published, they are the subject of intense debate amongst modern scholars.

The *Aqwāl Qatāda* has never been part of the legal literature of the Ibāḍiyyah in Oman. However, the manuscript of the *Aqwāl Qatāda* has repeatedly attracted particular interest among modern scholars as it raises questions concerning the early development of the Ibāḍī Baṣran community.

It is a unique document because it attests to the existence of a scholarly link between Sunnīs and Ibāḍīs during the early development of Islamic law. The fact that the legal responses and traditions of Qatāda are part of an Ibāḍī collection, in which the traditions of Jābir bin Zayd (one of the founders of Ibadism) have been transmitted through ʿAmr b. Harim and ʿAmr b. Dīnār, proves that Ibāḍī lawyers of the first generations considered Qatāda to be a faithful upholder of Jābir's doctrine.

This present study is based on two recently discovered manuscripts. One of these is in the Dār al-Kutub al-Miṣriyyah in Cairo, while the other is in the al-Bārūniyyah Library (*al-Khizānah al-Bārūniyyha*) on the Tunisian island of Djerba. We shall look at both of them in detail.[39] The narrations are composed of seven bundles; these are divided into seven parts with each part consist-

38 Josef Schacht, *Bibliotheques et manuscrits abadites, Revue Africaine* (Algiers), 100 (1956), 375-398; Josef van Ess, *Theologie und Gesellschaft im 2. und 3. Jahrhundert Hidschra*,vol. 1: 270-273; Van Ess, *Anfänge*, 122; W. Schwartz, "Die Anfänge der Ibāḍīten in Nordafrika - der Beitrag einer islamischen Minderheit zur Ausbreitung des Islams," in *Studien zum Minderheitenproblem im Islam* 8 (Wiesbaden: 1983), 30, 40, 309; A. Kh. Ennami, "A Description of New Ibāḍī Manuscripts from North Africa," *Journal of Semitic Studies* 15 (1970): 63-87; Ersilia Francesca, *Teoria e pratica del commercio nell'Islam medievale. I contratti di vendita e di commenda nel diritto ibāḍita* (Rome: Istituto per l'Oriente C.A. Nallino, 2002), 79-82; Ersilia Francesca, "The Formation and Early Development in the Ibāḍī Madhhab," *Jerusalem Studies in Arabic and Islam* 28 (2003): 260-277; Ersilia Francesca, "Investigating Early Ibāḍī Jurisprudence: Sources and Case Law," *Jerusalem Studies in Arabic and Islam* 30 (2005): 231-263; Ennami, *Studies in Ibāḍism*, I, Chap. IV, Ibāḍī Jurisprudence, 79-117, 136-140; Wilferd Madelung, "Aqwāl Qatāda and the Shuʿaybiyya and Nukkār," in *Ibāḍī Jurisprudence. Origins, Developments, and Cases*, ed. Barbara Michalak-Pikulska and Reinhard Eisener (Hildesheim-Zurich-New York: Olms Verlag, 2015), 25-29; Josef *vanEss, Actes du Colloque sur l'histoire de Jerba, avril 1982* (Tunis: L'Institut, 1986), 93ff.

39 Martin Custers, *Al-Ibāḍiyya, a Bibliography* (Muscat: 2008), vol. 1: 349.

ing of narrations, *ḥadīths*, and legal opinions. The texts show three important features: (1) *fiqh* legal opinions commonly held during the early Islamic period in Baṣra; (2) the approach used when collecting early Islamic religious traditions including *ḥadīths* of the Prophet and opinions on matters of *fiqh*; and (3) the development of Islamic jurisprudence during the first two centuries of the Islamic era.

Early Islamic law came into existence through the theoretical and practical efforts (*ra'y*) of the first Muslim jurists. But already in the 1st/7th century people acknowledged the rule of Qur'an and of the Prophet's narrations as sources of the law. Authentic traditions from the Prophet and the Companions can easily be detected in the early sources. A comparison of the early stocks of traditional material, as they appear in "virgin" sources like the *Aqwāl Qatāda*, with the later collections could contribute much to answering the question of how *ḥadīths* of the Prophet grew and acquired their continuous *isnād*.

In particular, the *Aqwāl Qatāda* displays a terrific informational value for questions on the origins and development of Islamic jurisprudence; therefore it is crucial to understand how old the material that it contains is, where it comes from, what characteristics it displays in terms of form and content, and in particular why old Ibāḍī material has been collected along with old Sunni material.

It must be noted that due to Qatāda's blindness, these texts were not actually written in his own hand, although the style indicates that they most probably originated from him. Qatāda used to dictate to his pupils while teaching, and these texts were thus transmitted orally to his students, who later reworded and transcribed them for posterity. They are attributed to Qatāda, but the actual transmitter who recorded them is unknown.[40]

The collector who put together the existing recensions is unknown and it is also difficult to determine with certainty whether all the strata contained in the manuscript were originally part of the work by Qatāda or were added at a later time. The question of the collection of the *Aqwāl Qatāda* is crucial in order both to date the material of the manuscript and to understand how the extant manuscript came into being.

Ennami believes that the person who collected the material was al-Rabīʿ b. Ḥabīb (d.c. 170/787) and that it was collated methodically under chapter headings by Abū Ghānim Bishar b. Ghānim al-Khurāsānī, the author of

40 Aḥmad b. 'Alī Ibn Ḥajar, *Tahdhīb al-Tahdhīb*, vol. 3: 328-30; Muḥammad b. Aḥmad b. 'Uthmān al-Dhahabī, *Siyar al-'Ālām al-Nubalā*, ed. Shu'ayb al-Ārnāwūṭ (Beirut: Mū'assasat al-Risālah, 2001), vol. 5: 269-283.

the *Mudawwanah*.[41] This view gained credence and was accepted by Ersilia Francesca, who examined the text and concluded that it consisted of statements by al-Rabīʿ and others of his ilk.[42]

Both Ennami and Ersilia Francesca believe that *Aqwāl Qatāda* was collated during the last third of the 2nd/8th century by al-Khurāsānī, whose works of jurisprudence contain early Ibāḍī writings on *fiqh* from Baṣra, Kufa, and Madinah. In their view, even if the collator and recorder of *Aqwāl Qatāda* is unknown, he was probably an Ibāḍī from Baṣra. However, they believe that it was al-Khurāsānī who took the collection from Baṣra to North Africa. Their argument is based on the fact that the *Aqwāl Qatāda* is included in a larger manuscript called *al-Diwān al-Maʿrūd ʿalā ʿUlamāʾ al-Ibāḍiyya*. Many works contained in that manuscript are related by the same transmitters as al-Khurāsānī in his *Mudawwanah*. The main problem with the *Aqwāl* is that it has been ignored by mediaeval Ibāḍī sources, which have recorded almost no information about it, with the result that no data about who could have collected itis available in those sources.[43]

On the other hand, Wilferd Madelung maintains that the opposite is the case. He reached this conclusion after a careful examination of the manuscripts of Abū Zayd b. ʿAbdal-Raḥmān b. ʿUmar b. Sālim b. Sulaymān b. Yadr b. ʿAlī b. Mūsā b. Yakhlaf b. ʿAbd al-ʿAzīz al-Sadrīnī and Ṣālih b. Sālim b. Sulaymān b. Yadr al-Sadrīnī, the two copyists who transcribed the text. Both were from the Tunisian island of Djerba and originally came from Zwāra in the Nafūsa Mountains. It appears that they were cousins and were among the last of the Ibāḍī *Nukkār* scholars during the 11th to 12th /17th to 18th centuries.[44] Of particular interest is Abū Zayd b. ʿAbdal-Raḥmān al-Sadrīnī, who was aware of

41 Ennami, *Studies in Ibāḍism*, 79-117, 136-40.

42 Francesca, *Teoria e pratica*, 72-82; Francesca, "The Formation and Early Development," 260-77; Francesca, "Investigating Early Ibāḍī Jurisprudence," 231-63.

43 T. Lewicki, "Ibn Ghānim: Abū Ghānim Bishr [b. Ghānim] al-Khurāsānī," in *EI2*, vol. 1: 120; and E. Francesca, "Ibn Ghānim: Abū Ghānim Bishr [b. Ghānim] al-Khurāsānī," in *EI3*, vol. 1: 14-16; *al-Mudawwanah al- ṣughrā*, 2 vols, Muscat: Ministry of National Heritage and Culture, 1984; and *Mudawwanah al-kubrā*, arranged by Muḥammad Aṭfayyish, 2 vols, Muscat: Ministry of National Heritage and Culture, 1984; Abū Ghānim Bishr [b. Ghānim] al-Khurāsānī, *Mudawwanah*, ed. Yaḥiyā b. ʿAbd Allāh al-Nabhānī and Ibrāhīm al-ʿAsākir (Muscat: 2006); another edition by Muṣṭafā Bajū (Muscat: Ministry of Heritage and Culture, 2007).

44 Wilferd Madelung, "*Aqwāl Qatāda*," 25-29; see also Martin Custers, *Al-Ibāḍiyya*, vol. 2: 370-1.

the importance of the early Ibāḍī heritage during its formative stage in Baṣra.[45] Indeed, both of these scholar-copyists played a significant role in collecting material related to Ibāḍism and its revival after the major schism that took place in the Maghrib around the year 168/785, at the beginning of the reign of the second Rustumid imam in Tāhirt – 'Abdal-Wahhāb b. 'Abdal-Raḥmān b. Rustum – under the leadership of Abū Qudāmah Yazīd b. Findīn al-Yifranī, who was a supporter of the first Rustumid imam, 'Abdal-Raḥmān b. Rustum.

Yazīd b. Findīn carried out a coup against the Imam 'Abd al-Wahhāb, on the grounds that he was not entitled to hold the position of imam. Subsequently, his group was referred to as the *Nukkār* (deniers).[46] While Imam 'Abd al-Wahhāb b. 'Abd al-Raḥmān was recognized as the legitimate imam by the Baṣran imam al-Rabī' b. Ḥabīb, Yazīd b. Findīn won an ally and supporter in the person of Abū 'l- Ma'rūf Shu'ayb b. al-Ma'arūf, who was living in Egypt at the time the dispute broke out. Shu'ayb then travelled to Tāhirt and joined Yazīd b. Findīn and the rebels against Imam 'Abd al-Wahhāb.

Very soon afterwards, the conflict spread to the community in Baṣra and subsequently produced a notable clash between Abū Ayyūb Wā'il b. Ayyūb, and later Maḥbūb b. al Raḥīl on one side, and Hārūn b. al-Yamān, 'Abd Allāh b. Yazīd al-Fazārī, Abū 'l- Mū'arrij 'Amr b. Muḥammad al-Sadūsī, and 'Abd Allāh b. 'Abd al-'Azīz on the other.[47] Ibāḍī sources have given us a complete picture of the controversy, with the exception of a "side-dispute" which took place through an exchange of letters between Maḥbūb b. al Raḥīl and the people of Ḥaḍramawt, Oman, and Hārūn b. al Yamān over the concept of sinful *khaṭī'ah*.

Later, Nūr al-Dīn 'Abd Allāh b Ḥumayd al-Sālimī (d. 1914) noted that in this dispute the Ibāḍīs of Yemen followed the views of Hārūn b. al-Yamān, while the people of Oman and Ḥaḍramawt followed Maḥbūb b. al-Raḥīl.[48] However, there are hardly any traces of the revised editions of the early Iraqi Shu'aybi authorities – namely Shu'ayb b. al-Ma'rūf, 'Abd Allāh b. 'Abd al-'Azīz, and Abū l-Mu'arrij 'Amr b. Muḥammad al-Sadūsi – in the *Aqwāl Qatāda*, though they

45 'Abd Allāh b. Yazīd Fazārī, *Early Ibāḍī Theology*, ed. 'Abdulrahman al-Salimi and Wilferd Madelung (Leiden: Brill, 2014), Introduction.

46 T. Lewicki, "Nukkār," in *EI2*, vol. 3: 112-14; John C. Wilkinson, *Ibāḍism*, 229-231; Werner Schwartz, "Die Anfänge der Ibāḍīten in Nordafrika – der Beitrag einer islamischen Minderheit zur Ausbreitung des Islams," in *Studien zum Minderheitenproblem im Islam* 8, (Wiesbaden: 1983); Ulrich Rebstock, *Die Ibāḍiten im Maghrib (2/8–4/10 Jh.): die Geschichte einer Berberbewegung im Gewand des Islam* (Berlin: Schwarz, 1983).

47 Crone and Zimmermann, *The Epistle of Sālim b. Dhakwān*, 309; Al-Salimi, "Themes of the Ibāḍī/Omani Siyar," 475-514; Wilkinson; *Ibāḍism*, 231-233.

48 Nūr al-Dīn 'Abd Allāh b. Ḥumayd al-Sālimī, *Tuḥfat al-Ā'iyān* (Cairo: 1962), vol. 1: 139; al-Salimi, "Early Ibāḍī Creed," 194-209.

can be found in the *Futyā al-Rabīʿ b. Ḥabīb* and in al-Khurāsānī's *Mudawwana*. This due to the fact that the *Aqwāl Qatāda* was written around half a century earlier than other collected works in the two manuscripts of our editions.

The historic legacy inherited by both groups of Ibāḍīs in North Africa from these notable early Ibāḍī scholars of Baṣra was subsequently determined geographically according to "areas of influence." Southern Tunisia – the region known today as the Jerid – remained under the influence of the *Nukkār*, and the teachings of ʿAbd Allāh b. Yazīd al Fazārī continued to dominate there until after the 3rd /9th century. His pupils traveled from far and wide to learn from him, and his teachings remained influential among the Ibāḍīs of Tunisia and some parts of Tripolitania, as well as Egypt.[49] Al-Maqrīzī (d.845/1441) notes that ʿAbd Allāh b. Yazīd al-Fazārī and his followers were the closest to the Sunni position.[50] There was also a rapprochement between the views of the Ibāḍī *Nukkār* in North Africa and the Ibāḍī *Shuʿaybiyyah* scholars in Baṣra, so that consequently the *Nukkār* were able to retain possession of a number of rare early Islamic writings on creedal and *fiqh* topics. It was thanks to the close intellectual relationship between Qatāda and the early Ibāḍī scholars that we have been able to retain these texts, since just as Qatāda is recognized as being a pupil of the Ibāḍī authoritative source Jābir b. Zayd, so too is he known as a pupil of other leading early Islamic figures or those close to them, such as ʿAmr b. Harim al-Āzdī, ʿAmr b. Dīnār, and ʿIkrimah b. ʿAbd Allāh.[51] These editing texts also refer to the *Aqwāl* of early Ibāḍī figures such as Ṣāliḥ al-Dahhān, Abū Ḥayyān al-Āʿraj al-Jawfī, and Abū Ḥassān al-Āʿraj Muslim, ʿAbd Allāh al-Āswad al-Nakhaʿī and their common position on *qadar*.[52]

Thus, these early Islamic texts reveal a number of significant points related to the rise of Islam that are still being viewed with skepticism by philologists and historians. Meanwhile, the Ibāḍī works that have come down to us are considered to be the most reliable and credible sources for that early period, particularly in Baṣra, which was the centre of Islamic scholarship at the time. They also provide the basis for our understanding of Ibāḍī *fiqh*, which grew out of historic roots distinct from those of the Sunni and Shiite schools.

Madelung's interpretation gives us a clearer picture of the ideas put forward in the works of ʿAbd Allāh b. Yazid al-Fazārī and the approach to schol-

49 ʿAbd Allāh b. Yazīd Fazārī, *Early Ibāḍī Theology*, Introduction.

50 Abū al-ʿAbbās Aḥmad b. ʿAlī b. ʿAbd al-Qādir al-Maqrīzī, *al-Mawāʿiẓ wa al-Iʿtibār bi Dhikr al-Khiṭaṭ wa al-Āthār* (Cairo: 1968), vol. 2: 354.

51 Josef van Ess, *Theologie und Gesellschaft*, vol. 2: 206-7.

52 ʿAlī b. al-Jaʿd al-Jawharī, *Musnad Ibn al-Jaʿd*, ed. Āmir Aḥmad Ḥaydr (Beirut: Mūʾassasat Nādir, 1990), 154; Aḥmad b. ʿAlī Ibn Ḥajar, *Tahdhīb al-Tahdhīb*, vol. 3: 428-30.

arly authorship in Iraq – between Baṣra and Kufa – at that time.[53] These two manuscripts show that Ibāḍī scholarship was not confined to Baṣra and that there were also people writing in Kufa during the mid-2nd/8th century, indicating that there were Ibāḍī scholars in both of those cities. It is the view of this paper that the texts were written before ʿAbd Allāh b. Yazīd al-Fazārī moved to Baghdad and became a business partner of Hishām b. al-Ḥakam, where he was subsequently known as "al Baghdādī" and established his academy.[54] This indiscriminate "collective classification" could be the reason for Wilkinson's confusion in his compilation of Ibāḍī *ḥadīth* narrations. The fact that this confusion has continued is due to Sunni influence in the period following this Baṣra era, as there were no changes in the approach to scholarly authorship in the Ibāḍī school after the 5th /11th century.[55] Hence a more critical view of the way in which early Ibāḍī scholars compiled *ḥadīth* narrations is required.

The present manuscript can therefore be considered a "virgin text" that represents a new departure in the concept of scholarly authorship and the compilation of Islamic narrations and traditions dating from before the year 150 AH. This means that it should be assessed not only on the basis of its scholarship and its method of organizing and classifying data under chapter headings for the purposes of circulation, but also in comparison with other works which have come down to us and were copied by Abū Zayd b. ʿAbd al-Raḥmān al-Zuwārī. This assessment should be made in spite of the fact that the text itself has never been used by the Ibāḍīs of the Mashriq and was rarely referred to by the Ibāḍīs of the Maghrib.[56]

III

To examine the transmission of these texts in order to find the connections between Qatāda and the Ibāḍī, we shall begin by taking a close look at Qatāda's narration on the basis of the texts that contain his views as narrated from his teachers. This is mentioned in the fifth section:

53 ʿAbd Allāh b. Yazīd Fazārī, *Early Ibāḍī Theology*, Introduction.

54 Wilferd Madelung, *Aḥmad al-Nāṣir li-Dīn Allāh; Streitschrift des Zaiditenimams Aḥmad an-Nāṣir wider die ibaditische Prädestinationslehre* (Wiesbaden: Orient-Institut der Deutsche Morgenländischen Gesellschaft, 1985), 4-12.

55 John C. Wilkinson, *"Ibāḍī Ḥadīth: an Essay on Normalization," Der Islam* 62 (1985): 231-59.

56 See Abū Zayd; Martin Custers, *Al-Ibāḍiyyah*, vol. 2: 370-1.

A. Narrations from ʿAmr b. Dīnār (46–116/666–744). These consist of teachings that ʿAmr b. Dīnār states came from his contemporaries or from people who acquired reports from them. They are: ʿAbd Allāh b. al-ʿAbbās, Abū al-Shaʿthāʾ, Jabir b. Zayd, Ṭāwūs b. Kisān (d. 106/724), and ʿAtāʾ b. Abī Rabāḥ (d. 114/732). These narrations seem to have come from the Hejaz.

B. Narrations from ʿAmr b. Harim (d. 107/725). He was one of Qatāda's teachers and a leading Ibāḍī scholar. It is reported that Qatāda prayed over him when he died.[57] These narrations, which came from Jābir b. Zayd, ʿIkrimah b. ʿAbd Allāh (*mawlā* of ʿAbd Allāh b. al-ʿAbbās), al-Ḥasan b. Abī ʾl-Ḥasan al-Baṣrī, and Muḥammad b. ʿAbd al-Raḥmān al-Ānṣārī, appear to have been written down in Baṣra.

These are the two main direct chains of transmission: via Qatāda from ʿAmr b. Dīnār or via Qatāda from ʿAmr b. Haram al-Āzdī. There is also a third class of direct narrations from Qatāda, which were written down by al Rabīʿ b. Ḥabīb and attributed to Qatāda. These appear in the second and last sections of the book as narrations of traditions, either *ḥadīth*s of the Prophet or narrations from the Companions.

The texts show the forms of transmission from Qatāda, as follows:

a. *ḥaddatha Qatāda* ("Qatāda reported").
b. *ḥaddathanā Qatāda* ("Qatāda reported to us").
c. *ḥaddathnī Qatāda* ("Qatāda told me").
d. *kāna Qatāda yaqūl* ("Qatāda used to say").
e. *qāla Qatāda* ("Qatāda's says").
f. *rāʾī Qatāda* ("Qatāda's opinion").

Sometimes this is by way of *irsāl* without a link between the "Follower" and the Prophet, with no indication as to the person from whom the narration has come. Hence, the text has a wide range of *ḥadīth* narrations from Qatāda in various forms – *irsāl* as well as direct chains of authority. If the narrations were collected together as a single collection they could be classed as *Musnad Qatāda*. In addition, the forms of the narration also give a broad picture of narrators in Baṣra, Kufa, and Madinah.

As we have seen, the texts consist of a hodgepodge of *ḥadīth* narrations and legal opinions, so that as a result a researcher is likely to feel he is dealing with a preliminary draft or a mass of raw data that has not yet been subjected to analysis. Where traditions or *ḥadīth* narrations from an Ibāḍī perspective are con-

57 Al-Mazzī, *Tadhīb al-Kamāl*, vol. 22: 276.

cerned, Ersilia Francesca views Qatāda as bridging the gap between Ibāḍī and Sunni Islam during that early Islamic period of the 1st-2nd /7th-8th centuries.[58] However, this paper presents a different view, contending that the opposite is the case. During the time of Qatāda, the Sunni schools of *fiqh* did not yet exist in the true meaning of the word; this did not happen till the 3rd /9th century, in contrast to Schacht's view on the emergence of Islamic jurisprudence. Thus, Ennami and E. Francesca use Qatāda's texts as a means of responding to Joseph Schacht's denial that early Ibāḍī *fiqh* made any contribution to the established body of *fiqh* and in order to rebut his claim that both the Ibāḍī and Shiite jurisprudence traditions were influenced by Sunni *fiqh*.[59] The Ibāḍī situation was indeed quite different from the one Schacht portrays because the Ibāḍīs succeeded in propagating their school of thought and establishing states in North Africa, Yemen, Ḥaḍramawt, Oman, and Central Asia from the beginning of the 2nd /8th century; this meant that they needed practical rules to enable them to administer the day-to-day business of government in their emerging states. Moreover, their jurisprudence began to establish its own traditions, particularly when it was applied to previously unfamiliar cases in various fields as rulings were given on new situations.[60]

However, the problematic issue here is basically that narrations from the traditions of the Prophet and the Companions were written down or circulated during the 3rd /9th century and began to reshape the Sunni schools. Subsequently, the personalities and narrations concerned were classified according to their biographical categories or chains of transmission, making it impossible for a researcher today to disprove them.[61] We therefore find ourselves closer to the position of Joseph van Ess, whose encyclopedic work states that the Islamic milieu during the second and third centuries was more intellectually diverse and pluralistic than was previously thought and that consequently we need to revise our views on many of the creedal trends and personalities of that time.

A comparison of this text with similar early texts indicates that it has retained the character and narrations of that early period, the 2nd/8th century, and that it has remained untouched by the hands of editors and recorders of

58 Francesca, *Teoria e pratica*, 79-82.

59 Schacht, *Origin*, 256-7, 261-4.

60 Abdulrahman Al-Salimi, "Early Islamic Theological Influence in Jurisprudence. An Ibāḍī Perspective," in *Ibāḍī Jurisprudence. Origins, Developments, and Cases*, eds. Barbara Michalak-Pikulska and Reinhard Eisener (Hildesheim-Zurich-New York: Olms Verlag, 2015), 55-73.

61 Schacht, *Origin*, 40-53.

chains of transmission. This is in contrast to what happened in the 3rd/9th century, when the narrations were reclassified according to their subject category, as happened with Mālik b. Anas's *Muwaṭṭā'*.[62] It appears that these texts have remained unchanged since they arrived in North Africa and, consequently, the narrations in these texts have maintained their rather haphazard organization without having been changed or reclassified in a fashion similar to what happened to other works. Thus, we are drawn to speculate on what these texts reveal regarding the practice of recording jurisprudence in that period.

Another thing we can learn from this text is how narrations and chains of transmission were recorded. Hence, we find ourselves close to Fuat Sezgin's view on how the early Muslims recorded narrations and chains of transmission in this text – i.e. that they relied on other texts which Qatāda had used as sources.[63] In other words, this particular text is a stereotypical model of early Islamic writing.

Qatāda used to narrate recorded material to his pupils. His narrations have generally been transmitted without being classified into these seven texts as Prophetic traditions or juridical legal opinions. The texts include Qatāda transmissions from ʿAmr b. Dīnār and ʿAmr b. Haram as monographs within the texts, while the final text consists of narrations by al Rabīʿ b. Ḥabīb from Qatāda, who may have met each other according to the reports in the fourth section of the book. Legal opinions or questions from al Rabīʿ were then added; the style of these questions shows that some *fiqh* issues were presented as "*sū'il*" ("he was asked"), then referred to as narrations from Qatāda.

At this point we should like to refer to the writings of al Rabīʿ b. Ḥabīb, including his *Musnad al-Imām Rabīʿ b. Ḥabīb*, which was re-collated by Abū Yaʿqūb al Warjlani and issued as *Al-Jāmiʿ al-Ṣaḥīḥ: Musnad al-Imām Rabīʿ b. Ḥabīb*. The text of the original *Musnad* no longer exists, but Abū Yaʿqub al-Warjlani's version of *al-Jāmiʿ al-Ṣaḥīḥ: Musnad al-Imām Rabīʿ b. Ḥabīb* is accessible with several commentaries.[64] In addition, Nūr al Dīn ʿAbd Allāh b. Humayd al Sālimī (d.

62 Miklos Muranyi, *Materialien zur Mālikitischen Rechtsliteratur* (Wiesbaden: Harrassowitz, 1984), 40-71; Harlod Motzki, *Die Anfänge der Islamischen Jurisprudenz: Ihre Entwicklung in Mekka bis zur Mitte des 2./8. Jahrhunerts* (Stuttgart: Abhandlungen für die Kunde des Morgenlandes, 1991); Harlod Motzki, "The Prophet and the Cat: On Dating Mālik's Muwaṭṭā' and Legal Traditions," *Jerusalem Studies in Arabic and Islam* 22 (1998): 18-83.

63 Maʿmar b. al-Muthannā, *Majāz al-Qur'ān*, ed. Muḥammad Fū'ād Sizjīn (M. Fuad Sezgin) (Cairo: Maktabat al-Khanjī, 1954),17-20.

64 Abū al-ʿAbbās Aḥmad b. Saʿīd al-Darjīnī, *Kitāb Ṭabaqāt al-Mashā'ikh bi-l-Maghrib*, ed. Ibrāhīm Ṭallāy, 2 vols. (Constantine, Algeria: 1394/1974), vol. 2: 273-277; Abū 'l-ʿAbbās Aḥmad al-Shammākhī, *Kitāb al-siyar*, vol. 1: 102-5. According to Brockelmann, al-Rabīʿ died in about 170/786 (G.A.L., Suppl., II, 823); Michael Cook agrees with him

1914) comprehensively re-edited the work. Moreover, another recent discovery is al Rabiʿ's *Athar* (*Traditions*), recorded by Abū Ṣufrah ʿAbd al-Malik b. Ṣufrah.[65]

The important point here is that both manuscripts include al-Rabīʿ's *Traditions*, as well as the texts of the *Aqwāl Qatāda* and al-Rabīʿ's *fatwas*. Al-Rabīʿ b. Ḥabīb is the common denominator between the texts in both collections. Hence, he and his traditions form an important link in the transmission of Ibāḍī traditions and scholarly authorship in Baṣra, Oman, and North Africa. The fact that these drafts have been passed down unchanged from generation to generation is important for two reasons: firstly, for our understanding of issues affecting the Islamic community of that time in southern Iraq and, secondly, in showing how narrations and other material were recorded during the early Islamic period in the middle of the 2nd/8th century.

IV

The two manuscripts we have relied upon for our source material are to be found in:

1. Egyptian *Public* Authority: Dār Al-Kutub al-Miṣriyya (National Library) in Cairo, (D) –د-.
2. Al-Bārūniyya Library, Djerba-Tunisia, (B)– ب -.

in *Early Muslim Dogma*, 56, as does John C. Wilkinson in "Ibāḍī Ḥadīth: an Essay on Normalization," *Der Islam* 62 (1985): 231-59. On the contrary, Josef van Ess fixes the date of al-Rabīʿ's death between 180/796 and 190/806, see "Untersuchungen zu einigen ibāḍitischen Handschriften," *Zeitschriften der Deutschen Morgenländischen Gesellschaft* (1976): 32-3 and *Theologie und Gesellschaft im 2. und 3. Jahrhundert Hidschra*, vol. 2: 199. Also see the bibliography of al-Rabīʿ in Muḥammad b. Ismāʿīl al-Jaʿfī al-Bukhārī, *al-Tārīkh al-Kabīr* (Beirut: Dār al-Fikr, 1986), vol. 3: 277; Muḥammad b. Ḥabbān al-Bustī, *al-Thiqāt* (Beirut: Dār al-Fikr, 1975). However, there is also a mixing of the *ḥadīth* bibliographies between al-Rabīʿ b. Ḥabīb and two other authors who had similar names, namely al-Rabīʿ b. Ḥabīb al-Kūfī and al-Rabīʿ b. Ḥabīb al-Ḥanafī; for further details see Abū Muḥammad ʿAbd al-Raḥmān b. Abī Ḥātim Muḥammad al-Rāzī, *al-Jarḥwaal-Taʿdīl*, vol. 3: 457; al-Mazzī, *Tadhībal-Kamāl*, vol. 9: 67-70; Aḥmad b. ʿAlī Ibn Ḥajar, *Taqrībal-Tadhīb* (Aleppo: Dār al-Rashīd, 1986), 206.

65 Kahlan Kharusi, *Āthār al-Rabīʿ b. Ḥabīb, Edition and Study* (PhD thesis, University of Oxford, Faculty of Oriental Studies, 2003); Ersilia Francesca, "La fabbricazione degli isnād nella scuola ibāḍita: il Musnad di ar-Rabīʿ b. Ḥabīb," in *Law, Christianity, and Modernism in Islamic Society, Proceedings of the 18th Congress of the Union Europeenne des Arabisants et Islamisants held at the Katholieke Universiteit Leuven (Sep. 3-9, 1996)*, ed. U. Vermeulen and J. M. F. Van Reeth (Leuven: Peeters, 1998), 39-59.

Through a comparison of these two manuscripts, we can conclude the following points:

1. It is clear that there were other copies available to the Al-Bārūniyya copyist, who stated that he had transcribed the book from several copies in his possession. It appears that copy (D) was one of them. He also relied on two manuscripts from an author named ʿIsā b. Aḥmad. In copy (B), Al-Sadrīnī mentions him at the end of Part Four of *Aqwāl Qatāda*, stating: "the words I am writing have ended." Then he noted that this part was incomplete. He writes: "ʿIsā b. Aḥmad wrote by hand in his transcription that he saw the remaining passage in some other copies that had been written down before. He could not write a copy because of the corruption of the words."
2. The copyist of manuscript (B) reveals that he did not use copy (D) while transcribing the texts, but rather used other manuscripts as transcription sources. This is indicated when al-Sidrīnī mentions Abū Zayd's arguments in marginal notes on certain pages that are not available in manuscript (D). Al-Sidrīnī was influenced by Abū Zayd's arguments, although they never met. Thus it is possible to argue that there are missing manuscripts still to be discovered.
3. Al-Sidrīnī – the copyist of (B) – added marginal notes on the pages in order to explain his arguments on whether he agreed or disagreed. These notes appear in the footnotes.
4. Abū Zayd may have added later classified sections in all seven volumes (*bāb*) in order to identify each part and ensure that they were not mixed.

Nevertheless, apart from these two copies, there are no other copies which include the seven texts written by Qatāda. They comprise the following:

1. Part I of *Āthār al-Rabīʿ b. Ḥabīb* (Ruwayāt Ḍamām).
2. Part II of *Futyā al-Rabīʿ b. Ḥabīb*.
3. *K. Nikāḥ al-Shighār* of *ʿAbd Allāh b. ʿAbd al-Azīz*. (Four Chapters).
4. *K. al-Nikāḥ* of *Jābir b. Zayd*.
5. *K. al-Ṣiyām*. This begins with a discussion about Abū l-Muʾarrij's legal narratives; he composed them as questions and answers with his teacher Abū ʿUbaydah. Many scholars held differing views on this topic (the chapter addresses a scholar's dispute with fasting), with reference to the views of the Ibāḍī Imams' confirmation.

6. *K. al-Mumtanai'in min al-Ḥudūd min al-Imām*. In the Cairo MS: *K. al-ʿUmmal wa-man-yalī ʾlā al-nās*. Primarily, it deals with the administrative and other duties of Imams and rulers and their relations with people. This is clearly part of an Imamate work that addressed similar topics, but it is not in the Cairo manuscript and it is incomplete in the al-Bārūniyya copy.
7. *K. Kaffārāt al-imān*, attributed to the Kūfans.
8. *K. al-Waṣiyah*, narrations of Abū ʿUbaydah Muslim b. Abī Karīmah al-Tamīmī.
9. *K. al-Dīyāt*.
10. *K. al-Qismah wa-Tafnīn Uṣūlihā*. Opinions ascribed to the Kūfans.
11. *K. al-Buyūʿ*.
12. *Abwāb al-Ḥudūd*.
13. *al-Aḥkām*.
14. *K. al-Shufʾa wa- Tafnīn/Taqnīn Uṣūlihā*.
15. *K. al-Jaʾl wa ʾl- Ijārāt*. Opinions ascribed to the Madīna authorities.
16. *K. al-Qaḍāʾ fī al-Qirāḍ*. Opinions ascribed to the Madīna authorities.
17. *K. al-Qaḍāʾ fī al-Taflīs wa al-ʿUyūb*.
18. *K. al-Dīyāt*. Opinions ascribed to the Kūfans.
19. *K. Kafālāt*.
20. *K. al-Wadāʿiʾ wa al-ʿĀriya*. Sayings of the Kūfans.
21. *K. al-ʿĀriya*.
22. *K. al- Shahādāt*.
23. The letter of Abū ʿUbaydah Muslim regarding *Zakāt* (alms tax).
24. A book about the ritual purity of women. Unknown author of this work. It appears that the author wrote this after completing a number of previous works.

The *Aqwāl Qatāda* from the two sources manuscripts is divided into seven parts as follows:

Part I: On the ritual purity of women and prayer.
Part II: On fasting, *zakāt*, the division of spoils, atonement for having broken a vow (*bāb kaffārat al-īmān*), and the ban on alcoholic beverages (*bāb al-āshriba*).
Part III: On marriage, divorce, repudiation (*bāb al-ẓihār*), exchange (*ṣarf*), sales (*buyūʿ*), ships, what the Polytheists took from the Muslims funds in *jihād*, a part which Al-Rabīʿ b. Ḥabīb was consulted, other legal opinions on compensation (*dīya*), the ban of alcoholic beverages (*bāb al-āshriba*), and giving testimony.

Part IV: On problems relating to morals and customs, as well as the ban on alcohol, ritual butchery and hunting, punishment (*ḥadd*), divorce, birth, and contracts for freeing a slave.
Part V: This part deals with traditions from ʿAmr b. Harim.
Part VI: This part includes traditions from ʿAmr b. Dīnār from Jābir on the subject of pilgrimage, ablutions, *salaf* (special kind of sale involving the ordering of goods to be delivered later for a price paid immediately), and repudiation; and from ʿAmr b. Harim concerning inheritance and repudiation. From f. 10616 we find responses by al-Rabīʿ under the title *bāb al-khiyār mimmā sūʾila ʿanhu al-Rabīʿ min bāb al-ṭalāq*, which resemble those preserved in part II.
Part VII: On legal opinions, ablutions, and prayers. According to the writer this part concludes with the book of Ḥabīb b. Abī Ḥabīb al-Jarmī al-Baṣrī (d. 162/778).

This part contains the *Kitab al-Salat* from Jabir b. Zayd from ʿAmr b. Harim from Ḥabīb b. Abī Ḥabīb al-Jarmī al-Baṣrī.[66]

Description of the two manuscripts[67]:

(D/ د) copy: This is available at the Egyptian Public Authority: *Dār Al-Kutub al-Miṣriyya* (National Library) in Cairo.

Manuscript Public Number: 4564
Private Number: B/21582Number of Pages: 328 pages
Size: 23 × 17 cm
Ruler: 36 lines
Calligraphy: Maghārībī
Colours: Text in black ink and headlines in red ink
Copyist: Abū Zayd b. Abd al-Raḥmān b. ʿUmar b. Muḥammad b. ʿUmar al-Zawārī
Date: Thursday of Ramaḍān 1041 / March 1632

The seven parts of the Aqwāl can be found in this source text under these pages:

66 Francesca, "Early Ibāḍī Jurisprudence: Sources and Case Law," *Jerusalem Studies in Arabic and Islam* 30 (2005): 236; Ennami, *Studies*, 84 (chapter on Ibāḍī jurisprudence).

67 For a further description of the two manuscripts, see Kahlan Kharusi, *Āthār al-Rabīʿ b. Ḥabīb* (Wiesbaden: Harrassowitz Verlag, 2016) 4-10; Martin Custers, *al-Ibaḍiyyah*, vol. 1: 39-40; Francesca, "La fabbricazione degli isnād," 39-59.

Part I: 74–88
Part II: 88–96
Part III: 96–109
Part IV: 109–119
Part V: 120–127
Part VI: 127–139
Part VII: 139–143

Al-Bārūniyya (B/ب):
Title of Manuscript: Mudawwanat Abī Ghānim /Al-Dīwān al-Maʿrūḍ
Private Number: 120. 42.
Number of Pages: 280 pages
Size: 33 × 23 cm
Ruler: 29 lines
Calligraphy: Maghāribī
Colours: Text in black ink and headlines in red ink
Copyist: Ṣāliḥ b. Sālim b. Sulaymān b. Yadar b. ʿAlī b. Mūsā b. Yakhlaf b. ʿAbdal-Azīz Al-Sadrīnī
Date: 15 Shawwāl 1191 / 16 November 1777
Location of the Copy: al-Māʾī mosque, Djerba-Tunisia

The seven parts of the *Aqwāl* can be found in this source text under these pages:

Part I: 1–27
Part II: 27–46
Part III: 46–67
Part IV: 67–87
Part V: 88–104
Part VI: 105–130
Part VII: 131–140

الجزء الأوَّل

من مسائل الحيض من قول قتادة[1].

بسم الله الرحمن الرحيم

وصلَّى الله على النبيّ الكريم وعلى آله وصحبه[2].

سئل عن المستحاضة؟

فقال: المستحاضة[3] تقعد أيّام أقرائها؛ ثُمَّ تنظر[4] يوما أو يومين، ثُمَّ تغتسل للصلاة[5] الأولى والعصر غسلا واحدا وتجمع بينهما، ثُمَّ تغتسل[6] لصلاة المغرب والعشاء غسلاً واحدًا وتجمع بينهما، وتغتسل لصلاة الغداة غسلا، ويكره لزوجها غشيانها ماكان دما سائلا، وإن كانت صفرة أوحمرة فلا بأس.

وقال: المستحاضة تصلِّي وتصوم رمضان وتطوف بالبيت، ويغشاها زوجها إلاَّ في الدم الكثير، فإنَّه يكره ذلك.

وسئل عن الحامل ترى الدم؟

---

1 لأبي زيد بن عبد الرحمن بن عمر بن مُحمَّد الزواري غفر الله له ولوالديه ولمن دعا له: +،د.

2 بسم الله الرحمن الرحيم، وصلَّى الله على النبيّ الكريم وعلى آله وصحبه: بسم الله الرحمن الرحيم صلى الله على سيدنا محمد وآله وصحبه وسلم تسليما كثيرا إلى يوم الدين الجزء الأول من قول قتادة، ب.

3 المستحاضة: -،د.

4 تنظر: تنتظر، ب.

5 للصلاة: لصلاة، ب،د.

6 ثم تغتسل: وتغتسل، ب.

قال: لا تدع الصلاة، فإن تركتها فعليها الإعادة لما تركت[7].

وقال: الحامل تصلّي وتقعد أيّام أقرائها وتجمع بين الصلاتين وتغتسل لكلِّ صلاتين إذا كان دما سائلا، وإن كان صفرة توضّأت لكلِّ صلاة ويغشاها زوجها في الصفرة والحمرة ويكره في الدم إذا كان كثيرا سائلا[8].

عن قتادة عن حفصة عن أمِّ عطيّة الأنصارية أنّها قالت: كنّا لا نعد الصفرة والكدرة بعد الطهر شيئا.

قال: إذا كانت في غير القروء فليس بشيء، إلاّ أنّها تتوضأ لكلِّ صلاة وليس عليها غسل[9].

سئل عن المرأة ترى الطهر في السفر وليس معها ماء؟

قال: تتيمّم كتيمّم الرجل للصلاة وليس عليها غسل[10].

سئل عن الحائض إذا رأت الطهر فأخّرت الغسل[11] يوما؟

قال: إذا فرّطت فإنّها تقضي صلاة ذلك اليوم، وإذا كانت بها جنابة فإنّها تغتسل للحيض غسلا وتغتسل[12] لجنابتها غسلا[13]، لا يجزئها غسل الحيض عن[14] غسل الجنابة.

---

7 لما تركت: -، ب.

8 في الدم إذا كان كثيرا سائلا: في الدم الكثير السائل، ب.

9 انظر: آثار الربيع، مسألة ٣٦، ص ٣١.

10 وليس عليها غسل: -، ب.

11 فأخرت الغسل: فأخرته، ب.

12 تغتسل: -،د.

13 غسلا: -،د.

14 عن: من،د.

سئل عن المرأة إذا حاضت وقد صلت ركعة أو ركعتين، أتقضي تلك الصلاة؟

قال: إن كانت أخَّرت الصلاة فعليها أن تعيد.

سئل عن التي قعدت عن الحيض ثُمَّ يستمر بها الدم؟

قال: تغتسل وتصلِّي فإنه ليس بحيض؛ إنما هو داء وتصنع كما تصنع المستحاضة[15].

سئل عن المرأة تؤخر الصلاة وقد حضر وقتها فأدركها الحيض.

قال: عليها القضاء إذا فرطت[16] عن الوقت، فإن لم تكن فرطت فلا قضاء عليها.

وسئل جابر بن زيد عمَّن يأتي امرأته وهي حائض؟

فقال: ما[17] أقول فيمن تعدى حدود الله شيئا[18]، قالها[19] ثلاث مرَّات.

سئل عمَّن غشي امرأته وهي نفساء قبل أن تأتي[20] عليها أربعون ليلة؟

قال: إذا طهرت في الأربعين أو قبلها طهرا بينا فليغشاها زوجها إن شاء، فإن لم تر[21] طهرا فلا يقربها.

15 سئل: عن التي قعدت عن الحيض ثُمَّ يستمر بها الدم، قال تغتسل وتصلِّي فإنه ليس بحيض إنما هو داء وتصنع كما تصنع المستحاضة: -،د.

16 فرطت: أخرت، ب.

17 ما: لا، ب.

18 شيئا: -،د.

19 قالها: يقولها، ب.

20 تأتي: يأتي، ب،د.

21 تَرَ: ترى، ب،د.

سئل عن الحائض تتناول من المسجد أو تضع فيه شيئا[22]؟

قال: يكره لها أن تتناول من المسجد شيئا أو تضعه فيه. وكان أبو عبيدة يكره أن تتناول شيئا[23].

وسئل عن الحائض هل تخضب؟

قال: نعم.

عن قتادة عن لاحق بن حميد قال: سألت ابن عبّاس عن الخضاب؟ فقال: أمّا نساؤنا فيخضبن من صلاة العشاء إلى صلاة الصبح، ثُمَّ يطلقن ذلك عن أيديهن[24]، ثُمَّ يعدن عليه من صلاة الصبح إلى صلاة الظهر، وهو أحسن الخضاب، ولا يمنعهن ذلك[25] من الصلاة.

وسئل عن المرأة تسافر مع غير ذي[26] محرم؟

قال: يكره للمرأة أن تسافر يوما إلاَّ مع ذي محرم.

عن قتادة عن أبي العالية الرياحي[27] عن عبد الله بن عبّاس أنّه قال: شهد عندي رجال مرضيون من أصحاب النبيّ ﷺ فيهم عمر، وأرضاهم عندي عمر: «أنَّ رسول الله ﷺ نهى عن الصلاة بعد العصر، حتّى تغرب الشمس وعن الصلاة بعد الفجر

22 شيئا: –، ب.

23 أن تتناول شيئا: –، ب؛ لذلك: –،د.

24 عن أيديهن: –،د.

25 ذلك: –، ب.

26 ذي: –،د.

27 الرياحي: الراحي، ب.

حتَّى تطلع الشمس»[28].

قال: بلغنا هذا، وقال بعضهم: نصف[29] النهار حتَّى تزول الشمس.

عن قتادة عن أبي رياح: أنَّ عمر طاف حول البيت[30] بعد الغداة، فلم[31] يصلِّ ركعتي الطواف[32] إلاَّ بعدما أشرقت الشمس. وقال غيره: بلغنا[33] ذلك.

وسئل عن الصلاة نصف النهار؟

قال: قال أبو النظر: يكره[34] نصف النهار في الصيف، وربما فعلناه في الشتاء، وقال: يكره[35] نصف النهار حتَّى تزول الشمس والشتاء ليس كالصيف.

وسئل عمَّن نسي الصلاة أو نام عنها؟

قال: يصلِّيها في ساعة واحدة الأُولى فالأُولى ولا يتطوّع بينهنَّ.

وسئل عمَّن نسي صلاة الظهر حتَّى دخل صلاة العصر؟

قال: إذا ذكر ذلك وقد صلَّى ثلاث ركعات فليقطعها وليصلِّ[36] الأولى ثُمَّ يصلِّ[37]

---

28 رواه الربيع، باب جامع الصلاة، ر٢٩٥، والبخاري، باب الصلاة بعد الفجر حتى ترتفع الشمس، ر٥٥٩.

29 نصف: ونصف، ب.

30 البيت: بالبيت، ب.

31 فلم: ولم، ب.

32 ركعتي الطواف: الركعتين، ب.

33 بلغنا: قد بلغنا، ب.

34 يكره: تكره، ب.

35 يكره: وتكره، ب.

36 وليُصَلِّ: وليصلي، ب د.

37 يُصَلِّ: يصلي، ب د.

العصر، وإن كان لم يتذكر حتَّى فرغ من العصر فليصلِّ[38] الظهر وقد مضت العصر.

وسئل عمَّن نسي العصر حتَّى غابت[39] الشمس؟
قال: يبدأ فيصلِّي العصر ثُمَّ يصلِّي المغرب.

وسئل عمَّن نسي العشاء حتَّى أصبح جدا، ثُمَّ ذكرها؟
قال: يبدأ بالعشاء وإن طلعت الشمس ثُمَّ يصلِّي الغداة، وهذا قول أبي عبيدة والربيع[40].
عن قتادة عن أبي الحرّ: أنَّ المسور[41] بن مخرمة دخل على ابن عبَّاس فأطال معه الحديث، ثُمَّ خرج من عنده ونام ابن عبَّاس فما[42] استيقظ ابن عبَّاس حتَّى سمع نداء الفجر[43]، فصلَّى العشاء ثُمَّ الوتر[44] ثُمَّ صلَّى ركعتي الفجر، ثُمَّ صلَّى الغداة، وقد كادت الشمس أن تطلع. وقال غيره: بلغنا ذلك.

عن قتادة عن معمر عن الزهري عن سعيد بن المسيب: أنَّ رسول الله ﷺ عرس بأصحابه في مرجعه من خيبر، وقال لبلال: «احفظ علينا[45] الصبح»، فما استيقظ حتَّى أشرقت الشمس، فقال رسول الله[46] ﷺ: «تحولوا من هذا المكان الذي أصابكم فيه

38 فليُصلِّ: فليصلي، ب د.
39 غابت: تغيب، ب.
40 والربيع: -،د.
41 المسور: المشهر،د.
42 فما: فلما،د.
43 الفجر: الضحى، ب.
44 ثم الوتر: أوتر، ب.
45 علينا: عنا، ب.
46 فقال رسول الله: نمت يا بلال؟ فقال: يا رسول الله، أخذ بنفسي ما أخذ بأنفسكم، ب.

هذه الغفلة»، ثُمَّ أمر رسول الله ﷺ مناديه، فأقام[47]: فصلَّى الصبح ثُمَّ قال: «من نسي صلاة فليصلِّها إذا ذكرها»؛ لأنَّ الله تعالى[48] يقول: ﴿وَأَقِمِ الصَّلَاةَ لِذِكْرِي﴾[49].

وقال غيره: كان أصحابنا يأخذون بهذا الحديث[50].

عن قتادة عن عبد الله بن رباح[51] عن أبي قتادة الأنصاري قال: بينما نحن مع رسول الله صلى الله عليه وسلم في بعض أسفاره إذ مال رسول الله صلى الله عليه وسلم عن راحلته فدعمته بيدي، ثُمَّ سرنا، فمال رسول الله صلى الله عليه وسلم عن راحلته فدعمته[52] فاستيقظ، فقال أبو قتادة: قلت: نعم، يا رسول الله. فقال: حفظك الله كما حفظتنا[53] منذ الليلة[54] فإني ما أرانا إلاَّ شققنا عليك، ثُمَّ قال رسول الله صلى الله عليه وسلم: «تنح بنا عن الطريق، أو مل بنا عن الطريق» وأناخ رسول الله صلى الله عليه وسلم راحلته، وأنخنا وتوسد كلّ واحد منا ذراع راحلته، فما استيقظنا حتَّى أشرقت الشمس[55].

قال: فذكرت صوت الصرد[56] فقلت: يا رسول الله، هلكنا[57] فاتتنا الصلاة، فقال

---

47 فأقام: فقال، ب.

48 تعالى: -،د.

49 سورة طه: ١٤؛ رواه البخاري، باب من نسي الصلاة فليصل إذا ذكرها، ر٥٧٢، ومسلم، باب قضاء الصلاة الفائتة واستحباب تعجيل قضائها، ر١٥٩٢. [وانظر: المدونة الكبرى لأبي غانم الخراساني، تحقيق:د. مصطفى باجو، ١/١٩٥].

50 بهذا الحديث: -، ب.

51 رباح: رياح، ب.

52 فدعمته: فدعمه، ب،د.

53 حفظتنا: حفظتني، ب.

54 منذ الليلة: من ذي الليلة،د،؛ من ذا الليلة، ب.

55 رواه عبد الرزاق، باب من نسي صلاة أو نام عنها، ر٢٢٤٠.

56 الصرد: السر، ب د.

57 هلكنا: أهلكنا، ب.

رسول الله ﷺ: «لم تهلكوا ولم تفتكم الصلاة، وإنّما تفوت اليقظان ولا تفوت[58] النائم»، ثُمَّ قال رسول الله: «هل من ماء؟» فأتيته بميضة[59] فيها ماء، ثُمَّ توضّأ رسول الله ﷺ ثُمَّ دفعها إليّ وفيها بقية من الماء، ثُمَّ قال: «احتفظ بها، فإنّه كائن لها نبأ» فأمر رسول الله ﷺ، بلالاً فأذن، فصلّى رسول الله ركعتين ثُمَّ تحول من مكانه فأمره فأقام الصلاة فصلّى صلاة الصبح، ثُمَّ قال رسول الله ﷺ: «إن كان الناس قد أطاعوا أبا بكر وعمر فقد رفقوا بأنفسهم، وإن كانوا خالفوهم فقد عنفوا بأنفسهم»[60].

قال: وكان[61] أبو بكر وعمر حين فقدوا رسول الله ﷺ، فقالا للناس: أقيموا بالماء حتّى تصبحوا، فأبوا عليهم فانتهى إليهم رسول الله ﷺ من آخر النهار وقد كادوا[62] يهلكون[63] عطشا، وقالوا: يا رسول الله، قد هلكنا، «فدعا رسول الله ﷺ بالميضة فأبطأها[64]، ثُمَّ دعا[65] بإناء فوق القدح ودون القعب[66] فجعل يصبّ في الإناء»، وشربنا حتّى شرب القوم كلّهم[67]، ثُمَّ نادى منادي[68] رسول الله ﷺ: «هل اكتفيتم[69]؟»

---

58 ولا تفوت: تفت، د؛ رواه أحمد،د، ر ٢٢٥٧٥.

59 المِيضَة والمِيضاة، تصحيف من المِيْضَأة بالهمز، وجمعها: مَواضِئ، وتعني: المَطْهَرة. انظر: الصفدي: تصحيح التصحيف وتحرير التحريف، ص: ١٠٢.

60 رواه أحمد، ر٢٢٦٢٨، وعبد الرزاق، باب النبوة، ر٢٠٥٣٨.

61 وكان: -، ب.

62 كادوا: كانوا، ب،د.

63 يهلكون: كادوا أن يهلكوا، ب.

64 فأبطأها: فأفضاها، ب.

65 دعا: أتى، ب.

66 القعب: -، ب. العقب:د.

67 وشربنا حتّى شرب القوم كلّهم: ويشرب القوم حتى شربنا وشربوا كلهم، ب.

68 منادي: -، ب.

69 اكتفيتم: من عال؟، ب.

فقالوا: بلى[70]، ثُمَّ رفع[71] النبيّ عليه الصلاة والسلام الميضة وفيها نحو مِمَّا كان فيها، قال: فسألناه كم كنتم؟ قال: مع أبي بكر وعمر ثمانون، وكنا مع رسول الله ﷺ اثنا عشر[72]»[73].

عن قتادة، عن أنس بن مالك[74] أن رسول الله ﷺ كان بالزوراء[75]، وقد حان وقت الصلاة فالتمس الناس وضوءا[76] فلم يجدوه[77]، فأُتي[78] رسول الله بإناء فيه ماء لا يغمر أصابعه ولا يواري أصابعه،[79] فوضع أصابع[80] كفِّه في الماء فجعل الماء ينبع من بين أصابع رسول الله ﷺ حتَّى توضَّأ القوم كلهم. فقلنا لأنس: كم كنتم؟ قال: كنَّا ثلاثمائة وأزيد[81] عن ثلاثمائة[82].

وعن صاحب له عن أبي الزبير عن جبير[83] بن مطعم عن أبي عبيدة عن عبد الله بن

70 فقالوا بلى: -، ب

71 رفع: دفع، ب.

72 مع أبي بكر وعمر ثمانون ألفا وكنا مع النبي اثنا عشر ألفا، هامش ب.

73 رواه أحمد، ر٢٢٦٢٨.

74 قال: +،د.

75 أن رسول الله ﷺ كان بالزوراء: -، ب.

76 وضوءا: وضوء، ب،د.

77 حان وقت الصلاة فالتمس الناس وضوء فلم يجدوه: -، ب.

78 فأتي: فأوتي، ب،د.

79 فأمر أصحابه فقال: توضؤوا: +، ب.

80 أصابع: -،د.

81 وأزيد: وأنها، ب.

82 رواه الربيع، باب جامع الوضوء، ر١٣١، والبخاري، باب علامات النبوة في الإسلام، ر٣٣٧٩.

83 نافع: -،د.

مسعود قال: «كنا مع رسول الله ﷺ فحبسنا عن صلاة الظهر والعصر والمغرب والعشاء، فاشتد ذلك علي فقلت: نحن مع رسول الله ﷺ وفي سبيل الله، فأمر رسول الله ﷺ بلالا فأقام فصلى بنا الظهر، ثم أقام فصلى العصر، ثم أقام فصلى المغرب، ثم أقام فصلى العشاء، ثم طاف علينا فقال: ما على الأرض عصابة يذكرون الله غيركم»[84].

سئل عن رجل سبقه الإمام بركعة أو ركعتين؟

قال: ما أدركت فصله مع الإمام وإذا سلم الإمام قمت وقضيت ما سبقك به، إن كان فيه قراءة وبدأت بأوّل الصلاة حتّى تنتهي إلى ما أدركت مع الإمام.

عن قتادة عن [أبي] رافع عن أبي هريرة: أنَّ رسول الله ﷺ قال: «إذا أقيمت[85] الصلاة فلا يَسعَ أحدكم، وليمش وعليه السكينة والوقار، فليصل ما أدرك وليقض ما سبق به»[86].

وقال غيره: قد بلغنا ذلك.

وسئل عن رجل أدرك سجدة واحدة مع الإمام ولم يدرك غيرها؟

قال: يلحق ما فاته إلى ما أدرك مع الإمام سجدة أو ركعة أو أقل من ذلك أو أكثر.

سئل عن رجل يسبقه الإمام ببعض صلاته فينهض إذا سلم الإمام؟

قال: حدَّثني[87] أيُّوب عن نافع أنَّ ابن عمر كان إذا سبق بشيء من صلاته قام إذا سلم

---

84 رواه النسائي، كيف يقضي الفائت من الصلاة، ر١٥٨٩، وأحمد، ر٤٠١٣.

85 أقيمت: أقامت، ب.

86 رواه الربيع، باب في صلاة الجماعة والقضاء في الصلاة، ر٢١٧، والبخاري، باب لا يسعى إلى الصلاة وليأت بالسكينة والوقار، ر٦١٠.

87 عن: +، د.

الإمام فإذا لم يسبقه الإمام لم ينهض حتَّى يكون من الإمام تحرك وانفتال أو أقوال[88].

[89]وبلغنا عن عثمان بن عتَّاب – شيخ من بني راشد – أن طلحة والزبير صليّا في مسجد من مساجدهم، فلمَّا قام المؤذِّن قلنا لهم: ليتقدّم أحدكما، قالا: أين إمامكم؟ فلم يتقدّم أحدهما حتَّى تقدّم الإمام، فلمَّا صلوا قالا: كلّ صلاتكم كانت حسنة إلاَّ شيئا رأيناكم تصنعونه، قام أحدكم قبل أن يكون من الإمام تحرك أو انفتال[90].

قال: يكره أن يقوم أحدكم حتَّى يحرف[91] الإمام أو ينفتل[92]، سبق أو لم يسبق، ويؤمّر الإمام إذا سلم أن ينفتل أو يحرف[93] من مجلسه أو يقوم.

سئل عن رجل صلَّى الظهر أو العصر، ثُمَّ أدرك الصلاة مع الإمام، أيصلِّي معه؟

قال: نعم، صنع ذلك جابر بن زيد.

سئل عن رجل صلَّى في جماعة، ثُمَّ قعد في مسجد قوم فأقيمت الصلاة وهو فيه[94].

قال: إذا حضرته[95] الإقامة فليصلِّ معهم.

سئل عن قوم انتهوا إلى مسجد، وقد صلَّى أهله جماعة؟

---

88 تحرك وانتقال أو أقوال: تحريك أو انفتال أو إقبال، ب.

89 وقال غيره بلغنا ذلك: +، ب.

90 انتقال: انفتال، ب.

91 يحرف: يتحرف، ب.

92 ينفتل: يتقبل، ب.

93 يحرف: يتحرف، ب،د.

94 فيه: فيها، ب.

95 حضرته: اضطرته، ب.

قال: يصلون فرادى وليس عليهم أذان[96] ولا إقامة.

قال أبو النضر: لا بأس إذا كان المسجد على ظهر الطريق، وليس له[97] مؤذن ولا إمام أن يجيء قوم فيؤذنوا ويقيموا[98] الصلاة[99] ويصلوا، ثُمَّ يجيء آخرون فيقيموا[100] ويصلوا[101]، فأما مسجد على غير طريق، فليس لقوم أن يجمعوا فيه[102] وعسى ألا[103] يكون بذلك بأس، فأما مسجد تجمع فيه الصلوات فلا.

سئل عن رجل سبقه الإمام بركعة، فنسي أن يقضي حتَّى تطوّع؟

قال: يعيد صلاته.

سئل عن رجل نسي ركعة من صلاته حتَّى قام في التطوّع.

قال: عليه الإعادة إن كان ركع أو سجد أو انصرف[104]، فإن كان[105] ذكرها حين قام ولم يقرأ[106] فليصلها وليعتدَّ بها.

وسئل عن رجل سبقه الإمام بركعة فظنَّ أن الإمام قد سلم فقام يقضي الركعة؟

---

96 أذان: آذان، ب،د.

97 له: لها، ب،د.

98 فيؤذنوا ويقيموا: فيؤذنون ويقيمون، ب د.

99 الصلاة: -،د.

100 فيقيموا: فيأذنون، ب؛ فيقيمون،د.

101 ويصلوا: ويصلون، ب د.

102 فيه: فيها، ب،د.

103 ألا: أن لا ، ب د.

104 انصرف: فانصرف، ب.

105 كان: -، ب.

106 يقرأ: فيها، ب.

قال: يعتد بها وليسجد سجدتي الوهم ما لم يتشهد وهو ينويها تطوّعا.

سئل عن رجل يلقن الإمام في صلاته؟

قال: لا بأس.

سئل عن سجدتي الوهم؟

قال: هما على من قرأ وهو لا ينبغي له أن يقرأ، أو سكت وهو ينبغي له أن يقرأ، أو قام وهو ينبغي له أن يقعد، أو قعد وهو ينبغي له أن يقوم، فليسجد سجدتي الوهم.

سئل عن رجل شك في صلاته فلم يدر ثلاثا صلّى أم اثنتين؟

قال: يعتد بما يستيقن[107] ويسجد سجدتي الوهم.

سئل عمّن سها خلف الإمام؟

قال: عليه سجدتا[108] الوهم إن كان خلف الإمام.

قلت: فإن وهم الإمام ولم يوهم المأموم[109]؟

قال: على الإمام الوهم وليس على من خلفه، إنّمَا الوهم على من نسي أو وهم.

سئل عن سجدتي الوهم: أيتشهد فيهما[110]؟

قال: ليس فيهما تشهد، إنّمَا يسلم على النبيّ عليه الصلاة والسلام وينصرف.

107 يستيقن: استيقن، ب.

108 سجدتا: سجدتي، ب.

109 المأموم: من خلفه، ب.

110 فيهما: لهما، ب.

سئل عمَّن وهم ونسي وقام ولم يسجد سجدتي الوهم حتَّى خرج من المسجد؟
قال: يقضيهما في دبر صلاة أخرى فريضة أو تطوّع[111].

سئل عمَّن سبقه الإمام بركعة في أيَّام التشريق: أيُكبِّر إذا انصرف الإمام، ثُمَّ يقضي الركعة أم يقضي الركعة ثُمَّ يُكبِّر؟
قال: يقضي ما فاته من صلاته، ولم يكن جابر يرى[112] ذلك التكبير لازما[113].
ولا عليه من وهم الإمام شيء فليقم وليتم صلاته.

سئل عن إمام قوم أحدث في صلاته؟
قال: ينفتل فيقدم رَجُلا فيصلِّي بهم ما بقي من صلاتهم[114].

سئل عن رجل صلَّى بقوم وهو غير طاهر؟
قال: أجزت عنهم[115] ويعيد هو صلاته، وإن ذكر وقد صلَّى ركعة أو ركعتين انفتل، وقدم رجلا واعتدوا بما مضى من صلاتهم ما لم يكن من جنابة، فإن كان من جنابة[116]

---

111 +: ب: قال أبو زيد عبد الرحمن بن سليمان الزواري – رحمه –: هذا قول قتادة ولم يأخذ أصحابنا بهذا من قوله بل قول أبيّ –رحمه الله–، من أصحابنا أن يعيد صلاته ولا يعبد الله على الشك ولا يجوز الزيادة في الصلاة ولا النقصان منها إلا أنه يبني على اليقين في الأولى ثُمَّ يعيدها أيضا انتهى وجدته بخطه: هامش، ب.

112 جابر يرى: –،د.

113 لازما: لازم،د؛ لازم: –، ب.

114 ثم يتشهد ثُمَّ يقوم فيصلي ما سبق به ثُمَّ يقعد فيسلم بهم ولا يسلمون، حتى يفرغ مهما بقي عليه حين فرغ من صلاته ثُمَّ يسلم بهم: +، ب. قال أبو زيد –رحمه الله–: هذا أيضا لا يؤخذ به وهو قول الربيع المتقدم: هامش، ب.

115 عنهم: عليهم، ب.

116 من جنابة: –،د.

أعاد الإمام وأعادوا. وبلغني أنَّ عمر بن الخطّاب رضي الله عنه وعليًا[117] صنعا ذلك، وإن كان من غير جنابة أعاد الإمام ومضت صلاة من خلفه.

سئل عن رجل دخل مع قوم في صلاتهم فنعس حتَّى ركع الإمام وسجد؟
قال: يتبع الإمام في صلاته وليعتد بها؛ لأنَّه قد صنع الناس ذلك في الجمعة والزحام.

سئل عن رجل انتهى إلى قوم في آخر صلاتهم؟
فحدّثنا عن قتادة قال: إذا أدركهم في آخر صلاتهم فليقعد ولا يُكبّر، وقال غيره مثل ذلك، وإن كبر ودخل في صلاتهم فقد دخل، وقد يقال: من أدرك تشهد إمام يوم الجمعة فكبر وتشهد فعليه ركعتان[118].
وكان قتادة يقول[119]: إذا أدرك الإمام جالسا في الركعتين الأوليين كبر ثُمَّ جلس، وإذا أدركهم في آخر صلاتهم جلس من غير أن يُكبّر، فإذا فرغ الإمام قام[120] يستأنف الصلاة، وقال غيره: أي ذلك فعل فهو جائز.

سئل عن رجل انتهى إلى قوم وهم يصلون العصر، فدخل معهم في صلاتهم وهو يرى أنَّها الظهر ولم يكن صلَّى الظهر؟
قال: إن صلَّى معهم العصر وهو يرى أنَّها الظهر فليعد الظهر والعصر، وإن ذكر وعرف أنَّهم يصلون العصر فلينصرف ثُمَّ يصلِّ الأولى ثُمَّ العصر ما لم يتشهد فذلك عليه، إلاَّ أن يكون قد انصرف من العصر ويرى أنَّها العصر، فإن كان دخل وهو ينوي

117 وعليا: وعلي، ب.
118 ركعتان: ركعتين، ب.
119 يقول: –، ب.
120 فرغ الإمام قام: –، ب. سلم: +، ب.

الأو لى وهم يصلو ن العصر فليعد هما جميعا.

سئل عن إمام قام في الركعتين؟

قال: [121] حدَّثني عن عليّ بن ثابت عن نافع بن الزبير: أنَّ الزبير [122] قام في الركعتين فسبح القوم فلم يجلس، ومضى في صلاته، فلمّا قضى صلاته سجد سجدتي الوهم.

قال: فذكر ثابت [123] لابن عمر فما أعاب عليه شيئا وكان [124] ينبغي أن يقعد فيتشهد ويسجد سجدتي الوهم إذا سلم؛ لأنّه لا تتمّ صلاته إلاَّ بالتشهُّد.

عن أبي معشر عن النخعي قال: يجلس ما لم يفتتح القراءة. قال: وإن افتتح القراءة، قال يقعد أحبّ إليَّ.

سئل عن رجل وهم في صلاته فلم يدر [125] أزاد أو نقص؟

قال [126]: عن يحيى بن [أبي] كثير عن عياض بن هلال عن أبي سعيد الخدري: أنَّ رسول الله ﷺ قال: «إذا جاء أحدكم الشيطان في صلاته [127]، فقال قد أحدثت، فليقل قد كذبت إلاَّ من وجد ريحًا نافحة أو صوتا باديا» [128].

قال: نعم، قد بلغنا هذا عن أصحابنا.

121 قال: -، ب.

122 أن الزبير: -،د.

123 ثابت: ذلك، ب.

124 قال: -،د.

125 يدر: يدري، ب،د.

126 قال: -، ب.

127 في صلاته: -،د.

128 رواه أبو داود، باب من قال يتم على أكبر ظنه، ر١٠٣١، وابن حبان، باب سجود السهو، ر٢٦٦٥. بلفظ: «... فَلْيَقُلْ كَذَبْتَ إِلاَّ مَا وَجَدَ رِيحًا بِأَنْفِهِ أَوْ صَوْتًا بِأُذُنِهِ».

سئل عن إمام صلَّى الظهر خمس ركعات؟

قال: يعيد ولا زيادة فيها ولا نقصان، ويسجد سجدتي الوهم.

سئل عن رجل تكلم، وقد بقي عليه من صلاته وهو يحسب أنَّه قد فرغ؟

قال: من تكلم أو أدبر بالقبلة فليعد صلاته.

سئل عن رجل نسي أن يسجد[129] سجدة من أوَّل صلاته؟

قال: يعيد صلاته.

سئل عن رجل صلَّى ثلاث ركعات، ثُمَّ انفتل فدخل في التطوّع؟

قال: إذا دخل في التطوّع وقرأ؛ فليعد صلاته.

سئل عن رجل أمَّ قوما في صلاة المغرب، فقرأ في نفسه؟

قال: أجزته وأجزتهم جميعا[130].

عن قتادة: أنَّ عمر بن الخطَّاب صلَّى بالناس المغرب فلم يقرأ فيها[131]، فلمَّا انصرف، قال رجل: يا أمير المؤمنين، صلَّيت ولم تقرأ، فقال عمر: عير جهزتها إلى الشام، وأنزلتها منازلها حتَّى أقدمتها إلى الشام أو دمشق، فرجع وأعاد بالناس الصلاة وقرأ فيها.

وبلغنا: أنَّه قيل له: يا أمير المؤمنين، قرأت في نفسك. قال: لا. ولو قرأ في نفسه لاجتزأ بها[132].

129 أن يسجد: -، ب.

130 أجزته وأجزتهم جميعا: إن كان قرأ في نفسه أجزاه وأجزاهم جميعا، ب.

131 فيها: -، ب.

132 لأجزته، ب. بها: -، ب.

سئل عن القراءة في الظهر والعصر؟

قال: ليس فيهما قراءة إلاّ بفاتحة القرآن[133]؟ قال: لا تجوز صلاته إلاّ بفاتحة الكتاب[134].

سئل عن رجل صلّى الصبح فقرأ في الركعة الواحدة[135] ونسي أن يقرأ في الأخرى؟

قال: عليه الإعادة، وفي المغرب مثل ذلك.

سئل عن رجل قرأ سورة في صلاته، فلمّا فرغ ذكر أنّه لم يقرأ فاتحة الكتاب؟

قال: لا تجوز صلاته إلاّ بفاتحة الكتاب، فإن ذكرها قبل أن يركع فليقرأها وليقرأ سورة معها.

سئل عن رجل صلّى ركعتين من المكتوبة، ثمّ انصرف ناسيا؟

قال: يصلّي ما بقي عليه من صلاته، ما لم يتكلم، ويسجد سجدتي الوهم وهو جالس، وكان يقال إذا انصرف وأدبر بالقبلة فليعد.

سئل هل يحتبي الرجل[136] في صلاته صلاة التطوّع[137]؟

قال: إذا كان يصلّي جالسا فليحتبِ[138] إن شاء.

وقال: دخلت على أبي عبيدة وهو يصلّي محتبيا.

---

133 القران: الكتاب، ب.

134 قال: لا تجوز صلاته إلاّ بفاتحة الكتاب: –، د.

135 الواحدة: الأولى، ب.

136 هل يحتبي الرجل: عن الرجل هل يحتبي، ب.

137 صلاة التطوع: –، ب.

138 فليحتب: فليحتبي، ب، د.

سئل عن صلاة الليل والنهار تطوّعا؟

قال: يصلّي ما فتح الله[139] له.

عن أيُّوب عن نافع عن ابن عمر أن رسول الله ﷺ كان يصلّي ركعتين قبل الظهر، وركعتين بعد الظهر، وركعتين بعد المغرب إذا رجع إلى بيته[140]، وركعتين بعد العشاء في بيته[141] وركعتين قبل الغداة عند طلوع الفجر، وركعتين بعد الجمعة في بيته[142].

قال: كان أصحابنا يستحبّون من ذلك عشر ركعات.

سئل عن رجل يصلّي الفجر[143] وهو يجد الأذى من الغائط والبول؟

قال: حدّثنا عن قتادة: أنَّ عمر بن الخطّاب رضي الله عنه قال: لا يصلِّ أحدكم وهو يدافع الأخبثين من الغائط والبول[144]. قال: مالم يعجله عن صلاته فلا بأس.

سئل عن دعاء الرجل[145] في صلاته؟

قال: القراءة في القيام[146]، والتسبيح في الركوع والسجود،[147] والدعاء في الجلوس،

---

139 الله: -، ب.

140 إلى بيته: -، ب.

141 في بيته: -، ب.

142 في بيته: -، ب. رواه الربيع، باب في سبحة الضحى وتبردة الظهر، ر١٩٨، والبخاري، باب الصلاة بعد الجمعة وقبلها، ر٨٩٥.

143 الفجر: -، ب.

144 رواه الربيع عن ابن عباس، باب جامع الصلاة، ر٢٩٨.

145 عن دعاء الرجل: عن رجل يدعو، ب.

146 القيام: القنوت، ب.

147 الخشوع: -، ب.

إذا فرغت من التشهُّد في آخر الصلاة، فاسأل[148] عما ما بدا لك من أمر الآخرة، فإذا فرغت فاسأل[149] عن دينك ودنياك. وفي التطوّع اسأل قائما أو جالسا[150] أو كيف شئت لآخرتك.

سئل عن الرجل يرفع يديه في الدعاء؟

قال: لم أرَ[151] أحدا من أصحابنا يرفع يديه رفعا شديدا، إلاَّ حاجبا[152] كان يرفع يديه في الموقف رفعا شديدا وقال: كان أحدهم يشير بأصبعه[153].

عن قتادة عن سعيد بن المسيب قال: ثلاثة مِمَّا أحدث الناس: اختصار السجود، ورفع الأيدي، والأصوات في الدعاء.

قال: كان هذا مكروها عند الفقهاء.

سئل عن الرجل يؤمّ القوم في بيت غيره؟

قال: إذا أذن له ربّ البيت فلا بأس.

عن قتادة عن أبي مضرة عن أبي سعيد[154] الأنصاري: أنَّه دعا أبا ذرّ وابن مسعود وحذيفة، فحضرت الصلاة فتقدّم أبو ذرّ فقال حذيفة: وراءك ربّ البيت أحقّ بالإمامة منك، قال أبو ذرّ: كذلك يا بن مسعود؟ قال: نعم، فتأخر وتقدّم ربّ البيت فصلّى بهم.

148 فاسأل: فسأل، ب،د.
149 فاسأل: فسأل، ب،د.
150 ساجدا: –، ب.
151 أر: أرى، ب،د.
152 حاجبا: حاجب، ب.
153 وقال: كان أحدهم يشير بأصبعه: –،د.
154 الأنصاري صنع طعاما فدعا: + هامش، ب.

قال: كانوا لا يستحبّون ذلك إلاَّ بإذن ربّ البيت، وقد كان ابن عمر يصلّي بنا في منازلنا إذا أمرناه بذلك.

سئل عن العبد: هل يؤمّ بالقوم؟
قال: إذا كان العبد أقرأهم لكتاب الله أمهم.

سئل عن الثلاثة يجتمعون فتحضرهم الصلاة أو الاثنين؟
قال: فليؤمّهم أقرؤهم.

سئل عن ثلاثة حضرتهم الصلاة وهم في القراءة سواء؟
قال: يؤمّهم أسنهم، فإن كانوا في السن سواء. قال: أفقههم أحقّ أن يؤمّهم.

سئل عن الإمام تحضره الصلاة ولا يحضر معه إلاَّ رجل واحد[155] وامرأة؟
قال: قال صالح الدهان[156]: يكونون مثل عرف الديك، يقف الرجل وراء الرجل والمرأة خلف ذلك.

سئل: متى يؤمر الصبيّ بالصلاة؟
قال: يؤمّر ابن سبع سنين وثمان وتسع، ويضرب ابن عشر على تركها.
عن يونس بن عبيد [157] [بن دينار] عن أبي العالية الرياحي: أنَّ عمر بن الخطّاب رضي الله عنه قال: «الطفل لا تكتب حسناته ولا تكتب سيئاته إلى اثنتي عشرة سنة، فإذا

155 واحد: -،د.
156 الدهان: -، ب.
157 عبيد: عبيدة، ب د.

بلغها كتبت عليه جميعا»[158].

قال: الله أعلم، أمّا أصحابنا فإنّهم يقولون: إذا بلغ الحلُم أو بلغ أترابه.

سئل عن الرجل: كيف يفتتح الصلاة؟

قال: عن أبي معشر عن النخعي عن علقمة بن قيس عن أيُّوب بن يزيد: أنّ عمر بن الخطّاب رضي الله عنه كان إذا كبّر قال: «سبحانك اللّهمّ وبحمدك، تبارك اسمك، وتعالى جدّك ولا إله غيرك»، يسمع من يليه.

قال: يفتتح بهذا، ثمّ يُكبّر، ثمّ يستعيذ[159] من الشيطان الرجيم.

عن أبي عبيدة سئل عن رجل يصلّي[160] فيفتتح السورة ولا يقرأ بسم الله الرحمن الرحيم؟

قال: كانوا يجُوّزون إذا قرأ سورتين في الركعة.

سئل عن قول[161] أبي معشر النخعي: أربعة يخفيهن الإمام: بسم الله الرحمن الرحيم، والاستعاذة، وآمين عند خاتمة فاتحة الكتاب،[162] و(ربنا ولك الحمد) عند رفع رأسه من الركوع؟

قال: يجهر ببسم الله الرحمن الرحيم، وأمّا (آمين) فلا نعرفه، وإن جهر باسم (ربنا ولك الحمد)، حتّى يسمع من على يمينه فلا بأس.

---

158 تكتب حسنات الصبي ولا تكتب سيئاته إلى اثني عشر سنة، ب؛ رواه أبو يوسف في الآثار، ر٨٧٩، بلفظ: عن الحسن، أنه قال في الصبي: «إذا كان ابن اثنتي عشرة سنة كتب له حسناته، ولم يكتب عليه سيئاته، حتى إذا أدرك كتب له حسناته وكتب عليه سيئاته».

159 يتعوذ بالله، ب.

160 يصلي: -، د.

161 سئل عن قول: -، ب.

162 اللّهم: +، ب.

سئل عن الاستعاذة؛ متى هي؟

قال: الاستعاذة بعد التوجيه وقبل فاتحة الكتاب.

عن أبي يزيد المدني عن عكرمة: أنَّ رجلا سأل ابن عبّاس عن القراءة في الظهر والعصر؟ قال: «قرأ رسول الله صلى الله عليه وسلم في الصلوات وسكت»[163]، فتقرأ فيما فيه قرأ، وتسكت فيما سكت فيه.

فقال له الرجل: لعلَّ رسول الله صلى الله عليه وسلم كان يقرأ في نفسه؟ فغضب ابن عبّاس، فقال له: أتتَّهم رسول الله عليه الصلاة والسلام؟

قال: نعم[164] قال: كانوا يقولون لو كان فيهما قراءة الجهر لجهر فيهما كما يجهر في غيرهما، وقال: الإمام ومن خلفه يقرأون بفاتحة الكتاب وحدها في الظهر والعصر[165] ويسبح ما بدا له.

عن قتادة: أنَّ عمر بن الخطَّاب قال: «لا بُدَّ للمسلم من ستِّ سُور يتعلَّمهنَّ: سورتين لصلاة الغداة، وسورتين لصلاة المغرب، وسورتين لصلاة العشاء».

قال: هذا كلّه حسن ينبغي له أن يفعله.

عن قتادة: أنَّ[166] أنس بن مالك صلَّى بالناس الصبح فقرأ آل عمران، وقد كادت الشمس أن تطلع. فقال: لو طلعت ما وجدتنا غافلين. قال: وبلغنا عن أبي بكر أنَّه قرأ بالبقرة.

163 رواه أحمد، ر٣٠٩٢، والطبراني: المعجم الكبير، ر١٢٠٠٥.

164 قال نعم: +، ب. رواه أحمد، ر١٨٨٧، بدون ذكر: «قال: نعم».

165 وحدها في الظهر والعصر: +، ب.

166 أن: عن، ب.

عن قتادة عن أيّوب: أنّ عمر بن الخطّاب كان يكثر القراءة في صلاة الصبح بالأحزاب[167].

سئل عن القراءة خلف الإمام؟

قال: إذا أدركت الإمام وقد فرغ من فاتحة الكتاب لا تقرأها وإذا دخلت وهو يقرأها[168] إذا سبقك بها فأنصت إلى القرآن.

وكان يقول[169]: كلّ صلاة لا يقرأ فيها بأم القرآن[170] فهي خداج[171] لم تتم.

عن أيّوب عن أبي قلابة: أنّ رسول الله ﷺ صلّى بأصحابه، فلمّا فرغ من صلاته أقبل عليهم بوجهه فقال: «لعلكم[172] تقرؤون في صلاتكم خلف الإمام والإمام يقرأ»، قال لهم ذلك ثلاث مرّات، فقال بعضهم: «إنا نفعل ذلك يا رسول الله، « . قال: «فلا تفعلوا ولكن ليقرأ أحدكم بفاتحة الكتاب في نفسه»[173].

سئل عن رفع الأيدي في التكبير[174]؟

قال: ما رأيت أحدا من الفقهاء يرفع يديه حين يدخل في الصلاة، ولا بعد ذلك، إلاّ المغيرة المصري، فقد كان يفعل ذلك.

---

167 يقول يا نساء النبي: +، ب.

168 يقرأها: فاقرأها، ب.

169 يقول: يقال، ب.

170 بأم القران: بفاتحة الكتاب، ب.

171 خداج: خداجة أي، ب.

172 لعلكم: -، ب.

173 رواه أحمد، ر١٨٠٩٥، وابن حبان، باب صفة الصلاة، ر١٨٤٤.

174 التكبير: الصلاة، ب.

عن قتادة عن عكرمة قال: قلت لابن عبَّاس: صلَّيت بالأبطح خلف الشيخ، وجمع صلاة الظهر والعصر[175] فكبر فيهما اثنتين وعشرين تكبيرة، يُكبّر إذا سجد وإذا رفع رأسه من السجود كبر[176].

قال ابن عبَّاس: لا أم لك، تلك صلاة أبي القاسم. قال: نعم، يُكبّر كلما رفع رأسه وسجد[177].

سئل عن تسبيح الرجل في صلاته؟

قال: حدَّثنا الربيع أن تسبيح الرجل في الركوع والسجود: سبحان الله وبحمده، كانوا لا[178] يزيدون على ذلك شيئا.

سئل عن حدّ السجود ما هو؟

قال: إذا أمكن الرجل جبهته من الأرض، فقد قضى ما عليه من السجود.

سئل عن النفخ في الصلاة والتمطي؟

قال: يكره ذلك.

سئل عن كيفية[179] السجود؟

قال: عن عمرو بن دينار عن طاؤوس عن ابن عبَّاس: أنَّ رسول الله ﷺ قال:

---

175 والعصر: –، ب.

176 كبر: –، ب.

177 وسجد: ويسجد، ب.

178 كانوا لا: لم يكونوا، ب.

179 كيفية: كم، ب.

أُمِرتُ أَن أَسجُدَ عَلَى سَبعَةِ أعضَاءٍ ولاَ أَكُفَّ شَعرًا ولاَ ثَوبًا»[180]، يعني بالسبعة: الكفين، والركبتين، والقدمين، والجبهة.

قال: كذلك بلغنا عن عمر بن الخطّاب رضي الله عنه أنَّ نبيَّ الله ﷺ قال: «إنَّ الله أمر[181] ابن آدم أن يسجد[182] للعبادة[183] على سبعة أعضاء؛ على جبهته وقدميه وركبتيه وكفيه»[184].

سئل عن السجود على الثوب إذا كان الحصى حارا؟

قال: لا بأس. وفي الثلج مثل ذلك.

سئل عن الرجل يسوي الحصباء[185] لجبهته إذا أراد أن يسجد؟

قال: لا بأس بالتسوية، وكان[186] قتادة يسويه مرة واحدة في الصلاة[187].

عن عبد الله بن دينار عن الحسن: أنَّ النبيّ ﷺ، إذا سجد انتصب على[188] أطراف أصابعه وركبتيه، وجافى بين يديه حتَّى يرى بياض إبطيه[189].

---

180 رواه البخاري، كتاب صفة الصلاة، باب لا يكف ثوبه في الصلاة، ر٧٨٣. ومسلم، كتاب الصلاة، باب أعضاء السجود والنهي عن كف الشعر...، ر١١٢٤.

181 أمر: وجه، ب.

182 أن يسجد: -، ب.

183 في السجود: +، ب.

184 البخاري بمعناه، كتاب صفة الصلاة، باب السجود على سبعة أعظم، ر٧٨٣. ومسلم، كتاب الصلاة، باب أعضاء السجود والنهي عن كف الشعر...، ر١١٢٤.

185 الحصباء: الحصاء، ب.

186 وكان: وعن، ب.

187 قال نعم: +، ب.

188 على: -، ب.

189 رواه البخاري، باب صفة النبي صلى الله عليه وسلم، ر٣٣٧١، ومسلم، باب مَا يَجْمَعُ صِفَةَ الصَّلَاةِ

قال: يتجافى، يفسح يديه عن جنبيه لا يضمهما[190] على فخذيه.

عن قتادة: [191] أنَّ ابن مسعود رأى رجلين أحدهما يجر إزاره والآخر يصلِّي ولا يركع، فضحك، فقالوا: ما أضحكك[192] يا أبا عبد الرحمن؟ قال[193]: أضحكني رجلان؛ أمَّا أحدهما لا ينظر الله إليه[194]، والآخر لا يقبل الله صلاته[195].

قال أبو النضر: صاحب الإزار هو الذي لا ينظر الله إليه، قال[196] بلغنا هذا عن ابن مسعود وهو كما قال.

عن القاسم بن عمرو عن مُحَمَّد بن عليّ: أنَّ رسول الله ﷺ مر برجل يقنع برأسه[197]. فقال: «إن مات هذا وهكذا صلاته، لمات على غير دين[198]» [199]. قال أبو النضر: بلغني أنَّه كان ينكت في صلاته.

وَمَا يُفْتَتَحُ بِهِ وَيُخْتَمُ بِهِ، ر١١٣٤.

190 يضمهما: ويضعهما، ب.

191 عن حذيفة بن اليماني، رأى رجلا يصلي ولا يركع كأنه بعير نافر، فقال: لو مات هذا أو هكذا صلاته، لمات على غير سنة الإسلام. قال: نعم، ب.

192 أضحكك: يضحكك، ب.

193 قال: فقال، ب.

194 في الدنيا ولا في الآخرة: +، ب.

195 والآخر لا يقبل الله صلاته: وأما الآخر فلا يقبل الله منه صلاته، ب.

196 قد: +، ب.

197 قال أبو النضر: يعني ينكث في صلاته: +، ب.

198 الإسلام، قال: نعم: +، ب.

199 رواه ابن أبي شيبة، في الرجل ينقص صلاته وما ذكر فيه وكيف يصنع، ر٢٩٦٩.

عن قتادة قال: ذكر لنا[200]: أنّ رسول الله ﷺ قال: «شرُّ[201] الناس سرقةً: الذي[202] يسرق من صلاته»، قالوا: كيف يسرق من صلاته؟[203] قال: «لا يتمّ ركوعها ولا سجودها»[204]. قال: نعم[205].

عن قتادة قال: ذكر لنا: أنّ رسول الله ﷺ قال: «إنّ أوّل ما يحاسب به العبد من عمله[206] يوم القيامة: صلاته، فإن صلحت فقد أفلح وأنجح، وإن فسدت فقد خاب وخسر»[207]. قال: نعم[208].

عن قتادة عن جابر بن عبد الله الأنصاري: عن[209] رسول الله ﷺ أنّه[210] قال: «لَيسَ بَيْنَ الْعَبدِ وَالْكُفرِ إلاّ تَركُهُ الصَّلاَة»[211].

سئل عن رجل رفع رأسه من الركوع، فلم يقم قائمًا حتّى سجد أو رفع رأسه من السجود

200 قال: ذكر لنا: -، ب.

201 شر: أشر، ب.

202 الذي: من، ب.

203 قالوا: كيف يسرق من صلاته؟: -، د.

204 رواه أحمد، ر١١٥٤٩، ٣/٥٦، والبيهقي، كتاب الصلاة، باب ما روي فيمن يسرق من صلاته فلا يتمها، ر٣٨٠٩.

205 قال نعم: -، د.

206 عمله: غدا، ب.

207 رواه الترمذي، أبواب الصلاة، باب ما جاء أن أول ما يحاسب به العبد يوم القيامة الصلاة، ر٤١٣. والنسائي، كتاب الصلاة، باب المحاسبة على الصلاة، ر٤٦٥.

208 قال: نعم: -، د.

209 عن: أن، ب.

210 أنه: -، ب.

211 رواه الربيع، عن ابن عباس بلفظه، كتاب الصلاة ووجوبها، باب جامع الصلاة، ر٣٠٣، ١/٧٨. وأبو داود، عن جابر بن عبد الله مثله، كتاب السنة، باب في رد الإرجاء، ر٤٦٧٨، ٤/٢١٩.

فلم يستوِ[212] جالسا حتّى سجد؟

قال: يعيد صلاته.

سئل عمَّن سجد ويداه في الثوب ولا يفضي بهما إلى الأرض؟

قال: لا بأس بذلك ما لم يكن ذلك اتقاء على يديه من التراب.

سئل عن الرجل يسجد على البساط؟

فحدَّث[213] قتادة قال: سألت سعيد بن المسيب عن الصلاة على الطنفسة؟ قال: مُحدَث. قال: قلت فالحصيرة؟ قال: سنة. قال: ما كان من نبات الأرض فلا بأس عليه، وما كان من صوف أو شعر فإنّه يكره.

سئل عن السجود على كور العمامة؟

قال: يكره.

سئل عن رجل كان بجبهته جرح؟

قال: إن خاف على جرحه صلَّى قاعدا أو أومأ برأسه إيماء.

سئل عن رجل يثني رجليه[214] في صلاته؟

قال: لا، ولكن يقعد على الأرض، وتكون رجله اليسرى تحت أليته اليمنى.

سئل عن المرأة: كيف تسجد؟

---

212 يستوِ: يستوي، ب،د.

213 عن: +، ب.

214 رجليه: رجله، ب.

قال: إذا سجدت التصقت[215] بالأرض وتتورّك إذا قعدت.

عن قتادة قال: ذكر لنا أنَّ نبيَّ الله عليه الصلاة والسلام: «نهى أن يصلّي الرجل وهو مختصر بيديه على حقويه»[216]. وكان يقال: إنَّه مختصر[217] اليهود، وكان ينهى أن يصلّي وهو عاقد شعره من ورائه[218]. وكان يقال: إنَّه كفل الشيطان، وكان ينهى أن يقعيَ[219] الرجل في صلاته[220]، وكان يقال: إنَّها قعية الشيطان.

قال: نعم، هذا كله يكره.

سئل عن التشهُّد؟

قال: كان الفقهاء يقولون: «التحيَّات المباركات لله، والصلوات الطيِّبات، السلام على النبيّ ورحمة الله وبركاته، وسلام علينا وعلى عباد الله الصالحين، أشهد أن لا إله إلاَّ الله وحده لا شريك له، وأشهد أن محمَّدًا عبده ورسوله»[221]. هذا عن ابن عبَّاس وجابر بن زيد، وكان يستحبّ إذا سلّم أن يدعو بدعاء ما في كتاب الله: ﴿رَبَّنَا[222] آتِنَا فِي الدُّنْيَا حَسَنَةً وَفِي الْآخِرَةِ حَسَنَةً وَقِنَا عَذَابَ النَّارِ﴾[223]، وزيِّن الإيمان في قلوبنا،

---

215 التصقت: لصقت، ب.

216 رواه البخاري، بلفظ: «نهي أن يصلي الرجل مختصرا» دون ذكر: «حقويه»، باب الخصر في الصلاة، ر١١٦٢، ومسلم، باب كراهة الاختصار في الصلاة، ر١٢٤٦.

217 مختصر: محشر، ب.

218 رواه الربيع، باب جامع الصلاة، ر٢٩٩.

219 يقعيَ: يقع، ب،د.

220 رواه الربيع، باب القعود في الصلاة والتحيات، ر٢٣٨.

221 رواه البخاري، باب التشهد في الآخرة، ر٧٩٧، ومسلم، باب التشهد في الصلاة، ر٩٢٩.

222 ربنا: اللّهم،د.

223 سورة البقرة: ٢٠١.

وكرِّه إلينا الكفر والفسوق والعصيان، ونحو هذا[224] مِمَّا في القرآن[225]، فهذا أفضل الدعاء في الصلاة المفروضة.

سئل ما يقول الإمام إذا أراد أن يسلم؟

قال: يقول: سبحان ربك ربّ العزة عما يصفون وسلام على المرسلين والحمد لله ربّ العالمين.

قال: كان الربيع حدَّثني بهذا الحديث أنَّه يستحبّ.

سئل عن التسليم؟

قال: واحدة عن يمينه ثُمَّ يرد وجهه عن يساره، ويكره للإمام أن يقعد بعد التسليم حتَّى ينحرف أو يقوم من مقعده.

سئل كيف ينفتل الإمام؟

قال: فحدَّث عن حسين عن عمرو بن شعيب عن أبيه عن جده قال: رأيت رسول الله ﷺ ينفتل عن يمينه وعن شماله، ورأيته يصلِّي حافيا ومنتعلا، ورأيته يصوم في السفر ويفطر، ورأيته يشرب قائما وقاعدا[226].

عن قتادة عن أنس بن مالك: أنَّه كان يكره أن يستدبر أحدهم القبلة كما يستدبر الحمار[227].

---

224 هذا ونحوه، ب؛ سورة الحجرات: ٧.

225 مما في القرآن: -،د.

226 قال نعم، لا بأس بذلك: +، ب. رواه أحمد، ر٦٦٢٧، والبيهقي، باب انصراف المصلي، ر٣٤٢٧.

227 أن يستدبر أحدهم القبلة كما يستدبر الحمار: أن يستدير أحدكم كما يستدير الحمار، ب.

سئل عن رد السلام على الإمام؟

قال: يقول من خلف الإمام، السلام على أنبياء الله ورسوله والسلام علينا وعلى عباد الله الصالحين.

سئل عمَّن أدرك بعض صلاة الإمام فسلم الإمام؟

قال: لا يرد السلام ولا[228] يُكبّر إذا نهض لبعض[229] ما سبق به.

سئل عما يقطع الصلاة؟

عن قتادة عن جابر بن زيد قال: قلت لابن عبَّاس: ما يقطع الصلاة؟ قال: الكلب الأسود والمرأة الحائض، قال قتادة: كان يقول ثلاثة[230]، قلت: وما ذاك؟[231] قال: الحمار. قال: قلت: كان يقال أربع، العلج الكافر. قال: إن استطعت ألا[232] يمر بين يديك كافر ولا مسلم فافعل. وقال: يقطع الصلاة الكلب والمرأة الحائض والمجوسيّ إذا كان قريبا.

سئل عن سترة[233] المصلِّي؟

قال: سترة[234] الإمام قدر واسطة الرحل، وقدر طوله وهو قاعد.

---

228 لا: -، ب.

229 لبعض: يقضي، ب.

230 يقول ثلاثة: يقال ثلاث، ب.

231 قلت وما ذاك: قلت: الحمار، قال: رويدك، ب.

232 ألا: أن لا، ب د

233 عن سترة: عما يستر، ب.

234 سترة: يستر، ب.

سئل عما يقطع على الإمام الصلاة، هل يقطع على من خلفه[235]؟

قال: نراه إذا قطع على الإمام أن يقطع على من خلفه.

سئل عن كم[236] تقطع إذا مر بنا ما يقطعها؟

قال: خمسة عشر ذراعا[237] ونحوه.

وقال: لا يقطع الصلاة إذا كان بينك وبين ما يقطع الصلاة نهر جارٍ[238].

سئل عن قوم كانوا على سطح يصلون فمر كلب على سطح آخر بينهم طريق؟

قال: لا يقطع عليهم، ومن كان على دكان مرتفع قدر قعدة الرجل لم يقطع صلاته.

سئل عن صلاة الجنائز؟

قال: لا يقطع المار إلاَّ صلاة فيها ركوع وسجود.

سئل عن رجل يأتَمّ بالإمام وهو على ظهر بيت من خلفه؟

قال: يكره ذلك في الفريضة، إذا كان بينهما طريق نافذ.

وقال: كان الربيع يكره إذا كان في الفريضة أن يأتَمّ الرجل[239] برجل وبينهما طريق، ولا بأس في رمضان إذا سمع التكبير.

---

235 على من خلفه: -، ب. .

236 لا: +، ب.

237 أو عشرين ذراعا: +، ب.

238 لم يقطع الصلاة: +،د.

239 الرجل: -،د.

سئل عن رجل يصلِّي في بيته[240] والناس[241] والنساء يصلون قدام البيت بصلاته؟ قال: نعم، إذا لم يكن بينهما طريق نافذ.

عن قتادة عن خالد بن درديرٍ: أنَّ عمر بن الخطَّاب رضي الله عنه قال: لو يعلم المار بين يدي المصلِّي ماذا عليه، لكان أن يقيم حولا أحبّ إليَّه من أن يمر بين يديه، ولو يعلم المصلِّي بغير سترة ما انتقص من[242] صلاته ما صلَّى إلاَّ بالسترة[243].

عن قتادة عن عبد الله بن يزيد أنَّ ابن مسعود قال: أربعة من الجفاء: أن يسمع الرجل النداء ثُمَّ لا يجيبه في تهليله وتكبيره، وأن يصلِّي والناس يمرون بين يديه وليس بين يديه ما يستره، وأن يمسح التراب عن وجهه[244] قبل أن يسلم، وأن يبول قائماً[245].

عن قتادة عن سعيد بن المسيب عن عائشة رضي الله عنها أنَّها قالت: إن رسول الله ﷺ قال: «لعن الله قوما اتخذوا قبور أنبيائهم مساجد»[246] وقال: تكره الصلاة على القبور والمشي عليها.

---

240 بيته: بيت، ب.

241 الناس: -، ب.

242 من: +، ب.

243 من الناس: +، ب. رواه عبد الرزاق، باب المار بين يدي المصلي، ر٢٣٢٤، والطبراني: المعجم الصغير، ر٤٢٠.

244 وجهه: جبهته، ب.

245 قال: نعم، هذا من الجفاء: +، ب.

246 قال: نعم: +، ب. رواه الربيع، في الأخبار المقاطيع عن جابر بن زيد، ر٩٨٠، والبخاري، باب الصلاة في البيعة، ر٤٢٥.

عن قتادة عن الحسن عن عبد الله بن معقل أنّ نبيّ الله ﷺ قال: «إن أدركت[247] الصلاة وأنت في معاطن الإبل فلا تصل، وإذا أدركتك في مرابض الغنم فصل إن شئت»[248].

سئل عن المسجد يكون على النهر[249]؟

قال: إن كان من تحته ماء جارٍ[250] فلا بأس به، وإن كان تحته نتن أو خبث فلا تصلِّ فيه.

سئل عن المسجد يكون قبلته الرجس؟

قال: فكره الصلاة فيه، إلاّ أن يكون بينهما حائطان[251].

سئل عن المسجد يكنس بكنس ليس بنظيف؟

قال: يكره ذلك.

سئل عن الصلاة عند كسوف الشمس والقمر؟

قال: عن قتادة[252] عن النخعي عن علقمة بن قيس عن ابن مسعود: أن الشمس انكسفت على عهد النبيّ -عليه الصلاة والسلام- فقال الناس: إنّمَا انكسفت لوفاة[253] إبراهيم ابن النبيّ -عليه الصلاة والسلام- فقام رسول الله فخطب الناس فقال: «إن الشمس

247 أدركت: أدركتك، ب.

248 قال: نعم، هذا مستقيم: +، ب. رواه أحمد، ر٢٠٥٦٠، والبيهقي، باب كراهية الصلاة في أعطان الإبل دون مراح الغنم، ر٤١٤٩.

249 النهر: القنطرة، ب.

250 جارٍ: جاري، ب،د.

251 حائطان: حائطين، ب.

252 قتادة: حماد، ب.

253 لوفاة: لموت، ب.

والقمر لا ينكسفان لموت أحد[254]، ولكنهما آيتان من آيات الله، فإذا رأيتم ذلك، فاحمدوا الله وكبّروه، وسبّحوه وصلّوا حتّى ينجلي كسوف أيهما انكسف[255]» [256]ثُمَّ نزل رسول الله ﷺ فصلّى بنا ركعتين[257].

قال: الصلاة حسن، والذكر حسن، والدعاء حسن، وقد[258] بلغنا أنَّ جابر بن زيد رأى بعض ذلك وبعض الأقوام[259] يصلون[260]، فقعد في ناحية المسجد حتّى انجلى ثُمَّ تلى[261] الآية: ﴿ يَوْمَ يَأْتِي بَعْضُ آيَاتِ رَبِّكَ لَا يَنفَعُ نَفْسًا إِيمَانُهَا لَمْ تَكُنْ آمَنَتْ مِن قَبْلُ أَوْ كَسَبَتْ فِي إِيمَانِهَا خَيْرًا ﴾[262].

وقال:[263] إذا انكسفت الشمس بعد العصر فإنَّهم يقومون يدعون[264] ولا يصلون، وقال في صلاة [265] كسوف الشمس والقمر: يصلّي كما يصلّي في سائر الأيّام قراءة وركوعًا وسجودًا[266].

254 أحد: بشر، ب.
255 كسوف أيهما انكسف: فكسف أحديهما انكسف، ب.
256 قال: +، ب.
257 رواه البخاري، باب الصدقة في الكسوف، ر٩٩٧، ومسلم، باب صلاة الكسوف، ر٢١٢٧.
258 وقد: فقد، ب.
259 الأقوام: الأفراد، ب.
260 يصلون: -، ب.
261 تلى: قال، ب؛ ألا وتأويل هذه الآية: +، ب.
262 سورة الأنعام: ١٥٨.
263 وقال: -، ب.
264 يدعون: ويودعون، ب،د.
265 في الصلاة: الصلاة عند، ب.
266 وركوعًا وسجودًا: وركوع وسجود، ب د

سئل عن صلاة الخوف؟

قال: يقوم الإمام وتقوم طائفة خلفه وطائفة قدام العدو وفي نحور العدو، فيُكبّر الإمام ويكبرون جميعا: الذين خلفه والذين كانوا بين يديه، فيقرأ ويركع ويسجد الإمام ومن خلفه والآخرون قيام في نحور العدو، فإذا فرغ الإمام ومن خلفه من الركعة الأولى[267] تقدّم من خلفه وتأخر الذين هم في نحور العدو[268] حتَّى يكونوا[269] خلف الإمام فيصلِّي بهم الركعة[270] الأخرى والآخرون قيام[271] في نحور العدو، و[272] يتشهد، فإذا فرغ سلم وسلمت الطائفتان جميعا، فيكون للإمام ركعتان ولأصحابه[273] ركعة ركعة، فهذه صلاة الخوف. وهذا قول الربيع عن أبي عبيدة وهو قول جابر وضمام.

سئل[274] عن قوله عز وجل[275]: ﴿فإنْ خِفْتُمْ فَرِجالاً أَوْ رُكْبَانًا﴾[276]؟

قال: قال قتادة: ذلك عند الضرب بالسيوف. قال: الصلاة عند الضراب والطعان خمس تكبيرات أمام وجهك، حيث ماكان، وقدكان حاجب يقول: ست تكبيرات

---

267 الأولى: -، ب.

268 خلفه وتأخر الذي هم في نحور العدو: تقدموا وتأخر الذين في نحور العدو، ب.

269 يكونوا: يكونون، د.

270 الركعة: ركعة، ب.

271 قيام: وقوف، ب.

272 لم: +، ب.

273 ولأصحابه: ولهولاء، ب.

274 سئل: -، ب.

275 عز وجل: -، ب.

276 سورة البقرة: ٢٣٩.

واحدة للإحرام[277] وخمس للركعات[278]، وإن كنت منهزما فكذلك، وإن كنت تطلب عدوك فركعتان[279] تقرأ وتركع وتسجد[280].

سئل عن رجل يصلِّي لغير القبلة؟

قال: إذا كان جاهلا بالقبلة مضت صلاته، وإن كان قد صلَّى ركعتين لغير القبلة ثُمَّ عرف القبلة تحرف إلى القبلة، وصلَّى ما بقي عليه، واعتد بما مضى.

سئل عن المغمى عليه؟

قال: إذا مضى[281] الوقت وهو مغمى عليه، فليس عليه إعادة تلك الصلاة، وإن أفاق في الوقت قضى تلك الصلاة التي أفاق في وقتها، وإن مضى اليوم كله لم يعد صلاة ذلك اليوم.

سئل عن رجل سلم عليه وهو يصلِّي[282]؟

قال: لا يرد[283] وهو في الصلاة، فإذا فرغ من الصلاة رد[284]، فإن في الصلاة شغلا.

---

277 واحدة للإحرام: للإحرام واحدة، ب.

278 في هامش (ب: «الجزء الأول من آثار الربيع، حدثني ابن الأزور عن يزيد أنه قال: خمس تكبيرات تجزيه الرجل في الحرب، إذا كان طالبا أو مطلوبا تلقاء وجهه».

279 فركعتان: فركعتين، ب.

280 في هامش (ب: «صلاة المسايفة إذا كنت تطلب العدو تصلي ركعتين وإذا».

281 مضى: ذهب، ب.

282 يصلي: في الصلاة، ب.

283 السلام: +، ب.

284 السلام: +، ب.

سئل عن رجل يشير في صلاته لحاجة[285]؟

قال: يكره ذلك.

سئل عن رجل يتفل في المسجد؟

قال: يكره أن يتفل قدامه، ولكن تحت قدمه أو عن يساره.

عن قتادة عن أنس بن مالك: أنَّ رسول الله صلى الله عليه وسلم قال: «لا يتفل أحدكم عن يمينه وهو يصلِّي ولا أمامه فإنَّه يناجي ربه، ولكن يتفل عن يساره أو تحت قدمه»[286].

عن قتادة عن أنس بن مالك: أنَّ رسول الله صلى الله عليه وسلم قال[287]: «النخامة[288] في المسجد خطيئة وكفَّارتها دفنها»[289].

قال[290]: قد بلغنا ذلك.

سئل عن رجل يرى القملة في ثوبه فيدفنها في المسجد، فحدث عن قتادة عن سعيد بن المسيب: سئل عن ذلك؟[291]

---

285 لحاجة: في الحاجة، ب.

286 رواه أحمد، ر١٣٢٦٦، وابن حبان، ذكر الزجر عن تنخم المصلي في قبلته أو عن يمينه، ر٢٢٦٧.

287 لا يتفل أحدكم عن يمينه وهو يصلي ولا أمامه، فإنه يناجي ربه، ولكن يتفل عن يساره أو تحت قدمه: +ب.

288 النخامة: النخاعة، ب، د.

289 رواه ابن حبان، ذكر الزجر للمرء أن يتنخم في المسجد من غير أن يدفن نخامته، ر١٦٣٥، وعبد الرزاق، باب الرجل يبصق في المسجد ولا يدفن، ر١٦٩٧.

290 نعم: +، ب.

291 سئل عن رجل يرى القملة في ثوبه فيدفنها في المسجد، فحدث عن قتادة عن سعيد بن

قال: نعم، إنك تدفن في المسجد ما هو أنتن منها، وقال[292] النخامة[293] يكره أن تشتغل بها في صلاتك، وقال: [294] إذا انصرفت فادفنها إن شئت.

سئل عن الرجل يصلِّي قاعدا؟

قال: إذا لم يستطع أن يصلِّي قائما فليصل قاعدا.

سئل عن الرجل يعتمد على حائط المسجد؟

قال: يكره ذلك، وكان أبو عبيدة حين كبر يضع يده[295] على وتد في مسجده، حدَّثني الربيع عن هذا. فقال: وقد كان يكرهه في أهل[296] الشباب والقوة.

سئل عن رجل يصلِّي جالسا؟

قال: إذا ابتدأ صلاته قائما، ثُمَّ جلس فليقم إذا أراد أن يركع، يقوم فيقرأ[297] ما بدا له ثُمَّ يركع قائما، فإذا ابتدأ صلاته[298] قاعدا استفتح قاعدا وأومأ[299] إيماء، وقد كان صالح الدهان يسجد وهو قاعد، وكان الربيع لا يرى به بأسا، إذا كان لا يحفظ الصلاة بالإيماء فليسجد إن شاء فلا بأس به.

المسيب سئل عن ذلك؟: –،د.

292 قال: –، ب.

293 النخامة: النخاعة، ب،د.

294 قال: –، ب.

295 يده: يديه، ب.

296 أهل: –، ب.

297 يقوم فيقرأ: قام فقرأ، ب،د.

298 استفتح: +، ب.

299 أومأ: –، ب.

عن مُحَمَّد بن سيرين عن بديل عن عبد الله بن شقيق عن عائشة زوج النبيّ عليه الصلاة والسلام أنَّ رسول الله ﷺ كان يكثر الصلاة قائما وقاعدا، فإذا صلَّى قائما ركع قائما وإذا صلَّى قاعدا ركع قاعدا[300].

قال: نعم، إذا كان قاعدا فيومئ إيماء وإن سجد فلا بأس.

سئل عن الرجل يصلِّي في الثوب الواحد؟

قال: حدَّثني الربيع عن أبي عبيدة أنَّه صلَّى في ثوب واحد وعنده ثياب، وبلغنا: أنَّ حذيفة[301] صلَّى في ثوب واحد وإلى جانبه ثياب على المِشْجَب، وهذا إذا صلَّى وحده، وأمَّا الإمام فلا بُدَّ له[302] من إزار ورداء.

سئل عن الرجل يصلِّي في القميص أو في الجبة إذا لم يجد غيرها؟

قال: ما لم يكن إماما فلا بأس.

سئل عن الرجل يؤمّ بقوم وعليه إزار وقميص.

فذكر أن أبا عبيدة كان يخرج يديه من تحت القميص، ويلقيه على عاتقه ويؤمّ أصحابه.

سئل هل يصلَّى في شعار المرأة؟

قال: إذا كان نظيفا فلا بأس[303].

---

300 رواه مسلم، باب جواز النافلة قائما وقاعدا، ر١٧٣٤، وأبو داود، باب في صلاة القاعد، ر٩٥٦.

301 بن اليمان: +، ب.

302 له: -، ب.

303 سئل: هل يصلَّى في شعار المرأة؟ قال: إذا كان نظيفا فلا بأس: -، د. شعار الشيء أقرب الأشياء إليه فشعار المرأة ثوبها الذي يلي بدنها: هامش، ب.

سئل في كم تصلّي المرأة من الثياب[304]؟

قال: كان أبو عبيدة لا يرى بأسا بالدرع إذا كان صفيقا، وكان عنده الخمار مستحبا[305] مع الدرع. ويقول: أكره أن تكون مثل أم ربيعة المجنونة[306].

سئل عن الجارية التي قد حاضت إذا لم تختمر[307]؟

عن قتادة عن صفية بنت الحارث أن عائشة زوج النبيّ ﷺ نزلت عليها فرأت بناتها قد حضن أو حاض بعضهن، فقالت: مري بناتك أن يختمرن فإنّهن قد[308] حضن، وإن[309] لم يختمرن فالله[310] لا يقبل لهن صلاة[311].

قال: يستحبّ لهن أن يختمرن.

سئل عن المملوكة[312] يطأها سيدها أعليها: أن تختمر؟

قال: لا، إلاَّ أن تحبّ[313].

عن قتادة عن أنس بن مالك: أنَّ عمر بن الخطّاب رضي الله عنه رأى أمة عليها قناع

304 من الثياب: -، ب.
305 الخمار مستحبا: مستحب الخمار، ب،د.
306 أبو عبيدة لا يرى بأسا لصلاة المرأة في الدرع: هامش، ب.
307 بحدث: +، ب.
308 قد: إذا، ب.
309 وإن: -، ب.
310 فالله: والله، ب،د.
311 «لم يقبل الله لهن صلاة»، رواه أحمد، ر٢٤٦٩٠، وإسحاق بن راهويه في مسنده، ر١٣٤٤، بدون ذكر: «فوالله لا يقبل لهن صلاة».
312 التي: +، ب.
313 ذلك: +، ب.

فأوقع[314] الخمار فضربها بِالدِرَّةِ، وقال: لا تتشبهن[315] بالحرائر.

سئل عن الرجل يصلِّي وهو متلثم بالعمامة؟

قال: يكره ذلك في الصلاة، ولا بأس أن يقرأ القرآن وهو متلثم.

سئل عن السدل في الصلاة؟

قال: يكره.

سئل عن الأعمى يؤمّ القوم؟

قال: فحدث قتادة: «أن النبيّ ﷺ استخلف ابن أمّ مكتوم سنين، فصلَّى بالناس وكان أعمى»[316].

سئل عن تخفيف الصلاة؟

قال: فحدث[317] عن قتادة: أنَّ جابر بن عبد الله الأنصاري حدَّث: أنَّ رسول الله ﷺ قال: «من كان إمام الناس[318] في الصلاة[319] فليقصد بهم، فإنَّه يكون فيهم الكبير والضعيف وذو الحاجة»[320]. وقد بلغنا ذلك، ولا بأس بالتخفيف إذا أتم، غير

314 فأوقع: –،د.

315 لا تتشبهن: لا تشبهي، ب.

316 رواه أبو داود، كتاب الصلاة، باب إمامة الأعمى، ر٥٩٥. وابن حبان، ذكر جواز إمامة الأعمى بالمأمومين إذا لم يكونوا عماة، ر٢١٣٥.

317 فحدث: –،د.

318 إمام الناس أمة، ب.

319 الصلاة: سبيل، ب.

320 رواه البخاري، كتاب الأذان، باب من شكى إمامه إذا طول...، ر٦٧٢ ومسلم، كتاب الصلاة، باب أمر الأئمة بتخفيف الصلاة في تمام، ر١٠٧٢.

أنَّه يستحبّ طول القراءة في الفجر[321] .

سئل عن الرجل يؤمّ القوم وهو في مكان أرفع من أصحابه؟

قال: فحدث أنَّه صلَّى خلف الحسن في بيته، فأمهم في مسجد بيته وهو عن يسار الصف الأوَّل، ورأيت قتادة يفعل مثل ذلك في بيته، وقال: لا بأس، وأن يكون في وسط القوم[322] أحبّ إليّنا.

سئل عن الرجل يقرأ السورة في الركعتين والسورتين في الركعة؟

قال: لا بأس أن يقرأ سورتين أو ثلاثا في الركعة والسورة في الركعتين[323] .

سئل عن قراءة[324] سورة ثُمَّ أراد أن يقرأ سورة أخرى، أيقرأ: بسم الله الرحمن الرحيم؟

قال: حدَّثني الربيع رفع الحديث إلى جابر بن زيد: أنَّه[325] لقي ابن عمر في المسجد الحرام فسأله عن ذلك؟ فقال: إنَّها آية من كتاب الله اختلسها منهم الشيطان، صلَّيت مع النبيّ عليه الصلاة والسلام فقرأها حتَّى مات، ثُمَّ صلَّيت مع أبي بكر فقرأها حتَّى مات، ثُمَّ صلَّيت مع عمر فقرأها حتَّى مات، وأنا أقرأها حتَّى أموت»[326] .

سئل عن الصفوف بين سواري المسجد؟

قال: يكره.

---

321 إمام على مكان أرفع من أصحابه: هامش، ب.

322 القوم: الصف، ب.

323 من قرأ سورة في ركعتين أو قرأ سورتين في ركعة: هامش، ب.

324 عن قرأة: من قرأ، ب.

325 أنه: -، ب.

326 لم أجد له تخريج.

عن قتادة عن أنس بن مالك: أنَّ رسول الله ﷺ قال: «ما بال أقوام يرفعون أبصارهم إلى السماء في صلاتهم»، حتَّى اشتد في ذلك قوله: «لينتهن عن ذلك أو ليخطف الله أبصارَهم[327]»[328].

قال: كان الفقهاء يذكرون[329] هذا.

عن قتادة قال: ذكر لنا أنَّ نبيَّ الله ﷺ قال: «راصوا[330] بين صُفوفكم، وقاربوا بينها وحاذُوا بالأعناق، والذي نفس مُحمَّد بيده[331] إنِّي لأرى الشيطان يتخلل الصفوف كأنه الحذف»[332].

قال: يستحبّ ذلك[333].

وكان يقال: خير صفوف الرجال المقدّم، وخير صفوف النساء المؤخَّر.

سئل عن تقليب الحصى في الصلاة، والالتفات في الصلاة؟

قال: يكره ذلك.

سئل عمَّن رفع رأسه قبل الإمام؟

327 ليخطفُ الله أبصارَهم: أو ليخطفن أبصارهم، ب.

328 رواه البخاري، باب رفع البصر إلى السماء في الصلاة، ر٧١٧، ومسلم، باب النهي عن رفع البصر إلى السماء في الصلاة، ر٩٩٥.

329 يذكرون: يكرهون، ب.

330 راصوا: واسطوا، د؛ أرصوا، ب.

331 لقد رأيت: +، ب.

332 رواه أحمد، ر١٤٠٤٩.

333 قال: يستحبّ ذلك: -، د.

قال: بلغنا: أن من رفع رأسه قبل الإمام أو سجد قبله: أنَّه لم يصلِّ وحده ولا مع الإمام؛ فليعد، ومن صنعه ساهيا فليسجد سجدتي الوهم.

عن ثابت بن مُحمَّد بن زيادة عن أبي هريرة: أنَّ رسول الله ﷺ قال: «أما يخاف أحدهم إذا رفع رأسه قبل الإمام أن يحول الله رأسه رأس حمار؟»[334] قال[335]: بلغنا ذلك[336].

سئل عن الرجل يصلِّي وفي فيه الدراهم أو الخاتم أو الشيء؟

قال[337]: فكره ذلك وفي يده أيضا[338].

سئل عن الرجل ينفض أصابعه في الصلاة؟

قال: يكره ذلك.

سئل عن الرجل يدخل المسجد وقد ركع الإمام فركع دون الصف وقد جاوز[339] صف النساء فمشى على حاله حتَّى دخل الصف؟

قال: قد[340] كره ذلك، وقد بلغنا: أنَّ ابن مسعود فعل ذلك، ولو فعله اليوم رجل لم

334 رواه البخاري، كتاب الأذان، باب إثم من رفع رأسه قبل الإمام، ر٦٥٩. ومسلم، كتاب الصلاة، باب تحريم سبق الإمام بركوع أو سجود ونحوهما، ر٩٩١.

335 قد: +، ب.

336 قال الشيخ أبو زيد (رحمه الله: ومن صنعه لا يؤخذ بهذا من قول قتادة والحق ما عليه أصحابنا، أن عليه الإعادة سهى أو تعمد: هامش، ب.

337 قال: -، ب.

338 قال: قد بلغنا ذلك: +، ب.

339 جاوز: جاوزا، د.

340 قد: -، ب.

يكن به[341] بأس.

سئل عن الرجل يدخل المسجد وقد ركع الإمام، فركع دون الصف، فلمّا رفع الإمام رأسه مشى حتَّى دخل الصف. أيعتد بها؟

قال: نعم.

سئل عن رجل انتهى إلى المسجد[342] وقدتم الصف؟

قال: كان يقال: يدخل في الصف وإلاَّ فليؤخر رَجُلا من الصف يقوم معه ولا يقوم وحده.

سئل عن رجل انتهى إلى الإمام وهو راكع فكبر تكبيرة وركع؟

قال: تجزيه تكبيرة واحدة.

سئل عمَّن أدرك الإمام وقد ركع ورفع رأسه وسجد معه؟

قال: يصلِّي[343] ما فاته ويعتد بما أدرك، وبلغنا: أنَّ جابرًا أدرك الصلاة في المغرب وقد رفع الإمام رأسه من الركوع، فلمَّا سلم الإمام قام فقرأ وركع، ثُمَّ انصرف قائمًا[344].

سئل عن الرجل ينتهي إلى المسجد والإمام والقوم جلوس في آخر صلاتهم فكبر وجلس ثُمَّ سلم الإمام؟

قال: إن كبّروا الإمام في التشهُّد وتشهد هو فليقض ما فاته، فإذا كان في آخر صلاته

341 به: –، ب.

342 المسجد: رجل، ب.

343 يصلي: يلحق، ب.

344 انظر الانصراف والصلاة قائما: هامش، ب.

وقد[345] رفع رأسه من السجود وصلَّى على النبيّ ﷺ قام فيصلِّي مبتدئا صلاته[346].

سئل عن رجل انتهى إلى الإمام وهو راكع فركع معه؟

قال: قد ثبتت ركعة[347] فإن انتهى إليه أيضا وهو ساجد فليسجد، فإذا سلم الإمام قام فلحق ما فاته واعتد بما أدرك، فإن الصلاة ليس فيها زيادة ولا نقصان.

سئل هل ينتظر الإمام أحدا[348] وهو راكع أو ساجد، إذا سمع وطأه مقبلا؟

قال: يكره للإمام أن ينتظر أحدا في ركوع أو سجود من المسجد ولا من[349] الطريق[350].

سئل عن قوم يصفون قبل أن يأتي الإمام؟

قال: إذا أقيمت الصلاة تقدّم رجل من القوم، فإن كان الإمام قد دخل المسجد فانتظروه فلا بأس[351].

سئل عن صلاة الجماعة؟

قال: حدَّث عن خالد بن ميمون عن أبي إسحاق[352] عن عبد الله بن أبي نضير عن أبيه عن أُبيّ بن كعب قال: صلَّى رسول الله ﷺ: صلاة الصبح، ثُمَّ قال: «أشهد فلان؟ أشهد

345 وقد: قد، ب.

346 قام فيصلي مبتدئا صلاته: -، ب.

347 ركعته: ركعته، ب.

348 أحدا: -، ب.

349 في: +، ب.

350 لا ينتظر إمام راكعا أو ساجدا المقبل: هامش، ب.

351 إذا أقيمت الصلاة تقدم رجل وصلى بهم قبل مجيء الإمام: هامش، ب.

352 المهدي: +، ب.

فلان؟ لنفرٍ من المنافقين لم يشهدوا تلك الصلاة»، ثُمَّ قال: «إن هاتين الصلاتين أثقل على المنافقين من سائر الصلوات: صلاة الصبح وصلاة العشاء، لو يعلمون ما فيهما لأتوهما ولو حبوا»، ثُمَّ قال: ﷺ «عليكم بالصف المقدم فإنَّه على مثل صف الملائكة ولو تعلمون ما فيه لا بتدرتموه»، ثُمَّ قال: «صلاتك مع الرجل الواحد، أزكى من صلاتك وحدك، وصلاتك مع الرجلين أزكى من صلاتك مع رجل واحد[353] وما كثر[354] فهو أحب إلى الله»[355].

قال: قد بلغنا ذلك[356].

وقد ذكر لنا أن النبيّ ﷺ قال: «لو يعلم المتخلفون عن صلاة العشاء وصلاة الصبح ما فيهما من الأجر لأتوهما ولو حبوا على أيديهم وأرجلهم»[357].

عن قتادة عن عمر بن الخطَّاب قال: لأن أشهد العشاء والغداة في جماعة أحبّ إليَّ من أن أحيي الليل كله.

عن قتادة: أنَّ كعبا قال: إن في التوراة مكتوبا إن بيوتي في أرضي[358] المساجد، فمن توضَّأ فأحسن الوضوء، ثُمَّ زارني في بيتي أكرمته، وحق على المزار كرامة الزائر.

عن قتادة عن أبي الدرداء عن النبيّ ﷺ قال: «خمس من جاء بهنَّ يوم القيامة مع

353 واحد: -،د.

354 وما كثر: وكلما أكثر، ب.

355 رواه النسائي، الجماعة إذا كانوا اثنين، ر٨٤٣.

356 ذلك: -، ب.

357 رواه الربيع، باب في فضل الصلاة وخشوعها، ر٢٩٢، والبخاري، باب فضل العشاء في الجماعة، ر٦٢٦.

358 أرضي: أرض، ب،د.

إيمان دخل الجنَّة: من[359] حافظ على الصلوات المكتوبة ووضوئها ومواقيتها وركوعها وسجودها، وأعطى الزكاة طيبة بها نفسه»[360]. ثُمَّ قال: «وايم الله لا يفعل ذلك إلاَّ مؤمن، وصام شهر رمضان، وحجّ البيت[361] إن استطاع إليه سبيلا، وأدّى[362] الأمانة».

قالوا: يا رسول الله،[363] وما الأمانة؟

قال: «الاغتسال من الجنابة، فإنَّ الله تعالى لم يؤمّن ابن آدم[364] على شيء من دينه غيرها»[365]. قال: من حافظ على هذا من المسلمين فله الجنَّة إن شاء الله، ومن ضيع هذا لم يؤد حق الله الذي عليه، وهذه عُرى الإسلام.

وقال:[366] يكره للمسلم أن يأتي عليه ليل لا يصيب في أوله وآخره شيئًا يتقرب به إلى الله[367]، وهو في تفسير قوله ﷻ[368]: ﴿ كَانُواْ قَلِيلاً مِّن اللَّيْلِ مَا يَهْجَعُونَ ﴾[369] قال: كان القوم قليلا من الليل ما ينامون[370].

---

359 من: -، ب.

360 رواه أبو داود، باب في المحافظة على وقت الصلوات، ر٤٢٩. وانظر: المدونة الكبرى لأبي غانم الخراساني، تحقيق: د. مصطفى باجو، ١/١٩١، بلفظ قريب.

361 البيت: بيت الله، ب.

362 أدى: أداء، ب.

363 يا رسول الله: -، ب.

364 ابن آدم: -، د.

365 رواه البيهقي: شعب الإيمان، فضل الوضوء - وفي ذلك تنبيه على فضل الغسل لأنه أكمل، ر٢٧٥٠.

366 إنه: +، ب.

367 يتقرب به إلى الله: -، ب.

368 قوله عز وجل: -، ب.

369 سورة الذاريات: ١٧.

370 : قليل من الليل ما ينامون: قليلا ما من الليل ينامون، د.

وقال: كان يقال: مائة آية من صلّى بهنّ لم يكتب من الغافلين.

سئل عن قوله تعالى[371]: ﴿إِنَّ نَاشِئَةَ اللَّيْلِ هِيَ أَشَدُّ وَطْئًا وَأَقْوَمُ قِيلاً﴾[372].
قال: ناشئة الليل أوله، وقد كان يقال: أفضل قيام الليل[373] وسطه.

عن قتادة عن سالم بن[374] أبي الجعد عن معدان بن[375] أبي طلحة اليعمري عن أبي الدرداء أنّ نبيّ الله ﷺ قال: أما[376] يستطيع أحدكم كلّ ليلة أن يقرأ ثلث القرآن؟» قالوا: يارسول الله، نحن أعجز وأضعف عن ذلك مرّتين أو[377] ثلاثا، قال ﷺ: «إنّ الله جزأ القرآن ثلاثة أجزاء، فجعل ﴿قل هو الله أحد﴾ جزءًا من أجزاء القرآن، وقال: إنّها تعدل ثلث القرآن[378]»[379].

[380]عن قتادة: أنّ رجلا أتى أبا الدرداء فقال: يا أبا[381] الدرداء كيف تأمرني في قيام الليل؟

---

371 تعالى: الله، ب.
372 سورة المزمل: ٦.
373 فتح الليل يقال: +، ب.
374 بن: عن، ب د.
375 بن: عن، ب د
376 أما: ألا، ب.
377 أو: وما، ب د.
378 وقال إنّها تعدل ثلث القرآن: وقال قد يقال إنها ثلث القرآن، ب.
379 رواه الربيع، باب في ذكر القرآن، ر٨، والنسائي، ما يستحب للإنسان أن يقرأ كل ليلة، ر١٠٥٣٧، وأحمد، ر٢٧٥٣٨.
380 قال ذكر لنا: +، ب.
381 أبا: أيها، ب،د.

قال: نم، فإذا استيقظت فاتق الله. قال: يا أبا الدرداء، كيف تأمرني في قيام الليل؟
قال: نم، فإذا استيقظت فاتق الله. قال: يا أبا الدرداء، كيف تأمرني في قيام الليل؟
قال: من خاف أدلج.

عن قتادة عن أنس بن مالك قال: جمع القرآن ستة[382] نفر على عهد رسول الله ﷺ: أُبيّ بن كعب، ومعاذ بن جبل، وزيد بن ثابت، وأبو زيد الأنصاري، وأبو أيُّوب، وعثمان بن حنيف[383].

عن قتادة عن الحسن: أنَّ رسول الله ﷺ قال لأُبيّ: إنَّ الله أمرني أن أقرئك القرآن. قال: [384]الله سماني لك فجعل يبكي[385].

عن حمَّاد عن النخعي: أنَّ أُبيًّا وعبد الله بن مسعود قرأ أحدهما على الآخر. قال: من أقرأك؟ قال نبيّ الله أقرأني، وقال الآخر: نبيّ[386] الله أقرأني، فليس هكذا أقرأني، فأتيا نبيّ الله، قال: إنّي قرأت آية من القرآن[387] فقال: ليس هكذا أقرأني نبيّ الله، فقال النبيّ ﷺ لأحدهما: اقرأ؛ فقرأ، قال: قد أحسنت. وقال للآخر: اقرأ، فقرأ، فقال رسول الله[388] ﷺ: كلاكما قد أحسن[389]. قال أُبَيّ: فدخل عليَّ من الشكِّ أشد مِمَّا كان في الجاهلية،

---

382 ستة: أربعة، ب.

383 أبو أيوب، وعثمان بن حنيف: –، ب.

384 إن: +، ب.

385 رواه البخاري، باب تفسير سورة البينة، ر٤٦٧٧، وأحمد، ر١٣٣١٠.

386 نبي: –، د.

387 القران: كتاب الله، ب.

388 رسول الله: –، ب.

389 رواه أحمد، ر٣٩٠٨.

فوضع نبيّ الله يده على صدري حتّى تصببت عرقًا، فكأني أنظر إلى ربي، فوجدت بردها على فؤادي. فقال: إن جبريل أتاني فقال[390]: يا محمّد، اقرأ القرآن على حرفٍ، فقلتُ: اللّهمَّ خفف على أمّتي. قال: فأتاني الثانية، فقال لي: يا محمّد، اقرأ القرآن على حرف، فقلت: اللّهمَّ خفف عن أمّتي، فأتاني الثالثة، فقال[391]: يا محمّد، اقرأ القرآن على سبعة أحرف، ولكل دعوة سؤالها. قال: فقلت اللّهمَّ اغفر لأمّتي، اللّهمَّ ارحم أمتي[392]، وأخرت دعوتي إلى يوم القيامة، حتّى إن إبراهيم[393] يحتاج إلى تلك الدعوة.

عن قتادة قال: ذكر لنا أنَّ نبيَّ الله ﷺ قال: «إن أرحم أمّتي بأمّتي أبو بكر الصديق، وأشدهم في دين الله عمر بن الخطّاب، وأعلمهم بالحلال والحرام معاذ بن جبل، وأقرؤهم لكتاب الله أُبيّ بن كعب، والأمين أبو عبيدة بن الجراح»[394]. قال: قد بلغنا هذا.

عن قتادة قال: بلغنا أنَّ عمر بن الخطاب قال: أقرؤنا: أُبيّ بن كعب، وأفضلنا عليّ بن أبي طالب. قال: بلغنا هذا[395].

عن قتادة عن الحسن: أنَّ رسول الله ﷺ سئل: أيَّ الصلاة أفضل؟ قال:

---

390 لي: +، ب.

391 لي: +، ب.

392 أمتي: -، د.

393 خليل الرحمن: +، ب. رواه أحمد، ر٢١٢١٧.

394 رواه الترمذي، باب مناقب معاذ بن جبل وزيد بن ثابت وأبي وأبي عبيدة بن الجراح رضي الله عنهم، ر٣٧٩٠، وابن ماجه، باب فضائل خباب، ر١٥٤. وانظر: المدونة الكبرى لأبي غانم الخراساني، تحقيق: د. مصطفى باجو، ٣/٣٣٠.

395 عن قتادة قال: بلغنا: أنَّ عمر بن الخطاب قال: أقرؤنا أبيّ بن كعب، وأفضلنا عليّ بن أبي طالب. قال: بلغنا هذا: -، د.

«طول القنوت»[396].

قال: قد بلغنا هذا، وأطولها قنوتا أطولها قياما.

عن قتادة عن الحسن: «أنَّ نبيَّ الله عليه الصلاة والسلام كان إذا قام من الليل قال: الله أكبر[397] لا إله إلاَّ الله، لا إله إلاَّ الله، الله أكبر الله أكبر كبيرا، أعوذ بالله من الشيطان الرجيم؛ من همزه ونفخه ونفثه»، قيل: يا رسول الله، ما همزه ونفخه ونفثه؟ قال: «همزه: الغيبة[398]، ونفخه: الكبر، ونفثه: الشعر»[399].

عن قتادة قال: كان يقال: «ما من مسلم يأوي إلى فراشه حين يأوي، إلاَّ وعند رأسه ثلاث عقدات، فإن استيقظ فذكر الله انحلت عقدة، وإن توضَّأ انحلت عقدة، فإن صلَّى ركعتين انحلت العقدة الثالثة، فولى الشيطان يركض برجله غضبان[400] فارا، وإن رقد ولم يذكر الله حتَّى أصبح بال الشيطان في أذنيه ومنخريه». حدَّثني بهذا الربيع.

عن قتادة عن الحسن: أنَّ رسول الله ﷺ مر برجل وهو نائم. فقال:[401] قم فصلِّ[402]. قال: إنَّما أصلِّي إذا قدر لي، فقال النبيّ ﷺ: وكان الإنسان

396 رواه مسلم، باب أفضل الصلاة طول القنوت، ر١٨٠٤، والترمذي، باب ما جاء في طول القيام في الصلاة، ر٣٨٧.

397 الله أكبر: –، د.

398 الغيبة: المؤونة، ب.

399 رواه ابن ماجه، باب الاستعاذة في الصلاة، ر٨٠٧، وابن حبان، باب صفة الصلاة، ر١٧٨٠.

400 غضبان: غضبانا، ب، د.

401 له: +، ب.

402 فصلِ: فصلي، ب، د.

أكثر شيء جدلاً[403].

عن قتادة قال: ذكر لنا أن هَرِم بن حيان قال: لم أر مثل النار نام هاربها[404]، ولا مثل الجنَّة نام طالبها. قال: قد بلغنا ذلك.

سئل عن السجود؟

قال: في القرآن إحدى عشرة سجدة، في الْحجّ الأولى منها سجدة[405]، وفي ﴿حم السجدة﴾ الآخرة من الاثنتين[406].

سئل عن الرجل يقرأ آية[407] السجدة وهو في صلاة فنسي أن يسجدها؟

فحدَّث عن قتادة: أنَّه قال: إذا ذكرها قرأ آية وسجدها، فإن كان قد ركع وذكرها لما رفع رأسه من الركوع سجد ثلاث سجدات، فإذا سلم سجد سجدتي الوهم[408].

وسئل عمَّن يتعلَّم القرآن فيمر بالسجدة؟

قال: يسجدها مرة أو مرَّتين[409]، ولا يعددها[410]، ولا يسجدها ما كان في ذلك المكان.

---

403 رواه البخاري، باب تحريض النبي صلى الله عليه وسلم على صلاة الليل والنوافل من غير إيجاب، ر١٠٧٥، ومسلم، باب مَا رُوِيَ فِيمَنْ نَامَ اللَّيْلَ أَجْمَعَ حَتَّى أَصْبَحَ، ر١٨٥٤.

404 هاربها: هاويها،د.

405 منها سجدة: -،د.

406 سجدة: +، ب. الاثنتين: الاثنين، ب،د.

407 آية: -، ب.

408 قال: إن شاء اجتزى بها، وإلا فليتم سجوده. وإذا سلم قرأ سجدة وسجد سجدتي الوهم: +، ب.

409 مرتين: واحدة، ب.

410 يعددها: ثم يعيدها، ب.

سئل عن القنوت؟

فحدَّث عن قتادة عن أنس بن مالك: أنَّ رسول الله عليه الصلاة والسلام أتاه بنو لحيان وعصبة[411]، فزعموا أنَّهم قد أسلموا واستمدوه على قومهم، فأمدهم رسول الله[412] صلى الله عليه وسلم بسبعين رجلا من الأنصار كلهم يعدهم في[413] القراء، فكانوا يحطبون النهار ويصلون الليل، فلمّا بلغوا[414] بئر معونة[415] غدروا بهم فقتلوهم فبلغ ذلك النبيّ عليه الصلاة والسلام، فقنت في صلاة الصبح فدعا عليهم فقرأنا عليهم قرآنا أن بلغوا عنا قومنا أنا قد لقينا ربنا ورضي عنا وأرضانا[416] ثُمَّ من بعد ذلك رجع عن القنوت.

قال: وبلغنا أنَّ النبيّ عليه الصلاة والسلام لم يقنت قبلها ولا بعدها.

عن أبي معشر عن النخعي عن سلمة بن قيس والأسود بن يزيد، قالا: صلّينا خلف عمر حولين لم يقنت في صلاة الصبح[417].

عن أبي معشر عن النخعي: أنَّ ابن مسعود كان لا يقنت في صلاة الصبح.

عن قتادة عن لاحق بن حميد؛ قال: صلّيت خلف ابن عمر صلاة الصبح فلم يقنت، فقلت: يا أبا عبد الرحمن الكِبَرُ ما منعك من القنوت؟ قال: ما أحفظه عن أحد من أصحابنا.

---

411 أتاه بنو لحيان وعصبة: أتاه عصوان ودكوان وهما حيان، ب.

412 رسول الله: -، ب.

413 زمام: +، ب.

414 بلغوا: وصلوا، ب.

415 معونة: معاوية، ب.

416 فقرأنا عليهم قرآنا أن بلغوا عنا قومنا أنا قد لقينا ربنا ورضي عنا وأرضانا: -، د. رواه البخاري، باب العون بالمدد، ر٢٨٩٩، وأحمد، ر١٢٠٨٣.

417 عن أبي معشر... صلاة الصبح: -، ب.

عن أيُّوب عن نافع أنَّ ابن عمر كان لا يقنت في شيء من صلاته[418].

عن قتادة عن لاحق بن حميد أنَّ ابن عبَّاس كان لا يقنت في صلاة الصبح.

قال: بلغنا أنَّ القنوت الذي قنته النبيّ عليه الصلاة والسلام كان قبل الركوع.

عن قتادة: أنَّه كان يقول: اللّهم إنا[419] نستعينك ونستغفرك ونثني عليك، ولا نكفر بك ونخلع ونترك من يكفر بك، اللّهم إياك نعبد ولك نصلي ونسجد، وإليك نسعى ونحفد، نخشى عذابك ونرجو رحمتك، إن عذابك للكافرين لاحق[420]، اللّهمَّ عذب الكفرة الفجرة، وألقِ في قلوبهم الرعب، وخالف بين كلّ منهم، وأنزل عليهم زجرك[421] وعذابك، اللّهمَّ عذِّب كفرة أهل الكتاب الذين يكذِّبون رسلك، ويصدُّون عن سبيلك. اللّهمَّ اغفر للمؤمنين والمؤمنات، والمسلمين والمسلمات، وأصلح ذات بينهم وألف بين قلوبهم، واجعل في قلوبهم الإيمان والحكمة، وثبتهم على مناهجك وملَّة رسولك وأوزعهم أن يوفوا بعهدك الذي عاهدتهم به، وانصرهم على عدوهم وعدوك إن وعدك[422] الحق.

سئل عن رجل مريض لا يستطيع السجود؟

فحدَّث عن قتادة عن عمرو بن دينار: أنَّ ابن عمر دخل على عبد الله بن صفوان يعوده وهو بمكة فحضرت الصلاة، فصلَّى بهم ابن عمر ركعتين، وقال: من كان من أهل

---

418 عن علقمة بن قيس والأسود بن زيد أنهما قالا: صلينا خلف عمر حولين لم يقنت في صلاة الصبح. عن أبي معشر عن النخعي: هامش، ب.

419 اللّهم إنا: -،د.

420 لاحق: ملحق، ب.

421 زجرك: +، ب.

422 إن وعدك: إنك الحق، ب.

مكة فليتم الصلاة، ورأى[423] عبد الله بن صفوان، وكان يسجد[424] على وسادة أو مُرَفَّعة[425]، فنهاه عن ذلك، وأمره أن يومئ في صلاته برأسه إيماءً[426].

قال: وكان جابر يأمر بالإيماء في الوجع ومن كان في طين أو سبخة[427].

عن سالم الغاري قال: دخلت على أبي قلابة، ووجدته وهو على سرير أو فراش له، فرأيته يصلي و يومئ برأسه إيماء. قال: نعم[428].

عن خالد بن ميمون عن أبي إسحاق الهمداني عن علقمة بن قيس أنَّ ابن مسعود عاد قريبا له، فرآه يسجد على وسادة أو على عود فتناوله منه، وأمره أن يومئ إيماء، وأن يجعل السجود أخفض من الركوع[429].

سئل عن الرجل تحضره الصلاة وهو في ماء وطين لا يقدر على الأرض؟

فحدث قتادة عن جابر بن زيد أنه قال: يومئ إيماء ويجعل السجود أخفض من الركوع[430].

سئل عن الصلاة على الدابة أو في الطين؟

---

423 ورأى: وراء،د.

424 يسجد: بمسجد،د. أن يسجد، ب.

425 مرفعة: مرفقة، ب.

426 أن يومىء في صلاته برأسه إيماءً: يوميء برأسه في صلاته إيماءً، ب.

427 قال: وكان جابر يأمر بالإيماء في الوجع ومن كان في طين أوسبخة: -،د.

428 عن سالم الغاري قال: دخلت على أبي قلابة، ووجدته وهوعلى سريرأوفراش له، فرأيته يصلي و يوميء برأسه غيماء. قال: نعم: -،د.

429 قال: نعم: +، ب.

430 أخفض من الركوع: -، ب.

قال: إذا أراد أن يصلِّي وهو على دابته وهي تسير[431] فإنّه يوجه نحو القبلة، وينصرف بالدابة[432] حيث تشاء[433] فإن قدر على الأرض للفريضة صلّى وسجد، وإن لم يقدر وكان طينا صلّى قائما يومئ برأسه إيماء.

وقال: كان الربيع يقول: يبدأ وجهه إلى القبلة ثُمَّ يوجه دابته حيث شاء.

عن رجل عن يحي[434] عن عمرو بن يحيي عن سعيد بن يسار عن ابن عمر أن رسول الله صلى الله عليه وسلم صلَّى وهو يتوجه إلى خيبر على حمار يومئ إيماء[435].

عن قتادة: أنَّه قال: لا يصلِّي الرجل الفريضة على الدابة إلاَّ من خوف أو مرض، قال الربيع: و في السبخة والمطر والرِّدَاغ[436] والمرأة التي ليس معها محرم.

عن قتادة في القوم إذا كانوا في سفينة فانكسرت بهم في البحر فخرجوا عراة، أيصلون جميعا ويؤمّهم أحدهم وهم قعود يومئون إيماء، ويكون إمامهم أوسطهم؟

قال: نعم.

عن قتادة قال: إذا كان الرجل عاريا فإنّه يصلِّي قاعدا يومئ إيماء.

سئل عن الصلاة في السفينة؟

431 تسير: به، ب.

432 بالدابة: بدابته، ب.

433 تشاء: شاء، ب.

434 رجل عن يحي: -، د.

435 الصلاة على الدابة تجوز النافلة دون الفريضة، إلا لخوف أو مرض فإنه تجوز الفريضة أيضًا. وأما هل يتوجه إلى القبلة، أو حيث هو متوجه؟ قولان: أصحهما الأول فيما أرى قاله أبا الربيع رحمه الله ورضي عنه: هامش، ب. رواه مسلم، باب جواز صلاة النافلة على الدابة في السفر حيث توجهت، ر١٦٤٨، وأحمد، ر١٦٠٨٤.

436 الرِّداغ: مفردها ردَغَة، وهو الطين والوحل الكثير.

عن قتادة عن سعيد بن المسيب قال: إن استطعت فصل قائما وإلاَّ فقاعدا، ولا تسجد إلاَّ على قرار منها، وقال: من صلَّى قاعدا فليومئ، ومن سجد فلا بأس، وقد كان صالح الدهان[437] يسجد ولا يرى بأسا.

عن قتادة قال: صلِّ في السفينة ولا تشق على أصحابك، وإن علمت أن خروجك إلى الأرض لا يشق عليهم فاخرج[438].

سئل عن قصر الصلاة في السفر؟

قال: كان جابر بن زيد يقصر إذا سافر[439] فرسخين.

عن قتادة عن الحسن: أنَّ المسافر يصلِّي ركعتين حتَّى يرجع إلى أهله وإن طال المقام.

عن قتادة عن الحسن: أنَّ أنس بن مالك كان بنيسابور عاملا يصلِّي ركعتين حتَّى رجع. قال: قد بلغنا ذلك، وكان أبو عبيدة يرى[440] العامل إذا استقر أتم صلاته ولا بأس. قال: قد بلغنا ذلك.

عن أيُّوب عن نافع: أنَّ ابن عمر أقام في أذربجان أشهرا[441]، وكان يصلِّي ركعتين حتَّى رجع. قال: قد بلغنا ذلك.

عن أبي معشر عن النخعي: أنَّ علقمة بن قيس سافر إلى خراسان فغاب سنين وصلَّى ركعتين ركعتين[442] حتَّى رجع.

---

437 الدهان: -، ب.

438 قال: نعم: +، ب.

439 سافر: سار، ب.

440 أن: +، ب.

441 أشهرا: +، ب.

442 ركعتين: -، ب.

سئل عن رجل مسافر أدرك شيئا[443] من صلاة المقيمين؟

قال: يصلّي صلاتهم، فإن لم يدرك صلَّى صلاة المسافر.

عن قتادة: أنَّ النبيّ عليه الصلاة والسلام حج فصلَّى ركعتين ماكان بمنى، وصلَّى أبو بكر وعمر ركعتين[444]، وعثمان ركعتين صدرا من خلافته، ثُمَّ صلَّى[445] أربع ركعات بمنى، فبلغ ذلك ابن مسعود فاسترجع. قال: بلغنا ذلك[446].

سئل عن رجل نسي الصلاة في السفر حتَّى قدم أو نسي الصلاة في الحضر حتَّى سافر.

قال: يصلِّي صلاة المسافر ركعتين وصلاة المقيم أربعا.

عن قتادة عن مؤرق العجلي أنَّ ابن عمر سئل عن الصلاة في السفر. قال: ركعتين ومن خالف السنة كفر.

سئل عن رجل سافر فجعل يصلِّي المغرب ركعتين ركعتين حتَّى رجع؟

قال: يعيد صلاته كلّها ما ذكر منها، يصلِّي لكلِّ صلاة ثلاث ركعات، ويصلِّي ذلك في ليلة إن شاء أو في يوم واحد إذا كان في وقتٍ يصلَّى فيه.

سئل عن الرجل يتطوّع في السفر؟

عن قتادة: أنَّ عليّ بن أبي طالب وابن عبَّاس وابن مسعود وعائشة زوج النبيّ عليه الصلاة والسلام كانوا يتطوّعون في السفر ويصلون المكتوبة ركعتين.

---

443 شيئا: -، ب.

444 ركعتين: -، ب.

445 ثم صلى: -، ب.

446 قال: بلغنا ذلك: -، د. رواه البخاري، باب الصلاة بمنى، ر١٠٣٤، ومسلم، باب قصر الصلاة بمنى، ر١٦٢٨.

عن عاصم الأحول عن أبي عثمان النهدي قال: سافرنا مع سعد بن مالك من الكوفة إلى مكة، وكان يجمع بين الصلاتين حتَّى قدم[447] مكة. قال: كان الفقهاء يجمعون.

عن قتادة عن جابر بن زيد أنَّ ابن عبَّاس كان يجمع بين الصلاتين في السفر ويقول: هي من السنة[448].

سئل عمن جمع بين المغرب والعشاء[449]، هل يتطوّع بين المغرب والعشاء؟ قال: لا، ولا بين الظهر والعصر.

عن قتادة عن عطاء بن أبي رباح قال: يجمع بين الصلاتين بأذان[450] واحد وإقامتين. قال: نعم[451].

عن قتادة: أنَّ سعد بن مالك كان يوتر بركعة، فبلغه أن معاوية يوتر بركعة، فقال ابن عامر: صلِّ[452] بها فبلغنا عن[453] ابن عبَّاس أنه قال: ويحه من أين يعرف[454] هذا لا أم له، أمَّا ذا عرف هذا فلا يزيد على ركعة[455].

---

447 قدم: دخل، ب.

448 ويقول هي من السنة: -،د. ابن عباس كان يجمع الصلاة في السفر ويقول هي من السنة: هامش، ب.

449 عمن جمع بين المغرب والعشاء: -،د.

450 بأذان: بآذان، ب،د.

451 قال نعم: -،د.

452 صل: صلي، ب،د.

453 عن: أن، ب.

454 يعرف: يحرف، ب،د.

455 فبلغه أن معاوية يوتر بركعة، فقال ابن عامر: صلّي بها فبلغنا: أنَّ ابن عبَّاس أنه قال: ويحه من أين يحرف هذا لا أم له، أمَّا ذا عرف هذا فلا يزيد على ركعة: -،د.

عن عبد السلام[456] عن حمَّاد عن النخعي: أنَّ ابن مسعود بلغه أن سعد بن مالك يوتر بركعة فقال: هذا الأبتر من الوتر، ومن أوتر بثلاث ركعات فلا يسلم إلاَّ في آخرهن. قال: هكذا بلغنا ومن أوتر بركعة أجزأ[457].

وبلغنا: أنَّ جابر بن زيد أوتر بركعة فقال: هذا وتر العاجز، ثُمَّ صلَّى حتَّى أصبح وأراد أن يري أصحابه أن ذلك واسع لهم.

عن قتادة عن عروة عن سعيد بن[458] عبد العزيز، عن أبيه: أنَّ رسول الله عليه الصلاة والسلام كان يوتر بسبح اسم ربك الأعلى، وبقل يا أيُّها الكافرون، وبقل هو الله أحد، ويقول: سبحان الملك القدوس ثلاث مرَّات بعد التسليم[459]، وبأي من القرآن أوتر فحسن جائز، إنَّمَا هي صلاة.

عن قتادة عن سعيد بن المسيب أنَّه قال: ضحى رسول الله عليه الصلاة والسلام وليس عليكم، وأوتر[460] وليس عليكم، وصلَّى ركعتين قبل الظهر وليس عليكم، وصلَّى الضحى وليس عليكم، فقلت: يا أبا مُحَمَّد، هذا كله قد[461] عرفناه ما خلا الوتر. فقال: أما إنَّه بلغنا: أنَّ نبيَّ الله عليه الصلاة والسلام قال: «يا أهل القرآن، أوتروا فإنَّ الله وتر يحب الوتر»[462]، وقال: الوتر على أهل القبلة كلهم فهو سنة، والسنة على أهل القبلة[463].

---

456 عن عبد السلام: -، د.

457 أجزاء: أجزاه، ب.

458 أبي امرؤ: +، ب.

459 وبلغنا هذا: +، ب. رواه النسائي، التسبيح بعد الفراغ من الوتر، ر١٧٥٠، وأحمد، ر١٥٣٩٢.

460 رسول الله صلة الله عليه وسلم: +، ب.

461 قد: -، ب.

462 رواه أبو داود، باب استحباب الوتر، ر١٤١٨، والنسائي، باب الأمر بالوتر، ر١٦٧٥.

463 كلهم فهو سنة والسنة على أهل القبلة: -، د.

عن أبي العالية أنَّه رأى ابن عبَّاس أوتر، ثُمَّ صلَّى ركعتين بعد ذلك.

قال: لا بأس، صلِّ قبل أو بعد ما شئت.

سئل متى يوتر من الليل؟[464]

قال: حدث قتادة: أنَّ أبابكر رضي الله عنه كان يوتر من أوّل الليل، وأن عمر بن الخطَّاب كان يوتر في آخر الليل، فبلغ ذلك النبيّ صلى الله عليه وسلم فقال: أبو بكر حذر كيس وعمر قوي معالٌ[465]. وكان مِمَّا ضرب لهما مثلا: مثل رجلين دفعا إلى مفازة فقال أحدهما: لا أنام حتَّى أقطعها، وقال الآخر: أنام[466] نومة ثم أقوم فأقطعها[467] وأنا أقدر عليها، فأصبحا وكلّ واحد قريب من صاحبه. قال: بلغنا هذا، وهو جائز لمن فعله.

وقد كان أبو عمرو الربيع يقول: من قدر على قيام آخر الليل فليوتر في آخر الليل فإنّه أفضل، ومن خاف ألاَّ يقوم في آخر الليل، فليوتر في أوّل الليل ثُمَّ ينام.

عن قتادة: أنَّه قال: إذا أدركه الصبح ولم يوتر فليوتر بركعة؟ قال: نعم[468].

عن زرارة بن أبي أوفى عن سعيد بن هشام[469]، وكان حبرًا لنا، وكان نازلا في بني عديّ ثُمَّ طلّق امرأته، ثُمَّ انطلق إلى المدينة يبيع عقاره ويجعله في السلاح والعدَّة[470]، ثُمَّ

---

464 سئل: متى يوتر من الليل: سئل عن في أتى الليل أوتر؟، ب.

465 رواه عبد الرزاق، باب أي ساعة يستحب فيها الوتر، ر٤٦١٥.

466 ثم أقوم: +، ب.

467 وأنا جام فأقطعها: -،د. انظر: مصنف عبد الرزاق، باب في أي ساعة يستحب فيها الوتر، ر٤٦١٦.

468 قال: نعم: -،د.

469 هشام: مسلم، ب.

470 تاعدة: الكراع، ب.

يجاهد الروم حتّى يموت.

قال: فلقي رهطا من قومه من الأنصار فأخبروه أن رهطا منهم[471] ستة أرادوا ذلك، فأتوا النبيّ عليه الصلاة والسلام فسألوه عن ذلك فنهاهم. فقال: أليست لكم أسوة فيّ؟ فراجع امرأته عند ذلك.

فلما أتانا أخبرنا أنّه لقي ابن عبّاس فسأله عن الوتر، فقال: ألاّ أدلك بأعلم أهل الأرض بوتر رسول الله عليه الصلاة والسلام؟ قلت: بلى. قال: فأتِ عائشة فاسألها عن ذلك، ثُمّ ارجع إلي فأخبرني بما تقول. قال: فأتيت إلى حكيم بن أفلح فاستحلفته، فقال: ما أنا بقاربها قد نهيتها[472] أن تقول في هاتين الشيعتين شيئًا، فأبيت إلاّ الإمضاء[473]، وأقسمت عليه فجاء معي فانطلقنا حتّى دخلنا عليها، فقالت: حكيم وعرفته. قال: نعم، قالت: من هذا معك؟ قال: سعيد بن هشام، قالت: ابن عامر، قلت: نعم، قالت: نِعْم المرء كان عامر، وترجّعت[474] عليه، وقالت خيرًا، وكان قتادة يقول: أصيب يوم أحد مع رسول الله عليه الصلاة والسلام. قلت: يا أم المؤمنين، أنبئيني عن خلق رسول الله صلى الله عليه وسلم؟ قالت: ألست تقرأ القرآن؟ قلت: بلى، قالت: فإن خلق رسول الله عليه الصلاة والسلام كان القرآن[475].

قال: فهممت أن أقوم ولا أسأل أحدًا عن شيء حتّى أموت، ثُمّ بدا لي قيام رسول الله. قال: يا أم المؤمنين أنبئيني عن قيام رسول الله، قالت: أتقرأ هذه السورة «يا أيُّها

---

471 منهم: –،د.

472 نهيتها: لأني نهيتها، ب.

473 قال: فأبى، ب.

474 والمعنى: قالت: إنا لله وإنا إليه راجعون.

475 رواه النسائي، سورة المؤمنون، ر١١٣٥٠، وأحمد، ٢٤٦٤٥.

المزمل» ؟ قلت: نعم، قالت: فإن رسول الله افترض القيام في أوّل هذه السورة، فقام رسول الله عليه الصلاة والسلام وأصحابه حولا حتَّى انتفخت أقدامهم، وأمسك الله خاتمتها اثني عشر شهرا، في السماء، ثُمَّ[476] أنزل التخفيف في آخر السورة، فكان قيام الليل تطوّعا بعد الفريضة[477].

قال: فهممت[478] أن أقوم ولا أسأل عن شيء حتَّى أموت، ثُمَّ بدا لي وتر رسول الله عليه الصلاة والسلام، فسألتها[479]، فقالت: كنَّا نعدّ لرسول الله صلى الله عليه وسلم سواكه وطهوره فيبعثه الله لما يشاء أن يبعثه، فيقوم فيتسوك ويتوضأ ويصلِّي ثماني ركعات لا يقعد إلاَّ في آخرهن فيحمد الله ويدعوه ويستغفره ثُمَّ ينهض، ولا يسلم ثُمَّ يصلِّي التاسعة ثُمَّ يقعد فيحمد الله ويدعوه ويستغفره ثُمَّ يسلم تسليما[480] ثُمَّ يصلِّي ركعتين جالسا، فذلك إحدى عشرة ركعة يا بنيّ[481].

قالت: فلمَّا أسن رسول الله وأخذ اللحم أوتر بسبع ركعات، ثُمَّ يصلِّي ركعتين وهو جالس بعد التسليم، فتلك تسع ركعات يا بنيّ، وكان رسول الله عليه الصلاة والسلام إذا صلَّى صلاة أحب أن يداوم عليها. وكان رسول الله صلى الله عليه وسلم إذا شغله عن صلاة الليل نوم أو وجع صلَّى ثلاث عشرة ركعة[482] من النهار لا

476 ثم: حتى، ب.

477 رواه النسائي، سورة المزمل، ر١١٦٢٧، وابن حبان، باب النوافل، ر٢٥٢٥.

478 فهممت: فهمت، ب،د.

479 فسألتها: -، ب.

480 تسميحا: +، ب.

481 رواه مسلم، باب جَامِعِ صَلاَةِ اللَّيْلِ وَمَنْ نَامَ عَنْهُ أَوْ مَرِضَ، ر١٧٧٣، والنسائي، الوتر بتسع، ر٤٤٨.

482 ركعة: ركعات، ب.

نعلم أنَّ رسول الله عليه الصلاة والسلام نام[483] ليلة حتَّى أصبح، ولا قرأ القرآن كله في ليلة قط، ولا صام شهراً كاملاً قط إلاَّ رمضان[484].

فأتيت ابن عبَّاس فأخبرته بذلك. قال: صدقت، أمَّا أنِّي لو كنت أدخل عليها لأتيتها فشافهتها مشافهة، قلت[485]: أما إنِّي لو أعلم[486] أنك لا تدخل عليها ما نبأتك[487] بحديثها.

سئل عن رجل أوتر على راحلته؟

قال: يصلِّي عليها تطوّعاً فإذا أراد أن يوتر أناخ فأوتر.

سئل عن الرجل ينتهي إلى المسجد والصلاة تقام ولم يصلِّ[488] ركعتي الفجر؟

قال: كان أصحابنا يكرهون أن يصلِّيها في المسجد، والناس يصلّون الفريضة، ولكن يخرج إن شاء، فإن خاف أن تفوته الفريضة مع الإمام فليصل الفريضة مع الإمام[489] ويصلِّي الركعتين بعد طلوع الشمس، وإن كان[490] صلَّى آخر الليل أجزاه ذلك.

سئل عن رجل انتهى إلى المسجد والمؤذِّن يقيم لصلاة الصبح ولم يركع ركعتي الفجر؟

---

483 نام: قام، ب.

484 رواه النسائي، ذكر اختلاف الناقدين لخبر عائشة في ذلك، ر٤٢٥، وأحمد، ر٢٤٣١٤.

485 قلت: قال، ب.

486 أعلم: كنت، ب.

487 نبأتك: أتيتك، ب.

488 يصل: يصلي، ب، د.

489 فليصل الفريضة مع الإمام: +، ب.

490 قد: +، ب.

قال: إن قدر على أن يصلّيهما قبل أن يفرغ المؤذّن من الإقامة فليتنحَّ[491] وليصلِّهما في الخارج، ثُمَّ يدخل معهم في صلاتهم. وإن لم يقدر فليصلِّهما[492] إذا طلعت الشمس.

عن قتادة أنَّه كان يستحبّ أن يقرأ في ركعتي الفجر: ﴿قل يا أيُّها الكافرون﴾، و﴿قل هو الله أحد﴾.

سئل: هل يضطجع الإنسان بعد أن يركع[493] ركعتي الفجر قبل أن يصلِّي الصبح؟
قال: لا، إلاَّ أن يكون مضطرا، فإن فعل فليس عليه شيء.
عن أيُّوب عن نافع عن ابن عمر أنه رأى[494] رجلا يصلِّي، فصلَّى ركعتي الفجر ثُمَّ اضطجع، فقال له[495]: ما يحملك على هذا؟ قال: الفصل بينها وبين صلاة الصبح.
قال: كفى بالتسليم فصل[496].
عن قتادة: أنَّ عمر بن الخطَّاب رضي الله عنه قال: هما أحبّ إليَّ من حمر النعم.

سئل عن رجل صلَّى من المغرب ركعة قبل أن يسقط قرن الشمس، وركعتين بعد ما غابت الشمس؟

قال: يعيد صلاته.

---

491 فليتنح: فليتنحي، ب،د.

492 فليصلهما: فليصليهما،د؛ ثم يصليها، ب.

493 يركع: يصلي، ب.

494 رأى: أن، ب.

495 له: –، ب.

496 فصل: فصلي، ب،د.

سئل عن صلاة الضحى؟

قال: فحدث[497] عن صاحب له عن عكرمة أنَّ ابن عبَّاس كان يصلِّي الضحى يوما ولا يصلِّيها عشرة أيَّام. قال: كان أبو عبيدة يصلِّيها يوما ويتركها زمانا.

قال: حدَّثني الربيع أنه لقي أبا عبيدة وهو في[498] طريقه بعد أن خرج من سجن الحجاج[499]. فقال: أنظرني[500] حتَّى أصلِّي ركعتين فلا عهد لي بهما منذ حين.

عن قتادة عن قاسم الشيباني[501] عن زيد بن أرقم: أنَّ نبيَّ الله عليه الصلاة والسلام مرَّ بمسجد قباء ودخل المسجد[502]، فصلَّى الضحى[503] بعد ما أشرقت الشمس. فقال: إنَّ الأوَّابين كانوا يصلُّونها إذا رمضت الفصال[504].

وقال: بلغنا أنَّ نبيَّ الله عليه الصلاة والسلام لم[505] يصلِّهما[506] إلاَّ أن يقدم من سفر فيصلِّي الضحى من قبل أن يدخل إلى أهله[507].

عن الحسن: أنَّ نبيَّ الله عليه الصلاة والسلام صلَّى الضحى ذات يوم فأطال فيها، فقيل: يا نبيّ الله، لقد رأيناك تصلِّي صلاة ما رأيناك تصليها. قال: إنَّها صلاة

---

497 فحدث: +، ب.

498 وهو في: الجنان، ب.

499 بعد أن خرج من سجن الحجاج: –، ب.

500 انظرني: انتظر، ب.

501 الشيباني: السماني، د.

502 قباء، بعد ما أشرقت الشمس: +، ب.

503 فصلى الضحى: –، ب.

504 رواه مسلم، باب صلاة الأوابين حين ترمض الفصال، ر١٧٨١، وأحمد، ر١٩٢٨٤.

505 يكن: +، ب.

506 يصلهما: يصليهما، ب، د.

507 رواه أحمد، ر١٥، وابن حبان، باب الحوض والشفاعة، ر٦٤٧٦.

رغبة ورهبة، وإني سألت ربي فيها ثلاثا، فأعطاني اثنتين ومنعني واحدة[508]، سألت ربي ألاَّ يسلط على أمَّتي السّيّئة[509] فيهلكهم، فأعطانيها، وسألته ألاَّ يسلط عليهم العدو من غيرهم، فأعطانيها، وسألته ألاَّ يلبسهم شيعا ويذيق بعضهم بأس بعض فمنعنيها[510].

عن أيُّوب عن أبي صفوان عن عبد الله بن الحارث بن نوفل: أنَّ ابن عبَّاس كان لا يصلِّي الضحى، فدخلت[511] على أم هانئ فقلت: أخبري هذا بما أخبرتني به، فقالت أم هانئ: دخل عليّ رسول الله صلى الله عليه وسلم يوم الفتح، فأمر بماء فصب في قصعة، ثُمَّ أمر بثوب فأخذه بيني وبينه فاغتسل ثُمَّ مشى ناحية البيت، فصلَّى ثمان ركعات قيامهن وركوعهن وسجودهن وجلوسهن سواء قريب بعضهم من بعض، فخرج ابن عبَّاس وهو يقول: لقد قرأت ما بين اللوحين فما عرفت[512] إلاَّ الساعة يسبحن بالعشي والإشراق[513].

سئل عن صلاة الفطر والنحر؟

قال: بلغنا أنَّ رسول الله عليه الصلاة والسلام وأبا بكر وعمر وعثمان – صدرا من خلافته –، كانوا يصلون قبل الخطبة[514]، ثُمَّ إن الناس كثروا على عهد عثمان فقالوا: لو

508 واحدة: الثالثة، ب.

509 السيئة: +، ب.

510 رواه أحمد، ر١٢٥٠٨، وابن خزيمة، باب استحباب مسألة الله عز وجل في صلاة الضحى رجاء الإجابة، ر١٢٢٨.

511 فدخلت: فأدخلته، ب.

512 قطُّ: +، ب.

513 ثم هي صلاة الإشراق: –، د.

514 رواه البخاري، باب الخطبة بعد العيد، ر٩١٩، ومسلم، صلاة العيدين، ر٢٠٨١.

جعلنا الخطبة قبل الصلاة لأدرك الناس، ففعل[515] وكانوا لا يؤذنون ولا يقيمون. قال: وأوّل من أحدث الأذان يوم الفطر والأضحى[516] معاوية بن أبي سفيان، وأوّل من أفرد الإقامة معاوية؛ لأنّه كان يطول عليه القعود على المنبر، حتّى يفرغ من الإقامة فأفردها.

عن حمّاد عن النخعي: أنّ الوليد بن عقبة بن أبي معيط[517] جاء إلى حلقة فيها ابن مسعود وحذيفة بن اليماني وأبو موسى الأشعري، وهو يومئذ أمير على الكوفة، فقال: إن هذا العيد قد حضر، فكيف الصلاة والتكبير فيه؟
فقال ابن مسعود: تبدأ فتُكبِّر تكبيرة تفتتح بها الصلاة، وتحمد الله وتصلّي على النبيّ عليه الصلاة والسلام، ثُمّ تدعو، ثُمّ تُكبِّر وتفعل مثل ذلك، ثُمّ تُكبِّر ثُمّ تفعل مثل ذلك، ثُمّ تُكبِّر وتقرأ ثُمّ تُكبِّر وتركع، فإذا نهضت واليت بين القراءتين ثُمّ تُكبِّر، وتحمد الله وتصلّي على النبيّ وتدعو ثُمّ تُكبِّر وتفعل مثل ذلك، ثُمّ تُكبِّر وتفعل مثل ذلك ثُمّ تُكبِّر[518] وتركع.
قال حذيفة وأبو موسى: أحسن أبو عبد الرحمن؟[519] قال: لم نسمع بالدعاء[520]، وأنّه أمره بالتكبيرة التي يفتتح بها الصلاة، ثُمّ يُكبّر أربعا ثُمّ يقرأ ويركع ويسجد، ثُمّ يقوم فيقرأ، ثُمّ يُكبّر ثلاثا ثُمّ يركع ويسجد.

---

515 ففعل: ففعلوا، د.
516 الأضحى: النحر، ب.
517 معيط: سعيد، ب.
518 وتفعل مثل ذلك ثم تكبر: -، د.
519 قال حذيفة وأبو موسى: أحسن أبو عبد الرحمن؟: -، د.
520 بلغنا: +، ب.

عن قتادة عن عكرمة عن ابن عبّاس أنّه قال:[521] كبّر سبعا أو تسعا أو إحدى عشرة أو ثلاث عشرة.

سئل عن الصلاة قبل الإمام وبعده يوم الفطر والأضحى؟
قال: أمّا الفطر فلم يكن أصحابنا يرون بأسا قبلها وبعدها، وأمّا الأضحى فقبلها وليس بعدها شيء، وكان بعض أصحابنا يقولون: لو صلّيت قبلها ماباليت ألاّ أصلّي مع الإمام، فأما الربيع فكان لا[522] يرى قبلها ولا بعدها.

عن قتادة: أنّه كان يكره الكلام يوم الفطر والأضحى والإمام يخطب؟ قال: ذكر ذلك[523].

عن قتادة: أنّه كان يعجبه الغسل يوم الفطر والنحر. قال: نعم، يستحبّ وليس بواجب[524].

سئل عن صلاة الفطر والأضحى؟[525]
عن جابر بن زيد: أنّ الصلاة كانت[526] في الفطر والأضحى قبل الخطبة ولا أذان[527]

---

521 أنه: +، ب.
522 لا: -، ب.
523 قال: فذكر ذلك: -،د.
524 عن قتادة: أنّه كان يعجبه الغسل يوم الفطر والنحر. قال: نعم، يستحبّ وليس بواجب: -، د.
525 سئل: عن صلاة الفطر والأضحى: -،د.
526 كانت: -، ب.
527 أذان: آذان، ب،د.

فيها ولا إقامة، ومن أراد في صلاة الفطر[528] أن يُكبّر سبعا كبر في الركعة الأولى أربعا قبل القراءة ثُمَّ يركع ويسجد، فإذا قام قرأ فإذا فرغ من قراءته كبَّر ثلاثا، ومن أراد تسعا كبر في الركعة الأولى أربعا وفي الثانية خمسا، ومن أراد الإحدى عشرة بدأ فأحرم ثُمَّ كبَّر ستا، ثُمَّ قرأ وركع وسجد ثُمَّ قام فقرأ فإذا فرغ من قراءته كبر خمسا وركع بالسادسة، ومن أراد ثلاث عشرة بدأ فأحرم ثُمَّ كبَّر[529] خمسا ثم قرأ[530]، فإذا فرغ من قراءته ركع بالسادسة ثُمَّ سجد، ثُمَّ قام فقرأ، ثُمَّ كبر خمسا ثُمَّ ركع، فإذا رفع رأسه كبر ثلاثا ثُمَّ سجد[531].

عن قتادة: أنَّه كان يعجبه أن يخرج أهل القرى فيصلي بهم رجلٌ[532] منهم. قال: نعم[533]، وإذا[534] كان القوم في سفر أن يجتمعوا فيصلوا جميعا. قال: نعم، إذا كانوا عشرة ونحو ذلك.

---

528 صلاة الفطر: –، د.

529 كبر: تكبر، ب، د.

530 ثم قرأ: ثُمَّ قرأ، ب، د.

531 من أراد السبعة بدأ فأحرم، ثُمَّ يكبر أربعة، ثُمَّ قرأ وركع وسجد، ثُمَّ قام فقرأ حتى إذا فرغ من قراءته كبر ثلاثة ثُمَّ ركع في الرابعة. ومن أراد تسعة بدأ فأحرم، ثُمَّ كبر أربعة ثُمَّ يقرأ، ثُمَّ يكبر الخامسة ثُمَّ يركع ويسجد، وإذا قام قرأ فإذا فرغ من قراءته كبر خمسة، ثُمَّ كبر السادسة وركع وسجد. ومن أراد الأحدى عشر بدأ فأحرم ثُمَّ، كبر ستة ثُمَّ قرأ وركع وسجد، وقام وقرأ فإذا فرغ من قراءته كبر خمسة ثُمَّ يركع بالسادسة. ومن أراد الثلاثة عشر، بدأ فأحرم ثُمَّ كبر خمسة، ثُمَّ قام فقرأ فإذا فرغ من قراءته ركع بالسادسة، فسجد فإذا قام قرأ، فإذا فرغ من قراءته كبر خمسة ثُمَّ ركع، فإذا رفع رأسه كبر ثلاثة ثُمَّ سجد، ب.

532 رجل: رجلا، ب، د.

533 أن يخرج أهل القرى فيصلي بهم رجلا منهم. قال: نعم: –، د.

534 وإذا: إذا، ب، د.

عن قتادة قال: كان يعجبه أن يخرج الرجل وأهله[535] يوم الفطر والأضحى إلى الصلاة؟ قال: نعم[536].

عن صاحب له عن نافع أنَّ عمر بن الخطَّاب رضي الله عنه قال: لا تمنعوا إماء[537] الله أن يخرجن إلى الصلاة[538]..

قال: نعم، في الفطر والأضحى.

سئل عن رجل لم يدرك الصلاة مع الإمام يوم الفطر والأضحى؟

قال: يصلِّي كما يصلِّي الضحى.

سئل عن التكبير أيَّام التشريق في دبر كلّ صلاة؟

قال: أمَّا جابر بن زيد فلم يكن يُكبّر في التشريق شيئًا، ومن صنعه فهو حسن[539].

سئل عن صلاة التراويح؟

قال: عن سلام[540] بن تميم[541] عن الحسن عن أُبيّ بن كعب أنَّه صلَّى بهم أربعين ركعة فسلم في كلّ ركعتين إلاَّ في ركعة الوتر فإنَّه كان ينهض ولا يسلم.

قال: نعم، من صلَّى الوتر ثلاثا فهي مثل صلاة المغرب ومن صلَّى واحدة فحسن.

---

535 بيته: +، ب.

536 قال: نعم: -،د.

537 إماء: إيماء، ب،د.

538 رواه البخاري عن ابن عمر مرفوعا إلى النبي صلى الله عليه وسلم، باب هل على من لم يشهد الجمعة غسل من النساء والصبيان وغيرهم، ر٨٥٨.

539 انظر: آثار الربيع، مسألة ٢٤٥، ص ٥٩.

540 سلام: سالم، ب.

541 تميم: غنيم، ب.

سئل عن القوم يؤمّهم الرجل وهو يقرأ[542] في المصحف؟

قال: إن أصابوا غيره وإلاّ أجزأعنهم.

عن قتادة[543] عن سعيد بن المسيب قال: إذا كان مع الإمام ما يقرأ به ليلة، فلا يقرأ في المصحف يكرر ما معه؟ قال: نعم[544].

سئل عن الرجل يصلّي فيما بين الترويحتين في رمضان فيقوم الإمام إلى الصلاة وهو كذلك؟

قال: يكره أن يصلّي الرجل في رمضان، والإمام قاعد إلاّ رجلا فاته شيء فيقضيه ويدخل معهم بتكبيرة.

سئل عن رجل يصلّي بظهر بيته بصلاة الإمام وهو عن يمين الإمام أو عن شماله أو من خلفه أو من قدامه.

قال: أمّا الفريضة فإنّه[545] يكره، ولا بأس بالتطوّع.

سئل أيصلّي الرجل بعد الوتر؟

قال: نعم.

سئل عن رجل يؤمّ النساء، ليس فيهن[546] ذو محرم.

542 وهو يقرأ: -، ب.

543 عن قتادة: -، ب.

544 قال: نعم: -،د.

545 أنه: +، ب.

546 فيهن: معهن، ب.

قال: لا بأس إذا كان النساء جماعة، وأمّا الواحدة فإنّه يكره إلاّ أن تكون محرمته.

سئل عن ليلة القدر؟

قال: فحدث قتادة: أنّ أعرابيا من جهينة أتى إلى النبيّ عليه الصلاة والسلام فذكر له بُعد منزله، وسأله عن ليلة القدر فأسر إليه النبيّ حديثا لا يدري القوم ما هو يريد أن يشهدها في أهله، يقال[547]: ليلة أربع[548] وعشرين، ويقال: ليلة ثلاث وعشرين، أو سبع[549] وعشرين.

عن قتادة قال: ذكر لنا أنّ نبيّ الله عليه الصلاة والسلام قال ذات يوم: إن هذا الشهر قد حضر، وهو شهر مبارك افترض الله صيامه، تفتح فيه أبواب الجنّة، وتغلق فيه أبواب الجحيم، ويغل فيه الشياطين، وفيه ليلة القدر خير من ألف شهر، من حرم خيرها فقد حرم[550].

عن قتادة قال: ذكر لنا أن ليالي رمضان ونهاره تفتح فيه أبواب السماء، وينادي كلّ ليلة من أوّل الليل مناد: هل من داع فيستجاب له؟ هل من سائل فيعطى؟ وهل من مستغفر فيغفر له؟ هل من تائب يتوب فيتاب عليه إلى آخر الليلة من رمضان؟ قال: نعم[551].

547 يقال: -، ب.

548 أربع: أربعة، ب،د.

549 سبع: سبعة، ب،د.

550 رواه النسائي: السنن الكبرى، كتاب الصيام، ر٢٤١٦. وابن ماجه، باب ما جاء في فضل شهر رمضان، ر١٦٤٤,

551 قال: نعم: -،د.

وسئل[552] عن قوله تعالى ﴿فِيهَا يُفْرَقُ كلّ أَمْرٍ حَكِيمٍ﴾[553].

عن قتادة قال: كنّا نحدث أنّه يفرق فيها أمر السنة إلى السنة. قال: قد بلغنا ذلك[554].

باب الجمعة

سئل عن الجمعة؟ فحدّث[555] عن قتادة: أنّ نبيّ الله عليه الصلاة والسلام كان يخطب يوم الجمعة[556] فجعل يخطب الناس ويعظهم ويذكرهم، وجعلوا يتسللون ويقومون حتّى بقيت منهم عصابة. قال: كم أنتم؟ فعدوا أنفسهم فإذا هم اثنا عشر رجلا وامرأة، ثمّ قام يوم الجمعة الثانية فجعل يخطبهم ويعظهم[557]، وجعلوا يتسللون ويقومون حتّى بقيت منهم عصابة. قال: كم أنتم، فعدوا أنفسهم[558] فإذا هم اثنا عشر رجلا وامرأة، فقال رسول الله عليه الصلاة والسلام ـ: والذي نفسي بيده، لو اتبع آخركم أولكم لالتهب عليكم هذا الوادي نارا[559].

قال: ثمّ أنزل الله تعالى: ﴿وَإِذَا رَأَوْا تِجَارَةً أَوْ لَهْوًا انْفَضُّوا إِلَيْهَا وَتَرَكُوكَ قَائِمًا﴾[560].

قال: هذا والذي بلغنا: أنّها كانت جمعة واحدة، جاءت عير من الشام فخرجوا إليها

552 وسئل: قد يقال ذلك، ب.

553 سورة الدخان: ٤.

554 قال: قد بلغنا ذلك: -، د.

555 سئل: عن الجمعة؟ فحدث: -، د.

556 يخطب يوم الجمعة: الناس، بدل يوم الجمعة، ب.

557 ويذكرهم: +، ب.

558 فعدوا أنفسهم: -، ب.

559 رواه البيهقي: شعب الإيمان، فضل الجمعة، ر٣٠١٩.

560 سورة الجمعة: ١١.

وتركوا النبيّ عليه الصلاة والسلام في اثني عشر رجلا وامرأة؟ فقال هذه المقالة[561].

سئل عن الغسل يوم الجمعة؟

فقال: ذكروا أنَّ عمر بن الخطَّاب رضي الله عنه إذا عاب[562] بعض أهله فيقول له: لأنّك أعجز من تارك الغسل يوم الجمعة.

عن قتادة: أنَّ كعبا وأبا هريرة[563] وعبد الله بن عبَّاس اجتمعوا فقال كعب: خلق الله آدم يوم الجمعة، وأسكنه في الجنَّة يوم الجمعة، وتاب عليه يوم الجمعة وتقوم الساعة يوم الجمعة، ويحق على كلّ مسلم أن يستحم[564] يوم الجمعة، قال أبو هريرة: يا ابن عبَّاس اسمع مايقول أبو إسحاق: فقال: ابن عبَّاس: نعم، ويمس من طيب أهله.

قال: نعم، يستحبّ الغسل يوم الجمعة[565] وليس بواجب، ويستحبّ الطيب والزينة يوم الجمعة[566].

عن قتادة عن الحسن: أنَّ رسول الله عليه الصلاة والسلام قال: من توضَّأ يوم الجمعة فبها[567] فضل ونعمة، ومن اغتسل فذلك أفضل؟[568] قال: نعم[569].

561 فقال هذه المقالة: –،د.

562 عاب: عاتب، ب.

563 أبا هريرة: –، ب.

564 يستحم: يغتسل، ب.

565 يوم الجمعة: –،د.

566 يستحب ذلك: +، ب.

567 فبها: فذلك، ب.

568 رواه أبو داود، باب في الرخصة في ترك الغسل يوم الجمعة، ر٣٥٤.

569 قال نعم: –،د.

عن قتادة عن[570] أبي رافع عن أبي هريرة: أنَّ رسول الله عليه الصلاة والسلام قال: إن في الجمعة ساعة لا يوافقها رجل مسلم فيصلِّي ويسأل الله فيها[571] خيرًا إلاَّ أعطاه[572].
وقال: إن جابرا كان يقول: إذا أقام الناس للصلاة عند الإقامة.

سئل عن الخطبة يوم الجمعة؟

قال: عن قتادة: أنَّ رسول الله عليه الصلاة والسلام وأبا بكر وعمر وعثمان، كانوا يخطبون قياما يوم الجمعة، ثُمَّ إن عثمان لما كبر جعل يقعد يتروح ولا يتكلم حتَّى ينهض. قال: نعم[573]، وأوّل من أحدث القعود فيما بلغنا عثمان[574].

عن قتادة عن عبد الملك بن يعلى قال: من ترك الجمعة[575] ثلاث جمعات من غير عذر لم تجز له شهادة[576].

قال: نعم، إذا تركها من غير عذر[577]، فهو أهل ألاَّ تجوز له شهادة[578]. قال: كذلك[579] رأي أبي عمرو الربيع[580].

---

570 الحسن: +، ب.

571 فيها: -، ب.

572 رواه الربيع، باب في صلاة الجمعة وفضل يومها، ر٢٨٠. والبخاري، باب الساعة التي في يوم الجمعة، ر٨٩٣.

573 نعم: -،د.

574 رواه عبد الرزاق، باب الخطبة قائما، ر٥٢٥٨.

575 الجمعة: -، ب.

576 شهادة: شهادته، ب.

577 عذر: قهر، ب.

578 شهادة: شهادته، ب.

579 كذلك: وكان ذلك، ب.

580 الربيع: ابن عامر، ب.

سئل عمَّن لا تجب عليه الجمعة؟

قال: حدث[581] قتادة قال: [582] ليس لأحد أن يتخلف عن الجمعة، إلاَّ رجل مريض أو صاحب جنازة.

قال: وكذلك في الحر الشديد، والمطر والبرد الشديد.

عن قتادة: أنَّه قال: ليس على المرأة جمعة، فإن جمعت[583] مع الإمام فقد أجزأ عنها صلاتها مع الإمام؟ قال: نعم[584].

سئل هل على العبد جمعة؟

قال: ليس على العبد جمعة، ولا على المرأة ولا على المسافر، والجمعة على من قدر أن يأوي إلى أهله فلا يتخلف عنها وهو يستطيع.

عن قتادة: أنَّ عمر بن عبد العزيز كتب إلى أهل الصدقة[585] أن يجمعوا. قال: ليس عليهم جمعة.

سئل متى يقطع الكلام يوم الجمعة؟

قال: من حين[586] يخرج الإمام إلى أن يفرغ من صلاته، ويكره ذلك أيضا للإمام.

سئل عن الكلام والصحف تقرأ.

581 عن: +، ب.

582 كان يقال: +، ب.

583 جمعت: أجمعت، ب.

584 قال: نعم: -، د.

585 الصدقة: الصوبة، ب.

586 حين: حيث، ب.

قال: أمَّا كتب أهل العدل فلا يتكلمون حتَّى يفرغ الذي يقرأ.

عن يوسف عن عمرو بن شعيب عن أبيه عن جده: أنَّ رسول الله عليه الصلاة والسلام قال: قال يحضر الجمعة ثلاثة رجال، رجل بدعاء وصلاة، فذلك رجل يدعو ربه إن شاء أعطاه وإن شاء منعه، ورجل يحضرها بإنصات وسكون فذلك حقها، ورجل يحضرها بلغو فذلك خطأ منه[587].

عن قتادة عن الحسن: أنَّ رسول الله عليه الصلاة والسلام كان يخطب، وجاء رجل يتخطَّى رقاب الناس حتَّى جلس، فلمَّا فرغ[588] رسول الله عليه الصلاة والسلام من صلاته قال للرجل: أما جمعت يا فلان، أو قال: ما منعك أن تجمع، إمَّا مرَّتين وإما ثلاثا، كلّ ذلك يقول: أمَا رأيتني[589] يا رسول الله؟ قال: بلى أتيت وآذيت[590].

قال: يكره أن يتخطَّى رقاب الناس، ويستحبّ أن يقعد حيث وجد مجلسا من خلف الناس.

سئل عن الإمام إذا لم يخطب الناس يوم الجمعة: أيصلِّي ركعتين أم يصلّي أربعا؟

قال: يصلَّى ركعتين خطب أو لم يخطب.

سئل عن الصلاة في رحبة المسجد؟

قال: الصلاة في المسجد أفضل والرحبة جائزة[591].

---

587 رواه أحمد، ر٦٧٠١.

588 فرغ: فضى، ب.

589 أما رأيتني: أمّا رأيتن، ب،د.

590 رواه ابن أبي شيبة، باب في تخطي الرقاب يوم الجمعة، ر٥٥١٥.

591 فالصلاة في المسجد أفضل من رحبتها: هامش، ب.

سئل عن رجل يصلِّي أمام الإمام يوم الجمعة، أو عن يمينه أو عن شماله إذا لم يقدر على المسجد؟

قال: ما أحب ذلك إلاَّ أن يدخل المسجد وهو أفضل، وكان يستحبّ أن يدنو من الإمام ويسمع الخطبة، ويكره أن يقوم أمام الإمام.

سئل عن الرجل يأتي يوم الجمعة والإمام يخطب؟

قال: يجلس ولا يصلِّي.

سئل: هل يصلِّي إذا خرج الإمام؟ أم يكره ذلك إلاَّ أن يخرج من المسجد؟

قال: كان أصحابنا يكرهون أن يصلِّي أحد والإمام يخطب ولكن ليخرج إن شاء فليصل.

سئل عن صلاة الجمعة في اليوم المطير[592] والحر الشديد والبرد الشديد والخوف والمرض[593]؟

فحدث عن قتادة عن ابن عبَّاس في يوم مطير، أمر مناديه فنادى: الصلاة في الرحال[594]. قال: فدبروا أصحابنا[595].

قال: لا جمعة في هذه الخصال.

592 المطير: المطر، ب.

593 والحر الشديد والبرد الشديد والخوف والمريض: -، ب.

594 الرحال: الرجال، ب،د.

595 فحدث عن قتادة عن ابن عبَّاس في يوم مطير، أمر مناديه فنادى الصلاة في الرحال. قال: فدبروا أصحابنا: -،د.

عن أيُّوب عن عبد الله بن الحارث: أنَّ[596] ابن عبَّاس قال لمؤذنه يوم جمعة مطيرة: إذا بلغت (حيّ على الفلاح) فأمسك حتَّى أكلمك[597]، فلمَّا بلغ «حيّ على الفلاح». قال: «نادِ: الصلاة في الرحال»، فنظر الناس. فقال: ما شأنكم؟ كأنكم تنكرون، فعله من هو خير مني. وإنها عزيمة أكره أن أخرجكم فتمشوا في الطين[598]. قال: بلغنا هذا[599].

عن قتادة عن أبي المليح عن أبيه: أنَّه شهد رسول الله عليه الصلاة والسلام في يوم مطير فأمر مناد[600] ينادي: الصلاة في الرحال[601].

عن قتادة عن سعيد بن المسيب قال: جمعة أحبّ إليَّ من حج تطوّع. قال:[602] بعد هذا القول هذه فريضة والحجّ بعد أداء الفريضة تطوّعًا.

عن قتادة والحسن: أنَّهما كانا لا يريان[603] بأسا أن يخوض الرجل الماء والطين يوم الجمعة، ثُمَّ يصلّي على حاله تلك غير أنَّه يميطه.

قال: بلغنا: أنَّ جابر بن زيد كان[604] يمشي في الطين فإذا بلغ باب المسجد مسح رجليه بالأرض ثُمَّ دخل فصلَّى.

عن قتادة قال: ذكر لنا أنَّه يبعث يوم الجمعة ملائكة على أبواب المساجد، يكتبون مجيء كلّ

---

596 عبد الله: +، ب.

597 أكلمك: آمرك، ب.

598 أخرجكم فتمشون في الطين: أوتمهم، ب د؛ رواه البخاري، ر٥٢١

599 وإنها عزيمة أكره إن أوتمهم. قال: بلغنا هذا: -،د.

600 مناد: مناديه، ب.

601 رواه أبو داود، باب الجمعة في اليوم المطير، ر١٠٥٩.

602 ما: +، ب.

603 يريان: يريا، ب.

604 كان: -، ب.

امرئ في ساعة كذا وكذا، حتّى يكتبوا: أدرك فلان الصلاة وفاتته الجمعة. قال: بلغنا أنّهم يكتبون حتّى يخطب الإمام، فإذا خطب الإمام لم يكتبوا، إذ[605] يكتبون السابق لسبقه.

عن قتادة عن ابن مسعود كان يصلّي في بيته يوم الجمعة ركعتين، فإذا جاء المسجد صلّى ركعتين وبعدها أربع ركعات وقال: يستحبّ أربع قبلها وأربع بعدها.
عن أبي معشر عن النخعي: أنّ ابن مسعود كان يصلّي بعدها أربعا وقبلها أربعا.

سئل عن الرجل يدرك ركعة مع الإمام يوم الجمعة: أيصلّي ركعتين أم يصلّي أربعا؟
قال: كان يقال: إن من أدرك التشهُّد مع الإمام حين يرفع رأسه فدخل معه صلّى ركعتين، وإن فاته تشهد الإمام صلّى أربعا.

سئل عمّن دخل في صلاة الإمام فركع ومنعه الزحام من الركوع والسجود؟
قال: يقوم حين ينصرف الإمام فيصلّي ركعتين صلاة[606] الجمعة.

سئل عن رجل كبّر مع الإمام ثمّ لم يقدر على ركوع ولا سجود من الزحام؟
قال: يصلّي ركعتي الجمعة إذا انصرف الإمام.

سئل عن رجل زحم يوم الجمعة حتّى خرج من المسجد وقد كبر مع الإمام من غير أن يركع؟
قال: إن كان خرج من المسجد وأدبر بالقبلة فليصلّ أربعا.

605 إذ: أحدا، ب.

606 صلاة: -، ب.

سئل عن الاحتباء يوم الجمعة؟

قال: لا بأس[607].

سئل عن العيد إذا وافق[608] يوم الجمعة[609]؟

قال: كان أبو عبيدة يرى إذا اجتمعا[610] والرجل[611] يضعف عنهما أن يترك العيد ويصلِّي الجمعة.

سئل عن الرجل يسافر يوم الجمعة؟

قال: بلغنا عن حاجب أنَّه يكره أن يخرج حتَّى يجمع، وقد خرج أصحابه فأدركهم في الطريق بعد يومين.

باب في غسل المَيِّت

سئل عن غسل المِيِّت؟

قال: عن[612] قتادة: أنَّ رسول الله عليه الصلاة والسلام غسله الفضل بن عبَّاس وعليّ بن أبي طالب، وكان أسامة بن زيد يصبّ الماء عليهما[613].

607 : سئل: عن الاحتباء يوم الجمعة؟ قال: لا بأس: -، د.

608 وافق: اجتمعا، ب.

609 يوم الجمعة: -، ب.

610 فخاف: +، ب.

611 أن: +، ب.

612 حدث، ب.

613 رواه الطبراني: المعجم الكبير، ر١٢١٤٧.

وقال: يُوضَّأ المَيِّت وضوء الصلاة، [614] يغسل بماء قراح ثُمَّ يغسل بالسدر، ثُمَّ يغسل بالماء حتَّى ينقيه، ويجعل الكافور في آخر غسلة.

سئل عن الْمَيِّت إذا غسل فخرج منه شيء بعد غسله؟

قال: إن كان سائلا أو قاطرا يعاد الغسل إلى خمس مرَّات، وإن لم يكن سائلا ولا قاطرا غسل ذلك المكان ولا يعاد.

سئل عن المرأة: هل تغسل زوجها؟

قال[615]: حدث أبو نوح أن امرأة جابر بن زيد أوصاها أن تغسله[616]، وقال: هي أحقّ بذلك من غيرها. وكان يرى أنَّ الرجل أحقّ بغسل امرأته، وبلغنا: أنَّ أبا بكر الصديق [617] أمر امرأته أن تغسله.

سئل عن الرجل يموت في النسوة وليس معهن ذو محرم؟

قال: لا أرى بأسا أن تغسله أمه أو امرأته أو ذات محرم ويتقين فرجه [618].

سئل عن امرأة تموت مع قوم ليس معهم إلاَّ [619] يهوديّة أو نصرانيّة؟

قال: تغسل اليهوديّة والنصرانيّة يدها غسلا نظيفا ثُمَّ تتعلم فتغسلها.

---

614 ثم: +، ب.

615 قال: -، ب.

616 انظر: آثار الربيع، مسألة ٦، ص ٢٨.

617 أنه: +، ب.

618 انظر إذا ماتت المرأة معها وليس معها من يغسلها من النساء: هامش، ب.

619 امرأة: +، ب.

وسئل[620] عن المرأة تموت وليس معها امرأة ولا زوج ومعها ذو محرم؟

قال: كان الربيع يبسط عليها[621] ثوبا ثُمَّ يدلكها[622] من تحت الثوب ولا يمس فرجها، وإن لم يكن معها محرم صبوا عليها الماء من فوق الثياب[623].

سئل عن غسل الشهيد؟

قال: إن أصابته جراحة فمات في المعركة لم يغسل، وإن رفع وبه رمق ثُمَّ مات غسل.

سئل عن الشهيد؟

قال: لا يغسل ولا ينزع من ثيابه[624] إلاَّ الكمة والخفين والسيف، ولا يغسل ولا يحنط.

سئل عن الذي يغسل المِّيت: هل عليه غسل؟

قال: لا، ولكن يتوضأ وضوء الصلاة.

سئل عن المسك للميت؟

قال: لا بأس به للميت والحي.

سئل عن كفن المَيِّت[625]؟

قال: ثلاثة: درع وإزار ولفافة يجزيه[626]. قال: وبلغنا أنَّ حمزة كفن في ثوب واحد.

---

620 سئل: -، ب.

621 عليها: +، ب.

622 يدلكها: ليدلكها، ب،د.

623 فوق الثوب: تحت الثياب،د.

624 شيء: +، ب.

625 الميت: المرأة، ب.

626 يجزيه: تجزيها، ب.

قال: وبلغنا: أنَّ رسول الله -عليه الصلاة والسلام- قال: عليكم بالبياض ألبسوه أحياءكم[627] وكفنوا فيه موتاكم، فإنّه من خير ثيابكم[628].

عن يعلى بن حكيم عن عبد الرحمن بن القاسم بن مُحمَّد أن أبا بكر[629] كفن في ثلاث لفائف إحداهن غسيل.

وقال: إذا لم يكن قميص فإزار ولفافتان[630]، وإن كان قميص فإزار ولفافة والإزار فوق القميص.

قال: كان يعجبهم القميص، ويكرهون أن يوزر القميص.

سئل عن الكفن: كم يجمر؟

قال: يجمر ثلاث مرّات.

سئل عن النساء: هل يتبعن الجنائز؟

قال: رأينا النساء يتبعن الجنائز ومعهن الفقهاء، ولم يعيبوا[631] ذلك ولم ينهوا عنه، ولو كرهوه لعابوا عليهن.

سئل عن الذي يحمل الجنازة من أين يبدأ حملها؟

قال: رأيتهم يحاذون[632] الجنازة من حيث تليهم.

627 أحياكم: في حياتكم، ب.

628 رواه الربيع، باب الكفن والغسل، ر٤٧١، وأبو داود، باب في البياض، ر٤٠٦٣.

629 أنه: +، ب.

630 لفافتان: لفافة، ب؛ ولفافتين، د.

631 يعيبوا: يغيروا، ب.

632 يحاذون: يحادون، د؛ يحملون، ب.

سئل عن الجنازة تمر على قوم وهم جلوس[633]: هل عليهم قيام حتَّى تمضي؟

قال:[634] عليهم القيام، وإن كانوا يريدون أن يتبعوها فلا يجلسوا حتَّى توضع[635].

سئل عن الرجل تمر عليه الجنازة وهو يمشي: هل عليه أن يقف أو يقعد حتَّى تمضي؟

قال: لا.

سئل: هل يقعد الرجل إذا وضعت الجنازة عند القبر قبل أن توضع في اللحد؟

قال: نعم[636].

سئل[637]: أين يقوم الإمام إذا صلَّى على الجنازة؟

قال: يقوم مقابل الصدر.

سئل عن الصلاة على الميِّت؟

قال: تُكبِّر، ثُمَّ تقرأ الفاتحة[638]، ثُمَّ تُكبِّر[639] ثُمَّ تصلِّي على النبيّ عليه الصلاة والسلام وتدعو للمؤمنين والمؤمنات، ثُمَّ تُكبِّر الثالثة، وتصلِّي على النبيّ وتدعو للميّت[640]، وتدعو له[641] تقول: اللّهمَّ هذا عبدك وابن عبدك وابن أمتك، توفيته وأبقيتنا بعده،

633 جلوس: قعود، ب.

634 ليس: +، ب.

635 فلا يجلسوا حتى توضع: -، ب.

636 صلاة الجنازة وتكبيرها ودعائها: هامش، ب.

637 عن الإمام: +، ب.

638 الكتاب: +، ب.

639 ثم تقرأ: +، ب.

640 للميت: له، ب.

641 وتدعو: يدعو، ب. وتدعو له: -، د.

اللّهمَّ لا تحرمنا أجره، ولا تفتنا بعده، اللّهمَّ ألحقه بنبيه، واغفر له ذنبه، ونور له قبره، وافسح له في الجنَّة، اللّهمَّ اكفنا فقده، واخلف علينا بعده بالإسلام، اللّهمَّ بدل له قرارا خيرا من قراره، ودارا خيرا من داره، وأهلا خيرا من أهله، ثُمَّ تُكبِّر وتسلم[642].

وكان ابن عمر يقول: لم نسمع فيه شيئا مؤقتًا.

سئل عن الصلاة على السقط؟

قال: إن وقع حيا فصلِّ عليه، وإن وقع ميتا لم يصلَّ[643] عليه.

عن قتادة عن الحسن قال: لا يصلَّى عليه ولا يورث حتَّى يستهلَّ صارخًا.

سئل عن الصلاة على ولدِ الزنا؟

قال مُحَمَّد بن كعب عن ميمون بن مهران: إنَّ ابن عمر كان في جنازةٍ فجعلوا يتوشوشون أنَّه لزانية. قال: وكان يقال: إنَّه لشر الثلاثة، فانتهى ذلك إلى ابن[644] عمر فصلَّى عليه، فقال: بل هو خير الثلاثة، وقال: يا مسور إن كان ما يقول أبو هريرة حقًّا لقد لقيت شرًّا، قال يصلَّى عليه، وأمَّا شرّ الثلاثة فحدَّثني الربيع أن رجلا أسلم أبوه[645] ولم يسلم هو فبلغ النبيّ عليه الصلاة والسلام فقال: شرّ الثلاثة.

642 ثم تُكبِّر وتسلم: -، ب.

643 يصل: يصلي، ب،د.

644 ابن: -، ب.

645 أسلم أبوه: أبويه أسلاما، ب.

سئل عن المشي أمام الجنازة؟

قال: [646] يكره، إنَّمَا يتبع الجنازة من كان خلفها، وقد ذكر عن أبي بكر وعمر أنَّهما كانا يمشيان [647] أمامها يرخّصون ذلك للناس.

سئل عن الصلاة على المرجوم؟

قال: إذا جاء تائبا صُلِّي عليه، وإن أُخذ وهو زانٍ [648] لم يصلَّ [649] عليه [650].

سئل عن الرجل يموت والده مشركًا: أيصلّي عليه ويقوم [651] عليه [652] ويلي دفنه؟

قال: لا يصلّي عليه، ولا يتبع جنازته، ولكنه يتقدّم ويدفنه [653].

سئل عن الرجل يفوته بعض التكبير على الجنازة؟

قال: يُكبّر ما أدرك ولا يقضي ما سبق به.

سئل عن الرجل يسبق بالصلاة على الجنازة؟

قال: إذا فاته التكبير أتى القبر فدعا [654] ولم يُكبّر.

---

646 كان ذلك: +، ب.

647 يمشيان: −، ب.

648 زان: زاني، ب،د.

649 يصل: يصلي، ب،د.

650 المرجوم إذا جاء تائبا صُلي عليه، وإن أخذ وهو زانٍ لم يصلَّ عليه: هامش، ب.

651 خلفه: +، ب.

652 عليه: −، ب.

653 من مات والده مشركا لا يتبع جنازته، ولكن يدفنه: هامش، ب.

654 فدعا: فيدعو، ب.

عن قتادة عن عطاء عن جابر بن عبد الله: أنَّ رسول الله صلى الله عليه وسلم لما بلغه موت النجاشي. قال: صلوا على أخ[655] لكم مات في غير بلادكم[656]. قال: فصلَّى عليه رسول الله صلى الله عليه وسلم وأصحابه. قال: فصففنا خلفه صفوفا، قال جابر: فكنت في الصف الثاني أو الثالث. قال: وكان اسم النجاشي أصحمة[657].

عن معمر عن الزهري: «أنَّ رسول الله عليه الصلاة والسلام صلَّى على النجاشِي، فكبّر أربعا»[658].

التكبير على المَيِّت[659]

سئل عن التكبير على المَيِّت؟

قال: فحدث قتادة: أنَّ عليّ بن أبي طالب رضي الله عنه صلَّى على رجل من أهل بدر فكبر خمساً[660]، وقال: لو زدت لكان لذلك أهلاً.

وقال: بلغنا: أنَّ أناسا[661] يُكبِّرون أربعا وخمسا[662] أو ستا أو سبعا حتَّى كان زمان عمر فجمع الناس ثُمَّ قال: إن الناس بعدكم يقتدون بكم، فاجتمعوا في صلاة المَيِّت على أمر يقتدى به من بعدكم، فاجتمعوا على أربع تكبيرات.

655 أخ: أخيكم، ب.

656 رواه البخاري، باب موت النجاشي، ر٣٦٦٤.

657 أصحمة: صحبة، ب.

658 رواه الربيع، باب صلاة الجنائز، ر٤٧٨، والبخاري، باب التكبير على الجنازة أربعا، ر١٢٦٨.

659 التكبير على الميت: -،د.

660 فكبر خمسا: -، ب.

661 كانوا: +، ب.

662 وخمسا: وخمسة: ب. وخمسا: -،د.

سئل عن التسليم بعد الصلاة على الجنازة؟

فقال: واحدة.

سئل: هل يقطع الصلاة على الجنازة شيءٌ؟

قال: لا.

سئل عن الرجل تحضره الصلاة على الجنازة وهو غير متوضئ؟

قال: إذا لم يقدر على الماء، وخشي أن يسبق بالجنازة تيمّم وصلَّى.

سئل عن الجنازة يؤتى بها وقد حضرت صلاة المغرب؟

قال: يصلّي المغرب وإن شاء بدأ بالجنازة.

سئل عن الصلاة على الجنازة قبل طلوع الشمس وبعد العصر؟

قال: صل عليها[663] ما لم يطلع قرن من الشمس، أو يغيب قرن ما كنت في وقت الصلاة، لو نسيتها أو شغلت.

سئل عن الجنائز إذا اجتمعت رجالا ونساء؟

قال: يقدم الرجال أمام النساء مِمَّا يلي القبلة، ثُمَّ النساء بين الإمام وجنائز الرجال.

سئل كيف تصف الجنائز إذا وضعت ليصلَّى عليها؟

قال: تصف كعرف الديك بعضها خلف بعض، الرجال قدام النساء والصبيان خلف الرجال والنساء خلفهم جميعا.

663 عليها: عليهما، د.

سئل عمَّن أحقّ[664] بالصلاة على الْمَيِّت؟
قال: الأب أولاهم ثُمَّ الزوج ثُمَّ الابن ثُمَّ العم.

سئل عن الإذن في الجنائز؟
قال[665]: لا يستأذنون[666]، فإذا صلوا وبلغوا القبر ووضعت الجنازة في القبر فلا سلطان لهم، ومن اتبعها بعد الصلاة كرهوا له أن يرجع حتَّى توضع في القبر.

سئل عن الْمَيِّت إذا وضع في اللحد: ما يقال؟
قال: يقال: بسم الله وعلى سنة رسول الله وملَّة رسول الله، ثُمَّ يدعو له.

سئل عن الثلاثة يدفنون في قبر جميعا؟
قال: ما نرى بذلك بأسا، إذا لم نجد بدا ويقدم أقرؤهم، فإن كانوا في القراءة سواء[667] فأسنهم.

سئل: [668]كم يدخل القبر من الرجال شفعا أو وترا؟
قال: لا يضر أي ذلك كان.

سئل: هل يجصص القبر أو يبنى عليه[669]؟

664 أحق: أخص، د.
665 يقال: +، ب.
666 يسيأذنون: يأذنون، ب.
667 قدم: +، ب.
668 عن: +، ب.
669 عليه: -، ب.

قال: ذلك يكره، ويكره[670] أن يزاد عليه غير ترابه الذي أخرج من القبر، ويكره أن يوطأ عليه إلا أن[671] لا تجد بدًا.

سئل عن المحرم يموت؟

قال: يكره أن يحنط، ولا يغطى وجهه ولكن يغسل غسلا رفيقا ويصب[672] عليه الماء.

سئل عن النواح[673]؟

قال[674]: حدَّث عن أبي يزيد المدني قال: اجتمع ابن عمر وابن عبَّاس في جنازةٍ رافع بن خديج فسمعا صوتا باكيا، فقال ابن عمر: إن صاحبكم كان شيخا كبيرا ولا طاقة له بعذاب الله، وإن المَيِّت ليعذب[675] بقول هذا الحي.

فقال ابن عبَّاس: يرحمك الله يا أبا عبد الرحمن، أمَّا إنك وأباك تقولان ذلك، وأي[676] كتاب الله عليكما نص، فالله يقول في كتابه: ﴿وَأَنَّهُ هُوَ أَضْحَكَ وَأَبْكَى . وَأَنَّهُ هُوَ أَمَاتَ وَأَحْيَا . وَأَنَّهُ خَلَقَ الزَّوْجَيْنِ الذَّكَرَ وَالْأُنثَى﴾[677]. وقال: ﴿وَلَا تَزِرُ وَازِرَةٌ وِزْرَ أُخْرَى﴾[678]، وقال: ﴿وَأَن لَّيْسَ لِلْإِنسَانِ إِلَّا مَا سَعَى﴾[679]. والله عز

670 يكره: -، ب.

671 إلا أن: ألا، ب د.

672 رفيقا ويصب: ورفيقا يصب، ب،د.

673 النواح: النوح، ب.

674 قال: -، ب.

675 ليعذب: ليؤذى، ب.

676 وأي: يأبى، ب.

677 سورة النجم: ٤٣-٤٥.

678 سورة الإسراء: ١٥. فاطر: ١٨.

679 سورة النجم: ٥٣. الآية: - ب.

وجل [680] أعدل من أن يؤاخذ هذا المَيِّت بصوت هذا الحي.

قال: بلغنا قول ابن عمر وابن عبَّاس وقول الله أعدل في كتابه حيث يقول: ﴿وَلَا تَزِرُ وَازِرَةٌ وِزْرَ أُخْرَى﴾.

نجز السفر المبارك من قول قتادة، بحمد الله وحسن عونه. والصلاة والسلام على سيدنا مُحَمَّد نبيه والرضى عن أصحابه، آمين [681].

680 عز وجل: أعز و، ب.

681 وكان الفراغ ليلة الاثنين لاثنتي عشرة خلون من شهر شعبان من سنة إحدى وتسعين ومائة وألف بجامع الماي الكبير الأعظم عظم الله شأنه وأعان عماره ودمر خرابه وكثر فيه أولياءه وأذهب من أعدائه بجاه من بلغ لهم دينه... آمين على يد عبيد الله وأحوج خلقه إلى توفيقه صالح بن سالم بن سليمان بن يدر بن عليّ بن موسى بن يخلف بن عبد العزيز السدريني، تاب الله عليه توبة نصوحًا وأحسن عواقبه... آمين بجاه الأمين: +، ب.

بسم الله الرحمن الرحيم

وصلَّى الله على محمَّد وآله وأصحابه الطاهرين[1]

كتاب الجزء الثاني

في الزكاة وقسمة الغنيمة من قول قتادة وفيه أبواب أخرى في غير ذلك كتاب الصيام، وباب النذور، وباب كفَّارات اليمين[2].

سئل عن قول الله تعالى: ﴿وَاعْلَمُوا أَنَّمَا غَنِمْتُم مِن شَيْءٍ فَأَنَّ لِلَّهِ خُمُسَهُ وَلِلرَّسُولِ وَلِذِي الْقُرْبَى وَالْيَتَامَى وَالْمَسَاكِينِ﴾[3].

حدث قتادة: أنه قال: تقسم الغنائم على خمسة أخماس، فأربعة أخماس لمن قاتل عليها، ويقسم الخمس الباقي على خمسة أخماس، فخمس منها لله وللرسول، وخمس لقرابة رسول الله، وخمس للمساكين، وخمس لابن السبيل، وخمس لليتامى.

وقال بعضهم: يقسم الخمس على أربعة أرباع، لله وللرسول ولذي القربى سهم، أمَّا سهم ذوي القربى فإن أبابكر وعمر حملا عليه في سبيل الله، قال[4]: سهم ذوي القربى طعمة لرسول الله، وقال غيره: بلغنا: أنَّ أبابكر كان يُزوِّج[5] الأيم ويخدم من لا خدم له

1 بسم الله الرحمن الرحيم وصلَّى الله على محمَّد وآله وأصحابه الطاهرين: -،د.

2 وفيه أبواب أخرى في غير ذلك كتاب الصيام، وباب النذور، وباب كفَّارات اليمين: -، ب؛ بسم الله الرحمن الرحيم وصلَّى الله على سيدنا ومولانا مُحَمَّد النبيّ الكريم وعلى آله وصحبه وسلم تسليما: +،د.

3 سورة الأنفال: ٤١.

4 الحسن: +، ب.

5 يتزوج: يزوج، ب،د.

وينفق على أهل المقتول[6] من سهم ذوي القربى.

قال غيره: بلغنا: أنَّ أبا بكر كان يجعل سهم ذوي القربى لمن هو له[7].

عن قيس بن سعد[8] أن نجدة كتب إلى ابن عبَّاس يسأله: عن سهم ذوي القربى أطعمة لرسول الله[9]؟ وعن اليتيم ماينقض يتمه؟ وعن أطفال المشركين؟
فقال ابن عبَّاس: لولا أن أرده [عن ضلالة وقع فيها] ما أجبته فكتب إليه: كتبت تسألني عن سهم ذوي القربى لمن هو؟ فإنا كنَّا نراه لقرابة رسول الله، فأبى ذلك علينا قومنا. وعن اليتيم متى[10] ينقضي[11] يتمه، فإنَّه ينقض يتمه إذا احتلم وأونس منه خير، وعن المرأة والعبد يشهدان الغنيمة، قال: ليس لهما شيء ولكنهما يجديان، وعن قتل أطفال المشركين فإن رسول الله عليه السلام لم يقتلهم، وأنت فلا تقتلهم إلاَّ أن تعلم منهم ما علم الخضر من الغلام الذي قتله[12].

عن ربيعة بن شهاب قال: كنت بخراسان فكتب يزيد بن معاوية إلى أمير خراسان: إذا أصبتم مغنمًا، فاجعلوه خمسة أخماس، أوقال: خمسة أسهم، فما وقع عليه سهمنا فأعط

6 المقتول: المقتر، ب.
7 قال غيره: بلغنا: أنَّ أبا بكر كان يجعل سهم ذوي القربى لمن هوله: -، ب.
8 سعد: سعيد، ب.
9 لرسول الله: لمن هو؟، ب.
10 متى: ما، ب،د.
11 ينقضي: ينقض،د، ب.
12 أظن أن قوله: عن قتل الحر مقدم عن قوله: وعن المرأة إلى آخره، والله أعلم: هامش، ب. الحديث رواه الطبراني: المعجم الأوسط، رقم ٧٠٢٦.

منه حق[13] الجلاوزة والقرابة[14] حتّى ولو من نصيبنا فإنّه بلغنا: أنّ رجلا سأل النبيّ عليه السلام زماما من الغنائم قبل أن تقسم فقال: ما لك أني تسألنيه ومالي أن أعطيكه ولو أعطيتكه لم أعطك[15] إلاّ زماما من نار أو كالذي قال: ونحو هذا.

عن قتادة قال: ذكر لنا أنّ نبيّ الله -عليه السلام- كان يبعث مناديه عند الغنائم فيقول:[16] ألاّ لا يغُلّن رجل مخيطا فما دونه[17]، ألاّ لا يعرفن رجل يغلّ بعيرا إلاّ أوتي به يوم القيامة، حامله على عنقه له رغاء، ألاّلا يعرفن[18] رجل يغل فرسا إلاّ أوتي بها يوم القيامة حاملها على عنقه لها حمحمة[19]، ألاّ لا يعرفن رجل يغل شاة إلاّ أتى بها يوم القيامة حاملها على رقبته لها ثغاء، فيتبع من ذلك ما شاء أن يتبع.

قال غيره: قد ذكر الله: ﴿وَمَنْ يَغْلُلْ يَأْتِ بِمَا غَلَّ يَوْمَ الْقِيَامَةِ﴾[20].

وبلغنا في شأن المخيط أنّه كره غلوله.

باب الصدقة

وعن قوله عزّ وجل: ﴿إِنَّمَا الصَّدَقَاتُ لِلْفُقَرَاءِ وَالْمَسَاكِينِ وَالْعَامِلِينَ عَلَيْهَا وَالْمُؤَلَّفَةِ قُلُوبُهُمْ وَفِي الرِّقَابِ وَالْغَارِمِينَ وَفِي سَبِيلِ اللَّهِ وَابْنِ السَّبِيلِ فَرِيضَةً

---

13 حق: -، ب.

14 القرابة: المعرفة، ب.

15 لم أعطك: لأعطك، ب.

16 فيقول: -،د.

17 دونه: فوقه، ب.

18 يعرفن: عرفن، ب،د.

19 رواه عبد الرزاق، باب الغلول، ر٩٤٩٣.

20 سورة آل عمران: ١٦١.

﴿مِّنَ اللَّهِ وَاللَّهُ عَلِيمٌ حَكِيمٌ﴾[21]

عن قتادة قال: ثمانية أسهم، أمّا الفقراء فإن الفقير الذي به زمنة[22] في بعض جسده، وهو فقير وبه حاجة، والمساكين مسكين وليست به زمانة وهو محتاج، ﴿والعاملين عليها﴾: الذين يسعون في جمعها جعل الله لهم فيها سهما، والمؤلفة قلوبهم: أناس كان نبيّ الله يعطيهم يتألفهم؛ لكي يسلموا جعل الله لهم سهما.

وذكر قتادة: أنّ أبا سفيان بن حرب وصفوان بن أميّة بن خلف وسهيل بن عمرو والأقرع بن حابس وعيينة بن حصين بن حذيفة بن بدر والحارث بن هشام كانوا من المؤلفة قلوبهم وأعطاهم رسول الله يوم خيبر[23]، أعطى أبا سفيان بن حرب ورهطا معه مائة من الإبل، وأعطى الأقرع بن حابس وعيينة بن حصن خمسين من الإبل، وأمّا الغارمون[24] وفي الرقاب جعل الله لهم فيها سهمين[25]. والغارمون[26]: أناس عليهم دين وغرم من غير فساد ولا إملاق، فجعل الله لهم فيها سهمين[27]، وفي سبيل الله قال: يحمل من ليس له حملان ويعطى منها، وابن السبيل، قال: الضعيف والمسافر إذا قطع به ليس له شيء جعل الله له فيها سهما، ويحمل الرجل في سبيل الله من الصدقة أو يعطى إذا كان لا شيء له ولم يكن له سهم مع المسلمين، والمؤلفة نزع منهم سهمهم عمر وقال: بيننا وبينهم السيف، وابن السبيل يعطى ما يبلغ

21 سورة التوبة: ٦٠.

22 فهو فقير: +، ب.

23 يوم خيبر: –، د.

24 الغارمون: الغارمين، د، السائلين، ب.

25 سهمين: سهمًا، ب.

26 الغارمون: الغارمين، د.

27 سهمين: سهمًا، ب.

بـه بلده إذا كـان فيها فضـل.

عن قتـادة قال: ذكـر لنـا أنَّـ نبيَّ الله عليه السلام قال: لأعطي الرجل وأمنع الرجل وهو أحبّ إليَّ منه، ولكني إنَّمَا أعطي هـذا لتألفـة الإسلام وأَكِلُ هذا الما في قلبـه[28].

عن قتـادة قال: ذكـر لنـا أنّـ[29] نبي الله عليه الصلاة والسـلام[30] أتـاه طعـام ذات ليـلة فخصّ به أناسا من أهل الصفّـة، ثُمَّ أتاهم فقال: إنَّـه أتـانا البـارحة طعام فخصصنا به أقوامًا ووكلنا أقوامًا إلى ما فيـ قلوبهم، ألاَّ وإن منهم[31] عمـر بن ثعلب، قـال[32] عمر: إنـ هذا القول أحبّ إليَّ من حمر النعم.

عن هشام بن عروة عن أبيه أن العبَّاس السلمي قال: أتجعل نهبي ونهب العبيد بين عينية والأقرع في شعر قاله، قال نبيّ الله عليه السلام: «لأقطعن لسانك، اذهب به يا بلال فاقطع لسانه»[33]. قال: فبم يقطع لساني يا رسول الله؟ قال: «بالعطية» فجعل يقول جعلني الله فداك. قال: بلغنا هذا.

وعنـ قول الله: ﴿الَّذِينَ يَلْمِزُونَ الْمُطَّوِّعِينَ مِنَ الْمُؤْمِنِينَ فِي الصَّدَقَاتِ

28 رواه أحمد، ر٢٤٢٩٥.

29 أن: -، ب،د.

30 قال: إنِّي لأعطي الرجل وأمنع الرجل وهو أحب إليَّ منه لكن إنما أعطي هذا التألفه الإسلام وأكل هذا الما في قلبه عن قتادة قال: ذكرلنا نبي الله ـ عليه الصلاة والسلام: +، ب.

31 منهم: -،د.

32 فقال: +، ب.

33 رواه الهندي: كنز العمال، غزوة فتح، ر٣٠١٨٦.

وَالَّذِينَ لا يَجِدُونَ إلاَّ جُهْدَهُمْ فَيَسْخَرُونَ مِنْهُمْ سَخِرَ اللَّهُ مِنْهُمْ وَلَهُمْ عَذَابٌ أَلِيمٌ ﴾[34] نزلت فيما بلغنا في عبد الرحمن بن عوف، جاء بأربعة آلاف وجاء رجل من الأنصار بصاع من تمر، فلمزهما المنافقون، فقالوا: أمّا عبد الرحمن يُري[35] الناس أن له مالا، وأمّا هذا فيذكر بنفسه.

قال قتادة: ذكر لنا أنّ عبد الرحمن بن عوف جاء بنصف ماله إلى رسول الله عليه السلام يتقرب به إلى الله[36] فقال: يا رسول الله، هذا نصف مالي أتيتك به وتركت النصف لعيالي، فدعا الله أن يبارك له فيما أعطى وفيما أمسك. فلمزه المنافقون فقالوا: ما أعطى هذا ماله إلاّ رياء وسمعة، وأقبل رجل من فقراء المسلمين من الأنصار يقال له الحبحاب أبو عقيل فقال: يا نبيّ الله، بتّ أجرّ الجريد الليل كلّه[37] على صاعين من تمر، فأما صاع منها فأمسكته لأهلي، وأمّا صاع فهو ذا، فقال له النبيّ عليه الصلاة والسلام خيرا[38]، فقال المنافقون: والله إن كان الله ورسوله لغنيان عن صاع أبي عقيل، فأنزل الله فيهم ﴿ اسْتَغْفِرْ لَهُمْ أَوْلاَ تَسْتَغْفِرْ لَهُمْ إِن تَسْتَغْفِرْ لَهُمْ سَبْعِينَ مَرَّةً فَلَن يَغْفِرَ اللَّهُ لَهُمْ ﴾[39] قال: بلغنا هذا[40]، وقال نبيّ الله: قد خيرني ربي والله لأزيدن على السبعين فأنزل الله ﴿ سَوَاءٌ عَلَيْهِمْ أَسْتَغْفَرْتَ لَهُمْ أَمْ لَمْ تَسْتَغْفِرْ لَهُمْ لَن يَغْفِرَ اللَّهُ لَهُمْ ﴾[41] قال: بلغنا هذا.

---

34 سورة التوبة: ٧٩.

35 يري: يرائي، ب.

36 يتقرب به إلى الله: -، ب.

37 الليل كله: -، ب.

38 فقال له النبيّ ـ عليه الصلاة والسلام ـ: خيرا: -،د. ذكره ابن حجر في فتح الباري، ٨/٣٣١.

39 سورة التوبة: ٨٠.

40 قال: بلغنا هذا: -، ب.

41 سورة المنافقون: ٦. الحديث رواه المتقي الهندي في كنز العمال، ر٤٣٩٣.

وكان بعض الفقهاء يقولون: إن نبيّ الله عليه السلام أعلم بالله من أن يزيدهم على السبعين التي وقت الله.

وعن قوله عزّ وجل: ﴿ وَإِذَا حَضَرَ الْقِسْمَةَ أُوْلُواْ الْقُرْبَى وَالْيَتَامَى وَالْمَسَاكِينُ فَارْزُقُوهُم مِّنْهُ وَقُولُواْ لَهُمْ قَوْلاً مَّعْرُوفًا ﴾[42].

عن قتادة عن سعيد بن المسيب قال: [43] هذا قبل الفرائض وقسمة الميراث، فلمّا ألحق الله لأهل الميراث ميراثهم جعلت الوصيّة لذوي القربى الذين يحرمون. قال: نعم.

عن قتادة قال: لا تحلّ الصدقة[44] إلاّ في ثلاثة: رجل تحمل بِحمَالة بين قوم فلا عليه أن يسأل حتّى يؤديها، و رجل أصابته جائحة فلا عليه أن يسأل حتّى يجبرها، و رجل عضته الفاقة حتّى يشهد له جيرانه أنّه قد حلت له الصدقة.

قال: وكان يقال: لا تحل الصدقة لغني ولا لذي مرة سوي ولا لمن ركبه دين من سرف.

عن قتادة قال: ذكر لنا أنَّ نبيَّ الله عليه السلام كان يقول: «يحبّ الله الغني الحليم المتعفف، ويبغض الفاحش البذيء السائل الملحف»[45]. قال: نعم، بلغنا هذا.

عن قتادة قال: ذكر لنا أنَّ نبيَّ الله عليه السلام كان يقول: «إنَّ الله كره لكم ثلاثة: قيل

42 سورة النساء: ٨.

43 كان: +، ب.

44 الصدقة: المسألة، ب

45 رواه ابن أبي شيبة، بلفظ: «إن الله يحب الحييَّ العفيف الحليم...»، ما ذكر في الحياء وما جاء فيه، ر٢٥٣٤٤.

وقال، وإضاعة المال، وكثرة السؤال»[46]. قال: بلغنا هذا.

عن قتادة قال: ذكر لنا أنَّ نبيَّ الله عليه السلام كان يقول: لأن يأخذ أحدكم جبلا فيتحامل على عنقه خير من مسألة الناس أعطوه أو منعوه[47]. وقال: تكره المسألة.

عن قتادة عن[48] ثوبان مولى رسول الله عليه السلام قال: من سأل مسألةً وهو عنها غني كانت شيئًا في وجهه إلى يوم القيامةِ[49].

عن قتادة عن خالد النضري[50] قال: بلغنا: أنَّ المؤمن عفيفٌ سؤولٌ[51]، وتلقاه[52] غنيًا فقيرًا وتلقاه[53] ذليلاً عزيزًا، تلقاه سؤولا لربه عفيفا عن الناس، تلقاه غنيا في نفسه فقيرا إلى ربه، تلقاه عزيزًا في نفسه ذليلا لربه.

عن قتادة عن هلال بن حصين عن عليّ بن قرة[54] بن عباد عن أبي سعيد الخدري قال: غزونا مرة وأصابنا جهد شديدٌ، فقال أهلي: لو أتيت النبيّ عليه السلام وسألته فانطلقت إليه فكان أوّل شيء واجهني به أنّه قال: من استعفف أعفه الله، ومن استغنى أغناه

---

46 رواه البخاري، باب قول الله تعالى: ﴿لا يسألون الناس إلحافا﴾، ر١٤٠٧.

47 رواه البخاري، باب الاستعفاف عن المسألة، ر١٤٠٢.

48 عن: قال ذكر لنا، ب.

49 رواه أحمد عن ثوبان مرفوعا إلى النبي صلى الله عليه وسلم، ر٢٢٤٧٣.

50 النضري: القصري، ب.

51 عفيف سؤول: عفيفا سؤولا، ب،د.

52 المؤمن: +، ب.

53 وتلقاه: -،د.

54 علي بن قرة: أخ ابن مرة، ب.

الله[55]، ومن سألنا لم ندخر عنه شيئًا وجدناه. قال: [56] فقلت في نفسي: أستغني فيغنيني الله، وأستعفف فيعفني الله، فوالله ما رجعت إلى نبيّ الله بعد ذلك أسأله شيئا من الفاقة حتَّى مالت علينا الدنيا فأهلكتنا إلاَّ من عصم الله. قال: بلغنا هذا الحديث.

عن قتادة قال: ذكر لنا أنَّ نبيَّ الله عليه السلام قال: «خير الصدقة ما أبقت[57] غنى، وابدأ بمن تعول، واليد العليا خير من اليد السفلى»[58].

يقول: المعطي خير من المانع، ولا يلوم الله أحدا على الكفاف. قال: بلغنا هذا. وبلغنا: أنَّ المعطي خير من المعطى له، فكل هذا صواب، والمعطي خير من المانع.

عن قتادة قال: ذكر لنا أن امرأة جاءت إلى رسول الله صلى الله عليه وسلم وفي حجرها يتامى[59] لها، فقالت: يا رسول الله، ما زلتَ تحث على الصدقةِ حتَّى هممتُ أن آخذ من أموالِ اليتامى فأتصدق بهِ. فقال: ما هو؟ قالت: كفافُ عيشهم. قال: فأمسكيهِ عليهم فإنَّهم أحقّ به.

عن قتادة: أنَّ عائشة زوج النبيّ عليه السلام جاءها سائلٌ فأمرت له بتمرة، وقال قائل: يا أم المؤمنين: إنك تتصدقين بتمرة! قالت: نعم، والله إن الخلق لكثير فلا يشبعهم[60] إلاَّ الله،

55 رواه النسائي: السنن الكبرى، باب من الملحف، ر٢٣٧٦.

56 قال: –، د.

57 أبقت: بقيت، ب.

58 رواه الطبراني: المعجم الكبير، ر١٢٧٢٦.

59 يتامى: يتيم، ب.

60 يشبعهم: يسعهم: يسع له، ب.

أوليس فيها مثاقيل ذر[61] كثير[62]؟! قال: بلغنا: أنَّه إنما[63] كان فلقة[64] تمر.

عن قتادة عن الحسن[65] قال: ذكر لنا أن الصدقة تطفئ الخطايا كما يطفئ الماء النار[66].

قال: بلغنا ذلك.

عن قتادة عن أنس[67] رضي الله عنه قال: إذا أنفقت[68] زكاتك في الفقراء[69] أجزى ذلك عنك. قال: نعم، وبلغنا: أنَّ رجلا أتى حاجبا بأربعمائة درهمٍ[70] من زكاته فقال: إنِّي أريد أن أعين بهذه بعض شيوخ المسلمين، فقال حاجب: بل افرقها. فقال: لا، فأعطاها رجلا واحدا[71].

سئل عما يحلّ لوليّ اليتيم من ماله؟

قال: اللبن، وركوب الدابة، وخدمة الخادم، وتخلط طعامه مع طعامك فتأكلان جميعا.

سئل عن قول الله: ﴿ يَا أَيُّهَا الَّذِينَ آمَنُواْ مَن يَرْتَدَّ مِنكُمْ عَن دِينِهِ فَسَوْفَ يَأْتِي اللّهُ بِقَوْمٍ

61 ذر: در، ب.

62 ذر كثير: -، د.

63 إنما: لما، ب.

64 حقه: فلقة، ب.

65 عن الحسن: -، ب.

66 رواه الترمذي، عن كعب بن عجرة، باب ما ذكر في فضل الصلاة، ر٦١٤.

67 عن أنس: عن الحسن، ب.

68 أنفقت: وضعت، ب.

69 المساكين: +، ب.

70 درهم: درهما، ب. + -، د.

71 رجلا واحدا: رجل واحد، ب، د.

يُحِبُّهُمْ وَيُحِبُّونَهُ أَذِلَّةٍ عَلَى الْمُؤْمِنِينَ أَعِزَّةٍ عَلَى الْكَافِرِينَ يُجَاهِدُونَ فِي سَبِيلِ اللَّهِ وَلَا يَخَافُونَ لَوْمَةَ لَائِمٍ ذَلِكَ فَضْلُ اللَّهِ يُؤْتِيهِ مَن يَشَاءُ وَاللَّهُ وَاسِعٌ عَلِيمٌ﴾[72].

عن قتادة قال: نزلت هذه الآية وقد علم الله[73] أنّه سيرتد المرتدون من الناس، فلمّا قبض رسول الله -صلى الله عليه وسلم- ارتدّ الناس عن الإسلام إلاّ أهل ثلاثة مساجد: المدينة، ومكة، وأهل جواثا[74] من عبد القيس[75]، فقالت العرب: أمّا الصلاة فنصليها، وأمّا الزكاة فوالله ما نوسط أموالنا. قال: فكلم أبو بكر أن يتجاوز عنهم، ويخلي عنهم وقيل: أما إنّهم لو قد فهموا أعطوا[76] الزكاة طائعين فأبى عليهم أبو بكر، وقال: والله لا أفرق بين شيء جمع الله به لهم[77]، والله لو منعوني عقالاً مماّ فرض عليهم رسول الله -صلى الله عليه وسلم- لجاهدتهم[78] عليه، ولقاتلتهم عليه[79]، فقاتلوا على ما قاتل عليه نبيهم حتّى أقروا بالماعون، وهي الزكاة المفروضة، ثُمّ إن وفود العرب أتوه بعد ذلك فخيرهم بين خطة مخزية، وحرب مجلية، فاختاروا الخطة المخزية، وكانت أهون عليهم أن يشهدوا أن قتلاهم في النار، وأن قتلى المسلمين في الجنّة، وما أصاب المسلمون من أموالهم فهو حلال وما أصابوا من أموال[80] المسلمين ردوه عليهم.

---

72 سورة المائدة: ٥٤.

73 الله: -، ب.

74 جواثا: حوايا، ب.

75 من نجران: +، ب.

76 أعطوا: -،د.

77 لهم: بينه، ب.

78 لجاهدتهم: لقاتلتهم، ب.

79 ولقاتلتهم عليه: -، ب.

80 أموال: -،د.

قال: بلغنا بعض هذا الحديث، لو منعوني[81] عقالاً لقاتلتهم عليه[82].

سئل أين توضع الزكاة؟[83]

قال: بلغنا عن مُحَمَّد بن سيرين قال: كانت الزكاة تدفع إلى رسول الله وإلى عُمَّاله، ليس لها وجه غيره، وإلى أبي بكر وعُمَّاله ليس لها وجه غيره، وإلى عمر وعُمَّاله ليس لها وجه غيره، وإلى عثمان وعُمَّاله ليس لها وجه غيره، فلمّا قتل[84] عثمان رضي الله عنه اختلف الناس فيها. قال: كان ما قالوه في أبي بكر وعمر وعثمان في الاستقامةِ فلمّا جاء الاختلاف أحبوا أن يضعوها في مواضعها[85] التي أمر الله بها.

سئل على ما زاد على مائتي درهم هل فيه زكاة؟

قال: في مائتي درهم خمسة دراهم، فإذا زادت أربعين درهما ففيها درهم.

سئل عن زكاة الحليّ؟

قال: إنّ عبد الله بن عمر كان يكتب إلى خازنه أن يخرج زكاة حليّ بناته كلّ سنة، وكتب إليه في زكاة رمضان أن يعطي عن الصغير والكبير وعن الحر والعبد. قال: نعم، قول الفقهاء مثل قول ابن[86] عمر.

عن أبي معشر عن النخعي: أنّ امرأة ابن مسعود سألته: عن طوق لها فيه عشرون

---

81 منعوني: منعني، ب.

82 قال: بلغنا بعض هذا الحديث، لو منعوني عقالاً لقاتلتهم عليه: -،د.

83 سئل: أين توضع الزكاة؟: -،د.

84 قتل: مات، ب

85 مواضعها: موضعها، ب،د.

86 ابن: -، ب.

مثقالا. قالت: أتزكيه؟ قال لها: نعم. فقالت له: أتعطيه لابن أخ لها يتيم[87] في حجرها، قال: نعم، إن شاءت[88].

وقال غيره: لا بأس إلاَّ أن تكون تلزمها نفقته فإن لزمتها نفقته[89] فلا تعطيه من زكاتها شيئا.

سئل عن زكاة الخيل؟

قال: لا زكاة فيها.

سئل عن زكاة الرقيق؟

قال: إن كانوا للتجارة ففيهم الزكاة، وإن كانوا للخدمة وأداء الغلة ففيهم صاع كلّ سنة[90] على كلّ رأس يوم الفطر زكاة الفطر.

سئل عن قوله جَلَّالَهُ ﴿وَابْتَلُواْ الْيَتَامَى حتَّى إِذَا بَلَغُواْ النِّكَاحَ فَإِنْ آنَسْتُم مِّنْهُمْ رُشْدًا فَادْفَعُواْ إِلَيْهِمْ أَمْوَالَهُمْ وَلاَ تَأْكُلُوهَآ إِسْرَافًا وَبِدَارًا أَن يكبروا وَمَن كَانَ غَنِيًّا فَلْيَسْتَعْفِفْ وَمَن كَانَ فَقِيرًا فَلْيَأْكُلْ بِالْمَعْرُوفِ﴾[91].

قال: زعم الفقهاء شرب اللبن وركوب الدابة في حاجة اليتيم وخدمة الخادم، وأن يخلط طعام اليتيم مع طعامه فيأكلوا[92] جميعًا.

وقال غيره: إذا أتى أرض اليتيم وأقام في ضيعته أكل مالا بُدَّ منه.

---

87 يتيم: -، ب.

88 إن شاءت: إن شئت، ب،د.

89 فإن لزمتها نفقته: -،د.

90 صاع كلّ سنة: -،د.

91 سورة النساء: ٦.

92 فيأكلوا: فيأكلون، ب د.

باب زكاة الأموال

سئل عن زكاة مال اليتيم؟

قال: بلغنا: أنَّ عائشة أم المؤمنين رضي الله عنها كانت تزكِّي مال أيتام لها، وصنع ذلك جابر بن زيد وامرأته، وقال: قبح الله مالا لا يزكَّى، وقبح[93] أهله لا يُزكوه.

سئل عن الابتغاء بأموال اليتامى؟

قال: كان أصحابنا يكرهون أن يحرّك أموال اليتامى، وكان أبو عبيدة يقول: إذا حركت فما كان من ربح[94] فلهم، وما كان من وضيعة فعلى الذي حركه[95].

سئل عن الذي يخرج زكاة ماله قبل حلها؟

فحدث قتادة عن الحسن أنَّه كان لا يرى به بأسا أن يعطيها قبل حلها بشهر أو شهرين، وزكاته على الوقت الأوَّل الذي يعطي فيه.

قال: وكان الربيع يقول: إذا كانت حاجة أو فاقة فلا بأس أن يعطيها[96] لشهر أو شهرين، وكذلك زكاة رمضان لا بأس إذا كانت حاجة أن تعجل أوَّل الشهر، شهر رمضان[97][98].

سئل عن الرجل يخرج زكاة ماله فتضيع؟

93 لا يزكَّى، وقبح: -، د.

94 فهو: +، ب.

95 يكره التجارة بمال اليتيم: هامش، ب.

96 يعطيها: يعجلها، ب.

97 شهر رمضان: -، ب.

98 لا بأس بتعجيل الزكاة قبل حلها بشهر أو شهرين: هامش، ب.

قال: لا تجزئ عنه حتَّى تصل إلى أهلها، إلاَّ أن يكون صاحب المال دفعها إلى من يلي قسمها فإن ضاعت فليس على أحد منهما غرم.

سئل عن رجل تحل عليه زكاة وعليه دين؟

قال: إن كان له فضل[99] عن دينه زكَّاه، وإن لم يكن له فضل فلا شيء عليه.[100]

سئل عن رجل تحل عليه الزكاة وعنده متاع أو رقيق للتجارة كيف يزكيه؟

قال: يزكي على رأس ماله. عند أبي عبيدة وكان ضمام يقول: بسعر يومه.[101]

سئل عن رجل يزكي[102] فيمر عليه العشار، فيأخذ منه أيضا أيحسب له فيما يستقبل؟

قال: لا يحاسب له إنَّمَا هو ظلم ظلمه.

سئل عن رجل له[103] مال مضاربة فيمر عليه العشار فيأخذ منه من مال من يكون؟

قال: من رأس المال.

سئل عن رجل يستعير البرواة[104] أو يعيرها؟

قال: أمَّا اليوم فاستعرها وأعرها[105] إذا كنت تخرج زكاتك يخرجها من أعرتها منه،

---

99 زكاة: +،د.

100 من أخرج زكاة وضاعت قبل أن تصل أهلها لا تجوز: هامش، ب.

101 من حلت عليه الزكاة للتجارة يحسبه برأس ماله: هامش، ب.

102 ماله: +، ب.

103 له: كان، ب.

104 البرواة: لم أجد معناها في اللغة، ولعله يقصد البروة، وهي الخلخال، أو الحلقة في أنف البعير (انظر: لسان العرب، مادة: «برى».

105 فاستعرها وأعرها: فأستعيرها وأعيرها، ب،د.

فيضعها في موضعها التي أمره الله بها.

سئل عن رجلٍ يكون له مال لا يرجوه[106] ثُمَّ أخذه: كيف يزكيه؟

قال: يستأنف به إذا كان على أناس مفلسين، ولا يقدر عليه فلا يحسبه عليهم إلاَّ أن يستعدى عليهم.

عن قتادة عن الحسن أنَّه قال: إذا[107] كان في مال زكَّاه، وإن كان ديونا[108] لم يزكّه فإذا أخذه زكَّاه مرة واحدة. قال: نعم[109].

سئل عن رجل يستفيد مالا؟

قال: كانوا يرون إن كان له سنة فما حال الحول وهو عنده زكّاه، إلاَّ أن يكون له مال قد حلت فيه الزكاة فيزكيهما.

عن قتادة: أنَّ عمر بن عبد العزيز كتب إلى عدي بن أرطأة إذا زكى الرجل ماله ثُمَّ أصاب فيه ربحا فليس فيه شيء حتَّى يأتي الشهر الذي يزكي فيه ماله.

قال: نعم، ولكن إذا أصاب ربحا قبل أن يزكي رأس ماله زكى الربح أيضًا، وإن أصاب الربح بعد أن أخرج الزكاة فليس عليه شيءٌ إلى الحول.

عن قتادة أن ابن عمر قال: ليس فيه زكاة حتَّى يحول عليه الحول. قال: نعم. إلاَّ أن يكون له ماله قد حلت فيه الزكاة فيزكيه معه.

106 لا يرجوه: لا يزكيه، د.

107 إذا: إن، ب.

108 وإن كان ديونا: -، د.

109 قال: نعم: -، د.

عن قتادة[110] سئل عن الرجل يعطي من زكاة ماله يهوديًا أو نصرانيًا؟

قال: يكره أن يعطوا ما لم تكن[111] زكاة مفروضة فهم المساكين.

سئل عن الرجل يخرج الشيء يتصدق به فيسبقه السائل فذهب يأكله؟

قال: يستحبّ إذا[112] أكله أن يعيد مثله.

ذكر ما سقت السماء والعيون والنضح وخراج الأرض

سئل عما سقت السماء؟

حدَّث عن قتادة قال: «سنَّ رسول الله -صلى الله عليه وسلم- فيما سقت السماء والعيون والسايحة والبعل وما كان بعلا العشر كاملا، وما سقي بالرشا وهي الدوالي والسواقي نصف العشر»[113].

وكان يقال: إذا بلغ من الثمرة ما كان[114] منها خمسة أوساق وذلك ثلاثمائة صاع ففيه الزكاة.

عن قتادة قال: كان يعجبهم أن يعطوا على ما يكال من الثمرة على قدر ذلك، وقد كان أبو عبيدة يقول: الزكاة في البر والشعير والذرة والتمر والزبيب والسلت فما بلغ من هذه خمسة أوساق ففيه الزكاة ولا نرى فيما دون ذلك زكاة.

---

110 قتادة: يكال، ب؛ -، د.

111 لا: +، ب.

112 إذا: وإن، ب.

113 رواه ابن أبي شيبة، ما قالوا فيما يسقى سحيا وبالدوالي، ر١٠٠٧٩. انظر: آثار الربيع، مسألة ١١٤، ص ٣٩.

114 ما كان: -، د.

سئل عن أرض الدهقان إذا أسلم؟

قال: على أرضه وماله صدقة، إلاَّ أن يجعلوه عبدالهم صلَّى أو لم يصلِّ، فإن[115] عتقه إسلامه فإن في ماله الصدقة وذهبت عنهم الجزية.

عن قتادة عن لاحق بن حميد: بعث عمر بن الخطَّاب عمار بن ياسر وابن مسعود وعثمان بن حنيف إلى الكوفة، فبعث عمارا على الصلاة وعلى الجيوش، وبعث ابن مسعود على القضاء وعلى بيت المال، وعثمان بن حنيف على مساحة الأرض، وجعل بينهم كلّ يوم شاة نصفها وسواقطها[116] لعمار بن ياسر والنصف بين[117] هذين، ثُمَّ قال: إنما[118] نزلتكم وإياي من هذا المال منزلة ولي اليتيم. من كان غنيا فليستعفف، ومن كان فقيرا فليأكل بالمعروف، وما أرى قرية يؤخذ منها كلّ يوم شاة إلاَّكان ذلك سريعًا[119] في خرابها، فوضع عثمان بن حنيف على جريب الكرم عشرة دراهم، وعلى جريب النخل ثمانية دراهم وعلى جريب القصب ستة دراهم وعلى[120] جريب الحنطة أربعة دراهم، وعلى جريب الشعير درهمين وعلى رأس كلّ رجل درهمين. قال: وبلغنا هذا كلّ رجل أربعة وعشرون درهما كلّ سنة وعزل من ذلك النساء والصبيان، و[121] ما يختلفون به من تجارتهم نصف العشر، ثُمَّ كتب بذلك إلى عمر بن الخطَّاب رضي الله عنه فجوز ذلك. قال: وبلغنا هذا وكان أصحابنا يرون أنَّه إذا عجز أحد منهم حملت جزيته على أغنيائهم.

115 فإن: وإن، ب.

116 وسواقطها: -،د.

117 بين: -،د.

118 إنما: -، ب.

119 سريعًا: واقع،د.

120 جريب القصب ستة دراهم وعلى: -،د.

121 في: +، ب.

ما يجب على تجار أهل الحرب

قيل[122] لعمر بن الخطّاب: كيف نأخذ من تجار أهل الحرب؟
قال عمر: كيف يأخذون منكم إذا أتيتم بلدهم؟ قالوا: العشر؟ قال: نعم.

عن قتادة: أنّ خالد بن الوليد صالح بني تغلب[123] من مواشيهم وأموالهم من عشرين درهما درهم في خلافة عمر وأضعف عليهم.
قال: بلغنا: أنّه ضعف على بني تغلب[124] وعلى بني[125] عبد القيس.

عن قتادة فرض رسول الله عليه السلام على أناس من أهل اليمن على كلّ حالم وحالمة دينارا أو قيمته من المعافرية[126]. قال: بلغنا هذا.

سئل هل يزكي المكاتب؟
قال: المكاتب حرّ وإن كان عنده فضل عن دينه أخذت منه الزكاة وإذا كان ماله كفافا لدينه فلا زكاة عليه.

سئل عن العبد هل يزكي ماله؟
قال: يزكي ما لم ينهه سيده، وقال: الزكاة على مواليه[127, 128]

122 قيل: سئل، ب.
123 تغلب: ثعلب، ب.
124 تغلب: ثعلب، ب.
125 بني: -، ب.
126 رواه عبد الرزاق، باب كم يؤخذ منهم في الجزية، ر١٩٢٦٨.
127 ماليه: ماله، ب.
128 زكاة العبد على مواليه: هامش، ب.

سئل عن زكاة رمضان؟

قال: هي على الكبير والصغير والحر والعبد صاعا من كلّ نوع.

سئل عن زكاة المعادن؟

قال: ماكان من ركاز ذهب أو فضّة فالخمس، وماكان من تراب يعالج بالنار ففي كلّ أربعين درهما درهم.

سئل عن قوله عزّ وجل: ﴿وَالَّذِينَ يَكْنِزُونَ الذَّهَبَ وَالْفِضَّةَ وَلاَ يُنفِقُونَهَا فِي سَبِيلِ اللهِ فَبَشِّرْهُم بِعَذَابٍ أَلِيمٍ﴾[129].

قال: بلغنا أنّ من أعطى زكاة ماله لم يكن من المكنزين[130]، وكان يقال: من أخرج حق الله منه فليس بكنز.

وكان ضمّام يقول: من أدّى مع زكاة ماله مثلها فقد أدى الحَقّ الذي عليه، وكان يقول: ألاّ فقد أدى الحَقّ الذي عليه، وقال الله: ﴿وَالَّذِينَ فِي أَمْوَالِهِمْ حَقٌّ مَّعْلُومٌ، لِّلسَّائِلِ وَالْمَحْرُومِ﴾[131].

عن قتادة: أنّ نبيّ الله عليه السلام سئل عن الإبل فقال: «عزّ لأهلها»[132].

وسئل عن الخيل؟ فقال: «عقد في نواصيها الخير والأجر والبركة»[133].

---

129 سورة التوبة: ٣٤.

130 لم يكن من المكنزين: لم يكن ماله كنزا، ب.

131 سورة المعارج: ٢٥. انظر ما قال في الإبل والخيل والغنم مدحا لهم: هامش، ب.

132 رواه ابن ماجه، باب اتخاذ الماشية، ر٢٣٠٥.

133 رواه البخاري، باب الخيل معقود في نواصيها الخير إلى يوم القيامة، ر٢٦٩٦.

وسئل عن الغنم؟ فقال: «مباركة، وإذا رأى أحدكم عبده مطلوبا فليعنه[134]»[135].

باب صدقة الإبل

سئل عن صدقة الإبل؟

فقال: «في كلّ[136] خمس شاة، وفي عشر شاتان، وفي خمس عشرة ثلاث شياه، وفي عشرين أربع شياه، وفي خمس وعشرين بنت مخاض، فإن لم توجد بنت مخاض فابن لبون ذكر إلى خمس وثلاثين، فإن زادت واحدة؛ ففيها بنت لبون، إلى خمس وأربعين، فإن زادت واحدة ففيها حقّة طروقة الفحل إلى ستّين، فإن زادت واحدة ففيها جذعة إلى خمس وسبعين، فإن زادت واحدة ففيها بنتا لبون إلى التسعين، فإن زادت واحدة ففيها حقتان طروقتا الفحل إلى عشرين ومائة، فإذا زادت واحدة ففيها ثلاث بنات لبون حتّى تبلغ تسعا وعشرين، فإذا زادت واحدة ففيها حقة وبنتا لبون حتّى تبلغ أربعين ومائة، ففيها حقتان وبنت لبون حتّى تبلغ خمسين ومائة ففيها ثلاث حقائق، حتّى تبلغ ستّين ومائة ففيها أربع بنات لبون، حتّى تبلغ سبعين ومائة ففيها حقة وثلاث بنات لبون، حتّى تبلغ ثمانين ومائة ففيها حقتان وبنتا لبون، حتّى تبلغ تسعين ومائة ففيها ثلاث حقائق وبنت لبون، حتّى تبلغ مائتين ففيها خمس بنات لبون أو أربع حقائق، ثُمّ في كلّ خمسين حقّة، وفي كلّ أربعين بنت لبون»[137].

---

134 مطلوبا فليعنه: مغلوبا فلعنه، ب.

135 لم أجد من خرجه.

136 كل: –، د.

137 رواه البخاري، باب زكاة الغنم، ر١٣٨٦.

سئل إذا كان عليه بنت مخاض فلم يجدها فأخذ بنت لبون؟

قال: يردّ فضل ما بينهما، وقال: إن[138] المصدّق إذا لم يجد بنت مخاض أخذ ابن لبون ذكر، وهي من السنّة.

سئل عن الناقة إذا أنتجت: أيحسب ولدها؟

قال: إذا قطع الوادي عدّه المصدق.

سئل عن الإبل يطحن عليها ويقل[139] عليها؟

قال: في كلّ خمس شاة، وما سقى الزرع فلا صدقة عليه.

باب الصيام

بسم الله الرحمن الرحيم

وصلّى الله على سيّدنا ومولانا محمّد، وعلى آله وصحبه وسلم تسليما[140]

سئل عن قوله عزّ وجل: ﴿ يَا أَيُّهَا الَّذِينَ آمَنُوا كُتِبَ عَلَيْكُمُ الصِّيَامُ كَمَا كُتِبَ عَلَى الَّذِينَ مِن قَبْلِكُمْ لَعَلَّكُمْ تَتَّقُونَ ﴾[141].

حدث عن[142] قتادة قال: هو رمضان، كتبه الله على من كان قبلكم.

---

138 إن: –، ب.

139 ويقل: أو يقل، ب.

140 بسم الله الرحمن الرحيم وصلّى الله على سيّدنا ومولانا محمّد، وعلى آله وصحبه وسلم تسليما: –، ب.

141 سورة البقرة: ١٨٣.

142 عن: –،د.

وعن قوله: ﴿أَيَّامًا مَعْدُودَاتٍ﴾[143].

فحدَّث عن[144] قتادة عن الحسن: أنَّ نبيَّ الله عليه السلام قال: «إذا رأيتم[145] الهلال فصوموا، وإذا رأيتموه فأفطروا، فإن غمّ[146] عليكم فأتموا العدَّة ثلاثين يوما»[147].

وكذلك قال غيره عن صاحب له بلغه أن[148] عبد الرحمن بن زيد بن الخطَّاب أنَّه[149] خطب الناس بمنى[150]. فقال: «أيُّها الناس إنا قد[151] لقينا أصحاب محمَّد عليه السلام، وسمعنا منهم وأخذنا عنهم فحدثونا: أنَّ نبيَّ الله عليه السلام قال: «إذا رأيتم الهلال فصوموا، وإذا رأيتموه فأفطروا، فإن غمّ[152] عليكم فأكملوا العدَّة ثلاثين يوما، إلاَّ أن يشهد اثنان ذوا عدل منكم أنَّهما رأياه بالأمس فصوموا لرؤيتهما، وأفطروا لرؤيتهما، وأمسكوا لرؤيتهما[153]»»[154]. قال: نعم.

عن أيُّوب عن أبي قلابة: أنَّ رجلين قدما على عمر بن الخطَّاب، أحدهما صائم والآخر مفطر، فقال للمفطر: لم أفطرت؟ فقال: رأيت الهلال فأفطرت. وقال للصائم:

---

143 سورة البقرة: ١٨٤.

144 عن: -،د.

145 رأيتم: رأيتموا، ب،د.

146 غم: أغمي، ب.

147 رواه البخاري بمعناه، باب قول النبي صلى الله عليه وسلم: إذا رأيتم الهلال فصوموا وإذا رأيتموه فأفطروا، ر١٨٠٧.

148 أن: عن، ب.

149 أنه: -،د.

150 بمنى: يوما، ب.

151 قد: -،د.

152 غم: أغمي، ب.

153 وأمسكوا لرؤيتهما: -،د.

154 رواه الهيثمي: مسند الحارث- زوائد الهيثمي، باب صوموا لرؤيته، ر٣١٦.

ما حملك على الصوم؟ فقال: أما إنِّي قد رأيت الهلال، ولكني قدمت المدينة ورأيت الناس صياما فكرهت أن أخالفهم.

فقال عمر[155] للمفطر: لولا هذا الصائم لأوجعت لك رأسا، ثُمَّ أمر الناس بالإفطار[156] وقد ارتفع النهار أن يخرجوا إلى الصلاة فخرجوا فأفطروا[157]. قال: إذا شهد شاهدان عادلان[158] على رؤيته أفطر الناس.

سئل عن الصوم في السفر؟

قال: الإفطار فيه[159] رخصة، ومن قدر على الصيام فهو أفضل.

و[160] بلغنا: «أنَّ رسول الله -عليه السلام- صام وأفطر، وصام أصحابه وأفطروا، فلم يغيّر بعضهم على بعض»[161].

سئل عن الركعتين في السفر؟

قال: رأينا من صلاَّهما ومن[162] يدع.

وبلغنا أنَّ أبا عبيدة لم يكن يزيد في العشاء على ركعتين، ويوتر بركعة.

---

155 عمر: -،د.

156 بالإفطار: -، ب.

157 أن يخرجوا إلى الصلاة فخرجوا فأفطروا: -،د.

158 عادلان: -،د.

159 فيه: -،د.

160 قال: +، ب.

161 رواه الطبراني: المعجم الكبير، ر١١٠٥٣

162 من: -، ب.

قال[163]: بلغنا أنَّ أبا عبيدة لم يصم في السفر تطوّعا قط.

سئل عن الحامل والمرضع؟

قال: إذا خافتا على أولادهما أفطرتا.

وسئل[164] عن قوله عزّ وجل: ﴿وَعَلَى الَّذِينَ يُطِيقُونَهُ فِدْيَةٌ طَعَامُ مِسْكِينٍ﴾[165]؟.

حدَّثني الربيع أنَّه قال: الشيخ الكبير والعجوز الكبيرة إذا عجزوا عن الصوم، والغلام المراهق الذي قد[166] صام أترابه، واشتهى الصيام فلم يطقه؛ فهؤلاء يطعم عنهم. وكانت عجوز كبيرة في زمان جابر بن زيد لا تطيق الصوم، وكان يأمرهم أن يصوموا عنها سنة، ويطعموا عنها سنة.

سئل عن الشيخ الكبير إذا لم يطق الصوم؟

قال: يطعم عن كلّ يوم مسكينا فطوره وسحوره.

وقد[167] كان أبو عبيدة حين ضربه الفالج يطعم[168] في رمضان كلّ يوم مسكينا فطوره وسحوره، فلمّا جاء رمضان آخر وجد بعض القوّة فصام رمضان، وشوال قضاء للشهر الذي أطعم فيه.

سئل عمَّن يخرج في رمضان؟

163 قال: –، د.

164 وسئل: –، ب.

165 سورة البقرة: ١٨٤.

166 قد: –، د.

167 قد: –، ب.

168 يطعم: أطعم، ب.

قال: يكره له فيه[169] الخروج إلاَّ أن تكون حاجة لا بد منها إن تركها فاتته.

عن محمَّد بن سيرين قال: سألت أبا عبيدة عن رجل يرى هلال رمضان، وهو مقيم ثُمَّ سافر؟

فقال: ألم يقل الله تعالى[170]: ﴿فَمَن شَهِدَ مِنكُمُ الشَّهْرَ فَلْيَصُمْهُ﴾[171]. قال: كان أصحابنا يكرهون الخروج إلاَّ لِما لا بدَّ منه.

سئل عن قوله عزّ وجل: ﴿أُحِلَّ لَكُمْ لَيْلَةَ الصِّيَامِ الرَّفَثُ إِلَى نِسَائِكُمْ﴾[172]؟.

عن قتادة قال: الرفث: الغشيان.

وعن قوله: ﴿أُحِلَّ لَكُمْ لَيْلَةَ الصِّيَامِ الرَّفَثُ إِلَى نِسَائِكُمْ هُنَّ لِبَاسٌ لَكُمْ وَأَنْتُمْ لِبَاسٌ لَهُنَّ﴾. قال: هن سكن لكم، وأنتم سكن لهن. ﴿عَلِمَ اللَّهُ أَنَّكُمْ كُنتُمْ تَخْتَانُونَ أَنْفُسَكُمْ﴾[173].

وعن قتادة قال[174]: أمروا أن يصوموا ثلاثة أيَّام من كلّ شهر، فكان ذلك بدء الصوم، فكانوا في صيامهم ذلك وبعد ما افترض عليهم الصيام[175] إذا رقدوا لم يحلّ لهم

169 فيه: –، ب.

170 تعالى: –،د.

171 سورة البقرة: ١٨٥.

172 سورة البقرة: ١٨٧.

173 سورة البقرة: ١٨٧.

174 الرفث: الغشيان. وعن قوله: ﴿أُحِلَّ لَكُمْ لَيْلَةَ الصِّيَامِ الرَّفَثُ إِلَى نِسَائِكُمْ هُنَّ لِبَاسٌ لَكُمْ وَأَنْتُمْ لِبَاسٌ لَهُنَّ﴾. قال: هن سكن لكم وأنتم سكن لهن. ﴿عَلِمَ اللَّهُ أَنَّكُمْ كُنتُمْ تَخْتَانُونَ أَنْفُسَكُمْ﴾(. وعن قتادة قال: –،د.

175 افترض عليهم الصيام: افترض رمضان، ب.

الطعام ولا[176] الشراب ولا[177] النساء إلى مثلها من قابل[178]، فكان قوم يأكلون[179] بعد رقادهم، فكانت تلك خيانة القوم لأنفسهم، فتاب الله عليهم بعد ذلك، وأحل لهم ذلك إلى طلوع الفجر، وعفا عنهم، وقال: ﴿فَالآنَ بَاشِرُوهُنَّ وَابْتَغُواْ مَا كَتَبَ اللّهُ لَكُمْ﴾[180] من الإباحة بعد الحظر، ﴿وَكُلُواْ وَاشْرَبُواْ حَتَّى يَتَبَيَّنَ لَكُمُ الْخَيْطُ الأَبْيَضُ مِنَ الْخَيْطِ الأَسْوَدِ مِنَ الْفَجْرِ﴾.

عن قتادة عن أبي معشر عن النخعي[181] قال: سألت ابن عبّاس قلت[182]: آكل حتّى أشك؟

قال: كلْ حتّى لا تشكّ.

قال غيره: قد يشرب الرجل من القدح فيحلّ له أوله ويحرم عليه آخره، يشرب ما لم يتبيّن له الصبح فإذا استبان أمسك، وهو قول أصحابنا.

وعن قوله عزّ وجل[183]: ﴿وَلاَ تُبَاشِرُوهُنَّ وَأَنتُمْ عَاكِفُونَ فِي الْمَسَاجِدِ﴾[184]؟

قال: كان الرجل يعتكف، فإذا خرج من مصلاّه ولقي امرأته غشيها، فنهاهم الله عن

---

176 لا: -، د.

177 لا: -، د.

178 قابل: القابلة، ب.

179 فكان قوم يأكلون: القوم يصيبون من ذلك، ب.

180 سورة البقرة: ١٨٧.

181 عن أبي معشر: قال: بلغنا هذا عن رجل أبي الضحاك، ب.

182 قلت: -، د.

183 عزّ وجل: -، ب.

184 سورة البقرة: ١٨٧.

ذلك حتّى يفرغوا من اعتكافهم. قال: نعم[185].

سئل عن الرجل يتقدّم رمضان بصوم؟

عن قتادة عن الحسن: أنّه قال: لأن أفطر يوما من رمضان ولا أتعمده أحبّ إليَّ من أن أصوم يوما من شعبان أتعمده. قال: نعم، إلاّ أن يكون صام[186] شعبان كله، فلا بأس أن يصوم إلى رمضان. قال: وكان أصحابنا لا يرون بذلك بأسا.

سئل عن الوصال؟

عن قتادة عن أنس بن مالك: أنّ نبيّ الله عليه السلام قال: «لا تواصلوا»، فقيل له: يا نبيّ الله، إنك تواصل؟ قال: «إنّي لست كأحد منكم[187]، إن ربي يطعمني ويسقيني»[188]. وقال غيره: بلغنا هذا عن قتادة عن الحسن بن عبد الرحمن عن رجل آخر[189] أنّ معاذ بن جبل قال: ليصومنّ الدهر كلّه. قالوا: كيف ذلك؟ قال: صوموا ثلاثة أيّام من كلّ شهر. قال: بلغنا هذا.

وكان جابر بن زيد يتأوّل قول الله: ﴿مَنْ جَاءَ بِالْحَسَنَةِ فَلَهُ عَشْرُ أَمْثَالِهَا﴾[190]، وتأولها فيمن يتصدق بماله كلّه، يقول[191]: العشر يجزيه.

185 قال: نعم: –،د.

186 صام: يصوم، ب.

187 كأحد منكم: كأحدكم، ب.

188 رواه البخاري، باب الوصال ومن قال ليس في الليل صيام، ر١٨٦٠.

189 عن رجل آخر: –،د.

190 سورة الأنعام: ١٦٠.

191 يقول: قال، ب.

وبلغنا أنَّ عليًّا رضي الله عنه كان يصوم يوم الخميس ويوم الاثنين[192] ويوما آخر.

قال: كان يكره أن تقصد ليوم معلوم كأنه فريضة عليك[193]، ولكن تصوم إذا فتح الله عليك[194].

سئل عن صوم الدهر؟

قال: أدركنا رجالا و[195]عجائز لا يفطرون إلاَّ يوما لا يصام فيه.

سئل عن صوم أيَّام التشريق؟

حدَّث عن قتادة عن سليمان بن يسار عن حمزة الأسلمي[196]: أن رجلا كان على جمل[197] آدم يتبع رحال الناس[198] بمنى: يقول [ألا] لا تصوموا هذه الأيَّام؛ لأنَّها أيَّام أكل وشرب، ونبيّ الله بين أظهركم[199].

قال: زعم الربيع: أنّ من جعل على نفسه صيام الدهر صامهنَّ[200].

وبلغنا أنَّ أبا الحر كان يصومهن، وعسى أن يكون كره صيامهنّ[201] بمنى، فإن أيَّام منى أيَّام

192 يوم الخميس ويوم الأثنين: يوم الاثنين ويوم الخميس، ب.
193 أن تقصد ليوم معلوم كأنه فريضة عليك: أن يقصد... عليه، ب.
194 من صام ثلاثة أيام من كل شهر كمن صام الدهر كله: هامش، ب.
195 رجالا و: -، د.
196 الأسلمي: بن الأسلم، ب، د.
197 جمل: جبال، ب.
198 الناس: النازلين، د.
199 رواه النسائي: السنن الكبرى، النهي عن صيام أيام التشريق...، ر ٢٨٧٥
200 صامهن: صامهم، د.
201 صيامهن: صومهن، ب.

أكل وشرب، فأمّا بمنى فيكره[202]، فعسى أن يكره إلاّ من كان عليه صيام الدهر.

عن قتادة قال: ذكر لنا أنَّ نبيَّ الله عليه السلام نهى عن صوم يوم الفطر ويوم النحر[203]

قال: نعم.

سئل عن صوم يوم عاشوراء؟

فحدَّث عن قتادة قال: بلغنا: أنَّ نبيَّ الله عليه السلام دخل المدينة فوجد اليهود صياماً فقال[204]: مالهم صاموا هذا اليوم؟[205]

قالوا: هذا يوم قطع فيه موسى البحر وأغرق فيه فرعون فصامه موسى عليه السلام شكرا لله وأمر بصومه، قال رسول الله عليه السلام أنا أولى بموسى منهم وأحق به، فصامه رسول الله عليه السلام، وأمر أصحابه أن يصوموا[206] حتَّى أنَّه[207] أمر أناسا قد كانوا أكلوا من أوَّل النهار أن يصوموا آخره.

قال: الله ورسوله أعلم، قد أدركنا أصحابنا وهم يرغبون في صيامه، ومنهم من يفطر فلا يعيب عليه بعض، ويقولون: من أصبح صائما لم يفطر، فإن أفطر فعليه قضاؤه، ومن أصبح مفطرا لم يصم والصيام من الليل إلى الليل.

عن رجل عن يحيى بن [أبي] كثير عن عبد الله بن يزيد عن ابن عبَّاس: أنَّ رسول

---

202 فيكره: -، د.

203 رواه الربيع، باب النهي عن صيام العيدين ويوم الشك، ر٣٢٤، ومسلم، باب النهي عن صوم يوم الفطر ويوم الأضحى، ر٢٧٢٨.

204 فقال: فقالوا، ب، د.

205 رواه مسلم، باب صوم يوم عاشوراء، ر٢٧١٤.

206 رواه البخاري، باب قول الله تعالى: (وهل أتاك حديث موسى، ر٣٢١٦.

207 أنه: -، ب.

الله صلى الله عليه وسلم لم يكن يتوخى فضل صوم يوم على يوم بعد رمضان إلاَّ يوم عاشوراء[208].

قال: هكذا كان أصحابنا يصنعون لا يقصدون إلى يوم معلوم، ولكن إذا وجدوا روح الصيام صاموا.

عن قتادة قال: ذكر لنا أن اليوم الذي تاب [الله] فيه على آدم يوم عاشوراء، وهبط نوح إلى الأرض يوم عاشوراء.

سئل عن صوم يوم الجمعة فحدّث عن صاحب له عن عبد الحميد بن جبير أن مُحَمَّد بن عباد سأل جابر بن عبد الله: هل سمعت رسول الله نهى أن يختص يوم الجمعة؟[209]
قال: نعم، ورب الكعبة. قال: كان الفقهاء يكرهون ذلك: وأحب الصيام إليهم إذا وجدوا روح الصيام.

سئل عن السواك؟
قال: كان أصحابنا يقولون: السواك للصائم أوّل النهار وما رأيت ربيعا تسوك عند الأولى وهو صائم. قال: وكان يكره عند الفطر حتَّى يفطر، ويستحبّ أن يشرب على الرائحة التي تكون في الفم، ولا بأس به في أوّل النهار، وكان بعض الفقهاء يكرهون آخر النهار.
عن قتادة قال: ذكر لنا أنَّ نبيَّ الله عليه السلام قال: لقد أمرت بالسواك حتَّى خشيت أن يكتب علي[210].

208 رواه الطبراني: المعجم الكبير، ر١١٢٥٥.
209 رواه البخاري، باب صوم يوم الجمعة، ر١٨٨٣.
210 رواه ابن ماجه، باب السواك، ر٢٨٩.

سئل عن الرجل يجعل الماء في فيه[211] وهو صائم ثُمَّ يَمجّه؟

قال: يكره، ولو صنعه لم يكن عليه بأس.

سئل عن الرجل يصبح وهو لا يريد الصيام ثُمَّ يبد وله؟

قال: لا يصوم إلاَّ أن يكون قد نوى ذلك[212] من الليل، ولا يفطر إذا كان نوى الصيام إلاَّ أن ينوي الإفطار من الليل.

سئل عن الرجل يصبح صائما في غير رمضان ثُمَّ يفطر من غير عذر؟

قال: يصوم يوما مكانه، وبئسما صنع إلاَّ أن يكون من عذر.

عن قتادة: أنَّ ابن عبَّاس أخبر أصحابه أنَّه صائم، ثُمَّ خرج عليهم برأسه يقطر، فقالوا: ألم تكن صائما. قال: بلى، ولكن مرت بي جارية[213] فأعجبتني فأصبتها، وكانت حسنة هممت بها وأنا أقضيه بيوم آخر.

قال غيره: ويكره أن يفطر إلاَّ من ضرورة.

سئل عن رجل يصوم شيئا من التطوّع وعليه قضاء يوم من رمضان؟

قال: يكره له[214] إلاَّ اليوم واليومين ونحو ذلك[215].

سئل عن الصائم إذا تقيأ؟

---

211 يجعل الماء في فيه: يجعل في فيه الماء، ب.

212 ذلك: -، د.

213 جارية: -، ب.

214 له: -، د.

215 من علي القضاء لا يصوم التطوع إلا ليوم واليومين: هامش، ب.

قال: إن سبقه[216] القيء فليس عليه شيء، وإن تقيأ [217]عمدا صام يوما مكانه.

سئل عن رجل يأكل ناسيا في صومه؟

قال: من أكل أو شرب ناسيا فقدتم صومه، فإنّ الله أطعمه وسقاه.

سئل عن الرجل يجعل على نفسه يمينا[218] صوم شهر؟

قال: يصوم شهرا كما جعل على نفسه، فإن استهل[219] الصوم وقد مضى من الشهر أيّام[220] صام ثلاثين يوما، وإن استهل[221] الشهر من أوله فعليه صيامه إلى[222] أن يتم له شهر[223].

سئل عن قضاء رمضان في الأيّام العشر؟

قال: لا بأس أن يقضيه في العشرة ولا يقضيه[224] متفرّقا، وإن كان عليه شهر واستأنف العشرة أفطر يوم النحر ثُمّ صام من الغد[225].

216 إن سبقه: سبقه، د؛ إذا أدرعه، ب.
217 تقيأ: استقيأ نفسه، ب.
218 يمينا: -، ب.
219 أستهل: أستقبل، ب.
220 أيام: أياما، ب، د.
221 أستهل: أستأنف، ب.
222 الشهر من أوله فعليه صيامه إلى: -، ب.
223 أو نقص: +، ب.
224 يقضيه: يقضيها، ب، د.
225 من الغد: -، د.

باب في الحجامة

سئل عن الحجامة للصائم؟

قال: لا بأس بها، إلاَّ أن يخاف الضعف عن الصوم.

سئل عن رجل مرض في رمضان فلم يفق حتَّى مات؟

قال: لا صيام عليه ولا إطعام، فإن صح ثُمَّ فرط فعليه الصيام والطعام.

سئل عن رجل جعل على نفسه نذر صوم[226] يوم[227] فمرض[228] ثُمَّ هلك؟

قال: عليه على كلّ حال.

سئل عمَّن مات وعليه رمضان[229]؟

قال: يطعم عنه[230]، أو يصام عنه شهر[231]. وكذلك أمر جابر بن زيد في عجوز كانت قد طعنت في السن، وأمر أهلها أن يصوموا شهرا ويطعموا شهرا[232] وإن كان لم يزل مريضا حتَّى مات فليس عليه قضاء[233] صيام ولا إطعام، الله أولى بالعذر، إنَّما ذلك

226 صوم: -، د.

227 يوم: شهر، ب.

228 فمرض: -، ب.

229 رمضان: رمضانان، ب.

230 شهرا: +، ب.

231 شهر: شهرا، ب،د.

232 وأمر أهلها أن يصوموا شهرا ويطعموا شهرا: -، د.

233 قضاء: -، ب.

على من صح ففرط، فإن صح وعاش فعليه صوم[234] الرمضانين جميعًا[235].

سئل عن رجل تتابع عليه صوم رمضانين ففرط في صومهما؟
قال: عليه الصوم والإطعام ولو صام سنة ثُمَّ أفلت بذلك لكان قليلا فيه، وإن أفلت فصام سنة لكلِّ شهر فهو صالح.

سئل عن الرجل يقبل وهو صائم؟
قال: يكره للشباب، لما يخاف أن يسبقه، وأمَّا الشيخ فلا بأس، وإن خاف على نفسه شيخا كان أو شبابا فلا يعرض صومه.

سئل عن رجل قبل امرأته أو باشرها في رمضان؟
عن قتادة: أنَّه كان يكره ذلك ولا يجعل عليه شيئا. قال: نعم، ما لم تجئه النطفة فإذا جاءت النطفة فعليه ما مضى من الشهر وإن أفلت فهو صالح.

سئل عمَّن أدركه الصبح وهو جنب؟
قال: [236] أصحابنا يقولون: من أدركه الصبح وهو جنب فعليه ما مضى من الشهر، ولا يفطر ذلك اليوم، وعليه بدله، وإن أفاض الماء على جسده، قبل أن يصبح الصبح، ثُمَّ أصبح ولم يتم غسله فلا شيء عليه[237].

---

234 صوم: الصوم، ب،د.
235 الرمضانين جميعا: -،د.
236 أما: +، ب.
237 وإن أفاض الماء على جسده، قبل أن يصبح الصبح، ثُمَّ أصبح ولم يتم غسله فلا شيء عليه: -،د.

سئل عمَّن أدركه الصبح وهو جنب؟

قال: إن كان تطوّعا أفطر وأعاد[238] يوما مكانه.

سئل عمَّن أفطر يوما من رمضان متعمّدا؟

قال: كان صالح الدهان[239] يقول: لو صام سنة ثُمَّ أفلت بذلك لكان يسيرًا.

سئل عمَّن أكل وغشي امرأته في رمضان؟

قال: إن أفلت بعتق رقبة وصيام سنة، فقد أفلت.

سئل عن رجل عالج امرأته أوغمزها أو قبلها في رمضان حتَّى دفق الماء الأعظم[240] وأمذى؟

قال: أمَّا المذي فلا شيء عليه، وأمَّا النطفة[241] فعليه أن يستأنف ما بقي ويقضي ما مضى[242].

سئل عن رجل غشي امرأته وهو يقضي رمضان؟

قال: يعيد أيَّامه التي مضت من قضائه[243]، ويستأنف أيَّامه تلك التي بقيت عليه[244] من رمضان كلها.

---

238 أعاد: أبدل، ب.

239 دهان: -، ب.

240 الأعظم: -،د.

241 النطفة: المني، ب.

242 من عالج امرأته حتى خرج منه المذي أو المني: هامش، ب.

243 قضائه: قضاءه، ب،د.

244 عليه: -، ب.

سئل عن رجل صام شهرين من كفَّارة الظهار، أو قتل نفسا خطأ ثُمَّ مرض؟

قال: إن أفطر من عذر فعليه صيام يوم مكانه، وإن أفطر من غير عذر استأنف صيامه، فليس أشد من رمضان.

سئل عن رجل غشي امرأته وهي حائض؟

قال: كان ضمام بن السائب يقول: إن كان خلقا منه وعادة، فلا أرى لمسلمة أن تقيم مع رجل يصنع بها هذا، وإن كان مرة أخطأ بها فلا نرى بأسا، وقد كان غيره يقول: إذا صنع ذلك مرة أخرى لم نأمره أن يقيم عليها ولا أن يفارقها، وإن يفارقها أحبّ إليّنا.

باب الاعتكاف

سئل عمَّن غشي امرأته في رمضان وهو معتكف؟

قال: عليه أن يستأنف رمضان ولو صام لذلك شهرا لكان يسيرا.

سئل عمَّن غشي امرأته في رمضان وهو معتكف، وهي حائض وأكل طعاما؟

قال: يكره أن يراجعها بعد هذا.

سئل عمَّن غشي امرأته في رمضان وهما معتكفان؟

قال: إن طاوعته فعليهما أن يستأنفا اعتكافهما، وقد كان الفقهاء يشددون في ذلك.

سئل عمَّن غشي امرأته وهي معتكفة وهو غير معتكف؟

قال: إن استكرهها فعليه كفّارتها، وإن طاوعته فعليها الكفّارة وليس عليه شيء.

سئل عن رجل غشي امرأته، أو غشيها وهي حائض أو لاعبها حتّى نزل الماء الأعظم[245] وأكل طعاما؟

قال: هو بمنزلة الذي يغشى في رمضان[246].

سئل عن الاعتكاف بغير صوم؟

قال: لا اعتكاف إلاّ بصوم ومن سمّى الاعتكاف ولم يسمِ الصوم فعليه الصوم.

سئل هل للمعتكف أن يتعشّى في أهله إذا اشترط ذلك؟

قال: ليس فيه شرط، يتعشى ويتسحر في المسجد، وقال: للمعتكف حضور[247] الجمعة، وجنازة أبيه وأمه، وليس له حضور[248] سواهما من الجنائز.

سئل عن المعتكفة إذا حاضت؟

قال: إذا حاضت رجعت لمنزلها، وإن طهرت رجعت فقضت الأيّام التي حاضت ،فليس بأشد من رمضان.

عن قتادة والحسن وجابر بن زيد وابن عبّاس وعكرمة أنّهم قالوا: لا اعتكاف إلاّ في مسجد تقيم الصلاة فيه. قال: نعم، والاحتصان في البيوت.

سئل عن رجل يدعى وهو صائم؟

245 الأعظم: -،د.

246 الذي غشي امرأته في الاعتكاف بمنزلة رمضان: هامش، ب.

247 حضور: -، ب.

248 حضور: -، ب.

قال: يستحبّ أن يجيب وإن لم يفعل فلا بأس.

سئل عن المرأة تصوم تطوّعا؟

قال: لا تصوم تطوّعا إلاّ بإذن زوجها، وتقضي رمضان بغير إذنه.

سئل: هل يكتحل الصائم؟

قال: لا بأس بذلك.

قال قتادة: ذكر لنا أنّ نبيّ الله عليه السلام قال: إذا صام أحدكم فلا يرفث ولا يفسق[249] يومئذ ولا يجهل[250]، فإن أمروه وشقوا عليه فليقل: إني صائم[251]، أي يحجر بذلك صيامه.

سئل عن الصوم يوم التروية؟

قال: كان[252] أبو عبيدة لا يأمر[253] به.

عن قتادة قال[254]: ذكر لنا أنّ نبيّ الله عليه السلام قال: قال الله عز وجل «الصوم جنّة يجتن بها عبدي من النار، والصوم لي وأنا أجازي به، يدع طعامه وشرابه وشهوته من أجلي، والذي نفس محمّد بيده لخلوف فم الصائم عند الله أطيب من ريح المسك»[255].

249 ولا يفسق: -، د.

250 ذلك: +، د.

251 رواه الربيع، باب في فضل رمضان، ر٣٢٩. والبخاري، باب فضل الصوم، ر١٧٩٥.

252 كان: -، ب.

253 لا يأمر: لا بأس، ب.

254 عن قتادة قال: -، ب.

255 رواه البخاري، باب ما يذكر في المسك، ر٥٥٨٣.

عن قتادة قال: ذكر لنا أنَّ نبيَّ الله عليه السلام قال: «صوموا يوم الصبر وثلاثة أيَّام من كلّ شهر يذهبن وحر[256] الصدر»[257].

باب النذر

سئل عن رجل جعل عليه[258] نذرا، ولم يسمّ شيئا؟

قال: يقال: إطعام مسكين أو اثنين، أو صيام يوم أو يومين، بلغنا ذلك عن جابر بن زيد[259] وأبي عبيدة.

سئل عن امرأة جعلت ثوبها عليها هديا إن لبسته؟

قال: لتهدِ ثوبها ذلك كما سمت، فإن بلغ ثمن ثوبها دما فلتبعه ثُمَّ لتذبح ما بلغ.

سئل عن رجل قال: كلّ مالي في رتاج الكعبة[260]؟

قال: أمَّا أصحابنا فيلزمونه العشر مِمَّا يملك يهديه للكعبة.

سئل عمَّن نذر بشيء لا يملكه؟

قال: عليه شراؤه فيما يقول أصحابنا.

256 وحر: بوحد، ب؛ بوجد، د.

257 رواه أحمد، ر ٢٣١٢٠.

258 عليه: -، ب.

259 بن زيد: -، ب. انظر: آثار الربيع، مسألة ١٦٨، ص ٤٥.

260 الرتج والرِّتاجُ: البابُ العظيم. وقيل: هو الباب الْمُغْلَقُ، ومنه: رِتاجُ الكعبة. وفي الحديث: «جَعَلَ مالَه في رِتاجِ الكعبة» أي: فيها؛ فكنى عنها بالباب؛ لأَن منه يُدخل إِليها، وجمع الرِّتاج رُتُجٌ. انظر: لسان العرب، مادة: (رتج.

سئل عن الرجل يبقِ غلا مه فيجعل لله على[261] إن قد ر عليه أن يقطع منه أصبعه[262]؟

قال: يكفر يمينه، فإن مثّل به فهو حر.

سئل عن رجل نذر ألاَّ يتكلم ولا يقعد ولا يستظل وأن يصوم يومه؟

قال: ليطعم للكلام وليتكلم، وليمض في صومه ويطعم للقيام مسكينا.

عن قتادة[263] قال: كان أبو الشعثاء يقول: فيمن قال: كل[264] مالي للكعبة أو للمساكين فليهد عشرة دراهم[265] أو ليتصدق بعشره.

قال قتادة[266]: بلغنا عن الفقهاء أنَّه من حلف على يمين فحنث في غضب أو رضا لزمته تلك اليمين مهما كانت.

سئل عن امرأة حلفت[267] أن تحج ماشية ناشرة شعرها؟

قال: عليها المشي وعليها أن تغطي شعرها[268] وتكفر عن ذلك وتطعم مسكينا أو اثنين.

سئل عن رجل جعل على نفسه هديا؟

قال: يهدي بدنة أو بقرة.

---

261 على: عليه، ب.

262 أصبعه: طائفة، ب.

263 عن قتادة: -، ب.

264 كل: -، ب.

265 دراهم: -،د.

266 عن قتادة: -، ب.

267 حلفت: نذرت، ب.

268 شعرها: رأسها، ب.

سئل عن رجل قال: هو يهدي فلانا أو قال: هو يهدي فلانة[269]؟

قال: إذا قال: هو يهدي فلانا فليس بشيء، وإن قال: هو على هدي أو هدي من ماله؛ فعليه أن[270] يهدي قيمته مملوكا.

سئل عن رجل قال: هو يهدي دار فلان؟

قال: يهدي قيمتها دراهم ويجعلها بدنة.

سئل عن رجل جعل على نفسه سواري مثل سواري المسجد ذهبا؟

قال: لا يجمع عنده مال إلاَّ أهداه ويمسك منه قدر[271] قوته[272].

سئل عن رجل قال: كلّ مالي هدي؟

عن قتادة عن جابر بن زيد أنَّه قال: إن كان كثيرا أهدى عشره، وإن كان وسطا أهدى سبعه، وإن كان قليلا أهدى خمسه، وهو قول قتادة، والكثير عند قتادة ألفان والوسط ألف والقليل خمسمائة.

قال: بلغنا هذا عن جابر، غير أنَّه لم يوقت الألف والألفين ولا شيء.

سئل عن رجل قال: هو محرم بحجّ أو بألف حجّة؟

قال: يحجّ ما استطاع حتَّى يموت. قال: حدَّثني[273] عن أبي عبيدة أنَّه قال: يحجّ حتَّى

---

269 فلانة: غلامه، ب.

270 فعليه أن: -، د.

271 قدر: -، ب.

272 من قال مالي كله هدي عليه أن يهدي عشره: هامش، ب.

273 رجل: +، ب.

يموت، وقال: من جعل على نفسه شيئا فهولازم له في رضى أوسخط[274]،

سئل عمّن قال: هو يهوديّ أو نصرانيّ أو مجوسيّ، فحنث؟

قال الربيع: عليه يمين مغلّظة تحرير رقبة، أو صيام شهرين، أو إطعام ستّين مسكينًا.

سئل عمّن حلف على يمين فرأى ما هو[275] خير منها؟

قال: ليفعل الذي هو خير، وليكفّر عن يمينه.

وعن أبي معشر عن النخعي: أنّ معقل بن مقرن أتى ابن مسعود فقال: إنّي حلفت أن أضع خدّي على فراش كذا وكذا.

قال ابن مسعود: إنّ الله يقول في كتابه: ﴿ يا أيُّها الَّذِينَ آمَنُواْ لاَ تُحَرِّمُواْ طَيِّبَاتِ مَآ أَحَلَّ اللّهُ لَكُمْ وَلاَ تعتدوا إنَّ الله لاَ يُحِبُّ الْمُعْتَدِينَ ﴾[276]. فقال: لولا هذه الآية ما سألتك.

فقال: كفّر عن يمينك. فقال: إنّي غني فهات. قال: اعتق رقبة.

قال: هو مخيّر بين العتق والكسوة والإطعام، فمن لم يجد فصيام ثلاثة أيّام.

سئل عمّن نذر أن يحجّ ولم يحجّ قط؟

قال: يبدأ بحجّة الإسلام، ثمّ يحجّ لنذره.

سئل عن رجل نذر أو حلف ليصومن شهرين متتابعين أو أكثر من ذلك؟

قال: يطعم عدد الأيّام التي حلف كلّ يوم مسكينا إن لم يستطع الصوم.

---

274 من جعل على نفسه شيئا يدوم لازم له في رضى كان أم سخط: هامش، ب.

275 ماهو: -، ب.

276 سورة المائدة: ٨٧.

سئل عن رجل جعل على نفسه[277] صيام كلّ يوم اثنين أو خميس، فوافق ذلك يوم الأضحى أو يوم الفطر؟

قال: فحدّث عن قتادة قال: يكفر يمينه ويصوم يوما مكان يوم، ليس عليه أكثر من صيام يوم مكانه. سألت عنه أبا عبيدة فقال: هذا إلاّ أن يكون حلف بالله، فعليه كفّارة يمين وصيام يوم مكانه.

سئل عن رجل جعل على نفسه[278] أن يصوم كلّ يوم اثنين فأراد أن يدع ذلك؟

قال أبو النظر: لا يدع ذلك فإن مرض فإنّه يطعم كلّ يوم اثنين مسكينا، وقال: يصوم يوما مكان يومه.

سئل عن رجل جعل على نفسه صوم شهر[279]؟

قال: من سمّى شهرا فعليه شهر متتابع ولا يقطعه فإن قطعه استأنف، ومن سمّى شهرين متتابعين فعليه صوم[280] شهرين متتابعين.

سئل عن المرأة يكون عليها صوم شهرين متتابعين فتحيض أو تمرض؟

قال: تقضي يوما مكان يوم ليس بأعظم من رمضان.

سئل عن رجل قال[281]: عليّ لله أو قال: لله علي؟

---

277 نفسه: حلف، ب.

278 نفسه: حلف، ب.

279 شهر: شهرين، ب.

280 صوم: -، ب.

281 قال: -،د.

قال: يمين يكفِّرها.

سئل عن رجل قال: علي عهد الله لأفعلنَّ كذا وكذا؟

قال: هي يمين مغلَّظة.

سئل عن رجل قال: والله لأفعلنَّ كذا وكذا ثمَّ سكت ساعة ثُمَّ استثنى؟

قال: إن كان الكلام موصولا بعضه ببعض فله ثنياه، وإن لم يصل الكلام وأطال السكوت فلا ثنيا له.

سئل عن رجل استحلفه السلطان ليد له على رجل أو مال، فحلف بالله ماله علم، وهو يعلم مكانه؟

قال: ليحلف وليكفر يمينه، ولا يدل على مسلم ولا على كافر ولا على مالهم[282].

سئل عمَّن حلف بملَّة غير ملَّة الإسلام؟

فحدَّث عن أبي معشر كتب إليه[283] رفع الحديث إلى رسول الله ﷺ أنَّه قال: من حلف بملَّة غير ملَّة الإسلام[284] كذبا متعمّدا فهو كما قال. وقال فيمن قتل نفسه متعمّدا[285] بشيء: عذبه الله به في نار جهنَّم[286]، وقال: هو كما قال[287] النخعي: كفّارة[288] يمين مغلَّظة.

282 من استخلفه السلطان ليد له على مسلم أو مال يحلف: هامش، ب.

283 كتب إليه: –،د.

284 ملة الإسلام: –،د.

285 نفسه متعمدا: –،د.

286 رواه البخاري، باب ما جاء في قاتل النفس، ر١٢٩٧.

287 هو كما قال: –،د.

288 كفار: كفر، ب د.

سئل عن رجل[289] يقول: هو ينحر ابنه؟

قال: أمَّا الذي يروى عن أصحابنا عن جابر بن زيد ينحر بدنة أو يعتق نسمة[290].

سئل عن الذي[291] يقول: أقسمت لأفعلنَّ كذا وكذا؟

قال: بلغنا أنَّ جابرا دعا رجلا إلى طعامه فأبى[292]، فقال: أقسمت، فأبى فقال: إنِّي أخاف أن تكون يمينا فجاء الرجل[293].

سئل عن رجل قال: حلفت لأفعلنَّ؟

قال: أمَّا حلفت فليس بشيء، وهي كذبة.

سئل عن رجل قال: أشهد لأفعلنَّ كذا وكذا؟

قال: ليس في ذلك شيء حتَّى يقول: أشهد بالله.

سئل عن رجل قال: أخزاه الله أو لعنه الله[294] إن لم يفعل كذا وكذا؟

قال: حدَّثني الربيع أن من قال: لعنه الله وأدخله نار جهنَّم إن لم يفعل كذا وكذا[295]، فإنَّه يستحبّ[296] له أن يصوم أو يتصدق ولم يوقت لذلك شيئًا، وقال: اليهوديّ يحلف

289 رجل: –، د.

290 من قال أقسمت بالله سبعين يمين ومن قال أقسمت أخاف أن يكون: +، ب.

291 الذي: رجل، ب.

292 فأبى: فأبا، ب، د.

293 الرجل: –، د.

294 الله: –، د.

295 كذا وكذا: –، د.

296 يستحب: يجب، ب.

بربِّ التوراة، والنصارى يستحلفون[297] بربِّ الإنجيل، والمجوس[298] يستحلفون[299] بربِّ النار والشمس والقمر[300].

سئل عن رجل يقول: معاذ الله إن فعلت كذا وكذا؟

قال: ليس يمين. وهوكقوله: أعوذ بالله.

سئل عن رجل يقول: والله لأ فعل كذا وكذا، ثُمَّ بدا له أن يكفر يمينه ويفعل ذلك؟

قال: يكفر قبل أن يفعل أو بعد أن يفعل أي ذلك شاء[301].

سئل عن رجل يقول: الطعام علي حرام إن فعلت كذا وكذا؟

قال: يمين يكفِّرها.

سئل عن رجل [أوجب] على نفسه تحريرا ولم يسم شيئا؟

قال: عليه تحرير.

سئل عن رجل حلف في مقاعد شتى في شيء واحد؟

قال: إذا حلف في مقاعد شتى فعليه كفَّارات شتى، وإن حلف في مقعد واحد، فردد يمينه: والله والله فإنَّما هي يمين واحدة.

297 يستحلفون: –،د.

298 المجوس: المجوسي، ب،د.

299 يستحلفون: –،د.

300 استحلاف اليهود والنصارى والمجوس: هامش، ب.

301 من أراد أن يكفر فليكفر قبل الحنث أو بعده على سواء: هامش، ب.

عن صاحب له عن ابن عمر كان إذا أكد اليمين أعجبه أن يعتق إذا كان واجدا.

وقال غيره: الميسر بالعتق أفضل له، وأي الثلاثة فعل أجزأ عنه: العتق أو الطعام أو الكسوة، فمن لم يجد فصيام ثلاثة أيّامٍ[302].

سئل عن رجل أعتق في كفّارة اليمين صبيًّا؟

قال: جائز، وعليه نفقته حتّى يكفي نفسه، و ليس له أن يتركه عالة[303] على الناس.

سئل عن قول الله. ﴿لَا يُؤَاخِذُكُمُ اللَّهُ بِاللَّغْوِ فِي أَيْمَانِكُمْ. . .﴾[304]؟

قال: اللغو أن يقول: لا والله، و بلى والله، وإنّما أن يحلف الرجل على الشيء وهو يرى[305] أنّه كما حلف فقد يلزمه اليمين.

عن قتادة قال: يكره أن يقول الرجل لعمر الله ولا يعلم فيها يمينا. قال: نعم[306].

سئل عن الرجل يقول: الحلال علي حرام إن فعلت كذا وكذا.

قال: يمين يكفّرها[307].

302 من حلف في مقاعد شتى كفارته: هامش، ب.

303 عالة: عيال، ب.

304 سورة المائدة: ٨٩، وتمامها: ﴿وَلَكِن يُؤَاخِذُكُم بِمَا عَقَّدتُّمُ الْأَيْمَانَ فَكَفَّارَتُهُ إِطْعَامُ عَشَرَةِ مَسَاكِينَ مِنْ أَوْسَطِ مَا تُطْعِمُونَ أَهْلِيكُمْ أَوْ كِسْوَتُهُمْ أَوْ تَحْرِيرُ رَقَبَةٍ فَمَن لَّمْ يَجِدْ فَصِيَامُ ثَلَاثَةِ أَيَّامٍ ذَٰلِكَ كَفَّارَةُ أَيْمَانِكُمْ إِذَا حَلَفْتُمْ وَاحْفَظُوا أَيْمَانَكُمْ كَذَٰلِكَ يُبَيِّنُ اللَّهُ لَكُمْ آيَاتِهِ لَعَلَّكُمْ تَشْكُرُونَ﴾.

305 يرى: يراه، ب.

306 قال: نعم: –، د.

307 قال: لا تحلفوا بأبيكم ولا بالطاغوت فإن أحب إلى الله ألاّ تحلفوا إلا به: هامش، ب.

عن قتادة عن الحسن عن النبيّ -عليه السلام- أنّه[308] سمع عمر يقول: وأبيك. قال: لا[309] تحلفوا بآبائكم ولا بالطواغيت[310]، فإنّه أحب إلى الله ألاّ تحلفوا إلاّ بالله، فإذا حلفتم بالله فاصدقوا. قال: نعم، بلغنا هذا، وكان الفقهاء يكرهونه، وأن يقول الرجل بحياة فلان، وحدث أن الزبير سابق رجلا فسبقه. قال: سبقتك والكعبة[311]، وقال عمر رضي الله عنه: لا أم لك الكعبة ترزقك وتطعمك وتسقيك؟ قال: لا تحلفوا إلاّ بالله، فإذا حلفتم بالله فاصدقوا. قال: نعم، إن قال[312]: ورب الكعبة لزمته اليمين.
عن قتادة عن ابن عبّاس مرّ برجل وهو يحلف بالكعبة. فقال: لأن أحلف بالله فأحنث أحبّ إليَّ [من] أن أحلف بغيره فأصدَّق. قال: نعم[313].

عن قتادة: أنَّ عمر بن الخطّاب ومعاذ بن جبل تداريا في حق فحكّما أُبيّ بن كعب، فكانت اليمين على عمر. فقال: إنّي أعفي[314] أمير المؤمنين، فأبى عمر إلاّ أن يحلف، فحلف ثُمَّ رده عليه فقال: ألاّ كان هذا قبل أن تحلف. فقال: إنّي كرهت أن يكون سنة فلا يحلف أحد على حقّ هو له.

عن عديّ بن عديّ: أنَّ رجلا من حضرموت خاصم رجلا من كنده، يقال له امرؤ

308 أنه: -،د.

309 لا: -،د.

310 الطاغوت، ب. رواه الربيع، باب الأيمان، ر٦٥٥. والبخاري، باب لا تحلفوا بآبائكم، ر٦٢٧٠.

311 والكعبة: ورب الكعبة، ب د.

312 إن قال: -، ب.

313 عن قتادة عن ابن عبّاس مرَّ برجل وهو يحلف بالكعبة. فقال: أحب لأن أحلف بالله فأحنث، أحبّ إليَّ أن أحلف بغيره فأصدق. قال: نعم: -،د.

314 أعفي: أعف، ب،د.

القيس بن عبّاس إلى النبيّ -عليه السلام- في أرض كانت بينهما فكلف الحضرمي البيّنة وجعل على الكندي اليمين، فقال الحضرمي: أمكنته من اليمين يا نبيّ الله، ذهبت والله أرضي، فقال رسول الله صلى الله عليه وسلم: «من حلف على يمين كاذبة ليقطع[315] بها مال أخيه لقي الله يوم القيامة وهو غضبان عليه[316]»[317] وتلا هذه الآية: ﴿ إِنَّ الَّذِينَ يَشْتَرُونَ بِعَهْدِ اللهِ وَأَيْمَانِهِم ثَمَنًا قَلِيلاً أُولَئِكَ لاَ خَلاَقَ لَهُمْ فِي الآخِرَةِ ﴾[318] قال: فما لمن تركها يا نبيّ الله؟ قال: «الجنَّة». قال: أشهدك أنّي تركتها. قال: نعم، بلغنا هذا.

باب كفّارة اليمين

قال: لكلّ مسكين أكلتان[319] يشبع فيهما غدوّا وعشيّة، غداء وعشاء ولم يذكر تمرا.

سئل عن الكسوة؟

قال: لكل مسكين ثوب؛ إزار[320] أو رداء، وللمرأة خمار وثوب، أي ذلك شاء.

سئل عن الرجل تكون عليه رقبة واجبة؟

قال: يكره أن تكون [بها] عوار أو عرج أو جذم أو وشال، أو طفلا أو معتقا عن دابر أو يهوديّا أو نصرانيّا، وإن أنفق على الصبي[321] ما أعتقه حتّى يستكفي نفسه أجزى عنه،

315 ليقطع: ليقتطع، ب.

316 عليه: -، ب.

317 رواه البخاري، باب عهد الله عز وجل، ر٦٢٨٣.

318 سورة آل عمران: ٧٧.

319 أكلتان: أكلتين، ب،د.

320 إزار: إزارا، ب،د.

321 الصبي: الصبر، ب،د.

فإما أن يعتقه ويخلي سبيله يسأل الناس فلا.

سئل عن الرجل عليه عتق رقبة أن يعتق ذا رقبة؟

قال: إن كان عبده أعتقه إن شاء، وإن كان اشتراه أعتقه إلاّ أن يكون والداً أو ولداً أو عماً أو خالاً؛ فإنه إذا ملك هؤلاء عتقوا وإن لم يعتقهم.

عن أبي نهيك عن ابن عبّاس أن رسول الله -صلى الله عليه وسلم- قال: من أعاذ بالله فأعيذوه[322]، ومن سأل[323] لوجه الله أعطوه[324]. قال: إنه يستحبّ ذلك إلاّ أن يسأل مالا يستطاع أو حراما أو يطلبوا منه مالا يجد، فإن سأل معروفا فليفعل[325].

عن قتادة عن أبي نهيك بن إبراهيم: أن مكاتبا سأل ابن عمر لوجه الله. قال: كم عليك. قال: كذا وكذا، فأعطاه. قال: يكره أن يسأل لوجه الله، وإن سأل مالا ينبغي لم أعطه[326].

باب فيما سئل عنه من باب الأشربة

سئل عن قول الله: ﴿يَسۡـَٔلُونَكَ عَنِ ٱلۡخَمۡرِ وَٱلۡمَيۡسِرِۖ قُلۡ فِيهِمَآ إِثۡمٞ كَبِيرٞ وَمَنَٰفِعُ لِلنَّاسِ وَإِثۡمُهُمَآ أَكۡبَرُ مِن نَّفۡعِهِمَا﴾[327].

---

322 من أعاذ بالله فأعيذوه: من أعاد بالله فأعيدوه، ب،د.

323 سأل: سئل، ب،د.

324 رواه أبو داود، باب عطية من سأل بالله، ر١٦٧٤.

325 عدا القرابة الذين إذا ملكهم قريبهم عتقوا حتمًا: هامش، ب.

326 أعطه: أعطيه، ب. قال: عمن أعاذ بالسفا عيذوه ومن سأل لوجه الله أعطوه، ما سئل: هامش، ب. باب: كفّارة اليمين. . . . . وإن سأل ما لا ينبغي لم أعطه: -،د.

327 سورة البقرة: ٢١٩.

قال: إنَّ الله عزّ وجل [328] ذمهما ولم يحرمهما وهي يومئذ حلال، ثُمَّ أنزل الله [329] بعد ذلك هذه الآية وهي أشدُّ منها: ﴿ يَا أَيُّهَا الَّذِينَ آمَنُوا لَا تَقْرَبُوا الصَّلَاةَ وَأَنْتُمْ سُكَارَى حَتَّى تَعْلَمُوا مَا تَقُولُونَ ﴾ [330] فكان السكر عليهم فيها حرام. فأنزل الآية التي في المائدة: ﴿ يَا أَيُّهَا الَّذِينَ آمَنُوا إِنَّمَا الْخَمْرُ وَالْمَيْسِرُ وَالْأَنْصَابُ وَالْأَزْلَامُ رِجْسٌ مِنْ عَمَلِ الشَّيْطَانِ فَاجْتَنِبُوهُ لَعَلَّكُمْ تُفْلِحُونَ ﴾ [331] فجاء تحريمها في هذه الآية لقليلها وكثيرها ما أسكر منها وما لم يسكر.

قال: نعم، من شرب الخمر قليلا أوكثيرا شرب حرامًا وعليه الحدّ، ومن شرب نبيذا فسكر ضرب الحد؛ لأنّه مكروه، وقد نهى النبيّ -صلى الله عليه وسلم- عنه فإن سكر جلد، وإن لم يسكر لم يجلد، وما نهى عنه النبيّ -عليه السلام- فهو حرام.

وأما قوله: الخمر والميسر والأنصاب والأزلام. قال: الميسر هو القمار، والأنصاب هي الحجارة كانوا يعبدونها ويذبحون لها، والأزلام: أقداح كانوا يستقسمون بها الأمور، وكان الرجل إذا أراد سفرا أخذ قدحا فقال: هذا يأمر بالخروج ومصيب في سفره خيرا، ويأخذ قدحا آخر وقال: هذا يأمر بالمكث وليس مصيبًا في سفره خيرا، والمنبج بينهما، فنهى الله عن ذلك وقدم فيه ما قدم.

عن قتادة: أنَّ نبيَّ الله نهى عن اللعب بالكعبين وقال: هي ميسر الأعاجم، وقال قتادة: يكره اللعب كله حتَّى اللعب بالحصى [332]. قال: نعم.

328 قال: إن الله عزّ وجل: –، ب.

329 الله: –، د.

330 سورة النساء: ٤٣.

331 سورة المائدة: ٩٠.

332 رواه ابن أبي شيبة، في اللعب بالنرد وما جاء فيه، ر٢٦١٤٤.

عن قتادة عن أيُّوب[333] بن عبد الله بن عمرو بن العاص قال: مثل الذي يلعب بالكعبين ويقامر بهما كمن أكل لحم الخنزير، ومثل الذي يلعب بهما ولا يقامر بهما كالمدهن بشحمه.

عن قتادة قال: ذكر لنا أن هذه الآية لما نزلت: ﴿يَا أَيُّهَا الَّذِينَ آمَنُواْ إِنَّمَا الْخَمْرُ وَالْمَيْسِرُ وَالأَنصَابُ وَالأَزْلاَمُ رِجْسٌ مِّنْ عَمَلِ الشَّيْطَانِ فَاجْتَنِبُوهُ لَعَلَّكُمْ تُفْلِحُونَ﴾[334]، قال رسول الله صلى الله عليه وسلم: «يا أيُّها الناس، إنَّ الله قد حرم الخمر فمن كان عنده شيء منها فلا يطعمه ولا يشربه ولا يبعه»[335]. قال: فأهرقوه، حتَّى جعل ريحها يوجد من طريق المدينة زمانًا. قال: بلغنا هذا، وبلغنا أنَّها كانت من التمر والبسر كانوا يسمون على كلّ شيء اختمر فهو عندهم خمر، وهي التي أهرقت فيما بلغنا يومئذ.

عن قتادة عن أنس بن مالك قال: كنت أسقي أبا طلحة وأُبي بن كعب وأبا دجانة الأنصاري، فدخل علينا داخل فقال: حدث خبر، نزل تحريم الخمر فهرقناها[336] وما هي يومئذ إلاَّ الفضيخ؛ خليط البسر والتمر. قال: بلغنا هذا، إنَّما كانت يومئذ الفضيخ.

عن قتادة قال: ذكر لنا أن رجلا سأل[337] ابن عمر عن الخمر؟

فقال: عن أي الخمر تسأل؟ فوالله إن من العنب لخمرا، وإن من التمر لخمرا، وإن من

333 عن أيوب: –، ب.

334 سورة المائدة: ٩٠.

335 رواه مسلم، باب تحريم بيع الخمر، ر٤١٢٦.

336 فهرقناها: فكفاناه، ب.

337 سأل: سئل، ب،د.

الأرز لخمرا، وإن من الشعير لخمرا، وإنَّ من العسل لخمرا، يُسمَّى كذا ويُسمَّى[338] كذا.
قال: كلّ شيء اختمر فهو خمر.

عن قتادة أنَّ رجلا سأل ابن عمر عن بيع الخمر.
قال: خبيث خبيث من باعها.
قال: كان يقال: لعن الله عاصرها وبائعها ومشتريها وحاملها والمحمولة إليه.

قال: سألت الربيع عن رجل يشرب الخمر ويدمنه، وله امرأة مسلمة هل تقيم معه؟
قال: ما أحب لها أن تقيم عند رجل مدمن للخمر.

عن أيُّوب عن نافع أن رواحل كانت لابن عمر وكان فيها غلام له، فجاء فقال: إن بعض القلائص مرضت، فنعتوا لي أن أواجرها[339] خمرا، فقال ابن عمر: أفعلت؟ فقال: لا. وكان قد فعل. فقال: لو فعلت لأوجعت لك رأسك.
[340] قال: يكره أن يسقي الدواب الخمر، ولو شربت دابة الخمر ثُمَّ ذكِّيت من ساعتها ما أكل لحمها.

سئل عن الطلاء؟
فحدث عن قتادة عن لاحق بن حميد: أن عمر بن الخطاب كتب إلى عمار بن ياسر، أمَّا بعد: فإنه أتتنا عير من الشام تحمل شرابا أسودَ[341] كأنه طلاء الإبل قد طبخ حتَّى

---

338 يسمى: –، د.
339 أواجرها: أوجدها، ب.
340 كان: +، ب.
341 أسود: أسودا، ب، د.

ذهب ثلثاه الخبيثان اللذان فيهما ريح الشيطان، وبقي ثلثه الطيب؛ فمر من قبلك أن يتخذوه ويصنعوه. قال: إذا صار العشرة ثلاثة وكان يصنع به الخبيص، ويصنعه على الأرض ولا يتعلَّق بها فاشربه ولا بأس به.

سئل عن نبيذ الجرِّ؟

قال: بلغنا: أنَّ نبيَّ الله عليه السلام نهى عن نبيذ الجر والحنتم والنقير والمزفت، وقال: كلّ مسكر حرام[342].

عن أبي يزيد المدني: أنَّ عمر بن الخطَّاب رضي الله عنه قال: لأن أشرب ماء قمقم محمي أحرق من بطني ما أحرق، وأبقي ما أبقي: أحبّ إليَّ من أن أشرب نبيذ الجرِّ.

قال: بلغنا هذا، وهو قول أصحابنا.

سئل عمَّن أعتق شقصا[343] له من مملوك عند موته؟

عن قتادة قال: عليه عتق ما بقي من ثلث ماله. قال: هذا رأينا[344].

سئل عن بيع الولاء وهبته[345]؟

عن قتادة عن عطاء بن أبي رباح. قال: إن عمر قال: إن الولاء مثل الرحم لا يباع ولا يوهب. قال: هذا رأينا.

---

342 رواه مسلم، باب الأمر بالإيمان بالله ورسوله، ر١٢٥. انظر: آثار الربيع، مسألة ٢٣٨، ص ٥٨.

343 شِقْصًا: أي جزءا.

344 قال: هذا رأينا: -،د.

345 وهبته: وهيبته، ب،د.

سئل عن ابن مسعود قال: الولاء كلحمة النسب لا يباع ولا يوهب قال: هذا رأينا.

سئل عن بيع المكاتب وهبته[346]؟

قال: إن المكاتب لا يباع ولا يوهب.

سئل عن العبد إذا أعتق وله أولاد من حرّة، أيجوزوا لهم؟[347] قال: نعم، هذا رأينا.

سئل عن رجل قال لمملوكة له: إن ولدت غلاما فأنت حرّة، فولدت غلاما ثمّ أتبعته جارية، قال: عتقت حين ولدت غلاما، فصارت هي والجارية حرتين. والغلام مملوك.

وقال: إن ولدت الجارية ثمّ ولدت الغلام فهي حرّة والغلام مملوك والجارية جميعا، فإن[348] ولدت غلمانا، فالأول منهم مملوك، والآخر حرّ كأنّها قد ولدته وقد عتقت قال: هذا رأينا.

سئل عن رجل أعتق مملوكا وله مال؟

قال: ماله له إلاّ أن يشترطه السيد.

سئل عن الرجل أنه أعتق مملوكا وعلى المملوك دين؟

قال: ينظر قيمة الغلام يوم أعتقه فيدفع إلى غرمائه، ليس عليه أكثر من قيمته.

وسئل عن رجل ملك ذا رحم؟

---

346 وهبته: وهيبته، ب،د.

347 أيجوزوا لهم: أن يجوزوا لهم، ب د.

348 فإن: فأي، ب،د.

قال: من ملك ذا رحم محرم عليه نكاحه فهو[349] حر[350].

سئل عن المعتق عن دبر أمن الثلث، أم من جميع المال؟

قال: يلزم من جميع المال.

وسئل عن المعتق عن دبر[351] أيبيعه صاحبه إذا احتاج؟

قال: لا يباع المدبر[352].

سئل عن أولاد المعتقات عن دبر؟

قال: مماليك وكلّ شيء وردت حتَّى يموت سيدها فما كان في بطنها فهو[353] حر.

سئل عن عبد بين[354] رجلين أعتقه أحدهما وكاتبه الآخر، لمن الولاء؟

قال: للذي أعتق؛ لأن علته خلاصه في ماله.

سئل عن عبد بين[355] ثلاثة نفر أعتقه أحدهم وكاتبه[356] الآخر وأمسكه الثالث؟

قال: عن الذي أعتق خلاص في ماله إن كان له مال، فإن لم يكن له مال استسعَ[357]

---

349 فهو: هو، ب د.

350 وهو حر: وحر، ب،د.

351 دبر: دبرا، ب،د.

352 انظر: آثار الربيع، مسألة ١٠٩، ص ٣٩.

353 فهو: هو، ب د.

354 عبد بين: عبدين، ب،د.

355 عبد بين: عبدين، ب،د.

356 وكاتبه: وكتبه، ب،د.

357 استسع: استمع، ب،د.

العبد من مكاتبه والذي[358] أمسك، وكان الولاء للذي أعتق.

وسئل عن رجل قال لآخر: إن بعتك غلامي فهو حر، قال الآخر: إن اشتريته فهو حرّ ثُمَّ باعه فاشتراه؟

قال: هو حرّ من مال الأول؛ لأنه أعتقه وهو في ملكه، وليس للآخر شيء؛ لأنه أعتقه، وهو ليس في ملكه.

سئل عن رجل أعتق رؤوسا عند موته، وليس له مال غيرهم

قال: يعتق من كلّ واحد الثلث ويستدفعون من بقية أثمانهم.

سئل عن رجل يهب امرأته لأهلها؟

قال: إذا وهب لأهلها طلاقها فهو واحد بائن[359].

باب الخيار

مِمّا سئل الربيع من باب الطلاق:

سئل عن الخيار. قال: إن اختارت نفسها فواحد وهو أحقّ بها، وإن اختارته فلا شيء، وهو رأي عمر بن الخطاب رضي الله عنه.

وسئل عن رجل يقول لامرأته: اختاري ثلاث مرّات، فقالت: قد اخترت نفسي؟

قال: إذا قال الرجل: اختاري، ينوي الطلاق، فهي واحدة وما نوى، وإن لم يكن

358 مكاتبه والذي: مكاتب وللذي، ب،د.

359 يعني: إذا وهب لأهلها طلاقها كان طلاقا واحدا بائنا.

ينوي طلاقا فلا شيء.

عن جابر إذا خير الرجل زوجته ثُمَّ جامعها قبل أن تختار، أو رجع في أمره، أو تفرقا[360]، فلا خيار لها.

سئل عن الرجل يجعل أمر امرأته بيدها، ثُمَّ توفي قبل أن يقضيَ شيئًا؟

قال: الميراث بينهما إذا لم يقضِ[361] بشيء في حياته.

وسئل عن رجل جعل أمر امرأته بيد رجلين فطلق أحدهما؟

قال: لا، حتَّى يجتمع.

وسئل عن الرجل قال لامرأته: يمين عليَّ حرام؟

عن عكرمة عن عمر بن الخطاب قال: في الحرام يمين يكفِّرها، وعن ابن مسعود وعبَّاس وجابر بن زيد -رضي الله عنهم- أنهم يقولون: يمين يكفِّرها[362].

كمل الجزء الثاني[363] من قول قتادة، ونحمد الله ربّ العالمين وصلَّى الله على سيدنا مُحَمَّد وعلى آله وصحبه وسلم تسليما.

سئل عن الرجل قال: كلّ حلال عليَّ حرام؟

قال: يمين يكفِّرها.

وسئل عن البريَّة والخليَّة والبيتة والحرام للبائنة؟

---

360 تفرقا: تفرق، ب،د.

361 يقض: تقضي، ب،د.

362 الحرام يمين يكفرها ولو قال لأمرته: أنت عليَّ حرام كانت عليه: هامش، ب.

363 سيكتمل الجزء الثاني بعد صفحة من ها هنا، ولا أدري لماذا نص على نهاية هذا الجزء هنا؟

قال: واحد بائن وما نوى إن كان ينوي الطلاق.

وعن عطاء بن أبي رياح عن ابن عبّاس -رضي الله عنه- قال: «لا طلاق إلاّ بعد النكاح، ولا عتق إلاّ بعد الملك»[364]. قال: هذا رأينا.

عن جبير عن الضحاك بن مزاحم عن البر بن شبرمة بن أبي شبرمة عن المسروق بن الأجدع: أن عليّ بن أبي طالب قال: «لا وصال في الصوم، ولا رضاعة بعد فطام، ولا صَمْتَ يومٍ إلى الليل، ولا يُتم بعد احتلام، ولا طلاق إلاّ بعد نكاح»[365]. قال: هذا رأينا.

سئل عن الرجل طلق امرأته قبل أن يدخل بها؟
قال: نرى[366] أن طلاق من لم يدخل واحدٌ فرّق طلاقَه أو جمعَه.

سئل عن الرجل طلق امرأته من قبل أن يمسها ثُمّ غشيها، وظن أن عليه الرجعة.
قال: لها صداق ونصف صداق.[367]

سئل عن الرجل كتب على وسادته طلاق امرأته؟
قال: فهو جائز عليه[368].

---

364 رواه الربيع عن ابن عباس مرفوعا إلى النبي صلى الله عليه وسلم، باب في الأولياء، ر٥١٠.
365 رواه أبو داود، رقم: ٢٨٧٣. والطبراني في الأوسط، رقم: ٧٣٣١.
366 نرى: نوى، ب،د.
367 من طلق امرأته ثُمّ غشيها ظنا أن عليها الرجعة صداق ونصف: +، ب.
368 رجل كتب على وسادته طلاق امرأته جاز عليه: هامش، ب.

سئل عمّن طلّق امرأته أو مات عنها وهو غائب فمتى تعتدّ؟

قال: تعتدّ من يوم مات أو من يوم طلق إذا أقامت بيّنة.

سئل عمن طلق امرأته ثمّ تركها أشهرا، ثمّ طلقها ثمّ تركها شهرا، ثمّ طلقها؟

قال: تعتد من أول طلاقها.

سئل عن الأمة تطلق اثنين ثمّ تُطلَق قبل أن تقضي عدّتها؟

قال: إذا طلقت تطليقتين فعدّتها عدّة الأمة ولا تحل له حتّى تنكح زوجا غيره.

سئل عن عدّة الأمة؟

قال: حيضتان[369]. قال: فإن لم تكن تحيض فشهر ونصف.

وسئل عن امرأة لا تحيض إلاّ مرة في كلّ سنة؟

قال: عدّتها في الحيض إلاّ أن يعلم أنه قطعه مرض.

بلغنا أنّ علقمة[370] بن قيس طلّق امرأته تطليقة[371] أو اثنتين فلبثت سنة غير شهر لا تحيض فماتت، فانطلق علقمة إلى ابن مسعود -رضي الله عنه- فسأله عن ميراثيها؟

قال: دونك ميراثها، فإنما حبسه الله عنك. قال: هذا رأينا.

عدّتها في الحيض وإن طال بينهما[372].

369 حيضتان: حيضتين، ب د.

370 علقمة: عن قمة، ب،د.

371 تطليقة: تطليقا، ب،د.

372 عدّتها في الحيض وإن طال بينهما: -،د.

سئل عن المستحاضة إذا طلقت؟

قال: تعتدّ أيّام أقرائها.

سئل عن رجل طلق امرأته وأشهد، ثمَّ غشيها ولم يشهد على مراجعتها؟

قال: إن غشيها قبل أن يشهد على مراجعتها، فرق بينهما ثمَّ لا يجتمعان أبدا.

سئل عن رجل طلق امرأته علانية ثمَّ راجعها سرًا؟

عن قتادة عن عروة عن الحسن العدني أن شريحا قال: من أعلن الطلاق ثمَّ أسر المراجعة فلا رجعة له. قال: فقلت لقتادة: فكيف هذا؟ قال: إذا طلق علانية فراجعها سرا لم يعلمها ذلك حتَّى تنقضي عدَّتها أنها قد بانت منه. قال: هذا رأينا. ورأينا أيّما رجل طلق امرأته ثمَّ راجعها ولم يعلمها حتَّى تنقضي عدَّتها أنَّها قد بانت منه.

سئل عن المراجعة قبل أن تطهر من الحيضة الثالثة[373]؟

عن أبي معشر عن النخعي: أنَّ عمر سأل عنها ابن مسعود فقال له: قل فيها، فقال ابن[374] مسعود: أنت أحقّ أن تقول فيها. فقال: أقسمت عليك لتقولن فيها. قال: زوجها أحقّ بها ما لم تغتسل. قال عمر: وافقت ما[375] نفسي يا ابن مسعود. قال: هذا رأينا.

وقال: إن المطلقة لا تنتقل من بيتها في واحد ولا اثنين، قال الله تعالى: ﴿لاَ تُخْرِجُوهُنَّ مِن بُيُوتِهِنَّ وَلاَ يَخْرُجْنَ﴾[376].

373 الثالثة: الثلاثة، ب،د.

374 فقال ابن: فقال له لابن، ب،د.

375 ما: فيما، ب د.

376 سورة الطلاق: ١. وتمامها: ﴿إِلاَّ أَن يَأْتِينَ بِفَاحِشَةٍ مُّبَيِّنَةٍ وَتِلْكَ حُدُودُ اللَّهِ وَمَن يَتَعَدَّ

عن مضر عن الحسن: أنَّ زوجا طلَّق امرأته، ثُمَّ وكَّل بعض أهله فتمهل[377] حتَّى وضعت غسلها لتغتسل من حيضتها الثالثة، فأتاه فأخبره فأقبل إليها وهي في مغتسلها فناداها يا فلانة، فقالت: ما تشاء؟ قال: إنِّي راجعتك، قالت: والله ما ذلك لك، حتَّى تحالفا وارتفعت أصواتهما فارتفعا إلى أبي موسى الأشعري، واستحلفها بالله إن كنت قد اغتسلت حين ناداك. قال: لا ماكنت اغتسلت بعد، فقضى[378] حفظا أنه أحقّ بها ما لم تغتسل من الحيضة الثالثة. قال: هذا رأينا.

عن مضر عن عمرو بن شعيب عن أبيه عن جده أن عمر سأل أبا موسى عنها، وكان قد بلغه قضاه قال: كيف قضيت فيها؟ قال أبو موسى: قضيت أنه أحقّ بها ما لم تغتسل. قال: إنك لو قضيت بغير ذلك لأوجعت لك رأسا.

تمَّ الجزء الثاني من قول قتادة والحمد لله رب العالمين[379].

حُدُودَ اللَّهِ فَقَدْ ظَلَمَ نَفْسَهُ لَا تَدْرِي لَعَلَّ اللَّهَ يُحْدِثُ بَعْدَ ذَلِكَ أَمْرًا﴾.

377 فتمهل: قد هل، ب،د. وورد في موضع آخر: فذهل عنها. وروي عن مطرف وليس عن مضر.

378 فقضى: –، ب،د.

379 بحمد الله وحسن عونه على يد العبد الفقير إلى الله: صالح بن سالم بن سليمان بن يدر يرجو ثواب الله عنه ،غفر له. آمين، وكان الفراغ ظهيرة يوم الخميس من خامس عشر يوم من شعبان سنة إحدى وتسعين ومائة ألف بجامع الماي، عمره الله آمين وكان الفراغ ظهيرة يوم الخميس من خامس عشر يوم من شعبان سنة إحدى وتسعين ومائة ألف بجامع الماي، عمره الله آمين: +، ب.

كتاب الجزء الثالث من قول قتادة

بسم الله الرحمن الرحيم

وصلّى الله على سيدنا مُحمَّد النبيّ الكريم وعلى آله وصحبه تسليما.

سئل عن رجل قال لرجل: زوّجتك ابنتي أو وهبتك ابنتي أو تصدقت بها عليك، ويقول الزوج: قد قبلت.

قال: لا يجوز أن توهب المرأة، إنّما كان ذلك للنبيّ -عليه السلام- خاصة دون المؤمنين.

سئل عن رجل وهب مهر ابنته لختنه؟

قال: لا تجوز هبته لختنه ويغرم مهر ابنته لها[1].

سئل عن امرأة وهبت لرجل دارهم ليتزوّجها بها؟

قال: إذا وهبتها له فلا بأس. [2]

سئل عن رجل تزوّج أمة فأمهرها مائة درهم، ثُمَّ اشتراها فأعتقها لمن ما على ظهره؟

قال: لسيدها الأول.

سئل عن رجل أغلق بابا وأرخى سترا؟

قال: إذا نظر إلى فرج امرأته [3] فطلقها فلها صداقها ولا عدّة عليها، إنّما العدّة من الماء،

---

1 لها: -، د.

2 امرأة وهبت لرجل دراهم ليتزوجها بها لا بأس عليه: هامش، ب.

3 ثم: هامش، ب.

فإن قالت: قد مسني فالقول قولها.

سئل[4] عن عدَّة أم الولد إذا أعتقت؟

قال: إذا أعتقت في حياة سيدها فثلاث حيض، وإن أعتقت بعد موته وأعتقها ولدها فأربعة أشهر وعشر[5].

سئل عن رجل كفر بعد إسلامه وكان مجوسيّا[6]؟

قال: تعتدّ عدَّة المطلقة، فإن أدركها قبل أن تتزوّج، وإن أتى لها عشرون سنة فهو أحقّ بها، وإن تزوّجت بعد العدَّة فذلك لها. وقال: إذا كفر بعد إسلامه وكان مجوسيّا. قال: إذا مضت ثلاثة قروء أوثلاثة أشهر إن كانت مِمَّن لا تحيض تزوّجت إن شاءت وإن أدركها فهو أحقّ بها[7].

سئل عن العبد تكون تحته الحرَّة فيطلقها تطليقتين؟

قال: الحرَّة تعتدّ ثلاث حيض أوثلاثة أشهر من الحر والعبد، والأمة من الحر والعبد حيضتان أوخمسة وأربعين يوما[8] إن كانت مِمَّن لا تحيض.

سئل عن مملوك استكره حرَّة على نفسها؟

قال: صداقها في رقبته، فإن شاء مولاه أن يفديه فعل وإلاَّ دفعه برمته، وقال: إن

---

4 سئل: -، هامش ب.

5 رجل كفر بعد إسلامه تعتد امرأته عدة المطلقة: هامش، ب.

6 كان مجوسيا: -، هامش ب.

7 بها: -،د.

8 ليلة: هامش، ب.

أفلت فهو هين.

سئل عن الحر يستكره حرّة؟

قال: كان قتادة يقول: عليه الحدّ والصداق في ماله. قال: نعم[9].

سئل عن رجلين ادعيا غلاما اجتمعا عليه في طهر واحد؟

قال: بلغنا: أنَّ رجلين ادعيا غلاما اجتمعا عليه في طهر واحد في الجاهلية على عهد عمر بن الخطّاب فدعا عمر ثلاثة من القافة ففرق بينهم، ثُمَّ أدخل أحدهم على الغلام فاستقبل واستدبر فقال: قد اشتركا فيه جميعا، ثُمَّ دعا بآخر فاستقبل واستدبر ثُمَّ قال: أعلن أم أسر؟ قال: بل أعلن. فقال: قد اشتركا فيه جميعا، وأخذ من شبههما جميعا[10]، قال: قد وافقت صاحبك، ثُمَّ دعا الآخر فقال مثل قولهما. قال: قد رأيت مثل الذي رأيتم، فقضى عمر به بينهما يرثهما ويرثانه، قال: الله أعلم. أمَّا أصحابنا فيرونه للأوّل الذي تزوّج حلالاً ويروون عن النبيّ -عليه السلام- أنَّه قال: الولد للفراش[11]، والفراش للأول.

سئل عن رجل تزوّج امرأة فرأى بها جنونا، أو[12] جذاما، أو برصا، فلم يشعر حتَّى دخل بها؟

قال: فعليه المهر، وإن كان وليها قد علم فدلسه فهو ضامن، وإن لم يعلم فلا شيء عليه، وإن لم يدخل بها فرق بينهما، وأمَّا البرص فلا ترد به إلاَّ من شيء فاحش.

9 قال: نعم: -، د.

10 جميعا: -، ب.

11 رواه الربيع، باب في الرجم والحدود، ر٦٠٩، والبخاري، باب تفسير المشبهات، ر١٩٤٨.

12 أو: و، ب، د.

سئل عن المجذوم يتزوّج امرأة ولم تعلم به حتَّى دخل عليها؟

قال: إن اختارت نفسها فلها الصداق.

عن مُحمَّد بن سيرين: أنَّ عمر بعث مصدقا فتزوّج امرأة وكان عقيما، وقال عمر: أعلمتها أنك عقيم؟ قال: لا. قال: أعلمها وهي بالخيار. قال: بلغنا هذا[13]. وإن رضيت فذلك لها، والخصي مثل ذلك.

سئل عن عبد تزوّج حرَّة ولا تعلم أنَّه عبد حتَّى دخل بها؟

عن قتادة قال: إن[14] كان بإذن مولاه فهي بالخيار فإن شاءت أقامت معه وإن كرهت فلها الصداق، وإن كان تزوّج بغير إذن سيده فرق بينهما، ولها الخمسان من الصداق[15]، وإن كان طلقها[16] زوج قبله ثلاثا لم ترجع إليه بنكاح هذا؛ لأنَّه تزوّج بغير إذن سيده.

قيل له: فإن كان بإذن سيده، أترجع إلى[17] زوجها الأول؟ قال: لا يعجبني[18].

باب الظهار

سئل عن رجل ظاهر من أربع نسوة ولم يجد ما يعتق؟

قال: يصوم شهرين ثُمَّ يسمّي أيتهن شاء يجعل لها ثُمَّ يجامعها، وإن قدر أن يصوم على

13 هذا: ذلك، ب.

14 إن: عن، ب، د.

15 ولها الخمسان من الصداق: -، د.

16 طلقها: تطلقها، ب، د.

17 سيدها: +، ب.

18 نكاح العبد لا يهتك الزوج الأول إذا كان: هامش، ب.

أخرى قبل أن تنقضي أربعة أشهر فعل، وإن مضت أربعة أشهر بانت بالإيلاء.

سئل عن رجل ظاهر ثُمَّ غشي[19] قبل أن يكفِّر؟

قال: إذا غشي[20] قبل أن يكفر بعتق أو صوم أو إطعام؛ فإن جابرا ومسلما يقولان: فسدت عليه إلى آخر الدهر.

سئل عن المظاهر إذا ماتت امرأته؟

قال: الميراث بينهما ما لم تنقضِ[21] أربعة أشهر قبل أن يكفِّر فإن مضت أربعة أشهر قبل أن يكفِّر ثمَّ[22] ماتت لم يكن بينهما الميراث؛ لأنَّها لو كانت حية لم يكن له عليها سبيل.

سئل عن الظهار؟

قال: الظهار من كلّ ذات محرم ولو ظاهر من الرِّجْل كان ظهارا.

سئل عن الرجل قال لزوجته: يا أماه متعمّدا؟

قال: ليس عليه شيء، إنَّمَا هو من الجفا.

سئل عن رجل ظاهر من امرأته فتركها أشهرا؟

قال: إذا مضت أربعة أشهر قبل أن يكفِّر بانت منه بالإيلاء[23].

19 غشي: غشا، ب،د.

20 غشي: غشا، ب،د.

21 تنقض: تنقضي، ب،د.

22 ثمّ: -،د.

23 انظر: آثار الربيع، مسألة ٣١، ص ٣١، ومسألة ١٣٨، ص ٤٢.

سئل عن رجل قال لامرأته: إن قربتها سنة فهي علي كظهر أمي؟

قال: إن كفر قبل مضي[24] أربعة أشهر فهي امرأته، وإن مضت أربعة أشهر قبل أن يكفر بانت بالإيلاء، وإن تزوّجها فعليه الكفّارة وإن تركها حتّى تمضي السنة فلا كفّارة عليه، وإن تزوّجها إذا مضت[25] أربعة أشهر بعد الإيلاء ثُمَّ تركها أربعة أشهر أخر بانت بتطليقة أخرى، ولكن إن تركها حتّى تمضي السنة ثُمَّ تزوّجها كانت عنده على تطليقتين، ولا يدخل الإيلاء فإن قربها في السنة فسدت عليه آخر الدهر[26].

سئل عن الإيلاء؟

قال: إذا مضت أربعة أشهر فهي تطليقة بائنة.

سئل عن رجل قال لامرأته: والله لا أقربك في أهلك[27]؟

قال: إن كانت خرجت من بيت زوجها إلى أهلها فأبت أن ترجع لم يدخل عليه إيلاء، وإن كانت نازلة في بيت أبيها وهو معها ثُمَّ اعتزلها لذلك اليمين دخل عليه الإيلاء.

سئل عن رجل كانت له امرأة مرضعة فخشي على ولدها فحلف لا يقربها حتّى يشب ولدها؟

قال جابر وأبو عبيدة: إذا مضت أربعة أشهر بانت منه بالإيلاء، ولكن إن اعتزلها على غير يمين حتّى يفصل ولدها لم يدخل عليه إيلاء.

24 مضي: أربعة، ب.

25 مضت: -،د.

26 فإن قربها في السنة فسدت عليه آخر الدهر: -،د.

27 والله لا أقربك في أهلك: والله لا أقربها في أهلها، ب.

باب في القرض وفي اقتضاء الذهب عن الورق أو عكسه بسعر يومها

سئل عن رجل أقرض لرجل شيئا فيعطيه أكثر مِمَّا أقرض منه؟
قال: إذا لم يكن بينهما شرط فلا بأس بذلك، إنَّمَا هو[28] له من ماله[29].

سئل عن رجل كان له على رجل دراهم بيضاء فتقاضاه فقال له[30]: ما عندي بيض ولكن خذ مني دراهم سودا فاقض بها حاجتك، فإذا أصبت البيض أخذت السود منك وأعطيتك البيض؟
قال: إن رهن له السود أو أقرضها له حتَّى يرد عليه مثل دراهمه فلا بأس، وإن حلله صاحبه فلا بأس أن يأخذ دون حقه، ويكره أن يأخذ أفضل من حقه؛ يقولون[31]: لأنَّه سلف جرَّ منفعة.

سئل عن رجل أقرض رجلا مائة درهم فخرج عطاؤه فبعث إليه مائة درهم من عطائه، عددا فوزنها فوجدها تزيد درهمين فكره ذلك؟
قال: إن وجدها ناقصة فسمحت نفسه بنقصانها فلا بأس بذلك[32].

سئل عن رجل ابتاع دنانير واتزنها منه فاشترط عليه إن نقصت فعليه نقصانها؟
قال: يكره الشرط وأن يفترقا وبينهما عمل فإن نقصت أو رَدَي[33] عليه شيء منها فعليه

---

28 هو: وهب، ب.
29 من استقرض شيئا ثُمَّ رده وزاد معه شيئا لا بأس إذا لم يشترط: هامش، ب.
30 له: –،د.
31 يقولون: –،د.
32 بذلك: –،د.
33 أو رَدَيَ: أو رد، ب د.

بدلها ما ورد منها[34].

سئل عمَّن اشترى من رجل دراهم بدنانير فردّ عليه بعضها: هل يردها كلها؟
قال: إذا لم يكن بينهما شرط فلا بأس.

سئل عن رجل انطلق بفضَّة ليبيعها فلم يجد وزنها إلاَّ أن يجعل له فيها زيادة؟
قال: إذا تراضيا يدا بيد فلا بأس.

سئل عن رجل كانت له عند رجل دراهم فتقاضاه، ثُمَّ ابتاع منه بها دنانير؟
قال: إن أخذ بسوق يومه دنانير بدراهم أو دراهم بدنانير يدا بيد[35] فلا بأس.

سئل عن السفتجة؟
قال: لا بأس إنَّمَا هو قرض أقرضه إيّاه.

سئل عن الرجل يقبض الدنانير من الورق؟
عن أيُّوب عن نافع أنَّ ابن عمر كان يقبض الدنانير من الورق بقيمة يومها؟ قال: نعم[36].

سئل عن رجل باع خادما له بذهب أو فضَّة فأراد أن يأخذ أحدهما؟
قال: لا بأس بذلك.

سئل عن بيع تراب الذهب والفضَّة؟

34 ما ورد منها: –،د.
35 يدا بيد: –،د.
36 قال نعم: –،د.

قال: إن كان ترابا فاشتره بما شئت، وإن كان فيه ذهب أو فضّة فاشتره[37] يدا[38] بيد، بذهب إن[39] شئت أو بفضّة وتكره النسيئة.

باب في المضاربة

سئل عن رجل دفع إلى رجل مالا مضاربة فدفعه الأوّل إلى[40] مقارض آخر: هل يضمن؟

قال: إذا دفعه إلى غيره فهو ضامن، فإن كان فيه ربح فنصف الربح للمضاربين والنصف لصاحب المال، فإن تلف[41] المال فالأوّل ضامن ولا ضمان على الآخر.

سئل عن رجل دفع إلى رجل متاعا مضاربة؟

قال: كان الربيع وأبو عبيدة يكرهان المضاربة إلاّ بالذهب والفضّة ويكرهان المتاع.

سئل عن رجل عنده مال مضاربة فباع من رجل بيعا فخشي أن يماطله فوضع عنه على من تكون الوضيعة؟

قال: على جميع المال؛ لأنّه أمين ينظر لنفسه ولصاحبه.

سئل عن رجل دفع إلى رجل مالا مضاربة فقال: لا تأخذ بنسيئة، فأخذ بيعا بألفي درهم فربح؟

---

37 فاشتره: فاشتريه، ب. + –،د.

38 يدا: فيدا، ب،د.

39 إن: –،د.

40 إلى: –، ب.

41 تلف: هلك، ب.

قال: إن أخذه على المال فالربح بينهما، والوضيعة على المضارب، وإن كان صاحب المال أمره أن يأخذ على المال فالوضيعة على المال والربح بينهما، وإن كان لم يأمره فالربح بينهما والوضيعة على المضارب.

سئل عن رجل دفع إلى رجل مالا مضاربة ثُمَّ حوله قرضا أو كان قرضا ثُمَّ حوله مضاربة أو كانت وديعة فحولها مضاربة؟

قال: هما على الأمر الأوّل الذي دفعه إليه إن كان المال قرضا فهو قرض حتَّى يقبضه، أو كان مضاربة فهو مضاربة حتَّى يقبضه، وإن وديعة فهو وديعة حتَّى يقبضها، لا تحول الأمانة ضمانة ولا الضمانة أمانة إلاَّ بعد قبضها[42].

قال: وإن أخذت مال مضاربة فشخصت أو أقمت فإنّه يستحبّ أن يذكر النفقة عند دفع المال، وأن يشترطها على صاحب المال.

وقال: النفقة والكراء وأجر الأجراء وكراء البيوت والدواب فهو على المال، ويستحبّ ألا[43] يذكر النفقة، فإن باع من أخذ مرابحة فكان هذا من رأس المال إلاَّ النفقة.

سئل عن رجل يعمل بيده فأخذ مالا مضاربة فعمل وأخذ عمالة يده وقاسم الربح؟

قال: يكره ذلك.

سئل عن رجل دفع إلى رجلٍ مالا مضاربة فضاع بعضه، أو ذهب فلم يخبر صاحب المال بما كان من أمره حتَّى ضرب بالمال فربح؟

قال: ليس له ربح حتَّى يكمل رأس المال، فإن فضل شيء فهو بينهما وإن أخبره

---

42 لا تحول... بعد قبضه: –، ب.

43 لا: +، ب د.

بالوضيعة أو بما ذهب أو ضاع ثُمَّ تركه عنده فالوضيعة على رأس المال، وأمّا الربح بعد ذلك فهو بينهما.

سئل عن رجل دفع إلى رجل مالا مضاربة فقال له: لا تخرج به[44] فخرج به؟
قال الربيع عن أبي عبيدة إن دفع إليه المال فقال: لا تخرج به فخرج به فهو ضامن.

سئل عن رجل دفع إلى رجل مضاربة واشترط عليه الضمان؟
قال: لا ضمان عليه إلاّ أن يتعدّى ما أمره به.

سئل عن رجل دفع إلى رجل مالا مضاربة، واشترط عليه أن يبضعه؟
قال: تكره البضاعة.

سئل عن رجل دفع إلى رجل مالا مضاربة فابتاع به بيعا بنسيئة فهلك المال أو لحقه دَينٌ؟
قال: لا يلحق صاحب المال بعد رأس ماله شيء، فإن قال صاحب المال: خذ بنسيئة، فما كان من الوضيعة فعلي وعليك، فإن يذهب رأس المال فما كان من دين لحقه بعد ذلك فهو بينهما كما اشترط.

سئل عن رجل دفع مالا مضاربة إلى رجل فدفعه إلى آخر مضاربة؟
قال: الربح بين صاحب المال وبين الأول، فإن تلف المال فالأوّل ضامن.

سئل عن رجل باع متاعا مرابحة ولم ير الرجل المتاع؟
قال: إذا ابتاعه ولم يره فهو بالخيار إذا رآه إن شاء أخذ، وإن شاء ترك.

44 به: –، د.

سئل عن بيع العشرة والاثني عشر ؟

قال: يأخذ النفقة على المتاع وكراء الدواب ربحا[45] .

سئل عن رجل مات وعليه دين وعنده مال مضاربة وودائع ومهر امرأته؟

قال: يكون ما ترك بينهم بالحصص، إلاَّ أن تكون لأحدهم بيِّنة أن هذا ماله بعينه.

عن صاحب له عن حمَّاد: أنَّه كان يقال: إنَّ[46] الربا ثمانون بابا، وأهونها أن يأكل الرجل في بيت غريمه.

قال: كان أصحابنا يكرهون أن يأكل الرجل في بيت غريمه إلاَّ أن يحسبه من دينه[47] .

باب في السلف

عن جعفر بن أبي وحشية عن سعيد بن جبير عن ابن عمر أنَّه قال: الرهن في السلف هو الربا المضمون. قال: أمَّا الربا فالله أعلم، غير أن الفقهاء يكرهونه.

سئل عن الرهن والقبيل؟

قال: كانوا يكرهون الرهن، ولا يرون بالقبيل بأسا.

عن قتادة عن أبي حسان قال: قلت لعبد الله بن عمر: ورِقي أسلفها في رأس إلى أجل. قال: لا بأس، قلت: ورقي أسلفها في عرض إلى أجل. قال: لا بأس، قلت:

---

45 سئل: عن بيع العشرة والاثني عشر ؟ قال: يأخذ النفقة على المتاع وكراء الدواب ربحا: –، د.

46 إن: –، د.

47 الربا ثمانون بابا أهونها أن يأكل الرجل في بيت غريمه: هامش (ب:

فقبضت الرأس فبعثه[48] إلى أجل مسمى. قال: لا بأس به، وعرضك بعه إلى أجل مسمى. قال: نعم.[49]

سئل عن رجل أسلف رجلا في طعام بالبصرة فلقيه بأرض أخرى: أله أن يأخذ سلفه؟ قال: لا يأخذه إلاَّ في أرضه، إلاَّ أن يكون الذي عليه السلف تحوّل إلى[50] تلك الأرض فيعطيه سلفه ويشتريه في تلك الأرض التي كان فيها، إلاَّ أن يرضى صاحب السلف أن يرد عليه دراهمه.

سئل عن رجل أسلف في غنم ثني أو رباع فأعطاه جذاعا؟
قال: خذ شرطك، أو درهمك[51].

سئل عن رجل أسلف في تمر برني: أله أن يأخذ دقلا، أو يأخذ دون الذي أسلف فيه؟ قال: أمَّا السلف فيكره إلاَّ شرطك أو درهمك، وإنَّما رخص أن يأخذ دون شرطك ولا[52] تزدد عليه.

سئل عن رجل أسلف رجلا خمسين درهما في كرٍّ من طعام فلم يجد عنده إلاَّ نصف الكر: أيأخذ نصف الكر وخمسة وعشرين درهما؟

48 فبعثه: فتبيعه، ب.
49 الكلام في السلف: هامش، ب.
50 إلى: من، ب.
51 يأخذ شرطه ودراهمه، ب؛ من أسلف على شيء لا يأخذ إلا شرطه أو دراهمه والرخصة: هامش، ب.
52 لا: -، د.

قال: يكره، إلاَّ أن يأخذ الكرجميعه أو دراهمه أجمع، إلاَّ أن يكون حين[53] سلفه سمىَّ لكلِّ درهم كذا وكذا كيلا مسمى فيأخذ من ذلك ما شاء، ويؤخره بما شاء ولا يأخذ كسرا نصفا ولا ثلثا، أو يأخذ تلك[54] الدراهم فيشتري بها طعاما فيوفيه بقية طعامه[55].

سئل عن رجل أسلف رجلا[56] في طعام[57] فأخذ منه قبيلا؟

قال: أمَّا القبيل فلا بأس ويكره الرهن.

سئل عن رجل أسلف في طعام فلم[58] يجد عنده طعام الذي أسلف فيه؟

قال: يأخذ الذي أسلف فيه أو دراهم لا يجاوز ذلك.

سئل عن رجل أسلف في خفاف على أن يعطيه الأوَّل فالأوَّل وليس عنده يومئذ منها[59] شيء؟

قال: إذا أسلف فيها إلى أجل على أن يعطيه الأوَّل فالأوَّل فلا بأس.

سئل عن رجل أسلف في كري[60] إلى مكة: أله أن يأخذ رهنا أو قبيلا؟

قال: لا بأس بذلك. وإن أولاه فلا بأس، وإنَّما يكره الكيل والوزن

---

53 حين: جزء، د.

54 تلك: -، د.

55 من أسلف على كيل ليأخذ نصفه ويرد نصف الدراهم: هامش، ب

56 رجلا: -، د.

57 طعام: متاع، ب.

58 فلم: لا، ب.

59 منها: منا، ب، د.

60 كري: كر، ب، د.

والمتكاري في ذلك[61] بالخيار إن شاء فعل، وإن كره لم يلزمه ذلك.

سئل عن رجل كان له على رجل دين إلى أجل مسمى، فقال له: أعجل لك قبل محل الذي لك وتضع عني.

قال: كان الربيع يكرهه وينهى عنه.

سئل عن رجل اشترى من رجل بعيرا بنسيئة فحل الأجل، فقال: أخر عني وأزيدك؟

قال: هذا الرباء الذي لا اختلاف فيه.

سئل عن رجل أسلف دراهما في بيع، فقال له[62] المبتاع: آخذ متاعا بنسيئة فتقبل عني فأقضيك؟

قال: مُكْرُوه، إنَّمَا له متاعه الذي أسلف فيه أو دراهمه.

سئل عن رجل يطلب رجلا بدراهم، فقال له المطلوب: خذ على[63] حريرًا ففعل؟

قال: هذا مكروه ولكن يذهب هو فيأخذ ما شاء.

سئل عن رجل أسلف رجلا[64] فحل سلفه[65]: أيبيعه من قبل أن يقبضه؟

قال: يكره حتَّى يقبض إلاَّ أن يكون قد رأى وقلب ثُمَّ تركها عند صاحبها فلا بأس.

---

61 في ذلك: -، د.

62 له: -، د.

63 على: -، ب.

64 قد أسلفه: +، ب.

65 فحل سلفه: -، ب.

سئل عن بيع ما ليس عندك، أيصلح للمبتاع؟

قال: يكره ذلك.

عن قتادة عن أبي حسان: أنَّ عبد الله بن عبَّاس وعبد الله بن عمر كانا لا يريان بأسا بالسلف في كلّ شيء، و في الحيوان، إذا سميَّ أسنانا معلومة إلى أجل معلوم[66].

سئل عن رجل يطلب رجلا بطعام معلوم فاستوفاه المطلوب من رجل آخر والطالب حاضر، أيأخذه بما اكتال وهو شاهد؟

قال: لا بُدَّ من كيلين.

سئل عن رجل ابتاع طعاما واستوفاه ثُمَّ باعه من رجل بكيله وقبضه الرجل.

قال: لا بُدَّ من كيلين[67].

باب في الرهن

سئل عن رجل ارتهن حيوانا فهلك أو دارا فاحترقت، هل يستوفي حقه منه؟

قال: أمَّا الحيوان فإنَّهم يكرهونه في الرهن، وأمَّا الدار والمتاع فلا بأس، فإن احترقت الدار فهي على[68] المرتهن.

سئل عن رجل ارتهن دارا فيها صاحبها وأشهد له إن أحدث بها حدثا فهي له حتَّى يستوفي حقه؟

---

66 انظر: آثار الربيع، مسألة ٢٧٩، ص ٦٣.

67 عن قتادة عن أبي حسان... لا بد من كيلين: -، ب.

68 على: من، جميع النسخ.

قال: لا يعد مقبوضا حتَّى يتحوَّل عنها صاحبها[69]، ويقبضها صاحب الْحَقِّ ويؤجرها بما شاء قل أو أكثر.

سئل عن رجل ارتهن رهنا وأمره صاحبه أن يلبسه أو يعيره؟

قال: لا يلبس الرهن ولا يعيره، قيل: فإن أذن له فلبسه فهلك. قال: يضمنه.

وقال: إذا وضع الرهن على يد عدل فهلك فليس بما فيه، وإن أمره أن يبيعه فليس له أن يبيعه دون السلطان.

سئل عن رجل ارتهن شاة فأصاب من لبنها وهو يعلفها؟

قال: لا بأس أن يصيب من لبنها، بقدر علفها أو يبيع الفضل.

سئل عمَّن ارتهن جارية فوقع عليها سيدها فحملت؟

قال: لا رق على ولدها ويبيعها المرتهن إن شاء.

باب كراء الأرض، وفي بيع الحرث قبل أن يطعم، وما أكله صاحب الأرض قبل الحصاد

سئل عن كراء الأرض بذهب أو فضَّة إلى أجل معلوم؟

قال: [لا] إلاَّ أن يعطي رجل لرجل أرضا فينفقا ويعملا جميعا ولا يأخذ للأرض ولا للماء أجرا والنفقة بينهما سواء[70].

---

69 صاحبها: -،د.

70 يكره كراء الأرض بالذهب والفضة إلا أن ينتفع جميعا: هامش، ب. انظر: آثار الربيع، مسألة ٣١٥، ص ٦٨.

سئل عن الرجل يستأجر النفر في أرضه على الثلث أو الربع[71] ولا ينفقون شيئا[72]؟
قال: مكروه ذلك؛ لأنّه إن لم يخرج من الأرض شيء ذهب عناؤهم ونفقتهم.

سئل عن رجلين يشتركان جميعا[73] فينفقان جميعا والأرض لأحدهما فما خرج فهو بينهما؟
قال: إذا أنفقا بالسوية فلا بأس ويكره أن يأخذ للأرض والماء أجرا.

سئل عن رجل منح أخاه أرضا أو دارا، واشترط عليه أن يردها إليه عامرة؟
قال: يكره ذلك، ولكن إن ردها إليه عامرة بغير شرط فلا بأس.

سئل عن رجل احترث حرثا، فقال له رجل قبل أن يطعم الحرث: أعطني هذا الحرث وأعطيك النفقة؟
قال: يكره، إلاّ أن يبيعه منه بعد أن يطعم أو يشتريه بقلا فيعلفه لدوابه ويبقى منه طائفة فلا بأس.

سئل عن رجل باع من رجل ثمرة أرضه، واشترط عليه أن يعطي زكاتها؟
قال: يكره أن تولي زكاتك إلاّ من يوثق به، ويكره أن تبيع زكاتك.

سئل عن السنبل: هل يحل شراؤه؟
قال: إذا أدرك فاشتره.

71 الثلث أو الربع: -، ب.
72 الثلث أو الربع: +، ب.
73 جميعا: -، ب.

سئل عن رجل يكون في أرضه ومعه أهله فيأكل منها هو وأهله[74]، ولا يعطي عما يأكل الصدقة؟ قال: يأكل الرطب والبسر ليس فيه صدقة، فإذا اجتمع وصرم فما أكل منه ففيه الصدقة، والزرع على مثل ذلك ماكان في الحصاد، ويعطى أجر العمال فليس فيه شيء، فإذا اجتمع فما أكل منه ففيه الصدقة[75].

باب في البيوع

سئل عن رجل باع بعيرا إلى أجل بمائة درهم فسافر عليه صاحبه، فلمّا حلّ الأجل وقد صار البعير نضوًا اشتراه[76] بخمسين درهما، وأخذ منه خمسين درهما بقية ثمن البعير؟
قال: لا بأس بذلك.

سئل عن رجل اشترى بعيرا أو دابة فندم فيها، فأراد أن يردها ويرد[77] عليه دراهمه؟
قال: تكره الدراهم إلاّ أن يشتري منه ببيع صحيح بزيادة أو نقصان يتراضيان على ذلك.

سئل عن رجل اشترى شاة بشاتين إلى الربيع؟
قال: يكره ذلك، إلاّ أن يختلف النوعان.

سئل عن بيع عشرة جزور بشاة؟
قال[78]: فكره ذلك.

---

74 أهله: +، ب.
75 ما أكل في أوان الحصاد وأجر العمال ليس فيه صدقة: هامش، ب.
76 اشتراه: فاشتراه، ب د.
77 ويرد: ويزيد، ب.
78 قال: –،د.

عن قتادة عن أبي حسان: أن عبد الله بن عمر وعبد الله بن عبّاس كانا لا يريان بأسا بالسلف في كلّ شيء وفي الحيوان إذا سمىَّ أسنانا معلومة إلى أجل معلوم. قال: نعم.

سئل عن منيحة الدهقان؟

قال: إذا أعطى الدهقان الخراج فلا بأس[79].

سئل عن بيع ألبان الغنم يباع لبن كلّ شاة بدرهم[80] كلّ شهر؟

قال: مكروه.

سئل عن بيع الحشيش سنتين أو أكثر من ذلك؟

قال: لا يشتري إلاَّ ما ظهر من النبات.

سئل عن رجل اشترى ثمرة فباعها قبل أن يصرمها؟

قال: لا بأس بذلك قبل وبعد.

سئل عن قوم ابتاعوا نخلا أيبيع أحدهم نصيبه قبل أن يبيعوا جميعا؟

قال: لا بأس.

سئل عن رجل ابتاع سلعة ثُمَّ أشرك فيها [غيره]، فذهب المبيع أو كانت وضيعة؟

قال: الوضيعة على الأوّل والربح بينهما، إلاَّ أن يقول: الثمن علي وعليك، فإنّه إن أشركه وقد نقد فهلك، فالربح والوضيعة بينهما.

---

79 الجواب: -، ب.

80 بدرهم: بدراهم، ب.

سئل عن رجل كان له طعام يبيعه فبعث إليه صاحب له، فقال له: ابعث لي من طعامك[81] كراء[82]، فإذا قام طعامك على سعر بعثت إليك بثمنه؟

قال: لا بأس بذلك ما لم ينفد ثمنه، فإن نفد ثمن الكراء فليعطِ[83] الثمن.

سئل عن رجل اشترى طعاما فاستوفاه بالجريب، أيبيعه بالقفيز؟

قال: يكيل كما اكتال ويكتال بما شاء، إلاَّ أن يكون القفيز دون الجريب، أو يقول: أبيعه بهذا المكيال كذا وكذا بدينار، ثُمَّ يوفي الكيل كما استوفى.

سئل عن رجل باع[84] طعاما بنقد ثُمَّ لم يوفه إيَّاه أيَّاما[85]؟

قال: لا بأس بذلك.

سئل عن رجل يطلب رجلا بطعام معلوم فاستوفاه المطلوب والطالب حاضر فيأخذه بما اكتاله وهو شاهد؟

قال: لا بد من كيلين.

سئل عن رجل ابتاع طعاما فاستوفاه ثُمَّ باعه من رجل بكيله وقبضه الرجل؟

قال: لا بُدَّ من كيلين[86].

---

81 طعامك: الطعام، د.

82 كرى: كرا، ب، د.

83 فليعط: فليعطي، د. فاليقطع، ب.

84 ابتاع، ب.

85 أياما: –، د.

86 سئل: عن رجل يطلب رجلا بطعام معلوم فاستوفاه المطلوب والطالب حاضر فيأخذه بما اكتاله وهو شاهد؟ قال: لا بد من كيلين. سئل: عن رجل ابتاع طعاما فاستوفاه ثُمَّ باعه من رجل بكيله

سئل عن رجل باع بيعا[87] ما قد عرف كيله؟

قال: لا يبعه إلاّ كيلا، إلاّ أن يقول: قد اكلته وهو كذا وكذا، فلا أدري زاد أم نقص وأنا أبيعه جزافا.

سئل عن رجل ابتاع طعاما من رجل واشترط عليه أن ينقيه له فعمد إلى قفيز[88] منه ونقاه، أله أن يأخذ ما بقي بحساب ذلك؟

قال: ذلك مكروه.

سئل عن رجل ابتاع من رجل طعاما، فأعطاه ما كان عنده وبقيت منه بقية. فقال: أنظرني؟

فقال: ذلك مكروه[89].

سئل عن رجل له طعام فأشرك فيه رجلا وقبض منه الثمن؟

قال: إذا أشركه فهما على شركتهما، فما كان من ربح فبينهما وإن كانت وضيعة فعلى المال.

سئل عن رجل ابتاع من رجل كراء[90] من طعام فاكتاله وقبضه[91]، أله أن يأخذ مكانه شعيرا أو ثمرا مكان كلّ قفيز قفيزين؟

فكره ذلك، وقال: ليأخذ بقيمته دراهم إن شاء.

وقبضه الرجل؟ قال: لا بُدَّ من كيلين: –،د.

87 لعله بيعا أو مبيعا، وفي ب: باعا، + –،د.

88 قفيز: أقفزة، ب.

89 السوأل والجواب: –، ب.

90 كرى: كرا، ب،د.

91 وقبضه: فنقص، ب.

سئل عن اللبن يشاب بالماء؟

قال: يكره بيعه إلاَّ أن يعلم بذلك.

سئل عن رجل ابتاع بيعا نَقَدَ[92] ثمنه، فإذا دراهمه دراهم سود، فلم يرض صاحبه فقال: أزيدك أو تعفيني؟

قال: يقول: أشتري منك بهذه الدراهم ويزيده ما شاء.

سئل عن رجل يولي لرجل بيعا قبل أن يقبضه؟

قال: إذا ولاه فلا بأس به.

سئل عن رجل يساوم على سوم أخيه أو يخطب على خطبة أخيه؟

فكره ذلك.

سئل عن رجل اشترى ثيابا فوجد في ثوب منها[93] عيبا[94] في شيء منها؟

قال: يرده بالقيمة.

سئل عن رجل دفع إلى رجل ثوبا يبيعه له بعشرة دراهم نقدا فباعه بخمسة عشر نسيئة؟

قال: ليس للبائع منه شيء، ولكن صاحب الثوب بالخيار؛ إن شاء أخذ منه ثوبه، وإن شاء أخذ منه عشرة أو يرد عليه ثوبه.

---

92 نقد: فقد، ب،د.

93 في ثوب منها: –،د.

94 عيبا: عورا، ب.

سئل عن رجل دفع إلى رجل ثوبا أو متاعا فقال له: بعه بكذا وكذا، ولا تنقص من ذلك، فباعه بدون ما قال[95]؟

قال: هو ضامن.

سئل عن شريكين افترقا وكان لهما دين، فاتبع كلّ واحد منهما طائفة من الغرماء، ورضيا بذلك فتوَى[96] ما صار لأحدهما؟

قال: ما أصابوا فهو بينهما وما توى فعليهما.

سئل عن رجل اشترى منه شريكان متاعا فأراد أن يضع عن أحدهما، هل يجوز ذلك؟

قال: ما وضع فهو بينهما إلاَّ أن يقبض الثمن فإذا قبض الثمن وهب منه له ما شاء[97].

سئل عن المساومة بالدراهم البيض كذا وكذا، والسود كذا وكذا، وبالنقد كذا وكذا والنسيئة كذا وكذا؟

قال: كان أبو عبيدة يقول: في النسيئة والنقد أدنى الأجلين وأغلا الثمنين.

سئل عن رجل اشترى عبدا من رجل فيشترط[98] ثلاثة أيَّام فمات في الشرط؟

قال: إن قطعا الثمن فمات فهو من مال الذي في يده، وإن لم يقطعا الثمن فهو من مال البائع.

---

95 قال: ذلك، ب.

96 تَوِيَ المالُ: ذَهَبَ فَلَمْ يُرْجَ.

97 ما توافه بين الشركاء وما خرج فهو بينهما: هامش، ب.

98 فيشترط: بشرط، ب.

سئل عن رجل باع بيعا لرجل[99]، ثُمَّ باعه لآخر[100]، فاستوفى الآخر منهما؟

قال: يكلف أن يرده إن قد عرفه، وإلاَّ فعلى البائع أن يبتاع مثله فيوفيه الأول.

سئل عن رجل ابتاع غلاما فمر لينظر إليه فأبق الغلام؟

قال: يضمن إن كان قطعا[101] الثمن[102].

سئل عن رجل دفع إلى رجل ثوبا ليبيعه فقال له: بعه بعشرة فما زاد فهو لك؟

قال: يكره ذلك، إلاَّ أن يقول له[103]: بعه بعشرة ولك منه درهم أو لك ما فضل[104].

سئل عن المسلم يشارك اليهوديّ أو النصرانيّ؟

قال: يكره ذلك، إلاَّ أن يكون المسلم يلي البيع والشراء فلا بأس بذلك.

سئل عمَّن باع[105] دهنا مَنًّا بِمَنَّين؟

قال: إن كان الأصل واحدا فلا بأس يدا بيد، ويكره بالنسيئة، وإن كان الأصل شتى فلا بأس بذلك في النسيئة.

سئل عن بيع السلف قبل أن يقبض؟

قال: لا يباع السلف، ولا يولي حتَّى يقبض.

99 لرجل: من رجلين، ب.
100 ثم باعه لآخر: -، ب.
101 قطعا: قطع، ب.
102 من اشترى عبدا فأبقى غرمه عليه إن قطع الثمن ولولم يقضه: هامش، ب.
103 له: -، د.
104 بعه بكذا وكذا ثُمَّ زاد فهو لك يكره إلا أن يقول بعه بكذا ولك منه: هامش، ب.
105 باع: -، ب.

سئل عن رجل اشترى جارية فوضعت على يدي عدل ليستبرئ رحمها، فماتت الجارية على تلك الحال؟

قال: إن وضعاها جميعا فهي من مال البائع، وإن كان المشتري وضعها فهي من ماله.

عن قتادة: أنه كان يقول: إذا كان عبد بين رجلين أو متاع أو دابة فغاب أحدهما. قال: إن شاء الشاهد أن يبيع نصيبه فعل، وكان يقول: الشفعة في التربة[106]؟ قال: نعم[107]، وكان الربيع يستحب أن يجعل ذلك في الرقيق[108].

سئل عن رجل بعث إلى رجل بألف درهم ليشتري له بها جارية، فزاد من عنده خمسمائة فاشترى له جارية فبعث بها إليه؟

قال: إن ماتت في الطريق فهي من مال[109] المشتري، وإن وصلت فهو بالخيار، إن شاء أخذها وإن شاء ردها.

سئل عن الغيلة والخبثة؟

قال: الغيلة الإباق والزنى والسرقة، والخِبثةُ [بيع] أهل عهد المسلمين[110].

سئل عن رجل ابتاع دابة ونقد ثمنها، فقال له رجل: أشركني فيها على أن أبتاع بيعا وأشركك فيه.

---

106 التربة: التربة، ب،د.

107 قال نعم: -،د.

108 عبد بين شريكين أو متاع لأحدهما أن يبيع نصيبه بغير: هامش، ب.

109 مال: -،د.

110 سئل: عن الغيلة والخبثة؟ قال: الغيلة الإباق والزنى والسرقة والخبثة [بيع] أهل عهد المسلمين: -،د.

عن قتادة: أنَّه كان يكره ذلك إذا كان فيه الشرط. قال: الله أعلم.

سئل عن رجل ابتاع[111] دابة من رجل، فقال له المبتاع: بعتني دابة سوء، فقال البائع: قد قبلتها. قال: فاقبضها فنفقت قبل أن يقبضها؟

قال: هو ضامن لها[112] حتَّى يردها كما أخذها.

سئل عن رجل ابتاع بيعا مِمَّا يكال أو يوزن، وقال البائع: خذ بيعك فإذا استيسرت فأنقدني الثمن، فقال المشتري: لا أقبضه حتَّى أنقدك، فأشهد البائع عليه أنِّي دعوته إلى بيعه ليقبضه فأبى فهلك المبيع؟

قال: هو من مال البائع مالم[113] يقبضه المبتاع فإن قبضه المبتاع فأرهنه للبائع فهو من ماله أيضا، وإن استودعه المبتاع عند البائع فهو من مال المشتري.

سئل عن بيع التمر بالتمر[114] نسيئة؟

قال: مكروه.

حدَّث عن قتادة عن الحسن بن أبي الحسن عن أبي معشر عن النخعي: أنَّه قال: كلّ شيء يكال أو يوزن فهو بمنزلة واحدة[115] في النسيئة، وهو قول الربيع.

عن الحسن عن أبي معشر عن النخعي: أنَّه كان لا يرى بأسا أن يبتاع الرجل ثوبا

111 ابتاع: باع، ب.

112 لها: -،د.

113 مالم: ما، ب،د.

114 بالتمر: بالنوى، ب.

115 واحدة: -، ب.

بثوبين إذا خالف صنفه[116]، وكان كتانا بقطن، أو كانا بصوف، أو صوفا بقطن إذا اختلف[117] الصنفان.

سئل عن شريكين متفاوضين اشترى أحدهما غلاما وأشهد أنّه من ماله فأبى ذلك شريكه؟

قال: إذا اشتراه من شركتهما فهو بينهما، وإن اشتراه مِمّا سوى ذلك فهو له.

سئل عن شريكين متفاوضين؟

قال أحدهما لصاحبه: لا تبع بنسيئة فما بعت بنسيئة فأنت له ضامن، فباع بنسيئة.

قال: هما على شرطهما، وما باع بنسيئة فهو له ضامن[118] وهذا بريء منه.

سئل عن رجل قال لرجل: عند فلان بيع كذا وكذا، فاشتره منه فيما بيني وبينك، فاشتراه فوضع فيه أو هلك؟

قال: هو من مال الذي أنقد، والربح بينهما على ما اشترطا.

سئل عن رجلين اشتركا مع كلّ واحد منهما ألف درهم، فقال أحدهما لصاحبه: أنا أبصر بالبيع منك، فلا أرضى أن يكون الربح بيني وبينك حتّى تعطيني عشرة دراهم في كلّ شهر والربح بيني وبينك؟

قال: هما على شرطهما، له عشرة دراهم وما بقي من الربح فهو بينهما.

---

116 صنفه: صنعه،د.

117 اختلف: خالف، ب.

118 ضامن: –، ب.

سئل عن رجلين اشتركا، و رأس مال أحدهما أكثر من الآخر فلحقهما دين بعد رأس المال؟

قال: هو على رأس المال إلاّ أن يكون اشترطا أن الربح والوضيعة بينهما سواء، فالربح بينهما سواء والوضيعة على رأس المال.

سئل عن شريكين انطلق أحدهما إلى أرض فابتاع بها بيعا و ليس له رأس المال و للمقيم رأس المال فأمره أن يأخذ بنسيئة، فأخذ، فاتهمه شريكه. أيكلف البيّنة؟

قال: إذا اتهمه فله يمينه، وكل مؤتمن إذا اتهم استحلف.

سئل عن رجل يبيع الثوب بالنقد ثُمَّ يندم المبتاع فقال: أعطيك عشرة دراهم وآخذ ثوبك؟

قال: مكروه.

سئل عن رجل طلب إلى آخر شراء بر[119] أو تمر[120] ولم يكن ذلك عند المبتاع، فابتاعه ثُمَّ باعه له؟

قال: مالم يساوم أو يقول: آخذ لك فلا بأس.

سئل عن رجل باع من رجل سلعة، واشترط البائع إذا أدركني فيها شيء أعطيك عشرة دراهم وتردها علي؟

قال: مكروه.

---

119 برا: بزا، ب.

120 تمرا: متاعا، ب.

سئل عن رجل ابتاع ثوبا وله الخيار إلى[121] نصف النهار فعرض له ربح فأراد بيعه؟

قال: إن كان قد رضيه فالربح له، وإن كان لم يرضه فلا يبعه، فإن باعه فالربح لصاحب الثوب الأول.

سئل عن رجل باع بيعا فضمن للمبتاع حملان المتاع، فقال للمبتاع: اذهب فاستأجر أجيرًا يحمل المتاع؟

قال: له شرطه.

سئل عن ثمن الكلب والسنور وكلب الصيد؟

قال: يكره بيع السباع[122].

سئل عن رجل باع بيعا إلى أن يجبى من أرض كذا وكذا أو إلى أن يخرج العطاء؟

قال: إن[123] كان العطاء مرة جائزا وأمّا اليوم فلا، ولكن يسمّي أجلا معلوما شهرا أو سنة معلومة.

سئل عن رجل ابتاع شحما في بطن شاة قد سلخت ولم يشق بطنها؟

قال: يكره الشحم؛ لأنّه شيء[124] متغيب فإن استثنى بطنها أوما في بطنها من ولد فلا بأس.

سئل عن رجل يشتري السخلة في بطن أمها؟

قال: ذلك مكروه.

121 وله الخيار: –، ب.

122 يكره بيع السباع: هامش، ب.

123 إن: –، د.

124 شيء: –، ب.

سئل عن البيع والمباع غير حاضر[125]؟

قال: كلّ شيء ابتاعه وهو لم يره فهو بالخيار حتَّى يراه، فإن كان رآه فقد جاز عليه، إلاَّ أن يحدث فيه عيب أو عور لم يكن رآه وليس مِمَّا يحدث فهو مردود.

سئل عن رجل طلب إلى رجل ثيابا ليبيعها له، فقال له الرجل: ليست عندي، ولكن هل لك أن أعطيك دراهم فتبتاع لي بها ثيابا؟

فقال: نعم، فأعطاه دراهم فابتاع له بها ثيابا ولا يدري أيكون بينهما بيع أم لا، ولم يساومه قبل ذلك، ثُمَّ إنَّه ابتاعها منه أو بعضها بالنسيئة.

قال: لا بأس.

سئل عن رجل باع من رجل دابة يقضي دابة فكره أن يأخذ دابة من ذلك البيع؟

قال: اشترها[126] منه، فلا بأس إذا كان البيع صحيحا.

سئل عن رجل يطلب رجلا بدراهم فلم يجدها عنده، فقال له المطلوب: أبيعك[127] ثيابا أعطيك بعضها، ولم يرها الآخر. قال: نعم، ادفعها إلى أبي[128] بأرض كذا وكذا، أو ببرية[129]، فانطلق بها إلى أبيه، فأبى أن يقبلها فباعها بربح، لمن يكون الربح؟

قال: إن كان حين[130] قبضها رضيها فالربح له، وإن كان أخذها على رضى أبيه فوجد ربحا

---

125 والمباع غير حاضر: -، ب.

126 اشترها: اشتريها، ب،د.

127 أبيعك: إني قد ابتعت، ب.

128 إليَّ، ب.

129 ببرية: ببيرية، ب،د.

130 حين: -، ب.

قبل أن يراها أبوه فالربح للأوّل، فإن رضيها فالربح للآخر.

سئل عن بيع أهل البيت جميعا؟

قال: يكره أن يفرق بين المرأة وولدها، وقدكان الربيع يكره تفريق[131] الأخوين.

سئل عن رجلين بينهما بيع من البيوع أو جارية أو دابة، هل لأحدهما أن يبيع نصيبه مِمَّن شاء؟

قال: نعم، وكان الربيع يحب أن يكون شريكه أحقّ به إن أراد.

سئل عن رجل اشترى جارية فوطئها فرأى بها عيبا؟

قال: كان أبو عبيدة والربيع يريان أنَّه إذا وطئها لزمه البيع ووضع عنه أرش العيب إلاَّ أن يقول البائع لا أضع عنك، ولكني أقبلها فذلك له.

سئل عن رجل كانت له جارية فتقاضاه غرماؤه، فأرادوا أخذ الجارية، فقال: قد أعتقتها؟

قال: إن[132] كان له مال وفاء لدينه مضى[133] عتقه، وإن لم يكن له وفاء لم يجز له عتق، وإن كان قد ظهر إفلاسه لم يجز له بيع ولا عتق.

سئل عن مملوك يؤدي الضريبة إلى مواليه فاشترى بدين، هل على مواليه من دينه شيء؟

131 تفريق: -، ب.

132 إن: إذا، د.

133 مضى: أجاز، ب.

قال: ليس على مواليه من دينه شيء إلاَّ أن يكون يشتري فهو على رقبته لا يجر على سيده أكثر من ذلك، إلاَّ أن يقول: خذ في مالي بدين، فما أخذ من شيء فهو على سيده.

سئل عن رجل أفلس بمال قوم؟

قال: إن كان أخذ قبل أن يظهر إفلاسه فهو أسوة الغرماء، وإن كان الأخذ بعد أن ظهر[134] إفلاسه[135] فإنَّمَا هي خيانة، صاحبه أحقّ به.

سئل عن رجل كان له دين على رجل فاحتال عليه رجل[136] فأفلس؟

قال: إن كان غنيا فتركه متعمّدا حتَّى أفلس، فهو ممَّن احتال عليه.

سئل عن العارية والوديعة؟

قال: إن حول المستودع المال أو أقرضه ثُمَّ قدم صاحبه فتلف فهو ضامن حتَّى يؤديه لصاحبه، وأمَّا العارية فهو مؤتمن إلاَّ أن يعيرها لغيره، فهو ضامن حتَّى يؤديها لصاحبها وهو قول الربيع[137].

باب في ضمان صاحب السفينة

سئل عن رجل يحمل الطعام في السفن ويضمن الملاح؟

قال: ليس له زيادة ولا عليه نقصان إذا ائتمنه، إلاَّ أن يتهم فيستحلف بالله.

وقال: إذا غرقت السفينة أو جاء الريح أو شيء لا يملكه فليس على الملاح ضمان،

134 ظهر: -، ب.

135 إفلاسه: أفلس، ب.

136 رجل: -،د.

137 العارية إذا أعارها لغيره فهو ضامن وكذا الوديعة إذا لعلة أيضمن: هامش، ب.

وإذا كان فيها خرق أو شيء من الملاح فهو ضامن.

سئل عن السفينة تكسر أخرى؟

قال: إذا كانت السفينة فيها ركاب فكسرت سفينة أخرى[138] واقفة، فالتي فيها الركاب ضامنة، وإذا لم يكن فيها أحد فليس على واحدة منها ضمان، وإذا كان في الواقفة أناس وليس في التي جاءت عليها أحد فكسرتها فليس عليها شيء، وإن كانتا تسيران جميعا فإن أدركتها من خلفها فكسرتا فهي ضامنة، وإن انكسرت هي فلا ضمان على المتقدّمة، وإن كانتا تسيران جميعا فاستقبلت أحداهن الأخرى فانكسرتا جميعا فهما ضامنتان بعضهما البعض[139].

باب فيما أصابه المشركون من مال المسلمين

سئل عما أصاب المشركون من المسلمين ثُمَّ أصابه المسلمون بعد ذلك فعرف[140] رجل متاعه بعينه؟

قال: كان أبو عبيدة يقول: هو أحق[141] به قسم أو لم يقسم، فإن قسم ترادّ المسلمون وأعطى الرجل متاعه، وإن لم يقسم فهو أحقّ به.

سئل عن عبد أصابه المشركون فاشتراه رجل من المسلمين؟

قال: مولاه أحقّ به بالثمن، فإن كان العبد قال له: لا تشترني فإني أخرج إلى مولاي، فاشتراه بعد هذا فلا شيء له، وهو لمولاه الأول.

---

138 أخرى: –، ب.

139 من اعترف رزقه مما أخذه المسلمون منهم وقد كان أخذه العدو وقبل: هامش، ب.

140 فعرف: فاعترف، ب.

141 أحق: أولى، د.

سئل عن شراء[142] عقار المشركين وأرضهم؟

قال: يكره أن تشتري ذلك من أجل أن على أرضهم خراج المسلمين.

سئل عن شراء رقيق أهل الذمّة؟

قال: لا تشتروهم فإنّهم أهل خراج، يبيع بعضهم من بعض، ولا تشتروا من أرضهم شيئا. قال[143]: إلاّ رقيقا أصابوه من غيرهم، زنجيا[144] أو خرسانيا، أو سنديا، أو غير ذلك مِمّن سواهم.

باب فيما سئل عنه أبو عمر و الربيع بن حبيب رضي الله عنه

سئل هل يتكلم المؤذِن في أذانه أو إقامته قبل أن يفرغ؟

قال: يكره ذلك.

سئل هل يؤخذ الأجر على تعليم القرآن؟

قال: يكره ذلك، وبلغنا -والله أعلم- أن بلالاً مؤذن النبيّ عليه السلام أمر أن يتثوب في صلاة الصبح ولا يتثوب في غيرها من الصلوات[145]. قال: ذلك رأينا[146].

سئل هل يستنجي بروثة أو عظم؟

قال: يكره ذلك.

---

142 شراء: -، ب.

143 قال: -،د.

144 زنجيا: ونجيا،د.

145 الصلوات: -،د.

146 أخذ الأجر على تعلم القرآن: هامش، ب.

سئل هل تسافر المرأة و ليس معها[147] محرم؟

قال بعض الفقهاء: جماعة المسلمين محرم لمن لا محرم له[148].

سئل عن إمام قوم صلَّى بهم وهو غير طاهر؟

قال: إن كان جنبا فليعد وليعيدوا، وإن كان على غير وضوء أعاد هو ولا إعادة عليهم.

سئل هل في الظهر والعصر قراءة؟

فذكر أنَّ جابر بن زيد والحسن قرأوا في الظهر والعصر بفاتحة الكتاب[149].

سئل هل يقرأ المصلِّي[150] خلف الإمام؟

قال: يقرأ الإمام ومن خلفه بفاتحة الكتاب، وإذا قرأ الإمام وجهر فأنصتْ كما قال الله، وإن لم تقرأ فاتحة الكتاب خلف الإمام فلا بأس[151].

سئل عن الصلاة عند كسوف الشمس والقمر؟

قال: ليصلِّ ما بدا له أو يقعد فيدعو، وبلغنا: أنَّ جابر بن زيد قعد ودعا حتَّى انجلى كسوف الشمس.

سئل عن قول الله: ﴿فَإِنْ خِفْتُمْ فَرِجَالاً أَوْ رُكْبَانًا﴾[152]؟

147 ذي: +، ب.

148 لا تسافر المرأة مع غير ذي محرم أو مع جماعة من المسلمين: هامش، ب.

149 انظر: آثار الربيع، مسألة ١٠، ص ٢٨.

150 المصلي: -، ب.

151 قال الشيخ أبو زيد عبد الرحمن ـ رحمه الله ـ: هذا قول الربيع وروايته ولا يؤخذ بهذا من قوله والحق الذي عليه أصحابنا أن يعيد ويعيدوا جميعا في الحالتين معا: هامش، ب.

152 سورة البقرة: ٢٣٩.

قال: ذلك عند الضرب بالسيوف فيُكبّر خمس تكبيرات حيث ما كان وجهه[153].

سئل عن رجل صلّى لغير القبلة؟

قال: ينحرف إلى القبلة التي أبصرها وهو في الصلاة، ويعتد بما كان صلّى قبل ذلك.

سئل عن رجل أتى يوم الجمعة وقد جلس الناس؟

قال: يكره له أن يتخطّى رقاب الناس. قال: بلغنا هذا[154].

وبلغنا: أنّه سئل الحسن عن الأمصار؟

فقال: هي سبعة: مكة، والمدينة، ومصر، والبصرة، والكوفة، والجزيرة، والبحرين[155].

وكان أبو عبيدة رحمة الله عليه[156] لا يرى في شيء من أرض الأعاجم جمعة. وكان ضمام يقول: كلّ أرض من أرض العجمة[157] والعرب أقيمت فيها الحد وجمع فيها.

سئل عن المرأة هل تغسل زوجها إذا مات؟

قال: نعم. وقد ذكر لنا أن أسماء[158] غسلت زوجها أبا بكر الصديق رضي الله عنه، وأنّ جابر بن زيد أمر زوجته آمنة أن تغسله[159].

---

153 رجل صلى لغير القبلة يرى أنها قبلة يحرف إذا تذكر: هامش، ب.

154 قال: بلغنا هذا: -،د.

155 عدد الأمصار السبعة ولا يرى أبو عبيدة جمعة في أرض: هامش، ب.

156 الترحم: -، ب.

157 العجمة: الذمة، ب.

158 أسماء بنت عميس.

159 والمرأة تغسل زوجها إذا مات: هامش، ب. انظر: آثار الربيع، مسألة ٦، ص ٢٨.

سئل عن رجل جعل على نفسه مثل سواري المسجد ذهبا؟

عن جابر بن زيد أنَّه كان يقول: من جعل ماله هديا أهدى عُشره إن كان قانعا، وإن كان وسطا سُبعه، وإن كان مقلا خُمسه.

وذكر أنَّ جابرا[160] كان يرى في النذر الذي لم يسم صوم يوم أو يومين أو طعام[161] مسكين أو مسكينين، وكل نذر نذره الناس وليس بمعصية الله أمروا بالوفاء به.

سئل عن رجل قال: والله لأفعلنَّ كذا وكذا ثُمَّ سكت ساعة ثُمَّ استثنى؟

عن قتادة: أنَّه قال: إن كان في طاعة الله فليفعل، وإن كان معصية فلا يفعل، وله ثنياه ما لم يتكلم بينهما بشيء. قال: هذا[162] رأينا.

وبلغنا: أنَّ رجلا جعل ابنه هديًا، فقال جابر بن زيد: يعتق نسمة أو يهدي بدنة[163].

سئل عن الصيد يصيده[164] قوم فيقطعونه بأسيافهم؟

قال: لا يؤكل.

سئل عن صيد ضرب فقطع منه عضو؟

قال قتادة: إن وقعا جميعا فلا بأس، وإن وقع[165] منه عضو ثُمَّ مشى ثُمَّ مات فكل الذي يلي الرأس، وقال الحسن: يأكلهما جميعا، وقول قتادة أحبّ إلينا، ولا يؤكل ما سقط منه[166].

160 جابرا: جابر بن زيد، ب.

161 طعام: -، ب.

162 هذا: ذلك، ب.

163 حلف وسكت ثُمَّ استثنى قتادة إن كان طاعةً فليفعل وإن معصية فلا وله: هامش، ب.

164 يصيده: يصيدونه، ب.

165 وقع: قطع، ب.

166 صيد ضرب فقطع منه عضولا يأكل إلا ما يلي الرأس. قتادة وبه لا يجاز: هامش، ب.

سئل عن الصدقة يرثها صاحبها بعد ما يتصدق بها؟

قال: لا بأس.

سئل عن البعير يتردَّى في البئر أيطعنه صاحبه حيثما نال منه؟

قال: لا، إلاَّ ما وافق بين المنحر والمذبح.

سئل عن جلود المَيّتة؟

قال: بلغنا: أنَّ دباغها طهورها.

سئل عن لحوم الجلالة وألبانها؟

فقال: لا يؤكل لحومها ولا تشرب ألبانها.

سئل عن لحوم الحمير الأهلية؟

قال: كان جابر لا يرى بلحومها وألبانها بأسا، وقال: إنَّمَا نهى رسول الله صلى الله عليه وسلم عن لحومها[167] يوم خيبر[168]، كره أن يشرعوا في كراعهم ولم يحرم لحومها[169].

167 عن لحومها: -،د.

168 رواه البخاري، باب غزوة خيبر، ر٣٩٧٨.

169 قال الشيخ [أبو] زيد - رحمه الله -: هذا قول الربيع وروايته ولا يؤخذ بهذا. من قوله الحق الذي علي أصحابنا تحريم لحوم الحمير الأهلية: هامش، ب. الحديث رواه الربيع عن علي، باب أدب الطعام والشراب، ر٣٨٨ بلفظ: «نهى رسول الله صلى الله عليه وسلم عن متعة النساء يوم خيبر وعن أكل لحوم الحمر الإنسية».

باب في الديات وأرش الجروح

سئل عن قول الله تعالى: ﴿فَمَنِ اعْتَدَى بَعْدَ ذَلِكَ فَلَهُ عَذَابٌ أَلِيمٌ﴾[170]؟

قال: من اعتدى بعد أخذ الدية فقتل، فله عذاب أليم. والعذاب الأليم: ألا يعفى ولا يؤخذ منه دية وليس للحاكم إلاّ قتله.

سئل عن جذع أنفه؟

قال: إن جذع أنفه فقيمته، وإن قطع يده فنصف ثمنه.

سئل عن دية الجنين؟

قال: في الجنين مالم يستهل غرة: عبد أو أمة، وقتل العمد على القاتل في ماله، ومن قتل خطأً عقل عنه قومه، وأمّا العمد فيقتل به.

سئل عن رجل ضرب أم ولده فألقت جنينا، ثمّ استهل ثمّ مات؟

قال: فعليه عتق رقبة وعليه الدية لا يرث أبوه منه شيئا وهو لأخوته أو لعصبته[171].

دية النفس في الخطأ عشرون جذعة وعشرون حقة وعشرون بنات لبون وعشرون بنو لبون ذكر وعشرون بنات مخاض[172].

سئل عن جنين اليهوديّة والنصرانيّة؟

170 سورة البقرة: ١٧٨.

171 دية الخطأ على العاقلة، ودية العمد في مال القاتل: هامش، ب.

172 انظر: آثار الربيع، مسألة ١٤، ص ٢٩.

قال: عشر دية أمة وإن استهل ففيه ثلث دية[173] المسلم[174].

تؤخذ هذه الأجزاء الخمسة من قيمة الإبل[175] على هذه الأسنان يوم يقضى فيها، على أهل الإبل الإبل[176]، وعلى أهل البقر البقر[177] [178] بقيمة الإبل[179]، وعلى أهل الشياه الشياه بقيمة الإبل، وعلى أهل الدراهم بقيمتها من الإبل، وعلى أهل الدنانير الدنانير[180]، كلّ ذلك بقيمة الإبل يوم يقضى فيها على هذه الأسنان التي سميناها[181] فيؤتى في ذلك اليوم لسوق الإبل، فتقوّم هذه الإبل فيؤخذ من كلّ قوم من أموالهم التي لا يقدرون على غيرها بقيمة الإبل.

وأما العمد: ففي النفس مائة من الإبل، أربعون ما بين جذعة إلى بازل عامها كلّها خلفات حوامل، وثلاثون حقة، وثلاثون بنات لبون فتؤخذ دية النفس يوم يقضى فيها مائة من هذه الأسنان ومن قيمتها، إن غلت رفع من قيمتها وإذا هاجت ورخصت نقص من قيمتها[182].

---

173 ثلث دية: دية ثلث، ب، د.

174 سئل: عن قول الله تعالى: ﴿فَمَنِ اعْتَدَى بَعْدَ ذَلِكَ فَلَهُ عَذَابٌ أَلِيمٌ﴾... قال: عشر دية أمة وإن استهل ففيه دية ثلث المسلم: -، د.

175 من قيمة الإبل: -، د.

176 الإبل: -، ب، د.

177 البقر: -، ب.

178 بهذه: -، ب.

179 الأبل: -، ب.

180 الدنانير: -، ب.

181 ها: -، د.

182 إن غلت رفع من قيمتها وإذا هاجت ورخصت نقص من قيمتها: إن غلت رفعت، وإن هانت خفضت، ب.

وموضحة العمد: تؤخذ قيمتها من أربعين ما بين جذعة إلى بازل عامها كلّها خلفات حوامل، وثلاثون حقة وثلاثون بنات لبون.

وتؤخذ قيمة الموضحة من هذه الأجزاء التي سميناها[183]، يؤتى بسوق الإبل فيؤخذ منها ثلاثة أباعر، ومثل ثلثي أثمانهن ناقة مسنة خلفة وحقة، وبنت لبون فتقوّم هؤلاء قيمة عدل ثُمَّ تجمع أثمانهن ثُمَّ تزيد على أثمانهن مثل ثلثي أثمانهن، فيكون ذلك جزاء[184]، فهذه دية التغليظ في موضحة العمد.

وإن كانت الشجة سمحاقا فأربعة أخماس من دية الموضحة، وإن كانت متلاحمة فثلاثة أخماس من دية الموضحة، وإن كانت باضعة فثلثا دية الموضحة، وإن كانت دامية ففيها خمس دية الموضحة، فهذا تفسير شجاج العمد.

وفي الأمة والجائفة في كلّ واحدة منهما ثلث الدية من جميع أسنان الإبل التي في دية المغلَّظة في العمد.

وكل جرح أصيب عمدا فإن الدية على نحو هذه الأسنان في المغلظ، والجمجمة صفيحتان مثل صفيحة الضلع بينهما مشاش، فإذا خرق اللحم كله حتَّى يضحو العظم فهي الموضحة، وإذا هشمت الصفيحة العليا والمشاش والصفيحة السفلى حتَّى يفضي إلى الدماغ فهي الأمة، وإذا هشمت الصفيحة العليا ثُمَّ نقلت ولم تفض إلى الدماغ فهي منقلة، وإذا هشمت ولم تنقل فعشرة من الإبل، وإذا انقلب العظم ولم تفض إلى الدماغ ولم تنقل فعشرة من الإبل، فإن كان عمدا غلظت ديته على أسنان الإبل، وإن كانت خطأ فديتها دية الخطأ من الخمسة الأسنان التي سميت لك. والموضحة في

---

183 ها: –، د.

184 جزاء: أجزاء، ب.

الوجه ضعف الموضحة في الرأس فيها عشرة من الإبل والموضحة التي تؤخذ فيها الدية إذا كانت بقدر مفصل الإبهام طولها[185] وعرضها، ففيها خمس من الإبل، فما نقص من أنملَّة الإبهام فبقدر ذلك، والأمة ثلث الدية، وإن ذهب العقل فالدية[186] كاملة[187]، وفي المنقلة خمس عشرة من الإبل إذا انقلت عظامها. وفي الناقبة عشر من الإبل، وفي الهاشمة عشر[188] من الإبل، وفي الموضحة خمس من الإبل، وفي السمحاق أربع من الإبل، وفي المتلاحمة ثلاث من الإبل وفي الباضعة بعيران، وفي الدامية بعير، وفي الحاجبين إذا استؤصلا مع الشعر[189] الدية كاملة، وإذا أصيب أحدهما فنصف الدية، وإن أصيب بعضها فبحساب ما أصيب منها.

وفي العينين الديـة كاملة إذا فقئـتا[190]، فإن فقئت إحداهما فنصف الديـة، وفي أجفان العين إذا استؤصلا دية العين كاملة، والجفن الأعلى ثلث[191] الدية، وفي الأسفل الثلث، وفي الأنف إذا استؤصل من المارن[192] الديـة كاملة، وما أصيب منه فبحساب ما ذهب منه، وفي أحد المنخرين نصف الديـة إذا استؤصل. وفي الشفتين الديـة كامـلة إذا استؤصلا، فإن أصيب أحدهما فنصف الديـة، وفي الشدقين الديـة كاملة، فإن استؤصل أحدهما فنصف الدية.

185 طولها: -،د.

186 فالدية: بالدية، ب،د.

187 وإن ذهب العقل العقل فالدية كاملة: -،د.

188 عشر: عشرة، ب،د.

189 مع الشعر:، -د.

190 فقئتا: افقيتان،د. افقيتا، ب.

191 ثلث: ثلثي، ب.

192 المارن: المارون،د.

والأسنان وضح الفم وغيرها سواء في كل[193] سن خمس من الإبل، فإن أصيب فتحرك انتظر به حولا كاملا، فإن اسودت وهي قائمة فديتها كاملة خمس من الإبل، فإن أصيب منها طائفة وبقيت طائفة[194] فبحسب ما بقي[195] منها ثلثا أو ربعا.

و في اليدين الدية كاملة، فإن أصيب إحداهما فنصف الدية، فإن قطعت الكف فدية اليد كاملة، و في أصابع اليد في كلّ أصبع عشر من الإبل[196]، وأصابع الكف على ثلاثة أركان في كلّ ركن ثلث دية الأصبع ثلاثة أبعرة وثلث بعير، و في الظفر إذا أصيب و لم ينبت بعير[197].

والكف على ثلاث منازل، إبهام اليد إذا استؤصل من ثلاثة أركان ثلث دية اليد، وفي الظفر بعير ولا شيء بين ذلك، والكف على ثلاث منازل إذا استؤصلت من ثلاثة أركان ثلث دية اليد[198]؛ لأنّها أفضل الأصابع، وموضحة العضد نصف موضحة الرأس، بعيران ونصف، وفي منقلة العضد نصف منقلة الرأس، وفي هاشمة العضد نصف هاشمة الرأس، وفي نافذة[199] العضد نصف نافذة الرأس، وفي سمحاق العضد نصف سمحاق الرأس، وفي متلاحمة العضد نصف متلاحمة الرأس، وفي باضعة العضد نصف باضعة الرأس، وفي دامية العضد نصف دامية الرأس، والعضد فيه نصف دية

193 كل: -،د.

194 وبقيت طائفة: -،د.

195 ذهب، ب.

196 انظر: آثار الربيع، مسألة ٤٨، ص ٣٣.

197 بعير: بعر، ب،د.

198 وفي الظفر بعير ولا شيء بين ذلك والكف على ثلاث منازل إذا استوصلت من ثلاث أركان ثلث دية اليد: +، ب.

199 نافذة: ناقذة،د؛ ناقبة، ب.

جراحات الرأس التي يكون مثلها في العضد؛ وذلك أن في الرأس الدية كاملة، وأنّ[200] في اليد نصف الدية، وإذا كانت هذه الجراحات أيضا في الساعد وكانت في الزندين كليهما فإن فيهما من الدية مثل ما في جراحات العضد، دية كلّ جرح منها نصف دية ذلك الجراح في الرأس إن كانت موضحة أو شيئا من تلك الجراحات التي سميت بعد أن تكون في الساعد وفي الزندين كليهما، فهي على[201] نصف دية ذلك الجرح في الرأس، فإن كان في أحد الزندين فإن دية كلّ جرح يكون في الساعد في أحد الزندين نصف جرح دية العضد؛ لأن الساعد قصبتان[202] إن كانت موضحة أو شيئا من هذه الجراحات التي سميت فتكون في الساعد في أحد الزندين فإنّ دية كلّ جرح من ذلك تكون نصف دية جرح العضد وتكون ربع جراحات الرأس.

وفي موضحة الأصبع نصف عشر دية الأصبع، وفي الجنبين الدية كاملة، وفي أحدهما نصف الدية، فإن أصيبت طائفة من الجنب وبقيت طائفة فبحساب ما أصيب من الضلوع.

وزعم بعض الناس أن التي تلي الصدر من الضلوع لها فضل في الدية على ما سواها من الضلوع.

وفي جائفة البطن إذا خرقت الجلد والصفاق فلها ثلث الدية، فإن كانت نافذة ففيها ثلث الدية، وفي الذكر الدية كاملة، وفي الحشفة الدية كاملة، فما أصيب منها فبقدر ذلك، فإن قطعت الحشفة فاستؤصلت ثُمّ قطع الذكر بعد ذلك فما أصيب منه بعد الحشفة فهو جرح كبعض الجراحات.

---

200 أن: -، د.

201 على: كل، ب.

202 قصبتين: عظمين، ب.

و في البيضتين[203] الدية كاملة، فإن أصيب إحداهما فنصف الدية، و في الصلب إذا انكسر فحدب صاحبه الدية كاملة فإذا انكسر ثُمَّ جبر فلم يحمل[204] فله الدية كاملة، فإن حمل فنصف الدية.

و في اللسان إذا قطع فلم يتكلم صاحبه الدية كاملة، فإذا قطع و تكلم صاحبه فنصف الدية.

و في الرجلين الدية كاملة، فإن أصيب إحداهما فنصف الدية.

و في كلّ أصبع من الرجل عشر من الإبل، و في أنملَّة الرجل ثلث دية ذلك الأصبع.

وقضى عمر بن الخطَّاب في الموضحة التي تكون في جسد الإنسان لا[205] في رأسه أن كلّ عظم كان له عقل مسمى أن موضحته نصف عشر عقله إن كان عضدا أو ذراعا أو أصبعا أو ساقا أو فخذا.

و في حلمتي ثدي الرجل عشر من الإبل و في إحداهما خمس من الإبل، وما كان من منقلة تنقل عظامها في الذراع أو العضد أو الفخذ أو الساق فهي نصف منقلة الرأس سبع قلائص و نصف.

فإن أصيب الذراع أو الفخذ أو الساق أو العضد حتَّى يخرج مخها أو تهنّ عظمها[206]

203 البيضتين: الإثنتين، ب.
204 يحمل: يجمل، ب.
205 لا: ليست، ب.
206 عظمها: –، د.

أو لا يجتمع فنصف مأمومة الرأس.

و في ثدي المرأة إذا استؤصل نصف الدية، و في حلمة ثدي المرأة عشر من الإبل.

ويقال: في أنف العبد ثمنه كاملا، وإذا قطع منه طائفة ففيه قياس[207] من الأرنبة إلى قصبة الأنف، فما قطع منه حسب على قدر ذلك من ثمنه[208]، والعين نصف ثمنه، والأذن نصف ثمنه، والشَفة نصف ثمنه، واليد نصف ثمنه، والرجل نصف ثمنه، والأصبع عشر ثمنه والأصابع من اليدين والرجلين سواء إلا إبهام اليد فإنه ثلث دية[209] يده، والسن نصف عشر ثمنه[210] وأسنان وضح الفم والأضراس كلّها سواء، كلّ سن نصف عشر ثمنه، والأمة ثلث ثمنه، والجائفة ثلث ثمنه، والموضحة نصف عشر ثمنه[211].

ويقال في خرم أذن الحر إذا لم يلتئم: ثلث دية الأذن، وجفن العين إذا خرم ثلث دية ذلك الجفن.

ويقال إذا سقط شعر أحد الجفنين الأعلى أو الأسفل: ربع الدية، و في خرم الأنف إذا لم يلتئم[212] ثلث دية المنخر، والمنخر نصف الأنف، و في الشفاه إذا خرمت فلم تلتئم ثلث دية الشفة.

207 قياس: فيقاس، ب.

208 ثمنه: قيمته،د.

209 دية: ديته، ب،د.

210 والأصبع عشر ثمنه والأصابع من اليدين والرجلين سواء إلا إبهام اليد فإنه ثلث ديته يده والسن نصف عشر ثمنه: -،د.

211 نصف عشر ثمنه: -،د.

212 يلتئم: يلتأم، ب،د.

ويقال في نافذة الكف والعضد والفخذ والساق ثلث ديته.

ويقال إذا أصيب قصبة الأنف ويقال في نافذة الكف والعضد والفخذ والساق ثلث ديته، ويقال إذا أصيبت قصبة[213] الأنف فخافت الأنف[214] وبه يبس ولا يجد ريح شيء ففيه الدية، وفي عين الأعور الدية كاملة، وفي يد الأجذم إذا قطعت الدية كاملة.

و في العين القائمة التي لا يبصر بها صاحبها والسن القائمة التي اسودت واليد الشلاء[215] والرجل الشلاء، فما أصيب من هذه الأشياء[216] التي سميت ففيها ثلث ديتها صحيحة.

وإذا قطعت اليد أو الرِّجل أو فقئت العين أو انكسرت[217] السن فإن دية كلّ واحد منها[218] ثلث ديته صحيحا، وإن أصيب منه شيء وبقي شيء فبحساب ما ذهب منه وما بقي فيقاس فينظر فيه.

وفي[219] رجل أعور فقأ عين رجل ليس بأعور، فأراد الرجل أن يقتص منه رد عليه نصف الدية.

وسئل[220] عن رجل قُتل وله أولاد صغار وإن الولي قَبِل الدية؟

---

213 ويقال نافذة الكف والعضد والفخذ والساق ثلث ديته ويقال إذا أصيبت قصبة: –،د.

214 فخافت الأنف: –،د.

215 الشلاء: العشماء، ب؛ العلاء،د.

216 الأشياء: –،د.

217 انكسرت: تكسر،د.

218 منها: منهم، ب.

219 وفي: وعن، ب.

220 سئل: –، ب.

قال: قال إن لم[221] يعلم أنَّه حافَ على اليتامى أو ضارّ بهم[222] فإنَّه يُجاز[223].

وعن رجل قتل وله أولاد صغار وإن الولي عفا عن الدم.

قال: ليس له ذلك.

وعن امرأة قتلت؟

قال: عقلها ومالها بين ورثتها على فرائض الميراث[224]، والمرأة نصف عقل الرجل وعقل المرأة تعقله عصبتها وقومها، ولا يرث العصبة إلاَّ ما فضل عن ورثتها، وعصَبتها يقيدون بها[225] ويقتلون قاتلها، والمال والعقل بين الورثة على ما قسم الله.

والمرأة ترث زوجها من ماله وعقله، وهو يرثها من مالها وعقلها ما لم يقتل أحدهما الآخر، وأيّما وارث قتل وارثه فإنَّه يؤدي ديته مسلَّمة إلى أهله ولا يرثه[226].

وروي[227] عن النبيّ قال: «من قتل قتيلا فإنَّه لا يرثه[228]، وإن كان والده أو ولده، وإن لم يكن له وارث غيره»[229].

---

221 لم: –،د.

222 ضار بهم: ضارهم، ب.

223 يجوز: يجوز، ب.

224 قال: عقلها ومالها بين ورثتها على فرائض الميراث: –، ب.

225 بها: لها، ب.

226 إلى أهله ولا يرثه: –، ب.

227 وروي: زعم، ب.

228 لا يرثه: لا يديه، ب،د.

229 رواه البيهقي، باب لا يرث القاتل، ر١٢٠٢٢.

وقال: «ليس لقاتل خطأ ولا عمد اميراثٌ»[230]، وقضى ألاّ[231] يقتل مؤمن بمشرك ولا حرّ بعبد، وجعل عقل اليهوديّ والنصرانيّ ثلث عقل المسلم، ثُمَّ أمر ألاّ[232] يستقيد من به جرح من صاحبه حتَّى يبرأ.

وفي الشفة والأذن إذا استؤصلا نصف العقل، وما أصيب منه فبحساب ما أصيب، والجرح على ما بلغ حتَّى يبرأ، وما كان من شلل أو عرج بعد البرء فلا قود فيه وهو عقل، فإن كان الجرح[233] والشلل من الجرح قبل أن يبرأ المجروح فإنَّه يأخذ أرش ذلك كله، وما كان بعد البرء من شلل أو عرج أو غير ذلك فلا شيء فيه.

ومن استقاد بجرح فأصيب المستقاد منه فهو عقل يلقى على المستقيد ما جرح من صاحبه واستقد منه، وبرئ ما فضل من ديته عن جرح صاحبه.

سئل عن رجل قتل عبدا؟
قال: يقوم قيمة عدل فيأخذ مولاه ثمنه.

سئل عن المسلم يقتل اليهوديّ أو النصرانيّ؟
قال: لا يقاد مسلم بمشرك، وإنَّما دية المشرك ثلث دية المسلم إذا كان من أهل الذمَّة[234].
عن قيس بن سعد عن مكحول: أنَّ عمر بن الخطَّاب لمَّا ورد الشام انطلق رجل من

230 رواه الربيع، باب في المواريث، ر٦٦٨.
231 ألا: أن لا، ب د.
232 ألا: أن لا، ب د.
233 الجرح: العرج، ب.
234 انظر: آثار الربيع، مسألة ٩٥، ص ٣٧.

المسلمين فناول دابته علجا أو نبطيا يمسكها، فأهوى[235] إليه فشجه، فانطلق إلى عمر فاستقاده فأراد عمر أن يقيده، فقال له زيد بن ثابت: مالك ذلك، أتقيد لعبدك من أخيك؟ فغرمه الدية ولم يقده. قال: نعم، عليه الغرم، تقاس شجته فما بلغت جعلت ديتها ثلث[236] دية شجة مثلها من شجاج المسلمين ولا يقاد له.

سئل عن رجل قتل امرأة عمدا أيقاد بها؟

قال: نعم[237] يقتل بها إن أحب أولياء المرأة، ويردون نصف الدية، وإلاَّ فلهم نصف دية الرجل[238]؛ لأن دية المرأة نصف دية الرجل.

عن قتادة: أنَّ عمر بن الخطَّاب قَتَل في غلام[239] قُتل غيلة ثلاثة نفر، وذلك في قصة الصنعانية[240]، وقال: لو اشتركوا فيها لأبيدنهم[241] -يعني أهل صنعاء - قال: نعم، بلغنا هذا، وهو قول أصحابنا.

قال: وبلغنا أنَّ عمر بن الخطَّاب قال: لو اجتمع أهل صنعاء على قتل رجل لقتلتهم به، وهو قول الفقهاء، لو اجتمع أناس على قتل رجل متعمّدين لقتله لقتلوا[242] به ولم يعف عنهم[243] ثُمَّ إلى النار.

---

235 فأهد، ب. أما في الهامش: فأهوى.

236 ثلث: -،د.

237 نعم: -،د.

238 الرجل، -،د.

239 بالصنعانية، ب.

240 الصنعانية: الصنعنية، ب،د.

241 لأبيدنهم: ليقدَّنهم بها، ب.

242 لقتله لقتلوا: لقتله لقتلتهم،د. لقتلوا، ب.

243 ولم يعف عنهم: -، ب.

سئل عن قوله عزّ وجل: ﴿فَمَنْ عُفِيَ لَهُ مِنْ أَخِيهِ شَيْءٌ فَاتِّبَاعٌ بِالْمَعْرُوفِ وَأَدَاءٌ إِلَيْهِ بِإِحْسَانٍ﴾[244]؟

عن قتادة قال: من قَتل عمدا فعُفي عنه وقبلت منه الدية فاتباع بالمعروف وأداء إليه بإحسان، أمر الطالب أن يحسن الطلب وأمر المطلوب أن يحسن الأداء، أي: أمر المتبع أن يتبع بالمعروف وأمر المؤدي أن يؤدي إليه[245] بإحسان. وقال: ذلك تخفيف من ربكم ورحمة، رحم بها هذه الأمة فأطعمهم الدية ولم تحل لأحد قبلهم. قال: كان أهل التوراة إنّمَا هو قصاص أو عفو ليس بينهم أرش، وكان أهل الإنجيل إنّمَا هو عفو، وجعل لهذه الأمة العفو أو القصاص أو الأرش. قال: نعم[246].

سئل عن قول الله: ﴿فَمَنِ اعْتَدَى بَعْدَ ذَلِكَ فَلَهُ عَذَابٌ أَلِيمٌ﴾[247]؟

عن قتادة قال[248]: من اعتدى بعد أخذ الدية فقتل فله عذاب أليم. قال: نعم[249].

والعذاب الأليم ألا[250] يعفى عنه، ولا تؤخذ منه الدية، وليس للحاكم إلاّ قتله.

قال: نعم، بل يقتل ثُمّ إلى النار[251].

عن قتادة من اعتدى [بعد] أخذ الدية فقتل فله عذاب أليم.

244 سورة البقرة: ١٧٨.

245 إليه: -، ب.

246 قال: نعم: -،د.

247 سورة البقرة: ١٧٨.

248 قال: -،د.

249 : نعم: -،د.

250 ألا: أن لا، ب د.

251 قال: نعم، بل يقتل ثُمّ إلى النار: -، ب.

قال: والعذاب الأليم أن لا يعفى عنه ولا تؤخذ منه الدية وليس للحاكم إلاّ قتله.

قال: نعم، بل يقتل، ثُمَّ إلى النار[252].

عن قتادة قال: ذكر لنا أنَّ نبيَّ الله عليه السلام قال: لا أعافي رجلا قتل بعد أخذ الدية[253].

قال: نعم، يقتل ثُمَّ إلى النار[254]

سئل في كم تؤخذ الدية؟

قال: في ثلاثة أعوام كلّ سنة ثلث الدية[255].

سئل عن العبد يقتل عبداً خطأ؟

قال: إنَّمَا هو مال غير أنَّه لا يبلغ دية الحر، فإن كان القاتل أكثر ثمنا فإن أحب مواليه أن يؤدوا ثمن المقتول[256] فلهم ذلك، وإن كان المقتول أكثر ثمنا لم يكن[257] على مواليه أكثر من رقبته، فهو لهم إن شاؤوا قتلوه وإن شاؤوا[258] أخذوا ثمنه، وإن كرهوا أن يعطوهم[259] الثمن فإنَّمَا لهم رقبته.

252 قال: نعم، بل يقتل ثُمَّ إلى النار: -، ب.

253 رواه البيهقي، باب من قتل بعد أخذه الدية، ر١٥٨٢٤.

254 قال: نعم، يقتل ثُمَّ إلى النار: -،د.

255 الدية: -، ب.

256 المقتول: الْمَيِّت، ب.

257 لم يكن: يجرؤ القاتل، ب.

258 قتلوه وإن شاؤوا: -،د.

259 أن يعطوهم: إن يعطونهم، ب،د.

سئل عن عبد جُدع أنفه؟

قال: إن جدع[260] أنفه أو قطعت يده فنصف قيمته[261].

سئل عن دية[262] الجنين إذا استهل ثُمَّ مات؟

قال في الجنين ما لم يستهل غرة: عبد أو أمة[263].

عن الحسن: أنَّ امرأة كانت مُغِيبةً[264]، فبلغ ذلك عمر بن الخطَّاب رضي الله عنه فأرسل إليها، وكان مهابا، فلمَّا جاءها الرسول، قال: أجيبي عمر. قالت: يا ويلها[265] ما لها ولعمر، فأخذها المخاض، فشدت عليها ثيابها ثُمَّ أقبلت، فأتت على نسوة فعرفن ما في وجهها، فاختلجنها، فولدت جنينا فاستهل ثُمَّ مات، فانطلق الرسول إلى عمر فأخبره ففزع من ذلك. فقال: أنت والله صاحبه أنت والله صاحبه[266]، أنت والله قتلته يعني نفسه، فسأل عمر أصحابه عن ذلك[267]، فقالوا: يا أمير المؤمنين، ما عليك من ذلك من شيء، إنَّمَا أنت مؤدب، إنَّمَا أنت معلم.

قال: وعلي رضي الله عنه ساكت، فقالوا: ما تقول يا أبا الحسن؟ فقال: إن كان القوم لحظوك[268]، فما نصحوك، وإن كانوا قد اجتهدوا فقد أخطأوا رأيهم، أنت صاحبه

260 جدع: جذ، ب،د.

261 السؤال والجواب: -، ب.

262 دية: -، ب.

263 الجواب: -، ب.

264 تتغدى: +، ب؛ المرأة المغيبة: التي غاب عنها زوجها.

265 ويلها: وليها، ب،د.

266 أنت والله صاحبه: -، ب.

267 عن ذلك: -،د.

268 لحظوك: لحظوا في هواك، ب.

وعليك ديته. قال: لا جرم، والله لا تجلس حتَّى تقسمها على قومك. قال: نعم، هي العشيرة، دية الخطأ[269].

سئل عن امرأة شربت دواء وهي حبلى فطرحت ما في بطنها؟

قال: إن كانت شربت الدواء لتقتل ما في بطنها[270] -ولدها- فخرج حيا فإذا مات فديته لأبيه، أو لورثته وليس للأم شيء، وإن كانت شربت الدواء ولا تعلم أنَّها حبلى فهو خطأ، إن خرج حيا فديته دية الخطأ على عشيرتها، وإن كان[271] خرج ميتا فغرة: عبد أو أمة في الوجهين جميعا، في العمد والخطأ[272].

سئل فيما توجب فيه[273] الدية كاملة؟

قال: في قتل الرجل خطأ الدية كاملة، وفي اللسان الدية كاملة وما نقص منه فبقدر ذلك، فإذا امنع الكلام فالدية كاملة، وفي الأنف الدية كاملة إذا قطع من المارون، وما نقص منه فبقدر ذلك، وإن وعى جذعا ففيه الدية لا يزاد عليها، وفي الأنثيين[274] الدية كاملة[275]، وفي الأسنان الدية كاملة[276]، وفي الذكر الدية كاملة، وفي الحشفة الدية كاملة، وما نقص من الحشفة فبقدر ذلك، وفي الشعر إذا صب عليه الماء الحار فلم ينبت الدية كاملة، وفي

269 رواه عبد الرزاق في مصنفه بمعناه، باب من أفزعه السلطان، ر ١٨٠١٠.

270 ما في بطنها: -، ب.

271 كان: -،د.

272 امرأة شربت الدواء وهي حامل فيه توجيه والأم: هامش، ب.

273 فيه: -، ب.

274 الأنثيين: الاثنتين، ب،د.

275 وإن وعى جذعا ففيه الدية لا يزاد عليها، وفي الاثنتين الدية كاملة: -،د.

276 وفي الأسنان الدية كاملة: -، ب.

شعر اللحية إذا ذهب ولم ينبت الدية كاملة، وفي الصلب إذا انكسر الدية كاملة، وفي الحدب إذا منع الجماع الدية كاملة، وفي الرجل يضرب حتّى ينقطع كلامه الدية كاملة، وفي الرجل يضرب حتّى يذهب عقله الدية كاملة، وفي الرجل يضرب حتّى يذهب سمعه الدية كاملة، وفي الرجل يضرب حتّى يذهب نكاحه الدية كاملة، وفي الرجل إذا فزع حتّى يذهب عقله الدية كاملة، وقتل العمد على القاتل في ماله إذا أخذت منه الدية ومن قتل خطأ عقل عنه قومه[277] .

سئل عن رجل رمي بحجر فذهب سمعه وبصره ولسانه وعقله؟

قال: في كلّ واحدة منهن الدية كاملة.

وفي الوترة ثلث الدية؛ لأنّها ثلاثة، فكل واحدة الثلث، وفي[278] الترقوة بعيران فإن كان فيها شين نظر في ذلك، وفي الكتف بعيران فإن كان فيها شين نظر في ذلك ذوا[279] عدل.

سئل عن عبد بين رجلين فقأ أحدهما عينه خطأ؟

قال: يغرم لشريكه ربع ثمنه وهو بينهما فإن فقأ عينه عمدا فإنّه يقوم من ماله ويغرم نصيب صاحبه.

سئل عن العين إذا أصيبت وقد كان صاحبها يبصر بها بصرا ضعيفا؟

قال: فيها القصاص أو ديتها كاملة.

---

277 وقتل العمد. . . عقل عنه قومه: –، ب.

278 الوترة ثلث الدية؛ لأنّها ثلاثة فكل واحدة الثلث وفي: –،د.

279 ذوا: ذوي، ب،د.

سئل عن طبيب قطع من عين رجل الظفر أو فقأ عينه؟

قال: هو ضامن وفيها ديتها كاملة، وقال الطبيب والبيطار ضامنان[280].

سئل عن ذنب الدابة إذا استؤصل[281].

سئل عن الحرّة تكون تحت العبد[282] المملوك[283] فيفقأ عينها؟

قال: ليس بينهما قصاص، وإن كان عمدا أخذ برمته[284] إن لم يكن ثمن العبد أكثر من دية عينها، فإن كان أكثر من دية عينها افتكَّهُ مولاه إن شاء فإن أخذته فصار لها حرم عليها، فإن أعتقته رجع[285] إلى نكاحها.

سئل عن رجل عض ذراع رجل آخر فانتزع ثنيته؟

قال: ليس عليه فيها دية، وقال: المرأة على النصف من دية الرجل في النفس وفي الجراحات.

سئل عن رجل قتله رجل بالغ وغلام لم يحتلم؟

قال: إن كانا قتلاه متعمّدين قتل به البالغ، وليس على الصبيّ قود في عمد ولا خطأ[286]

280 الطبيب والبيطار ضامنان: هامش، ب.

281 سئل: عن ذنب الدابة إذا استؤصل: –،د.

282 العبد: –،د.

283 المملوك: مملوك، ب،د.

284 بذمته، ب. وفي الهامش: برمته.

285 رجع: رجعا، ب د.

286 ولا خطأ: –،د.

وجنايات الصبيّ كلّها خطأ وجنايات العبد عمدها وخطأها في رقبته[287].

سئل عن رجل قتله رجلان مع أحدهما حديد ومع الآخر عصًا؟

قال: إذا اشتركا جميعا في قتله قتلوا به.

سئل عن رجل قتل رجلا فعفا عنه بعض الأولياء؟

قال: إذا عفا بعضهم لم يقتل وكانت عليه[288] الدية[289].

سئل عن رجل ضرب فعفا عند موته؟

قال: إن كان عمدا فعفوه جائز وإن كان[290] خطأ فليس له إلاّ الثلث.

سئل عن رجل أوصى بثلث ماله ثُمّ قتل خطأ؟

قال: إن ديته داخلة في ثلثه[291].

سئل عن عفو النساء؟

عن قتادة: أنّه كان لا يرى للنساء عفوا ولا قودا.

سئل عن عبد قتل رجلا فعفا عنه بعض الأولياء وأبى[292] بعض؟

287 الصبي لا قود عليه في العمد والخطأ والعبد جناياته كلها في رقبته هامش، ب.

288 عليه: -،د.

289 إذا عفى بعض الأولياء ليس للباقين إلا الدية إلا القتل: هامش، ب.

290 كان: -،د.

291 رجل ضرب وعفا عن ضاربه عند الموت إن كان في العبد جائز عفوه: هامش، ب.

292 أبى: أبا، ب،د.

قال: يرجع عفوا الذين عفوا إلى موالي[293] العبد، وليس عليه قتل.

سئل عن ثلاثة قتلوا رجلا عمدا؟

قال: للولي[294] أن يقتلهم جميعا إذا اشتركوا في دمه متعمّدين قتله، ويكره أن يُعفى عن هؤلاء، ولكن القتل ثُمَّ إلى النار[295].

سئل عن عبد قتل عبدا؟

قال: إن كان القاتل أكثر ثمنا فإن شاء مولاه أن يعطي ثمن العبد المقتول فعل، وإن كان المقتول أكثر ثمنا فلمولى المقتول أن يأخذ العبد وإن شاء قبل منه الثمن.

سئل عن عبد شجَّ رجلا ثُمَّ شج رجلا آخر؟

قال: ليس فيه حكومة حتَّى ينتهي إلى القاضي فيعطي كلّ رجل حصَّته، مالم يرفع[296] العبد إلى الحاكم وقد أصاب جراحات من أناس شتى فإنَّه يقسم ثمنه بينهم على قدر جراحاتهم[297].

عن قتادة عن جابر بن زيد أنَّه قال[298]: إذا قطعت اليد في سبيل الله ثُمَّ قطعت الأخرى ففيها الدية كاملة: دية النفس، فإن قطعت في حدّ ثُمَّ قطعت الأخرى ففيها نصف الدية، وذلك رأي ابن[299] عمر.

---

293 موالي: مولى، ب.

294 للولي: له، ب.

295 ثلاثة نفر قتلوا رجلا متعمدين يكره أن يعفى عنهم: هامش، ب.

296 مالم يرفع: إن رفع، ب.

297 إذا قطعت يد في سبيل الله، وقطعت الأخرى إلا بدية: هامش، ب.

298 أنه قال: -، ب.

299 ابن: أبي، ب.

عن قتادة: أنَّ عبد الملك بن مروان قضى في الظفر ببعير، فإن كان فيه شين فبعيران، وذلك رأي ابن[300] عمر.

سئل عن الطعنة النافذة؟

قال: إذا طعن الرجل ونفذت الطعنة إلى الجوف[301] ففيها ثلث الدية[302]، ثلاثة وثلاثون بعيرا وثلث بعير، إن كان عمدا فدية العمد وإن كان خطأً فدية الخطأ.

سئل عن الكسر يكون في الفخذ أو العضد أو الساق أو الذراع؟

قال: إذا جبرت على غير شين ولا عور ففيها بعيران.

سئل عن رجل ضرب فأصابه الفتق؟

قال: فيه ثلث الدية.

سئل عن رجل أصاب زوجته فأفضاها؟

قال: عليه ثلث الدية[303].

سئل عن رجل خنق رجلا فأحدث؟

قال: عليه ثلث الدية.

سئل عن رجل أعور فقئت عينه خطأً؟

عن قتادة عن لاحق بن حميد قال: سألت ابن عمر عنها فقال عبد الله بن صفوان:

300 ابن: أبي، ب.

301 إلى الجوف: -، ب.

302 ثلث الدية: جائفتان، ب.

303 سئل: عن رجل أصاب زوجته فأفضاها؟ قال: عليه ثلث الدية: -، د.

قضى عمر بن الخَطَّاب فيها بالدية كاملة، وهو رأي ابن[304] عمر.

سئل عن الأعور فقأ عين الصحيح؟[305]

سئل عن عبد بين[306] رجلين فقأ أحدهما عينه خطأ؟

قال: يغرم لشريكه ربع ثمنه وهو بينهما.

سئل عن العين إذا أصيبت وقد كان صاحبها يبصر بها بصرا ضعيفا؟

عن قتادة قال: فيها القصاص إن أحب أو الدية كاملة دية العين لا ينقص ضعف بصرها من ديتها شيئا، وذلك رأي ابن[307] عمر.

عن قتادة: أنَّ شُريحا قضى في عين الدابة ربع[308] ثمنها، وهو رأي ابن عمر.

عن قتادة: أنَّه قال: في ذنب الدابة إذا استؤصل الثمن وفي الاثنتين الثمن، ولكل قائمة من قوائمها الثمن.[309]

سئل عن رجل كانت في يده قصبة فضرب بها حمارا فطارت منها شظية ففقأت عين الحمار؟

قال: [310]

---

304 ابن: أبي، ب.

305 هذه المسألة جاءت هكذا من غير جواب.

306 عبد بين: عبدين، ب،د.

307 ابن: أبي، ب.

308 ربع: -، ب،د. انظر: مصنف عبد الرزاق، باب عين الدابة، ر١٨٤١٧.

309 دية كل قائمة من قوائم الدابة ثمنها: هامش، ب.

310 هذه المسألة جاءت هكذا من غير جواب.

سئل عن رجل ضرب فذهب بعض بصره، ثُمَّ ضربه آخر فذهب بصره كله؟

قال: ديته كاملة.

سئل عن رجل اقتص منه فمات؟

قال: لا يقتص من أحد حتَّى يبرأ فإذا[311] برئ اقتص منه، وإن هلك المقتص منه فهو عقل[312] على قوم المقتص له، وكل جرح يدرك قصاصه ففيه القصاص، وإن لم يقدر على القصاص ففيه الدية.

سئل عن القصاص متى يكون؟

عن عمرو بن دينار عن مُحَمَّد بن طلحة: أن رجلا طعن على ركبته[313] أو فخذه على عهد النبيّ فأتى النبي[314] عليه السلام فقال: يا نبيّ الله، أقدني من فلان فقال له: حتَّى تبرأ، ثُمَّ أتاه فقال: يا نبيّ الله، أقدني من فلان. فقال: حتَّى تبرأ، ثُمَّ أتاه الثالثة فقال له: أقدني[315] فأقاده، ثُمَّ أتاه بعد ذلك، فقال: إني عرجت وبرئ فلان فقال له النبيّ صلى الله عليه وسلم: قد أقدتك ولم يجعل له شيئا[316].

عن قتادة قال[317]: كان جابر بن زيد يقول: المرأة نصف الرجل في النفس وما دونها، وفي عين الدابة ربع ثمنها.

311 فإذا: فإن، ب.
312 عقل: تعقال، د.
313 ركبته: رجله، ب.
314 فأتى النبي: -، د.
315 فقال له: أقدني: -، د.
316 رواه البيهقي، باب ما جاء في الاستثناء بالقصاص من الجرح والقطع، ر١٥٨٩٣.
317 قتادة قال: -، ب.

سئل عن الحميل: هل يرث؟

قال: إذا أقر أحدهما أنه وارث صاحبه صدق، وورث عندنا بإقرارهما واعترافهما على أنفسهما[318].

عن مخلد بن سعيد عن الشعبي: أنَّ عمر بن الخطَّاب -رضي الله- عنه كتب إلى شريح: في عين الدابة ربع ثمنها[319].

سئل عما كان من دية[320] العمد بسلاح أو بغير سلاح؟

قال: هو على القاتل والجارح في أموالهما خاصة، إلاَّ أن تشاء العشيرة أن يعقلوا ذلك عنهما.

وسئل عن رجل أقر على نفسه بالقتل؟

قال: عليه الدية في ماله وليس على عاقلته شيء، إلاَّ أن يقيم البيِّنة على الذي أقر به[321].

سئل عن أمِّ الولد إذا جنت جناية؟

قال: أم الولد عندنا أمة حتَّى يعتقها سيدها.

318 سئل: عن الحميل هل يرث؟ قال: إذا أقر أحدهما أنه وارث صاحبه صدق وورث عندنا بإقرارهما واعترافهما على أنفسهما: -،د. الحميل هو الطفل الذي تجيء به المرأة تحمله من أرض الشرك فتقول هذا ولدك وقيل الحميل هم الذين يسبون فيقول بعضهم: هذا أخي وهذه أختي وهذا أبي وهذا جدي وهذه جدتي وهذه أمي قد أحال بدعواه نسبه على غيره انتهى من كتاب ابن عبيد رحمه الله: هامش، ب.

319 قول جابر: في عين الدابة ربع ثمنها: هامش، ب.

320 دية: -، ب.

321 رجل أقر على نفسه بالقتل ليس على عاقلته شيء إلا بينته: هامش، ب.

سئل عن أربعة شهد وا على رجل بحد فرجم ثمّ إن أحدهم أكذب نفسه؟

قال: يقتل به[322]، وليس على الثلاثة شيء.

سئل عن عفو النساء؟

عن قتادة: أنّه كان لا يرى للنساء عفوا ولا قودا. قال: ذلك رأينا[323].

سئل عن الجراحات بين العبيد؟

قال: قصاص العبيد إلى مواليهم، والموضحة من قيمة العبد[324] ألف درهم[325] نصف عشر ثمنه ويترادون.

باب فيمن شرب الخمر

سئل عمّن شرب الخمر؟

عن قتادة: أنّ النبيّ صلى الله عليه وسلم وأبا بكر جلدا على الخمر بالنعال[326] وبالدريد[327] أربعين جلدة[328]، وجلد عمر صدرا من خلافته أربعين، فلمّا رأى أن الناس لا ينتهون استشار أناسا من أصحابه في جلد ثمانين وهو أهون الحدود، فقال عبد الرحمن بن عوف:

---

322 به: –، د.

323 سئل: عن عفو النساء؟ عن قتادة: أنه كان لا يرى للنساء عفوا ولا قودا. قال: ذلك رأينا: –، د.

324 قيمة العبد: من قيمته، ب.

325 ألف درهم: –، د.

326 رواه البخاري، باب ما جاء في ضرب شارب الخمر، ر٦٣٩١.

327 الدريد: الجرائد، ب.

328 جلدة: –، ب.

متى يشرب يسكر ومتى يسكر يفجر ومتى يفجر يقذف، فأرى[329] أن يجلد ثمانين جلدة أخف الحدود[330]، وكان أول من جلد ثمانين قدامة بن مظعون[331].

عن حصين بن أبي أساس قال: خرج الوليد بن عقبة وهو عامل عثمان على الكوفة فصلّى بالناس الصبح أربع ركعات وهو سكران، ثُمَّ أقبل عليهم فقال: أفلا أزيدكم؟ فركب نفر منهم فأتوا عثمان بن عفان وهو يومئذ خليفة، فرفعوا ذلك إليه، فقال عثمان لعلي: اجلد ابن عمك، فأمر علي ابنه الحسن أنَّ يجلده. قال: فيما أنت من هذا؟ هذا ولي هذا[332]. فقال له علي: بل عجزت ووهنت وضعفت[333]، قم يا عبد الله بن جعفر فاجلده. قال: فجعل عبد الله يجلد وعلي يعد حتَّى بلغ أربعين فقال: أمسك جلد رسول الله عليه السلام أربعين، وجلد أبو بكر أربعين، فأكملها عمر ثمانين وكلٌّ سُنّة[334].

سئل عن الجلد في الحدود؟

عن قتادة قال: كلّ جلد من تعزير أو من[335] فرية أو من[336] شرب خمر ونحو هذا فإنَّمَا هو جلد بين الجلدين لا يوضع قميصه ولا يرفع الجلاد يده حتَّى يرى بياض إبطه. قال: هذا رأينا[337].

---

329 فأرى: فرأى، ب.

330 أخف الحدود: -، ب.

331 وكان أول من جلد ثمانين قدامة بن مظعون: -،د.

332 فيما أنت من هذا؟ هذا ولي هذا: وهذا لغيرك» مكان «هذا ولي هذا، ب.

333 وضعفت: -،د.

334 حد الخمر: هامش، ب. رواه مسلم، باب حد الخمر، ر٤٥٥١.

335 من: -،د.

336 من: -،د.

337 صفة جلد الحدود: هامش، ب.

سئل عمَّن يعمل عمل قوم لوط ؟

قال: يلقى من فوق جبل وترسل عليه الحجارة.

سئل عن رجل قال لرجل: يا لوطي ؟

عن فرقد الشيخ: أن رجلا يقال له عبد الله قيل له: يا لوطي، ثُمَّ سعى وأدرك فسأل الحسن وابن سيرين قالا: إن لوطا رجل صالح فإن كان قال لك: يا لوطي، فليس عليه الحدّ ولكن لو قال لك: أنت تعمل عمل قوم لوط كان لك[338] عليه الحد.

قال: ذلك رأينا[339].

سئل عن رجل قذف امرأة بنفسه؟

قال: عليه حدان، قيل فإن أكذب نفسه قال: عليه[340] حدّ واحد.

قال: هذا رأينا[341].

سئل عن عبد قذف حرّة؟

قال: كان جابر لا يرى على المملوك ولا على الذمي حدّا، ولكن يضربون ويعزرون دون الحد.

سئل عن صبيّ[342] يحصن فيصيب فاحشة الزنا؟

---

338 لك: -، ب.

339 حد اللواط: هامش، ب.

340 عليه: -، د.

341 رجل قذف امرأة بنفسه فيه حدان: هامش، ب.

342 صبي: غلام، ب.

قال: ليس عليه رجم.

وعن: الجارية تحصن ولم تحض فتصيب فاحشة الزنا[343]؟

قال: ليس عليها رجم[344].

عن قتادة عن الشعبي: أن شراحة الهمدانية أتت عليًا فأخبرته أنَّها قد زنت، فقال لها: لعلك رأيت ذلك في منامك أو استكرهت، كلّ ذلك تقول: لا، فجلدها يوم الخميس ورجمها يوم الجمعة، ثُمَّ قال: جلدتها بكتاب الله ورجمتها بسنة رسول الله عليه السلام.

قال: نرى[345] أن عليها الرجم إن كانت محصنة[346] ولا جلد عليها.

باب في مسائل متفرّقة

سئل عن الجدَّة إذا كانت من قبل الأب، أهي أقرب أو إذا كانت من جهة الأم؟

قال: إذا استويتا فهما سواء، وإن لم تستويا[347] فهو للأقرب منهما من قبل الأب أو من قبل الأم[348].

سئل عن ميراث الخنثى؟

---

343 الزنا: -، ب.

344 الغلام والجارية اللذان لم يبلغا إذا زنيا ليس عليهما حد: هامش، ب.

345 نرى: -، ب.

346 إن كانت محصنة: -، ب.

347 تستويا: يستويتا، ب،د.

348 مسائل المواريث: هامش، ب.

عن قتادة[349]: أنّ جابر بن زيد قال: من أيهما بال. قيل: فإن خرج منهما جميعا؟
قال: من أيهما سبق. قال: بلغنا هذا.

سئل عن ميراث الإخوة من الأم من الدية؟
قال: بلغنا أنّ الإخوة من الأم يرثون من الدية.

سئل عن قوم يموتون ولا يدرى أيهما مات قبل صاحبه؟
قال: بلغنا أنّ الناس إذا لم يدر أيهم مات قبل، ورث بعضهم من بعض من صلب أموالهم ولا يرثون مِمّا ورثوا شيئا.

عن عبد الله بن نجيح عن طاوس: أنّ رسول الله عليه السلام قال: لا رقبى[350]، ومن أرقب شيئا فهو لورثة المرقب[351]. قال: هذا رأينا[352].

سئل عن رجل أسكن داره رجلا عشر سنين، ثُمّ مات صاحب الدار؟
قال: له شرطه.

سئل عن رجل أجّر دابته عشر سنين ثُمّ مات؟
قال: لورثته أن يتموا شرط المِيّت، فإن باعوا فليشترطوا إلى المدّة.

سئل عن رجل قال لرجل: أسكنتك حياتك، أو عمرتك حياتك؟
قال: هي راجعة إلى صاحبها الأوّل، حتّى يقول: هي لك حياتك.

349 قتادة: مخلد، ب.

350 رقبى: رقبة، ب.

351 رواه ابن ماجه، باب الرقبى، ر ٢٣٨٢.

352 الشرطة السكنة: هامش، ب.

سئل عن رجل مات ولا عقب له ولا ولد ولا عمومة، وله أخت أو خالة أو عمّة أو أخت أب؟

عن قتادة: أنَّه كان يرى ماله كله لها. قال: هذا رأينا.

باب في الوصيَّة وغيرها

سئل عن رجل أوصى بعتق مملوكه[353]؟

قال: كان جابر بن زيد يقول: إذا قال في مرضه: إن مت فهو حر، فهو مدبر إلاَّ أن يقول: في مرضي هذا.

سئل عن رجل أوصى بوصيَّة فأحدث بعد ذلك وصيَّة أخرى تخالفها؟

قال: يؤخذ بآخر وصيته، وقال: يرد ثلثا الثلث على أقاربه الذين أوصى لهم ثلث الثلث[354] لا يرثونه[355].

سئل عن رجل أوصى بثلث ماله لغير أقاربه؟

عن جابر بن زيد قال: يرد ثلثا الثلث على أقاربه، ويجوز للذين أوصى لهم ثلث الثلث[356].

---

353 مملوكة: -، ب.

354 أوصى لهم ثلث الثلث: -،د.

355 لا يرثونه: -، ب. يبدو أن في هذه الفقرة سقطا، ورد في شرح النيل، ١٢/٣٨٠ ما نصه: «يَرُدُّ ثُلُثَيْ الثُّلُثِ أَيْ إذَا أَوْصَى بِالثُّلُثِ وَهُوَ مَا ذَكَرْته مِنْ مَذْهَبِ أَصْحَابِنَا، وَقَالَ طَاوُسٍ: يَرُدُّ الْأَقْرَبُ الثُّلُثَ كُلَّهُ، وَقَالَ قَتَادَةَ: ثُلُثَ الثُّلُثِ، وَذَلِكَ إذَا أَوْصَى بِالثُّلُثِ، وَقِيلَ: يَرُدُّ نِصْفَ الثُّلُثِ إذَا أَوْصَى بِالثُّلُثِ. . . ».

356 الكفن ليس من الثلث بل من جميع: هامش، ب.

سئل عن الكفن: أمن الثلث أم من جميع المال؟
قال: بل[357] من جميع المال.

سئل عن رجل أوصى لأقاربه ولم يسم أحدا منهم[358]؟
قال: ثلثا[359] الوصيّة لأعمامه، والثلث لأخواله، ويعطون الأقرب فالأقرب.

عن قتادة عن خلاس أنَّ عليًّا قال في رجل أوصى بثلث ماله ثُمَّ قتل خطأ: إن ثلثه داخل في ديته. قال: هذا رأينا.

سئل عن رجل مات ولا عقب له ولا ولد[360] ولا عصبة، وله أخت أو خالة أو عمة أو أخت لأب؟
عن قتادة: أنّه كان يرى ماله كله لها. قال: هذا رأينا[361].

سئل عن رجل مات ولم يترك وارثا[362] إلاّ عمة و[363] خالة؟
قال: الثلثان[364] للعمة والثلث للخالة.

---

357 بل: -،د.

358 منهم: -،د.

359 ثلثا: ثلثي، ب،د.

360 ولا ولد: ولا ولدا، ب،د.

361 سئل: عن رجل مات ولا عقب له ولا ولدا ولا عصبة وله أخت أو خالة أو عمة أو أخت لأب؟ عن قتادة: أنّه كان يرى ماله كله لها. قال: هذا راينا: -،د.

362 وارثا: -،د.

363 و: أو، ب د.

364 الثلثان: الثلثين، ب،د.

سئل عن ميراث ولد المتلاعنين[365]؟

ذكر عن جابر بن زيد أنّه قال: ولد المتلاعنين ميراثه لأبيه.

سئل عن ميراث المرتد عن دينه؟

قال: ميراثه لأهل دينه الذي اختار.

سئل عن رجل كاتب على نفسه وولده فمات أحدهما، هل يلقى عنه من كتابة المّيِّت شيئا؟
عن قتادة عن أبي المليح أن رجلا أعتق نصيبا له في غلام، فرفعوا ذلك إلى رسول الله عليه السلام فجعل خلاصه في ماله[366]، وقال: ليس لك[367] شريك. قال: هذا رأينا.

عن قتادة عن النضر بن أنس عن بشير بن نهيك عن الزهري: أنَّ رسول الله صلى الله عليه وسلم - قال: من أعتق شقصا له في مملوك فعليه خلاصه في ماله[368]، إن كان له مال، وإن لم يكن له مال قوّم المملوك قيمة عدل ثُمَّ يستسعى. قال: هذا رأينا.

تم[369] الجزء الثالث من قول قتادة، والحمد لله ربّ العالمين، ولا حول ولا قوة إلاَّ بالله العلي العظيم، وصلَّى الله على سيدنا مُحَمَّد وعلى آله وصحبه وسلم تسليما[370].

---

365 الملاعنة.، ب

366 رواه البخاري، باب تقويم الأشياء بين الشركاء بقيمة عدل، ر٢٣٦٠.

367 لك: لله، ب.

368 في ماله: -،د. رواه مسلم، باب ذكر سعاية العبد، ر٣٨٤٦.

369 تم: نجز،د.

370 بحمد الله وحسن عونه على يد العبد الفقير صالح بن سالم بن سليمان بن يدر السدريني تاب الله عنه. آمين. بجامع الصلت عمره الله آمين بالعلم والعمل من رجال المسلمين، ب.

الجزء الرابع من قول قتادة

وبالله العون والتوفيق[1]

بسم الله الرحمن الرحيم

وصلى الله على سيدنا محمد النبي الكريم، وعلى آله وصحبه وسلم تسليما كثيرا دائما[2].

سئل عن نبيذ السقاء[3]؟

عن قتادة قال: ذكر لنا أن وفدا من عبد القيس قدموا على رسول الله صلى الله عليه وسلم فيهم الأشجع. فقال: يا رسول[4] الله، إنا حيّ[5] من ربيعة وبيننا وبينك قفار مضر، وإنا لا نقدر عليك إلاّ في الأشهر الحرم، فأمرنا بأمر ندعو به من وراءنا، وإن عملنا به أدخلنا الله[6] الجنّة؟!

قال: «آمركم بأربع وأنهاكم عن أربع[7]: اعبدوا الله ولا تشركوا به شيئا، وأقيموا الصلاة وآتوا الزكاة، وصوموا رمضان وحجوا البيت[8]، وأعطوا الخمس من الغنائم. وأنهاكم عن الحنتم والدباء والنقير والمزفّت». قالوا: يا رسول الله، ما ندري ما

---

1 وبالله العون والتوفيق: -،د.

2 كثيرا دائما: -،د.

3 سئل: عن نبيذ السقاء: -،د.

4 يا رسول: لرسول، ب.

5 حي: -،د.

6 أدخلنا الله: عملنا ندخل به، ب.

7 آمركم بأربع وأنهاكم عن أربع: أمركم بأربعة وانهاكم عن أربع، ب.

8 وحجوا البيت: -، ب.

النقير[9]؟ قال: «جذع ينقرونه، يرفعون فيه من الفضيخ والماء حتَّى إذا سكن غليانه شربتموه، حتَّى إن أحدكم ليضرب ابن عمه بالسيف»[10].

قال: وفي القوم من قد أصابته جراحة. قال: فجعلنا نخبئها[11] حياء[12] من رسول الله عليه السلام. قال: فيم نشرب؟ قال: «في سقاء الأدم التي تلثّ[13] على أفواهها»[14].

قالوا: يا نبيّ الله، إنَّ أرضنا كثيرة الجرذان لا يتَّقى بها[15]؟ قال النبيّ عليه السلام[16]: «وإن أكلتها الجرذان»[17]. قال[18]: بلغنا أنَّه أمر به وفد احين قد مواعليه، وقال: «كل مسكر حرام»[19].

سئل عن نبيذ الجرّ؟ قال: إذا كان يوكأ عليها فلا بأس بها[20].

سئل عن الرجل يدخل على أخيه فيستقيه، أيسأله عن شرابه؟

---

9 ما ندري ما النقير: يا رسول الله وما النقير، ب.

10 رواه مسلم، باب الأمر بالإيمان بالله ورسوله، ر١٢٧.

11 فجعلنا نخبئها: فجعلت نخفاها، ب.

12 حياء: –، د.

13 تلث: تثلث، ب.

14 تكملة للحديث السابق.

15 لا يتقى بها: –، د.

16 قال النبي عليه السلام: قال رسول الله عليه الصلاة والسلام، ب.

17 رواه مسلم، باب الأمر بالإيمان بالله ورسوله، ر١٢٧.

18 قال: –، ب.

19 رواه البخاري، باب بعث أبي موسى ومعاذ بن جبل رضي الله عنهما إلى اليمن قبل حجة الوداع، ر٤٠٨٧.

20 سئل: عن نبيذ الجرّ؟ قال: إذا كان يوكأ عليها فلا بأس بها: –، د.

قال: إن[21] كان متَّهما[22] فلا تشرب، وإن كان غير متَّهم فلا تسأله إن وثقت به، فاشرب ولا تسأله[23].

سئل عن رجل قدَّم طعامه فيسكب من سقاء في جرّ[24] فيشرب منه؟

قال: كان[25] يكره أن تأكل مع قوم يديرون الكأس. وبلغنا: «أن كلّ مسكر حرام، وكل[26] ما أسكر كثيره فقليله حرام»[27].

سئل عن نبيذ نبذ على عكر؟ قال: يكره أن ينبذ على عكر مسكر[28].

باب ما سئل عنه من الذبائح

سئل عن قوله تعالى: ﴿حُرِّمَتْ عَلَيْكُمُ الْمَيْتَةُ وَالدَّمُ وَلَحْمُ الْخِنْزِيرِ وَمَآ أُهِلَّ لِغَيْرِ اللَّهِ بِهِ وَالْمُنْخَنِقَةُ وَالْمَوْقُوذَةُ وَالْمُتَرَدِّيَةُ وَالنَّطِيحَةُ وَمَآ أَكَلَ السَّبُعُ إِلَّا مَا ذَكَّيْتُمْ وَمَا ذُبِحَ عَلَى النُّصُبِ وَأَنْ تَسْتَقْسِمُواْ بِالأَزْلَامِ﴾[29].

قال: أمّا ﴿وَمَآ أُهِلَّ لِغَيْرِ اللَّهِ بِهِ﴾ فإنّه ما ذبح لغير الله، ﴿وَالْمُنْخَنِقَةُ﴾: تخنق بالحبل حتَّى تموت ثُمَّ يأكلونها، ﴿وَالْمَوْقُوذَةُ﴾: كانوا يضربونها بالخشب حتَّى تموت ثُمَّ يأكلونها.

21 إن: إذا، د.

22 متهما: متهم، ب، د.

23 وإن كان غير متهم ووثقت به فلا تأله واشرب، ب.

24 جر: خمر، د.

25 كان: -، د.

26 كل: -، د.

27 رواه ابن ماجه، باب ما أسكر كثيره فقليله حرام، ر٣٣٩٢.

28 سئل: عن نبيذ نبذ على عكر؟ قال: يكره أن ينبذ على عكر مسكر: -، د.

29 سورة المائدة: ٣.

﴿وَالْمُتَرَدِّيَةُ﴾: التي تتردى في البئر أو غيره[30] فتموت، فيأكلونها. ﴿وَالنَّطِيحَةُ﴾: التي يلتقي عليها الأكباش[31] فيتناطحان فيموت[32] أحدهما فيأكلونه. ﴿وَمَآ أَكَلَ السَّبُعُ إِلاَّ مَا ذَكَّيْتُمْ﴾ يقول: ما أدركتم من هذه الوجوه غير الخنزير وبه حياة أو تحرك[33] شيء منه فذبحته؛ فكُله، إذا ذكرت اسم الله عليه؟ قال: نعم[34].

سئل عن رجل نسي[35] أن يذكر اسم الله؟

قال: لا يؤكل[36] منها شيء[37]؛ لأنّ الله يقول: ﴿فَكُلُواْ مِمَّا ذُكِرَ اسْمُ اللّهِ عَلَيْهِ﴾[38]، وهذا لم يذكر اسم الله عليه[39]، وإنّما ذكر اسم الله باللسان وليس بالقلب[40, 41].

عن قتادة عن الحسن: أنّ رسول الله صلى الله عليه وسلم قال: «إذا ذبحتم فأودجوا، وإذا قتلتم فأحسنوا، فإنّ الله محسن يحبّ الإحسان»[42]؟ قال: يستحبّ ذلك.

---

30 أو غيره: –، ب.
31 الأكباش: الكباش، ب.
32 فيموت: فتموت، ب د.
33 تحرك: تحريك، ب.
34 قال: نعم: –،د. انظر: فتح الباري لابن حجر، ٩/٥٩٩: «... وما أكل السبع ما أخذ السبع الا ما ذكيتم الا ما أدركتم ذكاته من هذا كله يتحرك له ذنب أو تطرف له عين فاذبح واذكر اسم الله عليه فهو حلال».
35 نسي: ينسى، ب.
36 يؤكل: يأكل، ب.
37 شي: شيئا، ب.
38 سورة الأنعام: ١١٨.
39 عليه: –،د.
40 بالقلب: بالأكل،د.
41 سئل عمن لم يذكر اسم الله ناسيا؟ لا تؤكل تلك الذبيحة: +، ب.
42 رواه مسلم، بلفظ: «إِنَّ اللّهَ كَتَبَ الإِحْسَانَ عَلَى كُلِّ شَيْءٍ فَإِذَا قَتَلْتُمْ فَأَحْسِنُوا الْقِتْلَةَ وَإِذَا

سئل عن ذبيحة الغلام الذي لم يحتلم وقد عقل؟

قال: إذا عقل وذكر اسم الله، وأحسن الذبيحة؛ فكل فلا بأس[43].

عن قتادة عن عامر الشعبي عن جابر بن[44] عبد الله الأنصاري: أنَّ غلاما من قومه صاد أرنبا فذبحها فعلقها، فسأل رسول الله عليه السلام عن أكلها؟ فأمره[45] بأكلها[46].

قال: [47]تذبح الأرنب بالمروة، والطير بالقصبة. والمروة تجري مجرى[48] الحديد. والغنم بالمروة[49] فلا بأس بالمروة وتجزئ عن الحديد.

عن أيُّوب عن نافع: أن أمة سوداء كانت لكعب بن مالك ترعى غنما له فعدا سبع على شاة منها فخشيت عليها فذبحتها بمروة[50]، فأتت بها كعبا، فكره أن يأكلها حتَّى أتى إلى رسول الله عليه السلام فسأله عنها، فأمره بأكلها[51].

قال: إذا أحسنت الذبح وذكرت اسم الله فكل[52] فلا بأس.

ذَبَحْتُمْ فَأَحْسِنُوا الذَّبْحَ وَلْيُحِدَّ أَحَدُكُمْ شَفْرَتَهُ فَلْيُرِحْ ذَبِيحَتَهُ»، باب الأَمْرِ بِإِحْسَانِ الذَّبْحِ وَالْقَتْلِ وَتَحْدِيدِ الشَّفْرَةِ، ر٥١٦٧.

43 انظر: آثار الربيع، مسألة ٦٣، ص ٣٤.

44 جابر بن: -،د.

45 فأمره: فأمرها، ب،د.

46 رواه الترمذي، باب ما جاء في الذبيحة بالمروة، ر١٤٧٢.

47 لا: +،د.

48 مجرى: مجز، ب،د.

49 والغنم بالمروة: -،د.

50 بمروة: بمرة، ب،د.

51 رواه ابن حبان، كتاب الذبائح، ر٥٨٩٢.

52 كل: -، ب.

سئل عما يصح الذبح به[53]؟

قال: كان أصحابنا لا يرون الذبح إلاَّ بالحديد والمروة، والقصبة يذبح بها العصفور. وكان الربيع يقول: هي أخف عليه.

سئل عن ذبيحة المرأة؟

قال: إذا أحسنت الذبح وذكرت اسم الله فلا بأس[54].

سئل عن ذبيحة اليهوديّ والنصرانيّ؟

قال: لا بأس بذبيحتهما[55].

سئل عن الرجل يذبح الذبيحة ولا يستقبل بها القبلة؟

إذا ذكر اسم الله فلا بأس، وأحبّ إليّ أن يستقبل القبلة.

سئل عن ذبيحة نصارى بني تغلب[56] وتزويج نسائهم النصارى منهم؟

قال: كان الربيع لا يرى بأسا بمن قرأ الإنجيل ويكره من لم يقرأه، وقال: يؤخذ من أموالهم[57] الخمس ضعف ما يؤخذ على المسلمين في الصدقة.

سئل عن رجل مريض أمر مجوسيّا أن يذبح له ويذكر اسم الله عليه؟

---

53 الذبح به: عما يذبح، ب.

54 انظر: آثار الربيع، مسألة ٢٥، ص ٣٠.

55 انظر: آثار الربيع، مسألة ١٠٧، ص ٣٨.

56 تغلب: ثعلب، ب.

57 أموالهم: مالهم، ب.

قال: حرام لا يحل، وزعم الربيع أنك لو بعثت مع[58] المجوسي[59] بلحم اشتريته من السوق لم يؤكل ذلك اللحم إلاّ أن تكون معه لم تفارقه.

سئل عن ذبيحة الأقلف[60]؟

عن جابر بن زيد، عن ابن عبّاس قال: الأقلف لا تؤكل ذبيحته، ولا تجوز شهادته، ولا يقبل منه حج ولا صلاة. قال: بلغنا هذا وهو قول أصحابنا[61].

سئل عما سمّى المشركون لآلهتهم؟

قال: يكره أن يذبحها لهم رجل مسلم.

سئل عن جنين الأنعام؟

قال: كان يقال: ذكاته ذكاة أمه، غير أنّ أبا عبيدة قال: فيه شيء: قال ضع يدك عليه حين تذبح أمه، فإن تحرك فكله وإن لم يتحرك فلا تأكله. قال: إن كان قد نتن فلا تأكله[62].

سئل عمّن ذبح شاة فنخعها؟

قال: إن كان تعمد ذلك فلا تأكلها، وإن كان السكين سبقه[63] فكلها فلا بأس.

عن قتادة عن خلاس أنّ عليًّا رضي الله عنه قال: يكره من الشاة الطحال، وكل ذي مخلب

58 مع: معه، ب،د.

59 المجوسي: –،د.

60 الأقلف: الأقل،د.

61 الأقلف لا تؤكل ذبيحته ولا شهادته ولا يقبل له عمل: هامش، ب. انظر: آثار الربيع، مسألة ٣٢٣، ص ٧٠.

62 أحق النعام ذكاته: هامش، ب.

63 السيف: +، ب.

من الطير. قال: لا بأس بالطحال إذا لم يقذره، وكل ذي مخلب مكروه، ومن أكله لم يأكل حراما، وكان أبوعبيدة يتأول[64] هذه الآية ﴿قُل لَّآ أَجِدُ فِيمَآ أُوحِيَ إِلَيَّ مُحَرَّمًا﴾[65] الآية.

سئل عما يذبح به؟

قال: كان أصحابنا لا يرون الذبح إلاّ بالحديد والمروة والقصبة يذبح بها العصفور[66].

باب ما سئل عنه من باب الصيد

حدّث[67] عن أيّوب عن أبي قلابة عن الحسن عن أبي ثعلبة[68] أنّه أتى النبيّ عليه السلام فقال: يا نبيّ الله، اكتب لي بأرضي. فقال له نبيّ الله: كيف أكتب بأرض الشام أو بأرض الروم وهي أرض حرب؟ فقال: يا نبيّ الله، والذي بعثك بالحقّ بشيرا ونذيرا لتملكن ما تحت أقدامهم. قال: فأعجب من ذلك النبيّ ﷺ فجعل النبيّ -عليه السلام- ينظر إليه وأصحابه ينظرون إلى ما يقول أبوثعلبة فكتب رسول الله ﷺ له كتابا.

فقلت: يا رسول الله، إنّا بأرض صيد، فما يحل لنا من ذلك وما يحرم علينا؟

فقال نبيّ الله عليه السلام: إذا أرسلت كلبك المعلم والمكلب وذكرت اسم الله فأخذ وقتل فكل، وإذا أرسلت كلبك الذي ليس بمعلم، فما أدركت ذكاته فكله وما لم تدرك فلا تأكله، وما ردّ عليك سهمك فكل.

قال: فقلت: يا رسول الله، إنا بأرض أهلها أهل كتاب، وإنا نحتاج إلى قدورهم وآنيتهم.

---

64 يتأول: يتناول، ب د.

65 سورة الأنعام: ١٤٥.

66 عن قتادة. . . . .بها العصفور: -، ب.

67 حدّث: -،د.

68 ثعلبة: ثعلب، ب،د.

فقال نبيّ الله: «لا تقربوها ما وجدتم منها بدا، فإذا لم تجدوا بدا فاغسلوها بالماء ثمّ اطبخوا واشربوا»[69].

وزعموا أنّه لما ظهر المسلمون على الشام بعد وفاة النبيّ عليه السلام أخرج كتاب رسول الله عليه السلام- وأعطي ما فيه.

قال: وأمّا الكلب المعلم فما أمسك وقتل ولم يأكل منه شيئا فكل، وما أمسك وأكل منه فلا تأكل، فإنّما أخذه لنفسه، والذي لم يعلم فذكّه إن أدركت ذكاته، فإن قتل فلا تأكل.

قال: ونهى رسول الله -عليه السلام- عن لحوم الحمير الأهلية، وعن كلّ ذي ناب من السباع[70]. وأمّا الحمر الأهلية[71] فبلغنا أنّها كانت حمولتهم يومئذ، فخافوا أن يأكلوها ولا تبقى معهم حمولة، وكان أبو عبيدة رحمة الله عليه[72] يتأول[73] الآية: ﴿قُل لاَ أَجِدُ فِيمَا أُوحِيَ إِلَيَّ مُحَرَّمًا على طَاعِمٍ يَطْعَمُهُ إِلاَّ أَن يَكُونَ مَيْتَةً أَوْ دَمًا مَّسْفُوحًا أَوْ لَحْمَ خِنزِيرٍ . . . ﴾[74] الآية.

---

69 رواه الطبراني: المعجم الكبير، ر٦٠٤. لا تقربوا أواني أهل الكتاب إن لم يجد منها بد فحين إذ فليغسلوها: هامش، ب.

70 رواه الترمذي، باب ما جاء في كراهية كل ذي ناب وذي مخلب، ر١٤٧٨.

71 فإنه: -،د.

72 رحمة الله عليه: -، ب.

73 يتأول: يتناول، ب د.

74 سورة الأنعام: ١٤٥. وتمامها: ﴿ فَإِنَّهُ رِجْسٌ أَوْ فِسْقًا أُهِلَّ لِغَيْرِ اللّهِ بِهِ فَمَنِ اضْطُرَّ غَيْرَ بَاغٍ وَلاَ عَادٍ فَإِنَّ رَبَّكَ غَفُورٌ رَّحِيمٌ ﴾.

سئل عن صيد المعراض؟

قال: لا، إلاّ أن تدركه فتذكيه.

قال: وكان أصحابنا يقولون: في صيد الكلاب والسهم ما أمسكن عليك فما[75] لم يأكلن فكل، فإن قتلن أو تغيبن عنك ليلا فلا تأكل، فإنك لا تدري ما قتله كلبك أو سهمك أو غيرهما.

سئل عن رجل أرسل كلبه أو صقره فنسي أن يذكر اسم الله؟

قال: لا يؤكل ما لم يذكر اسم الله عليه، فإن ذكر اسم الله فكل ما لم يتغيب عنك ليلا.

سئل عن رجل أرسل كلبا غير معلم وذكر اسم الله فأخذ صيدا فأدركه صاحبه قد مات تحته؟

قال: لا يؤكل منه شيء إلاّ أن يدركه حيا فيذكيه.

سئل عن رجل أرسل كلبه على صيد فأخذ الصيد فأدركه الرجل وليس معه ما يذكيه؟

قال: إذا أدركه حيا ووقع في[76] يده ومات فلا يأكله، وإن كان معه حديدة فتوانى فلا يأكله إلاّ أن يكون في طلب الحديد أو كان يحدها فلا بأس بأكله.

75 فما: وما، ب، د.

76 في: –، د.

سئل عن رجل يرسل كلبه فيأخذ الصيد فينتهي إليه الرجل ومعه كلب آخر والصيد بينهما قتيل؟

قال: لا يأكله. وإذا رمى الصيد فوجد فيه سهما آخر فلا يأكله.

سئل عن رجل يرمي الصيد فيقع في الماء فيموت؟

قال: إن كان من[77] طير الماء فكل، وإلاّ فلا تأكل.

سئل عن رجل رمى صيدا وذكر اسم الله وأصاب اثنين؟

قال: يأكلهما جميعا وإن أصاب مائة بتلك الرمية فقتلها فكلها[78].

سئل عن رجل ذكر اسم الله وأرسل كلبه على الصيد فغاب عنه ثُمَّ وجده؟

عن قتادة قال: يؤكل[79] ما لم يجد فيه أثرا غير سهمه أو يجده في الماء أو يغيبه ليل.

سئل عمَّن يرمي بالبندق والحجّر؟

قال: لا يؤكله إلاَّ أن يدرك ذكاته.

سئل عن رجل رمى صيدا فتردى من رأس الجبل؟

قال: لا يؤكل[80].

سئل عن الرجل يستعير كلب المجوسيّ أو صقره؟

---

77 من: ‒، د.

78 إذا رميت صيدا بسهم وذكرت اسم الله فكله ولو قتلت ذكيت: هامش، ب.

79 يؤكل: يأكله، ب.

80 يؤكل: لا تأكله، ب.

قال: لا يؤكل ما صاد كلب المجوسيّ أو صقره.

سئل عن الرجل يصيد الصيد[81] بالحبال والمناجل؟

قال: لا يؤكل إلاَّ ما أدركت ذكاته.

سئل عن صيد أصابه قوم بينهم فقطعوه بأسياقهم؟

قال: إن كان حمارا وحشيا فضربه فكل، وإن ضربته نصفين فكل كليهما[82] وإن ضربت العنق فكلهما جميعا[83]، وإن ضربت العجز[84] وكان المقدم أكثر من المؤخر فكل المقدم واترك البقية وإن كان المقدم أكثر فكلهما جميعا، وبلغنا هذا عن الربيع.

سئل عن الضب؟

قال: لا بأس بأكله ما لم يقذره.

سئل عما يقذف البحر من السمك؟

عن نافع أن عبد الرحمن بن أبي هريرة قال لابن عمر: «إن البحر ليأت[85] بماء جار[86] وسمك كثير فما تقول فيما مات منه؟»

قال: لا تأكله، ثُمَّ انطلق إلى البيت فدعا بالمصحف فأتى على هذه الآية: ﴿ أُحِلَّ لَكُمْ صَيْدُ

81 يصيد الصيد: صاد صيدا، ب.

82 كليهما: كلاهما، ب،د.

83 جميعا: -، ب.

84 العجز: -،د.

85 إن البحر ليأت: لماله لا يأت البحر، ب.

86 بماء جار: -،د.

الْبَحْرِ وَطَعَامُهُ مَتَاعًا لَّكُمْ وَلِلسَّيَّارَةِ﴾[87] قال: فانطلق نافع إلى عبد الرحمن فأخبره أنّي وجدته في كتاب الله[88]. قال: وكان أبو عبيدة يقول: إذا لم يقذره فلا بأس بأكله. قال: وكان الفقهاء لا يكرهون منه شيئًا إلاّ أن يقذروه[89] لنتنه فيتركوه[90] من غير تحريم.

ما سئل عنه من باب الشراب

سئل عن لبس الحرير والديباج وآنية الفضّة، وعن[91] الشراب في آنية الفضّة؟ فحدث قتادة عن عروة عن الحسن العراقي أن حذيفة استسقى فأتاه دهقان بشراب في آنية من الفضّة فحذفه بها فأخطأه ثمّ اعتذر إلى القوم. فقال: إنّي كنت تقدّمت إليه أنّ رسول الله نهانا عن الشرب في آنية الفضّة وعن لبس الحرير والديباج، قال: «هي لهم في الدنيا وهي لنا في الآخرة»[92]. قال: بلغنا هذا. وأمّا النساء فلا بأس بالحرير والديباج[93]، وقد رخص المضبب[94] من الفضّة في الأواني[95]، وإنّما يكره الإناء المصمت[96].

---

87 سورة المائدة: ٩٦.

88 في كتاب الله: -، ب.

89 يقذروه: يقذرونه، ب د.

90 فيتركوه: فيتركونه، ب د.

91 عن لبس الحرير والديباج وآنية الفضّة وعن: -،د.

92 رواه البخاري، باب لبس الحرير وافتراشه للرجال وقدر ما يجوز منه، ر٥٤٩٣.

93 قال: «هي لهم في الدنيا وهي لنا في الآخرة»(. قال: بلغنا هذا. وأمّا النساء فلا بأس بالحرير والديباج: -،د.

94 المضبب: بالطبة، ب،د.

95 الأواني: الإيناء، ب.

96 نهى عليه الصلاة والسلام عن الشراب في آنية الفضة: هامش، ب. المصمت: المصمطة، ب،د.

عن قتادة عن أبي المتوكل الناجي عن أبي سعيد الخدري: أن رجلا أتى إلى النبيّ -عليه السلام- فقال: إنَّ أخي يشتكي بطنه. فقال: «اسقه عسلا» ثُمَّ أتاه فقال: إنِّي قد فعلت. فقال: «اسقه عسلا»، ثُمَّ أتاه فقال: إنِّي قد فعلت. قال: «اسقه عسلا»، ثُمَّ أتاه فقال: قد فعلت[97]. فقال: «صدق الله وكذب بطن أخيك، اسقه عسلا»، فسقاه فبرئ الرجل[98].[99]

باب ما سئل عنه من باب اللباس

سئل عن الجبن[100] والجراد والذهب والحرير؟

فحدّث عن قتادة عن عليّ بن عبد الله: أتتني امرأة من عبد القيس فسألتني عن الجبن[101] والجراد والحرير، فمر عبد الله بن عمر، فقلت: اسألي هذا فسألت المرأة ابن عمر عن الجراد فقال: ذِكّي كله، وسألته عن الجبن[102]؟ قال: وما الجبن[103]؟ فنعتته له، فقال: ما صنع المسلمون وأهل الكتاب حلال[104]. فسألته عن الذهب؟ فقال: أكرهه للرجال. فسألته عن الحرير، قال: لا تلبسيه فقالت: في كتاب الله أم نهى عنه رسول الله، قال: في كتاب الله يجد أن من لبسه في الدنيا لم يلبسه في الآخرة، وقال: حرمه الله عليه في

97 قال: «اسقه عسلا»، ثُمَّ أتاه فقال: قد فعلت: -،د.

98 الرجل: -،د.

99 انظر قوله - عليه الصلاة والسلام -: صدق الله وكذب بطن أخيك لرجل: هامش، ب. رواه البخاري، باب الدواء بالعسل، ر٥٣٦٠.

100 الجبن: الجين، ب،د.

101 الجبن: الجين، ب،د.

102 الجبن: الجيز، ب،د.

103 الجبن: الجيز، ب،د.

104 انظر: آثار الربيع، مسألة ١٧١، ص ٤٦.

الآخرة. قال: هو كما قال ابن عمر، إلاّ أن الحرير لا يكرهه الفقهاء للنساء.

عن قتادة عن خلاس أنّ علياً كان يكره من الشاة الطحال، ومن السمك الجرتي، وكل ذي مخلب من الطيور قال: لا بأس بالطحال إذا لم يقذره[105]، وكل ذي مخلب مكروه ومن أكله لم يأكل حراما. وكان أبو عبيدة يتناول هذه الآية: ﴿قُل لَا أَجِدُ فِيمَا أُوحِيَ إِلَيَّ مُحَرَّمًا على طَاعِمٍ يَطْعَمُهُ﴾[106].

سئل عن علم الحرير[107] بالثوب؟

قال: اختلف الناس في العلم في الثوب بالحرير[108]، عن قتادة عن الشعبي عن سويد[109] عن علقمة: أنّ عمر بن الخطّاب رضي الله عنه خطب الناس بالجابية. فقال: «إنّ رسول الله ﷺ نهانا عن لبس الحرير إلاّ موضع أصبع أو أصبعين أو ثلاثة وأشار بأصابعه»[110].

قال: بلغنا ذلك عن عمر بن الخطّاب وكان أصحابنا يكرهونه[111].

عن قتادة عن [أبي] النظر[112] عن الحسن: أنّ عمران[113] بن الحصين قال: إن رسول

105 يقذره: نقدره، ب،د. وقد سبقت هذه الفقرة في باب ما سئل عنه من الذبائح.

106 سورة الأنعام: ١٤٥. سئل: عن الجبن والجراد والذهب والحرير؟ . . . : ﴿قُل لَا أَجِدُ فِيمَا أُوحِيَ إِلَيَّ مُحَرَّمًا على طَاعِمٍ يَطْعَمُهُ﴾: -،د. كل ذي مخلب مكروه ومن المعلم لا يأكل حراما: هامش، ب.

107 الحرير: -، ب.

108 في الثوب بالحرير: -، ب.

109 سويد: مؤيد، ب.

110 رواه مسلم، باب تحريم استعمال إناء الذهب والفضة، ر٥٥٣٨.

111 قال عمر: لا بأس بموضع الأصبعين والثلاثة: هامش، ب.

112 عن أبي النظر: عن النظر، ب،د.

113 عمران: عمر، ب،د.

الله قال: «لا أركب الأرجوان، ولا ألبس المعصفر، ولا ألبس القميص[114] المكفف بالحرير» قال: وأهوى الحسن بيده[115] إلى جيب قميصه: ألا وطيب النساء لون[116] لا ريح فيه، ألا وطيب الرجال ريح لا لون فيه[117].

قال أبو النظر: إنَّمَا قوله في طيب النساء على أنَّها إذا خرجت وأمَّا عند زوجها فإنَّها تتطيب بما شاءت. قال: نعم، وكانوا يكرهون للمرأة أن تتطيب إذا خرجت[118]، وتتطيب لزوجها بما[119] شاءت[120].

سئل عن لبس الخز؟

قال: يكره ذلك للرجال وهو أيضا من السرف[121].

عن أيُّوب عن نافع عن مولى لآل عن ابن عبَّاس[122]: أنّ[123] عليًّا قال: نهاني رسول الله صلى الله عليه وسلم عن لبس المعصفر وعن القسي، وعن خاتم الذهب للرجال[124]، وأن

---

114 القميص: الثوب، ب.

115 بيده: -،د.

116 لون: -،د.

117 ريح: -،د. رواه أبو داود، باب من كرهه (لبس الحرير، ر٤٠٥٠.

118 إذا خرجت: -،د.

119 بما: إذا، ب.

120 طيب النساء لون لا ريح له وطيب الرجال ريح لا لون له: هامش، ب.

121 السرف: الشرف، ب.

122 عن أيوب عن نافع عن مولى لآل عن ابن عباس أن عليا: ب،د. رواه النسائي بهذا السند: «عن أيوب عن نافع عن مولى للعباس أن عليا»، باب خاتم الذهب، ر٥١٧٩.

123 عن ابن عباس أن: -،د.

124 للرجال: -،د.

أقـرأ قرآنا وأنا راكع[125].

قال: يكره خاتم الذهب للرجال، وليس في الركوع قراءة غير التسبيح، ولم نسمع أحدا يكره المعصفر. وقد رخص للمحرم في المعصفر مالم ينتفض[126]

حدَّث عن قتادة عن عليّ بن عبد الله البارقي[127] أنَّه قال: أتتني امرأة من عبد القيس فسألتني عن الجراد والجبن وعن الذهب والحرير فمر عبد الله بن عمر، فقلت: اسألي هذا، فسألت المرأة ابن عمر عن الجراد، فقال: ذكي كله، وسألته عن الجبن فقال: وما الجبن؟ فنعتته[128] له فقال: ما صنع المسلمون وأهل الكتاب فلا بأس بأكله، وسألته عن الذهب فقال: أكرهه للرجال، فسألته عن الحرير فقال: لا تلبسيه. فقالت: أفي كتاب الله أم نهي عنه رسول الله عليه السلام؟ فقال: يقال: إن من لبسه في الدنيا لم يلبسه في الآخرة، أوقال: حرمه الله عليه في الآخرة.

قال: هو كما قال ابن عمر إلاَّ أن الفقهاء لا يكرهون الحرير للنساء[129].

سئل عن الثوب فيه التصاليب؟

فكره لبس ثوب به[130] تصاليب.

125 وأن أقرأ قرآنا وأنا راكع: وأن تقرأ القرآن وأنت راكع، ب.

126 وقد رخص للمحرم في المعصفر مالم ينتفض: -،د.

127 البارقي: الباقي، ب،د.

128 فنعتته: فنعته، ب،د.

129 ذكر سابقا، ب. انظر: ص ١١٩.

130 ثوب به: -، ب.

قتادة عن أيُّوب أن[131] [132]عمرو بن العاص سأل عمر بن الخطّاب أن يرخّص له في لبس الحرير. فقال: لا آمرك. فقال: أليس قد رخص لعبد الرحمن بن عوف والزبير بن العوام. قال عمر[133]: ائت[134] مثلهما؟ قال: سمعنا العلماء يقولون: من جاهد في سبيل الله أو في الحج فما فضل فهو للذي جهد له إلاَّ أن يجعله لمن خرج[135].

سئل عن جائزة السلطان؟

قال: لا بأس بها ما لم يعلم أنَّها حرام بعينها إن[136] أخذ ها غصبا وظلما، والرشوة في الحكم كفر. عن عمر[137].

سئل عن التصاوير؟

قال: يكره إن كان منصوبا[138]، ولا أرى بأسا بما كان يوطأ عليه من بساط أو وسادة وشبه ذلك، مِمَّا يوطأ عليه وينام عليه، ويكره ما كان منه في الجدر والسقف. وبلغنا أنَّ من

131 قتادة عن أيوب: –، ب.
132 عن عمر وروى أيوب بن: +، ب.
133 عمر: –،د.
134 أئت: أن، ب.
135 قال: سمعنا العلماء يقولون من جاهد في سبيل الله أو في الحج فما فضل فهو للذي جهد له إلاَّ أن يجعله لمن خرج: –،د.
136 إن: إنما، ب،د.
137 جائزة السلطان لا بأس بها مالم يعلم أنها حرام بعينها ـ الرشوة في الحكم: هامش، ب. سئل: عن جائزة السلطان؟ قال: لا بأس بها مالم يعلم أنَّها حرام بعينها إنما أخذها غصبا وظلما والرشوة في الحكم كفر. عن عمر: –،د.
138 انظر: آثار الربيع، مسألة ١٨٨، ص ٤٨.

صور صورة في الدنيا كلف أن ينفخ فيها[139] الروح يوم القيامة[140] وليس بفاعل.

سئل عن نقش الخاتم؟

قال: انقش فيها ما شئت غير أنَّه يكره أن ينقش فيها آية من القرآن؛ لمكان[141] الخلاء والبول والجنابة[142].

سئل عن لبس خاتم الذهب والحديد للرجل[143]؟

قال: يكره خاتم الذهب للرجال، ويكره لبس خاتم الحديد إذا كان صاحبه يرى أنَّه يدفع عنه شيئا من الجن.

سئل عن لبس الفراء؟

قال: البسها بعد أن تدبغ، وقال: تكره جلود الأسود والنمور[144].

باب في الهبة وأخذ الأب من مال ولده

سئل هل للرجل أن يرجع في هبته[145]؟

قال: ليس له أن يرجع فيها[146] إذا خرجت من يده.

---

139 فيها: فيه، ب،د.

140 يوم القيامة: -، ب.

141 لمكان: -،د.

142 نقش الخاتم جائز إلا بآية فلا: هامش، ب.

143 للرجل: -،د.

144 سئل عن التصاوير... جلود الأسود والنمور: -، ب.

145 هل للرجل أن يرجع في هبته: عن رجل يرجع في هبته، ب.

146 فيها: -،د.

سئل عمّن[147] يتصدق بصدقة ثُمّ يرثها؟

حدث قتادة عن [عاصم] الأحول عن سلمة بن جنادة عن سفيان بن سلمة: أن رجلا من المهاجرين تصدق على أمه بأرض[148]، فماتت وليس لها وارث غيره. فأتى النبيّ -عليه السلام- فأخبره بذلك فقال له -عليه السلام-: قد وجب الله لك[149] أجرك، ورد الله إليك أرضك، اصنع بها ما شئت[150]. قال: نعم، ذلك له إذا ردها الميراث. وإن كان تصدق عليها لوجه الله ثُمّ ماتت فورثها[151] فهو له، ويقال: أحبّ إلينا أن يمضيها في ذلك الوجه[152].

عن أيُّوب أنّ عمر جعل فرسا في سبيل الله، فأراد أن يشتريها، فسأل عن ذلك النبيّ -عليه السلام- فكره ذلك. قال: يكره أن يرجع في شيء مِمّا يهبه[153].

سئل عن رجل تصدق على أمه بغلام فجعل يصيب من غلته؟

قال: إن كان لله فلا يقربه.

سئل عن جائزة السلطان؟

147 عمن: عن رجل، ب.

148 بأرض: -، د.

149 الله لك: -، د.

150 رواه النسائي: السنن الكبرى، ميراث الولد للوالد المنفرد، ر٦٣١٢.

151 فورثها: فورثتها، ب، د.

152 أن يمضيها في ذلك الوجه: أن يمضيها حيث كانت، ب.

153 ولا غيره: +، ب. الحديث رواه الربيع، باب في الخيل، ر٤٦٢، والبخاري، باب هل يشتري صدقته، ر١٤١٨.

قال: لا بأس بها ما لم يعلم أنّها حرام بعينها إن[154] أخذ ها غصبا وظلما[155] والرشوة في الحكم كفر[156].

سئل عن الضيافة؟

عن قتادة عن الحسن عن الأحنف بن قيس أن عمر بن الخطاب رحمه الله اشترط على الأعاجم للمسلمين يومًا وليلة أن يصلحوا لهم القناطر. قال: بلغنا[157] أنّهم صالحوا أهل السواد[158] أن يضيفوا من مر بهم من المسلمين، وأن يعلفوا دوابهم ويصلحوا لهم القناطر. وكان قتادة يقول: الضيافة ثلاث ليال فما أصاب فوق[159] ذلك فهو صدقة.

سئل هل للرجل أن يأخذ من مال ولده؟

عن عبد الله بن عمرو بن شعيب عن أبيه عن جده أن أعرابيا أتى إلى النبيّ عليه السلام فقال: إن أبي يريد أن يحتاز مالي، فقال له: أمّا علمت أنك ومالك لأبيك؟ ثُمّ قال: إن من أطيب أموالكم كسب أولادكم، فكلوه هنيئا مريئا[160]. قال: بلغنا هذا عن النبيّ عليه السلام.

154 إن: وإنما، ب،د.

155 وظلما: وظلمها، ب،د.

156 سبق ذكرها، د ب.

157 أن عمر بن الخطاب رحمه الله اشترط على الأعاجم للمسلمين يوم وليلة أن يصلحوا لهم القناطر. قال: بلغنا: –،د.

158 أهل السواد: –، ب.

159 فوق: بعد، ب.

160 رواه أبو داود، باب في الرجل يأكل من مال ولده، ر٣٥٣٢.

وهو كما قال[161]: وقد قال بعض الفقهاء: ما يحتاج إليه الوالد من مال ولده فهو له ما لم يضره[162]، وإن ضار فليس له أن يضار به[163]. [164]

عن قتادة عن الحسن أنّه قال: يأخذ الوالد من مال ولده ما شاء، ويغشى جاريته، ويتسرى ويعتق ويصنع ما شاء. قال: نعم، ما لم يضار بولده[165]: يعتق ويطأ ويهب ما لم يضارّ ولده[166]، فإذا غشي جاريته أشهد وأعلم ابنه ذلك؛ لئلا يغشاها بعده. والوالدة ليست بمنزلة الوالد في مال الولد[167]. [168]

سئل عن عتق ولد الزنا؟

قال: لا أرى به بأسا إذا كان متحرجا عفيفا[169].

سئل عن عتق اليهود والنصارى في الواجب؟

قال: لا بأس به.

ما سئل عنه من باب اللقطة

سئل عن اللقطة؟

---

161 وهو كما قال: –،د.

162 ما لم يضره: –،د.

163 يضار به: له مضارته، ب.

164 انظر هل يأخذ الرجل من مال ابنه أم لا: هامش، ب.

165 يضار بولده: يضر ولده، ب.

166 يعتق ويطأ ويهب مالم يضار ولده: –، ب.

167 الولد: الابن، ب.

168 سئل هل للرجل . . . في مال ولده» . ذكرلاحقا، ب.

169 سئل: عن عتق ولد الزنا؟ قال: لا أرى به بأسا إذا كان متحرجا عفيفا: –،د.

قال: يعرّفها بها[170] سنة فإن جاء صاحبها وإلاّ تصدق بها على ذوي الفاقة ممن[171] لا يعول، فإن جاء صاحبها بعد ذلك خيّره[172] بين الأجر أو الغرم.

قال: نعم، إذا تصدق بها على ذوي الحاجة[173] فيضعها حيث شاء في قرابة أو غيرها، فقد صار ضامنا لها إذا جاء صاحبها[174]. وقال: يعرفها سنة فإن جاء صاحبها وإلاّ تصدق بها على أهل الحاجة قرابة أو غيرهم فهو لها ضامن، وإن كان محتاجا أكلها. فإن جاء صاحبها خيره بين الأجر أو يرد عليه مثل[175] متاعه فما اختار فهو له.

وكان أصحابنا يقولون: كلّ لقطة توجد في السفر من عصا أو سوط أو مخرز أو أداة[176] ممّا لا يرجع إليها صاحبها انتفع به وعرفه، فإن وجدت[177] صاحبها فادفعها إليه، وإن لم[178] يوجد فهو لك إن احتجت إليه، وإلاّ فاعطه من يحتاج إليه[179].

سئل عن الضالّة[180]؟

عن قتادة عن سعيد بن المسيب أنّ عمر بن الخطّاب -رضي الله- عنه قال: «لا يأوي

170 بها: +، ب.

171 ممن: من، ب،د.

172 خيّره: فخيره، ب د.

173 على ذوي الحاجة: -،د.

174 إذا جاء صاحبها: -،د.

175 متاعه: -، ب.

176 أداة: دوات، ب.

177 وجدت، وجد، ب،د.

178 لم: -،د.

179 لا يضم الضوال إلا ضال: هامش، ب.

180 سئل: عن الضالة: -،د.

الضالّة إلاّ ضال»[181] . قال: يكره ذلك إلاّ ضالّة ليعرف بها صاحبها وما سميت لك مِمّا لا يرجع إليه صاحبه إن احتجت إليه[182] .

عن معمر عن الزهري عن سعيد بن المسيب أنّ عمر بن الخطّاب[183] رضي الله عنه كتب إلى عماله[184] : ألاّ تعارضوا الضوال من الإبل[185] ، فكانت تتناتج[186] هملا، وترد الماء لا يعرض لها، فلمّا ولي عثمان كتب إلى عُمّاله أن ضموها فعرفوا بها، فإن جاء صاحبها فادفعوها إليه، وإلاّ فبيعوها[187] واجعلوا ثمنها في بيت المال[188] ، وأخرجوا زكاتها كلّ عام حتّى يجيء[189] طالبها، فتدفعوها إليه، أو تأتي الزكاة على آخرها.

قال غيره: لا يعرف هذا، ومن قبل ضالّة فهو لها ضامن حتّى يؤديها إلاّ أن تموت أو يأكلها السبع في غير ضياع.

سئل عن قتل الحداة؟

قال: ما رأينا أحدا من[190] الفقهاء ينهون عن قتل شيء منها.

---

181 رواه الربيع عن ابن عباس مرفوعا إلى النبي صلى الله عليه وسلم، باب في الضالة، ر٦١٤.

182 إن احتجت إليه: –،د.

183 رحمه الله: +، ب.

184 عماله: عمال، ب،د.

185 من الإبل: –، ب.

186 تتناتج: تتناتج، ب د.

187 فبيعوها: فتبيعوها، ب د.

188 مال المسلمين: +، ب.

189 لها: +، ب.

190 أحدا من: –،د.

باب في وصيّة أبي بكر رضي الله عنه ليزيد بن أبي سفيان، وفي مسائل أخرى

عن قتادة[191] عن يزيد بن أبي مالك أنّه لما وجّه[192] أبو بكر بن أبي قحافة[193] رضي الله عنه يزيد بن أبي سفيان إلى الشام أميرا مشى معه وجعل يوصيه فقال يزيد[194]: يا خليفة رسول الله إمّا أن أنزل وإمّا أن تركب، فقال: ما أنت بنازل وما أنا براكب إني احتسبت خطاي هذه في سبيل الله. ثُمّ قال: إنك ستأتي إلى قوم حبسوا أنفسهم وزعموا أن ذلك[195] لله فذرهم وما حبسوا له أنفسهم وإنك ستأتي إلى[196] قوم قد فحصوا وسط رؤوسهم وتركوا ما[197] حولها كالعصائب فاضرب بالسيف ما فحصوا به عن رؤوسهم وإنك ستؤتى بطعام، فاذكر اسم الله على كلّ إناء تأكل منه، وإني أوصيك بعشر: لا تقتل طفلا صغيرا ولا شيخا هرما ولا امرأة ولا تعقرن[198] نخلا ولا تحرقنه، ولا تخربن عامرا، ولا تقطعن مثمرا ولا تقتلن شاة ولا بقرة، ولا تذبحن شاة ولا بقرة[199] إلاّ لمأكل أو حاجة ولا تجَبَّر ولا تغلل[200] اندفع باسم الله. قال: بلغنا هذا إلاّ ضرب السيف لم نسمع به.

---

191 عن قتادة: –، ب.

192 وجه: جهد، ب.

193 بن أبي قحافة: –،د.

194 يزيد: –، ب.

195 أن ذلك: –، ب.

196 إلى: على، ب.

197 ما: –،د.

198 تعقرن: تحقرن، ب.

199 ولا تذبحن شاة ولا بقرة: –، ب.

200 تغلل: تتعال، ب، تعال،د.

باب الطيرة[201]

سئل عن الطيرة؟

عن قتادة: أنَّ رسول الله عليه السلام قال: «لا عدوى ولا طيرة»[202]. قال: نعم، لا عدوى ولا طيرة.

عن قتادة: أنَّ ابن عبَّاس قال: إنَّمَا الطيرة على من أمرته أو نهته، فإن مضى على وجهه فهو متوكل، وإن نكس فهو متطيّر.

سئل عن رجل يلعن الريح؟

عن قتادة عن أبي العالية: أن رجلا خالجته الريح رداءه فلعنها، فقال رسول الله -عليه السلام-: «إنَّها مأمورة و[203] من لعن شيئا لا ينبغي له لعنه رجعت اللعنة على صاحبها»[204]؟. قال: بلغنا هذا عن النبيّ صلى الله عليه وسلم[205].

باب في الحيَّات والضيافة

سئل عن قتل الحيَّات

قال: ما رأينا أحدا من الفقهاء ينهون عن قتل شيء منها. وفي المردود قال عليه السلام: «اقتل الحيَّات صغارها وكبارها»[206].

---

201 باب الطيرة: -،د.

202 رواه البخاري، باب في الطيرة، ر٥٤٢١.

203 أنها مأمورة و: -،د.

204 رواه أبو داود، باب في اللعن، ر٤٩١٠.

205 لا يجوز لعن الريح: هامش، ب.

206 باب: في الحيَّات والضيافة سئل: عن قتل الحيَّات قال: ما رأينا أحدا من الفقهاء ينهون عن

باب في الحمى والاختتان

سئل عن الحمى والاختتان[207]؟

حدث قتادة: أنَّ النبيّ عليه السلام قال: الحمى فيح[208] من فيح[209] جهنَّم فنحوها عنكم بالماء البارد[210]. قال: بلغنا هذا[211] أنَّه قال[212]: أطفئوها عنكم[213] بالماء البارد.

سئل عن خفاض النساء؟

عن قتادة قال: هو للنساء مكروه وللرجال سنة؟ قال: نعم[214]، وليس النساء فيه[215] مثل الرجال؛ فالرجل إذا لم يختتن لم تقبل شهادته ولم توكل ذبيحته ولم يصلّ خلفه.

باب الكَمْأة[216]

سئل عن الكمأة؟

قتل شيء منها وفي المردود قال: اقتل الحيّات صغارها وكبارها: -،د. رواه الربيع، باب الحجة على من قال إن أهل الكبائر ليسوا بكافرين، ر٧٤٤.

207 باب في الحمى والاختتان: سئل: عن الحمى والاختتان: -،د.

208 فيح: -،د.

209 فيح من فيح: كير من كير، ب.

210 رواه البخاري، باب صفة النار وأنها مخلوقة، ر٣٠٨٨.

211 هذا: -،د.

212 كان: +، ب.

213 عنكم: -،د.

214 قال: نعم: -،د.

215 فيه: -،د.

216 باب: الكمية: -،د.

عن قتادة[217] عن شهر بن حوشب عن عبد الرحمن بن غانم عن أبي هريرة: أن أناسا قالوا[218]: إن الكمأة جُدَرِي في الأرض فبلغ ذلك[219] [220] النبيّ عليه السلام قال: «إن الكمأة[221] من المنّ، وماؤها شفاء للعين[222]، وإن[223] العجوة من شجر الجنّة، وأنّ العجوة[224] من الجنّة، وهو دواء من السمّ»[225].

سئل عن الكلب يكون في الدار، وفي الدار من هو له كاره؟

قال: وإنّما إثم ذلك على ربّ الدار الذي يملكها[226]. قال: كان أصحابنا يكرهون الكلاب إلاّ لزرع أو ضرع أو صيد، ويكرهون ما سوى ذلك[227].

سئل عن نصاب الجوز؟

قال: يكره ويقال هو الشيطان ورأيت الربيع يكره أكله إلا ما أعطيت منه بيدك.

---

217 عن قتادة: -،د.

218 قالوا: قال، ب،د.

219 أن أناسا قال: أن الكمأة جدري في الأرض فبلغ ذلك: -،د. رواه أحمد، ر ٨٣٠٧.

220 أن: +،د.

221 الكمأة: الكمة، ب،د.

222 رواه البخاري، باب المن شفاء للعين، ر ٣٥٨١.

223 إن: -،د.

224 العجوة: العجمة، في النسخ.

225 وأنّ العجمة من الجنّة وهو دواء من السم: -،د. رواه الترمذي، باب ما جاء في الكمأة والعجوة، ر ٢٠٦٨.

226 قال: وإنّما أثم ذلك على ربّ الدار الذي يملكها: -،د.

227 ويكرهون ما سوى ذلك: -،د. أصحابنا يكرهون الكلاب إلا لزرع أو ضرع وينكرون: هامش، ب.

سئل عن العطاس؟

قال: إذا عطس إنسان فحمد الله يقول من حوله[228]: يرحمك الله، قال[229] ويقول هو: يهديكم الله.[230]

سئل عن الرجل يكنى بأبي القاسم؟

قال: يكره أن يكنى بأبي القاسم؛ فيما بلغنا[231]؛ لأنّه كنية النبيّ عليه السلام.

باب في التسليم والاستئذان ومسائل أخرى

سئل عن التسليم على أهل الكتاب؟

قال: لا تبدؤوا أهل الكتاب بالسلام ولكن يرد عليهم، ولا يسلم على المجوسيّ ولا يرد عليه[232].

سئل عن الاستئذان؟

عن ميمون العناب[233] أن أبا موسى الأشعري أتى باب عمر بن الخطّاب رضي الله عنه فاستأذن ثلاثا فلم يؤذن له فرجع ثُمَّ لقي عمر، فقال: ما ردك عن بابنا؟ قال: سمعت رسول الله عليه السلام يقول: «الاستئذان ثلاثا فمن لم يؤذن له فيهن فليرجع»[234].

228 حوله: خلفه، د.

229 قال: –، د.

230 ما يقول العطاس وما يرد عليه: هامش، ب.

231 فيما بلغنا: –، د.

232 لا تبدوا أهل الكتاب بالسلام ولكن يرد عليهم بخلاف المجوسي: هامش، ب.

233 لم أجد ميمون بن العناب في سند هذا الأثر، ولعله عمرو بن ميمون.

234 رواه البخاري، باب التسليم والاستئذان ثلاثا، ر٥٨٩١.

فقال عمر: لتأتيني على ذلك ببيّنة، وإلاَّ عاقبتك[235]. فأتى حلقة في المسجد فيها طلحة بن عبيد الله والزبير بن العوام[236] فذكر ذلك لهما وناشدهما فجاء بهما[237] فشهدا عند عمر.

سئل هل للرجل أن يدخل الحوانيت بغير إذن؟

قال: ليس فيها إذن إذا افتحت للناس، ولا[238] في العرس إذا دعي الناس، وفتح الباب.

سئل عن الماشية تُحلب بغير إذن أهلها؟

قال: لا يحلّ أن تحلب بغير إذن أهلها إلاَّ أن يعلم أن صاحبها راض بذلك.

سئل عن الرجل يدخل الحائط ليأكل من ثمره؟

قال: إن اضطر إلى أكله فليأكل، وإن لم يضطر فلا يأكل إلاَّ بإذن [أهله]، إلاَّ أن يعلم أن أهل الحائط أذنوا بذلك ورضوا به[239].

سئل عن الخضاب؟

قال: كان أبو عبيدة[240] يكره الأسود[241] للشيخ ولا بأس به للشباب. بلغنا [ذلك]، وكان أبو عبيدة يكره الأسود للشيخ[242]. قال: هذا رأينا[243] وقد رأينا بعض الفقهاء

235 وإلا عاقبتك: -، د.
236 بن العوام: -، د.
237 فجاء معهما: فجاءا معه، ب.
238 ولا: كذلك، ب.
239 سئل عن الماشية... ورضوا به: -، ب.
240 كان أبو عبيدة: -، د
241 الأسود: السواد، ب.
242 بلغنا... للشيخ: -، ب.
243 قال: هذا رأينا: -، د.

يخضب وبعضهم يترك، وبلغنا: أنّ النبيّ عليه السلام أمر به.

باب ما سئل عنه في بيع جلود المَيْتَة ولحم الخيل

سئل عن جلود السباع؟

قال: يكره جلود الأسود والنسور.

سئل عن الفرو؟

قال: البسها إلاّ أنه يكره أن تدبغها أنت، إلاّ أن يدبغها غيرك[244] فلا بأس[245].

سئل عن بيع جلود المَيْتَة؟

قال: إذا دبغت فلا بأس ببيعها.

عن قتادة عن الحسن عن سلمة بن المحتم: أن النبيّ عليه السلام أتى يوم خيبر على قربة فيها ماء فدعا منها بماء، فقالت[246] امرأة: إنّها جلد[247] ميتة، فقال: اسألوها: أدبغت؟ قالت: نعم. فقال رسول الله صلى الله عليه وسلم: «دباغ الأديم طهارته[248]، فأوتي رسول الله عليه السلام منها بماء فقضى به حاجته».

سئل عن لحوم الجلاّلة وألبانها؟

244 غيرك: غيره، ب. + -،د.

245 سئل: عن جلود السباع؟ قال: يكره جلود الأسود والنسور. سئل: عن الفرو؟ قال: البسها إلاّ أنه يكره أن تدبغها أنت إلاّ أن يدبغها غيرك فلا بأس: -،د.

246 فقالت: وعندها، ب.

247 جلد: قربة، ب.

248 ذكاته، ب. رواه أحمد، ر٣٥٢١.

عن قتادة عن مجاهد عن عبد الرحمن بن أبي ليلى: أنَّ رسول الله صلى الله عليه وسلم نهى عن لحوم الجلاَّلة وألبانها[249]. قال: نعم، يكره ركوبها وأن يحجّ عليها[250]. وعن أبي الزبير عن مجاهد أنَّ ابن عمر كان يكره أن تركب الجلاَّلة وأن[251] يؤكل لحم الجلاَّلة[252] أو يشرب لبنها قال: نعم، إلاَّ أن تحصر أربعين ليلة في كلأ أو تعلف حتَّى يذهب عنها.

سئل عن لحوم الخيل؟

عن قتادة عن الحسن: أنَّه لم يكن يرى بأسًا بها[253]، وهو قول قتادة.

سئل عن أكل الثوم والبصل[254]؟

قال: يكره لرائحته[255] وأن يؤذي الناس[256] وأما الحرام فلا[257]، وبلغنا: أنَّ النبيّ عليه السلام قال: «من أكل من هذه[258] الشجرة الخبيثة[259] فلا يصلِّي معنا»[260]، من أجل رائحتها ولو كانت حراما لنهى عنها.

249 رواه أبو داود، باب النهي عن أكل الجلالة وألبانها، ر٣٧٨٧,
250 قال: نعم، يكره ركوبها وأن يحجّ عليها: -،د. في مصنف عبد الرزاق: «وكان يكره أن يحج عليها»، باب الجلاَّلة، ر٨٧١٢.
251 تركب الجلاَّلة وأن: -،د.
252 لحم الجلاَّلة: لحمها، ب.
253 بها: به، ب،د.
254 والبصل: -،د.
255 لرائحته: لأجل الرائحة، ب.
256 وأن يؤذي الناس: لئلا يؤذي به الناس، ب.
257 وأما الحرام فلا: -،د.
258 هذه: هاتين، ب.
259 الخبيثة: الخبيثتين، ب، + -د.
260 رواه مسلم، باب نَهْيِ مَنْ أَكَلَ ثُومًا أَوْ بَصَلاً أَوْ كُرَّاثًا أَوْ نَحْوَهَا عَنْ حُضُورِ الْمَسْجِدِ، ر١٢٨٤.

سئل عن الفأرة إذا وقعت في إدام قوم أو وزغة أو دابة من نحوها فماتت فيه[261] ؟

قال: إن شاؤوا دهنوا به الأدم وإن شاؤوا أسرجوا به إلاَّ أن يكون في سمن جامد فتلقى وما حولها ويؤكل ما بقي إن لم يقذروه.

سئل عن شاة تحلب بغير إذن أهلها؟

قال: لا يحلّ أن تحلب إلاَّ بإذن أهلها إلاَّ أن يعلم أن صاحبها راضٍ بذلك لا يكره[262] .

سئل عن فارة وقعت في قدر قوم؟

قال: إن غلت مع اللحم فلا يؤكل لحمه ولا مرقه؟

سئل عن الثمر يدخله الرجل ويأكل منه؟

قال: إن اضطر إليه فليأكل، وإن لم يضطر فلا يأكل إلاَّ بإذن أهله إلاَّ أن يعلم أن أهل الحائط أذنوا بذلك ورضوا[263] .[264]

261 فيه: -،د.

262 سئل: عن شاة تحلب بغير إذن أهلها؟ قال: لا يحلّ أن تحلب إلاَّ بأذن أهلها إلاَّ أن يعلم أن صاحبها راضٍ بذلك لا يكره: -،د.

263 سئل: عن الثمر يدخله الرجل ويأكل منه؟ قال: إن اضطرر إليه فليأكل، وإن لم يضطر فلا يأكل إلاَّ بأذن أهله إلاَّ أن يعلم أن أهل الحائط أذنوا بذلك ورضوا: -،د.

264 به فرحون، يجوز أخذ ما يبقى في الحائط والأمر به من الثمار والحب بهذا انتقال أهله عنه وتعصيبه وكذلك أخذ ما يسقط من الحب عند الحصاد مما لا يعتني صاحب الزرع بلقطه: هامش، ب

ما سئل عنه من باب الضمان والشهادة

سئل عن رجل حمل غلاما على فرس فأصاب الفرس إنسانا؟

قال: إن كان الذي ركب الفرس رجلا فهو ضامن. وإن كان غلاما[265] لم يبلغ فالضمان[266] على صاحب الفرس. فإن وقع الغلام وهلك أو جرح فصاحب الفرس ضامن.

سئل عن رجل ركب دابة فضربها رجل آخر فضربت برجلها رجلا[267] آخر؟

قال: الذي ضربها[268] ضامن. وقال: يضمن صاحب الدابة ما أصابت بمقدمتها فلا بأس عليه إلاّ أن يقيمها بلجام.

سئل عن جدار مائل أشهدوا[269] على صاحبه ثُمَّ وقع الجدار فأصاب إنسانا؟

قال: هو ضامن، وإن لم يشهدوا عليه فلا ضمان عليه.

سئل عن الكلب العقور يكون في الدار فيصيب إنسانا؟

قال: إن دخل بإذن ربّ الدار فعقره فصاحب الدار ضامن، وإن دخل بغير إذن فلا ضمان عليه[270].

---

265 غلاما: –، ب.

266 فالضمان: فهو، د.

267 رجلا: إنسانا، ب.

268 ضربها: ضرب الدابة، ب.

269 أشهدوا: شهدوا، ب.

270 الكلب العقور: هامش، ب.

سئل عن المجلود في القذف أتجوز شهادته؟

قال: كلّ مجلود في حد[271] إذا[272] علم منه خير أو تاب قبلت شهادته، ومن شهد في أموال الناس بزور لم تقبل شهادته ولو تاب حتّى يرد ذلك المال.

سئل عن شهادة السمع؟

قال: إذا كان الرجل مع قوم فشهد وسمع وحفظ ذلك، أدى[273] شهادته إذا كان عدلا[274].

سئل عن رجل قص عليه قوم قصة، فقالوا: لا تشهد علينا بما تسمع به؟

قال: إذا قالوا له ذلك فلا يشهد عليهم بشيء.

سئل عن شهادة الأب لابنه والابن لأبيه؟

قال: إذا كانوا عدولا جازت شهادتهم بعضهم لبعض[275].

سئل عن شهادة القاضي؟

قال: يرفع[276] إلى من هو فوقه وإن يشأ أقعد رجلا فحكم بين القوم وشهد بما يعلم.

---

271 حد: قذف، ب.

272 إذا: -، د.

273 أدى: فهي، ب.

274 شاهد الزور لم تقبل له توبة حتى يرد ما أتلف بها: هامش، ب.

275 انظر: آثار الربيع، مسألة ٢٥١، ص ٥٩.

276 يرفع: يدفع، ب.

سئل عن شهادة الأعمى؟

قال: يقال: إذا عرف الرجل الذي يشهد عليه كما يعرف ابنه[277] وكان عدلا جازت شهادته.

سئل عن شهادة الورثة بعضهم على بعض؟

قال: إذا شهد اثنان عدلان جازت شهادتهما على بقيتهم[278].

سئل عن شهادة من ترك الجمعة ثلاثا من غير عذر؟

قال: إنّه أهل ألاّ تجوز شهادته[279].

سئل عن نفر رأوا رجلا أصاب حدا فكتموا[280] ثمّ غضبوا عليه؟ فشهدوا عند غضبهم أنهم لا تقبل شهادتهم عند الغضب وقد كتموها[281] عند الرضا وهو إليها محتاج[282].

سئل عن شهادة الصبيان على الصبيان والمملوك على المملوك؟

قال: تكتب شهادتهم فإذا أدرك الصبيان وعتق المملوك فحفظوا الشهادة جازت شهادتهم، واليهود والنصارى مثل ذلك إذا أسلموا.

سئل عن شهادة اليهوديّ على النصرانيّ والنصرانيّ على اليهوديّ؟

277 ابنه: الله، ب.

278 شهادة الورثة بعضهم على بعض تجوز إذا كانوا عدولا: هامش، ب.

279 قال: لا تجوز شهادته، ب.

280 فكتموا: فكتبوا، ب د.

281 كتموها: كتبوها، ب د.

282 سئل: عن نفر رأوا رجلا أصاب حدا فكتّبوا ثمّ غضبوا عليه؟ فشهدوا عند غضبهم أنهم لا تقبل شهادتهم عند الغضب وقد كتبوها عند الرضا وهو إليها محتاج: –، د.

قال: شهادة اليهود على اليهود جائزة وشهادة النصرانيّ على النصرانيّ جائزة، ولا تجوز [شهادة] اليهوديّ على النصرانيّ ولا النصرانيّ على اليهوديّ، وشهادة المسلمين عليهم جائزة ولا تجوز شهادتهم على أحد من المسلمين.

سئل عن شهادة النساء فيما لا ينظر إليه الرجل؟

قال: شهادة[283] القابلة والمرضعة إذا كانتا من ذوات العدل جازت شهادتهما.

سئل فيم لا تقبل شهادة النساء؟

قال: لا تجوز شهادتهن في الحدود، وتجوز فيما سوى ذلك[284].

سئل عن شهادة المرأة على المرأة؟

قال: جائزة.

سئل عن رجل باع امرأته برضاها؟

قال: يعاقبان وينكلان ولا يجتمعان. وكل رجل سرق عبدا أو حرا، فإن كان العبد أو الحر كبيرين لم يقطع سارقهما؛ لأنهما لو شاءا[285] أنكرا ذلك فإن كان صغيرين فعليه القطع[286].

283 شهادة: -، ب.

284 انظر: آثار الربيع، مسألة ٢٣٦، ص ٥٧.

285 شاءا: سابا، ب،د.

286 سئل: عن رجل باع امرأته برضاها؟ قال: يعاقبان وينكلان ولا يجتمعان. وكل رجل سرق عبدا أو حر، فإن كان العبد أو الحر كبيرين لم يقطع سارقهما؛ لأنهما لو شاء أنكر ذلك فإن كان صغيرين فعليه القطع: -،د.

باب في المحارب والحدود

سئل عن قوله عزّ وجل: ﴿ إِنَّمَا جَزَآءُ ٱلَّذِينَ يُحَارِبُونَ ٱللَّهَ وَرَسُولَهُۥ وَيَسْعَوْنَ فِي ٱلْأَرْضِ فَسَادًا أَن يُقَتَّلُوٓاْ أَوْ يُصَلَّبُوٓاْ أَوْ تُقَطَّعَ أَيْدِيهِمْ وَأَرْجُلُهُم مِّنْ خِلَٰفٍ أَوْ يُنفَوْاْ مِنَ ٱلْأَرْضِ. . . ﴾[287] الآية.

قال: حدود الله أربعة أنزلها في هذه الآية[288]: أمّا من حارب الله فسفك الدماء وأصاب المال فعليه الصلب، وأمّا من حارب فسفك الدماء فعليه القتل، وأمّا من حارب الله وأصاب المال ولم يسفك الدماء فعليه القطع، وأمّا من حارب الله[289] ولم يسفك[290] الدماء ولم يصب مالا فعليه النفي.

سئل عن اللص إذا كانت معه حديدة؟

قال: إذا أشار بها قطعت يده ورجله وهو أخبث من السارق.

سئل عن السارق: في كم تقطع يده؟

قال: في ثلث دينار تقطع فيه يده.

سئل عن لص ثقب بنيانا[291] فأدخل رأسه وصدره؟

قال: لا يقطع حتّى يحمل المتاع فإذا جمع المتاع وحمله قطع خرج به أو لم يخرج، وقال

---

287 سورة المائدة: ٣٣. وتمامها: ﴿ ذَٰلِكَ لَهُمْ خِزْيٌ فِي ٱلدُّنْيَا وَلَهُمْ فِي ٱلْآخِرَةِ عَذَابٌ عَظِيمٌ ﴾.

288 في هذه الآية: –، ب.

289 الله: –، د.

290 يسفك: يصب، د.

291 بنيانا: بيتا، ب.

غيره: إذا جمع المتاع ولم يخرجه من حرزه فلا قطع عليه.

سئل عن رجل يسرق فتقطع يده ثمّ يسرق؟

قال: يكره أن تقطع اليدان[292] جميعا فيبقى[293] بغير يد ولكن تقطع الرجل اليسرى إذا قطعت اليد اليمنى، وكل من دخل بيتا بإذن أهله ثمّ سرق فلا قطع عليه.

عن قتادة قال: كل[294] من قذف المسلم من الناس أجمعين يهوديّا كان أو نصرانيّا أو حرا أو عبدا فعليه الحد، ومن سرق فعليه القطع والحد[295].

وقال: أمّا السارق من كان قطع.

وأمّا الحدود فإنّمَا هي على أهل الصلاة وأهل الكتاب، وليس على العبيد حدود[296].

قال: ليس على من دخل الحوائط فسرق قطع إلاّ أن يكون عليه حافظ وباب ومن سرق قيمة أربعة دراهم قطع.

سئل عن عبد سرق أهله؟

قال: ليس عليه قطع.

سئل عن المسروق له أهل[297] هل له أن يعفو عن السارق إذا أخذه؟

قال: نعم.

292 اليدان: اليدين، ب،د.

293 فيبقى: فيترك،د.

294 كل: -، ب.

295 فعليه القطع والحد: فعليه القطع،د.

296 حدود: الحدود، ب،د.

297 له أهل: -،د.

سئل عن السارق أخذ فاعترف ولم تقم[298] عليه بيّنة؟

قال: إذا اعترف وكان حرا قطعت يده، وإن كان مملوكا لم يجز اعترافه.

سئل عن الحدود إذا رفعت إلى الحاكم، هل فيها عفو؟

قال: لا يحلّ تركها، لا عفو حينئذ، والعفو قبل أن يرفع إلى الحاكم. قال: بلغنا هذا عن جابر بن زيد، وقال: بلغنا أيضا أنّه أتاه آت فذكر له أن سارقا سرق فقال: اتركوه قبل أن ينتهي إلى الحاكم فإنّه إذا انتهى إليه لم يكن له عفو.

سئل عن الخلسة: هل يقطع فيها؟

قال: لا يقطع فيها.

سئل عن رجل وجدت عنده سرقة فادعى أنّه اشتراها؟

حدّث عن قتادة: أنّ عمر بن عبد العزيز كتب في رجل إن قامت عليه البيّنة أخذت منه وأتبع صاحبه، وإن لم تكن بيّنة أخذت منه واستودع في[299] السجن. قال: الله أعلم. فأما القطع فليس عليه شيء[300].

سئل عن رجل سرق من الغنيمة؟

قال: إذا كان له فيها نصيب فلا قطع عليه، وإن لم يكن له فيها نصيب قطع.

سئل عن السارق: هل يغرم ما سرق إذا قطع[301]؟

298 تقم: يقام، ب.

299 في: -، د.

300 فليس عليه شيء: وليس عليه قطع، ب.

301 إذا قطع: -، ب.

قال: إذا قطعت يده فلا غرم عليه، إلاَّ أن يوجد[302] شيء من المتاع فيوجد بعينه فيؤخذ، وأمَّا ما استهلك فهو ثمن يده.

سئل عن رجل أقر بسرقة عند قوم ثمَّ أكذب نفسه عند السلطان؟

قال: إذا أقر من غير عقوبة قطع[303].

سئل عن رجل باع امرأته برضاها؟

قال: يعاقبان وينكلان ولا يجتمعان، وكل رجل سرق عبدا أو حرا، فإن كان الحر والعبد كبيرين[304] لم يقطع سارقهما؛ لأنَّهما لو شاءا أنكرا ذلك، فإن كانا صغيرين فعليه القطع[305].

سئل عن الرجل إذا اجتمعت عليه حدود وفيها قتلة؟

قال: يؤخذ بكل شيء أصابه من سرقة أو قذف أو مثلة مثلها ثمَّ يقتل ثمَّ إلى النار[306].

سئل عمَّن شرب خمرا ولم يسكر: أعليه حدّ أم لا؟

قال: من شرب الخمر سكر أم لم يسكر أقيم عليه[307] الحدّ، ومن سكر من غير الخمر أقيم عليه الحد.

302 يوجد: يأخذ، د.

303 والسارق إذا قطعت يده لا غرم عليه: هامش، ب.

304 كبيرين، كبيران، ب، د.

305 ذكر السوأل في مكان سابق، ب.

306 ثم يقتل ثم الى النار: ثمَّ يقبل إلى النار، ب.

307 أقيم عليه: -، ب.

سئل عن جلد الحدود، وعن قوله عزّ وجل: ﴿وَلَا تَأْخُذْكُمْ بِهِمَا رَأْفَةٌ فِي دِينِ اللَّهِ﴾[308] .

قال: هو[309] الجلد الشديد الفتل يتراوحه[310] الرجال كلّ رجل يجلده[311] عشرين سوطا على جسده كله ورأسه وظهره وبدنه .

سئل عن جلد الخمر وما سواه من التعزير والقذف؟

قال: جلد بين الجلدين لا يوضع ثوبه[312]، ولا يرفع الجلاد يده حتّى يرى بياض إبطيه .

سئل عمّن يعمل عمل قوم لوط؟

قال: يلقى من أطول شيء يقدر عليه ثمّ يرمى بالحجارة .

سئل عمّن زنا بذات محرم؟

قال: يقتل بالسيف ثمّ إلى النار .

سئل عن المرتد عن الإسلام؟

قال: إذا أخذ استتيب فإن لم يتب قتل، رجلا كان أو[313] امرأة[314] .

سئل عن العبد إذا ارتد عن دينه؟

قال: لا يقتل إنّما هو مال رجل، ولكن إن لم يتب بيع في الأعراب .

308 سورة النور: ٢ .

309 هو: –،د.

310 يتراوحه: يرى أوجه،د، يتراوجه، ب .

311 يجلده: يضربه،د.

312 ثوبه: قميصه، ب .

313 أو: –،د.

314 المرتد يقتل ولو كان امرأة ما خلا العبد فإنه يباع: هامش، ب .

سئل عن الساحر؟

قال: يستتاب فإن تاب وإلاَّ قتل.

سئل عن مشرك من أهل الحرب[315] دخل دار الإسلام تاجرا؟

قال: إذا دخل بأمان لم يعرض له[316].

سئل عن رجل قذف رجلا فجلد ثمَّ ادعى على ذلك القاذف فقذفه به؟

قال: يجلد الحدّ أبدا حتَّى ينتهي.

سئل عن رجل قال لرجل: لست بابن فلان؟

قال: عليه الحدّ وذلك قذف.

سئل عن رجل[317] رمى قوما مجتمعين بكلمة واحدة؟

قال: عليه يجلد[318] حدّا واحدا[319].

سئل عن رجل قال لامرأته: يا زانية؟

قال: إن تم على ذلك لاعنها، وإن أكذب نفسه جلد الحدّ وفرق بينهما[320]، وإن

315 من أهل الحرب: -،د.

316 لا بأس بدخول رجل من أهل الحرب إلى دار الإسلام على الأمان: هامش، ب.

317 رجل: -،د.

318 يجلد: -،د.

319 حدا واحدا: حد واحد، ب،د.

320 وفرق بينهما: -،د.

لاعنها[321] فرق بينهما ثُمَّ لا يجتمعان[322]، وإن قال ذلك ولم يسمعه أحد، ثُمَّ كذب نفسه ورجع لم يكن عليه لعان ولا فرقة.

سئل عن عبد أعتق نصفه فأصاب حدا؟

قال: إن كان مملوكا قد أحصن بحرة فعليه حدّ المملوك، وإن لم يحصن بحرة فلا حدّ عليه، وإذا أعتق نصفه فعليه الحد.

سئل عن عبد قذف حرا؟

قال: ليس عليه حد[323]، وعليه العقوبة.

سئل عن رجل يصيب الحدّ في الحرم؟

عن ابن عبَّاس أنَّه قال: إذا أصاب الحدّ في الحرم أقيم عليه الحدّ في الحرم، وإذا أصابه في غير الحرم ثُمَّ لجأ إلى الحرم فإنَّه لا يكلم ولا يجالس ولا يبايع حتَّى يخرج من الحرم ويقام عليه الحد.

سئل عن رجل غشي[324] جارية لم تحض؟

قال: إن كان اغتصبها أقيم عليه الحد، وإن طاوعته[325] وقد أدرك أترابها أقيم عليها وعليه الحد.

---

321 وإن كذب نفسه جلد الحدّ و: +،د.

322 انظر: آثار الربيع، مسألة ١٩٣، ص ٤٨، ومسألة ٢١٦، ص ٥٢.

323 حد: شيء، ب.

324 امرأته: +،د.

325 طاوعته: تابعته،د.

سئل عن صبيّ غشي امرأة؟

قال: يقام عليها الحدّ ولا حدّ عليه، إلاّ أن يكون قد أدرك أترابه واشتهى النساء.

سئل عن الصبيّ يفتض عذرة الصبية؟

قال: عليه في عذرتها مهر نسائها، ولا حدّ عليهما.

سئل عن امرأة تزوّجت ولها زوج آخر؟

قال: عليها الرجم، وله ما على ظهره، وما وجد مِمّاً أعطاها بعينه فهو له.

عن قتادة عن أبي حيان الأعرج: أن رجلا هاجر إلى الشام فقال: ما زنيت منذ هاجرت[326] إلاّ بربّة منزلي. فرفع ذلك إلى أبي عبيدة بن الجراح فكتب بذلك إلى عمر بن الخطّاب، فكتب عمر أن يسألوه عن الحدود فإن كان يعلمها أقيم عليه الحدّ وإن كان لا يعلمها فعلموا عباد الله.

قال: إذا كان مِمَّن أقر بالقرآن والصلاة ثُمّ زنى أقيم عليه الحدّ.

سئل عن حدود أهل الذمّة في الزنا؟

قال: إذا رفعوا إلى حكّامنا حكموا[327] عليهم بما في كتابنا.

عن أيُّوب عن ابن عمر: أن يهوديّين أصابا فاحشة فرفعا إلى النبيّ عليه السلام:

326 منذ هاجرت: -،د.

327 حكموا: اقيم،د.

«فقال[328]: ما تجدون[329] في التوراة في شأن[330] الرجم؟» فقالوا: نفضحهما[331] ويعاقبان. فقال عبد الله بن سلام: بل[332] كذبوا يا رسول الله، بل في كتابهم الرجم. قال: فأتوا بالتوراة فاتلوها إن كنتم صادقين، فجاؤوا بها وجاؤوا بقرائهم[333]، وجعل يقرأ ما قبلها وما بعدها[334] فقال عبد الله بن سلام: ارفع يدك، فباعدها فإذا هو[335] بآية الرجم تلوح «فأمر رسول الله ﷺ برجمهما»[336]. فقال ابن عمر: لقد رأيتهما وهما يرجمان وهو يقيها من الحجارة[337] بنفسه، قال: بلغنا هذا.

سئل عن مملوك تزوّج بغير إذن سيده؟

قال: إن شاء السيد أقرهما على نكاحهما وإن شاء فرق بينهما.

ما سئل عنه من باب الميراث والوصيّة

سئل عن قوله تعالى: ﴿كُتِبَ عَلَيْكُمْ إِذَا حَضَرَ أَحَدَكُمُ الْمَوْتُ إِن تَرَكَ خَيْرًا الْوَصِيَّةُ

---

328 فقال: -، د.

329 تجدون: -، ب.

330 شأن: ما في كتابكم، ب.

331 نفضحهما: يخزيان، ب.

332 بل: -، د.

333 وجاؤوا بقرائهم: -، د.

334 ما قبلها وما بعدها: -، ب.

335 هو: -، د.

336 رواه الربيع، باب في الرجم والحدود، ر٦٠٧. والبخاري، باب ما يجوز من تفسير التوراة وغيرها من كتب الله بالعربية وغيرها، ر٧١٠٤.

337 الحجارة: الرجم، ب.

لِلْوَالِدَيْنِ وَالأَقْرَبِينَ. . . ﴾[338] الآية.

قال: أمّا قوله: ﴿ إِن تَرَكَ خَيْرًا ﴾ أي مالا. وكان قتادة يقول: الخير ألف درهم.

وأما قوله: ﴿ الْوَصِيَّةُ لِلْوَالِدَيْنِ وَالأَقْرَبِينَ ﴾ فقد نسخ ذلك بآية الميراث[339] في سورة النساء، وألحق لأهل الميراث ميراثهم، للوالدين نصيبهما لكلّ واحد منهما السدس مِمّا ترك إن كان له ولد، فإن لم يكن له ولد وورثه أبواه فلأمه الثلث، فإن كان له إخوة فلأمه السدس، حجبوا الأم عن الثلث، ولا يرثون ولا يحجب الأخ الواحد ويحجب مافوق ذلك.

وقال: كان أبو عبيدة يرى[340] أنَّ أربعمائة فيها وصيَّة ونسخت وصيَّة[341] الوالدين كما قال قتادة.

وفي قوله: ﴿ فَمَنْ خَافَ مِن مُّوصٍ جَنَفًا أَوْ إِثْمًا فَأَصْلَحَ بَيْنَهُمْ فَلاَ إِثْمَ عَلَيْهِ ﴾[342].

عن قتادة: أنَّه قال: من أوصى بجنف أو جور في وصيته فردها ولي المِيِّت أو إمام من أئمة المسلمين[343] إلى كتاب الله وسنة نبيه عليه السلام فذلك له.

عن قتادة: أن سعد بن مالك قال: يا نبيّ الله، إنّه ليس لي ولد إلاّ ابنة[344] لي، أفأتصدق بثلثي مالي؟ قال: لا. قال: فبالشطر[345]. قال: لا. قال: فالثلث؟ قال: «نعم»[346]،

---

338 سورة البقرة: ١٨٠. وتمامها: ﴿ بِالْمَعْرُوفِ حَقًّا عَلَى الْمُتَّقِينَ ﴾.

339 بآية الميراث: -، ب.

340 يرى: -،د.

341 ونسخت وصية: ونسخ الوالدين، ب.

342 سورة البقرة: ١٨٢.

343 المسلمين: الهدى،د.

344 إلا ابنة: -، ب.

345 فبالشطر، فنصف، ب،د.

346 نعم: -،د. رواه الربيع، باب الوصية، ر٦٨٠، والبخاري، باب رثى النبي صلى الله عليه وسلم

والثلث جم[347]. قال: بلغنا أنّه قال: الثلث كثير.

قال: بلغنا ذلك وكان أصحابنا يرون أن من لم يكن له ولد ولا والد ولا إخوة أوصى بالثلث وإن كان له ورثة من هؤلاء أوصى[348] بالخمس[349] أو السدس، وإن كان المال كثيرا فالخمس عندهم كثير.

والكلالة الذي لا ولد له ولا والد ولا جد[350].

سئل عن العبد يعتق واليهوديّ والنصرانيّ يسلمان[351] قبل أن يقسم الميراث؟

قال: كان الربيع يقول: كلّ إنسان أسلم قبل أن يقسم الميراث فله سهمه وإن قسم الميراث قبل أن يعتق أو يسلم[352] فلا شيء له.

سئل عن رجل أوصى لوالديه بدين؟

عن قتادة عن الحسن قال: قال جابر بن زيد: أصدق ما يكون الإنسان[353] عند موته.

قال: نعم[354].

خزامة بن سعد، ر١٢٣٣.

347 جم: جما، ب. + –،د.

348 أوصى: –،د.

349 بالخمس، فالخمس، ب،د.

350 الكلالة: هامش، ب.

351 يسلمان: يسلما، ب د.

352 أو يسلم: –، ب.

353 الانسان: الناس، ب.

354 قال: نعم: –،د.

سئل عن صغير أسلم أبوه ولم تسلم أمه؟

قال: يرث المسلم منهما، وإذا بلغ عرض عليه الإسلام فإن قبل وإلاّ قتل.

سئل عن امرأة تركت بني عمها أحدهما زوجها والآخر أخوها لأمها؟

قال: يرث الزوج بالتزويج ويرث هذا[355] بالقرابة، وإذا اجتمع لرجل قرابتان فهو أحقّ من صاحب القرابة الواحدة.

سئل عن رجل ينحل امرأته نحلا فلا تقبضه[356]؟

قال: ليس بين الرجل وامرأته قبض إذا أشهد لها[357] جاز لها، قال[358]: ونحل الوالدة يجوز من غير حيازة.

سئل عن رجل أسكن رجلا سكنا ثُمَّ مات؟

قال: هي راجعة إلى الأوّل وإن كانت عمرى[359] فهي للذي في يده ولورثته من بعده.

سئل عن رجل أوصى بعتق وأوصى لقرابته، وجعل لأناس سماهم وآخرين لم يسمهم فزادت الوصيّة على الثلث؟

قال: يأخذون بالحصص ويستسعى الرقيق بالحصص[360].

355 هذا: الأخ، ب.

356 فلا تقبضه: ولم تقبضها، ب.

357 لها: -،د.

358 قال: -،د.

359 عمرى: عمرا، ب،د.

360 بالحصص: -، ب.

سئل عن رجل أهدى هدية فلم تصل الهدية إلى صاحبها حتّى مات؟

قال: إن كانت خرجت من يده والمهدى إليه حيّ فهي لورثته، وإن كان يوم خرجت من يده قد مات رجعت للأول.

سئل عن رجل يوصي بأكثر من الثلث؟

قال: إذا[361] أمضاه الورثة مضى، وإن أنكروا رجع ذلك[362] إلى الثلث ينقصون بالحصص، وإذا أقر الورثة[363] عند الوصيّة مضى عليهم، وليس لهم فيها رجعة، وإن لم يمضوا الوصيّة[364] فهم بالخيار.

سئل عن رجل أوصى بحجّ أو زكاة واجبة عليه؟

قال: هي من الثلث، إن شاء الورثة لم يعطوها، وإن أعطوها فهي من الثلث[365].

سئل عن رجل أوصى لقرابته ولم يسم؟

قال: للأعمام الثلثان من الثلث، وللأخوال الثلث من الثلث، إلاّ أن يقول هو: إنّها[366] بينهم بالسواء.

361 إذا: إن، ب.

362 ذلك: -، ب.

363 الوصية: +،د.

364 الوصية: -، ب.

365 إن شاء الورثة لم يعطوها وإن أعطوها فهي من الثلث: -،د؛ رجل أوصى بحج وشبيهه إن شاء الورثة لم يعطوه، وإن شاءوا أعطّوا: هامش، ب.

366 إنها: -، ب.

سئل عن وصيّة[367] الحبلى أو الذي يخاف الغرق[368] أو عند الزحف أو الذي بأرض الطاعون؟

قال: وصيتهم وصيّة الموت.

سئل عن الطاعون إذا وقع[369] بأرض قوم؟

عن قتادة عن عكرمة عن يحيى بن سعيد عن أبيه قال: إذا وقع الطاعون بأرض فلا تخرج منها، وإذا سمعت به بأرض تهبط عليه إن شئت، فإن الطاعون لا يقدم أجلا ولا يؤخره، قال تعالى: ﴿أَيْنَمَا تَكُونُوا يُدْرِكْكُمُ الْمَوْتُ وَلَوْ كُنْتُمْ فِي بُرُوجٍ مُشَيَّدَةٍ﴾[370].

عن قتادة عن زرارة بن أوفى عن سعيد بن هشام عن عائشة زوج النبيّ عليه السلام أنه قال: «من أحب لقاء الله أحب الله لقاءه ومن كره لقاء الله كره الله لقاءه». فقيل له[371]: يا رسول الله، كلنا نكره الموت. قال: «إنّما ذلك عند موته؛ إذا بشّر برحمة الله ومغفرته أحبَّ لقاء الله وأحبّ الله لقاءه، وإذا بشر بعذاب الله كره لقاء الله وكره الله لقاءه»[372].

سئل عن بيع الوصيّ؟

---

367 الوصية: -، ب.

368 لعله: كالغريق.

369 الطاعون: +، ب.

370 سورة النساء: ٧٨. ورد في مسند الربيع: «فإذا سمعتم به بأرض فلا تدخلوها عليه وإذا وقع في أرض وأنتم فيها فلا تخرجوا فرارا منه»، باب في الطاعون، ر ٦٤٠.

371 له: -، د.

372 رواه البخاري، باب من أحب لقاء الله أحب الله لقاءه، ر ٦١٤٢؛ تم قوله عما يبشر العبد عند موته بمغفرة الله أو بعذابه: هامش، ب.

قال: أعجب إلي أن يرفعوه إلى القاضي.

سئل عن رجل ترك مالا[373] وعليه دين وله أولاد وورثة[374]، فأنكر بعضهم الدَّين[375] وعرفه بعضهم؟

قال: إن عرف منهما اثنان فهو جائز عليهم، وإن كان واحدا جازت شهادته على قدر حصَّته.

سئل عن رجل مات ولا[376] عقب له ولا ولد، ولا والد ولا عصبة، وله[377] أخت وعمة وخالة؟

عن قتادة: أنَّه كان[378] يرى أن ماله كله لأخته، وهي أحقّ به.

سئل عن رجل مات ولم يدع إلاَّ عمة وخالة؟

عن قتادة عن بكر بن عبد الله المزني[379] عن بشير بن عبد الحميد عن زياد أنَّ عمر بن الخطَّاب -رضي الله عنه- قال: الثلثان لعمته، والثلث لخالته.

سئل عن ميراث أولاد الملاعنة؟

---

373 مالا: مات، ب.

374 وورثة: -،د.

375 الدين: -، ب.

376 ولا: -،د.

377 وله: إلا، ب.

378 كان: -،د.

379 المزني: المدني، ب،د.

قال: إن كان قد دخل بها فالولد[380] ولده وميراثه لعصبة أبيه، وإن لم يدخل بها فالولد لأمه وميراثه لعصبة أمه.

سئل عن ميراث المرتد عن دينه؟

قال: ميراثه لأهل دينه من أهل الذمّة ولا يرثه أهل الحرب.

سئل عن رجل اعترف بولد عند موته؟

قال: يرثه فإن كان[381] ادعاه من زنا لم يرثه.

باب ما سئل عنه في باب المكاتبة

سئل عن قوله تعالى: ﴿وَالَّذِينَ يَبْتَغُونَ الْكِتَابَ مِمَّا مَلَكَتْ أَيْمَانُكُمْ فَكَاتِبُوهُمْ إِنْ عَلِمْتُمْ فِيهِمْ خَيْرًا﴾[382].

قال: إن علمتم عندهم وفاء وصدقا وأمانة.

عن قتادة: أنَّه كان يكره للمكاتب أن يقول لمواليه: ضعوا عني وأعجل لكم، وكان لا يرى بالتعريض بأسًا. قال: نعم[383].

سئل عن رجل كاتب مملوكه على وصف؟

قال قتادة كان عمر بن عبد العزيز يكره ذلك، إلاَّ أن يكون يدا بيد.

380 فالولد: فالولد له، ب.

381 كان: –، د.

382 سورة النور: ٣٣.

383 قال: نعم: –، د.

سئل عن عبد بين رجلين كاتب أحدهما ولم يكاتب الآخر؟

قال هو على من كاتبه بقيمة عدل.

سئل عن رجل كاتب غلامه وله أم ولد وولده ولم يذكرهم في مكاتبته؟

قال: إن كان مواليه يعرفون ماله ولم يستثنوه فهو له، وإن استثنوا فهو لهم، وإن كان عنده شيء من المال خفي على مواليه ثُمَّ علموا[384] بعد ذلك فهو لهم. قال[385]: والولد وأم الولد والمال سواء في ذلك.

سئل عن مملوك[386] كاتب[387] على نفسه وعلى[388] ولده فمات واحد منهما؟

قال: إذا كاتبوا جميعا وكتب الكتاب عليهم جميعا، فعلى كلّ واحد حصّته[389] وإن كاتب عليهم أبوهم وضمن المال فهو عليه[390] لازم.

سئل عن رجل غشي مكاتبته؟

عن قتادة: أنّه قال: إن استكرهها فعليه العقر، وعليه[391] الحدّ مائة جلدة وهي على ما بقي من مكاتبتها، وإن طاوعته فلا عقر لها، وعليه وعليها الحدّ مائة جلدة، وهي على ما

384 علموا: عرفوا، ب.

385 قال: -، د.

386 مملوك: رجل، ب.

387 مملوكا: +، ب.

388 : وعلى -، د.

389 فعلى كل واحد حصته: -، ب.

390 عليه: -، ب.

391 وعليه: ويجلد، ب.

بقي من كتابتها. قال: نعم[392].

سئل عن رجل يقول لغلامه: اخدمني سنة وأنت حر؟

قال: هو على[393] شرطه.

سئل عن رجل قال لغلامه: أنت حرّ واخدمني سنة؟

قال: هو على[394] شرطه قدم الكلام أو أخره سواء، إلاّ أن يكون فصل بين كلامه أو سكت ساعة.

سئل عن بيع الولاء وهبته[395]؟

قال: لا يباع الولاء[396] ولا يوهب.

عن قتادة: أنّ جابر بن عبد الله قال: مكروه أن يباع المكاتب مرّتين. قال: نعم[397].

سئل عمّن اعتق شقصا له[398] من مملوك؟

عن الحسن وقتادة: أنّهما قالا: من أعتق شقصا من مملوك فعليه خلاصه في ماله، إن كان له مال، وإلاّ استسعى غير مشفوق عليه.

---

392 قال نعم: -،د. انظر: آثار الربيع، مسألة ١٩٥، ص ٤٩.

393 على: له، ب.

394 هو على: له،د.

395 وهبته: وهيبته، ب،د.

396 الولاء: الولي، ب،د.

397 سئل: عن بيع الولاء وهيبته؟ قال: لا يباع الوليّ ولا يوهب. عن قتادة: أنّ جابر بن عبد الله قال: مكروه أن يباع المكاتب مرّتين. قال: نعم: -،د.

398 له: -، ب.

عن قتادة عن أبي المليح: أن رجلا أعتق نصيبا له من غلام، فرفع ذلك [إلى] النبيّ عليه السلام، فجعل خلاصه في ماله، قال: «إنَّه ليس لله شريك»[399]. وعن عمر وأبي هريرة مثل ذلك.

سئل عن رجل أعتق شقصا له من مملوك عند موته؟
قال: إذا كان له مال يبلغ عتقه أعتق وإلاَّ استسعى.

سئل عن بيع الولاء وهبته؟
قال: لا يباع ولا يوهب، عن قتادة: أنَّ جابر بن عبد الله قال: أكره أن يباع[400] المكاتب مرَّتين[401].

سئل عن[402] عبد أعتق وله أولاد من حرَّة أيجوز ولاؤهم؟
قال: نعم.

سئل عن رجل أعتق مملوكته واستثنى ما في بطنها أله ذلك؟
قال: نعم.

سئل عن رجل قال لأمته: إن كان هذا الذي في بطنك غلاما فهو حرّ فولدت غلامين أو ثلاثة؟
قال: هم أحرار.

399 رواه أبو داود، باب فِيمَنْ أَعْتَقَ نَصِيبًا لَهُ مِنْ مَمْلُوكٍ، ر٣٩٣٥.
400 يباع: يبيع، ب د.
401 ذكر في مكان سابق، ب.
402 عن: عن بيع، ب.

سئل عن رجل أعتق مملوكا له مال؟

قال: إن كان يعرف ما له فتركه ولم يستثنه فهو للغلام، وإن استثناه فهو له، وإن لم يعرف بما كان له من مال ثُمَّ علم به فهو له إن شاء أخذه وإن شاء تركه.

سئل عن رجل أعتق غلاما وعلى الغلام دين؟

قال: إن أعتق فالدين عليه.

سئل عن رجل كانت تحته مملوكة فولدت ثُمَّ اشتراها، أله أن يبيعها؟

قال: هو قبيح فأما حرام فلا.

سئل عن رجل قال لمملوكه: إنَّمَا أنت حرّ إنَّمَا أنت عتيق؟

قال: هو حرّ كما قال[403].

سئل عمَّن[404] اشترى مملوكا على أن يعتقه ولم يفعل[405] وقد شرط عتقه؟

قال: يكره أن يبيعه وإن كان على عتق رقبة لازمة كره له أن يشتريه[406] بوضيعة من ثمنه.

سئل عن عبد[407] بين رجلين كاتب أحدهما وأعتق على[408] الآخر لمن الولاء؟

403 كما قال: -، ب.

404 عن رجل، ب.

405 ولم يفعل: -،د.

406 يشتريه: يستبد، ب.

407 عبد: عبدين، ب.

408 على: -،د.

قال: الولاء للذي أعتقه.

سئل عن عبد بين رجلين[409] [أو] ثلاثة أعتق أحدهم نصيبه، ثمّ كاتب الثاني[410] وأمسك الثالث؟

قال: على الذي أعتقه خلاصه في ماله، وإن لم يكن له مال استسعى العبد للمكاتب وللذي أمسك وللمعتق الولاء.

باب فيما سئل عنه من باب الطلاق[411]

سئل عن رجل يهب امرأته لأهلها؟

قال: إن قبلوها فواحد، وهو أحقّ بها، وإن ردوها فلا شيء. قال: نعم، هو قول أصحابنا[412].

سئل عن الخيار؟

عن أبي معشر عن النخعي: أنّ عمر بن الخطّاب وعبد الله بن مسعود قالا: إن اختارت[413] نفسها فواحد، وهو أحقّ بها، وإن اختارته فلا شيء. قال: نعم، هو قول أصحابنا.

سئل عن رجل يقول لامرأته: اختاري؟

---

409 رجلين، ـ د.

410 الثاني: الأخر، د.

411 الكلام في الخيار: هامش، ب.

412 قال: نعم، هو قول أصحابنا: ـ، د.

413 طلقت: +، ب.

قال: إن خيرها ثلاثا فاختارت ثلاثا فقد بانت منه، وإن كان خيرها واحدا فرددها[414] فإنما هي واحدة، وهو أملك بها.

سئل عن رجل قال لامرأته: أمرك بيدك؟

عن أبي معشر عن النخعي: أنّ عمر بن الخطّاب وعبد الله بن مسعود قالا: إذا طلقت نفسها ثلاثا فهو واحد وهو أحقّ[415] بها، وإن ردت الأمر إلى زوجها فليس بشيء، وكان أصحابنا يرون أنّها أشد من المخيّرة، وكان[416] ضمام يقول في التي يجعل أمرها بيدها: إن طلقت نفسها ثلاثا فهو ثلاث، وإن طلقت نفسها اثنين فهو اثنين، وإن طلقت نفسها واحدة فهي واحدة، وهو أحق[417] بها. وإن قالت: أنا طالق، ولم تسم شيئا؛ فهو طلاقها منه.

سئل عن رجل جعل أمر امرأته بيد رجلين وطلق أحدهما ولم يطلق الآخر؟

قال: لا يجوز إلاَّ منهما جميعا.

سئل عن رجل جعل أمر امرأته بيد رجل ثُمَّ غشيها بغير أذنه؟

قال: لا خيار للرجل، إلاَّ أن يكون يطلبه بحق فليس له أن يغشاها، فإن غشيها فسدت عليه[418].

414 فرددها: -،د.

415 أحق: أملك، ب.

416 وكان: عن، ب.

417 أحق: أملك، ب.

418 سئل: عن رجل جعل أمر امرأته بيد رجلين وطلق أحدهما ولم يطلق الآخر؟ قال: لا يجوز إلاَّ منهما جميعا. سئل: عن رجل جعل أمر امرأته بيد رجل ثُمَّ غشيها بغير أذنه؟ قال: لا خيار للرجل، إلاَّ أن يكون يطلبه بحق فليس له أن يغشاها فإن غشيها فسدت عليه: -،د.

سئل عن رجل جعل أمر امرأته بيدها أو بيد غيرها، ثُمَّ قذفها فردت الأمر إليه أو رده إليه؟

قال: إن اختارته فإنَّه يلاعنها، ولا حدّ عليه، وهي تطليقة، وإن طلقت نفسها ثلاثا أو طلقها الذي جعل[419] الأمر بيده أو اختارت نفسها جلد، ولا ملاعنة بينهما.

سئل عن رجل طلق امرأته ثلاثا قبل أن يدخل بها؟

قال: هو واحد بائن، ويخطبها إن شاء.

سئل عن رجل طلق امرأته ثلاثا[420] قبل أن يدخل بها، ثُمَّ غشيها وهو يرى أنَّه له عليها الرجعة[421]؟

قال: لها صداق ونصف، للنكاح الأوّل نصف الصداق، وللوطء صداق كامل، ولولا جهله لأقيم عليه الحد[422].

سئل عن أمّ الولد إذا توفي عنها سيدها وهي حامل: هل لها النفقة[423]؟

قال: لا نفقة لها إلاَّ من نصيب ذي بطنها إن خرج حيا، وإن خرج ميتا فهو دين عليها، إن شاء الورثة أخذوه، وإن شاؤوا تركوه.

سئل عن الأمة تكون تحت حرّ ثُمَّ يطلقها تطليقتين وهي حامل، أو الحرّة تكون[424] تحت

419 جعل: -، ب.

420 ثلاثا: -،د.

421 أن له عليها الرجعة: أن له عليه الرجعة، ب.

422 ولو جهله لأقيم عليه الحد: -،د.

423 هل لها النفقة: -، ب.

424 تكون: -،د.

العبد فطلقها[425] وهي حامل؟

قال: لها النفقة.

سئل عن نفقة المختلعة الحامل؟

قال: لها النفقة حتَّى تضع حملها إلاَّ أن يشترط أنَّه لا نفقة لها.

سئل عن عبد كانت تحته مملوكة فطلقها تطليقتين، وهو يحسب أن الطلاق أكثر من ذلك ثُمَّ غشيها جهلا؟

قال: لها الصداق[426] الأوّل والعقر مثل عقر مثلها ولا حدّ عليهما.

سئل عن رجل طلق امرأته تطليقة أو اثنتين، فتركها حتَّى انقضت عدَّتها فتزوّجها رجل آخر، ثُمَّ طلقها أو مات عنها ثُمَّ راجعها الأول؟

قال: هي عنده على ثلاث تطليقات وانهدم الأوّل، إن كان الآخر دخل بها، وإن لم يكن الآخر قد دخل بها فهي على ما بقي من طلاقها وفرق بينهما[427][428].

سئل عن رجل غشي امرأته في دبرها؟

قال: إن كان ذلك[429] عادة منه أمرت ألا تقيم معه، وإن كان مرة فقد كان ضمام يرخّص فيها وفي الحائض وأما غيره فقد كان يكره ذلك للمرأة ولغيرها[430].

---

425 فطلقها: فطلقه، ب،د.

426 الصداق: العقر، ب.

427 وفرق بينهما: -،د.

428 ينهدم الطلاق الأول بعد الزواج الثاني: هامش، ب.

429 ذلك: منه، ب.

430 وأما غيره فقد كان يكره ذلك للمرأة ولغيرها: -،د. انظر: خميس الشقصي: منهج الطالبين،

سئل عن متعة النساء؟

قال: كان يقال: أتموا الحجَّ والعمرة ومتعة النساء بشهود وولي وما سوى ذلك فهو زانٍ[431].

سئل عن رجل زنى بامرأة فأراد أن يتزوّج أمها أو ابنتها[432]؟

قال: حرمت عليه كان قبل التزويج أو بعده.

سئل عن عبد تحته حرَّة وأمة كيف يقسم بينهما؟

قال: للحرة يومان وللأمة يوم.

سئل عن عبد زنى وتحته أمة؟

قال: لا رجم عليه حتَّى يحصن[433] بحرة، وإن زنت هي فعليها نصف الحدّ خمسون[434] جلدة[435].

سئل عن بِكر زنى وله امرأة لم يدخل بها؟

قال: يفرق بينهما وعليه الحد[436] ولا صداق لها[437]، ويقول: أعظم الناس عليه الحدّ

.١٠١/١٦

431 سئل: عن متعة النساء؟ قال: كان يقال: أتموا الحجَّ والعمرة ومتعة النساء بشهود وولي وما سوى ذلك فهو زاني: –،د.

432 أو بنتها: وبنتها،د.

433 يحصن: فيحصن، ب د.

434 خمسون: خمسين، ب،د.

435 من تزوج أمة ثُمَّ زنا يرجم عليه، وإن زنت هي فلا: هامش، ب.

436 قال: يفرق بينهما وعليه الحد: قال: اختلف فيه في الحد والرجم، ب.

437 ولا صداق لها: –، ب.

ولا رجم عليه[438].

سئل عن بكر زنت ولها زوج ولم يدخل بها؟

قال: يفرق بينهما، وعليها[439] الحدّ، ولا صداق لها.

سئل عن رجل زنى وله جارية قد ولدت له أولادا؟

قال: عليه الحدّ ولا رجم عليه[440].

سئل عن امرأة كان لها زوج فكتمت ذلك وتزوجت[441] آخر؟

قال: إن كان الذي تزوّجها علم أن لها زوجا رجم إن كان محصنا.

سئل عن رجل طلق امرأته واحدا أو اثنين ثُمَّ قذفها؟

عن قتادة عن ابن عبّاس قال: يجلد ولا يتلاعنان[442].

سئل عن رجل قال لامرأته: رأيتك تزني قبل أن أتزوّجك؟

قال: يجلد الحدّ ولا ملاعنة بينهما ويفرق بينهما[443].

سئل عن رجل تزوّج امرأة في عدَّتها؟

---

438 ويقول: أعظم الناس عليه الحدّ ولا رجم عليه: -،د.

439 عليها: عليه، ب د.

440 سئل: عن بكر زنت ولها زوج ولم يدخل بها؟ قال: يفرق بينهما وعليه الحدّ ولا صداق لها.
سئل: عن رجل زنى وله جارية قد ولدت له أولادا؟ قال: عليه الحدّ ولا رجم عليه: -،د.

441 وتزوجت: وزوجت، ب،د.

442 إن طلق امرأته واحدة أو اثنتين ثُمَّ قذفها: هامش، ب. انظر: آثار الربيع، مسألة ٢٢٤، ص ٥٣.

443 ومن قال لامرأته رأيتك تزنين قبل أن أتزوجك: هامش، ب.

قال: إن تعمد ذلك فرق بينهما وألزما الحد، وإن جهلت بالعدَّة فرق بينهما واعتدَّت بقية أيَّامها التي بقيت من عدَّتها، فإن راجعها الأوَّل[444] فلا يدخل بها حتَّى تستبرئ رحمها من الآخر إن كان دخل بها، وإن[445] انقضت عدَّتها ولم يراجعها الأوَّل خطبها الآخر، فإن شاءت تزوّجته وإن شاءت تركته[446].

سئل عن رجل قذف امرأته ولم يدخل بها؟

قال: يتلاعنان ولها نصف الصداق.

سئل عن رجل قذف امرأته وهي أمة؟

قال: العبد والأمة ليس بينهما ملاعنة؛ لأنَّه لا شهادة لهما واليهوديّة والنصرانيّة مثل ذلك[447].

سئل عن رجل أقر بولده[448]، ثُمَّ أنكر؟

قال: إن علم منه الدخول فالولد للفراش وإن لم يعلم منه الدخول فالولد ولدها ويتلاعنان.

عن أنس بن معاوية أن جارية لامرأة المغيرة بن شعبة، كان المغيرة يغشاها، وكانت مولاتها لا تدعوها إلاَّ يا زانية، فأتت الجارية عمر، فقالت: إن المغيرة يغشاني، وإن فلانة

---

444 فإن راجعها الأول: -، ب.

445 وإن: إذا، ب.

446 من تزوج امرأة في عدتها: هامش، ب.

447 من قذف امرأته قبل أن يدخل بها يتلاعنان: هامش، ب.

448 بولده: بوليدة، ب.

لا تدعوني إلاَّ يا زانية[449]. فأرسل إليها، فقالت له[450]: إن كنت للمغيرة فانهها عن قولها، وإن كنت لها فانه[451] المغيرة[452] عن غشياني، فأرسل عمر إلى المغيرة[453]، فقال: ألك فلانة[454]؟ قال: نعم. قال: من أين كانت لك؟ قال: وهبتها لي[455] فلانة. قال: أتغشاها قال: نعم. قال: هل لك على هبتها بيِّنة؟ قال: لا. قال: والله لئن أنكرت[456] لا ترجع إلى أهلك إلاَّ وأنت مرجوم، فأرسل إليها رجلين رفيقين فحدثاها بقول عمر فقالت: أيرجم بعلي، والله لقد وهبتها له، فرجعا إلى عمر فأخبراه فخلي عنه. قال: بلغنا هذا[457].

بلغنا عن قتادة عن جابر بن زيد[458] عن قبيصة بن ذؤيب: أن رجلا تزوّج جارية غلامه ثُمَّ وقع عليها فرفع إلى عمر فجلده مائة جلدة نكالا[459].

سئل عن عبد يعتق وتحته أمة[460]، فيصيب فاحشة قبل أن يدخل بها[461]؟

قال: يرجم.

449 زانية: زنية، ب،د.

450 فقالت له: –، ب.

451 فانه: فانهاها، ب؛ فانته،د.

452 المغيرة: –،د.

453 فارسل عمر إلى المغيرة: –،د.

454 فلانة: –،د.

455 لي: –، ب.

456 لأن أنكرت: –،د.

457 قال: بلغنا هذا: –،د.

458 زيد: حمادة،د؛ حيادة، ب.

459 نكالا: –، ب.

460 أمة: حرة، ب.

461 بها: عليها،د.

سئل عن الأمة تكاتب ألها الخيار إن كانت متزوّجة؟

قال: لها الخيار يوم تُكاتب ويشهد الشهود[462].

سئل عن المعتقة عن دبر إذا مات سيدها ألها الخيار؟

قال: نعم.

سئل عن الأمة يدركها العتق قبل[463] أن يدخل بها زوجها فتختار نفسها؟

قال: لا صداق لها.

سئل عن طلاق السنة.

قال: يطلقها واحدة ثُمَّ يتركها حتَّى تحيض فيراجعها إن شاء في عدَّتها وإن تركها حتَّى تحيض ثلاث حيض بانت منه فيخطبها إن شاء في الخطاب[464].

سئل عن رجل ادعى على امرأته أنّه دفع إليها كذا وكذا[465] وقال: إن لم أكن دفعت إليك كذا وكذا[466] فأنت طالق؟

قال: إن قالت: إنَّه لم يدفع إليها شيئا، ولم تكن له بيِّنة فهي طالق.

سئل عن رجل قال لامرأته: إن دخلت دار فلان فأنت طالق فدخلت دار فلان وهو لا يشعر؟

462 الأمة لها الخيار عند العتق وكذا المدبرة: هامش، ب.

463 قبل: ثم، ب.

464 صفة طلاق السنة: هامش، ب.

465 كذا وكذا: -، ب.

466 كذا وكذا: -، ب.

قال: إن كان مسها بعد الدخول فقد بانت منه ولا تحل له أبدا.

سئل عن رجل قال لامرأته: أنت طالق إن لم أتزوّج عليك، فتزوّج امرأة ثُمّ طلقها قبل أن يدخل بها؟

قال: قد تزوّج إلاّ إن كان ينوي الدخول في قوله[467].

سئل عن رجل طلق امرأته تطليقة، فقال: إن راجعتك فأنت طالق؟

قال: إن راجعها ما دامت له عليها العدّة[468] فهي طالق وإن رجعها بعد ما تبين منه بتزويج جديد[469] فإنّه لا يدخل عليه شيء[470].

سئل عن رجل قال: إن كلم فلانا فامرأته طالق ثلاثا ثُمّ مر عليه في قوم فسلم عليهم؟

قال: إذا سلم عليه وحده فهو كلام، وإذا رد عليه وحده فهو كلام.

سئل عن رجل قال لامرأته: قد خليت سبيلك أو فارقتك أو سرحتك فلا سبيل لي عليك؟

قال: إن نوى طلاقا فهو واحد[471] وهو أملك بها[472]، وإن لم ينو[473] طلاقا[474] فلا شيء.

---

467 في قوله: -، ب.

468 العدة: الرجعة، ب.

469 بتزويج جديد: -، ب.

470 من قال لامراته: إن راجعتك فبانت طالق انظر كيف: هامش، ب.

471 وما نوى: +، ب د.

472 وهو أملك بها: -، د.

473 ينو: ينوي، ب، د.

474 طلاقا: -، ب.

سئل عن رجل قال لامرأته: ألحقي بأهلك؟

قال: هي تطليقة إن نوى طلاقا، وهو أملك بها[475]، وإن لم ينو طلاقا فلا شيء.

سئل عن رجل قال له رجل: ألك امرأة؟ قال: لا؟

قال: هي كذبة: وهو قول أبي عبيدة.

سئل عن رجل قال لامرأته: اذهبي فتزوّجي؟

قال: بئسما قال، ولا نعلم في ذلك طلاقا.

سئل عن رجل قال لامرأته: تعالي يا مطلقة.

قال: إن كانت طلقت مرة أو طلقها هو فهي تلك. قال: نعم، إن كان هو طلقها قبل ذلك معناه ذلك الطلاق الأول.

سئل عن رجل طلق امرأته فلقيه رجل فقال له: طلقت امرأتك؟ قال: نعم، ثُمَّ لقيه آخر فقال: طلقت امرأتك؟ قال: نعم، ثُمَّ لقيه آخر فقال: طلقت امرأتك؟ قال: نعم.

قال: هي واحدة وما نوى.

سئل عن رجل قال لامرأته: أنت طالق ثلاثا إن شئت، قالت: قد شئت ثلاثا.

قال: هو كما قالت، وإن قالت: لا أشاء شيئا، فلا شيء عليه.

سئل عن رجل كانت له امرأتان فخرجت[476] إحداهما فرآها في الطريق، قال: هذه فلانة؛

475 بها: واحد،د.

476 فخرجت:فخرج، ب،د.

للتي في البيت وليست هي، فقال: يا فلانة أنت طالق.

قال: بانت منه جميعا هذه بالإيماء إليها، وتلك بنيته.

سئل عن رجل له امرأتان لهما اسم واحد. فقال: فلانة طالق.

قال: له نيته تبين بذلك، فإن عنى فلانة بنت فلان فذلك له.

سئل عن رجل قال لامرأته: أنت طالق إن لم أنقلك من هذا البيت وإن لم أنتقل[477] أنا.

قال: ينتقل وينقل أهله ومتاعه حتَّى يتحول من ذلك المنزل ويبيت[478] في غيره، وإن مضت أربعة أشهر ولم ينتقل من ذلك المنزل فقد بانت بالإيلاء، ولا يقربها حتَّى ينتقل، فإن قربها فسدت عليه آخر الدهر، فإذا فعل فقد بر في يمينه.

سئل عن طلاق الرجل الذي به جنون.

عن قتادة عن سعيد بن المسيب قال: لا يجوز عند أخذه إيَّاه، فإذا أفاق جاز طلاقه، وكان ضمام يقول مثل قول سعيد، وكان أبو عبيدة يقول: المجنون مجنون، ولا يجوز طلاقه ولا غيره.

سئل عن رجل شهر عليه قوم السلاح وقالوا: لتطلقن امرأتك أو لنقتلنك فطلق.

قال: لا يجوز على مثل هذا طلاق ولا عتق ولا صدقة.

سئل عن رجل تزوّج امرأة وله امرأة أخرى فقالت له: أخبرت أنك تزوّجت، فقال: كلّ امرأة لي هي طالق وينوي التي تزوّج آخرا.

477 أنتقل: أنت قل، ب،د.

478 ويبيت: ويبت، ب،د.

قال: قد وقع عليهما الطلاق جميعا.

سئل عن رجل زوَّجه أبوه وهو غائب وله امرأة أخرى غيرها فخلفه السلطان فحلف.

قال: لا نراه إلاَّ إلى نيته إذا لم يعلم بالأخرى.

سئل عن أخوين قال أحدهما للأخر: إن كلمتك فامرأتي مني[479] بريئة[480].

قال: أمَّا البرية فهي إلى نيته، وإن نوى الطلاق فهو واحد.

سئل عن رجل له أربع نسوة فطلق واحدة منهن، ثُمَّ تزوّج أخرى ثُمَّ مات ولم يدر أيتهن طلق.

عن أبي معشر عن النخعي قال: ربع الثمن من الميراث للتي تزوّج آخرا وما بقي فهو بين الأربع.

سئل عن رجلين أبصرا طيرا فقال أحدهم: إن لم يكن هذا غرابا فامرأته طالق ثلاثا، وقال الآخر: إن لم يكن حماما فامرأته طالق ثلاثا فطار قبل أن يعلماه.

قال: هذا أمر مشتبه، لا يقرب أحدهما امرأته.

سئل عن رجل قال: إنِّي كنت طلقت أمتي[481] في نفسي.

قال: ليست نيته بشيء، فإذا أظهر ذلك بلسانه صارت طالقا.

سئل عن رجل طلق امرأته في مرضه قبل أن يدخل بها.

---

479 مني: منه، ب د.

480 فامرأتي مني بريئة: فامراته منه برية، ب د.

481 أمتي، أو امرأتي: أماتي، ب،د.

قال: لها نصف الصداق، وإن كان قد دخل بها فقد قال الله: ﴿وَلِلْمُطَلَّقَاتِ مَتَاعٌ بِالْمَعْرُوفِ﴾[482]

سئل عن المرأة تطلق وهي حامل بولدين، فوضعت أحدهما، هل لزوجها عليها الرجعة قبل أن تلد الآخر؟

قال: هو أحقّ بها ما لم تضع الآخر.

باب فيما سئل عنه في باب النكاح

سئل عن رجل زوج رجلا، فقال: ما أمرتك أن تزوّجني.

قال: إن كانت له بيّنة جاز عليه، وإلاَّ استحلف بالله ما أمره، ثُمَّ يلزم المزوج نصف الصداق.

سئل عن رجل أرسل رجلا ليزوجه فمات الرجل.

قال: إن كان زوجه قبل أن يموت الرجل فللمرأة الصداق والميراث، وإن كان التزويج بعد موت الرجل فلا ميراث ولا صداق.

سئل عن رجل أمر رجلا أن يزوجه على صداق مسمى فزاد من قبله.

قال: هو ضامن لما زاد.

سئل عن رجل طلق امرأته ثلاثا هل له أن يتزوّج أختها؟

قال: إن كان دخل بها فلا يتزوّج أختها حتَّى تنقضي عدَّتها، وإن كان لم يدخل

482 سورة البقرة: ٢٤١.

بها تزوّج أختها متى شاء.

سئل عن رجل مات ولم يسم لامرأته صداقا.

قال: كان جابر يقول: لها الميراث وعليها العدَّة ولا صداق لها، وكان يقول: ليس لها صداق إن طلقت ولم يفرض لها، فكيف يكون لها بعد موته، وإنّما لها في كتاب الله المتعة.

عن أيُّوب عن نافع أنَّ ابن عمر زوج ابنه من بعض آل عمر ولم يذكر لها صداقا، فمات قبل أن يدخل بها، فانطلقوا إليه يطلبون الصداق، فقال: مالكم عندي شيء، فلوكان لكم شيئًا لأعطيته لكم، فتحاكموا إلى زيد بن ثابت، فقضى لها بالميراث ولا صداق لها.

قال: هذا قول جابر بن زيد وأبي عبيدة والربيع؛ أن لها الميراث ولا صداق لها وعليها العدَّة.

سئل عن رجل تزوّج وهو مريض؟

قال: إن كان معه عقله ويحفظ الصلاة ويعلم ما يأخذ وما يعطي جاز تزويجه.

سئل عن رجل تزوّج على عاجل وآجل؟

قال: كان أبو عبيدة مسلم يقول: لا يحلّ الآجل[483] حتَّى يتزوّج عليها أو يتسرى أو تحتاج إلى خادم أو يموت، وإلاَّ فهو آجل[484] حتَّى يموت.

سئل عن رجل تزوّج امرأة فدخل بها ثُمَّ ماتت، فشهد أناس أنَّه أخوها لأمها قبل أن

483 الآجل: الأجل، ب،د.

484 آجل: أجل، ب،د.

يقسم الميراث؟

قال: إن كان قد دخل بها فلها الصداق كاملا، وإن لم يدخل بها فلا صداق لها ويتوارثان بالرحم ولا يتوارثان بالنكاح، وقال: لو قسم الميراث ثُمَّ علم أنَّها أخته نزع منها ما أخذت حيث إنَّها أخذت ما ليس لها.

سئل عمَّن تزوّج أخته لأمه أو أخت امرأته ودخل بها وهو لا يشعر؟

قال: إن كان دخل بها فلها الصداق كاملا لما أصاب منها، وإن لم يكن دخل بها فلا صداق لها.

عن أبي معشر عن النخعي قال: إذا كان أصل النكاح حراما فإن غشيها فلها صداق كامل العاجل والآجل، وإن لم يكن دخل بها فلا صداق لها.

سئل عن المرأة تطلق وفي بطنها اثنان[485]؟

قال: هو أحقّ بها ما لم تضع الآخر[486].

سئل عن رجل تزوّج امرأة ولم يستطع أن يغشاها؟

قال أبو عبيدة: يؤجل سنة، وإلاَّ فرق بينهما، وأخذت صداقها إن كان نظر إلى فرجها أو مسها.

عن قتادة قال: إذا غشيها مرة واحدة ثُمَّ لم يستطع فهي امرأته، إن شاء طلق وإن شاء أمسك[487].

485 اثنان: اثنين، ب،د.

486 سئل: عن المرأة تطلق وفي بطنها اثنين؟ قال: هو أحقّ بها ما لم تضع الآخر: -،د.

487 من تزوج امرأة ولم يستطع أن يغشاها يؤجل سنة: هامش، ب.

سئل عن رجل عجز عن نفقة امرأته؟

عن قتادة عن سعيد بن المسيب قال[488]: لا يقار[489] على ذلك؛ إما أن ينفق عليها[490]، وإما أن يطلق. قال: نعم[491].

سئل عن رجل كانت[492] له امرأة فخرج إلى أرض فتزوّج ابنتها أو أمها من الرضاع؟

عن قتادة[493] وعن الحسن أنّهما قالا: حرمت عليه[494]. قال: نعم[495].

سئل عن رجل تحته أختان ولم يعلم بذلك حتّى مات؟

عن حمّاد عن النخعي قال: الميراث للأولى منهما. قال: نعم[496]

سئل عن نكاح المحرِم؟

قال: لا بأس قد تزوّج رسول الله عليه السلام ميمونة[497] وهو محرم[498]، وأعرس بها بعد

488 قال: -،د.

489 تضاره، ب.

490 عليها: -،د.

491 قال: نعم: -،د.

492 كانت: -،د.

493 قتادة: -،د.

494 لا حرج عليه، ب.

495 قال: نعم: -،د.

496 سئل: عن رجل تحته أختان ولم يعلم بذلك حتّى مات؟ عن حمّاد عن النخعي قال: الميراث للأولى منهما. قال: نعم: -،د.

497 ميمونة: -،د.

498 وفي رواية أخرى أنه تزوجها وهو حلال، رواه مسلم، باب تَحْرِيمِ نِكَاحِ الْمُحْرِمِ وَكَرَاهَةِ خِطْبَتِهِ، ر٣٥١٧.

أن حل[499] بمكان[500] يقال له سرف.

عن قتادة: أنَّ أبا عيسى المازني حدَّث: أن[501] امرأة عمدت إلى جارية زوجها فأوجرتها من لبنها، فأتى الرجل عمر بن الخطَّاب رضي الله عنه فسأله فقال له عمر: عزمت عليك لتوجعن رأس امرأتك، ولتكونن جاريتك أوّل من تقع عليها، وقال[502]: لا رضاع بعد فصال.

عن قتادة: أنَّ رجلا وامرأة كانا في سفر ومعهما صبيّ فمات الصبيّ، فشق عليها بقاء اللبن، فجعل يمص ثديها ويمجه، وأحيانا يصل منه إلى بطنه، فشدد عليه أبو موسى قال: فأتى ابن مسعود فسأله، فأخبره أنه شدد عليه أبو موسى، فأخذ بيده فأتى به إلى أبي موسى فقال: أنت أفتيت هذا؟ قال: نعم[503]. فقال ابن مسعود إنه لا يحرم من الرضاع إلاَّ ما أنشأ العظم وأنبت[504] اللحم، قال أبو موسى: لا تسألوني عن شيء[505] ما دام هذا الحبر[506] فيكم. قال: نعم، وذلك ما كان من الرضاع غذاه[507] وأنبت اللحم[508].

---

499 حل: رحل،د.
500 بمكان: –، ب.
501 أن: –،د.
502 قال: –،د. و: –، ب.
503 فسأله فأخبره أنه شدد عليه ابو موسى فأخذ بيده فأتى به إلى أبي موسى فقال: أنت أفتيت هذا قال: نعم: –،د.
504 وأنبت: وأنبتت، ب،د.
505 عن شيء: –،د.
506 الحبر: الخبر، ب،د.
507 غذاة: غذاة، ب،د.
508 قال: نعم، وذلك ماكان من الرضاع غذاة وأنبت اللحم: –،د؛ لا رضاع بعد فصام: هامش، ب.

سئل عن لبن الفحل؟

عن قتادة عن الحسن عن سعيد بن المسيب أنهما لا يريا بأسا، قال: اللبن للفحل[509].

سئل عن مجوسيّ كانت تحته امرأة وأمها ثمّ أسلم وأسلمتا معه؟

قال: حرمتا[510] عليه جميعا.

سئل عن مجوسيّ أسلم وتحته أختان[511] فأسلمتا معه؟

قال: الأولى منهما امرأته.

سئل عن الإحصان؟

قال: قال الله تعالى: ﴿وَالْمُحْصَنَاتُ مِنَ الْمُؤْمِنَاتِ وَالْمُحْصَنَاتُ مِنَ الَّذِينَ أُوتُوا الْكِتَابَ مِن قَبْلِكُمْ﴾[512]، فإن كانت[513] من غير أهل الكتاب فلا إحصان لهن.

عن الحسن قال: يحكم بين أهل الكتاب بما في كتابنا. قال: نعم[514]. قال الله: ﴿فَإِن جَاءُوكَ فَاحْكُم بَيْنَهُم[515]﴾[516].

509 سئل: عن لبن الفحل؟ عن قتادة عن الحسن عن سعيد بن المسيب أنهما لا يريا باسا قال: اللبن للفحل: –،د.

510 حرمتا: حرمنا، ب،د.

511 أختان: أختين، ب د.

512 سورة المائدة: ٥.

513 كانت: كنّ، ب.

514 قال: نعم: –،د.

515 بما أنزل الله ولا تتبع أهواءهم: +،د.

516 سورة المائدة: ٤٢.

سئل عن الذي بيده عقدة النكاح؟

قال: اختلفوا في ذلك، فقال بعضهم: هي[517] المرأة تعفو عن النصف الذي وجب لها، أو يعفو الزوج عن جميع الصداق، وليس للولي هاهنا عفو.

عن قتادة: عن جابر بن زيد: عن ابن عبَّاس أنه قال[518]: البغايا اللاتي يُنكحن أنفسهن بغير بيِّنة.

سئل عن امرأة زوجها وليها سرًّا، وأشهد على ذلك رجلين؟

قال: إذا أشهد شاهدين جاز ذلك، وأنه يستحبّ كثرة الشهود.

سئل عن امرأة خطبها وليها؟

قال: كان يقال: إذا كان أولى الناس بها دعا شاهدين فأشهدهما على تزويجها[519].

سئل عن امرأة زوجها وليان لرجلين؟

قال: إن كانا في الولاء سواء فهي للأوّل، وإن كان أحدهما أقرب، فالأقرب نكاحه أجوز من غيره.

سئل عن امرأة زوجها وليان بغير إذنها لرجلين[520]؟

517 هي: -،د.

518 أنه قال: -،د.

519 على تزويجها: ثُمَّ تزوجها، ب.

520 لرجلين: -، ب.

قال: هي بالخيار، وأيهما شاءت فهو زوجها، وإن شاءت لم تختر[521] واحدا[522] منهما. وإن كانت أذنت لهما جميعا فالأوّل منهما أحقّ بها ولا خيار لها، فإن دخل بها الآخر منهما فإنَّه يفرق بينهما ولها الصداق كله، فإذا انقضت عدَّتها فهي امرأة الأوّل إن شاء طلق وإن شاء أمسك، ولكنه لا يقربها حتَّى تنقضي عدّتها، فإن تزوّجها الذي كان قد[523] فرق بينهما بعد ما طلقها الأوّل أو مات عنها فهي عنده على ثلاث.

عن قتادة قال: ذكر لنا أن النبيّ عليه السلام قال: لا شغار في الإسلام[524]، والشغار أن يبادل الرجل بأخته أو ابنته على غير صداق، ألا لا جَنَب ولا جَلَب، وهذا النهاب كرهه النبيّ عليه السلام، ونهى عنه وقدم فيه وقال: من أنهب فليس منا[525] والنهبة على كلّ شيء أكله. قال: يكره الشغار[526].

عن قتادة قال: ذكر لنا أنَّ عمر بن الخطَّاب خطب الناس[527] فقال في خطبته: أيُّها الناس إن غلاء المهور لو كان مكرمة في الدنيا وتقوى لله في الآخرة لخص به نبيه، وإنه والله[528] ما نعلم نبيّ الله أنكح أحدا من بناته بأكثر من اثنتي عشرة[529] أوقية وهي ثمانون وأربعمائة.

---

521 لم تختر: لن تجز، د.

522 واحدا: واحد، ب، د.

523 قد: –، ب.

524 رواه الربيع، باب في الأولياء، ر٥١٤، ومسلم، باب تحريم نكاح الشغار وبطلانه، ر٣٥٣٣.

525 ونهى عنه وقدم فيه وقال: من أنهب فليس منا: –، د. رواه أبو داود، بلفظ: «... وَمَنِ انْتَهَبَ نُهْبَةً مَشْهُورَةً فَلَيْسَ مِنَّا»، باب القطع في الخلسة والخيانة، ر٤٣٩٣.

526 قال: يكره الشغار: –، د.

527 خطب الناس: –، د.

528 إنه و: –، د.

529 عشرة: عشر، ب، د.

عن قتادة عن طلحة بن مصرف عن خثيمة بنت عبد الرحمن[530]: أنَّ رجلا تزوّج امرأة[531] على عهد رسول الله ﷺ وكان معسرا فأمرها رسول الله -عليه السلام- أن ترفق به فدخل بها[532] قبل أن يعطيها شيئا[533]. قال: إذا سمىَّ مهرا دخل بها، وإن دخل بها ولم يسمِّ[534] مهرا فمهر[535] نسائها لاكسر ولا شطر[536].

سئل عن رجل زوَّج إحدى بناته وسمى لها، ثُمَّ مات ومات الزوج ولم يدر الشهود أيتهن هي.

قال: لهن الثمن أو الربع سواء بينهنَّ ولا قرعة، وإن[537] مات الأب وقال الشهود: لا نحفظ أيتهن هي، فنرى أن يقول: إن امرأته طالق فتبين منه ثُمَّ يخطب أيتهن شاء فتكون عنده على تطليقتين[538].

سئل عن رجل زوج ابنته, واختلف الأب والزوج في الصداق؟

قال الأب: ألفان[539]. وقال الزوج: ألف؟ قال[540]: القول قول من كانت المراة

530 عن طلحة بن مصرف عن خيثمة بن عبد الرحمن: حليمة بنت عبد الرحمن: ب؛ -،د.

531 امرأة: -،د.

532 بها: عليها،د.

533 رواه البيهقي، باب المرأة ترضى بالدخول بها قبل أن يعطيها شيئا، ر١٤٢٤٣.

534 يسم: يسمي، ب،د.

535 فمهر: ومهر، ب،د.

536 قال: إذا سمَّى مهرا دخل بها، وإن دخل بها ولم يسمِّي مهرا ومهر نسائها لاكسر ولا شطر: -،د.

537 وإن: وإذا، ب.

538 تطليقتين: اثنتين، ب.

539 ألفان: ألفين، ب د.

540 الأب ألفين وقال الزوج: ألف قال: -،د.

عنده، إلاَّ أن يأتي الآخر ببيِّنة.

سئل عن رجل قال لرجل: قد زوجتك أو [541] وهبتك ابنتي أو تصدقت بها عليك، ويقول الآخر: قد[542] قبلت؟

قال: لا تجوز هبة المرأة لأحد، وإنَّما كان ذلك للنبي عليه السلام خاصة دون المؤمنين.

سئل عن رجل وهب مهر ابنته لختنه؟

قال: تجوز[543] هبته[544]، ويغرم لها مهرها.

سئل عن امرأة تدفع إلى رجل دراهم ليتزوّجها بها؟

قال: إذا وهبتها له فلا بأس.

سئل عمن تزوّج أمة فأمهرها مائة درهم، ثُمَّ اشتراها فأعتقها لما[545] عليها، فإن قالت: قد مسني فالقول قولها.

سئل عن أم الولد إذا أعتقت؟

قال: إذا أعتقها في حياته فثلاث حيضات وإن أعتقها بعد موته، أو[546] أعتقها ولدها فأربعة أشهر وعشر.

---

541 قد زوجتك أو: -،د.

542 قد: -، ب.

543 تجوز: يجوز، ب،د.

544 هبته: هيبته، ب. + -،د.

545 لما: لمن ما، ب،د.

546 أو: و، ب،د.

سئل عن رجل كفر بعد إسلامه؟

قال: تعتدّ امرأته عدّة المطلقة، فإن أدركها قبل أن تتزوّج وإن أتى لها عشرون[547] سنة أو أكثر فهو أحقّ بها، وإن تزوّجت بعد العدّة فذلك لها. قال: إذا كفر بعد إسلامه وكان مجوسيًا. قال: إذا حاضت ثلاثة قروء، أو ثلاثة أشهر إن كانت مِمَّن لا تحيض تزوّجت إن شاءت وإن أدركها قبل أن تتزوّج فهو أحقّ بها.

سئل عن عبد تكون تحته الحرّة فيطلقها تطليقتين؟

قال: الحرّة تعتدّ ثلاث[548] حيضات أو ثلاثة أشهر من الحر والعبد، والأمة تعتدّ من الحر والعبد حيضتين[549]، وخمسة وأربعين يوما إن كانت لا تحيض.

سئل عن مملوك استكره أمة على نفسها؟

قال: صداقها في رقبته، إن شاء مولاه أن يقر له[550] بصداقها وإلاَّ دفعه برمته. قال: إن افتداه فهو[551].

سئل عن رجل استكره حرّة؟

قال: كان قتادة يقول: عليه الحدّ وصداقها في ماله[552].

547 عشرون: عشرين، ب د.

548 ثلاث: ثلاثة، ب،د.

549 حيضتين: حيضتان، ب،د.

550 له: به، ب،د.

551 إن افتداه: : إن افتداهته فهو، ب د.

552 سئل: عمن تزوّج أمة فأمهرها مائة درهم ثُمَّ اشتراها فأعتقها لمن ما عليها، فإن قالت: قد مسني فالقول قولها. . . . . قال: كان قتادة يقول عليه الحدّ وصداقها في ماله: -،د.

كمل الجزء الرابع من قول قتادة، والحمد لله ربّ العالمين، وصلّى الله على سيدنا مُحَمَّد وعلى آله وصحبه، ويتلوه الجزء الخامس.[553]

553 انتهى ما وجدت فيما وقفت عليه من النسخ وذكر في نسخة أن هذا الجزء لم يتم. وقال وذكر المرحوم عيسى بن أحمد ـ رحمه الله ـ في نسخته التي نسخها بيده أنه رأى بقية في بعض النسخ من قبله فلم ينسخه بما فيه من كثرة التصحيف وفساد كلمه وكذا في نسخ أخرى أخبر أنه رأى بقيته فلم ينسخه وغالب النسخ ليس فيهن من هذا الشيء شيئا فإنا لله وإنا إليه راجعون، أقول: ولو نسخه -رحمه الله- على حاله لكان أحسن وأولى من أن يندرس كله فاندراس البعض أهون من اندراس الكل: +، ب.

الجزء الخامس من قول قتادة

بسم الله الرحمن الرحيم

وصلى الله على سيدنا محمد وعلى آله وصحبه وسلم

عن[1] عمرو[2] قال: سئل جابر بن زيد عن امرأة حملت، فأتى عليها خمسة أشهر، فتحرك الولد في بطنها، وأبصرت[3] النساء تحركه، ثُمَّ إن ولدها مات فمكث محشوشا سنة في بطنها، ثُمَّ إن زوجها مات، وانتظرت المرأة ولدها، فلم تلد سنتين[4] وشكَّت[5] في[6] حملها، بسبب[7] حبس ولدها في بطنها، قيل له: أيحل لها أن تتزوّج؟
قال: لا نكاح لها حتَّى تضع ما في بطنها، حيا كان أو ميتا.

قال عمرو: سئل جابر بن زيد عن رجل ملك امرأة، ثُمَّ قال لها: إن لم آتك[8] بنقدك إلى كذا وكذا فأمرك بيدك، طلقي نفسك إن شئت، واصنعي[9] ما شئت، وأشهد لها على ذلك، وانتظرت المرأة، فلمَّا حلّ الأجل، ولم يأتها بنقدها طلقت نفسها ثلاثا[10]، ثُمَّ

---

1 عن: -، ب،د.

2 عمرو: -،د.

3 وابصرت: وأبهر، ب.

4 سنتين: سنين،د.

5 وشكت: -،د.

6 في: من، ب،د.

7 بسبب: لأجل، ب.

8 آتك: آتيك، ب،د.

9 واصنعي: أو اصنعي، ب.

10 ثلاثا: -، ب.

أشهدت على ذلك، فسأله صاحب المرأة: ماذا ترى في هذه المرأة؟

قال: إن كنت جامعتها فلا تنكحها[11] حتَّى تنكح زوجا غيرك، وإن لم تكن جامعتها فاخطبها، فلا بأس.

قال عمرو: سئل جابر بن زيد عن رجل جعل طلاق امرأته بيدها؟

قال: إن طلقت نفسها حين جعل ذلك إليها فقد بانت منه، وإن لم تطلق نفسها[12] حتَّى رجع فيما أعطاها فلا أمر لها[13] في نفسها بعد أن يجامعها، أو يرجع فيما جعل إليها من طلاقها، والأمر بيده، ولو أن رجلا جعل طلاق امرأته بيد رجل فلم يطلقها ذلك الرجل حتَّى رجع زوجها فيما كان قد جعل لذلك الرجل من طلاق امرأته أو جامع امرأته، فلا أمر لذلك الرجل في طلاقها، والأمر بيد زوجها إن شاء طلق، وإن شاء أمسك.

قال عمرو: سئل جابر بن زيد عن رجل أخذ بأمر يطلب إليه، ثُمَّ قيل له: ائت قبيلا بنفسك، فقال: فلان وفلان يتقبلان بي، فقال الرجلان لا نتقبل بك حتَّى تجعل طلاق امرأتك بأيدينا إن فررت منا نطلقها إن شئنا، فجعل إليهما ذلك، وللرجل امرأتان لا يعلم القبيلان بإحداهن، ثُمَّ فر منهما.

قال: أَمَّا التي لا يعلم بها القبيلان، فليس لهما أن يطلقاها؛ لأَنَّهما لا يعلمان بها، ولم يشترطا طلاقها، أَمَّا التي عرفها القوم فإن طلاقهما يجوز عليها، إن لم يكن زوجها جامع بعد ما جعل الطلاق إليهما، أو رجع فيما جعل إليهما من طلاقها وأشهد أَنَّه رجع عن طلاق

11 تنكحها: تقربها، ب.

12 حين جعل ذلك . . . تطلق نفسها: -، ب.

13 فلا أمر لها: - ب.

امرأته، فأي ذلك فعل فلا طلاق لهما، فإن لم يكن فعل من ذلك شيئا وفرّ منها فطلقا امرأته، أو طلقها أحدهما، فإن طلاقهما[14] يجوز للتي عرفا من امرأتيه.

ومن حكّم قوما في طلاق امرأته ثمّ لم ينقض أمره بنكاحها أو يرجع فيما أعطاهم أو يشترط عليهم حين أعطاهم ذلك؛ إن طلق بعضهم وأبى البعض فلا أمر للذي يريد الطلاق منهم دون الآخر، فإن طلق منهم مطلق جاز، وإن اشترط عليهم حين أعطاهم وجعل أمر امرأته بأيديهم فلا أمر لرجل منهم دون الآخر في الطلاق.

قال عمرو بن هرم: سئل جابر بن زيد عن رجل ملك امرأة، وفرض عليه مهرا، ثُمّ توفي قبل أن يدخل بها، ما لها من المهر عليه، وماذا عليها من العدّة؟
قال: لها مهر كامل وترثه، وتعتدّ عدّة المتوفى عنها زوجها.

قال عمرو بن هرم[15]: سئل جابر بن زيد عن رجل ملك امرأة فتوفي عنها قبل أن يفرض لها مهرا؟
قال: أيهما توفي قبل صاحبه ورث الحي منهما الميِّت، وليس لها مهر إن لم يكن سمّى لها مهرا، إلاّ أن يكون قد وقع عليها أو أبصر عورتها أو مسها بيده أو بذكره، فلها[16] مثل مهر أمها أو بعض أخواتها[17].

قال عمرو: سئل جابر بن زيد عن رجل ملك امرأة ثُمّ طلقها قبل أن يدخل بها وقد فرض لها عليه مهرا، ما لها من المهر وما عليها من العدّة؟

---

14 طلاقهما: طلاقه، ب.
15 بن هرم: –، د.
16 فلها: لها، ب، د.
17 مهر المثل يعتبر بالنسب لا كما يقول مالك يعتبر بالشرف والضعة: هامش، ب.

قال: لا عدَّة عليها، تبين منه بتطليقة واحدة ولها نصف ما فرض لها ﴿ إلاَّ أَن يَعْفُونَ أَوْ يَعْفُوَاْ الَّذِي بِيَدِهِ عُقْدَةُ النِّكَاحِ ﴾[18]، وهو الزوج الذي يملك عقدة النكاح، وعفوه أن يعطيها مهرا كامل[19].

قال عمرو: سئل جابر بن زيد عن رجل طلَّق امرأته قبل أن يدخل بها وقد أبصر عورتها بعينيه أو مسها بيده أو بذكره؟

فقال: قد وجب عليه المهر كاملا إذا أبصر بعينه أو مس بيده أو بذكره قبلها، ولا تحلّ لأبيه ولا لابنه[20].

وسئل ماذا عليها من العدَّة؟

قال: إنَّمَا العدَّة من الجماع، وإنَّما نقول: إن الرجل إذا تزوّج ثُمَّ دخل بها وأبصر عورتها أو تفخذها أو أهرق على قبلها ماءه، ثُمَّ طلقها قبل أن يجامعها وجب لها مهر كامل[21]، وتعتدّ منه من أجل أنَّه كان قد أهرق ماءه على قبلها وقد تحمل المرأة من ذلك[22].

قال عمرو: سئل جابر بن زيد عن رجل ملك امرأة ثُمَّ طلقها قبل أن يدخل بها وقد أبصر بطنها ورأسها؟

قال: لها نصف ما فرض لها إن كان أبصر رأسها وبطنها ولا عدَّة عليها.

قال عمرو: سئل جابر بن زيد عن رجل ملك امرأة ثُمَّ طلقها قبل أن يدخل بها ولم

18 سورة البقرة: ٢٣٧.

19 الذي بيده عقدة النكاح هو الزوج: هامش، ب.

20 من نظر لعورتها أو لمسها بيده أو بذكره وجبت العدة: هامش، ب.

21 مهر كامل: مهرا كاملا، ب،د.

22 قد تحمل المرأة من إهراق الماء خارجا فسبحان الله: هامش، ب.

يفرض لها مهرا.

قال: لا عدَّة عليها ولا مهر لها إلاَّ متاعا بالمعروف.

قال عمرو: سئل جابر بن زيد عن رجل ملك[23] امرأة ثُمَّ طلقها واحدة قبل أن يدخل بها؟

قال: هي عنده على تطليقتين.

قال عمرو: سئل جابر بن زيد عن رجل ملك امرأة تزوّجها[24]، ثُمَّ طلقها قبل أن يدخل بها ثُمَّ تزوّجها، ثُمَّ طلقها أيضا قبل أن يدخل بها ثُمَّ تزوّجها؟

قال: هي عنده على تطليقة واحدة.

قال عمرو: سئل جابر بن زيد عن رجل ملك[25] امرأة، ثُمَّ طلقها قبل أن يدخل بها، ملكها ثلاث مرّات، يملك ويطلق؟

قال: لا تحل له حتَّى تنكح زوجا غيره.

قال عمرو: سئل جابر بن زيد عن رجل تزوّج امرأة ثُمَّ طلقها ثلاثا جميعا قبل أن يدخل بها، هل تحل له قبل أن تتزوّج غيره؟

قال: نعم، إن الرجل إذا ملك امرأة ثُمَّ طلقها واحدة قبل أن يدخل بها تبين منه وليس ما سوى ذلك من الطلاق شيئا، فإن خطبها بعد ذلك فتزوّجها فهي عنده على تطليقتين.

---

23 ملك: تزوج، ب.

24 تزوجها: تزوج، ب، + -، د.

25 ملك: تزوج، ب.

قال عمر و: سئل جابر بن زيد عن رجل ملك امرأة ولم يفرض لها عليه مهرا، هل يحل له منها ما يحل للرجل من امرأته؟

قال: نعم، فإن لم يمسها حتَّى يفرض عليه مهرها، فما تراضوا عليه من المهر، وإن مسها قبل أن يفرض لها مهرا فمهرها عليه كمهر إحدى نسائها.

قال عمر و: سئل جابر بن زيد عن رجل ملكت عليه امرأة وهو غائب وأدى صداقها، ثُمَّ جاء خبر الذي ملكت عليه أنَّه توفي؟

قال: يعد بين ملاك المرأة وموت الرجل الذي ملكت عليه المرأة، فإن كان ملك عصمتها قبل موته فلها المهر كاملا والميراث، وعليها عدَّة المتوفى عنها زوجها، وإن كانت ملكت عليه بعد موته فلا صداق لها ولا عدَّة عليها ولا ميراث لها، وقال: إذا تزوّج الرجل المرأة ثُمَّ عرس بها فهذا الدخول الذي ذكر الله، وتصدق المرأة على زوجها إذا دخل بها إذا زعمت أنَّه جامعها أو مس فرجها بيده أو بذكره فيجب مهرها كاملا عليه.

قال عمر و بن هرم[26]: سئل جابر بن زيد عن رجل قال وهو لاعب: قد أنكحتك يا فلان فلانة، وهو يملك نكاح تلك المرأة[27]»، فيقول الرجل: قد قبلت، والرجل يقول وهو لاعب: أنكحني يا فلان فلانة، فيقول له نعم[28] قد أنكحتك، جادا[29] أو لاعبا؟

قال: كان أبو الدرداء يقول: لا يلعب بثلاثة، من لعب بشيء منهن أو جدَّ فقد جاز

26 بن هرم: -،د.

27 وهو يملك نكاح تلك المرأة: لامرأة يملك نكاحها، ب.

28 نعم: -،د.

29 جادا: جاد، ب،د.

عليه: النكاح، والطلاق، والعتق[30].

قال عمرو بن هرم[31]: سئل جابر بن زيد عن رجل ملك امرأة وفرض لها عليه مهرها، ثُمَّ لم يجد الرجل ما ينقدها، فتجهزت المرأة من قبلها، أيصلح للرجل أن يدخل بها؟
قال: نعم.

قال: سئل جابر بن زيد عن رجل طلق امرأته تطليقة واحدة[32] ثُمَّ سكت عنها حتَّى تنقضي عدَّتها، فجعلت له المرأة ألف درهم على أن يتزوّجها، فتزوّجها على ذلك؟
قال: إن كان[33] تزوّجها بفريضة، فإن شاءت المرأة أن تقضي ألفَ[34] مهرها فعلت، وإن لم يكن تزوّجها بفريضة، فإن فريضتها تجب على الرجل من نحو فريضتها الأولى إذا جامعها إلاَّ أن ترضى المرأة بدون ذلك.
قال[35] عمرو بن هرم[36]: سئل جابر بن زيد عن رجل تزوّج امرأة، فاشترطت عليه قبل أن يملكها ألاَّ ينقلها من دارها، فاشترط لها غلام ثُمَّ بدا له بعد ما دخل بها لينقلها إلى داره[37]؟
قال: إن كان جعل ذلك من مهرها عليه حين تزوّجها، فلها ذلك، وإن كان إنَّمَا جعل

30 لا يلعب بثلاثة: هامش، ب.
31 بن هرم: -،د.
32 واحدة: -،د.
33 كان: -، ب.
34 : ألفَ: الألف من، ب،د.
35 قال: حدثني، ب.
36 بن هرم: -،د.
37 من دارها فاشترط لها غلام ثُمَّ بدا له بعد ما دخل بها لينقلها إلى داره: -،د.

لها ذلك على نفسه فإن له أن ينقلها إلى أهله و داره.

قال عمرو بن هرم[38]: سئل جابر بن زيد هل يصلح للرجل أن يتزوّج الأمة وهو يجد مهر الحرَّة؟
قال: إنَّمَا يتزوّج من الأحرار الأمة من لا يجد مهر الحرَّة وخشي العنت و أن يصبر فهو خير له[39].

قال عمرو بن هرم[40]: سئل جابر بن زيد هل يصلح للرجل أن يتزوّج الأمة على الحرَّة؟
قال: لا، و له أن يتزوّج الحرَّة على الأمة.

قال عمرو: وقد زعم الحسن أنَّه إذا تزوّج الحرَّة على الأمة قسم للأمة ليلة و للحرة ليلتين[41].

قال عمرو بن هرم[42]: سئل جابر بن زيد عن رجل تزوج أمة ثُمّ كاتب عليها إلى أجل، فإذا مكاتبها أقرّ[43] أنَّها مِمَّا ملكت اليمين، و أداه المولى في مغارم كانت تخرج عليهم، فسألته امرأته أن يطلقها لكيلا تؤخذ عليها[44]، فطلقها ثلاثا وهما يحسبان أنَّها أمته، و إن طلاقها ليس بشيء؟

---

38 بن هرم: -،د.
39 إنما يتزوج من الأحرار الأمة من لا يجد مهر الحرة وخشي العنة: هامش، ب.
40 بن هرم: -،د.
41 ليلتين: ليلتان، ب د.
42 بن هرم: -،د.
43 فإذا مكاتبها أقر: فإذا كاتب رأى عليها،د.
44 عليها: -،د.

قال: لا يقربها حتَّى تنكح زوجا غيره.

قال عمرو[45]: سئل جابر بن زيد عن رجل كانت تحته أمة فطلقها تطليقة واحدة، ثُمَّ عتقت الأمة ومضت عدَّتها، ثُمَّ إن زوجها الذي طلقها خطبها ثُمَّ تزوّجته؟
قال: هي عنده على تطليقتين، وتعتدّ بالطلقة التي كان قد طلقها وهي أمة.

قال عمرو: سئل جابر بن زيد عن رجل كانت تحته أمة فطلقها تطليقتين فبانت منه، ثُمَّ اشتراها بعد ذلك.
فقال: لا يحلّ له مجامعتها حتَّى تنكح زوجا غيره وهي وليدة[46].

قال عمرو: سئل جابر بن زيد عن رجل كانت تحته أمة فطلقها طلقة واحدة[47]، ثُمَّ اشتراها لامرأته[48]، ما منزلتها عنده؟
قال: إذا اشتراها فهي بمنزلة السرية إن غشيها[49].
قال عمرو: وقد أفتى بذلك عكرمة والحسن أيضا في هاتين الأمتين.

قال عمرو: سئل جابر بن زيد عن رجل أنكح عبده امرأة ثُمَّ أمره أن يطلقها، ثُمَّ إن سيده أراد أن يجمع بينهما بعد ذلك؟
قال: لا تحل لعبده إذا فارقها بأمر سيده حتَّى تنكح زوجا غيره.

45 قال: عمرو: -، ب.
46 وهي وليدة: -،د.
47 ثم أعتق العبد: +، ب.
48 لامرأته: -،د.
49 إن غشيها: -، ب.

قال عمرو: سئل جابر بن زيد عن امرأة لها زوج مملوك أبق وليس لها نفقة ففقد زمانا؟
قال: إذا فقد سنتين طلقها سيد زوجها، ثُمَّ لتعتدّ عدَّة المتوفى عنها زوجها، وقد أفتى بذلك الحسن البصري[50].

قال عمرو: سئل جابر بن زيد عن رجل كانت له امرأة مملوكة فطلقها تطليقتين[51]، ثُمَّ إن سيدها تسراها ثُمَّ تركها، هل تحل لزوجها الذي كان قد[52] طلقها أن يراجعها؟
قال: لا، حتَّى تنكح زوجا غيره.

قال عمرو: سئل جابر بن زيد عن عبد تحته امرأة حرَّة فتوفي العبد، كم تعتدّ امرأته؟
قال: تعتدّ أربعة أشهر وعشرا، وإن كانت امرأته أمة اعتدت شهرين وخمس ليالي.

قال عمرو بن هرم[53]: سئل جابر بن زيد عن رجل توفي وترك امرأته وهي أمة، كم تعتدّ؟
قال: شهرين وخمس ليالٍ[54].

قال عمرو: سئل جابر بن زيد عن رجل أعتق سريته واشترط نكاحها عتقها؟
قال: جائز نكاحها، وليصدقها صداقها، فإن له أن يتزوّجها إن شاء ولا عدَّة عليها منه، فإذا أعتق الرجل سريته وهو صحيح اعتدت ثلاثة قروء إن كانت مِمَّن تحيض، وإن

50 الحسن البصري: أيضًا البصري، ب.
51 تطليقتين: -، ب.
52 قد: -، ب.
53 بن هرم: -، د.
54 السؤال والجواب: -، ب.

كانت مِمَّن لا تحيض فعدَّتها ثلاثة أشهر إن تزوّجها غيره، وإن تزوّجها هو فلا عدَّة عليها منه، وإذا أعتق الرجل سريته عند موته اعتدت أربعة أشهر وعشرا.

قال عمرو: سئل جابر بن زيد عن رجل كانت له سرية، فولدت له، ثُمَّ تركها زمانا لا يغشاها، ثم مات عنها[55] فأعتقها عند موته ثُمَّ مات[56] ما عدَّتها؟
قال: عدَّتها أربعة أشهر وعشر.

قال عمرو: سئل جابر بن زيد عن رجل كانت له سرية فمات ولم يعتقها؟
قال: تعتدّ عدَّة الأمة الحائض[57].

قال عمرو: سئل جابر بن زيد عن رجل باع وليدة وهو[58] يقع عليها كم تعتدّ؟
قال: تعتدّ حيضة إن كانت تحيض، والتي قد حبست عن الحيض عدَّتها شهر ونصف، والجارية التي لم تحض عدَّتها خمس وأربعون ليلة.

قال عمرو: سئل جابر بن زيد عن رجل كانت له وليدة تخدمه وهو يقع عليها أحيانا فأعتقها عند موته، كم تعتدّ؟
قال: أربعة أشهر وعشر.

قال عمرو: سئل جابر بن زيد عن نساء اليهود والنصارى، أيحل للمسلمين أن يتزوّجوا شيئا منهن؟

---

55 ثم مات عنها: –، د.
56 ثم مات: –، ب.
57 الحائض: حيضة، ب.
58 وهو: –، ب.

قال: نعم، قد تزوّجهن المسلمون في خلافة عمر رضي الله عنه، فتزوّج حذيفة بن اليمان فيهم وغيره[59].

قال عمرو: سئل جابر بن زيد عن الصابئين: أمن أهل الكتاب هم؟

قال: نعم، ونساؤهم وطعامهم حلّ للمسلمين.

قال عمرو: سئل جابر بن زيد عن نصارى العرب، هل تحل نساؤهم للمسلمين؟

قال: ليسوا من أهل الكتاب، ولا تحل نساؤهم للمسلمين ولا طعامهم، وقد بلغنا عن عليّ بن أبي طالب رضي الله عنه أنه كان يمنع المسلمين من نساء أهل الجزيرة أن يتزوّجوهن[60]، وينهى عن ذبائحهم بأن تؤكل، ويرى أنّهم من العرب.

قال عمرو: سئل جابر بن زيد عن نصرانيّ كانت تحته امرأة نصرانيّة، فأسلمت المرأة وأبى[61] زوجها أن يسلم؟

قال: أرى أن يفرق بينهما، فإن كان قد دخل بها فلها مهرها كاملا وإن لم يكن دخل بها ردت إليه ما كان أعطاها.

قال عمرو: وقد زعم الحسن أنّ المسلم إذا تزوّج امرأة من أهل الكتاب طلقها كما تطلق الحرّة المسلمة، وتعتدّ كما تعتدّ الحرّة المسلمة[62].

59 تزويج نساء أهل الكتاب: هامش، ب.

60 يتزوجوهن: يتزوجونهن، ب،د.

61 وأبى: وأبا، ب،د.

62 نصرانية أسلمت وأبى زوجها: هامش، ب.

قال عمرو: في رجل[63] تزوّج امرأة وابنتها في أرض الحرب وهم مشركون، ثُمَّ ماتت الأم وهي في الشرك ثُمَّ سبي الزوج[64] وامرأته ابنة المرأة[65] الميِّتة، فأسلما جميعا.
قال عكرمة: لا تحل المرأة للرجل الذي ينكح أمها وإن كانا قد أسلما.

سئل جابر بن زيد عمن سبى على غرة وقد أعطين الأمانة هل يصلح أن يشتري منه شيئا؟
قال: لا وإن أعطيت شيئا منه فلا تقبله، وإن قبلت فأعتقت فلا تجامع شيئا منهنَّ[66].

قال عمرو: سئل جابر بن زيد عن رجل ملك امرأة ثُمَّ طلقها قبل أن يدخل بها، هل تحل له أمها؟
قال: لا، حرمت عليكم[67] ﴿أُمَّهَاتُ نِسَآئِكُمْ﴾[68].

قال عمرو: سئل جابر بن زيد عن ربيبة الرجل ابنة امرأته التي ليست في حجره، هل تحل للرجل الذي قد دخل بأمها؟
قال: لا، [69] فهي على من تزوّج أمها ودخل بها حرام.

---

63 في رجل: فيمن، د.
64 الزوج: الرجل، ب.
65 المرأة: -، د.
66 سئل جابر بن زيدعمن سبى على غرة وقد أعطين الأمانة هل يصلح أن يشتري منه شيئا؟ قال: لا، وإن أعطيت شيئا منه فلا تقبله، وإن قبلت فأعتقت فلا تجامع شيئا منهنَّ: -، د.
67 حرمت عليكم أمهات نسائكم: +، ب.
68 سورة النساء: ٢٣.
69 ابنتها كانت: +، ب.

قال عمرو: سئل جابر بن زيد هل يصلح للرجل أن يتزوّج امرأة وربيبتها؟
قال: يكره ذلك.

قال عمرو: سئل جابر بن زيد عن بنات الربائب؟
قال: حرمتهن حرمة أمهاتهن.

قال عمرو: سئل جابر بن زيد هل يصلح للرجل أن يتزوّج[70] امرأة وابنة أختها أو ابنة أخيها جميعا؟
قال: لا.
قال عمرو: وزعم سعيد بن المسيب أيضا أنّ رسول الله صلى الله عليه وسلم نهى عن ذلك[71].

قال عمرو: سئل جابر بن زيد هل يصلح للرجل أن يتزوّج[72] المرأة على ابنة عمتها؟
قال: تلك القطيعة ولا تصلح القطيعة.

قال عمرو: سئل جابر بن زيد هل يصلح للرجل أن يتزوّج امرأة كانت تحت زوج أمه ويتسرى سرية[73] زوج أمه؟
قال: كان ابن عبّاس يقول: لا تزاحم والدك زوج أمك، ولا تتسرى ما تسرى.

---

70 أن يتزوج: -،د.
71 في نسخة للمرأة أن تتزوج: هامش، ب. رواه النسائي: السنن الكبرى، تحريم الجمع بين الأختين، ر٥٤٣١.
72 للرجل أن يتزوج: -،د.
73 سرية: -،د.

قال عمرو: قال: وقد روي ذلك عن عكرمة ورواه عكرمة عنه[74] أيضًا.

قال عمرو: سئل جابر بن زيد عن رجلين ينكح أحدهما للآخر أخته بغير مهر بضع كلّ واحدة منهن موضع[75] صاحبتها.
قال: ذلك هو الشغار، وهو نكاح أهل الجاهلية، ولا يصلح ذلك في الإسلام.

قال عمرو: سئل جابر بن زيد عن الخصي يتزوّج المرأة الحرّة؟
قال: نهى عن ذلك.

قال عمرو: سئل جابر بن زيد عن وليدة أبصرت عورة سيدها أو مسته بيدها، هل يصلح لولد ذلك الرجل أن يطأها؟
أحب في ذلك إلي ألاّ يجامعها، وقد قال ذلك الحسن أيضا[76].

قال عمرو: سئل جابر بن زيد عن أمة كانت لرجل فمس قبلها بيده وأبصر عورتها ثُمّ وهبها لابن له، هل يصلح لابنه أن يطأها؟
قال: لا.

قال عمرو: سئل جابر بن زيد هل يصلح للرجل أن يطأ أمة[77] له قد وطئ أمها قبلها أو شيئا من بناتها؟
قال: لا يحلّ له ذلك.

74 ورواه عكرمة عنه: -،د.
75 موضع: ببضع، ب.
76 تعريف الشغار: هامش، ب.
77 أمة: وليدة، ب.

قال عمرو: سئل جابر بن زيد عن رجل كانت له سرية، فأعجبته أخت لها[78] فأرادها، هل له أن يجتنب التي عنده ويتخذ الأخرى التي أعجبته؟

قال: لا يصلح أن ينكح أختها حتَّى يعتق التي عنده، أو يهبها أو يزوجها رجلا أو تموت.

قال عمرو: سئل جابر بن زيد هل يصلح للرجل أن يجمع الأختين المملوكتين له؟

قال: لا يصلح ذلك.

قال عمرو: سئل جابر بن زيد عن رجل أنكح عبده وليدته[79]، ورغب فيها بعد ذلك لنفسه، هل يصلح ذلك[80] له أن ينزعها من زوجها[81]؟

قال: ما أرى أن يقع عليها حتَّى يطلقها زوجها عبده، وقد قضى بذلك عمر بن الخطَّاب رضي الله عنه.

قال عمرو: وسئل جابر بن زيد عن رجل أنكح وليدته عبد قوم آخرين، هل يحل[82] له أن ينزعها منه؟

قال: لا تحل حتَّى يطلقها زوجها. فقيل له: إن زوجها بيع وذهب إلى أرض أخرى، ولم يطلقها[83]؟

---

78 فأعجبته أخت له: فأعجبت أختا لها، ب،د.

79 وليدته: وليدة، ب.

80 ذلك: –، ب.

81 أن ينزعها من زوجها: –،د.

82 يحل: –،د.

83 ولم يطلقها: –،د.

قال: يطلقها عنه مولاه الذي باعه، فإن لم يوجد مولاه الذي باعه فلا يصلح لسيدها أن يمسها ولها زوج تزوّجها بفريضة وشهود.

قال عمرو: سئل جابر بن زيد عن رجل اشترى وليدة ولها زوج؟
قال: لا أرى أن يقع عليها الذي اشتراها حتَّى يطلقها زوجها، فإن كان زوجها عبدا فمولى العبد أملك بعبده وامرأته إن شاء جمع وإن شاء فرق.

قال عمرو: سئل جابر بن زيد عن رجل اشترى وليدة من السبي، أيقع عليها؟
قال: لا، حتَّى يعلمها الصلاة والغسل من الجنابة وحلق العانة إن كانت بكرا، وإن كانت ثيبا ذات زوج أمرها بذلك واستبرأ طهرها.

قال عمرو: سئل جابر بن زيد عن عبد كانت تحته أمة، فأعتقت الأمة، كيف يصنع بزوجها؟
قال: إن عائشة زوج النبيّ ﷺ اشترت وليدة يقال لها بريرة من رجل من الأنصار ولها زوج عبد فأعتقتها عائشة حين اشترتها فخيرها رسول الله ﷺ حين أعتقت بين أن تقيم عند زوجها وبين أن تفارقه[84]، فاختارت فرقته ففرق بينهما رسول الله ﷺ[85].

قال عمرو: سئل جابر بن زيد عن عبد أتى قوما فأخبرهم أنَّه حر، فزوجوه امرأة حرَّة، ثُمَّ علموا بعد ذلك أنَّه عبد[86] غرَّ بهم؟

84 تفارقه: يفارقها، د.

85 رواه البيهقي، باب عدة المعتقة تحت عبد إذا اختارت فراقه، ر ١٥٣٨٠.

86 عبد: -، د.

قال: إن شاءت مكثت عنده، وإن شاءت فارقته ولا حقّ لها عليه.

قال عمرو: سئل جابر بن زيد عن عبد أذن له مولاه أن يتزوّج، فأتى امرأة حرّة فتزوّجها، فهل على السيد من مهرها شيء؟

قال: لا، إلاّ أن يباع العبد فإن بيع العبد[87] فمهرها في ثمن العبد.

قال عمرو: سئل جابر بن زيد عن امرأة تزوّجها عبد فورثته عن ابن لها[88]، ففرق بينهما حين ملكته، ثُمّ إنّها[89] أعتقته بعد ما فرق بينهما، أيَحلّ[90] لها أن تتزوّجه بعد ذلك؟

قال: نعم، وقال عمرو: قال الحسن أيضا ذلك.

قال عمرو: سئل جابر بن زيد هل يصلح لرجل أن يقول لسريته إنها طالق؟

قال: ما يريد إلى ذلك ألاّ يذكره ما استطاع.

قال عمرو: سئل جابر بن زيد عن رجل أعتق سريته خطأ؟

قال: ليمسك عليه وليدته.

قال عمرو: سئل جابر بن زيد هل للرجل أن يجامع جاريتين له في جنابة واحدة؟

قال: لا بأس بذلك ما لم يجمع بينهما على فراش واحد، وأمّا أن يجامع إحداهما في بيت، ثُمّ

87 فإن بيع العبد: -، ب.

88 عن ابن لها: -،د.

89 إنها: -،د.

90 أيحل: -،د.

يخرج أو[91] يخرجها، ثُمَّ يدعو الأخرى فيقع عليها وهو جنب[92] قال[93]: لا بأس بذلك[94].

قال عمرو: سئل جابر بن زيد عن امرأة أنكحت نفسها سرا على شهادة امرأة ورجل[95]؟

قال: لا يصلح ذلك إلاَّ بأمر أوليائها وبشهادة رجلين أو رجل وامرأتين.

قال عمرو: سئل جابر بن زيد، سألته امرأة أنَّها رأت زوجها يأتي شاة؟

قال لها: فارقيه، فإنَّه لا يحلّ لك مجامعته.

قال عمرو: سئل جابر بن زيد عن وليدة كانت لرجل فزنى ذلك الرجل؟

قال: أرى[96] إن استطاعت أن تفتدي منه ولو ببيع فلتفعل، فإن كانت قد ولدت له فلتراجعه[97] على بيعها وإن بيعها يستقبحه أناس، ويزعم أناس أنَّه لا بأس به، فذلك خير لها من أن تقيم عند زانٍ.

قال: سئل جابر بن زيد عن رجل زنى بامرأة في الشرك هل يصلح له أن يتزوّجها في الإسلام؟

قال: ذلك الذي قال ابن عبَّاس: أوله سفاح وآخره نكاح.

---

91 يخرج أو: -، ب.

92 وهو جنب: أو يخرج هو عليها، ب.

93 قال: -، د.

94 لا يجمع بين جاريتين على فراش واحد: هامش، ب.

95 امرأة ورجل: -، ب.

96 أرى: -، ب.

97 له فلتراجعه: منه فلتراضه، ب.

قال عمرو: سئل جابر بن زيد عن رجل زنى بامرأة في الإسلام، هل له أن يتزوّجها[98] بعد ذلك؟

قال: لا.

قال عمرو: سئل جابر بن زيد عن بناتها هل يحللن له؟

قال: لا، وقد قال عكرمة أيضا ذلك[99].

قال عمرو: سئل جابر بن زيد عن رجل لامس امرأة فمس فرجها بيده أو بذكره أو أبصره بعينه ولم يجامعها، أيحل[100] له أن يتزوّجها؟

قال: لا.

قال عمرو[101]: سئل جابر بن زيد عن امرأة كان لها زوج فخرجت إلى قوم حرب لأهل الدين[102] فتزوّجت فيهم، ثُمَّ رجعت إلى أرض[103] الإسلام، هل يصلح لمسلم أن يتزوّجها بعد ذلك؟

قال: لا، إنَّها حرام على كلّ مسلم أن يتزوّجها بعد الذي فعلت.

قال عمرو: سئل جابر بن زيد عن امرأة كانت تجمع بين النساء والرجال، هل يحل

---

98 هل له أن يتزوجها: هل تحل له، ب.

99 قال عمرو: سئل جابر بن زيد عن بناتها هل يحلن له؟ قال: لا، وقد قال عكرمة أيضا ذلك: –،د.

100 أيحل: أيصلح، ب.

101 عمرو: –،د.

102 القبلة، ب.

103 أرض: –، ب.

نكاحها إن تابت من ذلك[104] ولم تقارف[105] شيئا منه؟

قال: لا أرى[106] أن يتزوّجها مسلم بعد الذي فعلت.

قال عمرو: سئل جابر بن زيد عن امرأة غاب عنها زوجها زمانا لا تعلم له حياة ولا موتا؟

قال: تتربص بنفسها على زوجها حتَّى تعلم أحي هو أم ميت.

قال عمرو: سئل جابر بن زيد عن رجل غاب عن أهله فنعى إليها فمكثت على ذلك زمانا[107]، فتزوّجت امرأته، ثُمَّ إن زوجها الأوّل رجع؟

قال: يخير زوجها الأوَّل بين امرأته وبين مهرها من زوجها الآخر، فإن اختار امرأته ردت إليه ولها المهر الذي كان أمهرها الآخر، وإن اختار[108] المهر كان له، وتتركه[109] المرأة عند الذي أخذها بعده[110]، قضى بذلك عثمان بن عفان[111] لصيفي بن قتيل[112] رجل من بني شيبان [كان في الجهاد] ثُمَّ [أشيع أنه قتل في قنديبل] من

104 من ذلك: -، ب.

105 تقارف: تقارب، د.

106 لا أرى: يكره، ب.

107 زمانا: سنة، ب.

108 اختار: اختارت، ب د.

109 وتتركه: وترد، ب.

110 الذي اخذها بعده: الذي تزوجها آخر بعد، د.

111 عثمان بن عفان: عمر بن الخطاب، ب د.

112 لصيفي بن قتيل: لطهر بن مبسيل، د؛ لصيفي بن سميدة، ب.

[أرض][113] الهند [و]، كانت له امرأة من بني شيبان[114] يقال لها سهيمة[115] بنت عمير، فنعي إليها زوجها صيفي، فتزوّجت العبّاس بن أوس العبسي[116]، [فأتوا عثمان بن عفان رضي الله عنه فقضى أن يخير الزوج الأول بين الصداق وبين امرأته، فاختار الصداق][117]، ثُمَّ أخذ [صيفي زوجة] من بني مرّة بن عباد من أهل البصرة[118].

قال عمرو: سئل جابر بن زيد عن امرأة فُقد زوجها ولم تعلم له موتا ولا حياة؟ قال: تتربص بنفسها على زوجها أربع سنين، فإن لم تعلم له موتا ولا حياة طلقها أولياء زوجها، ثُمَّ تعتدّ أربعة أشهر وعشرا، وينفق عليها من مال زوجها ما تربصت[119] في طلاقها بالمعروف.

قال عمرو: سئل جابر بن زيد: هل ينفق عليها من مال زوجها ما تربصت عليه؟

قال: سئل عن ذلك ابن عبّاس قال: إذا يكون ذلك من وراء الميراث ولا يحجب[120] ذلك بالورثة، ولكن تنفق على نفسها من ماله[121]، وكان ابن عمر يقول: إنّي لأحب أن ينفق عليها من مال زوجها بالمعروف ما تربصت عليه، ولا أرى ما قال ابن عمر لو طابت أنفس الورثة إلاَّ حسنا.

---

113 بني: +، ب.
114 من بني شيبان: –، ب.
115 سهيمة: سميرة، ب،د.
116 العباس بن أوس العبسي، والذي يذكره البيهقي العباس بن طريف القيسي.
117 انظر: السنن الكبرى للبيهقي، رقم. ١٥٩٨٥
118 قوله فنعي بالنبأ للمفعول أي فاعترف بموته فالنعي خبر الموت: هامش، ب.
119 ما تربصت: –،د.
120 يحجب: يجحف، ب.
121 ماله: مالها، ب د.

قال عمرو: إذا نعي إلى المرأة زوجها أو فقد، فطلقت، فتزوّجت زوجا آخر، فجاء زوجها الأوّل قبل أن يدخل بها زوجها الآخر، ردت إليه، وليس لها على زوجها الآخر صداق، وليس عليها منه عدّة، وإذا نعي إلى المرأة زوجها أو فقد فطلقها أولياء زوجها، فتزوّجت زوجا آخر، فجامعها، ثُمَّ رجع زوجها الأول؛ يخير بين امرأته وبين مهرها من زوجها الآخر، فإن اختار المهر فليس عليها طلاق ولا عدّة سوى الذي كان[122] من طلاق الأولياء وهي عند زوجها الآخر كما كانت.

قال عمرو[123]: سئل جابر بن زيد عن امرأة نعي إليها زوجها وفقد وطلقها أولياء زوجها، فتزوّجت زوجا آخر فجامعها ثُمَّ رجع زوجها الأول؟

قال: يخير بينها وبين مهرها من زوجها[124] الآخر، فإن اختار المرأة فلها مهرها كاملا من زوجها الآخر، وليس لزوجها الأوّل الذي ردت إليه أن يجامعها حتَّى يستبرأ طهرها، فإن حاضت وطهرت جامعها وإن كان بها حمل[125] فأجلها حتَّى تضع حملها.

قال عمرو: سئل جابر بن زيد عن امرأة نعي إليها زوجها أو فقد، فطلقها أولياء زوجها، فتزوّجت زوجا آخر فجامعها، ثُمَّ[126] إنَّ زوجها الأوّل خيّر بين امرأته وبين مهرها من زوجها الآخر فاختار امرأته، فماتت حين اختارها قبل أن يجامعها.

قال: يرثها زوجها الأول، وإن مات هو قبلها ورثته، واعتدت أربعة أشهر وعشرا،

---

122 كان: -،د.

123 قال عمرو: -،د.

124 من زوجها: -،د.

125 حمل: حبل،ب.

126 رجع: +،ب.

إلاَّ أن يكون لها من زوجها الآخر حمل، فإن كان لها[127] من زوجها الآخر حمل فعليها العدَّة[128] من زوجها الآخر حتَّى تضع، فإذا وضعت حملها اعتدت من زوجها الذي مات عنها أربعة أشهر وعشرا، وإن مات زوجها الأوَّل وليس لها من زوجها الآخر حمل، فالعدَّة من زوجها قبل أربعة أشهر وعشر، ولتعتدّ بعد ذلك من زوجها الآخر ثلاثة قروء، وإن كانت ممن[129] لا تحيض فثلاثة أشهر، ولزوجها الآخر أن يخطبها في الخطاب في عدَّتها منه إن شاء. فإن تزوّجته أمهرها آخر، وإن لم يردها هو أو أبت هي أن ترده[130]، فلا يحلّ لها أن تنكح زوجا آخر حتَّى تعتدّ منه ثلاثة قروء أو ثلاثة أشهر إن كانت مِمَّن لا تحيض، ثُمَّ يحل لها أن تتزوّج إن شاءت.

قال عمرو: سئل جابر بن زيد عن امرأة نعي إليها زوجها أو فقد فطلقها أولياء زوجها، فتزوّجت زوجا آخر فبلغها أن زوجها الأوَّل حي.

فقال: يعتزلها الذي تزوّجها آخرا حتَّى يعلم ما يصنع زوجها الأوَّل، أيختارها أم يختار[131] مهرها.

وقال عمرو والحسن: إن كان زوجها الغائب مات قبل أن يختارها هي أو مهرها فهي امرأة الذي تزوّجها بعده.

قال عمرو في العبد المملوك تكون تحته المرأة الحرَّة، فيباع العبد، فيغيب عنها أربع سنين،

127 لها: لها حبل، ب.

128 العدة: اعتدت، ب.

129 ممن: -، ب.

130 ترده: تريده، د.

131 مهرها: -، ب.

ثُمَّ ينعى إليها زوجها، فتتزوّج زوجا غيره، ثُمَّ يجيء زوجها الأول:
فقال عكرمة: إنَّه[132] يخيّر زوجها الأوّل بين امرأته وبين ما ساق إليها زوجها[133] الآخر، فإن اختار امرأته فهو أحقّ بها ولها مهرها من زوجها الآخر كاملا[134]، وإن اختار الصداق كان له من أجل أنَّها تزوّجته وهي تعلم أنَّه عبد مملوك.

قال عمرو: سئل جابر بن زيد هل تعتدّ المرأة على شهادة رجل واحد إذا نعي إليها زوجها؟
قال: لا، حتَّى يكونا رجلين ذوي عدل.
قلت: أرأيت إن مات في الطريق وليس معه غير رجل واحد أو أكله السبع.
قال: إن المرأة تأخذ[135] على شهادة رجل واحد الذي لا يتهم، تنعى خبر زوجها إذا نعي إليها.

قال عمرو: سئل جابر بن زيد هل يصدق غير أهل الصلاة إذا نعوا الرجل إلى أهله إن كانوا من أهل الكتاب أو من غيرهم، فتعتدّ المرأة على شهادتهم، ثُمَّ تتزوّج بعد عدَّتها؟
قال: لا يصدق غير أهل الصلاة، ومن اتهم من أهل الصلاة كذب، ومن تزوّج بشهادة أهل الكتاب أو من[136] يتهم من أهل الصلاة فرق بينهما من غير طلاق ويعاقبان.

---

132 عكرمة: إنه: –،د.

133 زوجها: زوجا، ب،د.

134 كاملا: –،د.

135 تأخذ: –،د.

136 من: –،ب.

قال عمرو: سئل جابر بن زيد هل تجوز شهادة امرأتين مع شهادة رجل على الطلاق والردة والنكاح إذا لم يكن رجلان.

قال: نعم.

قال عمرو: سئل جابر بن زيد عن رجل تزوّج امرأة في ليالي بقين من عدَّتها وهما لا يعلمان ذلك، فمكث سنة أو أقل أو أكثر، ثمَّ علم أنه تزوّجها في عدَّتها.

قال: يفرق بينهما بغير طلاق حين علم أنَّه تزوّجها في عدَّتها، فإن كان[137] دخل بها فلها مهرها كاملا، وإن لم يكن دخل بها فلا مهر لها عليه، وتصير حين يفرق بينهما في عدَّة زوجها الأوَّل الذي كان قد طلقها، فتعتدّ ماكان بقي عليها من عدَّة الأيَّام التي تزوّجت فيهن، إلاَّ أن يكون زوجها الذي كان طلقها توفي قبل أن ترد إلى عدَّتها منه أو توفي حين ردت إليها وهي في عدَّتها منه، فإنَّها تعتدّ عدَّة المتوفى عنها زوجها وترثه[138]. وإن كان حيا فله أن يراجعها في بقية من عدَّتها فإن راجعها[139] فليشهد على رجعتها، لا يمسها حتَّى يستبرئ طهرها، إن كان زوجها الذي تزوّجها في عدَّتها مسها، فإن لم يكن مسها فلزوجها أن يجامعها[140] إذا أشهد على رجعتها، وإن لم يرد مراجعتها[141] ولم يراجعها في عدَّتها منه حتَّى تخلو بقية[142] عدَّتها منه فلا سبيل له عليها، ولزوجها الذي كان تزوّجها في عدَّتها أن يخطبها، إذا خلت[143]

137 يعلم: +، ب.

138 وترثه: –،د.

139 فإن راجعها: –،د.

140 يجامعها: يعالجها،د.

141 مراجعتها: –، ب.

142 بقية: –،د.

143 خلت:دخلت، ب،د.

عدَّتها من زوجها الأول[144]، فإن تزوّجها فليمهرها مهرا آخر سوى صداقها الأول، وله أن يجامعها إذا ملك عصمتها، وليس عليها عدَّة من نكاحه الأول، فإن كان قد مسها ولم يتزوّجها ثانية[145] فلا يحلّ لها أن تتزوّج حتَّى تعتدّ منه عدَّة كاملة بعد عدَّتها من زوجها الأوَّل إن كان دخل بها، فإن لم يكن دخل بها فلا عدَّة عليها من بعد أن تخلو عدَّتها من زوجها الأول، ومن تزوّج امرأة من بقية من عدَّتها من زوج لها توفي وهما لا يعلمان ذلك فرق بينهما حين يعلم أنه تزوّجها في عدَّتها، وتوفى مهرها إن كان دخل بها، وإن لم يكن دخل بها[146] [فلا] مهر لها عليه، وترث زوجها المتوفى وتعتدّ عدَّة المتوفى أربعة أشهر وعشرا، إلاَّ أن يكون بها حمل من زوجها الذي كان تزوّجها في عدَّتها، فإن كان بها حمل فالعدَّة[147] منه حتَّى تضع حملها، ثُمَّ تعتدّ لزوجها المتوفى أربعة أشهر وعشرا، ثُمَّ يحل لها أن تتزوّج إن شاءت، وإن توفي زوجها الأوَّل وليس بها حمل من زوجها الآخر فالعدَّة من زوجها الأوَّل أربعة أشهر وعشر، ثُمَّ تعتدّ من زوجها الآخر بعد ذلك ثلاثة قروء، وإن كانت لا تحيض فثلاثة أشهر، ولزوجها الآخر[148] أن يخطبها في عدَّتها منه، فإن تزوّجها أمهرها مهرا آخر، ثُمَّ يدخل بها في عدَّتها منه، وإن لم يتزوّجها هو أو أبت هي أن تتزوّجه فلا يحلّ لها أن تتزوّج غيره حتَّى تستكمل عدَّتها منه ثلاثة

144 الأول: الآخر، ب.

145 ثانية: –، ب.

146 عدَّة عليها من بعد أن تخلو عدَّتها من زوجها الأول ومن تزوّج امرأة من بقية من عدَّتها من زوج لها توفي وهما لا يعلمان ذلك فرق بينهما حين يعلم أنه تزوّجها في عدَّتها وتوفي مهرها إن كان دخل بها، وإن لم يكن دخل بها: –،د.

147 فالعدة: فالتعدُدَّ، ب.

148 الآخر، –، ب،د.

قروء أو ثلاثة أشهر إن كانت لا تحيض، ثُمَّ تتزوّج إن شاءت، ومن تزوّج امرأة في عدَّتها وهما يعلمان ذلك فرق بينهما ثُمَّ لا يراجعها.

قال عمرو: قد زعم الحسن أنَّ عمر بن الخطَّاب رضي الله عنه قد فرق بين رجل وامرأة تزوّجها في عدَّتها وضربهما جميعا.

قال عمرو: سئل جابر بن زيد عن رجل طلق امرأته، فرأى أن عدَّتها قد انقضت، فتزوّج أختالها في ليالٍ من عدَّة المطلقة؟

قال: يفرق بينهما بغير طلاق يوم يعلم أنَّه تزوّجها في عدَّة أختها، فإن كان قد دخل بها فلها مهرها الذي كان تزوّج عليه، وتعتدّ عدَّة المطلقة، ولا تحل له ما بقيا.

قلت: أرأيت إن كانت المطلقة ماتت في عدَّتها قبل أن يعلم أنَّه تزوّج أختها في عدَّتها؟

قال: يرث المَيِّتة، ويفرق بينه وبين الحية على كلّ حال، وإن لم يكن دخل بها[149] فلا مهرلها ولا عدَّة عليها، ثُمَّ إن شاء أن يراجعها بعد الفرقة، بعد ما يخلو ما بقي من عدَّة أختها المَيِّتة.

قال عمرو: سئل جابر بن زيد عن رجل كانت تحته امرأتان، فأخبرته امرأة أنَّهَا أرضعتهما جميعا؟

قال: إن كانت المرأة مِمَّن لا يتهم صدقت، ويفرق بين الرجل والمرأتين بغير طلاق؛ لأنَّه جمع بين الأختين، وذلك من أكبر الحرام، ولا أرى أن يراجع واحدة منهن ما بقي بعد الفرقة، فإن كان قد دخل بهما فعليهما عدَّة المطلقة، وإن لم يكن دخل بهما فلا مهر لهما عليه ولا عدَّة عليهما منه.

ومن كانت تحته امرأة فتزوّج عليها أختالها من الرضاع، فعلم بعد ذلك أنَّهَا أخت امرأته

149 وإن لم يكن دخل بها: –،د.

من الرضاع فطلقها قبل أن يدخل بها فلا مهر لها عليه، ولا عدّة عليها منه، ولا بأس أن يمسك امرأته التي كانت تحته.

قال عمرو: سئل جابر بن زيد عن امرأة تزوّجها رجل ودخل بها، ثُمَّ جاءت امرأة مرضية مقنعة[150] فزعمت أنَّها أرضعتهما جميعا؟

قال: يفرق بينهما، ويوفي مهرها كاملا إن كان دخل بها، وإن لم يكن دخل بها فلا مهر لها عليه، وتجوز شهادة المرأة عليهما وحدها.

قال عمرو: سئل جابر بن زيد عن رجل كانت له ثلاث بنات وكان غازيا، وكان معه ابن أخ، فقال ابن أخيه: أنكحني إحدى بناتك، فقال له عمه[151]: قد أنكحتك إحداهن، فإذا قدمت المصر فانظر أحبهن إليك أن تتزوّج فهي امرأتك، وأشهد له على ذلك، وفرض لها صداقها عليه[152]، وأنقده ابن أخيه ألف درهم، ثُمَّ توفي ابن أخيه قبل أن يقدم المصر[153]، وقد سمّىَ المرأة التي يريد منهن، فسئل عن المهر والميراث: لأيتهن يؤول[154]؟

قال: ليس لواحدة منهن مهر ولا ميراث. من[155] المتوفى، ويرد إلى ورثة المتوفى الألف التي كان نقد؛ لأنّه لا يكون تزويجا حتَّى يُسمِّي المرأة التي تزوّج ويُشهد على نكاحها شهودا فيثبت الصداق ويحل النكاح، ولا يحلّ لرجل أن يملك عصمة ثلاث أخوات في الإسلام، ولا يكون لامرأة مهر على رجل ولا ترثه بعد موته حتَّى يحل له مجامعتها في حياته.

150 مرضية مقنعة: –،د.

151 عمه: –،د.

152 عليه، وعليه، ب،د.

153 المصر: المصروف، ب د. .

154 يؤول: هو، ب.

155 من: على، ب.

قال عمرو: سئل جابر بن زيد عن رجل طلق امرأته، ثُمَّ تزوّجها آخر، ثُمَّ طلقها قبل أن يدخل بها، هل يحل[156] لزوجها الأوّل الذي كان قد بت طلاقها أن يراجعها؟

قال: لا، حتَّى يجامعها زوجها الذي تزوّجها بعده، وقد بلغنا أنَّ امرأة من بني النظير يقال لها تميمة[157] بنت وهب[158] بن عتيق، كانت تحت رجل من قريظة يقال له رفاعة، قد بتَّ طلاقها[159]، فتزوّجها بعده رجل يقال له عبد الرحمن بن الزبير، فطلقها ابن الزبير قبل أن يدخل بها، فجاءت إلى رسول الله صلى الله عليه وسلم فقالت له: أأرجع إلى زوجي الأول؟ فقال لها رسول الله صلى الله عليه وسلم: هل مسك هذا الآخر منهما؟ فقالت: لا، فقال لها رسول الله صلى الله عليه وسلم: لا يحلّ لك أن تتزوّجيه حتَّى يكون قد جامعك الآخر منهما[160]، فذهبت المرأة ثُمَّ جاءته فقالت: إنَّه قد جامعها زوجها الآخر، فكذبها رسول الله صلى الله عليه وسلم ومنعها أن ترجع لزوجها الأول، ثُمَّ إنَّها جاءت إلى أبي بكر بعد خلافته فمنعها أن تتزوّجه، ثُمَّ جاءت إلى عمر في خلافته فمنعها أن تتزوّجه، كلهم منعوها أن تتزوّج زوجها الأوّل حتَّى تتزوّج زوجا يجامعها.

قال عمرو: سئل جابر بن زيد عن رجل طلق امرأته ثُمَّ تزوّجها رجل[161] ليحللها له،

156 يحل: تحل، ب.

157 تميمة: سمية، د.

158 بنت وهب: -، د.

159 طلاقها: فطلقها، ب.

160 رواه الترمذي، باب ما جاء فيمن يطلق امرأته ثلاثا فيتزوجها آخر فيطلقها قبل أن يدخل بها، ر١١١٨.

161 رجل: آخر، ب.

ولا يشعر زوجها الأول[162] الذي طلقها أنّه فعل ذلك ليحللها له؟

قال: لا تصح مراجعتها[163] وإن لم يشعر بعد أن يكون الآخر إنّمَا تزوّجها ليحلها له.

قال عمرو: سئل جابر بن زيد عن رجل خطب امرأة في عدّتها فتوافقا[164] على أمر بينهما، فلمَّا انقضت عدّتها أظهرا أمرهما ذلك؟

قال: إن ابن عبّاس كان يقول: بديا أمرهما بمعصية الله وأحب ذلك[165] أن يفرق بينهما.

قال عمرو: سئل جابر بن زيد عن رجل قال لامرأته: هي عليه[166] حرام؟

قال: إنّمَا هي يمين فليكفر يمينه وليمسك امرأته، وإن لم يكفر يمينه ويراجع امرأته حتَّى تمضي أربعة أشهر تبين منه امرأته، وهي تطليقة واحدة، وإن خطبها بعد ذلك فتزوّجته فهي عنده على تطليقتين[167].

باب في الإيلاء

قال عمرو: سئل جابر بن زيد عن رجل هجر امرأته حتَّى مضت[168] أربعة أشهر: أتحرم عليه امرأته؟

162 الأول: ـ،د.
163 تصح مراجعتها: تصلح مجامعتها، ب.
164 فتوافقا: فتواطن، ب.
165 ذلك: ـ،د.
166 عليه: علي،د.
167 من قال: لأمرأته هي عليه حرام، فعليه كفارة يمين: هامش، ب.
168 تمضي، ب.

قال: لا، إلاَّ أن يكون أقسم بالله ألا يمسها ولا يصالحها، فإن كان أقسم بذلك ولم يراجعها حتَّى مضت أربعة أشهر فقد بانت منه وهي إيلاء.

قال عمرو: قد زعم نافع مولى ابن عمر أن ابن عمر كان يقول من آلى من امرأته شهرا أو أقل أو أكثر فليس له أن يراجعها حتَّى يكفر عن يمينه التي آلى عليها.

قال عمرو: سئل جابر بن زيد عن رجل آلى من امرأته؟

قال: له أن يتربص أربعة أشهر، فإن فاء فيهن فكفر عن يمينه راجع امرأته وأشهد على رجعتها، فهي امرأته. وإن لم يكفر يمينه ولم يراجع امرأته حتَّى تنقضي[169] أربعة أشهر فقد حرمت عليه امرأته[170]، وهي تطليقة واحدة، ثُمَّ تعتدّ منه بعد أن تبين منه بثلاثة قروء إن كانت تحيض، وإن كانت مِمَّن لا تحيض فثلاثة أشهر، ولزوجها أن يخطبها في عدَّتها منه، فإن خطبها فتزوّجته فهي عنده على تطليقتين، ويكفر عن يمينه قبل أن يدخل بها، فإن خطبها فتزوّجها[171] فهي عنده على تطليقتين ويكفر عن يمينه قبل أن يدخل بها، فإن لم يراجعها فلا يحلّ لها أن تتزوّج غيره حتَّى تعتدّ منه ثلاثة قروء أو ثلاثة أشهر إن كانت ممن[172] لا تحيض بعد الأربعة أشهر، ثُمَّ إن شاءت تزوّجت.

قال عمرو: وكذلك قال الحسن أيضا.

169 تنقضي: تمضي، ب.

170 امرأته: -،د.

171 فتزوجها: فتزوجت، ب د.

172 ممن: -،د.

قال عمرو: ومن الإيلاء أن يقول الرجل: علي عهد الله وميثاقه ألاَّ آتي امرأتي[173].

قال عمرو: سئل جابر بن زيد عن رجل آلى من امرأته ثُمَّ سافر قبل أن يكفر عن يمينه ويراجع امرأته، هل يصلح أن يكفر عن يمينه في غيبته ويراجع امرأته وإن لم يجامعها؟ قال: نعم، يكفر عن يمينه ويشهد على رجعتها وهي امرأته وإن لم يجامعها.

قال عمرو: سئل جابر بن زيد عن رجل آلى من امرأته، ثُمَّ طلقها تطليقة واحدة؟ قال: إن أجل الإيلاء أربعة أشهر وأجل الطلاق ثلاثة قروء، فإن خلا أجل الإيلاء أربعة أشهر قبل أن يكفر يمينه ويشهد على رجعة امرأته فقد بانت منه بتطليقتين، وإن خلا أجل الطلاق ثلاثة قروء قبل أن يشهد على مراجعة امرأته فقد بانت منه بتطليقة واحدة، وإن راجعها قبل أن يخلو أحد الأجلين فليس له أن يجامعها حتَّى يكفر عن يمينه التي آلى عليها، وهي عنده على تطليقتين.

قال عمرو: سئل جابر بن زيد عن رجل آلى من امرأته، ثُمَّ لم يراجعها حتَّى مات قبل أن تقضي أربعة أشهر؟
قال: ترثه وتعتدّ عدَّة المتوفى عنها زوجها، وإن ماتت هي قبل أن تقضي[174] أربعة أشهر من الإيلاء ورثها زوجها، وإن لم يكن راجعها قبل موتها.

قال عمرو: سئل جابر بن زيد عن رجل آلى من سريته ما الذي يصنع؟
قال: إن كفر عن يمينه وراجعها قبل أن تقضي أربعة أشهر فلا بأس بذلك.

---

173 ألاَّ آتي امرأتي: أن لا يأتي امرأته، ب.

174 تقضي: تخلو، د.

قال عمرو: سئل جابر بن زيد عن امرأة فرت من زوجها، فحلف زوجها ألا يطأها حتَّى ترجع هي، فخلا أربعة أشهر قبل أن ترجع هي؟

قال الحسن: ليس ذلك بشيء، ولا هو إيلاء إذا كانت هي التي فرت منه، وزعم أنَّه كان يقال[175]: لا يقبل لها عمل حتَّى ترجع إلى زوجها فتضع يدها في يده، ثُمَّ تقول له: أنا هذه فاصنع ما شئت[176].

قال عمرو: سئل جابر بن زيد عن الكفَّارة لمن آلى من امرأته أو سريته أو من جعلهما عليه حراما، ماذا يصنع؟

قال: يطعم عشرة مساكين من أوسط ما تطعمون أهليكم أو كسوتهم أو تحرير رقبة فمن لم يجد فصيام ثلاثة أيَّام متتابعات.

قال عمرو: سئل جابر بن زيد عن رجل ظاهر من امرأته شهرا فمضى شهر ولم يراجعها؟

قال: إذا ظاهر الرجل شهرا أو أقل من ذلك أو أكثر، فليس له أن يجامعها حتَّى يكفر عن يمينه، فإن جامعها قبل أن يكفر عن يمينه فقد حرمت عليه أبدا ما بقيا[177]، وهو حدّ من حدود الله تعالى[178] تعداه، فإن كفر عن يمينه[179]، وراجع امرأته قبل أن تمضي أربعة أشهر فلا بأس بذلك، وإن مضت أربعة أشهر ولم يكفر ولم يراجع امرأته

175 كان يقال: -، د.

176 المرأة الهاربة من زوجها لا يقبل لها عمل حتى ترجع: هامش، ب.

177 ما بقيا: -، ب.

178 تعالى: -، د.

179 عن يمينه: -، ب.

فقد حرمت عليه، وهي تطليقة واحدة، وإن خطبها بعد ذلك فتزوّجته فلا يمسها حتَّى يكفر عن يمينه، فإن كفر يمينه[180] ودخل بها فهي عنده على تطليقتين[181].

حدَّثنا عمرو بن هرم قال: سئل جابر بن زيد عن رجل قال لامرأته: أنت علي كبطن أمي؟

قال: البطن والظهر بمنزلة واحدة في الظهار.

قال عمرو: سئل جابر بن زيد عن رجل قال لامرأته: أنت علي مثل ظهر أمي أو ابنتي؟

قال: إنه[182] منزلة من حرم الله عليه نكاحه مثل هذا على الرجل؛ إذ ظهر[183] الأم والابنة وجميع من حرم الله عليه سواء إن ظاهر في شيء منهن، وهن بمنزلة الأم كلهن في الحرمة سواء.

قال عمرو: سئل جابر بن زيد عن رجل عرضت عليه امرأة ليتزوّجها، فقال: هي علي كظهر أمي إن تزوّجتها، ثُمَّ رغب فيها بعد ذلك؟

قال: فليتزوّجها إن شاء، فلا بأس بذلك.

قال عمرو: سئل جابر بن زيد عن رجل ظاهر من امرأته مرارًا في مجالس شتى، ماذا عليه من الكفَّارة؟

قال: واحدة، وإن الظهار في الحرّة والأمة سواء في الكفَّارات إذا هو ظاهر منهما.

---

180 يمينه: -،د.

181 تطليقتين: تطليقة،د.

182 إنه: -،د.

183 ظهر: بمنزلة، ب.

قال عمرو: سئل جابر بن زيد عن رجل طلق امرأته طلاقا[184] واحدا، ثُمَّ حاضت بعد ذلك ثلاث[185] حيضات[186]، لا تستنكر من نفسها شيئا، ثُمَّ تزوّجت زوجا آخر وساق إليها صداقها، ثُمَّ توفي الرجل قبل أن يدخل بها، ثُمَّ استبان حمل المرأة بعد ذلك، فمرض زوجها الذي كان طلقها، فبلغه في مرضه أن فلانة المطلقة تزعم أنَّها حبلى منك، فأنكر ذلك وزعم أنَّها حاضت ثلاث حيضات بعد طلاقه إيَّاها، فكيف[187] حبلت منه؟ قال: أمَّا زوجها الآخر، فلا صداق لها عليه ولا ترثه، وأمَّا الأوَّل فإن وضعت ولدها وتبين ذلك لستة أشهر إلى تسعة من قبل أن المرأة تمكث سنة ثُمَّ تلد. قال: إن كان ذلك كذلك وكانت مِمَّن لا يتهم فإنَّها تصدق، وإن مكثت في حبلها سنة أو زيادة على ذلك فالولد ولده وترثه إن مات، وإن كان مجاحدته إيَّاها على شبهة من ظن لتزوّجها[188] الآخر فلا حدّ عليه، وله أن يراجعها في عدَّتها إن شاء، وإن كان إنَّمَا رماها بالزنى مخافة أن ترثه إن مات قبل أن تخلو عدَّتها، فإنَّها ترثه إن مات، وإن عاش جلد صاغرا. فقد زعم ابن عبَّاس أن رامي المطلقة يحد[189] ولا يتلاعنان وإن كان له عليها رجعة. وأمَّا ابن عمر فزعم أن العدَّة في ملاك مراجعة الرجل[190] امرأته تمحي عنه الحدّ ما دام له عليها الرجعة، وأمَّا أنا فلا أرى العدَّة بمنزلة العصمة، إنَّه رماها في ظهر الغيب، وإنَّما التلاعن

184 طلاقا: -، ب،د.

185 ثلاث: ثلاثة، ب،د.

186 حيضات: حيض، ب.

187 فكيف: فإن، ب.

188 لتزوجها: لتزويجها، ب.

189 يحد: يجلد، ب.

190 الرجل: -،د.

بين الزوجين بشهادة في غير أذى ولا أمر يتهم غيبته[191].

ومن رمى امرأته بالزنى، فإن أقام عليها أربعة شهود[192] أنّها زانية رجمت، وإن لم يقم عليها البيّنة جلد الحد، إلاّ أن يشهد ﴿ أَرْبَعُ شَهَادَاتٍ بِاللَّهِ إِنَّهُ لَمِنَ الصَّادِقِينَ وَالْخَامِسَةُ أَنَّ لَعْنَتَ اللَّهِ عَلَيْهِ إِن كَانَ مِنَ الْكَاذِبِينَ ﴾[193]، ويوجب على المرأة الرجم، إلاّ ﴿ أَن تَشْهَدَ أَرْبَعَ شَهَادَاتٍ بِاللَّهِ إِنَّهُ لَمِنَ الْكَاذِبِينَ وَالْخَامِسَةَ أَنَّ غَضَبَ اللَّهِ عَلَيْهَا إِن كَانَ مِنَ الصَّادِقِينَ ﴾[194]، ويدرأ عنها العذاب[195] بذلك وهو الرجم، ويفرق بينهما بغير طلاق، وتوفى مهرها كاملا، وتعتدّ عدّة المطلقة، فلا يحلّ له أن يراجعها بعد هذا أبدا ما بقيا، وإن كانت حاملا فزعم زوجها أن حملها ذلك من الزنا، فالولد لأمه يرثها وترثه[196]، وعصبته أولياؤها ،ولا يدعى إلى الذي انتفى منه من بعد ما انتفى منه[197]، ومن نفاه بعد ذلك فزعم أنّه ابن زانية جلد الحدّ، ومن رمى أمه بالزنى جلد الحد، وإن ادعى الذي انتفى منه من بعد ما انتفى منه وزعم أنّه ابن زانية جلد الحدّ برميه أمه بالزنى، والولد ولده، ويرث أحدهما الآخر، ولا سبيل له على المرأة بعد رميه إيّاها بالزنى وملاعنتها.

قال عمرو: سئل جابر بن زيد عن رجل رمى امرأته بالزنى وهي حبلى، وزعم أن حبلها ليس منه، ثمّ مات الرجل قبل أن يتلاعنا؟

191 بشهادة في غير أذى ولا أمر يتهم غيبته: -،د.

192 شهود: شهداء، ب.

193 سورة النور: ٦، ٧.

194 سورة النور: ٨، ٩.

195 العذاب: -، ب.

196 وترثه: -،د.

197 من بعد ما انتفى منه: -، ب.

قال: ابن عبَّاس كان يقول: هو الملعون[198] إذا لاعنت نفسها، وشهدت بالله أنَّه لمن الكاذبين ترثه وتأخذ صداقها كاملا والولد ولده وهو يرثه.

قال عمرو: سئل جابر بن زيد عن رجل نفى الابن بعد ذلك، وقال: نفاك أبوك وأنت ابن زانية؟

قال: يجلد الذي نفاه الحدّ ولو صدق لم يقم عليه الحدّ، والحدُّ على المرأة الرجم.

قال عمرو: سئل جابر بن زيد عن رجل رمى امرأته بالزنى، وبعث ثلاثة شهود فشهدوا عليها أنَّها زانية؟

قال عكرمة مولى ابن عبَّاس: روى عن ابن عبَّاس أنَّه كان يقول: إن حلفت جلد الثلاثة، ولم تقبل شهادتهم؛ لأنَّها لما حلفت برئت منه وكان الثلاثة بمنزلة من رماها.

قال عمرو: سئل جابر بن زيد عن امرأة زنت ثُمَّ رجمت[199] هل يرثها زوجها؟

قال: لا، وله ماله الذي كان قد أصدقها إيَّاه، كله عاجله وآجله، يؤخذ من مالها إن كان لها مال ويدفع إليه، وسائر مالها ميراث بين ورثتها، وقال: إن الزانية لا مهر لها ولا يرثها زوجها إذا رجعت.

قال عمرو: سئل جابر بن زيد عن رجل رمى سريته بالزنى؟

قال: كان ابن عبَّاس يحرمها عليه، ولا نراه إلاَّ قد صدق.

قال عمرو: سئل جابر بن زيد عن امرأة رمت زوجها بالزنى؟

---

198 هو الملعون: –،د.

199 رجمت: رجعت،د.

قال: إن بعثت عليه أربعة شهود[200] رجم، وإن لم تبعث عليه أربعة شهود جلدت الحد، وليس بينهما تلاعن، فإن شاء زوجها أن يمسكها بعد الحد، وإن شاء فارقها، وكان رجل من الأنصار واحد من بني واقف يقال له: هلال بن أميَّة، كانت تحته امرأة من قومه فظنها لرجل من قومه يقال له شريك بن سحماء، وكان أسود، فلاعن رسول الله -صلى الله عليه وسلم- بين هلال بن أميَّة وامرأته، وأمر أن يفرق بينهما، ثُمَّ إن المرأة بعد ذلك ولدت غلاما أسود شبيها بالذي رميت به أمه، وأنه أُتي به إلى رسول الله -صلى الله عليه وسلم- فزعموا: أنَّ رسول الله -صلى الله عليه وسلم- قال: لولا الذي كان من أمرها كان لي فيها أمر[201]. قال: إنَّمَا يعني بذلك التلاعن الذي كان بينهما[202]، ويقال: إنَّه قضى بالغلام لعصبة أمه، وإن الغلام عاش حتَّى بلغ مبلغ الرجال وأصاب المال[203]، ثُمَّ توفي في خلافة عمر بن الخطَّاب، فيقال إنَّه جاء أهل هلال بن أميَّة زوج أمه الذي كان انتفى منه ولاعن امرأته[204] يطلبون ميراثه، فقالوا: إنَّه ابن هلال، فأبى ذلك عليهم عمر ولم يورثهم شيئا وجعل ميراثه لعصبة أمه.

قال عمرو: سئل جابر بن زيد هل كان رسول الله صلى الله عليه وسلم فرض للنساء مهورا؟

قال: لا أعلمه إلاَّ ما اصطلح عليه الناس، قال عمرو: قد قال الحسن ذلك أيضا.

---

200 رجمت: -، ب.

201 رواه البخاري، باب ﴿وَيَدْرَأُ عَنْهَا الْعَذَابَ أَنْ تَشْهَدَ أَرْبَعَ شَهَادَاتٍ بِاللَّهِ إِنَّهُ لَمِنَ الْكَاذِبِينَ﴾، ر٤٤٧٠. ورواه البيهقي، السنن الكبرى، ر ١٥٣٥١.

202 الذي كان بينهما: -،د.

203 وأصاب المال: -،د.

204 ولعن امرأته: -،د.

فصل في الصدقات

«ثنا عمرو بن هرم حدثني محمد بن عبد الرحمن الأنصاري يعني أبا الرجال قال: لما استخلف عمر بن عبد العزيز أرسل إلى المدينة يلتمس كتاب رسول الله صلى الله عليه و سلم في الصدقات وكتاب عمر، فوجد عند آل عمرو بن حزم كتاب رسول الله صلى الله عليه و سلم إلى عمرو بن حزم في الصدقات، و وجد عند آل عمر كتاب عمر رضي الله عنه في الصدقات مثل كتاب رسول الله صلى الله عليه و سلم فنسخا له فحدثني عمرو أنه طلب إلى محمد بن عبد الرحمن أن ينسخ له ما في ذينك الكتابين»[205].

حدَّثني أنَّه طلب إلى مُحَمَّد بن عبد الرحمن أن ينسخ له ما في هذا الكتاب من صدقات[206] الإبل و البقر و الشياه و الذهب و الورق و التمر و الحب[207] و الزبيب.

صدقات الإبل: لا يؤخذ من دون الخمس منها شيء، فإذا بلغت خمسا ففيها شاة حتَّى تبلغ تسعا، فإذ زادت على تسع ففيها شاتان، حتَّى تبلغ أربع عشرة، فإذا زادت على أربع عشرة ففيها ثلاث شياه حتَّى تبلغ تسع عشرة، فإذا زادت على تسع عشرة ففيها أربع شياه حتَّى تبلغ خمسا وعشرين، ففيها بنت مخاض، فإن لم توجد بنت مخاض فابن لبون ذكر حتَّى تبلغ خمسا وثلاثين، فإذا زادت واحدة على خمس وثلاثين، ففيها بنت لبون حتَّى تبلغ خمسا وأربعين، فإذا زادت واحدة على خمس وأربعين ففيها حقة طروقة الفحل، حتَّى تبلغ ستِّين، فإن زادت واحدة ففيها جذعة حتَّى تبلغ خمسا

205 نقلت هذا الأثر من سنن البيهقي، باب إبانة قوله وفي كل أربعين ابنة لبون وفي كل خمسين حقة، ر٧٠٥٠؛ لأن النص في ب،د مضطرب وفيه حذف.

206 صدقات: صدقة، ب.

207 الحب: –،د.

وسبعين، فإن زادت واحدة ففيها ابنتا لبون حتَّى تبلغ تسعين، فإذا زادت على التسعين[208] واحدة ففيها حقتان حتَّى تبلغ عشرين ومائة، فإن زادت على عشرين ومائة ففيها ثلاث بنات لبون حتَّى تبلغ تسعا وعشرين ومائة، فإن زادت الإبل أكثر من ذلك فليس فيما لم يبلغ العشرة منها شيء حتَّى تبلغ العشرة، وفي الثلاثين ومائة ابنتا لبون وحقة، وفي الأربعين ومائة حقتان وبنت لبون، وفي خمسين ومائة ثلاثة حقائق، وفي الستِّين ومائة أربع بنات لبون، وفي سبعين ومائة ثلاث بنات لبون وحقة، وفي الثمانين ومائة حقتان وبنتا لبون، وفي التسعين ومائة ثلاث حقائق وبنت لبون، وفي مائتين خمس بنات لبون، أو أربع حقائق، وفي عشر ومائتين أربع بنات لبون وحقة، وفي عشرين ومائتين ثلاث بنات لبون وحقتان، وفي ثلاثين ومائتين ثلاث حقائق وبنتا لبون، وفي أربعين ومائتين ست[209] بنات لبون، أو أربع حقائق وبنت لبون، وفي خمسين ومائتين خمس حقائق، أو خمس بنات لبون وحقة، وفي ستِّين ومائتين أربع بنات لبون وحقتان، وفي السبعين ومائتين ثلاث حقائق وأربع[210] بنات لبون، وفي ثمانين ومائتين سبع بنات لبون، أو أربع حقائق وابنتا لبون، وفي تسعين ومائتين ست بنات لبون وحقة، وفي ثلاثمائة ست حقائق، أو خمس بنات لبون وحقتان.

في أي هذه السنن شاء المتصدق أخذ هذه الفرائض في[211] هذه العدَّة، فإن كانت الإبل أكثر من ذلك أخذ مِمَّا يبلغ منها خمسين حقة وفيما يبلغ الأربعين بنت لبون على نحو ما في الكتاب، لا يفرق بين مجتمع ولا يجمع بين مفترق حذار الصدقة، ومن أي سنٍ أخذت

208 على التسعين: -، ب.

209 ست: ستة، ب،د.

210 اربع: ثلاث، ب.

211 في: على، ب.

الفرائض فإن لرب الإبل أن يختار خير ذلك السنين بعيرا، ثُمَّ يختار المصدق بعيرا فإن كانت الإبل أكثر من ذلك فإن ربّ المال يختار منها بعيرا[212]. منها أربعين[213]، ثُمَّ المصدق آخر حتَّى يستو في عدَّة ما فيها من الفرائض على ذلك النحو إن شاء المصدق باع الفرائض قبل أن يقبضها من ربها إذا علمها ولربها إن شاء باعها.

قالوا[214]: والبقر يؤخذ منها ما يؤخذ من الإبل من الصدقة على عدَّتها، وقد سئل عن صدقتها إذا كثرت[215].

وقالوا: هي بمنزلة الإبل يؤخذ منها ما يؤخذ من الإبل من الصدقة على عدَّتها وقد سئل عن صدقتها غيره[216]، قالوا: هي بمنزلة الإبل يؤخذ منها ما يؤخذ من الإبل من الصدقة إذا كثرت أخذ من كلّ خمسين بقرة بقرة.

وصدقة الغنم: لا يؤخذ مِمَّا لم يبلغ أربعين شاة[217]، فإذا بلغت أربعين كان فيها شاة حتَّى تبلغ عشرين ومائة، فإن زادت على عشرين ومائة واحدة ففيها شاتان حتَّى تبلغ مائتين، فإذا زادت على المائتين واحدة ففيها ثلاث شياه حتَّى تبلغ ثلاثمائة، فإذا زادت على ثلاثمائة كان في كلّ مائة منها شاة لا يؤخذ من الزيادة على المائة، وإن بلغ تسعا وتسعين حتَّى تبلغ المائة بعد أن تزيد الغنم على ثلاثمائة لا يؤخذ هرما ولا ذكرا إلاَّ أن يشاء المتصدق، ولا يفرق بين مجتمع ولا يجمع بين مفترق حذار الصدقة.

212 خير ذلك السنين بعيرا، ثُمَّ يختار المصدق بعيرا فإن كانت الإبل أكثر من ذلك فإن ربّ المال يختار منها بعيرا: -،د.

213 منها أربعين: -، ب.

214 قالوا: -،د.

215 إذا كثرت: -،د.

216 وقالوا هي بمنزلة . . . صدقتها غيره: -، ب.

217 شاة: شي،د.

ويؤخذ من التمر والحب والزبيب ماكان سقي بالسماء والأنهار وماكان[218] من بعلٍ[219] العشر من كلّ عشرة واحد، ويؤخذ مِمّاَ يسقى بالنضح نصف العشر، فلا يؤخذ من التمر والحب والزبيب حتَّى تبلغ خمسة[220] أوساق[221].

وصدقة الذهب والورق لا يؤخذ من الذهب شيء حتَّى يبلغ عشرين دينارا فإذا بلغ عشرين دينارا ففيها نصف دينار ولا يؤخذ من الورق شيء حتَّى يبلغ مائتين، فإذا بلغ مائتين ففي كلّ أربعين درهما درهم.

قال عمرو: عن جابر بن زيد سئل عن زكاة الذهب والورق؟
قال: قال رسول الله -صلى الله عليه وسلم-: «اعلموا شهرا من السنة فأخرجوا فيه صدقة أموالكم، فما حدث لكم من أموال بعد إخراج الصدقة فلا صدقة فيها حتَّى يبلغ رأس السنة»[222].

قال عمرو: سئل جابر على من تجب الصدقة من الناس؟
قال: على أهل الأموال على أنفسهم زكاة الفطر وعلى[223] أموالهم.

قال عمرو: سئل جابر بن زيد عن الفقراء: هل على أنفسهم من الصدقة شيء؟
قال: إنَّمَا الصدقات للفقراء والمساكين والعاملين عليها[224]، فليست عليهم.

218 سقي: +، ب.
219 بعل: بعد،د.
220 خمسة: خمس، ب د.
221 أوساق: أوست،د.
222 لم أجد من خرجه.
223 زكاة الفطر وعلى: -، ب.
224 والعاملين عليها: -،د.

قال عمرو: سئل جابر بن زيد عن الصدقة كم من الذهب والورق؟

قال: في عشرين مثقالا نصف مثقال[225] وعلى مائتين من الورق خمسة دراهم، وعلى أهل الأموال على كلّ نفس صغير وكبير،ذكر وأنثى، حرّ وعبد، صاع من بر أو شعير[226] أوتمر، والأخيرة زكاة فطر[227]».

قال عمرو: سئل جابر بن زيد فيمن تجعل الصدقة؟

قال: في أهل الفقر[228] والمسكنة من الناس من المسلمين ومن أهل عهدهم.[229] وفي أهل الذمّة من الخمس والصدقة.

قال عمرو: سئل جابر بن زيد هل للرجل فضل في الصدقة على المرأة[230]؟

قال: ليس بميراث يفضل فيها الرجال على النساء، فالرجال والنساء فيها سواء إذا كانت الفاقة سواء[231].

قال عمرو: سئل جابر بن زيد عن حلي المرأة؟

قال: فيه الزكاة في كلّ سنة[232] إذا بلغ عشرين دينار أو مائتي درهم.

---

225 نصف مثقال: -، ب،د.

226 شعير: الشعير، ب،د.

227 والأخيرة زكاة فطر: -، ب.

228 الفقر: الفاقة، ب.

229 قال وقد كان في رسول الله - عليه الصلاة والسلام - يقسم: -،د.

230 المراءة: النساء، ب.

231 إذا كانت الفاقة سواء: -،د.

232 في كل سنة: -،د.

قال عمرو: سئل جابر بن زيد عن مال[233] الرجل المكنز[234]؟

قال: إذا أعطى زكاته كلّ سنة وعرف حق ذي قرابته[235]، وأتى من[236] ماله ما أمره الله به فليس بكنز وإن كنز.

قال عمرو: سئل جابر بن زيد عن ماشية كانت لرجل فصدقت، ثُمَّ مات الرجل ثُمَّ ورثها أهله هل عليهم فيها صدقة؟
قال: ما أعرف منها في الميراث أو عطية لم يؤخذ لها ثمن، فلا صدقة فيه دون الحول، وأمّا ما بيع منها فالصدقة فيه إلاَّ أن يكون الذي ابتاعها قد زكى ورقه الذي ابتاع بها قبل أن يبتاعها، فلا زكاة[237] فيها.

قال عمرو: سئل جابر بن زيد عن رجل أصاب مالا فابتاع رقيقين في يده وهو صدقة أو أوراق وفيها بعد ذلك ما كان على الرقيق؟[238]

قال عمرو: سئل جابر بن زيد عن رجل يبتاع بضاعة[239] البر، ثُمَّ يكسد عليه حتَّى يحول الحول، يرى أنَّه لو باعه لم يبلغ النصف من رأس ماله وحضرت صدقته؟

233 مال: -،د.
234 المكنز: المكنوز، ب.
235 قرابته: قرباته، ب،د.
236 من: -،د.
237 زكاة: صدقة، ب.
238 هذه المسألة جاءت هكذا من غير جواب.
239 بضاعة: -،د.

قال: لا أرى لو قوّمه بنحو ثمنه وكملت فيه الزكاة[240]، ثُمَّ أخذ[241] زكاته إلاَّ أنَّه أحسن، على أنَّ ابن عبَّاس كان يقول: لا بأس بالتربص حتَّى يبيع والزكاة عليه واجبة.

قال عمرو: سئل جابر بن زيد عن رجل يكون له الدين على الرجل؟

قال: أيّما دين يرجوه أهله فإنّه يؤدي زكاته، وما خفت تراه فالزكاة إذا قبضه زكاة السلف منه[242]. ومما لا يرجوه فالزكاة فيه إذا قبضه زكّاه[243].

قال عمرو: سئل جابر بن زيد عن رجل ورث من[244] أبيه مالا، أو أب ورث من[245] ابنه مالا ثم[246] لم يكن الميِّت زكّاه؟

قال: أمَّا ما كان من أمر جهالة جهله الميِّت، فأحب أن يزكيه الحي عن الميِّت، إذا ولي ذلك، وعلم أن الميِّت إنَّمَا ترك ذلك من قبل جهالة، وأمَّا من ترك ذلك عمدا وهو يعلم فلا يزكى عنه، وقد يترك الناس الزكاة من جهالة ثم[247] يكون للقوم الحلي لا يرون أن عليهم فيها زكاة فيكونون على عذر منه، فمن علم ذلك فليبتغ منه الحَقّ، من غير أن يركب من ذلك ما[248] يجحف بأهل الميراث فيذهب[249] بما في أيديهم منه.

---

240 قوّمه بنحو ثمنه وكملت فيه الزكاة: قومه بثمنه يوم حلت فيه الزكاة، ب.

241 أخذ: أخرج، ب.

242 وما خفت تراه فالزكاة إذا قبضه زكاة السلف منه: –،د.

243 ومما لا . . . قبضه الزكاة: –، ب.

244 من: عن، ب.

245 من: عن، ب.

246 ثم: –،د.

247 ثم: –،د.

248 يركب من ذلك ما: –،د.

249 فيذهب: –،د.

قال عمرو: سئل جابر بن زيد عن رجل زكى ثمرته يوم حصادها، ثُمَّ حالت السنة ولم يأكلها؟

قال: ليس عليه فيه زكاة ما لم تحول إلى بضاعة أخرى.

قال عمرو: سئل جابر بن زيد عن رجل يلي مال اليتيم، أيعطي زكاة ماله؟

قال: نعم.

قال عمرو: سئل جابر بن زيد عن رجل يصيب الدراهم وعليه من الدين أكثر منها؟

فقال: لا زكاة عليه فيها، وعليه الدين حتَّى يقضي منه[250] دينه.

تَمَّ الجزء الخامس من قول قتادة بحمد الله وجميل عونه، والحمد لله ربّ العالمين، وصلَّى الله على سيدنا مُحمَّد وعلى آله وصحبه أجمعين. [251]

250 دينه: -، ب.

251 انتهى ما وجد بحمد الله وحسن عونه على يد العبد الفقير إلى الله صالح بن سالم بن سليمان بن يدر السدريني تاب الله عليه آمين. وكان الفراغ الظهيرة يوم السبت الثالث والعشرين من شهر رمضان سنة إحدى وتسعين ومائة وألف بجامع الماي الكبير الأعظم عمره الله بالمسلمين وأعلى فيه كلمته ودنى المنافقين وشتت جمعهم وفرق شملهم وأذل كلمتهم إنه على ذلك قدير وبالإجابة جدير آمين، والحمد لله ربّ العالمين: +، ب.

كتاب الجزء السادس من قول قتادة

بسم الله الرحمن الرحيم

وصلّى الله على سيدنا محمّد وعلى آله وصحبه وسلّم

باب: بيع الولاء وهبته[1]

[سئل عن بيع الولاء وهبته؟

عن قتادة عن عطاء بن أبي رباح أنّ عمر قال: الولاء مثل الرحم لا يباع ولا يوهب.

قال: هذا رأينا.

وعن ابن مسعود قال: الولاء لحمة كلحمة النسب لا يباع ولا يوهب.

سئل عن بيع ولاء المكاتب وهبته؟

قال: إن[2] الولاء لا يباع ولا يوهب.

سئل عن العبد إذا أعتق وله أولاد من حرّة، أيجوز ولاؤهم؟

قال: نعم، هذا رأينا.

سئل عن رجل قال لمملوكته: إن ولدت غلاما فأنت حرّة فولدت غلاما ثمّ أتبعته جارية؟

قال: عتقت حين ولدت الغلام، وباتت[3] هي والجارية حرتين[4]، والغلام مملوك، وقال: إن

---

1 باب: بيع الولاء وهبته: –،د.

2 إن: –،د.

3 وباتت: وماتت، ب،د.

4 حرتين: أحرار، ب.

ولدت الجارية ثُمَّ ولدت الغلام فهي حرَّة، والغلام مملوك والجارية جميعا[5]، وإن ولدت غلامين فالأوّل منها مملوك والآخر حر، ولدته بعد ما أعتقت. قال: هذا كله رأينا.

سئل عن رجل أعتق مملوكا له وله مال؟

قال: ماله له، إلاَّ أن يشترطه السيد.

سئل عن رجل أعتق غلامه[6] وعلى الغلام دين؟

قال: ينظر إلى قيمة الغلام يوم أعتقه فيدفع إلى غرمائه ليس عليه أكثر من رقبته.

سئل عن رجل ملك ذا رحم؟

قال: من ملك ذا رحم محرم فهو حر.

سئل عن المعتق من دبر[7] من الثلث أم من جميع المال؟

قال: بل هو[8] من جميع المال.

سئل عن المعتق عن دبر: أيبيعه صاحبه إذا احتاج إليه؟

قال: لا أرى أن يبيع المدبر.

سئل عن أولاد المعتقة عن دبر؟

قال: مماليك، وكل ما ولدت حتّى يموت سيدها، فإذا مات سيدها فما كان في بطنها

5 جميعا: –، ب.

6 غلامه: مملوكه، ب.

7 أو: +، ب د.

8 هو: –، ب.

فهو حر .

سئل عن عبد بين رجلين أعتقه أحدهم وكاتبه الآخر لمن ولاؤه؟
قال: للذي أعتق؛ لأن عليه خلاصه من[9] ماله .

سئل عن عبد بين ثلاثة نفر أعتقه أحدهم وكاتبه الآخر وأمسك الثالث؟
قال: على الذي أعتقه خلاصه في ماله إن كان له مال، وإن لم يكن له مال استسعى العبد للمكاتب وللذي أمسك، وكان الولاء للذي أعتق .

سئل عن رجل قال لرجل: إن بعتك غلامي هذا[10] فهو حر، وقال الآخر: وأنا إن اشتريته فهو حر، فباعه فاشتراه؟
قال هو حرّ من مال الأوّل؛ لأنّه أعتقه وهو في ملكه وليس للآخر شيء؛ لأنّه أعتقه وليس في ملكه][11] .

سئل عن رجل أعتق عبيده عند موته وليس له مال غيرهم؟
قال: يعتق من كلّ واحد منهم الثلث، ويستسعون في بقية أثمانهم .

[سئل عن رجل يهب امرأته لأهلها؟
قال: إذا وهب طلاقها لأهلها فهي واحدة بائنة][12] .

---

9 من: في، ب .
10 هذا: –،د .
11 هذه الفقرة التي ما بين معكوفتين مكررة،ذكرت سابقا .
12 هذه الفقرة التي ما بين معكوفتين مكررة،ذكرت سابقا .

باب: الخيار

مِمّاَ سئل عنه الربيع من باب الطلاق:

[سئل عن الخيار؟ قال: إن اختارت نفسها فواحد وهو أحقّ بها، وإن اختارته فلا شيء، وهو رأي عمر بن الخطَّاب رضي الله عنه.

سئل عن رجل يقول لامرأته: اختاري، ثلاث مرَّات، فقالت: قد اخترت نفسي؟ قال: إذا قال الرجل: اختاري، ينوي الطلاق فهو واحد وما نوى، وإن لم ينو الطلاق فلا شيء.

عن جابر بن زيد[13] إذا خيّر الرجل امرأته ثُمَّ جامعها قبل أن تختار أو رجع في أمره أو تفرقا فلا خيار لها.

سئل عن رجل يجعل أمر امرأته بيدها ثُمَّ توفي قبل أن تقضي شيئا؟ قال: الميراث بينهما إذا لم تقض شيئا في حياته.

سئل عن رجل جعل أمر امرأته بيد رجلين فطلق أحدهما؟ قال: لا، حتَّى يجتمعا[14].

سئل عن رجل قال لامرأته هي علي حرام؟ عن عكرمة أنَّ عمر بن الخطَّاب قال في الحرام: يمين يكفِّرها، وعن ابن عبَّاس وابن

---

13 بن زيد: -،د.

14 يجتمعا: يجتمعان، ب د.

مسعود وجابر بن زيد أنَّهم يقولون: يمين يكفِّرها][15][16] .

سئل عن رجل قال: كلّ حلال علي حرام؟

قال: يمين يكفِّرها .

سئل عن الخلية والبرية والبتة والحرام والبائنة؟

قال: واحد بائن، وما نوى إن كان يعني الطلاق .

عن عطاء بن أبي رباح عن ابن عبَّاس أنَّه قال: لا طلاق ولا عتق إلاَّ بعد ملك، قال :هذا رأينا .

عن جبير عن الضحاك بن مزاحم عن النزال[17] بن سبرة عن مسروق بن الأجدع[18]: أنَّ عليًّا رضي الله عنه قال: «لا وصال في الصوم، ولا رضاع بعد فصال، ولا يُتمَ بعد احتلام أو بلوغ، ولا صَمْتَ يومٍ إلى الليل، ولا طلاق إلاَّ بعد نكاح»[19] .

قال: هذا رأينا .

سئل عن رجل طلق امرأته قبل أن يدخل بها؟

قال: نرى أن طلاق من لم يدخل بها واحد فرّق طلاقها أو جمعه .

---

15 هذه الفقرة التي ما بين معكوفتين مكررة،ذكرت سابقا .

16 مرتين: +، ب .

17 النزال: النوال، ب .

18 الأجدع: الأدع، ب .

19 رواه البيهقي، عن علي مرفوعا إلى النبي صلى الله عليه وسلم، باب رضاع الكبير، ر١٥٤٣٦ .

سئل عن رجل طلق امرأته واحدا قبل أن يمسها ثُمَّ غشيها وظن أنـــ له عليها[20] الرجعة عليها؟

قال: لها الصداق ونصف الصداق.

سئل عن رجل كتب على وسادته طلاق امرأته؟

قال: هو جائز عليه.

سئل عن رجل طلق امرأته أو مات عنها وهو غائب عنها: متى تعتدّ؟ من يوم مات أو من يوم طلق؟

قال: من يوم طلق أو من يوم مات[21] إذا قامت البيّنة.

سئل عن رجل طلق امرأته ثُمَّ تركها شهرا، ثُمَّ طلقها ثُمَّ تركها شهرًا ثُمَّ طلقها؟

قال: تعتدّ من أوَّل طلاقها.

سئل عن أمة تطلق اثنتين ثُمَّ تعتق قبل أن تنقضي عدَّتها؟

قال: إذا طلقت تطليقتين فعدَّتها عدَّة الأمة ولا تحل له حتَّى تنكح زوجا غيره.

سئل عن عدَّة الأمة؟

قال: حيضتان، فإن لم تحض فشهر ونصف.

سئل عن امرأة لا تحيض في كلّ سنة إلاَّ مرة واحدة[22]؟

---

20 عليها: –،د.

21 أو من يوم مات: –، ب.

22 واحدة: –،د.

قال: عدَّتها في الحيض إلاَّ أن تعلم أنَّه قطعه مرض. بلغنا: أنَّ علقمة بن قيس طلق امرأته تطليقة أو اثنتين فلبثت ستة عشر شهرا لا تحيض فماتت فانطلق علقمة إلى ابن مسعود فسأله عن ميراثها، فقال له: دونك ميراثها، فإنَّمَا حبسه الله عليك، قال هذا رأينا.

سئل عن المستحاضة إذا طلقت؟
قال: تعتدّ أيَّام أقرائها.

سئل عن رجل طلق امرأته وأشهد: ثُمَّ غشيها ولم يشهد على مراجعتها؟
قال: نرى إذا غشيها ولم يشهد على مراجعتها، فرق بينهما ثُمَّ لا يتراجعان أبدا.

سئل عن رجل طلق امرأته علانية وراجعها سرا؟
عن قتادة عن عروة عن الحسن [23]: حدَّثنا أن شريحا قال: من أعلن الطلاق وأسر المراجعة فلا رجعة له، قال[24]: قلت لقتادة: كيف هذا؟
قال: إذا طلق علانية وراجع سرا ولم يعلمها ذلك حتَّى تنقضي عدَّتها فقد بانت منه، ورأينا أيّما رجل طلق امرأته ثُمَّ راجعها ولم يعلمها حتَّى تنقضي عدَّتها فقد بانت منه.

سئل عن المراجعة قبل أن تطهر من الحيضة الثالثة؟
قال: عن أبي معشر عن النخعي: أنَّ عمر سأل عنها ابن مسعود فقال له: قل فيها، قال له ابن مسعود: أنت أحقّ أن تقول فيها، فقال له: أقسمت عليك لتقولن فيها، قال:

---

23 بن عدن العدي: +، ب.

24 قال: -،د.

زوجها أحقّ بها ما لم تغتسل من الحيضة الثالثة[25].

فقال عمر: وافقت ما في نفسي يا ابن مسعود. قال: هذا رأينا. ونرى أن المطلقة لا تنتقل من بيت زوجها في واحد ولا اثنين قال الله تعالى[26]: ﴿لاَ تُخْرِجُوهُنَّ مِن بُيُوتِهِنَّ وَلاَ يَخْرُجْنَ إلاَّ أَن يَأْتِينَ بِفَاحِشَةٍ مُّبَيِّنَةٍ﴾[27].

عن مطرف عن الحسن: أنَّ رجلا طلق امرأته ثُمَّ وكل بعض أهله لمراجعتها فذهل عنها[28] حتَّى وضعت غسلها لتغتسل من الحيضة الثالثة، فأتاه فأخبره فأقبل إليها وهي في مغتسلها فناداها: يا فلانة فقالت: ما تشاء؟ فقال: إنِّي قد راجعتك، قالت: والله ما ذلك لك، حتَّى تحالفا وارتفعت أصواتهما، فرفعت[29] إلى أبي موسى، واستحلفها بالله إن كنت قد اغتسلت حين ناداك، فقالت: لا، ماكنت اغتسلت بعد، فقضى أنَّه أحقّ بها ما لم تغتسل من الحيضة الثالثة. قال: هذا رأينا.

عن مطرف عن عمرو بن شعيب عن أبيه عن جده، أنَّ عمر سأل أبا موسى عنها وقد كان بلغه قضاؤه. قال: كيف قضيت فيها، قال أبو موسى: قضيت أنَّه أحقّ بها ما لم تغتسل من الحيضة الثالثة[30]. قال: أمَّا إنك لو قضيت بغير ذلك لأوجعت رأسك.

سئل عن المطلقة ثلاثا والمتوفى عنها زوجها: هل يتحولان؟

قال: نرى أن المتوفى عنها زوجها تنتقل إن[31] أحبت ذلك، ونرى أن المطلقة لا

25 من الحيضة الثالثة: –،د.

26 تعالى: –،د.

27 سورة الطلاق: ١.

28 عنها: –،د.

29 فرفعت: فارتفعا، ب.

30 من الحيضة الثالثة: –،د.

31 تنتقل إن: تنتقلان، ب،د.

تنتقل من بيتها في واحد ولا اثنين، قال الله: ﴿ لاَ تُخْرِجُوهُنَّ مِن بُيُوتِهِنَّ وَلاَ يَخْرُجْنَ إلاَّ أَن يَأْتِينَ بِفَاحِشَةٍ مُّبَيِّنَةٍ[32] ﴾[33].

سئل عن المتوفى عنها زوجها، هل تلبس الممشّق والمعصفر أو تكتحل بالإثمد أو تخضب أو تمتشط بطيب أو تمس طيبا؟ قال: لا.

سئل عن نفقة الحامل والمتوفى عنها زوجها: أمن جميع المال؟

قال: لا، ولكن من ميراثها.

سئل عن الأمة تكون تحت الحر فيطلقها تطليقتين وهي حامل والحرّة تحت العبد فيطلقها وهي حامل؟

قال: لهما عليهما النفقة حتى تضعا[34].

سئل عن الرجل يتزوّج المرأة: هل عليه نفقتها قبل أن يدخل بها؟

قال: نرى أن لها النفقة إذا طلبتها وإن لم يدخل بها.

سئل عن المرأة إذا اختلعت؟

قال: جاز خلعها، إنّما طلقها بما لها.

سئل عن المختلعة: هل يزداد زوجها على ما أعطاها؟

قال: لا.

---

32 وَلاَ يَخْرُجْنَ إلاَّ أَن يَأْتِينَ بِفَاحِشَةٍ مُّبَيِّنَةٍ: –،د.

33 سورة الطلاق: ١.

34 حتى تضعا: –،د.

سئل عن المختلعة إذا ندما في العدَّة وأراد مراجعتها وأرادت مراجعته؟

قال: يرد عليها ما أخذ منها وترد عليه نفسها، فإن انقضت العدَّة فلا سبيل له عليها ويخطبها في الخطاب.

سئل عن رجل خالع امرأته فردت عليه[35]، ثُمَّ طلقها بعد ذلك في عدَّتها؟

قال: كان جابر يقول: طلاق المختلعة منه امرأته[36] طلاق ولا نرى له فيها أمرا[37].

سئل عن رجل كانت له أمة فطلقها تطليقتين ثُمَّ أعتقها[38] في عدَّتها؟

قال: نرى أن عليها عدَّة الحرَّة، ولا تحل له حتَّى تنكح زوجا غيره ويدخل بها.

سئل عن الأمة يطلقها تطليقتين؟

قال: لا تحل له حتَّى تنكح زوجا غيره، فإن أعتقها ثُمَّ أراد أن يتزوّجها فلا تحل له حتَّى تنكح زوجا غيره.

سئل عن طلاق العبد؟

قال: طلاقه بيد سيده[39].

سئل عن عدَّة الحامل المتوفى عنها زوجها؟

---

35 فردت عليه: -، ب.

36 منه امرأته: -، ب.

37 يرى جابر أن الخلع فسخ وليس بطلاق. انظر: ابن بركة: الجامع، ٢/١٩٦. العوتبي: الضياء، ١٠/٤٧. الكندي: المصنف، ٣٨/٦٢.

38 أعتقها: عتقت، ب.

39 طلاقه بيد سيده: طلاق العبد بإذن سيده، ب.

قال: عدّتها أبعد الأجلين.

سئل عن رجل طلق امرأته تطليقة أو تطليقتين ثُمَّ تركها حتَّى انقضت عدّتها ثُمَّ تزوّجت رجلا آخر، ثُمَّ طلقها أو مات عنها فراجعها الأول؟

قال: إذا طلقها ثُمَّ تزوّجت ثم[40] دخل بها ثم فارقها أو مات عنها[41] الآخر[42] فنكاح جديد وطلاق جديد.

سئل عن رجل أصدق امرأته صداقا، ثُمَّ طلقها قبل أن يدخل بها؟

قال: إذا طلقها قبل أن يدخل بها وقد ساق إليها صداقها ترد إليه النصف وهي ضامنة حتَّى تؤديه إليه، وإن كانت اشترت متاعا وهو شاهد يراها تجهز[43] فنرى أن نصف المتاع له.

سئل عن رجل أعتق مملوكته وجعل عتقها صداقها، ثُمَّ طلقها قبل أن يدخل بها؟

قال: من أعتق لله كره له التزويج، ومن أعتق ليتزوّجها، فإن طلقها قبل أن يدخل[44] بها فلها نصف صداق مثلها.

سئل عن رجل زنى بأخت امرأته؟

عن جابر بن زيد: قال[45]: حرمت عليه امرأته وهو قول الربيع.

40 طلقها ثم تزوجت ثم: –،د.

41 ثم فارقها أو مات عنها: –،د.

42 الآخر: –، ب.

43 تجهز: تجه، ب،د.

44 قبل أن يدخل بها: –، ب.

45 قال: –،د.

سئل عن نكاح المرأة على عمتها أو خالتها؟

قال: يكره جمع المرأة مع[46] العمة والخالة.

سئل عن نكاح اليهوديّة؟

عن قتادة: أنَّ حذيفة وطلحة بن عبيد الله والجارود وأذينة العبدي تزوّج كلّ واحد منهما امرأة من أهل الكتاب، فقال عمر: طلقوهن، فطلقوهن إلاَّ حذيفة فقال له عمر: طلقها. فقال: أتشهد أنَّها حرام. قال: هي جمرة، فقال: أتشهد أنَّها حرام. قال: هي جمرة[47] قال: قد علمت أنَّها جمرة ولكن هي حلال، فأبى أن يطلقها، ولما[48] كان بعد ذلك طلقها، فقيل له: ألاَّ تطلقها حين أمرك عمر. قال: كرهت أن يظن الناس أنِّي ركبت[49] أمرا لا ينبغي. قال: هذا هكذا، ويشرط ألا تعلق صليبا ولا تأكل لحم الخنزير، ولا تشرب خمرا، وتغتسل من الجنابة.

سئل عن نكاح اليهوديّة والنصرانيّة على المسلمة والقسمة بينهما؟

قال: نرى أن القسمة بينهما، للمسلمة يومان وللنصرانيّة يوم.

سئل عن تزويج الأمة على الحرّة؟

قال: يفرق بينه وبين الأمة.

سئل عن تزويج الأمة على اليهوديّة والنصرانيّة؟

46 المرأة مع: -، ب.

47 فقال: أتشهد أنَّها حرام. قال: هي جمرة: -، د.

48 ولما: لما، ب، د.

49 ركبت: فعلت، ب.

قال: يتزوّج اليهوديّة والنصرانيّة على الأمة إن شاء، ويقسم يومان لليهوديّة والنصرانيّة، ويوم للأمة والنفقة على مثل[50] ذلك.

عن قتادة عن جابر بن زيد قال: إذا تزوّج الحرّة على الأمة، فذلك للأمة طلاق، ويروونه عن ابن عبّاس، قال هوكذلك.

عن جعفر بن أبي وحشية عن سعيد بن جبير قال: ما[51] نكاح المملوكة من الزنى إلاّ قريب.

سئل عن نكاح[52] البكر على الثيب؟

عن الحسن وسعيد بن المسيب أنهما[53] قالا: يقيم عند البكر ثلاثة ثُمَّ يقسم، وإن كانت ثيبا أقام[54] عندها يومين ثُمَّ يقسم. قال: قد بلغنا ذلك ولا بأس به.

سئل عن رجل طلق امرأته ثلاثا ثُمَّ جحد عليها[55]؟

عن قتادة عن جابر بن زيد: يفرق بينهما بشهادة الرجلين والثلاثة، وإن شهد عليه أربعة يقام عليه الحدّ إن كان غشيها. قال: نعم.

سئل عن رجل طلق امرأته ثلاثة ثُمَّ أنكر؟

عن حيان الأعرج عن جابر بن زيد قال: تفتدي منه بما لها كله أوتفر منه لا يسعها غير

50 مثل: قدر، ب.

51 أن يخف: +، ب.

52 عن نكاح: عن رجل ينكح، ب.

53 أنهما: -،د.

54 أقام: بقي، ب.

55 عليها: -،د.

ذلك. قال: هذا كله رأينا.

سئل عن رجل زنا وله جارية قد ولدت له أولادا؟

قال: يجلد ولا يرجم.

سئل عن رجل طلق امرأته تطليقة أو تطليقتين ثُمَّ قذفها؟

قال: يجلد ولا يلاعن.

سئل عن أربعة شهدوا على امرأة أنَّها زنت أحدهم زوجها؟

قال: ترجم.

سئل عن رجل تزوّج امرأة فوجدها حبلى قبل أن يدخل بها؟

قال: نرى أنَّه إن خلا بها وأرخى سترا فإن الولد ولده، ويتلاعنان إن انتفى منه، وإن لم تقم البيِّنة أنَّه خلا، بها تلاعنا والولد لأمه ولعصبتها.

سئل عن امرأة تزوّجت في عدَّتها ولم تعلم بها إلا بعد[56] سنة أو سنتين؟

قال: زوجها الأوّل أحقّ بها.

سئل عن رجل قذف امرأته ثُمَّ طلقها ثلاثة؟

قال: بينهما الملاعنة أيفر من شيء هو عليه.

سئل عن حرّ قذف امرأته وهي أمة؟

قال: لا ملاعنة بينهما وإن كان صادقا فلا يقيم على زانية وإن كان كاذبا يستغفر

56 ولم تعلم بها إلا بعد: تعلم بها بعد، ب،د.

الله ويقيم عليها.

سئل عن القاذف لامرأته[57] إذا كذب نفسه دون السلطان؟

قال: إذا كذب نفسه عند رهط تساكتا[58].

عن قتادة: أنَّ رجلا من عجلان يقال له هلال بن أميَّة أتى النبيّ عليه الصلاة والسلام فقال: يا رسول الله، إني بت أجر الجريد البارحة، حتَّى أصابني برد السحر فانطلقت إلى أهلي، فإذا أنا برجل مع امرأتي يغشاها.

قال: فأعرض عنه رسول الله ـ عليه الصلاة والسلام ـ، فأكب الصحابة، وخافوا على صاحبهم أن يحد، فقال الرجل: رأت عيني وسمعت أذني ووعى قلبي وعرفت أن الله لا يظلمني وإن رسول الله صلى الله عليه وسلم لن يجور علي.

قال: فبينما هما كذلك إذ نزلت آية التلاعن، فقال رسول الله صلى الله عليه وسلم: «إن أحدكما كاذب، فهل منكما تائب؟» فأبيا إلاَّ الإمضاء في التلاعن، ففرق بينهما[59].

عن عمرو بن دينار عن سعيد بن جبير: أنَّ رسول الله عليه الصلاة والسلام لما فرق بين المتلاعنين. قال: لا سبيل لك عليها[60].

قال الرجل[61]: يا رسول الله، مالي؟ فقال رسول الله صلى الله عليه وسلم: «لا مال لك إن كنت صادقا فيما قلت، فبما أصبت من فرجها وإن كنت كاذبا فذلك أبعد

---

57 لأمرأته: ـ، ب.

58 تساكتا: ـ،د.

59 رواه البخاري، باب صداق الملاعنة، ر٥٠٠٥.

60 رواه البخاري، باب المتعة للتي لم يفرض لها، ر٥٠٣٥.

61 الرجل: ـ،د.

لك منها، أمّا أحدكما كاذب وحسابكم على الله» [62] .

عن قتادة عن سعيد بن المسيب: أنَّ رسول الله عليه الصلاة والسلام ـ قال: «انظروا فإن جاءت به أجعد الشعر أكحل العينين خدلج[63] الساقين فهو للذي قذفت به» . فولدت جارية كحلاء، قال رسول الله صلى الله عليه وسلم: «لولا ما سلف من اليمين لكان لي ولها شأن» [64] . وأخبر[65] أيُّوب [عن] عكرمة[66] أنَّه قال: إنما ولدت غلاما [كأنه جمل أورق] فاستعمل بعد[67] ذلك على مصر[68] .

سئل عن ميراث ولد الملاعنة؟

قال: ميراثه لعصبة أمه وليس للمنتفي منه عندنا [69] . والله أعلم.

سئل عن قاذف اليهوديّة والنصرانيّة؟

قال: ليس على قاذفهما حدّ.

سئل عن قاذف أم الولد؟

---

62 رواه البخاري، باب قول الإمام للمتلاعنين: إن أحدكما كاذب فهل منكما من تائب، ر٥٠٠٦.

63 خدلج: خداج،د.

64 رواه البخاري، باب: ويدرأ عنها العذاب أن تشهد أربع شهادات بالله إنه لمن الكاذبين، ر٤٤٧٠.

65 وأخبر: عن، ب.

66 عكرمة: ـ،د.

67 فاستعمل بعد: فاستعلم على،د.

68 فاستعمل بعد ذلك على مصر: ـ،د.

69 وليس للمنتفي منه عندنا: وليس له الانتفاء، ب.

قال: ليس على قاذفها حد.

سئل عن الغلام يحصن قبل أن يحتلم، أو الجارية تحصن قبل أن تحيض، ثُمَّ يزني[70]؟
قال: ليس عليهما رجم حتَّى يحتلم وتحيض.

سئل عن رجل شهد عليه أربعة أنَّه زنى ثُمَّ رجم، ثُمَّ كذب أحدهم نفسه؟
قال: إن أراد أولياء المرجوم أخذوا منهم الدية، وحكم السلطان فيه بالعدل يتبع.
عن قتادة: أنَّ امرأة أتت أبا بكر فقالت له: إن غلامي أطوع لي من غيره وإني أريد أن أعتقه وأتزوّجه؟
قال: انطلقي إلى عمر، فإن رخص لك، فأنا له متابع[71]، فانطلقت إلى عمر فذكرت له ذلك فدعا بسوط فضربها حتَّى شاخت ببولها، فقال لا تزال العرب عربا ما منعت نساءها.
قال: إن أعتقته ورضي به أولياؤها فلا بأس بتزويجه.
عن قتادة عن الحسن: أنَّ عمر أراد أن يرجم امرأة مجنونة زنت، فنهاه عليّ بن أبي طالب رضي الله عنه، وقال: مالك ذلك، إن رسول الله صلى الله عليه وسلم قال: رفع القلم عن ثلاث: النائم حتَّى يستيقظ، والمجنون حتَّى يفيق، والصبيّ حتَّى يدرك، أي يعقل[72].
عن قتادة عن أبي حرب بن [أبي] الأسود: أن امرأة رفعت إلى عمر، ولدت لستة

70 ثم يزني: –، ب.
71 متابع: متبّع، ب.
72 رواه أبو داود، باب في المجنون يسرق أو يصيب حدا، ر٤٤٠٠

شهور، فأراد عمر[73] أن يرجمها،فجاءت أختها إلى عليّ بن أبي طالب، فقالت: إن عمر يريد أن يرجم أختي، أناشدك الله إن كنت تعلم لها عذرا إلاّ أخبرته، فقال علي: فإن لها عذرا فكبرت تكبيرة سمعها عمر ومن عنده، فجاءت إلى عمر، فقالت: إن عليا يزعم أن لها عذرا، فدعا عليا فسأله فقال: إنَّ الله يقول: ﴿وَالْوَالِداتُ يُرْضِعْنَ أَوْلادَهُنَّ حَوْلَيْنِ كامِلَيْنِ﴾[74] ثُمَّ قال أيضا: ﴿وَحَمْلُهُ وَفِصالُهُ ثَلاثُونَ شَهْرًا﴾[75]، ستة أشهر في البطن وأربعة وعشرون في الحجر،فخلى عنها عمر، ثُمَّ إنَّها[76] ولدت بعد ذلك لستة أشهر[77].

قال: بلغنا هذا وهو رأينا.

سئل عن رجل زنا بامرأة ثُمَّ أراد أن يتزوّجها؟

عن جابر بن زيد قال: لا يتزوّجها أبدا وليجعل بينهما البحر الأخضر. قال: هذا رأينا.

سئل عما يحل للعبد من النساء؟

قال: اثنتان.

سئل عن المملوك يزوجه سيده؟

قال: الطلاق بيد السيد.

---

73 عمر: -،د.

74 سورة البقرة: ٢٣٣.

75 سورة الأحقاف: ١٥.

76 إنها: -،د.

77 رواه عبد الرزاق في مصنفه، كتاب الطلاق، باب التي تضع لستة أشهر، رقم ١٣٠١٣.

سئل عن أمِّ الولد؟

قال: هي أمة حتَّى يعتقها سيدها.

سئل عن رجل زنا بأمة قوم ثُمَّ اشتراها؟

قال: لا يغشاها بملك اليمين.

سئل عن رجل تحته أمة بين رجلين اشترى نصيب أحدهما؟

قال: يكف عنها حتَّى يخلصها.

سئل عن المدبرة أيغشاها سيدها؟

قال: نعم، يغشاها.

سئل عن رجل كانت تحته جاريتان أختان يغشى إحداهما، ثُمَّ أمسك عنها أيغشى أختها[78]؟

قال: لا، حتَّى تخرج الأولى من ملكه ببيع أو عتق أو تزويج.

سئل عن رجل تزوّج امرأة واشترط أن يأتيها بالنهار؟

قال: إذا رضيت فلا بأس، وإن كرهت[79] قسم لها أو طلقها.

سئل هل يتزوّج الأعرابي مهاجرة ويخرج بها؟

قال: كره ذلك[80] إلاَّ أن يقيم بها في مصرها.

78 أختها: الأخرى، ب.

79 كرهت: لم ترضى، ب.

80 ذلك: بذلك، ب د.

سئل عن الأمة، أعتقت ولم تشعر أن لها الخيار؟

قال: إذا غشيها زوجها فلا خيار لها.

عن قتادة وعطاء الخراساني أنّهما قالا: إن رسول الله ﷺ قضى في بريرة أربع قضايا، أولهن: أن عائشة أرادت أن تشتريها وتعتقها وتشترط ولاءها لأهلها، فقال رسول الله ﷺ: «الولاء لمن أعتق». والثانية: أنّها خيرت. والثالثة: أنّ رسول الله ﷺ: «أمرها أن تعتدّ ثلاث حيضات». والرابعة أنّها أهدت إلى الرسول ﷺ لحما فدخل رسول الله على عائشة[81] فقال لها: «هل عندك من شيء؟» فقالت: يا رسول الله، ما عندنا شيء[82] إلاّ لحما أهدته لنا بريرة من شاة تصدق بها عليها. فقال رسول الله ﷺ: «هو صدقة عليها وهو لنا منها هدية»[83]. فأكل منها.

عن عاصم الأحول عن الشعبي أن عائشة زوج النبيّ عليه الصلاة والسلام قالت: إن زوج بريرة كان حرا يوم خيرت[84]. قال هذا رأينا.

عن قتادة: إذا أرادت المكاتبة كتابتها كان لها الخيار قبل أن يدخل بها.

وقال: إن المكاتبة عندنا حرّة، لها الخيار.

سئل عن أمة تعتق قبل أن يدخل بها زوجها فتختار نفسها؟

قال: لا صداق لها، وكذلك الذمّية إذا لم يدخل بها.

---

81 على عائشة: -، ب.

82 شيء: -، ب.

83 رواه الربيع، باب الحداد والعدة، ر٥٣٥. والبخاري، باب الصدقة على موالي أزواج النبي صلى الله عليه وسلم، ر١٤٢٢.

84 يوم خيرت: -،د.

سئل عن نصرانيّة أسلمت ثُمَّ أسلم زوجها في العدَّة؟
قال: هو أحقّ بها، ونرى أنَّه إذا أسلمت ثُمَّ أسلم زوجها قبل أن تتزوّج ولو بعد عشرين سنة فهو أحقّ بها، وإذا أسلم هو ولم يتزوّج أربع نسوة حتَّى تمضي عشرون سنة ثُمَّ أسلمت فهو أحقّ بها.

عن قتادة: أنَّه كان يقول في المرأة تطلق تطليقة فلزوجها أن يتنحنح ويسلم ولا يستأذن، وتتشوف له[85] وتتصنع، ولا يرى لها رأسا ولا بطنا ولا رجلا، ولكن ينام معها في البيت، قال هذا رأينا ويستأذن[86].

سئل عن رجل قال لامرأته: إن دخلت دار فلان فأنت طالق. فأدخلت رأسها ويديها؟
قال: لا، حتَّى تدخل رجليها، فإذا أدخلت[87] رجليها فقد دخلت لأن الجسد تبع الرجلين. قال: هذا رأينا.

سئل عن رجل قال لامرأته[88]: إن خرجت من باب الدار فأنت طالق، وإنَّما يعني في نيته إلى أهلها. فخرجت إلى غيرهم؟
قال: إذا خرجت من الباب[89] فهي طالق حتَّى يبين.

سئل عن رجل قال لامرأته: إن دخلت دار فلان هذه فأنت طالق؟

---

85 له: −،د.
86 ويستأذن: −،د.
87 أدخلت: دخلت، ب،د.
88 لامرأته: −، ب.
89 الباب: باب الدار، ب.

قال: إن دخلت فإنّـه يدخل عليه الطلاق.

سئل عن رجل قال لامرأته: إن لم أخرج إلى أرض كذا وكذا فأنت طالق؟
قال: لا يمسها حتَّى يخرج إلى الأرض التي سمىَّ فإن مضت أربعة أشهر قبل أن يخرج فقد وقع الطلاق.

سئل عن رجل قال لامرأته: إذا حملت فأنت طالق ثلاثا؟
قال: يقع عليها عند كلّ طهر من الحيض وقعة[90]، فإن حبلت[91] فهي طالق كما قال.

سئل عن رجل له أربع نسوة فقال: بينكن تطليقة؟
قال: إذا جعل بينهنّ تطليقة فلكل واحدة تطليقة، وإن قال: تطليقتان فإنَّه بلغنا: أنَّه لكلِّ واحدة تطليقتان، وإن قال: بينكن ثلاث فلكل واحدة ثلاث.

سئل عن رجل قال لزوجته: أنت طالق كم شئت أو ما شئت؟
قال: نرى إن قالت: ثلاثا فثلاثا وإن لم تقل شيئا فلا شيء.

سئل عن رجل مر على عاشر فاستحلفه بالطلاق ماكتمتني شيئا؟
قال: عن جابر بن زيد أنَّه قال: إن كان حلف ماكتمه شيئا وذلك علمه لا يعلم إلاَّ ذلك، ثُمّ كان فيه فضل، أنَّه لا يدخل عليه الطلاق، وإن كان قال: عدَّة مالي كذا وكذا، ثُمّ كان فيه فضل ولم يعلم ذلك فإنَّه يدخل عليه الطلاق.

90 وقعة: مرة، ب.
91 حبلت: حملت، د.

سئل عن رجل قال لامرأته: أنت طالق، ثمّ سكت ساعة فقال: إن لم يكن كذا وكذا[92]؟
قال: له ثنياه ما لم يتكلم.

عن قتادة: أنّ عمر بن الخطّاب رضي الله عنه قال: لا تزوّجوا اليتيمة إلاّ لكفئها ولا تعتدّوا[93] منها أمرها.

سئل عن متاع المطلقة؟
قال: المتاع على من وجد درعًا[94] وخمارًا وجلبابًا ومئزرًا، وقد كان الميسر يعطى الوصيف والخادم.

سئل عن رجل طلق امرأته ولم يدخل بها وقد فرض لها؟
قال: نرى أن من أعطى نصف الصداق فلا متاع.

سئل عن رجل طلق في مرضه قبل أن يدخل بها؟
قال: عن قتادة عن جابر بن زيد أنّهما قالا: لها الصداق كاملا ولا عدّة عليها.
قال: نرى أنّها إذا تزوّجت قبل موته[95] فلا شيء لها، وإن قامت فتوفي قبل أن تنقضي عدّتها فلها الميراث، وكذلك[96] عدّة الطلاق ثلاث حيضات إن كانت تحيض، وإن لم تكن مِمَّن تحيض فثلاثة أشهر، فإن انقضت عدّتها قبل وفاته[97] فلا ميراث لها.

92 وكذا: –، ب.
93 تعتدوا: تتعدوا، ب.
94 درعا: درع، د.
95 موته: –، د.
96 كذلك: –، د.
97 وفاته: موته، ب.

عن قتادة عن خلاس أن هشام بن هبيرة[98] كتب إلى شريح أن رجلا طلق امرأته ثلاثا في مرضه، وعن امرأة توفيت وتركت بني عمها ثلاثا[99] أحدهم زوجها، وعن مكاتب ترك دينا عليه[100] وبقية من مكاتبته، ورجل جلد في الخمر ثُمَّ أونس رشد منه هل تقبل شهادته؟

قال: فقدم كتاب شريح وأنا شاهد، فكان في كتابه: أمَّا المكاتب الذي مات وعليه دين وبقية من مكاتبته فإن ترك وفاء فلكل وفاء ولكل حق، وإن لم يترك وفاء يقاسم[101] بينهم بالحصص.

وأما المحدود في الخمر، فإن أونس منه رشد فإنَّ الله يقول: ﴿وَهُوَ الَّذِي يَقْبَلُ التَّوْبَةَ عَنْ عِبَادِهِ وَيَعْفُو عَنِ السَّيِّئَاتِ﴾[102].

وأما المرأة التي ماتت وتركت بني عمِّها أحدهم زوجها، فإن لزوجها النصف وما بقي فهو بينهم[103]. قال: هذا رأينا في هذه الأربع مسائل.

سئل عن رجل تزوّج امرأة ثُمَّ مات ثُمَّ قامت البيّنة أنَّها أخته قبل أن يقسم المال[104]؟

قال: نرى أنَّه إذا قامت البيِّنة أنَّها أخته من الرضاع أو من النسب، فإن كان[105] دخل

98 : هبيرة: عبيدة، د.

99 ثلاثا: –، د.

100 مكاتب عليه دين، ب.

101 يقاسم: فأقر، ب.

102 سورة الشورى: ٢٥.

103 بينهم: بينهما، ب د.

104 المال: الميراث، ب.

105 كان: –، ب، د.

بها فلها الصداق ولا ميراث لها، وإن لم[106] يدخل بها فلا صداق لها ولا ميراث.

سئل عن رجل[107] تزوّج أخته أو أخت امرأته وهو لا يشعر فدخل بها؟
قال: لها الصداق كاملا لغشيانه إيّاها.

سئل عن رجل طلق امرأته أو مات عنها وقد أحدث في بيته متاعا؟
قال: لها ما ساق إليها من متاع، وأمّا ما أحدث في بيتها من متاع من ماله[108] فهو أحقّ به حتّى يجعله لها.

سئل عن رجل تحته أختان لا يعلم بهما حتّى مات؟
قال: الميراث للأولى منهما.

سئل عن أختين أهديتا إلى أخوين، فأخطأوا بهما فدخلت هذه على غير زوجها والأخرى على غير زوجها؟
قال: عن قتادة عن خلاس[109] عن الحسن[110]: أنَّ عليًّا رضي الله عنه يقول: لكلٍّ منهما الصداق لغشيانه إيّاها وعلى وليهما أن يجهزهما، ولا يقرب كلّ واحد منهما امرأته حتّى تنقضي عدّتها. قال: هذا رأينا.

106 لم: –، ب،د.
107 رجل: زوج، ب.
108 من ماله: –،د.
109 عن قتادة عن خلاس: –،د.
110 عن الحسن: –، ب.

سئل عن رجل ينظر[111] إلى فرج المرأة هل تحل لأبيه؟[112]

قال: نرى إذا نظر إلى فرجها ولمسها حرمت على أبيه.

قال: قتادة عن ابن مسعود قال: «حرم الله عز وجل اثنتني عشرة امرأة، وأنا أكره اثنتني عشرة: الأمة وأمها، والأختين[113] يجمع بينهما، والأمة إذا وطئها أبوك، والأمة إذا وطئها ابنك، والأمة إذا زنت، والأمة في عدة غيرك، والأمة لها زوج، وأمتك مشركة، وعمتك وخالتك من الرضاعة»[114]. قال: هذا رأينا.

سئل عن الرضاع[115]؟

قال: إذا رضع الصبيّ قبل أن يفطم فهذا يحرم منه ما يحرم من النسب[116].

سئل عن رجل يشتري الجارية فيها شرط؟

قال: يكره أن يغشاها وفيها شرط.

سئل عن امرأة كانت تحت مملوك فملكت منه شقصا؟

قال: حرمت عليه، ولا نرى بأسا أن يتزوّجها في عدَّتها فتكون عنده على تطليقتين إن

---

111 ينظر: جرد، ب.

112 هل تحل لأبيه: -،د.

113 الأختين: الأختان، ب،د.

114 ذكر لفظ هذا الأثر مضطربا وفيه غموض فاستبدلته من المعجم الكبير للطبراني، ر٩٧٠٩، ٣٤٣/٩. وفي حاشية الترتيب لأبي ستة، وشرح النيل للشيخ اطفيش: «إحدى عشرة مملوكة».

115 سئل: عن الرضاع: -،د.

116 انظر: آثار الربيع، مسألة ٤٩، ص ٣٣.

خرج من ملكها[117].

سئل عن رجل أسلم وتحته عشر[118] نسوة؟
قال: الأربع[119] الأولى نرى أنّهن نساؤه.

سئل عن امرأة يزوجها[120] وليها بغير شهود، ثُمَّ أشهد به[121] وأخبر به وأعلنه؟
قال: جائز.

سئل عن امرأة زوجها وليها سرا وأشهد رجلين؟ قال: جائز.

سئل عمَّن زنى من اليهود والنصارى بعد إحصانه في دينه؟
قال: أقيم عليه الحدّ وإن لم يكن تزوّج بعد إسلامه، فأما المجوس وعبدة الأوثان فلا يقام عليهم الحدّ حتَّى يتزوّجوا[122] بعد إسلامهم.

سئل عن رجل يزوج أخته وأبوه غائب؟
قال: نكاحه جائز، وإن كان أبوه شاهدا وأنكح فليس بجائز إلاَّ بإذن والده.
عن قتادة: أنَّه كان يقول: لا يحلّ للمرأة أن تنكح ابنتها إلاَّ بولي، وإن كان الولي غائبا فأنكح

117 إن خرج من ملكها: -، ب.
118 عشر: عشرة، ب،د.
119 الأربع: الأربعة، ب،د.
120 يزوجها: تزوجها، ب.
121 أشهد به: خرج، ب.
122 يتزوجوا: يتزوجون، د؛ يحصن، ب.

ولي هو أبعد من[123] الغائب[124] فهو جائز، وينبغي أن يكون أولى الناس بالولي الغائب.

عن يحيى بن كثير عن أبي سلمة عن أبي هريرة أن النبيّ صلى الله عليه وسلم قال: لا تنكح البكر حتَّى تستأمر، ولا الثيب حتَّى تستأذن، قيل: وما إذنها يا رسول الله؟ قال: «إذنها أن تسكت»[125]. قال: هذا رأينا[126].

عن يحيى أن رجلا من الأنصار زوج ابنته، فكرهت ذلك، فأتت نبيّ الله عليه الصلاة والسلام فذكرت ذلك له فرد نكاحها[127].

سئل عن رجل نكح يتيمة يتيم[128]؟

قال: يكره نكاح الصغار حتَّى يبلغوا[129] ويستأذنوا.

سئل عن رجل زوج ابنته فاختلف الأب والزوج، قال الأب: إنَّمَا زوجتك فلانه، وقال الزوج: إنَّمَا زوجتني فلانة؟

قال: نرى أن يقول: امرأتي طالق واحدة فتبين منه، ثُمَّ يخطب بعد أيتهما شاء فتكون عنده على تطليقتين.

سئل عن قوم يزوجون ويقولون للشهود: قد تراضينا فيما بيننا على الصداق؟

123 من: منه، ب،د.

124 الغائب: -،د.

125 رواه البخاري، باب لا ينكح الأب وغيره البكر والثيب إلا برضاها، ر٤٨٤٣.

126 قال: هذا رأينا: -،د.

127 رواه الربيع، باب في الأولياء، ر٥١٢. والبخاري، باب إذا زوج ابنته وهي كارهة فنكاحهم مردود، ر٤٨٤٥.

128 يتيم: يتيمة، ب،د.

129 يبلغوا: يكبروا،د.

قال: لا بأس.

سئل عن رجل كفر بعد إسلامه وهو مجوسيّ أو نصرانيّ ثُمَّ مات[130]؟

قال: ميراثه لأهل دينه.

سئل عن استبراء أم الولد؟

قال: إن أعتقها فثلاث حيضات، وإن مات عنها فحيضة.

سئل عن العبد تكون تحته الحرّة فيطلقها تطليقتين؟

عن أبي معشر عن النخعي عن ابن مسعود قال: السنة بها في الطلاق والعدّة.

قال: نعم[131].

عن عمرو بن دينار عن جابر بن زيد: عن ابن عبّاس أنّه قال: الطلاق والعدّة بها.

عن أيُّوب عن سليمان بن يسار: أنَّ غلام أمّ سلمة طلق امرأة حرّة تطليقتين، فأراد مراجعتها، فنهاه عثمان بن عفان وزيد بن ثابت، وقالا له: ليس لك من الطلاق أكثر من ذلك. قال: نعم.

سئل عن العزل عن النساء؟

قال: اعزل عن الأمة إن شئت، ولا تعزل عن الحرّة إلاّ بإذنها.

عن ابن عبّاس قال: ما أبالي أعزلت أم تفلت، ماكان ابن آدم أن يتفل نسمة قضى الله

130 أن نصراني ثُمَّ مات: -، ب.

131 قال: نعم: -،د. انظر: مصنف عبد الرزاق، باب طلاق الحرة، ٧/٢٣٤ وما بعدها.

عليها، حرثك إن شئت سقيت وإن شئت عطّشت[132].

عن عمرو بن دينار عن جابر بن زيد: عن ابن عبّاس قال: أربعة لا يجزن في البيع والنكاح: الجنون، والجذام، والبرص، والعفل. وكان يقول: البرص الفاحش. قال: هذا رأينا[133].

سئل عن رجل اشترى جارية فغشيها وبها داء لا يشعر به؟
قال: إذا وطئها جازت عليه عند أصحابنا ورفع عنه قيمة[134] عيبها.

سئل عن رجل أعتق جارية لم يكن يغشاها، أيخطبها في العدَّة؟
قال: يخطب جاريته في عدَّتها، والمختلعة[135] يرد عليها ما أخذ منه إذا كانت في عدَّتها بشاهدين فلا بأس بذلك عندنا ولا تحل امرأة المتلاعن له إذا لاعنها أبدا.

سئل عن أمة أتت قوما فأخبرتهم أنَّها حرَّة فتزوّجها رجل منهم فولدت له أولادا ثُمَّ إن سيدها ظهر عليها؟
قال: عليه قيمة الولد[136] يستسعى فيهم.

باب المفقود

عن جعفر بن أبي وحشيّة عن عمرو بن هرم عن جابر بن زيد قال: تذاكر ابن عمر وابن

---

132 عطشت: ضمئت، د.

133 قال: نعم، ب.

134 ورفع عنه قيمة: ووضع عنه قيمة، ب.

135 المختلعة: المختلفة، د.

136 الولد: ولده، ب.

عبّاس المفقود فقالا: تتربص امرأته أربع سنين، ثُمَّ يطلقها ولي زوجها، ثُمَّ تعتدّ أربعة أشهر وعشرا[137]، وقال ابن عمر: لها النفقة لحبسها نفسها عليه، وقال ابن عبّاس: لا، ولكن تستدين عليه فإن رجع كان لها عليه في ماله وإن لم يرجع كان الدين على رقبتها.

سئل إن قدم زوجها فاختارها كم تعتدّ من الذي تزوّجت به؟

قال: فزعم قتادة قال: تعتدّ منه ثلاث حيضات يستبرئ رحمها. فإن اعتدت منه شهرين ثُمَّ مات الذي اختارها.

قال: ترثه[138]، نرى أن تكمل[139] ما بقي عليها من العدَّة، ثُمَّ تعتدّ من المتوفى عنها أربعة أشهر وعشرا. قال: هذا رأينا.

وإذا قدم المفقود، فمات قبل أن يختار.

عن قتادة قال: ترثه، ويفرق بينها وبين الآخر، وتعتدّ أربعة أشهر وعشرا، ثُمَّ تعتدّ ثلاث حيضات، ثُمَّ يتزوّجها الآخر إن شاء.

وإن كانت حاملا اعتدت من الحمل، ثُمَّ اعتدت أربعة أشهر وعشرا.

فإن مات الأخير قبل أن يعلم للأوّل حياة.

قال قتادة[140]: ترثه، ولها ما أخذت من الصداق؛ لأنّه نكاح شبهة ومات قبل أن تعلم له حياة. قال: نعم[141]

137 انظر: آثار الربيع، مسألة ٣٥، ص ٣١.

138 ترثه: -،د.

139 نرى أن تكمل: - ب.

140 قتادة: -،د.

141 قال نعم: -،د.

سئل عن المفقود إذا اختار امرأته وهي حامل ثُمَّ طلقها تطليقة؟

قال قتادة[142]: هو أحقّ بها حتَّى تحيض بعد الحمل ثلاث حيضات أو ثلاثة أشهر.

قال: نعم.

عن قتادة قال: إذا اختار المفقود الصداق، فقامت المرأة[143] عند زوجها الآخر، فلا عدَّة عليها ولا يزداد على ما أعطاها شيئا، فإن كان صداق الآخر أقل فهو للأول.

قال: نعم.

باب الظهار

سئل عن رجل ظاهر من امرأته؟

عن قتادة: أنَّ خولة بنت ثعلبة ظاهر منها زوجها وكان يقال له: أوس بن الصامت، فأتت النبيّ ﷺ فقالت: حين كبر سني ورقّ عظمي، وانثنى صلبي، ظاهر منِّي زوجي، فأنزل الله آي الظهار فدعاه النبيّ ﷺ فقال: «أتستطيع أن تحرر رقبة؟ فقال: لا أجد. فقال: «أتستطيع أن تصوم شهرين متتابعين؟». فقال: إنَّه والله، إنَّه إذا أخطأت الماء في اليوم ثلاث مرَّات لكلَّ بصري. فقال: «أتستطيع أن تطعم ستِّين مسكينا؟» قال: لا والله، إلاَّ أن تعينني منك بعون وصلة، فأعانه رسول الله ﷺ، وجمع الله له أهله[144] والله رؤوف رحيم»[145]. قال: نعم[146].

142 قتادة: ـ،د.

143 المرأة: ـ،د.

144 أهله: ـ،د.

145 رواه الترمذي، باب ومن سورة المجادلة، ر٣٢٩٩.

146 قال نعم: ـ،د.

سئل عن رجل ظاهر من امرأته في مقاعد شتى؟

قال: كفَّارة واحدة ما لم يكفر.

سئل عن رجل ظاهر من أربع نسوة؟

قال: إذا قال: أنتن[147] علي كظهر أمي، فكفَّارة واحدة، وإن قال لكلِّ واحدة منهن، أنت علي كظهر أمي فعليه أربع كفَّارات.

سئل عن المظاهر إذا ماتت امرأته؟

قال: يتوارثان ما لم تنقض أربعة أشهر.

سئل عن رجل ظاهر من امرأته ثُمَّ طلقها ثلاثا؟

عن الحسن وعن النخعي، قالا: كفَّارة الظهار عليه واجبة. قال: نعم.

سئل عن المملوك يظاهر من امرأته؟

قال: نرى نحن، -والله أعلم-، أنَّه لا يظاهر.

عن مطرف عن حيان الأعرج عن جابر بن زيد قال: إذا ظاهر بذات محرم فهو ظهار، ولو قال: هي علي كظهر رجل لكان ظهارا. قال: نعم[148] بلغني ذلك عن جابر.

سئل عن رجل ظاهر من امرأته وهو لا يطؤها؟

قال: إذا ظاهر وهي في ملكه فعليه الظهار ولا يقربها حتَّى يكفِّر.

---

147 أنتن: أنت، ب،د.

148 ولو قال: هي علي كظهر رجل لكان ظهارا. قال: نعم: -،د.

سئل عن رجل ظاهر من إمائه؟

قال: عليه العتق ولا وقت لها ولا يغشاها حتَّى يكفِر[149].

سئل عن رجل ظاهر فصام شهرا ثُمَّ مرض فأفطر؟

قال: يصوم يوما مكان يوم إذا كان من عذر قال[150]: وإذا أفطر من غير عذر استأنف.

سئل عن رجل ظاهر فصام ثُمَّ أيسر من[151] قبل أن يقضي صومه؟

قال: إذا أيسر قبل أن يقضي صومه أعتق.

باب في الإيلاء

سئل عن الإيلاء؟

قال: إن مضت أربعة أشهر عدَّة الإيلاء، فإنا نرى أن تتزوّج.

سئل عن رجل قال لامرأته: والله لا أقربك الليلة فتركها أربعة أشهر؟

قال: فهي تطليقة بائنة، وإن تركها لغير ذلك فلا يدخل عليه الإيلاء.

سئل عن رجل قال لامرأته: والله [لا] أقربك في بيتك هذا؟

قال: إن كانت مراغمة في أهلها، فإن ذلك لا يدخل عليه الإيلاء، وإن كانت في بيته فتركها أربعة أشهر دخل عليه الإيلاء.

149 سئل: عن رجل ظاهر من إمائه؟ قال: عليه العتق ولا وقت لها ولا يغشاها حتَّى يكفر: –، د.

150 قال: –، د.

151 من: –، د.

سئل عن رجل آلى من امرأته، وشغله مرض أو طرده سلطان.

قال: يشهد على مراجعتها.

قال أبو أيُّوب: إذا أشهد فقد فاء ولا بد من الكفَّارة، وعن قتادة عن الحسن عن عكرمة أنَّهم قالوا: إذا كان له عذر وأشهد على مراجعتها، فقد فاء. قال: نعم.

سئل عن رجل آلى من أربع نسوة وفرق؟

قال: كفَّارات شتى، فإذا آلى بقول واحدة فكفَّارة واحدة.

سئل عن رجل آلى، ثُمَّ طلق؟

قال: إذا آلى الرجل ثُمَّ طلق فانقضت عدَّة الإيلاء قبل عدَّة الطلاق فهما تطليقتان[152] إن كان طلق واحدا، وإن انقضت عدَّة الطلاق قبل عدَّة الإيلاء فهي واحدة.

سئل عن إيلاء العبد من الأمة؟

عن قتادة قال: تتربص شهرين، وإن كانت حرَّة في قولهما فالسنة بها[153]. قال: نعم.

سئل عن رجل آلى من امرأته فمضت أربعة أشهر فبانت منه، ثُمَّ تزوّجها في عدَّتها، ثُمَّ طلقها قبل أن يدخل بها؟

قال: لها نصف الصداق وتكمل ما عليها من العدَّة.

---

152 تطليقتان: تطليقتين، ب،د.

153 بها: لها، ب. رواه ابن ابي شيبة، في الرجل يتزوج الأمة فيفجر ما عليه، ر٢٨٧٤٥، بلفظ: «عن قتادة عن الحسن وهو قول قتادة أنهما كانا يقولان في الحرة تحت العبد تزني السنة بها ترجم وفي الحر تحته الأمة لا يرجم».

عن عمرو بن دينار عن ابن عبّاس قال[154]: لا يكون الإيلاء إلاَّ بحلف. قال: نعم.

سئل عن رجل تزوّج امرأة فمكثت عنده سنين[155]، ثُمَّ طلقها، ثُمَّ تزوّج أخرى، فلم يستطع أن يأتيها فقيل له: مكثت مع امرأتك الأولى سنين فلم تستطع أن تأتيها فكيف تأتي هذه؟ فقال: إن هذه طالق ثلاثا، لقد أتيت تلك. قال: سمعت ذلك له ليس لهم أن يعلموا ذلك من قبل الأولى.

باب في الربا

سئل عن قوله تعالى: ﴿يَا أَيُّهَا الَّذِينَ آمَنُوا اتَّقُوا اللَّهَ وَذَرُوا مَا بَقِيَ مِنَ الرِّبَا إِنْ كُنْتُمْ مُؤْمِنِينَ. فَإِنْ لَمْ تَفْعَلُوا فَأْذَنُوا بِحَرْبٍ مِنَ اللَّهِ وَرَسُولِهِ وَإِنْ تُبْتُمْ فَلَكُمْ رُؤُوسُ أَمْوَالِكُمْ لَا تَظْلِمُونَ وَلَا تُظْلَمُونَ﴾[156].

قال: آذنهم[157] بحرب عظيم من الله ورسوله أينما ثقفوا، فإن تبتم فلكم رؤوس أموالكم، لا تظلمون بالزيادة عليها، ولا تظلمون بنقصانها[158]، إياكم وما خالط البيوع من هذا الربا؛ لأنَّ الله قد وسع في الحلال وأطاله ولم يلجئكم إلى معصيته، فإنَّه قد ذكر أنَّ عمر بن الخطَّاب رضي الله عنه قال: الدنانير بالدنانير، والدراهم بالدراهم.

عن قتادة عن مسلم بن يسار عن شعبة الصنعاني عن عبادة بن الصامت – وكان نقيبا

---

154 قال: –، د.

155 سنين: سنتين، ب.

156 سورة البقرة: ٢٧٨ – ٢٧٩.

157 اذنهم: وعدهم بالقتل وجعلهم، ب.

158 فإن تبتم فلكم رؤوس أموالكم. قال: ماكان لكم من دين فأخذوا رؤوس اموالكم لا تظلمون ولا تظلمون، ب.

بدريا أحد نقباء الأنصار، بايع رسول الله ﷺ على ألا يخاف في الله لومة لائم، قام في الناس خطيبا بالشام. فقال: يا أيُّها الناس إنكم أحدثتم بيوعا ما ندري ما هي؟ ألا إن الذهب بالذهب وزنا بوزن تبره وعينه، ألا إن الفضَّة بالفضَّة وزنا بوزن تبرها وعينها ألا ولا بأس ببيع الذهب بالفضَّة يدا بيد والفضَّة أكثرهما ولا تصلح بنسيئة، والحنطة بالحنطة مدين بمدين والشعير بالشعير مدين بمدين، من زاد أو استزاد فقد أربى[159]. قال: نعم.

حديث عبادة بن الصامت صحيح، وكان جابر يروي عن ابن عبَّاس فيما بلغني أنَّه كان يقول: أحل الله البيع وحرم الربا، فلا بأس بالصرف أن يشتري بالدراهم والفضَّة المكسورة بوزنها، وذكر ابن عبَّاس أن أسامة بن زيد، وزيد بن أرقم كانا يأتيان وادي القرى، يشتريان الذهب والفضَّة التبر منه المنكسر بالنقصان من الوزن بزيادة[160] فعاب عليهما أناس من أصحاب رسول الله ﷺ فأتى أسامة إلى رسول الله ﷺ فسأله عن ذلك فقال النبيّ ﷺ: «يدا بيد»[161]. قال: نعم. قال: لا بأس، فأخذ بذلك ابن عبَّاس فيما بلغني وترك من خالفه، وكان زيد بن أرقم لا يرى بأسا به، والبراء بن عازب لا يرى بالصرف بأسا.

سئل عن قوم شهدوا على رجل مات وعليه دين؟

قال: إن كان في الصك جازت شهادتهم، وقال غيره: إن كانوا في الصك وغير الصك جازت شهادتهم، واستحلفوا الطالب أن الرجل مات وعليه حقك، وأنك لم تقبض منه شيئا، فإذا حلف أخذ له بحقه.

---

159 أربى: أربا، ب،د؛ البيهقي، السنن الكبرى، ر ٦١١٠.

160 يشتريان الذهب والفضَّة التبر منه المنكسر بالنقصان من الوزن بزيادة: -،د.

161 رواه مسلم، باب بيع الطعام مثلا بمثل، ر٤١٧٤.

سئل عن رجل له مملوك عليه كلّ شهر خمسة دراهم، فأعطى غلامه مائة درهم على أن يعطيه كلّ شهر عشرة دراهم؟

قال: ليس بين العبد وسيده ربا[162].

سئل عن رجلين يتدارآن[163] في بيع وليس بينهما بيِّنة؟

قال: إذا تدارآ البيعان في بيع فالقول ما قال البائع، إذا كان المباع في يده لم يقبضه المبتاع، فإن كان المبتاع قد قبضه وأقر البائع أنَّه قد باعه إيَّاه ولكنهما اختلفا في الثمن؛ فالقول قول المبتاع.

سئل عن رجلين اختلفا في متاع، فقال أحدهما: هو عندي رهن، وقال الآخر هو عندك وديعة؟

قال: يكلف الذي قال هو عندي رهن البيِّنة أنه رهن عنده، وإلاَّ دفعه إليه، فإن أقرا جميعا أنَّه رهن، وقال أحدهما: إنَّه بعشرة، وقال الآخر: إنَّه بدرهم. قال: إن ادعى المرتهن في الرهن شيئًا، وقال الراهن أقل من ذلك، فالقول قول الراهن حتَّى يقيم المرتهن البيِّنة.

سئل عن رجل ارتهن رهنا، فقال لصاحبه: إن مضى كذا وكذا ولم أقضك فهو لك؟

عن قتادة: أنَّ شريحا قال: ليس له ذلك. قال: هذا رأينا.

162 انظر: آثار الربيع، مسألة ٧٢، ص ٣٥.

163 يتداران: تداريا، ب.

سئل عن رجل وضع رهنه على يد عدل، فأفلس الغريم أومات. هل يشاركه الغرماء؟

قال: نعم، هم فيه سواء ولوكان في يد المرتهن لم يدخل عليه فيه أحد.

سئل عن رجل ارتهن جارية، هل لسيدها أن يطأها[164]؟

قال: كان ضمام يكره رهن الحيوان، ويقول: فرهان مقبوضة.

عن صاحب له عن[165] مُحَمَّد بن عبد الرحمن، عن سعيد بن المسيب، أنَّ عليًّا رضي الله عنه باع بعيرا بخمسة أبعرة فقيل نسيئة فقال: ولا ساعة؟

قال: نعم.

سئل عن بيع بعير والدراهم نسيئة[166]؟

قال: إن كان البعير يدا بيدا والدراهم نسيئة[167] فلا بأس، وإن كان البعير[168] نسيئة والدراهم يدا بيد[169] نقدا[170] فكره ذلك، وقال: الحيوان كله لا بأس به واحد باثنين يدا بيد.

سئل عن بيع[171] الحيوان واحد باثنين نسيئة؟

164 يطأها: يغشاها، ب.

165 صاحب له عن: -،د.

166 عن بيع بعير والدراهم نسيئة: عن بعير ببعيرين وزيادة دراهم، ب.

167 إن كان البعير يدا بيدا والدراهم نسيئة: -،د.

168 البعير: البعيران، ب.

169 يدا بيد: -،د.

170 نقدا: -، ب.

171 بيع: -، ب.

قال: فكره النسيئة في الحيوان وإن اختلف الصنفان، وكره بعير ببعيرين ونفس ذلك[172].

عن قتادة: أنَّ رجلا باع بعيرا مريضا وشرط على صاحبه رأسه وسواقطه، ثُمَّ إن البعير صحَّ، فاختصما إلى شريح فقضى بمثل ثمن[173] رأسه وسواقطه. قال: ما نرى بذلك بأسا.

عن قتادة: أنَّه كره بيع المصاحف وأجر كتَابتها وأجر عرضها، وكان يكره أن تنقط المصاحف بالنحو، وأجر الذين يقسمون الأرض، والرجل يحسب للرجال حسابا فيأخذ عليه أجرا، وأجر القنان، إلاَّ ما كان من غير شرط. قال: هذا رأينا.

سئل عن رجل باع مملوكا وله مال؟

قال: إذا باعه وله مال ظاهر تبعه ماله، إلاَّ أن يستثنيه البائع، إلاَّ أن يكون مالا لم يطلع عليه البائع فذلك للبائع.

وأما النخل إذا باعها صاحبها وقد أثمرت ولم تمنع ثمرتها فهي للبائع، وإذا أحل بيع ثمرتها فهي للبائع إلاَّ أن يشترطها[174] المبتاع، ويقال: إنَّمَا هي كسيمة[175] في رؤوسها.

سئل عن رجل باع إبريسما إلى أجل مسمى فحل الأجل ولم يجد عنده دراهم[176]، هل له أن يأخذ الإبريسم بدون الثمن الذي كان قد باعه به؟

قال: إذا لم يجد الدراهم فله أن يأخذ[177] الإبريسم بالثمن الذي يبتاع به الناس يومئذ،

172 وكره بعير ببعيرين ونفس ذلك: -،د.

173 ثمن: شرو، ب.

174 يشترطها: يستثنيها، ب.

175 كسيمة: -،د.

176 دراهم: دراهما، ب،د.

177 يأخذ: يشتري، ب.

ويتبعه بفضل الثمن، والبر مثل الإبريسم في ذلك.

سئل عن رجل أسلف دراهم في بيع إلى أجل بوزن أو كيل، ثُمَّ جاء الأجل، فلم يجد عنده؟

قال: لا تأخذ بدراهمك إلاَّ الذي أسلفت فيه أو رأس مالك، ولا تحوله في شيء من البيع حتَّى تقبضه.

وقال: إذا بعت بيعا بدراهم فخلت الدراهم فخذ بدراهمك ما شئت من عروض أو غيره.

عن قتادة عن سعيد بن المسيب أنَّه كان لا يرى بأسا بكل بيع ابتاعه رجل إلى أجل أن يبيعه قبل أن يقبضه ما خلا المكيل[178] والموزون[179]. قال: هذا رأينا، عن الحسن عن قتادة مثل ذلك.

عن يزيد بن أبي مالك الشامي: أنَّ رسول الله عليه الصلاة والسلام ـ قال: «مطل[180] الغني ظلم، ومن أحيل[181] إلى غنيّ[182] مليء فليحتل[183]»[184].

ونهى عن وطء الحبالى حتَّى يلدن. قال: هذا عدل وهو رأينا[185].

---

178 المكيل: الكيل، ب،د.

179 الموزون: الوزن، ب.

180 مطل: مطول، ب،د.

181 أجبل، ب.

182 غني: –،د.

183 فليحتل: فليحتال، ب،د.

184 رواه الربيع،دون ذكر: «ومن أحيل. . .»، باب الأحكام، ر٥٩٨. وأحمد، ر٩٩٧٤.

185 وهو رأينا: –،د.

عن قتادة عن الحسن: أنَّهما كرها إذا اشترى نفر تمرا على رؤوس النخل أن يبيع أحدهم حتَّى يبيعوا جميعا. قال: لا نرى به بأسا.

عن ابن سيرين أن رجلا ابتاع من رجل شاة بعشرين درهما، واستثنى البائع[186] نصفها، فباعها المشترى بدرهم وعشرين درهما، فهلك الثمن فاختصما إلى شريح. فقال: أردت أن تربي فلم يرب لك، إنَّماكان شريكك في درهم، يقول إنَّماكان شريكك في الربح. قال: هذا رأينا.

سئل عن رجل باع جلالا[187] من تمر. فقال: كلت فيها كذا وكذا؟

قال: إذا ذكر الكيل ولم يبع كيلا فباعه مجازفة فلا بأس[188].

سئل عن ألماسة يكون فيها البيع، وبينهم شرط يلقون للمساسة كذا وكذا مِمّاً يوزن ألماسة؟

فكره ذلك.

سئل عن الباسنة[189] يكون فيه البيع، وبينه شرط يلقون للباسنة كذا وكذا مِمّاً يوزن الباسنة؟

فكره ذلك[190].

186 البائع: -،د.

187 جلالا: هكذا في ب،د، ولعلها جدابا.

188 قاموس قفاف: هامش، ب.

189 الباسنة: وهي آلاتُ الصُنَّاع وقيل: هي الحَدِيدةُ التي تُحْرَثُ بها الأرضُ» (غريب الحديث لابن الجوزي، باب الباء مع الشين.

190 سئل: عن الباسنة يكون فيه البيع وبينه شرط يلقون للباسنة كذا وكذا مِمّا يوزن الباسنة؟ فكره ذلك: -،د؛ قاموس سكة الحراث، أو الآلات الصناع: هامش، ب.

سئل عن رجل اشترى سمنا وعسلا كيلا، أله أن يأخذه وزنا.

قال: إذا كان اشتراه كيلا فلا يأخذه إلاَّ كيلا، وإن اشتراه وزنا فلا يأخذ إلاَّ وزنا.

سئل عن الذي يعد البطيخ فمرت به صغيرتان[191] فجعلهما بدلا عن واحدة؟

فقال: ما أرى بأسا ببطيختين بواحدة، يدا بيد، ولم ير بأسا أن يعد حزم الشرط فيأخذ ما بقي بحسابه.

سئل عن رجل ابتاع من رجل طعاما فأعطاه ما كان عنده وبقيت بقية، فقال: أنظرني بقيمته[192] حتَّى أوفيك إذا تيسرنا؟

قال: أكره أن يبيع الرجل ما ليس عنده، فإن أسلفه إلى أجل فلا بأس أن يؤخره عنه.

سئل عن رجل له طعام فشرك رجلا فيه وقبض الثمن؟

قال: أكره حتَّى يكتاله؛ لأنَّه لو هلك كان من مال الأول.

سئل عن رجل يولي لرجل بيعا لم يقبضه؟

قال: لا نرى بأسا إن لم يأخذ ربحا.

سئل عن رجل يبتاع ثمرا[193]، ثُمَّ يكتاله ويضعه في البيت، ثُمَّ يستشرك فيه رجلا فيشركه فيقبض منه الثمن ويُقر أنَّه في البيت حتَّى يبيعاه ولا يقسماه حتَّى يقتسما الثمن؟

قال: لا تثبت شركته، حتَّى يقسماه بكيل أو وزن.

---

191 فمرت به صغيرتان: مر به صغيرين، ب.

192 بقيمته: في بقيته، ب.

193 ثمرا: -،د.

سئل عن رجل يبتاع تمرا بكذا وكذا، صاعا بدينار ثُمَّ يجريان عيارا[194] يأخذ صاعين أو أقل من ذلك أو أكثر فيكيلا ن به فيكون ذلك أهون عليهما من كيل الصاع، أيجوز ذلك؟ أو يعمل ذلك في الكراء إذا كرى الرجل على مكيله الصيعان؟

قال: لا بأس به في التمر إذا كان سواء.

سئل عن رجل كان له شركاء[195] في نخل فكان له ثلثها أو نصفها ولم يقاسم أصحابه حقهم، فأراد أن يبيع حقه من ثمر ذلك النخل. هل يجوز أن يبيع حقه إذا لم يكن مقسوما وإِنَّما يكون بيعه إيَّاه أني أبيعك حصتي[196] من هذا التمر إنَّمَا حقي منه الثلث أو النصف؟

قال: لا نرى بهذا بأسا.

سئل عن رجل ابتاع تمرا بنسيئة فاكتاله، ثُمَّ أشرك[197] فيه رجلا آخر، هل يجوز أن يشترك[198] ويكتاله[199] ويتركه[200] على حاله حتَّى يبيعه؟

قال: هذا مكروه حتَّى يكتاله.

سئل عن رجل قال لعبد بينه وبين إخوته: لو كاتبت[201] ثُمَّ استعنت مواليك لأعانوك

194 يجريان عيارا: بنقل أو غيره، ب.

195 شركاء: شريك، ب.

196 حصتي: حقك، د.

197 أشرك: اشترك، ب، د.

198 يشترك: يشترط، ب.

199 ويكتاله: -، د.

200 ويتركه: ويقره، ب.

201 كاتبت: أنكحت، ب.

وهولا يريد أن يعتقه ولا ينوي به.

قال: لا بأس لعمري إنّه مولاه.

سئل عن رجل اشترى سمنا واشترط كيلا غير كيل الناس ورأوه جميعا وتراضيا عليه؟

قال: لا بأس، ولكن يبيعه كما اكتاله.

سئل عن تمر اشتراه رجل فاستشرك فيه رجلا آخر بدينارين بكيل مسمى، ثُمَّ حبسوا التمر، ثُمَّ وزن تمره صاحب الدينارين فزاد أربعين رطلا على ما أخرج له شريكه؟

قال: لا بأس إلاَّ أن تكون زيادة بيِّنة.

سئل عن امرأة كان لها غلام أرادت بيعه، فقالت لها أختها: لا تبيعيه؛ أنا أشهد أنك حلفت بعتقه ثُمَّ حنثت، وإنّه لحر وإنَّها عندنا مصدقة؟

قال: لا بأس، قد تكون مصدقة.

سئل عن المحرم: هل يحتجم؟

قال: نعم.

سئل عن رجل هلك وترك مالا ولم يوجد له وارث، وادعى عليه رجل دينا بغير شهود وهو غير متهم.

قال: لا أرى شيئا أفضل من أن يعطى عنه دينه وإن فضل شيء كان للفقراء.

سئل عن رجل غضبت عليه امرأته ثُمَّ أرضاها فرضيت، فقال لها: والله لا أسرع ما طلقتك، يقول: ما أوشك ما أرضيك، فقالت: إنَّمَا عنيت طلاقي، فذهب إلى أبي

الشعثاء فأخبره فقال: لا شيء فيه، فذهب إلى امرأته[202] فأخبرها بما قال أبو الشعثاء، قالت: لا أفعل،فخرج إلى أبي الشعثاء فأخبره قال: أشهد على تطليقة واحدة ثُمَّ راجعها.

مسائل في الحج[203]

سئل عن رفع الصوت بالتكبير على الصفا والمروة؟

فقال: إن أبا الشعثاء كان يرفع صوته كأنه أعرابي، والتلبية رفعها أيضا، والرفع يوم المزدلفة قبل طلوع الشمس وإن أقام الأمير.

سئل عن الوقوف على[204] الصفا والمروة؟

قال: إذا وقفت أقمت على حجر واحد فلا بأس والسعي بينهما رَمَلٌ[205].

سئل عن الاستراحة بين الصفا والمروة؟

قال: لا، إلاَّ للمضطر.

سئل عن رجل طاف بامرأته بين الصفا والمروة فأعيت، فذهب يستكري لها حمارا فقطع طوافه؟

قال: لا بأس إذا كان من عذر.

202 فذهب إلى امرأته: -،د.

203 مسائل الحج: -،د.

204 الوقوف على: -، ب.

205 والسعي بينهما رمل: -،د.

سئل عن رجل طاف بالبيت، ثُمَّ ركع بعد العصر للإفاضة[206] وطاف بين الصفا والمروة ثُمَّ رجع إلى منى.

قال: يركع ركعتين فإنَّه لا صلاة بعد العصر، ولا أقول: إنَّه يبطل حجه.

سئل عن رجل طاف بالبيت[207] و[208] بين الصفا والمروة، ثم ركع بين الصفا والمروة[209] ثُمَّ دميت رجله؟

قال: يتم طوافه، والجمرة كذلك، والبيت ليس مثلهما.

سئل عن رجل رمى الجمرة ثُمَّ سقطت منه حصاة في الجمرة، أيأخذ مكانها من الجمرة؟

قال: نعم، إذا كان لا يعرف حصاته.

سئل عن امرأة قصرت قبل أن تذبح؟

قال: تعيد ذبحها[210].

سئل هل يصلِّي معهم العصر إذا أقاموا الصلاة ونحن معهم وقد صلَّينا إذا تخوفنا الشهوة[211]؟

قال: نعم.

206 للإفاضة في الإفاضة، ب،د.

207 بالبيت: -،د.

208 و: -، ب،د.

209 ثم ركع بين الصفا والمروة: -،د.

210 ذبحها:ذبيحها، ب،د.

211 الشهوة: -،د.

وسألته: عن رجل لي عليه سلف دراهم فقلت له[212]: أسلفكها في سمن؟

قال: لا، إلاَّ أن ينقده.

سئل عن رجل طاف بالبيت ثُمَّ خرج بعد العصر إلى منى؟

قال: يركع ركعتين قبل أن يخرج من الحرم.

سئل عن الغراب هل يؤكل؟

قال: فكره ذلك.

سئل عن رجل رمى طيرا[213] في الحل فذهب حتَّى دخل الحرم في طريقه؟

قال: لا تأخذه.

سئل عن رجل طلق امرأته اثنين فقالت: زد الثالثة. قال: قد زدت؟

قال: قد فرغ.

سئل عن عبد طلق حرَّة؟

قال: طلاقها ثلاثة وعدَّتها ثلاثة قروء، وطلاق الحر الأمة اثنان وعدَّتها حيضتان.

سئل عن رجل قال لامرأته: يا بنت[214] أمي؟

قال: لا بأس، أرأيت لو قال لها: يا أختي ما عليه شيء.

212 له: –،د.

213 غرابا، ب.

214 بنت: –،د.

سئل عن رجل قال له آخر: تزوّجت؟ قال: لا؟

قال: قد كذب وليس بشيء.

سئل عن أهل مربد يدخلون مكة بالعطر[215]، أيخرجون زكاتهم بمكة؟

قال: يخرجونها حيث شاؤوا بمكة أو بالمربد.

سئل لو أنّي أخرجت حماما شاميا من مكة؟

قال: جائز.

سئل عن المحرم يقطع الشجرة في الحل؟

قال: نعم، يقطعها[216]، ولا يقطعها في الحرم.

سئل عن رجل قال له رجل: ما لخادمك[217] يخاصم أباك؟ قال: أنا أشهد، ما يحسب إلاَّ أنَّه حرّ وما هو إلاَّ[218] حر؟

قال: لا أرى ذلك بشيء إذا كان يقول حرّ في نفسه.

سئل عن رجل قال لامرأته: أمرك بيدك، قالت: قد قبلت، قال لها ماذا كان في نفسك؟ قالت: واحد؟

قال: كان أبو الشعثاء يراها واحدا زمانا، ثُمَّ كأنه يكره ذلك. قال: يخطبها مع الخطاب.

---

215 بالعطر: بالعصر، ب.

216 يقطعها: -، ب.

217 لخادمك: لغلامك، ب.

218 إلا: -، د.

قال: لا، حتَّى تنكح زوجا غيره[219].

سئل عن رجل لم يرم الجمرة إلى الليل جهلا أو نسيانا؟

قال: يفعل خيرا، قلت: يذبح شاة؟ قال: كثير.

سئل عن رجل كانت معه بضاعة عشرة دراهم مصرورة في ثوبه، وكانت له تسعة دراهم في ثوبه ثُمَّ هلكت الدراهم كلّها إلاَّ خمسة لا يدري البضاعة هي أم لا؟

قال: تقسم بحصص الدراهم.

سئل عن رجل اشترى تمرا، ثُمَّ أشرك آخر فباعوا بنقد ودين، ثُمَّ خشي الشريك النقصان. فقال: أعفني من شركتي. قال: نعم[220] قد أعفيتك؟

قال: لا أرى بأسا.

سئل عن رجل كان له مع رجل سلف، ثُمَّ اشترى منه متاعا بسلفة؟

قال: جائز.

سئل عن رجل يقصر بين الصفا والمروة للحجَّة؟

قال: جائز.

219 قال: لا حتَّى تنكح زوجا غير: –،د.

220 نعم: –،د.

عن عمرو بن دينار عن جابر بن زيد قال: وقت الدفعة من المزدلفة[221] بعد[222] ما يرجع المصلّي من صلاة الصبح.

عن عمرو بن دينار عن جابر بن زيد قال في المرأة: لها شرطها بما[223] يستحل من فرجها.

عن عمرو بن دينار عن جابر بن زيد سئل عن رجل يعزب في أبله[224] وليس معه ماء؟ قال: إلى أن يأتي أهله يكفيه التيمّم.

في حكم أولاد المدبر ذكرا كان أو أنثى.

عن عمرو بن دينار عن أبي الشعثاء قال: [أولاد المُدَبَّرة مملوكون][225].

عن عمرو بن دينار عن جابر بن زيد قال: يلون المحرم بعيره ويطليه بالقطران. قال[226]: لا بأس.

عن عمرو بن دينار قال: قال رجل عند جابر بن زيد: إن أصحاب النبيّ -عليه الصلاة والسلام- كانوا لا يرون بالدخيل بأسا يعني بالرهان.

قال جابر: كانوا أعز من ذلك.

---

221 وقت الدفعة من المزدلفة: -،د.

222 بعد: قدر، ب.

223 في المرأة لها شرطها بما: -،د.

224 يعزب في أبله: -،د.

225 أولاد المُدَبَّرة مملوكون: -، ب،د. انظر الإضافة من: سنن البيهقي، باب ما جاء في ولد المدبرة من غير سيدها بعد تدبيرها، ر٢١٣٨٠.

226 قال: -،د.

عن عمرو بن دينار: أنَّه رأى جابر بن زيد أومأ في ماء وطين.

عن عمرو بن دينار عن جابر بن زيد قال: لا يصلح الخلع حتَّى يكون من قبل المرأة.

عن عمرو بن دينار قال: ما فراه الأوداج فكل.

قال سفيان: قلت لعمرو بن دينار: نبيع الطعام إلى أجل فإذا حلّ أتيت صاحبي أتقاضاه، فأخذ طعاما.
قال أبو الشعثاء: إذا حلّ الأجل فخذ به ما شئت.

قال عمرو عن طاؤوس عن ابن عبّاس: عن الرجل يطلق امرأته تطليقة أو تطليقتين ثُمَّ تزوّجت فمات عنها أو طلقها، ثُمَّ رجعت إلى زوجها الأول؟ قال: عنده على ثلاثة[227].

قال عمرو عن عطاء و[228] أبي الشعثاء أنَّهما قالا: هي واحد[229].

عن عمرو بن دينار عن جابر بن زيد قال: إذا أكلت من الهدي تطوّعا غرمته[230].

عن عمرو بن دينار عن جابر بن زيد قال: المرأة إقراؤها ما كانت تحيض وإن كان في كلّ سنة مرة.

227 قال: عنده على ثلاثة: –،د.

228 و: عن، ب،د.

229 هي واحد: –،د.

230 غرمته: غرمت، ب،د. رواه ابن أبي شيبة، في هدي التطوع يؤكل منه أم لا، ٤/٢٥١.

عن عمرو بن دينار عن أبي الشعثاء في المرأة تحيض في كلّ شهر مرة[231]؟ قال: عدتها أقراؤها ما كانت تحيض، قال طاؤوس: يكفيها ثلاثة أشهر.

عن عمرو بن دينار عن جابر بن زيد قال: إذا أقلد الحاج فقد أحرم.

عن عمرو بن دينار عن جابر بن زيد أخبره ابن عبَّاس عن خالته ميمونة أنَّها كانت تغتسل هي ورسول الله صلى الله عليه وسلم من إناء واحد[232].

عن عمرو بن دينار عن جابر بن زيد. قال: إذا أسلمت في شيء فلا تأخذ إلاَّ الذي أسلمت فيه أو رأس مالك.

عن عمرو بن دينار عن جابر بن زيد قال: إذا طلقت البكر قبل الدخول ثلاثا فهو واحد.

عن عمرو بن دينار عن عطاء وجابر بن زيد[233]: المتوفى عنها زوجها تخرج في عدَّتها[234] إن شاءت[235].

عن طاؤوس قال: لا تجوز في الهدي العوراء ولا الجرباء ولا العجفاء[236].

---

231 مرة: -،د.

232 رواه البخاري، باب الغسل بالصاع ونحوه، ر٢٥٠.

233 عمرو بن دينار عن عطاء وجابر بن زيد: -، ب.

234 في عدتها: -،د.

235 رواه ابن أبي شيبة، من رخص للمتوفى عنها زوجها أن تخرج، ٤/١٣٣.

236 العجفاء: الجذماء، ب.

قال عمرو: قال أبو الشعثاء: لا تجوز المصطلمة أذنها.

عن عمرو بن دينار عن جابر بن زيد: عن ابن عبَّاس أنَّه سمع رسول الله صلى الله عليه وسلم يخطب يقول: من لم يجد إزارا فليلبس سراويل[237]، ومن لم يجد نعلين فليلبس خفين[238].

عن عمرو بن دينار عن جابر بن زيد قال: ترث مع ابنها يعني الجدَّة.

عن عمرو بن دينار عن جابر بن زيد قال: لم نجد في ذلك الزمان[239] شيئا أنفع من الرشاء. قال: زمان زياد بن أبي سفيان.

عن عمرو بن دينار عن جابر بن زيد: قال: إذا خيّر الرجل امرأته فهو ما قالت في مجلسها، فإذا تفرقا فليس له بشيء[240]، ليس له أن يمشي في الناس وطلاق امرأته بيد غيره.

عن عمرو عن عطاء وأبي الشعثاء أنَّهما قالا في المتوفى عنها زوجها: تخرج في عدَّتها إن شاءت.

عمرو بن دينار عن جابر بن زيد قال[241]: سمعت ابن عبَّاس يقول: صلَّيت مع رسول الله صلى الله عليه وسلم ثمانيا جمعا وسبعا، قلت: «يا أبا الشعثاء أظنه أخر الظهر وعجل

237 سراويل: سروالا، ب.
238 رواه البخاري، باب لبس الخفين للمحرم إذا لم يجد النعلين، ر١٧٤٤.
239 في ذلك الزمان: -،د.
240 له بشيء: -،د.
241 قال: -،د.

العصر، وأخر المغرب وعجل العشاء. قال: وأنا أظن كذلك»[242].

عمرو عن عطاء عن جابر بن زيد أنّهما قالا: إذا تزوّج الرجل المرأة وفرض لها أو[243] مات ولم يفرض لها[244] فلها الميراث والصداق.

عن عمرو عن جابر بن زيد، سئل عن رجل باع طعاما ما بدينار أو دينارين لأجل، فلمّا حلّ الأجل قال: ليس عندي طعام؟
قال: جائز أن يأخذ بديناره ما شاء. وقال طاؤوس: لا يأخذ إلاّ طعاما.

عن عمرو بن دينار عن جابر بن زيد قال: [لا]تجوز عطيّة الرجل[245] المرأة وشَرْوَاها[246] في حال الولادة.

عمرو بن دينار عن جابر بن زيد قال: صلّيت مع ابن عبّاس بالبصرة فلم يكن يُكبّر هذا التكبير الذي تُكبِّرون[247].

عمرو بن دينار عن جابر بن زيد قال: إذا مضت الأربعة أشهر فليس عليها عدّة[248].

---

242 رواه البخاري، باب من لم يتطوع بعد المكتوبة، ر١١٢٠.
243 أو: ثم، ب،د.
244 ولم يفرض لها: –،د.
245 الرجل: –،د.
246 شرواها، ب. والشروى هي المثل والصنو.
247 رواه ابن المنذر في الأوسط، ر١٣٢٣، بلفظ: «صليت مع ابن عباس بالبصرة فلم يكبر هذا التكبير بالخفض والرفع».
248 عمرو بن دينار عن جابر بن زيد قال: إذا مضت الأربعة أشهر فليس عليها عدّة: –،د.

عمرو بن دينار عن جابر بن زيد: إذا مات الرجل وله ابن مملوك فأعتق قبل أن يقسم ميراثه فله الميراث.

عمرو بن دينار عن جابر بن زيد قال: أخبرني رجل عن ابن عبَّاس أن المسلم فيه اسم من أسماء الله، فإذا ذبح فنسي أن يذكر اسم الله فليذكر اسم الله وليأكل.

عمرو بن دينار عن جابر بن زيد قال: لا تجوز عطية المرأة إذا كانت ذات زوج[249] إلاَّ بإذنه.

عن عمرو بن دينار عن جابر بن زيد قال: إذا بلت فامسح ذكرك من أصله فإن البول ينقطع عنك.

انتهت مسائل عمرو بن دينار

249 إذا زادت شرواها، ب.

قال عمرو بن هرم: سئل جابر بن زيد عن امرأة ماتت وتركت زوجها وأمها وأخوتها لأبيها وأمها، وأخوتها لأمها.

قال: للزوج النصف ثلاثة أسهم، ولأمها السدس سهم، ولإخوتها لأمها الثلث سهمان، ويشترك معهم في سهم بني الأم بنو الأب[250] والأم؛ لأنَّهم كلهم بنو الأم، وكذلك قال ابن عبَّاس وزيد بن ثابت، قال عمرو: لوكانوا لأبيها ليسوا لأمها لم يرثوا شيئا؛ لأنَّهم عصبة ولا يرثون بفريضة.

قال عمرو: سئل جابر بن زيد عن رجل توفي وترك بني عمه أحدهما ابن عمه أخي[251] أبيه لأبيه وأمه، والآخر ابن عمه أخي[252] أبيه لأمه[253]؟

قال: ابن عمه أخو[254] أبيه لأبيه وأمه أحقّ بالمتوفى من ابن عمه أخي[255] أبيه الذي لأمه من أجل إنما قرب من أمه من الآخر لجدته[256].

أخبرنا عمرو قال: لا يرث اليهوديّ ولا النصرانيّ المسلم ولا يرثهما المسلم ولا يحجبون وتجوز لهم الوصيَّة.

وإن أسلم يهوديّ أو نصرانيّ أو غيرهم بعد موت ولي لهم من المسلمين فأدرك ميراثه قبل أن يقسم فإنّه يرث إن كانت فريضة بفريضته أو بعصبته إن كان عصبة،

250 الأب: -، ب.
251 أخي: أخ، ب،د.
252 أخي: أخ، ب،د.
253 لأمه: لصلته، ب؛ -،د.
254 أخو: أخ، ب،د.
255 أخي، أخ، ب،د.
256 الذي لعلة من أجل إنما قرب من أمه من ـ الآخر لجدته: -،د.

والمملوك لا يرث ولا يحجب، وإن مات له ولي حرّ وترك مالا فأعتق المملوك قبل أن يقسم المال فإنّه يرث إن كانت له فريضة أو بعصبته إن كانت له عصبة.

قال عمرو: سئل جابر بن زيد عن وصيَّة الغلام والجارية؛ أجائزة[257]؟

قال: نعم، إذا أوصيا بالمعروف. قال: ولا تجوز وصيَّة الرجل والمرأة إذا أوصيا[258] بالجنف والإثم.

ولا تجوز وصيَّة المملوك في ماله[259] إلاّ بإذن سيده، وإن مات للمالك ولي حرّ فأوصى للمملوك بوصيَّة من ماله يجوز للمملوك ما أوصى له به؟

قال: إذا مات رجلان أو قتلا وكل واحد منهما يرث من صاحبه، ولا يدرى أيهما مات قبل صاحبه[260]، فإنّه يرث كلّ واحد منهما من صاحبه بفريضته.

فقيل: أرأيت إن لم يكن لواحد منهما مال؟

قال: لا يرث الذي لا مال له من صاحبه، ولا يرث ذو المال من صاحبه شيئا.

قال عمرو: سئل جابر بن زيد عن رجل مات أو امرأة وأراد أن يوصي فلا استطاع فعلا[261]؟

قال عمرو: أرى أن يجعل مِمّا تركا وصيَّة معروفة ربعا أو خمسا لأقاربهما.

قال عمرو: سئل جابر بن زيد عن رجل أعتق مملوكا له[262] فمات المعتق ولم يترك ولدا

257 سئل جابر بن زيد عن وصيَّة الغلام والجارية أجائزة: جابر بن زيد هل تجوز وصية الغلام والجارية؟، ب

258 إذا أوصيا: –، ب.

259 ولا تجوز: +، ب.

260 صاحبه: –، د.

261 قال عمرو: سئل جابر بن عن رجل مات أو امرأة أن يوصي فلا استطاع فعلا: –، د.

262 مملوكا له: –، ب.

ولا ذا رحم يعلم مكانه، أيرثه مولاه الذي أعتقه؟

قال: لا، إلاَّ أن يوصي له بشيء من ماله جاز له[263]، وإن أوصى له بكل ماله جاز، وإن لم يكن له وارث ولم يوص للمولى بشيء ولا لغيره تصدق عنه بماله، قال[264]: وزعموا أنَّه مات مولى لعبد الله بن عمر بن الخطَّاب، وترك مائة ألف درهم. وأن[265] ابن عمر قال: هل له ولد أو ذوو[266] قرابة يعلمون مكانهم أو واحد من أهل قريته التي هو منها مسلم؟ فلم يجدوا له قرابة ولا ذا رحم ولا أحدا مِمَّن سئل عنهم، فكره ابن عمر أن يرثه، فاشترى بماله رقيقا فأعتقهم، وإذا أعتق رجلا منهم قال: هذا عبد الله ومال الله.

قال عمرو: سئل جابر بن زيد عن عبد كانت له ابنتان حرتان فاشترته إحداهما وأعتقته، ثُمَّ أصاب الأب مالا ثم مات[267]، وليس له ولد إلاَّ هما ولا وارث غيرهما كيف يقسم ماله؟

قال: ميراثه بينهما سواء.

قال عمرو: تجوز شهادة القابلة وحدها على الولد المنفوس إذا شهدت أنَّه ولد حيّا ثُمَّ مات ولم يعلم ذلك إلاَّ هي، فيرث إن كان مات والده أو والدته وهي حبلى.

قال عمرو: سئل جابر بن زيد عمَّن أسلم من العجم من رجال أو نساء يموت أحدهم وليس له وارث ذو فريضة ولا عصبة، ولا يعلم له ذو قرابة من الرجال والنساء إلاَّ نساء

263 له: -،د.

264 قال: -،د.

265 أن: -،د.

266 ذوو: ذو، ب،د.

267 ثم مات: -،د.

من تلقاء أمه أونساء من تلقاء أبيه.

قال: يجعل ميراثه لهم وإن كانت نفسا واحدة ذكرا أوانثى فهم أحقّ بميراثه، قضى الله أن أولي[268] الأرحام بعضهم أولى ببعض في كتاب الله إذاكانوا مسلمين، والله بكل شيء عليم. فأمر الله أحقّ أن يتبع.

وقضى عمر بن الخطّاب رضي الله عنه عنه في ميراث رجل لم يعلم له وارث ذو فريضة ولا ذو رحم إلاّ عمة له[269] وخالة بجعل عمر لعمته الثلثان ولخالته الثلث.

قال عمرو: قضى عليّ بن أبي طالب رضي الله عنه في امرأة توفيت ولا يعلم لها وارث ولا عصبة ولها زوج: أن للزوج ميراثها كله.

قال عمرو: قضى عليّ بن أبي طالب في مولى قتل وليس له وارث ولا عصبة يحوز ميراثه، وله أم وأخت من أب مملوكتان، فقضى بدية المولى كاملة، ثُمَّ أمر أن تشترى أمه وأخته شراء من ديته فتعتقا[270]، ثُمَّ يقسم ما بقي من ديته بينهما على نحو ما فرض الله لهما من الميراث على خمسة أخماس، بجعل للأخت ثلاثة أخماس وللأم الخمسان؛ وذلك لأن لأخته من ميراثه في الفريضة النصف ثلاثة أسهم ولأمه الثلث سهمان ثُمَّ رد عليهما السهم السادس على قسمة أنصبتهما[271].

وقضى في امرأة تركت ابنتها وابنة ابنها ولا عصبة لها ولا وارث غيرهما، أن لابنتها ثلاثة أرباع ولابنة ابنها الربع؛ وذلك لأنّ لابنتها من ميراثها النصف ثلاثة أسهم ولابنة ابنها السدس سهم بالفريضة، ثُمَّ يرد عليهما السدسان فيقسمانه

268 أولي: أولو: ب،د.

269 له: –،د.

270 فتعتقا: فتعتقا، ب،د

271 أنصبتهما: فريضتهما، ب.

على قسم فريضتهما.

قال عمرو: قضى عليّ بن أبي طالب في تركة رجل حرّمات وترك مالا يسيرا ولم يترك ولدا ولا عصبة يعلم مكانهما وله أم مملوكة أن تدفع تركته إلى أمه فتنتفع بها.

قال عمرو: سئل جابر بن زيد عن الأخ من الأم هل يرث عقلا من أخيه لأمه إن لم يكن من أبيه؟

قال: نعم، قد ورثه عمر بن الخطّاب وعليّ بن أبي طالب رضي الله عنه، فذلك للأخ[272] من الأم[273].

قال عمرو: قضى عمر بن الخطّاب رضي الله عنه في خلافته في مال رجل من دهاقين أهل[274] الشام، [275] مات وترك مالا كثيرا من أراضين ولم يترك وارثا غير ابنته، قضى عمر بميراثه كله لابنته.

قال عمرو: سئل جابر بن زيد عن رجل طلق امرأته ثلاث تطليقات جميعا ثُمَّ مات أحدهما في العدَّة: هل يرث الحي[276] منهما[277] الميِّت؟

قال: لا، إلاَّ أن يكون طلقها وهو مريض مضارًا بها، فإنَّها ترثه إن مات في مرضه قبل أن تخلو عدَّتها[278] قضى بذلك عمر بن الخطّاب.

---

272 للأخ: -،د.

273 للأم: +،د.

274 أهل: -،د.

275 ثم: +،ب.

276 الحي: -،د.

277 منهما: أحدهما،د.

278 انظر: آثار الربيع، مسألة ٥، ص ٢٨.

قال عمرو: من طلق امرأته وهي حائض فليست حيضتها بشيء من قروئها؛[279] لأن الله تعالى يقول: ﴿فَطَلِّقُوهُنَّ لِعدَّتهنَّ وَأَحْصُوا الْعدَّة﴾[280] والعدَّة الطهر أو الشهور إن كانت[281] مِمَّن لا تحيض، قضى بذلك ابن مسعود وابن عبَّاس رضي الله عنهما.

قال عمرو: سئل جابر بن زيد عن رجل طلق امرأته تطليقة، ثُمَّ استبان حملها بعد شهر، ثُمَّ أسقطت أيحرمها ذلك على زوجها؟

قال: كان ابن عبَّاس يقول: أحب في ذلك إليَّ أن تعتدّ شهورا من لدن [طلاقها] فإنَّها ليست عليها الأقراء[282]، وقد كانت حاملا فأسقطت ثُمَّ ثبت في ذلك الدم أربعين ليلة. قال: وأمَّا عليّ بن أبي طالب فبلغني أنَّه قال: حمل ووضع فإذا طهرت من الدم حلت، وليس[283] لصاحبها عليها رجعة إلاَّ أن يخطبها في الخطاب. واعلم أنَّه يعتد في نفس أمران تشاجرا فيهما: أحدهما فيه ريبة، والآخر لا ريبة فيه.

قال عمرو: إذا مات الرجل وترك امرأته حبلى فعدَّتها آخر الأجلين، فإن وضعت حملها قبل أربعة أشهر وعشرا أكملت أربعة أشهر وعشرا، وإن كان الحمل أبعد من ذلك فأجلها أن تضع حملها، قضى بذلك عليّ بن أبي طالب وأبي بن كعب وعبد الله بن عبَّاس رضي الله عنهم جميعا حدث بذلك عنهم عكرمة مولى ابن عبَّاس[284].

---

279 انظر: آثار الربيع، مسألة ١٤٧، ص ٤٣.

280 سورة الطلاق: ١.

281 إن كانت: -، ب.

282 الأقراء: القروء، ب.

283 لها الأزواج وليس: +، ب.

284 حدث بذلك عنهم عكرمة مولى ابن عبَّاس: -،د.

قال عمرو: سئل جابر بن زيد عن امرأة تطلق وهي ترضع ولا تحيض ما أرضعت حتَّى تفطم[285] ولدها: كم تعتدّ؟

قال: ثلاثة قروء، وإن لم تحض حتَّى تفطم[286] ولدها، وإذا حاضت فلتعتدّ ثلاثة قروء، وإن حاضت ثلاثة قروء في شهر أو شهرين فقد برئت منه.

قال عمرو: سئل جابر بن زيد عن جارية طلقت بعد ما دخل بها زوجها وهي لا تحيض، فاعتدت شهرين وخمسة وعشرين ليلة ثُمَّ حاضت؟

قال: تعتدّ أيضا ثلاثة قروء، كذلك قال ابن عبَّاس.

قال عمرو: عن عكرمة أن المطلقة إذا توفي عنها[287] زوجها وهي في عدَّتها من طلاق واحد أو اثنين اعتدت لوفاة زوجها عدَّة المتوفى عنها زوجها، إذا كانت[288] في عدَّتها قبل أن تحرم عليه، من أجل أنَّها ترثه، وإن ماتت هي ورثها، وإن طلقها ثُمَّ توفي قبل أن تخلو عدَّتها من قروءها فإنَّها تستأنف عدَّة المتوفى عنها زوجها أربعة أشهر وعشرا وترث زوجها، وإن كان أبانها[289] الطلاق ثلاثا ثُمَّ توفي في عدَّتها فلا ميراث لها، وتعتدّ بقية قروئها من طلاقها.

قال عمرو: سئل جابر بن زيد عن رجل كان تحته أربع نسوة فطلق إحداهن ثلاث تطليقات جميعا؟

---

285 تفطم: تفطن، ب،د.

286 تفطم: تفطن، ب،د.

287 عنها: –،د.

288 كانت: وهي، ب.

289 أبانها: –،د.

قال: لا يحلّ له أن يتزوّج امرأة أخرى حتَّى تخلو عدَّة امرأته التي طلق.

قال عمرو: سئل جابر بن زيد عن رجل تحته امرأة فطلقها ثلاث تطليقات جميعا: أيحل له أن يتزوّج أختها في عدّة أختها المطلقة؟
قال: لا.

قال عمرو: سئل جابر بن زيد عمَّن تخرج من النساء من بيوتهن إذا فارقهن أزواجهن؟
قال: التي توفي عنها زوجها والمختلعة والملاعنة والمخيرة التي تختار نفسها والتي جعل أمرها بيدها فطلقت نفسها.

قال عمرو: سئل جابر بن زيد عن امرأة قعدت عن المحيض[290] فطلقت ثُمَّ رأت الدم بعد ذلك؟
قال: إن كانت مِمَّن يئست من المحيض فعدَّتها ثلاثة أشهر، وإن لم تكن مِمَّن يئست من المحيض فعدَّتها ثلاثة قروء، وقد تحبس المرأة زمانا عن الحيض ثُمَّ تحيض بعد ذلك.

قال عمرو: سئل جابر بن زيد عن رجل قال لامرأته: يوم تسأليني الطلاق فأنت طالق؟
قال: إذا سألته الطلاق[291] فهي طالق وهي تطليقة واحدة.

قال عمرو: سئل جابر بن زيد عن رجل عاتب رجلا في أمر قد[292] بلغه عنه، فاعتذر إليه وزعم أنَّه لم يفعل ذلك[293]، فقال له الرجل: فامرأتك طالق ثلاثا إن كنت فعلت

290 المحيض: الحيض، ب.
291 إذا سألته الطلاق: -، ب.
292 قد: -،د.
293 ذلك: -،د.

قال: نعم، فظن الرجل أنَّه قد قاله.

قال: لا خير له[294] في حبسها.

قال عمرو: سئل جابر بن زيد عن رجل تزوّج امرأة، فافتضها[295] فحبس عنها زمانا ثُمَّ طلقها قال: العدَّة عليها بعد الطلاق[296] [297].

قال: سئل جابر بن زيد عن رجل طلق امرأة فحبس عنها فلبث زمانا ثمَّ طلقها؟ فقال[298]: لها المهر كاملا ولا عدَّة عليها[299].

قال عمرو: سئل جابر بن زيد عن رجل طلق امرأته تطليقة[300] واحدة على شهادة رجلين ولم يبين لها الطلاق ثُمَّ راجعها من قبل أن تنقضي عدَّتها على شهادة رجلين ثُمَّ أخبرها أنَّه كان قد طلقها ثُمَّ راجعها فكرهت المرأة أن تقيم عنده على ذلك[301]؟

قال: ليس عليها إن فارقته جناح.

قال عمرو: سئل جابر بن زيد عن رجل طلق امرأته بشهادة رجلين وأعلن طلاقها ثُمَّ راجعها من قبل أن تفرط عدَّتها سرا.

---

294 له: لك،د.

295 فافتضها: -،د؛ فافتضها ثم: ب.

296 زمانا ثُمَّ طلقها قال: العدَّة عليها بعد الطلاق: -،د.

297 فلبثت زمانًا ثم طلقها: +، ب د.

298 سئل جابر بن زيد عن رجل طلق امرأة فحبس عنها فلبث زمانا ثمَّ طلقها فقال: -،د.

299 ولا عدة عليها: -،د.

300 تطليقة: -،د.

301 على ذلك: -،د.

قال: لا يصلح أن يراجعها سرا حتَّى يعلمها مراجعتها على شهادة رجلين فقيل له: أرأيت إن كان الرجل الذي طلق غائبا عن امرأته حين طلق. فقال: وإن كان غائبا فلا تصلح مراجعتها حتَّى يعلمها ذلك.

قال عمرو: وقد قال الحسن ذلك أيضا.

قال عمرو: سئل جابر بن زيد عن رجل طلق امرأته، وهو غائب، ثُمَّ راجعها قبل أن تخلو عدَّتها، فأخبرت بعد سنة أو قبل ذلك أن زوجها قد كان طلقها ثُمَّ راجعها، وأتاها خبر طلاقه ورجعتها جميعا؟

قال: هي امرأته.

قال عمرو: سئل جابر بن زيد عن رجل له امرأتان فقالت له إحداهن: لا أرضى عليك[302] حتَّى تطلق فلانة لصاحبتها، فطلقها تطليقة[303] فقال لها: إنَّه قد كان طلقها تطليقتين وبقيت الثالثة، ولم يكن طلقها كما قال، ولكنَّه أراد أن يرضيها بذلك[304]؟

قال: قد بانت منه حين سمىَّ ثلاث تطليقات.

قال عمرو: سئل جابر بن زيد عن رجل يحلف بطلاق امرأته؟

قال: إذا حنث فقد برئت منه امرأته.

قال عمرو: سئل جابر بن زيد عن المرأة الناشزة، فقيل له: إنه يقال: لا يحلّ خلعها حتَّى تقول إنها لا تقيم لله حدا ولا تغتسل من الجنابة ما كانت عند زوجها ثُمَّ يحل خلعها.

---

302 عليك: عنك، ب.

303 تطليقة: -، د.

304 بذلك: -، ب.

قال: لا تفعل هذا مسلمة ولا تقوله ولا تكلف أن تقوله ولا يخف[305] النشوز، فإذا قبل الرجل خلع امرأته ولم يطلقها فقد بانت منه وهي أملك بنفسها، وعدَّتها عدَّة المطلقة، وإن شاءت رجعت إلى زوجها ما دامت في عدَّتها، ويرد إليها الذي أخذ منها إن أراد ذلك زوجها، وإن مات أو ماتت في عدَّتها قبل أن يراجعها فلا ترثه ولا يرثها ما لم يراجعها، وإن لم يراجعها حتَّى تخلو عدَّتها ثُمَّ أراد مراجعتها ففعلت فإنَّهما يصطلحان على ما شاء ا من المهر، وهي عنده على ثلاث تطليقات.

قال عمرو: سئل عكرمة مولى ابن عبَّاس عن المرأة التي يقبل الرجل فديتها ثُمَّ يطلقها بعد ذلك؟

فقال: لا طلاق بعد الفدية، وقد برئت منه حين قبل فديتها ولا يكون طلاقا بعد الفدية.

قال عمرو: سئل جابر بن زيد عن امرأة خافت من بعلها نشوزا أو إعراضا فاصطلحا على صلح من مهرها ليصلح إليها فصلح زمانا ثُمَّ طلقها؟

قال: كان ابن عبَّاس يقول: من قبل من امرأته مالا فإنَّه[306] لا أمر له في الطلاق حتَّى يرد إليها ما أخذ منها.

قال عمرو: سئل جابر بن زيد عن رجل يحدث نفسه بالطلاق؟

قال: إذا أفصح به لسان الرجل فقد طلق، وإن لم يفصح به لسانه فليس بشيء.

قال عمرو: سئل جابر بن زيد هل تجوز شهادة امرأتين مع رجل على الطلاق إذا لم

---

305 ولا يخف: خفاءً بالنشوز، ب.

306 فإنه: -، ب.

يكن رجلان؟
قال: نعم، ولا تجوز شهادة النساء وحدهن إلاَّ مع الرجال.

قال عمرو: سئل جابر بن زيد عن رجل حدث امرأته حديثا ثُمَّ قال لها: إن حدثت هذا الحديث لأحد من الناس فهي طالق وهي[307] عليه حرام وهي يومئذ حبلى ثُمَّ حدثت الحديث الذي نهاها عنه ووضعت حملها؟
قال: برئت منه حين ولدت ولدها، وإن أراد أن يكفر يمينه فعل لقوله: إنَّها عليه حرام، تحرير رقبة، فإن لم يجد فإطعام عشرة مساكين أوكسوتهم فإن لم يجد فصيام ثلاثة أيَّام متتابعات، ثُمَّ يخطبها، فإذا تزوّجها فهي عنده على تطليقتين.

قال عمرو: سئل جابر بن زيد عن رجل ائتمنه رجل على مال فسأله عن أشياء منه فاتهمه فيما حدثه فقال له: امرأتك طالق إن كنت كتمتني شيئا؟
قال: نعم، إن كان كتمه شيئا فقد حرمت عليه، وإن كان لم يكتمه شيئا فلا طلاق ولا بأس، قال عمرو[308]: قال الحسن ذلك أيضا.

قال عمرو: سئل جابر بن زيد عن رجل طلق امرأته وهو مبرسم يهذي ولا يعقل ما يقول؟
قال: لا يجوز له طلاق ولا عتق ما كان على هذا الحال.

قال عمرو: سئل جابر بن زيد عن رجل طلق امرأته وهو مجنون حين أخذه جنونه؟

307 هي: –،د.
308 قال عمرو: عمر، ب،د.

قال: لا يجوز طلاقه ولا عتقه حين يأخذه جنونه.

قال عمرو: سئل جابر بن زيد عن رجل سكران طلق امرأته؟

قال: يجوز طلاقه وعتقه وهو سكران ويؤخذ بما أجرم وأتى وهو سكران.

قال عمرو: سئل جابر بن زيد عن رجل غاب فأتى امرأته نعيه[309] متى تعتدّ امرأته؟

قال: من يوم نعي[310] إليها زوجها.

قال عمرو: سئل جابر بن زيد عن رجل طلق امرأته سرا[311] فكتمها طلاقها؟

قال: عليه نفقتها من يوم طلقها إلى يوم أعلمها طلاقها، وتتزوّج إن شاءت إن كانت عدَّتها من يوم طلقها إلى يوم أعلمها قد مضت، ولا سبيل له عليها.

قال عمرو: سئل جابر بن زيد عن رجل لزمته امرأته تسأله الطلاق[312]، فقال لها: اذهبي بريئة وأنا منك بريء لا ينوي بذلك طلاقا ولا يريده؟

قال: إن لم يكن نوى الطلاق فليس بطلاق وإن نوى طلاقا فهو واحد[313]، وله أن يراجعها في عدَّتها إن شاء.

قال عمرو: سئل جابر بن زيد عن رجل قال لقوم إن لم آتكم[314] إلى سنة فطلاق

309 نعيه: تطليقة، ب.

310 نعي: طلق، ب.

311 سرا: –، د.

312 الطلاق: الصداق، ب.

313 واحد: واحدا، ب، د.

314 آتكم: آتيكم، ب، د.

صاحبتكم بأيديكم، ثُمَّ خرج الرجل فغم عليهم خبره زمانا، فطلقوا المرأة فتزوّجت غيره، ثُمَّ بلغ المرأة وأهلها أن زوجها توفي بعد خروجه من عندهم[315] بأشهر دون السنة.

قال: أمَّا الطلاق بعد الوفاة فلا أراه بشيء، وترث زوجها فإن كانت المرأة تزوّجت زوجها الآخر وقد فرطت عدَّتها من زوجها المتوفى أُمضي تزويجها، وإن كانت تزوّجت[316] قبل أن تخلو عدَّتها من زوجها المتوفى فرق بينهما، فإن كان دخل بها غرم مهرها وإن كان لم يدخل بها فلا مهر عليه، ومن تزوّج امرأة في عدَّتها فالبراءة بينهما بغير طلاق ولا عدَّة له عليها.

قال عمرو: سئل جابر بن زيد عن رجل قال لامرأته: إذا أهلَّ الشهر شهر كذا وكذا فأنت طالق أو إلى رأس السنة؟

قال: إنَّها غير طالق إلى الأجل الذي سمىَّ: وتحل له فيما دون ذلك.

قال عمرو: سئل جابر بن زيد عن رجل قال لامرأته: اختاري بين الطلاق والإمساك؟ فقال: إن اختارت زوجها فلا طلاق ولا بأس، وإن سكتت فهو الرضى بزوجها ولا طلاق[317] وإن اختارت الطلاق فقد بانت منه، ولا أدري أواحدا أو ثلاثا، وهذا أمر لبس، وكل أمر فيه لبس لا يصلح النكاح فيه حتَّى يجيء أمر بين يصلح[318] النكاح فيه.

قال عمرو: سئل جابر بن زيد عن رجل خيّر امرأته فسكتت ولم تقل شيئا، فاجتنب

315 من عندهم: -،د.

316 تزوجت: -،د.

317 ولا طلاق: -،د. انظر: آثار الربيع، مسألة [١٢]، ص ٥٦.

318 يصلح: -، ب.

فراشها حتَّى أتى عليها أشهر؟

قال: هل اختارت المرأة شيئا؟ قال: لا. قال: ليس عليه جناح[319] وقد أحسن حين اعتزلها حتَّى يعلم أمرها.

قال عمرو: سئل جابر بن زيد عن رجل قال لامرأته: إن تزوّج عليها أوتسرى فأمرها بيدها ولها مهرها.

قال: لها ذلك إن تزوّج عليها أوتسرى، وأمَّا إذا ملك الرجل امرأته طلاقها فطلقت نفسها تبين بواحد منه كما تبين بثلاثة ولا يملك الرجعة عليها[320].

سئل جابر بن زيد عن رجل قال لامرأته: اعتدي[321]؟

قال: هي بنيته إن كان نوى الطلاق فهي تطليقة واحدة، وإن لم يكن نوى الطلاق فهو ما نوى وليس بطلاق.

قال عمرو: جاء رجل فقال له: لوأنِّي قلت في نفسي: إن امرأتي طالق ثلاثا؟

فقال: لقد أشهدتني الآن أن امرأتك طالق ثلاثة فقد برئت منك.

قال عمرو: سئل جابر بن زيد عن رجل طلق امرأته واحدا أو اثنين ثُمَّ غاب عنها، فقدم، فأشهد على رجعتها[322] شاهدين وأرسل إليها بذلك، فلم يبلغها الرسول حتَّى مضت عدَّتها وتزوّجت رجلا آخر، فجاء زوجها الأوّل فقال: امرأتي قد

319 جناح: شيء، ب.

320 ولا يملك الرجعة عليها: ولا عدة له عليها، ب.

321 سئل جابر بن زيد عن رجل قال لامرته: اعتدي: -، د.

322 رجعتها: مراجعتها، ب.

راجعتها في غيبتي، وأرسلت إليها وأشهدت[323] شاهدين على رجعتها؟
قال: لا أراها إلاَّ قد[324] برئت منه، ولا جناح عليها في أن تتزوّج[325].

قال عمرو: سئل جابر بن زيد عن رجل قال لامرأته: إذا تزوّج عليها أو تسرى[326] فهي منه بريئة؟
قال: إذا[327] تزوّج عليها أو تسرى فهي تطليقة[328] فليراجعها[329] إن شاء إلاَّ أن يكون جامعها بعد ما تزوّج عليها[330] أو تسرى قبل أن يراجعها فإن كان قد جامعها قبل أن يشهد على رجعتها، فقد حرمت عليه أبدا من أجل الذي أصاب منها من وطء[331] الحرام.

قال عمرو: سئل جابر بن زيد عن رجل قال لامرأته: إن دخلت دار فلان فهي[332] طالق فدخلت ولم يشعر، وكتمته ذلك حتّى جامعها ثُمَّ اطلع على دخولها بعد ما جامعها؟
قال: لا تحل له أبدا من أجل الذي أصاب منها من الحرام، ومن طلق امرأته ثُمَّ

323 وأشهدت: -،د.
324 قد: -،د.
325 تتزوج: تزوجت، ب.
326 أو تسرى: وتسى،د.
327 إذا: إن، ب.
328 فهي تطليقة: +،د؛ قبل أن: +، ب.
329 فليراجعها: يراجعها، ب.
330 عليها: -،د.
331 وطء: -،د.
332 فهي: فأنت، ب.

جامعها[333] قبل أن يشهد على رجعتها، أو ظاهر من امرأته ثُمَّ جامعها قبل أن يكفر يمينه أو رمى امرأته بالزنى فقد حرم عليه ما بقين[334].

قال عمرو: سئل جابر بن زيد في رجل جعل امرأته كأمها[335] إن جامعها في بيت ثُمَّ خرج إلى خراسان فجامعها في بيت؟
فقال: كم لها منذ جامعها؟ فقيل له: زمان. فقال: برئت منه.

قال عمرو: سئل جابر بن زيد عن رجل من الفرقاء كان قد حرم عطاء، وكان كتّاب امرأته عليه فخاف عند العطاء يحرم به فكتبها من عامل فلان باسمه فلانة بنت فلان فهي مطلقة يعني أن يخرج عطاؤها بذلك ولا ينوي طلاقها؟
قال: لا أرى بأسا فأمسك امرأتك[336].

قال: عمرو: سئل جابر بن زيد عمن[337] قال لامرأته: كلّ امرأة أتزوّجها عليك[338] فهي طالق وكل سرية يتسرى عليها فهي عتيقة؟
قال: ليس هذا بشيء، إنَّمَا يطلق الرجل ويعتق ما يملك، فأما من لا يملك[339] فليس له أن يطلق ولا يعتق، فإن شاء فليتزوّج وليتسَرَّ.

---

333 جامعها: غشيها، ب.
334 بقين: بقوا، ب.
335 كأمها: طالقا، ب.
336 قال عمرو: سئل: عن جابر بن زيد: عن رجل من الفرقاء... يعني أن يخرج عطاؤها بذلك ولا ينوي طلاقها؟ قال: لا أرى بأسا فأمسك امرأتك: -،د.
337 عمن: -، ب،د.
338 عليك: عليها، ب.
339 فأما من لا يملك: -، ب.

قال عمرو: وزعم عكرمة أن عبد الله بن عبّاس كان يقول ذلك.

قال عمرو: سئل جابر بن زيد عن رجل خطب امرأة فأبت أن تتزوّجه حتّى شرط لها أن كلّ امرأة يتزوّجها عليها فهي طالق وكل سرية يتسرى عليها فهي عتيقة فتزوّج عليها أو تسرى؟

قال: لا بأس بذلك، هو رجل أخلف امرأته.

قال عمرو: سئل جابر بن زيد عن رجل طلق امرأته وهو غائب عنها، فأشهد على طلاقها رجلين ثُمَّ رجع من سفره ذلك فأتى امرأته وكتمها طلاقها وجامعها ثُمَّ جاء الرجلان فشهدا عليه أنّه كان قد طلقها في غيبته عنها.

قال: يفرق بينه وبينها بشهادة رجلين ولا يجب عليه حدّ الزنى بشهادة رجلين، ولو شهد عليه أربعة أنّه كان قد طلقها ثُمَّ جامعها بعد الطلاق أقيم عليه الحد[340]؛ لأنّه لا يقام الحدّ على الزاني إلاّ بشهادة أربعة نفر أو اعتراف على نفسه.

قال عمرو: سئل جابر بن زيد عن رجل مازح امرأته فقال لها: إنّه يريد أن يتزوّج امرأة أخرى؛ لأنّه[341] قد أحل له ذلك، فقالت له امرأته: فأحل لي أن أتزوّج إذا تزوّجت، فقال لها: نعم، قد أحللت لك إذا تزوّجت أنا أن تتزوّجي[342]، فتزوّج الرجل؟

قال: كان يقال الرجل أعلم بنيته، فإن كان نوى طلاقا فهو طلاق، وقد برئت منه، وإن كان قال لها: هو لك حلال فليس له أن يحل ما حرم الله فليتق الله[343] صاحب

340 حد الزنا... عليه الحد: -، ب.

341 لأنه: لأن الله، ب.

342 أو تتزوجي: تتزوجني، ب،د.

343 الله: -،د.

هذا القول ولينظر ما ينوي.

قال عمرو: سئل جابر بن زيد عن رجل كانت له[344] امرأة فتزوّج عليها أخرى فقالت له امرأته الأولى[345]: والله لا آتيك حتَّى تطلق فلانة، فقال لها: إن هو طلق فلانة فالتي سألته الطلاق منه بريئة؟

فقال: إن لم يطلق الأخرى فلا بأس بذلك، وإن طلقها[346] ولم يكن دخل بها فله أن يخطبها في الخطاب، ويكون قوله لامرأته الأولى: إن طلق فلانة فهي بريئة منه تطليقة لها، وإن شاء راجعها.

قال عمرو: سئل جابر بن زيد عن رجل خطب امرأة فأبت أن تتزوّجه حتَّى يشترط لها إن تزوّج عليها أو تسرى فطلاقها بيدها ومهرها؟

قال: إن كان الشرط قبل أن يملكها فليس ذلك[347] بشيء، وإن كان أعطاها بعدما ملكها فلها ذلك.

قال عمرو: سئل جابر بن زيد عن قوم يسبون أهل أرض ثُمَّ يصير الرجل وامرأته لرجل كيف يصنع بنكاحهما إذا ملكهما[348] جميعا؟

قال: إن شاء مولاها أن يقرهما[349] على نكاحهما الأوّل، فعل[350]، وإن شاء فرق بينهما

344 له: تحته، ب.

345 الأولى: الأخرى، ب.

346 لامرأته تطليقة واحدة فقد برئت منه: +، ب.

347 ذلك: -، د.

348 ملكهما: أصابهما، ب.

349 يقرهما: يقربهما، د؛ أقرهما، ب.

350 فعل: -، ب.

وإن كان فرق بينهما فقد حلي في نكاحهما الأول فالطلاق والعدَّة بعد الطلاق[351] وإن كانت الفرقة قبل الطلاق[352] فلا طلاق عليهما، ويستبرئ طهرها.

قال عمرو: سئل جابر بن زيد عن رجل تزوّج امرأة فوجدها رتقاء[353] لا يستطيع أن يخلص إليها فأراد طلاقها وترد إليه ماله، فكره أهلها أن يبرأ من حقها وقالوا: الرتقاء تشق فتبرأ[354] المرأة فكره الرجل ذلك؟

فقال: تدفع المرأة إلى أهلها ويؤجلون[355] أجلا، فإن أبرؤوها وصارت بمنزلة النساء، فهي امرأته وإن طلقها بعد أن يبرئوها وقبل أن يمسها فلها نصف ما فرض لها، قالوا: فإن مس ذكره قبلها. فقال: إن مسها ولم يخلص إليها فليست يومئذ بمنزلة من يحل[356] لها المهر على هذا النحو، وإن لم يبرئوها[357] فلا مهر لها.

قال عمرو: سئل جابر بن زيد عن رجل كانت تحته ثلاث نسوة، فقال له رجل وهو يسأله بعض الأمور، إن لم تفعل فامرأتك طالق ثلاثا ولم يسم واحدة منهن فقال زوجهن: نعم، ثُمَّ أخلفه الذي قال له؟

قال: كان ابن عبَّاس يقول: الطلاق يعمهن إذا لم يخص بالطلاق امرأة دون أخرى ولم

351 وإن كان فرق بينهما فقد حلي في نكاحهما الأول فالطلاق والعدَّة بعد الطلاق: -،د.

352 الطلاق: الصلاة، ب،د.

353 ارتقاء: -،د.

354 فتبرأ: فتؤتى، ب.

355 ويؤجلون: ويؤجلوا، ب د.

356 يحل: يجب، ب.

357 يبرئوها: يبروها، ب،د.

يقصد به امرأة[358] دون صاحبتها فإن ذلك يعمهن كما يعمهن الميراث جميعا، إلاَّ أن يقول صاحبهن حين سئل عن الطلاق نويت طلاق فلانة إن لم أفعل فإن له الخيار قبل الطلاق، فأما إذا قال: امرأته طالق ولم يسمِّ امرأة دون أخرى؛ فإن ذلك يشملهن[359]، وليس له بعد الطلاق الخيار.

قال عمرو: سئل جابر بن زيد عن رجل تزوّج إلى قوم وأخبرهم أنَّه غني ثُمَّ بعد ذلك لم يجدوا له مالا، وسألوه الصداق فلم يجد شيئا ينقدهم فرفعوا أمره إلى الإمام فنزعها منه وأمره بطلاقها ثُمَّ تحرج القوم من الذي صنعوا؟

قال: إن الرجل إذا غرقوما جعلوا له أجلا يسعى في صداقها ويطلب فإن قدر على صداقها فهي امرأته، وإن لم يقدر على صداقها ولم يجيء إلى أجله فالقوم مالكون لأمرهم فإن طلقها ثلاثا قبل أن يمسها يصير إلى واحد،[360] في أن يسعى في صداقها[361]، وإن يكن مسها قبل الطلاق فقد مضى طلاقها ولا صداق لهم من أجل أنَّهم انتزعوها منه وهو كاره.

قال عمرو: سئل جابر بن زيد عن رجل طلق امرأته قبل أن يمسها فقيل له إنَّها لم تحرم عليك، فدخل بها بنكاحها الأوّل فمكثت عنده سنينَ[362] وولدت له أولادا ثُمَّ علم بعد ذلك أنَّها عليه حرام؟

---

358 إلا: +، ب د.

359 يشملهن: يعمهن، ب.

360 امرأته: امرأت، ب.

361 وله أن يعيد مهرها إليها ثُمَّ تكون امرأته في أن يسعى في صداقها: +، ب.

362 سنين: سنينا، ب،د.

قال: أنَّه يفرق بينهما وتعطى المرأة من نكاحها الأوَّل نصف مهرها ومن دخوله بها ومجامعته إيَّاها مهراكاملا.

قال عمرو: سئل جابر بن زيد عن رجل قال لامرأته أنت طالق ثلاثا، إن لم أتزوّج عليك، فقال ذلك ثلاث مرَّات؟

فقال: لا يقربها حتَّى يتزوّج عليها، فإن قربها قبل أن يتزوّج عليها بانت منه ولا تحل له أبدا؛ لأنَّه أصاب منها حراما[363]، فإن تزوّج عليها قبل أن تمضي أربعة أشهر فهي امرأته فلا طلاق ولا بأس، وإن مضت أربعة أشهر قبل أن يتزوّج عليها فقد برئت منه ولا تحل له حتَّى تنكح زوجا غيره، [364] ثُمَّ يطلقها الثاني قبل أن يجامعها الأول بزواج جديد، ولو أن رجلا قال لامرأته: هي طالق إن لم يتزوّج عليها حتَّى تنقضي أربعة أشهر[365]، فقد بانت منه ويخطبها في الخطاب إن شاء فإن تزوّجته فهي عنده على تطليقتين، وقيل إن رجلا كان غائبا وأشهد على طلاق امرأته[366] رجلين فقدم الرجلان فأتيا المرأة عند أهلها فشهدا أنَّه قد طلقها، وهما يومئذ لا تتهم شهادتهما فاعتدت المرأة حتَّى مضت عدَّتها فخطبها أحد الشاهدين، فقدم زوجها الذي كان شهد عليه الرجلان أنَّـه طلقهـا إلى امرأته وقد تزوّجت. فقال: والله ما طلقتها وإن اللذين شهدا، شهدا[367] على الكذب وإنَّما شهدا على هذا من أجل ما فعل، فقيل: إن كان يوم شهد عدلاً فقد جازت شهادته ونكاحه.

---

363 حراما: محرما، ب.

364 فيحللها له أو يتزوّج عليها امرأة: +، ب.

365 ولم يسم إلاَّ تطليقة واحدة وليس له أن يقربها حتَّى يتزوّج عليها، حتَّى تنقضي أربعة أشهر: -،د.

366 طلاق أمراته: طلاقها، ب.

367 شهدا: -، ب.

قال عمرو: سئل جابر بن زيد عن رجل آلى من سريته، ما الذي يصنع؟

قال: إن كفر عن يمينه وراجعها قبل أن تنتقض أربعة أشهر فلا بأس بذلك

قال عمرو: سئل جابر بن زيد عن الكفَّارة لمن آلى من امرأته أو سريته أو جعلهما عليه حراما، ما الذي يصنع؟

قال: يطعم عشرة مساكين من أوسط ما تطعمون أهليكم أوكسوتهم أو تحرير رقبة، فمن لم يجد فصيام ثلاثة أيَّام متتابعات.

قال عمرو: سئل جابر بن زيد عن كسوة المساكين وطعامهم؟

فقال: لكلِّ مسكين ثوب ومد[368] المكوك من البر للمسكين طعاما حسنا[369].

قال عمرو: زعم عكرمة والحسن ذلك.

تم الجزء السادس من قول قتادة من المسائل المعروضة، والحمد لله ربّ العالمين، وصلَّى الله على سيدنا محمَّد وعلى آله وصحبه وسلم تسليما.[370]

---

368 ومد: أو، ب.

369 رواه ابن أبي شيبة، «عن عثمان بن غياث قال: سألت جابر بن زيد عن كفارة اليمين قال إطعام عشرة مساكين مكوك لكل إنسان»، ٣/٤٠٦. والمكوك: مكيال لأهل العراق ومقداره صاع ونصف.

370 أنجز الجزء السادس من قول قتادة من المسائل المعروضة والحمد لله على ذلك كثيرا. وكان الفراغ صبيحة يوم الأربعاء الحادي عشر يوما خلون من شهر شوال إحدى وتسعين ومائة وألف بجامع الماي الكبير الأعظم عظم الله قدره وعمَّره بأوليائه، وأخرج منه أعداءه بجاه أنبيائه وأوليائه وأصفيائه، إنه على ذلك قدير وبالإجابة جدير اللّهم ألبس كلّ من يسعى في خرابه ذلا واجعل كيده في نحره وأضحد حجته وقِلّ أعوانه على الباطل إنك انت العليّ الحكيم وكفى بك وليا ونصيرا ولا حول ولا قوة إلاَّ بالله العلي العظيم وآخر دعوانا أن الحمد لله ربّ العالمين: +، ب.

كتاب الجزء السابع من قول قتادة

من المسائل المعروضة مِمَّا أفتى به قتادة ومن لله العون والتوفيق وهو حسبنا[1]

بسم الله الرحمن الرحيم

وصلَّى الله على سيدنا محمَّد وعلى آله وصحبه وسلَّم

سئل عن بدء الصلاة؟

قال: كان بدء الصلاة ركعتين غدوة وركعتين عشيَّة، وبدء الصيام ثلاثة أيَّام من كلّ شهر.

سئل عن مواقيت الصلاة؟

حدث[2] قتادة عن أبي العالية الرياحي أنَّ عمر بن الخطَّاب رضي الله عنه كتب إلى أبي موسى الأشعري أن يصلِّي صلاة الظهر إذا زالت الشمس عن بطن السماء، ويصلَّى صلاة العصر إذا تصوبت الشمس وهي بيضاء نقية، ويصلِّي صلاة المغرب إذا غربت الشمس، ويصلِّي العشاء إذا غاب الشفق إلى أي حين شئت.

وقال قتادة: وكان يقال: إلى نصف الليل درك، وما[3] فوق ذلك فرط، ويصلَّى صلاة الصبح والنجوم مشتبكة.

عن قتادة: أنَّ للصلاة وقتا كوقت الحج، فصلوا الصلاة لوقتها، وبلغنا عن عبد الله بن مسعود كان[4] إذا طلع الفجر ركع ركعتين، وكان يعز عليه أن يسمع متكلما يتكلم إذا صلَّى

1 من المسائل المعروضة مِمَّا أفتى به قتادة ومن لله العون والتوفيق وهو حسبنا: –،د.

2 حدث: حدث عن، ب.

3 ما: –،د.

4 كان: –،د.

ركعتي الفجر حتَّى يصلِّي الغداة إلاَّ بذكر الله.

قال أبو عبيدة: كما تحدث أن عندها يجتمع الحارسان[5] من ملائكة الله حارسا[6] الليل وحارسا[7] النهار، ويقرأ عنده الآية: ﴿وَقُرْآنَ الْفَجْرِ إِنَّ قُرْآنَ الْفَجْرِ كَانَ مَشْهُودًا﴾[8]، وكان ابن مسعود يقول: الصوت الحسن زينة القرآن. وفي نسخة الصلاة[9].

عن قتادة عن أبي أيُّوب عن ابن عمرو بن العاص قال: إذا زالت الشمس من بطن السماء فصلاة الظهر درك إلى أن تصلِّي العصر وصلاة العصر درك إلى أن يقع قرن الشمس الأول، فإذا غابت الشمس فصلاة المغرب درك إلى أن يغيب الشفق، فإذا غاب الشفق فصلاة العشاء درك إلى نصف الليل، فإذا طلع الفجر فصلاة الصبح درك إلى أن يطلع قرن الشمس الأول.

عن قتادة: أنَّ رجلا قام إلى النبيّ عليه الصلاة والسلام يسأله عن وقت صلاة الصبح، فأمر المؤذِّن[10] أن يقيم[11]، فأقام عند طلوع الفجر ثُمَّ أمره الغداة الثانية ألا يقيم حتَّى يأمره فخلى عنه حتَّى أصبح جدا، وأسفر[12] جدا، ثُمَّ أمره فأقام ثُمَّ صلَّى بهم فقال: أين السائل عن وقت الصلاة؟ فقام الرجل[13] فقال له: شهدت معنا هاتين الصلاتين؟ قال: نعم.

5 الحارسان: الحارصان، ب.
6 حارسا: حارسان، د؛ حارصان، ب.
7 حارسا: حارسان، ب، د.
8 سورة الإسراء: ٧٨.
9 وفي نسخة الصلاة: –، د.
10 المؤذن: مناديا، ب.
11 أن يقيم: –، ب.
12 وأسفر: وأبرز، ب د.
13 الرجل: –، د.

قال: إنّمَا بينهما وقت للصلاة[14].

قال غيره: وبلغني ذلك، وأوّل الوقت فضيلة.

حدَّثني عن قتادة[15] قال: كان بدء الأذان أن ينادى الصلاة جامعة[16] فقالوا ذات يوم[17]: يا رسول الله، لو اتخذنا ناقوسا أو كيرا. قال: فرأى زيد بن ثابت الأنصاري في منامه[18] رجلا بيده خشبة حسنة فأعجبته. قال: لو أعطيتنا هذه الخشبة. قال: ما تصنعون بها. قال: نتخذها ناقوسا، قال الرجل: أولا أدلك[19] بما هو خير من ذلك؟ قال: فما هو[20]؟ قال: تأمرون مناديكم[21] فيُكبّر، ثُمَّ يشهد شهادة الحق، ثُمَّ يشهد أن مُحَمَّدا رسول الله، ثُمَّ يدعو بالصلاة والفلاح، فأتى زيد نبيّ الله ﷺ فقص عليه ما رآه، قال رسول الله ﷺ: كذلك فاصنعوا، فأمرنا بهذا الآذان[22].

عن أبي معشر عن النخعي قال: كان أذان رسول الله عليه الصلاة والسلام مثنى مثنى، وإقامته مثنى مثنى[23]، فلمّا كان هؤلاء الملوك جعلوها[24] إذا خرجوا واحدة

14 للصلاة: -، ب.
15 عن قتادة: -،د.
16 جامعة: جماعة، ب.
17 ذات يوم: -،د.
18 الأنصاري في منامه: -،د.
19 أدلك: أنبوك، ب.
20 قال: فما هو: -،د.
21 مناديكم: -،د.
22 رواه أبو داود، باب بدء الأذان، ر٤٩٨.
23 رواه الترمذي، بلفظ: «... شفعا شفعا»، باب ما جاء أن الإقامة مثنى مثنى، ر١٩٤.
24 الإقامة: +، ب.

للسرعة، وقال غيره: بلغني ذلك وكان معاوية أوّل من أفرد الإقامة.

عن قتادة عن الحسن عن علي رضي الله عنه قال: من سمع الأذان من جيران المسجد فلم يجب من غير عذر فلا صلاة له، وقال غيره: أمّا إمام مسلم فلا أرى لك أن تترك الصلاة معه إذا سمعت الأذان.

سئل عن الكلام في الأذان؟
قال: رأينا أنّه يكره وكذلك في الإقامة أيضا.

سئل أيستقبل المؤذِّن القبلة إذا أذن؟
عن قتادة: أنّه كان يقول: يستقبل القبلة بوجهه حتّى إذا فرغ من الشهادتين صرف وجهه أين شاء وفي الإقامة يستقبل بوجهه القبلة؟
قال: نعم.

سئل عن المؤذِّن أيأخذ على أذانه أجرا[25]؟
عن قتادة: أنّه يكره ذلك إلاّ أن يعطى شيئا من غير شرط إذا كان محتاجا وقال غيره مثل ذلك.

عن قتادة عن الضحاك بن قيس قال له رجل: إني أحبك في الله فقال له: أبغضك أنا في الله، إنك تبتغي في أذانك وتأخذ عليه وعلى تعليم القرآن أجرا.

25 أجرا: جعلا، ب.

عن قتادة عن أبي هريرة أنّه كان يقول: المؤذِّنون أطول الناس أعناقا يوم القيامة[26].

عن قتادة قال: ذكر لنا أنّه قال: يغفر الله له مد صوته، وأنه سيدعو له من سمع صوته رطبا كان أو يابسا، وفضل آخر له أجر من صلّى معه ولا ينقص من أجورهم شيئا. قال: يقال للمسلم أفضل من ذلك.

عن قتادة قال: بلغني أن أوّل من يقضى له يوم القيامة، المؤذِّنون والشهداء، يبدأ بمؤذن الكعبة وبمؤذن بيت المقدس، ثُمَّ يتابع[27] المؤذِّنون، وقال غيره: والله أعلم.

عن قتادة: أنَّ إماما من أئمة المسلمين دعا مؤذنه فقال: للمسلمين عليك حقان اثنان: لا تؤذن لصلاة الصبح حتَّى يطلع الفجر لسحورهم، ولا تؤذن لصلاة المغرب حتَّى تغيب الشمس لإفطارهم.

وقال قتادة: المؤذِّنون أئمة يقتدى بهم.

سئل عن التثويب في الصبح؟
عن قتادة: أنَّ عثمان بن عفان رضي الله عنه كان إذا سمع المنادي ينادي يجيبه في قوله حتَّى إذا بلغ «حيّ على الصلاة، حيّ على الفلاح». قال: ما شاء الله ولا حول[28] ولا قوة إلاَّ بالله، فإذا قال: «قد قامت الصلاة» قال: مرحبا بالقائلين عدلا وبالصلاة مرحبا وأهلا، ثُمَّ ينهض.

26 رواه مسلم، باب فضل الأذان، ر٨٧٨، وابن حبان، باب الأذان، ر١٦٦٩.

27 سائر: +، ب.

28 ولا حول: –، د.

سئل عن الرجل هل تجزيه الإقامة[29]؟

قال: نعم، إذا كان وحده.

سئل عن رجل دخل مسجدا وقد صلَّى في أهله أيتطوّع أم يبدأ بالفريضة؟

قال: إذا لم يدرك الفريضة معهم إن شاء تطوّع وإن شاء بدأ بالفريضة.

سئل عن رجل دخل المسجد وقد صلَّى[30] أهله، أتجزئ[31] عنه إقامته في ذلك المسجد؟

قال: نعم.

سئل عن رجل صلَّى[32] في قرية، هل يجزئ عنه إذا سمع الإقامة أن يصلِّي في بيته بإقامتهم؟

قال: ما لم يتعمد ذلك فهي تجزيه إن سها عن أن يقيم للصلاة حتَّى صلَّى وقد سمع أذانهم وإقامتهم أجزأه ذلك.

سئل عن الصلاة في السفر أيؤذن المصلِّي ويقيم الصلاة؟

قال: إذا أذن وجعل الأذان ليؤتى، وإن أقام ولم يؤذن في السفر فلا بأس عليه.

سئل عن رجل سها عن الإقامة في صلاته؟

قال: عليه الإعادة إلاَّ أن يكون سمع أذان المؤذِّنين وإقامتهم في المسجد.

29 واحدة: +، ب.

30 في: +،د.

31 أتجزئ: أتجزأ، ب،د.

32 صلى: كان، ب.

سئل هل على النساء أذان وإقامة؟

فحدَّثني عن الحسن وابن المسيب أنَّهما قالا: ليس على النساء أذان ولا إقامة. وقال غيرهما مثل قولهما.

سئل عن الوضوء.

قال: بلغنا عن عمر أنَّه كان يحدث ويمسح مرة واحدة، وكان ضمام يقول: مرَّتين تجزئ، ولم يكن يرى الأذنين من الوجه ولا من الرأس وكان يرى تركهما كترك المضمضة والاستنشاق.

وسئل عن قول الله عزّ وجل[33]: ﴿يَا أَيُّهَا الَّذِينَ آمَنُوا إِذَا قُمْتُمْ إِلَى الصَّلَاةِ فَاغْسِلُوا وُجُوهَكُمْ وَأَيْدِيَكُمْ إِلَى الْمَرَافِقِ وَامْسَحُوا بِرُءُوسِكُمْ وَأَرْجُلَكُمْ إِلَى الْكَعْبَيْنِ﴾[34].

قال: يغسل الوجه واليدين والرجلين ويمسح الرأس.

عن قتادة عن جابر بن عبد الله الأنصاري: أنَّ رسول الله صلى الله عليه وسلم قال: إذا قام أحدكم من منامه فلا يغمس[35] يديه في الإناء حتَّى يغسلهما ثلاث مرَّات قبل أن يغمسها في[36] الإناء[37].

سئل عن الاستنشاق للجنابة والوضوء؟

قال: يستحبّ ثلاث مرَّات ويمضمض ثلاث مرَّات ويمسح مرة.

33 عز وجل: تعالى، ب.

34 سورة المائدة: ٦.

35 يغمس: يغمسنَّ، ب.

36 في: -، د.

37 رواه الربيع، باب في آداب الوضوء وفرضه، ر٨٧. ومسلم، باب كَرَاهَةِ غَمْسِ الْمُتَوَضِّئِ وَغَيْرِهِ يَدَهُ الْمَشْكُوكَ فِي نَجَاسَتِهَا فِي الإِنَاءِ قَبْلَ غَسْلِهَا ثَلَاثًا، ر٦٦٥.

عن قتادة قال: ذكر لنا أنَّ نبيَّ الله عليه الصلاة والسلام قال: لا يقبل الله صدقة من غلول ولا صلاة من غير طهور[38].

سئل عن رجل ترك موضعا له[39] في وضوئه لم يصبه بالماء[40]؟
قال: يغسل ما ترك ولا يعيد الوضوء.

عن قتادة كان يقال: إن[41] مفتاح الصلاة الطهور، وإحرامها التكبير، وإحلالها التسليم[42]. قال غيره: نعم[43].

سئل عن رجل يصلِّي الصلوات بوضوء واحد؟
قال: لا بأس بذلك ما لم يحدث.

سئل عن رجل نسي أن يستنشق أو يتمضمض أو يمسح أذنيه؟
قال: ينصرف من صلاته ف[44]يستنشق ويتمضمض.

سئل عمَّن نسي عضوا من أعضائه حتَّى دخل في صلاته.
قال: ينصرف فيغسل ذلك العضو ولا يعتد بما صلَّى.

---

38 رواه مسلم، باب وجوب الطهارة للصلاة، ر٥٥٧.

39 له: -،د.

40 لم يصبه الماء: لم يصبه الوضوء، ب.

41 إن: -، ب.

42 هذا حديث عن النبي صلى الله عليه وسلم، رواه أبو داود عن علي، بلفظ: «مِفْتَاحُ الصَّلَاةِ الطُّهُورُ وَتَحْرِيمُهَا التَّكْبِيرُ وَتَحْلِيلُهَا التَّسْلِيمُ»، باب في تحريم الصلاة وتحليلها، ر٦١٨.

43 قال غيره: نعم: -،د.

44 من صلاته ف: -،د.

وعن قتادة أنه[45] قال: إن جف عضو من أعضائه، فإنّه يستأنف الوضوء وإلاّ فإنّه يغسل ذلك إن كان من ساعته.

وقال غيره: جف أولم يجف ليس عليه إلاّ غسل ذلك العضو إلاّ أن يكون ذلك قد طال، وإن كان من ساعته فليغسل ذلك العضو.[46]

سئل عن رجل نسي أن يمسح برأسه حتّى دخل في صلاته؟

عن قتادة عن أبي معشر عن إبراهيم النخعي أنّه قال: إن كان في لحيته بلل مسح برأسه، وإلاّ انصرف ثُمّ يمسح برأسه. وقال غيره: نعم[47].

سئل عن رجل دخل في صلاته فشك في وضوئه؟

قال: إن شك بعد ما دخل في صلاته فإنّه يمضي في صلاته، فإذا سلم توضّأ لما[48] يستقبل من الصلوات، وتمت صلاته تلك، وإن كان شك قبل أن يدخل في صلاته تلك توضّأ[49].

سئل عن رجل توضّأ فقدم بعض أعضائه[50] قبل بعض؟

قال: إن كان تعمدا منه لذلك أعاد الوضوء.

---

45 أنه: –، د.

46 وفي نسخة أخرى: «إن كان غسل ذلك العضو من ساعته أجزى وإن جف استأنف الوضوء من أوله، وهذا مبني على القولة الأولى: هامش، ب.

47 وقال غيره: نعم: –، د.

48 لما: لم، ب، د.

49 بتلك الوضوء: –، ب.

50 أعضائه: وضوؤه، ب.

سئل عن رجل يتوضأ ويمسح وجهه بالمنديل؟

قال: كان مسلم والربيع يكرهان ذلك.

سئل عن المرأة كيف تمسح رأسها عند الوضوء؟

قال: يجزئها ما يجزي الرجل.

سئل عن رجل يقبل امرأته ويغمزها أينقض ذلك وضوءه؟

قال: ما لم يجئ[51] منه بلل فلا بأس، وقد كان بعض الناس يكرهون ذلك.

سئل عن الملامسة، ما هي؟

قال: بلغني أن سعيد بن جبير وعطاء بن [أبي] رباح[52] وعبيدة بن عمير الليثي اختلفوا في الملامسة.

قال عطاء وسعيد: هو اللمس والغمز. وقال عبيدة بن عمير: هو الجماع. فخرج عليهم ابن عبَّاس وهم في ذلك فسألوه واحدا واحدا بما قالوا. فقال: أخطأ الموالي وأصاب العربي، فالملامسة هو الجماع[53]، ولكن الله يكنّي ويعفف.

سئل عن رجل يرعف وهو في الصلاة؟

قال: ينفتل[54] ويتوضأ ثُمَّ يصلِّي ما بقي عليه من صلاته ولا يتكلم، فإن تكلم استأنف الصلاة.

51 يجيء: يكن، ب.

52 رباح: رياح، ب.

53 فالملامسة هو الجماع: -، د.

54 ينفتل: ينتفل، ب، د.

سئل عن رجل يخرج من جسده[55] الدم فيسيل ويقطر؟

قال: ينتقض وضوؤه، فإن لم يسل أو يقطر لم ينتقض عليه وضوؤه.

سئل عن رجل يتنخم، فيرى في ريقه الدم؟

قال: ليس عليه في ذلك وضوء إلاَّ أن يغلب الدم على الريق.

سئل عن رجل يقلس؟

قال: ما لم يبلغ اللسان فلا وضوء عليه.

سئل عن رجل يحتجم؟

قال: يتوضأ ويغسل أثر الحجام.

سئل عن رجل نسي أن يغسل أثر الحجام[56]؟

قال: إن مسح أثر الحجام مسحا نقيا فلا بأس عليه، وقال غيره: لا بُدَّ من غسل أثر الحجام ثُمَّ الوضوء.

سئل عن رجل يحدث أيجلس في المسجد؟

قال: نعم.

55 جسده: -، د.

56 الحجام: محاجم، ب.

سئل عن رجل يخرج منه الغائط، أيقعد في المسجد ولم يتوضأ؟

قال: بلغني أنَّ جابر بن زيد قال: إذا استنجى بالماء فلا بأس أن يقعد في المسجد.

قال: ولا بأس بمن بال أو خرج منه ريح أن يقعد في المسجد.

سئل عن الرجل الجنب، أيقعد في المسجد أو يمر فيه؟

قال: لا يقعد ولا يمر في المسجد وهو جنب.

سئل عن رجل يمس إبطيه أو ينتفه، أينتقض وضوؤه؟

قال: لا.

سئل عن رجل يمس ذكره؟

قال: عليه الوضوء، وهو قول أصحابنا ضمام وأبي عبيدة.

سئل عن رجل توضَّأ ثُمَّ نام؟

قال: لا ينقض عليه وضوؤه حتَّى يضع جنبه وينام[57].

سئل عن المسح على الخفين؟

قال: كره المسح على الخفين، ويكره إذا رأيته يمسح أن تصلِّي خلفه.

سئل أيغسل الرجل أثر الغائط والبول إذا توضَّأ للصلاة؟

قال: لا بد من غسل ذلك؛ لأن الناس فيما مضى كانوا يبعرون وهم اليوم على غير ذلك، فلا بد من الغسل.

---

57 وينام: -، ب.

عن قتادة، أنَّه لما نزلت هذه الآية: ﴿فِيهِ رِجَالٌ يُحِبُّونَ أَن يَتَطَهَّرُواْ﴾[58] قال رسول الله صلى الله عليه وسلم: يا أهل قباء إنَّ الله قد أحسن عليكم الثناء في الطهور، فما الذي تصنعون عند الوضوء وعند الغائط، فقالوا: يا رسول الله، نتبع الغائط الأحجار ثُمَّ نتبع الأحجار الماء تغسل علينا أثر الغائط والبول[59].

سئل عن رجل يطعم وهو غير طاهر؟

قال: يكره للجنب وأمَّا غير الجنب فلا بأس به.

سئل عن رجل يطعم بشماله؟

قال: حدَّثني معمر عن الزهري: أنَّ رسول الله صلى الله عليه وسلم قال: «إذا أكل أحدكم فليأكل بيمينه وإذا شرب فليشرب بيمينه، فإن الشيطان يأكل ويشرب بشماله»[60].

عن عمرو بن سلمة أنَّه دخل على النبيّ عليه الصلاة والسلام وهو يطعم. قال: «ادنُ[61] فكل[62] وسم الله وكل بيمينك وكل مِمَّا يليك»[63].

قال: حدَّثني الربيع أنَّ أبا عبيدة كان وهو وحده يأكل مِمَّا يليه.

عن أبي معشر عن النخعي عن عائشة أنَّها قالت: كان يمين رسول الله صلى الله

58 سورة التوبة: ١٠٨.

59 فقالوا يارسول الله. . . الغائط والبول: -، ب. رواه البيهقي، باب الاستنجاء بالماء، ر٥١٤.

60 رواه مسلم، باب آداب الطعام والشراب وأحكامهما، ر٥٣٨٤.

61 أدن: أذن، ب،د.

62 فكل: -،د.

63 رواه البخاري، باب الأكل مما يليه، ر٥٠٦٣.

عليه وسلم لطعامه ولطهوره، وكانت شماله للخلاء وماكان من أذى[64].

عن قتادة: أنَّ جن نصيبين[65] أتوا رسول الله صلى الله عليه وسلم فقالوا: زودنا يا رسول الله، فقال رسول الله صلى الله عليه وسلم: «كل روثة هي طعام لدوابكم[66]، وكل عظم لكم عرق، فقالوا إن أمتك ينجسوه علينا. فنهى رسول الله عليه الصلاة والسلام عند ذلك أن يستنجى بروث أو عظم[67]، وقال غيره: بلغني ذلك عن سويد بن عبد الله عن الحسن.

قال أبو النضر: وحدثت هند قالت: قد سمعت عن الحسن: أنَّ رسول الله عليه الصلاة والسلام قال: لا يباشر الرجل الرجل، ولا المرأة المرأة[68] ولا يمشي الرجل بالنعلة الواحدة[69] ولا يشربن وهو قائم، ولا يبولن وهو مستقبل القبلة[70]، وإذا دخل أحدكم الخلاء فيستنجي ثلاث مرَّات ولا يستنجي بروثة ولا بعظم[71]، ولا يحدث الرجل بما يخلو به من امرأته، ولا تحدث المرأة بما تخلو به من زوجها[72].

64 عن أبي معشر عن النخعي عن عائشة أنَّها قالت: كان يميل رسول الله ﷺ لطعامه ولطهوره، وكانت شماله للخلاء وماكان من أذى: -،د. رواه أبو داود عن حفصة، باب كَرَاهِيَةِ مَسِّ الذَّكَرِ بِالْيَمِينِ فِي الِاسْتِبْرَاءِ، ر٣٢.

65 نصيبين: -، ب.

66 لكم حضر، ب. رواه الهندي: كنز العمال، ر١٥١٨٢.

67 رواه النسائي: السنن الكبرى، ذكر نهي النبي صلى الله عليه وسلم عن الاستطابة بالعظم والروث، ر٣٨.

68 رواه ابن أبي شيبة، في مباشرة الرجل الرجل والمرأة المرأة، ر١٧٨٨٤.

69 رواه الربيع، باب في الثياب والصلاة فيها وما يستحب من ذلك، ر٢٧٠.

70 رواه أحمد، ر١١١٣٢.

71 رواه البيهقي، باب النهي عن استقبال القبلة واستدبارها، ر٤٣٦.

72 رواه ابن السماك والخلدي، ر٣٤.

فقالت امرأة: والله يا رسول الله، إنَّهم ليفعلون ذلك، وإنَّهن ليفعلن ذلك، فقال رسول الله صلى الله عليه وسلم لا تفعلوا، فإن ذلك مثل الشيطان لقي شيطانة في الطريق فقضى منها حاجته والناس ينظرون»[73].

قال غيره: بلغني ذلك وقد رأينا من الفقهاء[74] من يمشي بالنعلة الواحدة حتَّى يصلح الأخرى وكان يشرب قائما وقاعدا. قال: بلغني ذلك عن عمر أيضا.

عن قتادة عن القاسم الشيباني عن زيد بن أرقم قال: إن هذه الحشوش محتضرة[75] فإذا أراد أحدكم أن يدخلها فليقل أعوذ بالله من الخبث والخبائث.

سئل عن رجل يتوضأ ثُمَّ يصيب جسده بول أو دم، أيغسل ما أصاب أو يعيد الوضوء؟ قال: إن كان دما[76] سائلا أعاد الوضوء، وأمَّا البول فقليله وكثيره فإنَّه ينقض الوضوء.

سئل عن بول الغلام والجارية ما لم يطعما الطعام؟

قال: يغسل ويعيد الوضوء منهما جميعا طعما أم لم يطعما.

عن عمر بن عامر قال: حدَّثنا صاحب لنا قال: أتيت عطاء فسألته عن المسك؟ فقال: ألاَّ أدلك على من يخبرك عنه، انطلق إلى أم كلثوم فاسألها عنه، فأتيتها[77] فقالت: إنا[78] كنَّا نطبخ اللبان والمسك جميعا، وقالت عائشة: يا أم كلثوم لا تطبخيهما جميعا

73 رواه أبو داود، باب مَا يُكْرَهُ مِنْ ذِكْرِ الرَّجُلِ مَا يَكُونُ مِنْ إِصَابَةِ أَهْلِهِ، ر٢١٧٦.

74 من الفقهاء: -، ب.

75 الحشوش محتضرة: الخشوش محصرة، ب؛ رواه البيهقي، السنن الكبرى، ر ٩٨٢٢.

76 دما: -،د.

77 فأتيتها: فاسألها فإنها، ب.

78 إنا: -،د.

فيذهب ريح المسك، ولكن اطبخي ذلك اللبان، فإذا نعمت وتمت طبخه فأغليه بالمسك غليا، فإنَّه أزكى لريحه، قالت: فنحن نطبخه بعد ذلك[79].

قال: إن أسماء بنت أبي بكر انطلقت بعبد الله بن الزبير إلى عائشة، قالت: ما بالك؟ قالت: يا بنت أبي انطلقي به إلى رسول الله فليحنكه وليدعو له، فانطلقت به عائشة إلى رسول الله صلى الله عليه وسلم فبال عليها، فدحيته دحية، تقول: ضربته ضربة فحنكه وسماه عبد الله، ثُمَّ قال لعائشة: أنت أم عبد الله، وما ولدت ولدا قط، وقالت أسماء بنت أبي بكر: إنِّي رمدت عيني وأنا معتدة[80]، فقلت: يا بنت أبي بكر رمدت عيني فقالت: اكحليها بصبر، قال غيره: مثل ذلك يكتحل بصبر وغيره مِمَّا لا طيب فيه.

سئل عن الضحك في الصلاة والتبسم؟

قال: ما لم يكثر أو يقهقه فلا بأس، فإن ضحك وقهقه فإنَّه يعيد الوضوء إذا فعل ذلك في صلاته.

قال قتادة: عن أبي العالية أن رجلا أعمى جاء إلى المسجد، ورسول الله صلى الله عليه وسلم يصلِّي بأصحابه، فتردى في بئر فضحك بعض من كان يصلِّي مع رسول الله صلى الله عليه وسلم فأمر رسول الله صلى الله عليه وسلم من ضحك منهم[81] أن يعيدوا الوضوء والصلاة[82].

سئل عن السنور يلغ في الماء؟

79 ذلك: -، ب.

80 معتدة: حمومة، ب.

81 منهم: -، ب.

82 والصلاة: -،د. رواه الدارقطني، باب أحاديث القهقة في الصلاة وعللها، ر٦.

قال: لا بأس ما لم يقذره.

سئل عن الكلب يلغ في الإناء؟

فقال: يغسله سبع مرّات، الأولى بالتراب.

سئل عن سؤر الحمار، أيتوضأ منه؟

قال: نعم.

سئل عن الماء يكون في الحوض فتلغ فيه الكلاب والسباع، أيتوضأ به؟

قال: إذا كان قليلا فأنا أكره ذلك.

سئل عن الجب، يقطر فيه الدم؟

قال: ما لم يكن الدم أكثر[83] فلا بأس.

سئل عن الدابة[84] تقع في الإناء، كالعقرب والخنفساء والجعار[85] والوزغ، وما أشبه ذلك؟

قال: لا بأس به يتوضأ، ويشرب منه ما لم يقذره.

سئل عن البئر تقع فيه الدابة والجرادة[86] والفأرة والدجاجة والسنور والكلب وما أشبه ذلك؟

---

83 أكثر: قليلا، ب.

84 الدابة: -، ب.

85 الجعار: -، ب.

86 والجرادة: -، د.

قال: ينزع منه دلاء قدر قلة الماء، وكثرته قدر الماء الكثير[87] أربعون[88] دلوا فإذا وقع في البئر إنسان[89] فمات نزع الماء كله.

عن قتادة: أنَّ زنجيا وقع في بئر زمزم فمات فيها، فأمر ابن عبَّاس أن تسد عيونها ثُمَّ ينزف[90] ماؤها، ثُمَّ قال: افتح العين التي تلي الكعبة وتضع السجل عندها فإنَّها عين من عيون الجنَّة، فشرب منها ابن عبَّاس.

قال غيره: بلغني أن تلك العين عذبة ولا نراها إلاَّ كما قال ابن عبَّاس.

سئل عن سؤر المرأة الحائض وطهورها؟

قال: كان بعضهم[91] يكره شرب سؤر الحائض ولو توضَّأ به رجل لم يكن به بأس فهي تعجن وتخبز[92]، وكان الربيع يقول: إذا غسلت يديها فأنقتهما[93] ثُمَّ عجنت وخبزت ونضحت المسجد فإذا جاز هذا جاز الوضوء والشرب.

سئل عن رجل تصيبه الجنابة وبه جرح أو قروح؟

فحدَّثنا قتادة عن سعيد بن جبير وغيره رفعه إلى[94] بعض الصحابة إلى ابن عبَّاس

---

87 مائة: +،د.

88 ثبت في السنة أن الميتة إذا وقعت في بئر نزح منها أربعون دلوا. انظر: مصنف ابن أبي شيبة، ١/١٦٢.

89 إنسان: إنسانا، ب،د.

90 ينزف: تنزف، ب،د.

91 بعضهم: -، ب.

92 ويأكل وكان يكره عند بعض أصحابنا إن كانت حائضا إن فضل وضوئها: +، ب.

93 فأنقتهما: -،د.

94 إلى: -،د.

قال: إذا كانت بالرجل قروح أو جروح، فأصابته الجنابة فكبر عليه الغسل، فإنّه يتيمّم بالصعيد، وقال غيره: إن شاء تيمّم وإن شاء غسل جسده وأبقى موضع الجرح على حاله[95] إن كان الماء يفسد عليه جروحه وقروحه، ولا يمسه بالماء، وإن شق عليه الماء تيمّم، وكذلك الكسر لا يصب عليه الماء.

سئل عن رجل يصيبه الجرح فيعصب عليه الخرقة فيظهر الدم من فوق الخرقة؟
عن قتادة: أنّه قال: فاليعصبه[96] بخرقة أخرى ثُمَّ يمسح عليه إذا توضّأ، وقال غيره: إن شاء لم يمسح عليه شيئًا.

سئل عن رجل يصيبه الكسر ثُمَّ تصيبه الجنابة؟
قال: يغسل جسده ما خلا الكسر فإن خاف تيمّم.

سئل عن رجل غير متوضئ وهو يقرأ القرآن؟
قال: يكره أن يقرأ القرآن إلاَّ متوضئا، وقد رخص في الآية والآيتين، فأما أكثر من ذلك فلا.

سئل عن الحائض والجنب، هل يقرؤون القرآن؟
قال: لا.

سئل عن الحائض، تسمع السجدة أتسجدها[97]؟

---

95 حاله: ذلك، ب.

96 فليعصبه: فليصب –، د.

97 أتسجدها: –، د.

قال: لا تسجدها، وقد تترك الفريضة وهي أعظم من السجدة.

سئل عن رجل يمس الدراهم وقد كتب عليها شيء من[98] القرآن وهو جنب.

قال: يحفظ الدراهم ولا يضيعها.

سئل عن غسل الجنابة؟

قال: يغسل كفيه ثُمَّ يغسل فرجه ثُمَّ يغسل كفيه ثُمَّ يتوضأ وضوء الصلاة ثُمَّ يفيض عليه الماء ويغتسل.

عن قتادة عن صفية بنت شيبة عن عائشة زوج النبيّ عليه الصلاة والسلام ـ: أنَّ رسول الله صلى الله عليه وسلم كان يغتسل بصاع ويتوضأ بقدر مد من الماء[99]، وقال غيره: بلغنا ذلك.

سئل عن رجل يغتسل فيقطر من مائه في الإناء؟

قال: ليس بشيء وينقي[100] ذلك جهده.

سئل عن جنب غمس يده في الإناء قبل أن يغسلها؟

قال: إن كان بيده قذر فليرقه[101] وإلاَّ فلا بأس ولا يتعمد ذلك.

سئل عن رجل اغتسل ورأى في جسده جنابة بعد غسله من الجنابة؟

قال: يستحبّ أن يبدأ فيغسل جنابته ثُمَّ يغتسل.

98 شي من: يمس الدراهم وفيها، ب.

99 رواه البخاري عن أنس بن مالك، باب الوضوء بالمد، ر١٩٨.

100 وينقي: ويتقي، ب.

101 فليرقه: فليوقه، ب.

سئل عن رجل غسل رأسه بخطم أو سدر ثُمَّ تركه حتَّى جف ثُمَّ اغتسل؟

قال: يصب عليه الماء فيغسله.

سئل عن رجل جنب توضَّأ ثُمَّ قام؟

قال: إن كان توضَّأ ذلك الوضوء للجنابة أجزاه، فإن صب عليه الماء فلا بأس.

سئل عن الوضوء بعد الغسل من الجنابة؟

قال: أي وضوء أفضل من الغسل.

سئل عن رجل يصب على الجنب فيقطر عليه من مائه؟

قال: ليس عليه[102] شيء.

سئل عن البول في الماء الراكد؟

قال: يكره ذلك وينهى عنه[103].

سئل عن رجل يأتي إلى الماء الراكد فيغتسل فيه؟

قال: يغترف منه فيغتسل، وإن وقع فيه الماء كثير لا ينجسه[104].

سئل عن الرجل والمرأة تصيبهما الجنابة فيغتسلان من الإناء الواحد؟

عن قتادة عن عائشة رضي الله عنها أنَّها قالت: كنت أنا ورسول الله

---

102 عليه: -،د.

103 وينهى عنه: ولا ينجسه، ب.

104 البول في الماء الراكد: هامش، ب.

صلى الله عليه وسلم نغتسل من إناء واحد[105]. وقال غيره: بلغنا ذلك. وكان قتادة يكره أن تغتسل المرأة قبل الرجل. ويعجبه أن يبدأ الرجل قبلها.

سئل عن المرأة تغتسل: أتنقض رأسها؟

قال: لا، ولكن تنقي وتصب عليه الماء وتدلكه وتخلله.

سئل عن رجل يرى في ثوبه جنابة ولا يدري متى أصابته؟

قال: يرى إن كان أصابته قبل الصلاة فليعد صلاته، وإن كان نام ولم يدر أمن نومه ذلك فليس عليه إعادة إلاَّ أن يعيد آخر صلاته.

سئل عن رجل رأى في ثوبه جنابة ثُمَّ خفيت عليه؟

قال: إذا خفيت عليه غسل الثوب كله.

سئل عن رجل ينام وهو جنب؟

قال: إذا أراد أن يعاود أهله توضَّأ وضوء الصلاة، وإن لم يرد ذلك اغتسل قبل النوم.

سئل عن رجل يأكل وهو جنب أو ينام؟

قال: يتوضأ وضوء الصلاة ثُمَّ يأكل.

عن قتادة عن الحسن: أنَّ عليّاً رضي الله عنه أمر المقداد بن الأسود أن يسأل النبيّ عليه الصلاة والسلام عن المذي، وقال: إنِّي أستحيي أن أسأله

105 رواه الربيع، باب في كيفية الغسل من الجنابة، ر١٤٢.

لمكان فاطمة مني، فساله فقال رسول الله صلى الله عليه وسلم: «إذا رأى أحدكم ذلك فليغسل فرجه من المذي والوذي ثُمَّ يتوضأ»[106]. والودي يجري من[107] بعد البول.

سئل عن رجل يجد البلل في صلاته؟

قال: ينفتل[108] ويتوضَّأ[109] ويغسل ذلك البلل ويتوضأ.

سئل عن رجل يخرج من ذكره شيء بعد غسله من الجنابة؟

قال: إن كان بال قبل أن يغتسل فإنَّه يغسل فرجه ويتوضأ وضوء الصلاة، وإن كان اغتسل قبل أن يبول فليعد الغسل وهوقول أبي عبيدة.

سئل عن رجل يغشى امرأته ولا ينزل؟

قال: إذا التقى الختانان فقد وجب الغسل، وإذا جاءت النطفة من الرجل فعليه الغسل.

سئل عن المرأة ترى في منامها ما يرى الرجل في منامه؟

قال: لا غسل عليها[110].

106 رواه البيهقي، باب الوضوء من المذي والودي، ر٥٦١.

107 من: -،د.

108 ينفتل: ينتفل،د.

109 ويتوضأ: -،د.

110 ورد في مسند الربيع، باب فيما يكون منه غسل الجنابة، ر١٣٦: « . . . يا رسول الله المرأة ترى في النوم ما يرى الرجل فقال رسول الله صلى الله عليه وسلم عليها الغسل إذا أنزلت».

عن قتادة: أنَّه قال في رجل إذا قضى شهوته من امرأته فيما دون الفرج: فإنه يغتسل ولا غسل عليها[111]، إلاَّ أن تكون دخلت[112] النطفة أو[113] خرجت من فرجها فعليها الغسل.

سئل عن المرأة يخرج منها شيء بعد الغسل؟

قال: تتوضأ وتغسل فرجها ولا غسل عليها، وكان ذلك رأي جابر بن زيد.

سئل عن رجل تصيبه الجنابة وليس معه من الماء إلاَّ قدر ما يتوضأ به؟

قال: يستنجي[114] بالماء ثُمَّ يتيمّم.

سئل عن رجل لم يجد ماء إلاَّ الثلج؟

قال: فليذبه فإن لم يجد الماء ولم يستطع الوضوء منه فليضرب بيده وليتيمّم.

سئل عن رجل لم يجد الماء في ركية؟

قال: فليتيمّم.

سئل عن الماء الراكد يأتيه الجنب؟

قال: يتنحى عنه ناحية فليغتسل قال[115]: ويجعل عنه حاجزا ألاَّ يعود فيه، إلاَّ أن

111 عن قتادة: أنَّه قال: في رجل إذا قضى شهوته من امرأته فيما دون الفرج فإنه يغتسل ولا غسل عليها: –،د.

112 دخلت: –،د.

113 أو: – ب،د.

114 يستنجي: يستقي، ب،د.

115 قال: –،د.

يكون ماء كثيرا فإنّه لا ينجسه شيء[116] فإذا تنظف ثُمَّ دخل فلا بأس عليه وإن اغتسل فلا بأس وهو أحسن.

سئل عن التيمّم؟

قال: ضربة للوجه وأخرى للكفين، وليس عليه غير ذلك.

سئل عن الرجل المتيمّم[117] أيصلِّي صلاتين أو ثلاثا بتيمّم واحد؟

قال: يحدث لكلِّ صلاة تيمّما.

سئل عن قوم في سفر ولهم إمام فحضرتهم الصلاة وإمامهم قد تيمّم وفي القوم من توضَّأ؟

قال: يتقدّم من قد توضَّأ فيؤمّهم.

عن أبي قلابة[118] عن رجل من بني قيس قال: كنت أعزب عن أهلي فتصيبني الجنابة فلا أجد الماء فأتيمّم فوقع في نفسي شيء، فأتيت أبا ذرّ في منزله فلم أجده، فأتيت المسجد وقد وصف لي، فأتيته فإذا هو قائم يصلِّي فعرفت النعت، فسلمت عليه فلم يرد علي السلام[119] حتَّى انصرف من صلاته، فقلت: أنت أبو ذرّ؟ قال: إن أهلي ليقولون ذلك. فقلت: ما كان أحد من الناس أحب إلي رؤيته منك. فقال: قد رأيتني. فقلت: إن كنَّا نعزب عن الماء فتصيبني الجنابة، فلبثت أيَّاما أتيمّم فوقع

---

116 ويقول أربعين قلت: لا ينجسها شيء: +، ب.

117 المتيمم: -، ب.

118 قلابة: قتادة، ب.

119 السلام: -،د.

في نفسي أمر وظننت أنِّي أهلك. فقال: أتعرف أبا ذر، كنت بالمدينة فاجتويتها، فأمر رسول الله عليه الصلاة والسلام بنعم من نعم الصدقة، فكنت فيها، فأصابتني جنابة فتيمّمت بالصعيد، فصلَّيت أيَّاما فوقع في نفسي من ذلك الشيء حتَّى ظننت أنِّي هالك، فأمرت ببعير لي فشددت عليه وركبت حتَّى قدمت المدينة فوجدت رسول الله صلى الله عليه وسلم في المسجد مع انتصاف النهار في نفر من أصحابه فسلمت عليه فرفع رسول الله عليه الصلاة والسلام رأسه فقال: سبحان الله أبا ذر؟ قلت: نعم، يا رسول الله، إنَّمَا أصابتني جنابة فتيمّمت أيَّاما فوقع في نفسي شيء حتَّى ظننت أنِّي هالك. قال: فدعا رسول الله صلى الله عليه وسلم لي بماء فجاءت به أمة سوداء في عس يتخضخض[120]، فاستترت بالراحلة وأمر رجلا أن يسترني، فاغتسلت، ثُمَّ قال رسول الله صلى الله عليه وسلم: «يا أبا ذرّ إن الصعيد الطيب طهور صالح[121] ما لم تجد الماء، ولو إلى عشرين سنة، فإذا وجدت الماء فاغتسل به[122]»[123]. وقال غيره: هو كما قال رسول الله صلى الله عليه وسلم[124].

وحدث أيُّوب عن أبي قلابة[125]: أنَّه بلغه أن جنابة أبي ذرّ كانت من جماع.

سئل عن رجل يغشى امرأته وليس معه ماء؟

120 في عس يتخضخض: -، ب.

121 صالح: -،د.

122 فأغتسل به: فأمسكه، ب.

123 رواه الطبراني: المعجم الأوسط، ر١٣٣٣.

124 وقال غيره: هوكما قال رسول الله ﷺ: -،د.

125 قلابة: قتادة،د.

قال: كان الربيع يكره أن يقع الرجل على امرأته وليس معه ماء، إلاَّ أن يصيبه أمر يخاف على نفسه.

سئل عن رجل صلَّى و في ثوبه دم فأبصره في الوقت أو صلَّى لغير القبلة، أو صلَّى و في ثوبه جنابة أو صلَّى بتيمّم، ثُمَّ أدرك الماء في الوقت.

قال: أمَّا الدم فعليه أن يعيده، وأمَّا القبلة إذا كان لا يعرفها فإنَّمَا عليه الجهد فلا يعيد.

سئل عن رجل أصابته الجنابة فتيمّم بالصعيد ثُمَّ أدرك الماء وهو في الوقت؟

قال: يستحبّ إذا كان في الوقت أن يعيدها فإن اجتزأ بها أجزته.

سئل عن رجل صلَّى لغير القبلة لم يتعمد[126]؟

قال: ليس عليه إعادة، قال[127]: فإن أبصر القبلة وهو في صلاته انحرف إلى القبلة واعتد بما صلَّى.

سئل عن إمام صلَّى بقوم وهو جنب؟

قال: عليهم جميعا الإعادة.

عن أيُّوب عن سليمان أنَّ عمر بن الخطَّاب رضي الله عنه صلَّى بأصحابه ثُمَّ خرج إلى أرض له فبينما هو عند ربيع جدول، وقد أشرقت الشمس إذ أبصر على فخذيه وعلى ثوبه جنابة، قال: هذه جنابة قد حركت[128] علينا الاحتلام منذ أصابنا هذا الدسم، فاغتسل فصلَّى. وبلغنا: أنَّ عمر أمر الناس أن يعيدوا.

126 لم يتعمد: –،د.

127 قال: –،د.

128 حركت: حوطت، ب.

عن بكر بن عبد الله المدني: أنَّ رسول الله صلى الله عليه وسلم دخل في صلاته فكبر وكبر من خلفه، ثُمَّ انصرف فأشار إلى القوم أن كما أنتم فلم يزالوا قياما، وانطلق نبيّ الله عليه الصلاة والسلام ـ، ثُمَّ جاء[129] ورأسه يقطر ماء[130]، وقال غيره: بلغنا ذلك.

سئل عن الوضوء بماء البحر؟

قال: يتوضَّأ منه فلا بأس بذلك.

سئل عن رجل يصوم ثلاثة أيَّام من الشهر؟

قال: كان أصحابنا يكرهون أن يؤقِّتوا شيئا، ولكن من فتح الله له شيئا فليصم إذا وجد روح الصيام والصلاة.

تم الجزء السابع من قول قتادة ويتلوه كتاب جابر بن زيد انتهى وغالب النسخ يضمون إليه كتاب جابر بن زيد: عن حبيب بن أبي حبيب في الصلاة، ولا يقولون: انتهى الجزء السابع من قول قتادة إلاَّ بعده، والله أعلم. كتبه العبد الفقير إلى الله صالح بن سالم بن يدر السدريني بجامع الماي عمره الله لخمسة عشر يوما خلون من شوال سنة إحدى وتسعين ومائة وألف من هجرة الرسول الأعظم. تمت والحمد لله انتهى وغالب النسخ يضمون إليه كتاب جابر بن زيد.

129 جاء: فرجع، ب.

130 رواه البخاري، باب إذا ذكر في المسجد أنه جنب يخرج كما هو ولا يتيمم، ر٢٧١.

Index of Quranic Verses فهرس الآيات

سورة البقرة

﴿ كُتِبَ عَلَيْكُمْ إِذَا حَضَرَ أَحَدَكُمُ الْمَوْتُ إِن تَرَكَ خَيْرًا الْوَصِيَّةُ لِلْوَالِدَيْنِ وَالأَقْرَبِينَ... ﴾ (آية:180) 302

﴿ فَمَنْ خَافَ مِن مُّوصٍ جَنَفًا أَوْ إِثْمًا فَأَصْلَحَ بَيْنَهُمْ فَلاَ إِثْمَ عَلَيْهِ ﴾ (آية:182) 303

﴿ فَمَنْ عُفِيَ لَهُ مِنْ أَخِيهِ شَيْءٌ فَاتِّبَاعٌ بِالْمَعْرُوفِ وَأَدَاءٌ إِلَيْهِ بِإِحْسَانٍ ﴾ (آية:178) 236

﴿ فَمَنِ اعْتَدَى بَعْدَ ذَلِكَ فَلَهُ عَذَابٌ أَلِيمٌ ﴾ (آية:178) 224، 236

﴿ يَا أَيُّهَا الَّذِينَ آمَنُوا كُتِبَ عَلَيْكُمُ الصِّيَامُ كَمَا كُتِبَ عَلَى الَّذِينَ مِن قَبْلِكُمْ لَعَلَّكُمْ تَتَّقُونَ ﴾ (آية:183) 142

﴿ أَيَّامًا مَعْدُودَاتٍ ﴾ (آية:184) 143

﴿ وَعَلَى الَّذِينَ يُطِيقُونَهُ فِدْيَةٌ طَعَامُ مِسْكِينٍ ﴾ (آية:184) 145

﴿ فَمَنْ شَهِدَ مِنكُمُ الشَّهْرَ فَلْيَصُمْهُ ﴾ (آية:185) 146

﴿ أُحِلَّ لَكُمْ لَيْلَةَ الصِّيَامِ الرَّفَثُ إِلَى نِسَائِكُمْ هُنَّ لِبَاسٌ لَّكُمْ وَأَنتُمْ لِبَاسٌ لَّهُنَّ ﴾ (آية:187) 146

﴿ عَلِمَ اللَّهُ أَنَّكُمْ كُنتُمْ تَخْتَانُونَ أَنفُسَكُمْ ﴾ (آية:187) 146

﴿ فَالآنَ بَاشِرُوهُنَّ وَابْتَغُوا مَا كَتَبَ اللَّهُ لَكُمْ وَكُلُوا وَاشْرَبُوا حَتَّى يَتَبَيَّنَ لَكُمُ الْخَيْطُ الأَبْيَضُ مِنَ الْخَيْطِ الأَسْوَدِ مِنَ الْفَجْرِ ﴾ (آية:187) 147

﴿ وَلاَ تُبَاشِرُوهُنَّ وَأَنتُمْ عَاكِفُونَ فِي الْمَسَاجِدِ ﴾ (آية:187) 147

﴿ رَبَّنَا آتِنَا فِي الدُّنْيَا حَسَنَةً وَفِي الآخِرَةِ حَسَنَةً وَقِنَا عَذَابَ النَّارِ ﴾ (آية:201) 54

﴿ يَسْأَلُونَكَ عَنِ الْخَمْرِ وَالْمَيْسِرِ قُلْ فِيهِمَا إِثْمٌ كَبِيرٌ وَمَنَافِعُ لِلنَّاسِ وَإِثْمُهُمَا أَكْبَرُ مِن نَّفْعِهِمَا ﴾ (آية:219) 171

﴿ وَالْوَالِدَاتُ يُرْضِعْنَ أَوْلاَدَهُنَّ حَوْلَيْنِ كَامِلَيْنِ ﴾ (آية:233) 404

﴿ إِلاَّ أَن يَعْفُونَ أَوْ يَعْفُوَا الَّذِي بِيَدِهِ عُقْدَةُ النِّكَاحِ ﴾ (آية:237) 342

﴿ فَإِنْ خِفْتُمْ فَرِجَالاً أَوْ رُكْبَانًا ﴾ (آية:239) 61، 220

﴿ وَلِلْمُطَلَّقَاتِ مَتَاعٌ بِالْمَعْرُوفِ ﴾ (آية:241) 327

﴿ يَا أَيُّهَا الَّذِينَ آمَنُوا اتَّقُوا اللَّهَ وَذَرُوا مَا بَقِيَ مِنَ الرِّبَا إِن كُنتُم مُّؤْمِنِينَ، فَإِن لَّمْ تَفْعَلُوا فَأْذَنُوا بِحَرْبٍ مِّنَ اللَّهِ وَرَسُولِهِ وَإِن تُبْتُمْ فَلَكُمْ رُءُوسُ أَمْوَالِكُمْ لاَ تَظْلِمُونَ وَلاَ تُظْلَمُونَ ﴾ (آية:278-279) 422

سورة آل عمران

﴿ إِنَّ الَّذِينَ يَشْتَرُونَ بِعَهْدِ اللهِ وَأَيْمَانِهِم ثَمَنًا قَلِيلاً أُولَئِكَ لاَ خَلاَقَ لَهُمْ فِي الآخِرَةِ ﴾ (آية: 77) 170

﴿ وَمَن يَغْلُلْ يَأْتِ بِمَا غَلَّ يَوْمَ الْقِيَامَةِ ﴾ (آية: 161) 123

سورة النساء

﴿ وَابْتَلُوا الْيَتَامَى حَتَّى إِذَا بَلَغُوا النِّكَاحَ فَإِنْ آنَسْتُم مِّنْهُمْ رُشْدًا فَادْفَعُوا إِلَيْهِمْ أَمْوَالَهُمْ وَلاَ تَأْكُلُوهَا إِسْرَافًا وَبِدَارًا أَن يَكْبَرُوا وَمَن كَانَ غَنِيًّا فَلْيَسْتَعْفِفْ وَمَن كَانَ فَقِيرًا فَلْيَأْكُلْ بِالْمَعْرُوفِ ﴾ (آية:6) 133

﴿ وَإِذَا حَضَرَ الْقِسْمَةَ أُوْلُوا الْقُرْبَى وَالْيَتَامَى وَالْمَسَاكِينُ فَارْزُقُوهُم مِّنْهُ وَقُولُوا لَهُمْ قَوْلاً مَّعْرُوفًا ﴾ (آية:8) 127

﴿ وَأُمَّهَاتُ نِسَائِكُمْ ﴾ (آية:23) 351

﴿ يَا أَيُّهَا الَّذِينَ آمَنُوا لاَ تَقْرَبُوا الصَّلاَةَ وَأَنتُمْ سُكَارَى حَتَّى تَعْلَمُوا مَا تَقُولُونَ ﴾ (آية:43) 172

﴿ أَيْنَمَا تَكُونُوا يُدْرِككُّمُ الْمَوْتُ وَلَوْ كُنتُمْ فِي بُرُوجٍ مُّشَيَّدَةٍ ﴾ (آية:78) 307

سورة المائدة

﴿حُرِّمَتْ عَلَيْكُمُ الْمَيْتَةُ وَالدَّمُ وَلَحْمُ الْخِنْزِيرِ وَمَا أُهِلَّ لِغَيْرِ اللَّهِ بِهِ وَالْمُنْخَنِقَةُ وَالْمَوْقُوذَةُ وَالْمُتَرَدِّيَةُ وَالنَّطِيحَةُ وَمَا أَكَلَ السَّبُعُ إِلَّا مَا ذَكَّيْتُمْ وَمَا ذُبِحَ عَلَى النُّصُبِ وَأَنْ تَسْتَقْسِمُوا بِالْأَزْلَامِ﴾ (آية:3) 259

﴿وَالْمُحْصَنَاتُ مِنَ الْمُؤْمِنَاتِ وَالْمُحْصَنَاتُ مِنَ الَّذِينَ أُوتُوا الْكِتَابَ مِنْ قَبْلِكُمْ﴾ (آية:5) 332

﴿يَا أَيُّهَا الَّذِينَ آمَنُوا إِذَا قُمْتُمْ إِلَى الصَّلَاةِ فَاغْسِلُوا وُجُوهَكُمْ وَأَيْدِيَكُمْ إِلَى الْمَرَافِقِ وَامْسَحُوا بِرُءُوسِكُمْ وَأَرْجُلَكُمْ إِلَى الْكَعْبَيْنِ﴾ (آية:6) 473

﴿إِنَّمَا جَزَاءُ الَّذِينَ يُحَارِبُونَ اللَّهَ وَرَسُولَهُ وَيَسْعَوْنَ فِي الْأَرْضِ فَسَادًا أَنْ يُقَتَّلُوا أَوْ يُصَلَّبُوا أَوْ تُقَطَّعَ أَيْدِيهِمْ وَأَرْجُلُهُمْ مِنْ خِلَافٍ أَوْ يُنْفَوْا مِنَ الْأَرْضِ...﴾ (آية:33) 294

﴿فَإِنْ جَاءُوكَ فَاحْكُمْ بَيْنَهُمْ﴾ (آية:42) 332

﴿يَا أَيُّهَا الَّذِينَ آمَنُوا مَنْ يَرْتَدَّ مِنْكُمْ عَنْ دِينِهِ فَسَوْفَ يَأْتِي اللَّهُ بِقَوْمٍ يُحِبُّهُمْ وَيُحِبُّونَهُ أَذِلَّةٍ عَلَى الْمُؤْمِنِينَ أَعِزَّةٍ عَلَى الْكَافِرِينَ يُجَاهِدُونَ فِي سَبِيلِ اللَّهِ وَلَا يَخَافُونَ لَوْمَةَ لَائِمٍ ذَلِكَ فَضْلُ اللَّهِ يُؤْتِيهِ مَنْ يَشَاءُ وَاللَّهُ وَاسِعٌ عَلِيمٌ﴾ (آية:54) 130–131

﴿يَا أَيُّهَا الَّذِينَ آمَنُوا لَا تُحَرِّمُوا طَيِّبَاتِ مَا أَحَلَّ اللَّهُ لَكُمْ وَلَا تَعْتَدُوا إِنَّ اللَّهَ لَا يُحِبُّ الْمُعْتَدِينَ﴾ (آية:87) 163

﴿لَا يُؤَاخِذُكُمُ اللَّهُ بِاللَّغْوِ فِي أَيْمَانِكُمْ...﴾ (آية:89) 168

﴿يَا أَيُّهَا الَّذِينَ آمَنُوا إِنَّمَا الْخَمْرُ وَالْمَيْسِرُ وَالْأَنْصَابُ وَالْأَزْلَامُ رِجْسٌ مِنْ عَمَلِ الشَّيْطَانِ فَاجْتَنِبُوهُ لَعَلَّكُمْ تُفْلِحُونَ﴾ (آية:90) 173

﴿أُحِلَّ لَكُمْ صَيْدُ الْبَحْرِ وَطَعَامُهُ مَتَاعًا لَكُمْ وَلِلسَّيَّارَةِ﴾ (آية:96) 268–269

سورة الأنعام

﴿فَكُلُوا مِمَّا ذُكِرَ اسْمُ اللَّهِ عَلَيْهِ﴾ (آية:118) 260

﴿قُلْ لَا أَجِدُ فِي مَا أُوحِيَ إِلَيَّ مُحَرَّمًا عَلَى طَاعِمٍ يَطْعَمُهُ إِلَّا أَنْ يَكُونَ مَيْتَةً أَوْ دَمًا مَسْفُوحًا أَوْ لَحْمَ خِنْزِيرٍ..﴾ (آية:145) 264، 265، 271

﴿يَوْمَ يَأْتِي بَعْضُ آيَاتِ رَبِّكَ لَا يَنْفَعُ نَفْسًا إِيمَانُهَا لَمْ تَكُنْ آمَنَتْ مِنْ قَبْلُ أَوْ كَسَبَتْ فِي إِيمَانِهَا خَيْرًا﴾ (آية:158) 60

﴿مَنْ جَاءَ بِالْحَسَنَةِ فَلَهُ عَشْرُ أَمْثَالِهَا﴾ (آية:160) 148

سورة الأنفال

﴿وَاعْلَمُوا أَنَّمَا غَنِمْتُمْ مِنْ شَيْءٍ فَأَنَّ لِلَّهِ خُمُسَهُ وَلِلرَّسُولِ وَلِذِي الْقُرْبَى وَالْيَتَامَى وَالْمَسَاكِينِ﴾ (آية:41) 121

سورة التوبة

﴿وَالَّذِينَ يَكْنِزُونَ الذَّهَبَ وَالْفِضَّةَ وَلَا يُنْفِقُونَهَا فِي سَبِيلِ اللَّهِ فَبَشِّرْهُمْ بِعَذَابٍ أَلِيمٍ﴾ (آية:34) 140

﴿إِنَّمَا الصَّدَقَاتُ لِلْفُقَرَاءِ وَالْمَسَاكِينِ وَالْعَامِلِينَ عَلَيْهَا وَالْمُؤَلَّفَةِ قُلُوبُهُمْ وَفِي الرِّقَابِ وَالْغَارِمِينَ وَفِي سَبِيلِ اللَّهِ وَابْنِ السَّبِيلِ فَرِيضَةً مِنَ اللَّهِ وَاللَّهُ عَلِيمٌ حَكِيمٌ﴾ (آية:60) 123–124

﴿الَّذِينَ يَلْمِزُونَ الْمُطَّوِّعِينَ مِنَ الْمُؤْمِنِينَ فِي الصَّدَقَاتِ وَالَّذِينَ لَا يَجِدُونَ إِلَّا جُهْدَهُمْ فَيَسْخَرُونَ مِنْهُمْ سَخِرَ اللَّهُ مِنْهُمْ وَلَهُمْ عَذَابٌ أَلِيمٌ﴾ (آية:79) 125–126

﴿اسْتَغْفِرْ لَهُمْ أَوْ لَا تَسْتَغْفِرْ لَهُمْ إِنْ تَسْتَغْفِرْ لَهُمْ سَبْعِينَ مَرَّةً فَلَنْ يَغْفِرَ اللَّهُ لَهُمْ﴾ (آية:80) 126

﴿فِيهِ رِجَالٌ يُحِبُّونَ أَنْ يَتَطَهَّرُوا﴾ (آية:108) 479

سورة الإسراء

﴿وَلَا تَزِرُ وَازِرَةٌ وِزْرَ أُخْرَى﴾ (آية:15) 119، 120

﴿وَقُرْآنَ الْفَجْرِ إِنَّ قُرْآنَ الْفَجْرِ كَانَ مَشْهُودًا﴾ (آية:78) 468

سورة طه

﴿وَأَقِمِ الصَّلَاةَ لِذِكْرِي﴾ (آية:14) 31

سورة النور

﴿وَلَا تَأْخُذْكُمْ بِهِمَا رَأْفَةٌ فِي دِينِ اللَّهِ﴾ (آية:2) 298

﴿أَرْبَعُ شَهَادَاتٍ بِاللهِ إِنَّهُ لَمِنَ الصَّادِقِينَ وَالْخَامِسَةُ أَنَّ لَعْنَتَ اللهِ عَلَيْهِ إِن كَانَ مِنَ الْكَاذِبِينَ﴾ (آية:6-7) 375

﴿أَن تَشْهَدَ أَرْبَعَ شَهَادَاتٍ بِاللهِ إِنَّهُ لَمِنَ الْكَاذِبِينَ وَالْخَامِسَةُ أَنَّ غَضَبَ اللهِ عَلَيْهَا إِن كَانَ مِنَ الصَّادِقِينَ﴾ (آية:8-9) 375

﴿وَالَّذِينَ يَبْتَغُونَ الْكِتَابَ مِمَّا مَلَكَتْ أَيْمَانُكُمْ فَكَاتِبُوهُمْ إِنْ عَلِمْتُمْ فِيهِمْ خَيْرًا﴾ (آية:33) 309

سورة الشورى

﴿وَهُوَ الَّذِي يَقْبَلُ التَّوْبَةَ عَنْ عِبَادِهِ وَيَعْفُو عَنِ السَّيِّئَاتِ﴾ (آية:25) 410

سورة الدخان

﴿فِيهَا يُفْرَقُ كُلُّ أَمْرٍ حَكِيمٍ﴾ (آية:4) 101

سورة الأحقاف

﴿وَحَمْلُهُ وَفِصَالُهُ ثَلَاثُونَ شَهْرًا﴾ (آية:15) 404

سورة الذاريات

﴿كَانُوا قَلِيلًا مِّنَ اللَّيْلِ مَا يَهْجَعُونَ﴾ (آية:17) 74

سورة النجم

﴿وَأَنَّهُ هُوَ أَضْحَكَ وَأَبْكَى . وَأَنَّهُ هُوَ أَمَاتَ وَأَحْيَا . وَأَنَّهُ خَلَقَ الزَّوْجَيْنِ الذَّكَرَ وَالْأُنثَى﴾ (آية:43-45) 119

﴿وَأَن لَّيْسَ لِلْإِنسَانِ إِلَّا مَا سَعَى﴾ (آية:53) 119

سورة الجمعة

﴿وَإِذَا رَأَوْا تِجَارَةً أَوْ لَهْوًا انفَضُّوا إِلَيْهَا وَتَرَكُوكَ قَائِمًا﴾ (آية:11) 101

سورة المنافقون

﴿سَوَاءٌ عَلَيْهِمْ أَسْتَغْفَرْتَ لَهُمْ أَمْ لَمْ تَسْتَغْفِرْ لَهُمْ لَن يَغْفِرَ اللَّهُ لَهُمْ﴾ (آية:6) 126

سورة الطلاق

﴿فَطَلِّقُوهُنَّ لِعِدَّتِهِنَّ وَأَحْصُوا الْعِدَّةَ﴾ (آية:1) 448

﴿لَا تُخْرِجُوهُنَّ مِن بُيُوتِهِنَّ وَلَا يَخْرُجْنَ إِلَّا أَن يَأْتِينَ بِفَاحِشَةٍ مُّبَيِّنَةٍ﴾ (آية:1) 182، 394-395

سورة المعارج

﴿وَالَّذِينَ فِي أَمْوَالِهِمْ حَقٌّ مَّعْلُومٌ، لِّلسَّائِلِ وَالْمَحْرُومِ﴾ (آية:25) 140

سورة المزمل

﴿يَا أَيُّهَا المزَّمل﴾ (آية:1) 89

﴿إِنَّ نَاشِئَةَ اللَّيْلِ هِيَ أَشَدُّ وَطْئًا وَأَقْوَمُ قِيلًا﴾ (آية:6) 75

سورة الكافرون

﴿قل يا أيُّها الكافرون﴾ (آية:1) 92

سورة الإخلاص

﴿قل هو الله أحد﴾ (آية:1) 92

Index of Prophetic Tradition فهرس الأحاديث والآثار

«أبو بكر حذر كيّس وعمر قوي معالٌ» 88

«أدنُ فكل وسمّ الله وكل بيمينك وكل مِمّا يليك» 479

«إذا أقيمت الصلاة فلا يسعى أحدكم، وليمش وعليه السكينة والوقار، فليصل ما أدرك وليقض ما سبق به» 34

«إذا أكل أحدكم فليأكل بيمينه وإذا شرب فليشرب بيمينه، فإن الشيطان يأكل ويشرب بشماله» 479

«إذا جاء أحدكم الشيطان في صلاته، فقال قد أحدثت، فليقل قد كذبت إلاّ من وجد ريحا نافحة أو صوتا باديا». 40

«إذا ذبحتم فأودجوا، وإذا قتلتم فأحسنوا، فإنّ الله محسن يحبّ الإحسان» 260

«إذا رأى أحدكم ذلك فليغسل فرجه من المذي والوذي ثُمّ يتوضأ» 489

«إذا رأيتم الهلال فصوموا، وإذا رأيتموه فأفطروا، فإن غمّ عليكم فأتموا العدّة ثلاثين يوما» 143

«إذا رأيتم الهلال فصوموا، وإذا رأيتموه فأفطروا، فإن غمّ عليكم فأكملوا العدّة ثلاثين يوما، إلاّ أن يشهد اثنان ذوا عدل منكم أنّهما رأياه بالأمس فصوموا لرؤيتهما، وأفطروا لرؤيتهما، وأمسكوا لرؤيتهما» 143

«إذا سجد انتصب على أطراف أصابعه وركبتيه، وجافا بين يديه حتّى يرى بياض إبطيه». 50

«إذا صام أحدكم فلا يرفث ولا يفسق يومئذ ولا يجهل ذلك، فإن أمروه وشقوا عليه فليقل إني صائم» 159

«إذا قام أحدكم من منامه فلا يغمس يديه في الإناء حتّى يغسلهما ثلاث مرّات قبل أن يغمسها في الإناء» 473

«إذا وقع الطاعون بأرض فلا تخرج منها، وإذا سمعت به بأرض تهبط عليه إن شئت فإن الطاعون لا يقدم أجلا ولا يؤخره» 307

«أرصوا بين صُفوفكم، وقاربوا بينها وحاذُوا بالأعناق، والذي نفس مُحَمّد بيده إنّي لأرى الشيطان يتخلل الصفوف كأنه الحذف» 69

«أصيب يوم أحد مع رسول الله ﷺ، قلت: يا أم المؤمنين، أنبئيني عن خلق رسول الله ﷺ؟ قالت: ألست تقرأ القرآن؟ قلت: بلى، قالت: فإن خلق رسول الله ﷺ كان القرآن» 89

«أعلموا شهرا من السنة فأخرجوا فيه صدقة أموالكم، فما حدث لكم من أموال بعد إخراج الصدقة فلا صدقة فيها حتّى يبلغ رأس السنة» 381

«اقتل الحيّات صغارها وكبارها» 282

«اقرأ» فقرأ فقال: «قد أحسنت»، وقال للآخر: «اقرأ»، فقرأ، فقال رسول الله ﷺ: «كلا كما قد أحسن» 76

«الاستئذان ثلاثا فمن لم يؤذن له فيهن فليرجع» 285

«الاغتسال من الجنابة فإن الله تعالى لم يؤمن ابن آدم على شيء من دينه غيرها» 74

«الحمى فيح من فيح جهنّم فنحوها عنكم بالماء البارد» 283

«الصوم جنّة يجتن بها عبدي من النار، والصوم لي وأنا أجازي به، يدع طعامه وشرابه وشهوته من أجلي، والذي نفس مُحَمّد بيده لخلوف فم الصائم عند الله أطيب من ريح المسك» 159

«الطفل لا تكتب حسناته ولا تكتب سيئاته إلى اثني عشرة سنة، فإذا بلغها كتبت عليه جميعا». 46

«المتوفى عنها زوجها تخرج في عدّتها إن شاءت» 439
«المؤذنون أطول الناس أعناقا يوم القيامة» 471
«النخامة في المسجد خطيئة وكفّارتها دفنها» 63
«الولد للفراش» 187
«أمَّا علمت أنك ومالك لأبيك؟» ثُمَّ قال: «إن من أطيب أموالكم كسب أولادكم فكلوه هنيئا مريئا» 277
«أما يخاف أحدهم إذا رفع رأسه قبل الإمام أن يحول الله رأسه رأس حمار؟» 70
«أما يستطيع أحدكم كلّ ليلة أن يقرأ ثلث القرآن؟» 75
«أُمِرتُ أن أسجُدَ عَلَى سَبعَةِ أعضاء ولاَ أكُفَّ شَعرًا ولاَ ثَوبًا» 49
«آمركم بأربع وأنهاكم عن أربع: اعبدوا الله ولا تشركوا به شيئا، وأقيموا الصلاة وآتوا الزكاة، وصوموا رمضان وحجوا البيت وأعطوا الخمس من الغنائم، وأنهاكم عن الحنتم والدباء والنقير والمزفّت». قالوا: «يا رسول الله، ما ندري ما النقير؟» قال: «جذع ينقرونه، يرفعون فيه من الفضيخ والماء حتَّى إذا سكن غليانه شربتموه، حتَّى أن أحدكم ليضرب ابن عمه بالسيف» 257–258
«إن أدركت الصلاة وأنت في معاطن الإبل فلا تصل، وإذا أدركتك في مرابض الغنم فصل إن شئت» 59
«إن أرحم أُمَّتي بأمَّتي أبو بكر الصديق، وأشدهم في دين الله عمر بن الخطّاب، وأعلمهم بالحلال والحرام معاذ بن جبل، وأقرؤهم لكتاب الله أُبيّ بن كعب، والأمين أبو عبيدة بن الجراح» 77
«أنَّ أعرابيًّا من جهينة أتى النبي عليه الصلاة والسلام، فذكر له بُعد منزله، وسأله عن ليلة القدر، فأسرَّ إليه النبي حديثا لا يدري القوم ما هو، يريد أن يشهدها في أهله» 100
«إن الشمس والقمر لا ينكسفان لموت أحد، ولكنهما آيتان من آيات الله، فإذا رأيتم ذلك، فاحمدوا الله وكبّروه وسبّحوه وصلّوا حتَّى ينجلي كسوف أيهما انكسف»، ثُمَّ نزل رسول الله ﷺ فصلَّى بنا ركعتين 59–60
«أنَّ الصدقة تطفئ الخطايا كما يطفئ الماء النار» 130
«إن الكمأة من المن وماؤها شفاء للعين، وأن العجوة من شجر الجنَّة، وأنَّ العجوة من الجنَّة وهو دواء من السم» 284
«إنَّ الله أمر ابن آدم أن يسجد للعبادة على سبعة أعضاء، على جبهته وقدميه وركبتيه وكفيه» 50
«إنَّ الله أمرني أن أقرئك القرآن» 76
«إنَّ الله جزأ القرآن ثلاثة أجزاء، فجعل قل هو الله أحد جزءًا من أجزاء القرآن، وقال إنَّها تعدل ثلث القرآن» 75
«إنَّ الله كره لكم ثلاثة: قيل وقال وإضاعة المال وكثرة السؤال» 127–128
«أن النبي عليه السلام أتى يوم خيبر على قربة فيها ماء، فدعا منها بماء، فقالت امرأة: إنها جلد ميتة»، فقال: «اسألوها أدبغت؟»، قالت: «نعم»، فقال رسول الله ﷺ: «دباغ الأديم طهارته»، فأوتي رسول الله عليه السلام منها بماء فقضى به حاجته» 287
«أن النبيّ ﷺ استخلف ابن أمّ مكتوم سنين، فصلَّى بالناس وكان أعمى» 67
«أنَّ النبيّ ﷺ حج فصلَّى ركعتين ما كان بمنى، وصلَّى أبو بكر وعمر ركعتين، وعثمان ركعتين صدرا من خلافته، ثُمَّ صلَّى أربع ركعات بمنى» 85
«أنَّ النبيّ ﷺ وأبا بكر جلدا على الخمر بالنعال» 248
«أن أمة سوداء كانت لكعب بن مالك ترعى غنما له فعدا سبع على شاة منها فخشيت عليها فذبحتها بمروة فأتت

بها كعبا فكره أن يأكلها حتّى أتى إلى رسول الله عليه السلام فسأله عنها، فأمره بأكلها» 261

«أنّ امرأة جاءت إلى رسول الله ﷺ وفي حجرها يتامى لها، فقالت: «يا رسول الله، ما زلت تحث على الصدقة حتى هممت أن آخذ من أموال اليتامى فأتصدق به، فقال: «ما هو؟» قالت: «كفاف عيشهم»، قال: «فأمسكيه عليهم فإنهم أحقُّ به» 129

«إنّ أوّل ما يحاسب به العبد من عمله يوم القيامة صلاته، فإن صلحت فقد أفلح وأنجح، وإن فسدت فقد خاب وخسر» 52

«أن جن نصيبين أتوا رسول الله ﷺ، فقالوا: زودنا يا رسول الله، فقال رسول الله ﷺ: «كل روثة هي طعام لدوابكم وكل عظم لكم عرق»، فقالوا: إن أمتك يحسوه علينا، «فنهى رسول الله ﷺ عند ذلك أن يستنجى بروث أو عظم»» 480

«أن رجلا اتى إلى النبي عليه السلام فقال: «إن أخي يشتكي بطنه»، فقال: «اسقه عسلا»، ثمّ أتاه فقال: «إنّي قد فعلت»، ثمّ أتاه فقال: «إنّي قد فعلت». فقال: «اسقه عسلا»، ثمّ أتاه فقال: «إنّي قد فعلت». قال: «اسقه عسلا»، ثمّ أتاه فقال: قد فعلت. فقال: «صدق الله وكذب بطن أخيك اسقه عسلا»، فسقاه فبرئ الرجل» 270

«أن رجلا أسلم أبوه ولم يسلم هو، فبلغ ذلك النبي عليه الصلاة والسلام فقال: «شر التلادة» 114

«أنّ رجلا أعتق نصيبا له في غلام فرفع ذلك إلى النبيّ عليه السلام، فجعل خلاصه في ماله، قال: «إنّه ليس لله شريك» 255، 312

«أن رجلا أعمى جاء إلى المسجد، ورسول الله ﷺ يصلّي بأصحابه، فتردى في بئر، فضحك بعض من كان يصلّي مع رسول الله ﷺ، فأمر رسول الله ﷺ من ضحك منهم أن يعيدوا الوضوء والصلاة» 482

«أنّ رجلا تزوّج امرأة على عهد رسول الله ﷺ وكان معسرا، «فأمرها رسول الله عليه السلام أن ترفق به». فدخل عليها قبل أن يعطيها شيئا» 335

«أن رجلا طعن على ركبته أو فخذه على عهد النبيّ فأتى النبي عليه السلام فقال: «يا نبيّ الله، أقدني من فلان»، فقال له: «حتّى تبرأ»، ثمّ أتاه فقال: «يا نبيّ الله، أقدني من فلان». فقال: «حتّى تبرأ»، ثمّ أتاه الثالثة فقال له: «أقدني»، فأقاده، ثمّ أتاه بعد ذلك فقال: «إني عرجت وبرئ فلان»، فقال له النبيّ ﷺ: «قد أقدتك ولم يجعل له شيئا» 246

«أن رجلا قام إلى النبي عليه الصلاة والسلام يسأله عن وقت صلاة الصبح، فأمر المؤذن أن يقيم، فأقام عند طلوع الفجر، ثم أمره الغداة الثانية أن لا يقيم حتى يأمره، فخلى عنه حتى أصبح جدا، وأبرز جدا، ثمّ أمره فأقام ثمّ صلى بهم، فقال: «أين السائل عن وقت الصلاة؟»، فقام الرجل فقال له: «شهدت معنا هاتين الصلاتين؟»، قال: «نعم»، قال: «إنما بينهما وقت الصلاة» 468–469

«أن رجلا كان على جمل آدم يتبع رحال الناس بمنى: يقول ألا لا تصوموا هذه الأيّام؛ لأنّها أيّام أكل وشرب، ونبيّ الله بين أظهركم» 149

«أن رجلا من الأنصار زوج ابنته فكرهت ذلك فأتت نبيّ الله ﷺ فذكرت ذلك له فرد نكاحها» 414

«أنّ رسول الله عليه السلام صام وأفطر، وصام أصحابه وأفطروا، فلم يغيّر بعضهم على بعض» 144

«أنّ رسول الله ﷺ أتاه بنو لحيان وعصبة، فزعموا أنّهم قد أسلموا واستمدوه على قومهم، فأمدهم رسول الله ﷺ بسبعين رجلا من الأنصار كلهم يعدهم في

القراء، فكانوا يحطبون النهار ويصلون الليل، فلمّا بلغوا بئر معونة غدروا بهم فقتلوهم، فبلغ ذلك النبيّ ﷺ، فقنت في صلاة الصبح فدعا عليهم فقرأنا عليهم قرآنا أن بلغوا عنا قومنا أنا قد لقينا ربنا ورضي عنا وأرضانا» 80
«أنّ رسول الله ﷺ دخل في صلاته فكبر وكبر من خلفه، ثُمّ انصرف فأشار إلى القوم أن كما أنتم فلم يزالوا قياما، وانطلق نبيّ الله ﷺ، ثُمّ جاء ورأسه يقطر ماء» 494
«أنّ رسول الله ﷺ صلّى على النجاشي، فكبّر أربعا» 116
«أن رسول الله ﷺ صلّى وهو يتوجه إلى خيبر على حمار يومئ إيماء» 83
«أنّ رسول الله ﷺ غسله الفضل بن عبّاس وعليّ بن أبي طالب، وكان أسامة بن زيد يصبّ الماء عليهما» 109
«أن رسول الله ﷺ كان بالزوراء حان وقت الصلاة، فالتمس الناس وضوءا فلم يجدوه، فأوتي رسول الله بإناء فيه ماء لا يغمر أصابعه ولا يواري أصابعه، فوضع أصابع كفه في الماء فجعل الماء ينبع من بين أصابع رسول الله ﷺ حتّى توضّأ القوم كلهم، فقلنا لأنس: «كم كنتم؟» قال: «كنّا ثلاثمائة وأزيد عن ثلاثمائة» 33
«أنّ رسول الله ﷺ كان يخطب، وجاء رجل يتخطّى رقاب الناس حتّى جلس، فلمّا فرغ رسول الله ﷺ من صلاته قال للرجل: «أمّا جمعت يا فلان»، أو قال: «ما منعك أن تجمع، إمّا مرّتين وإما ثلاثا، كلّ ذلك يقول: أمَا رأيتني يا رسول الله؟ قال: بلى أتيت وآذيت» 105
«أن رسول الله ﷺ كان يصلّي ركعتين قبل الظهر، وركعتين بعد الظهر، وركعتين بعد المغرب إذا رجع إلى بيته، وركعتين بعد العشاء في بيته وركعتين قبل الغداة عند طلوع الفجر، وركعتين بعد الجمعة في بيته» 43
«أنّ رسول الله ﷺ كان يغتسل بصاع ويتوضأ بقدر مد من الماء» 486
«أنّ رسول الله ﷺ لما بلغه موت النجاشي. قال: «صلوا على أخ لكم مات في غير بلادكم» 116
«أنّ رسول الله ﷺ لما فرق بين المتلاعنين. قال: «لا سبيل لك عليها» 401
«إنّ رسول الله ﷺ نهانا عن لبس الحرير إلاّ موضع أصبع أو أصبعين أو ثلاثة وأشار بأصابعه» 271
«أنّ رسول الله ﷺ نهى عن الصلاة بعد العصر، حتّى تغرب الشمس وعن الصلاة بعد الفجر حتّى تطلع الشمس» 28
«أنّ رسول الله ﷺ نهى عن ذلك» 352
«أنّ رسول الله ﷺ نهى عن لحوم الجلالة وألبانها» 288
«أن رسول الله ﷺ وأبا بكر وعمر وعثمان صدرا من خلافته، كانوا يصلون قبل الخطبة» 94
«أنّ رسول الله ﷺ وأبا بكر وعمر وعثمان، كانوا يخطبون قياما يوم الجمعة» 103
«أنّ رسول الله ﷺ، لم يكن يتوخى فضل صوم يوم على يوم بعد رمضان إلاّ يوم عاشوراء» 150–151
«أنّ رسول الله سئل: «أيّ الصلاة أفضل؟» قال: «طول القنوت» 77–78
«أن رسول الله ﷺ عرس بأصحابه في مرجعه من خيبر، وقال لبلال: «احفظ علينا الصبح»، فما استيقظ حتّى أشرقت الشمس، فقال رسول الله ﷺ: «تحولوا من هذا المكان الذي أصابكم فيه هذه

الغفلة»، ثمّ أمر رسول الله ﷺ مناديه، فقال: فصلّى الصبح ثمّ قال: «من نسي صلاة فليصلّيها إذا ذكرها»؛ لأنّ الله تعالى يقول: ﴿وَأَقِمِ الصَّلَاةَ لِذِكْرِي﴾» 30–31

«إن رسول الله ﷺ قضى في بريرة أربع قضايا، أولهن: أن عائشة أرادت أن تشتريها وتعتقها، وتشترط ولاءها لأهلها، فقال رسول الله ﷺ: «الولاء لمن أعتق». والثانية: أنها خيرت. والثالثة: أن رسول الله ﷺ أمرها أن تعتد ثلاثة حيضات. والرابعة: أنها أهدت إلى رسول الله ﷺ لحما، فدخل رسول الله على عائشة فقال لها: «هل عندك من شيء؟»، فقالت: «يا رسول الله، ما عندنا من شيء إلا لحما أهدته لنا بريرة من شاة تصدق بها عليها»، فقال رسول الله ﷺ: «هو صدقة عليها وهو لنا منها هدية»، فأكل منها» 406

«أنّ رسول الله عليه الصلاة والسلام كان يوتر بسبح اسم ربك الأعلى، وبقل يا أيّها الكافرون، وبقل هو الله أحد، ويقول سبحان الملك القدوس ثلاث مرّات بعد التسليم» 87

«أنّ رسول الله عليه الصلاة والسلام مرّ برجل وهو نائم، فقال: «قم فصل»، قال: «إنما أصلي إذا قدر لي»، فقال النبي عليه الصلاة والسلام: «وكان الإنسان أكثر شيء جدلاً» 78–79

«أنّ رسول الله نهانا عن الشرب في آنية الفضّة، وعن لبس الحرير والديباج» 269

«إن عائشة زوج النبيّ ﷺ اشترت وليدة يقال لها بريرة من رجل من الأنصار ولها زوج عبد، فأعتقتها عائشة حين اشترتها، فخيرها رسول الله ﷺ حين أعتقت بين أن تقيم عند زوجها وبين أن يفارقها، فاختارت فرقته، ففرق بينهما رسول الله ﷺ» 355

«أن عبد الرحمن بن عوف جاء بنصف ماله إلى رسول الله عليه السلام يتقرب به إلى الله، فقال: «يا رسول الله هذا نصف مالي أتيتك به، وتركت النصف لعيالي»، فدعا الله أن يبارك له فيما أعطى وأمسك، فلمزه المنافقون فقالوا: «ما أعطى هذا ماله إلا رياء وسمعة»، وأقبل رجل من فقراء المسلمين من الأنصار يقال له الحبحاب أبو عقيل، فقال: «يا نبي الله، بت أجر الجريد الليل كله على صاعين من تمر، فأما صاع منه فأمسكته لأهلي، وأما صاع فهو ذا»، فقال له النبي عليه الصلاة والسلام خيرا» 126

«أن عمر جعل فرسا في سبيل الله، فأراد أن يشتريها، فسأل عن ذلك النبي عليه السلام فكره ذلك» 276

«أنّ غلاما من قومه صاد أرنبا فذبحها فعلقها، فسأل رسول الله عليه السلام عن أكلها؟ فأمره بأكلها» 261

«إن في الجمعة ساعة لا يوافقها رجل مسلم فيصلّي ويسأل الله فيها خيرا إلاّ أعطاه» 103

«أن كلّ مسكر حرام، وكل ما أسكر كثيره فقليله حرام» 259

«إن مات هذا وهكذا صلاته، لمات على غير دين» 51

«إن مفتاح الصلاة الطهور، وإحرامها التكبير وإحلالها التسليم» 474

«أنّ نبيّ الله عليه السلام دخل المدينة فوجد اليهود صياما فقال: «ما لهم صاموا هذا اليوم؟»، قالوا: «هذا يوم قطع موسى فيه البحر وأغرق فيه فرعون، فصامه موسى عليه السلام شكرا لله، وأمر بصومه»، قال رسول الله ﷺ: «أنا أولى بموسى منهم وأحق به»، فصامه رسول الله عليه السلام وأمر أصحابه أن يصوموا، حتى أنه أمر أناسا قد كانوا أكلوا من أول النهار أن يصوموا آخره» 150

«أنَّ نبيَّ الله عليه السلام سئل: عن الإبل فقال: «عزّ لأهلها» 140

«أنَّ نبيَّ الله عليه السلام كان يبعث مناديه عند الغنائم فيقول: ألاَّ لا يغلن رجل مخيطا فما دونه ألاَّ لا يعرفن رجل يغل بعيرا إلاَّ أوتي به يوم القيامة، حامله على عنقه له رغاء ألاَّ لا يعرفن رجل يغل فرسا إلاَّ أوتي بها يوم القيامة حاملها على عنقه لها حمحمة، ألا لا يعرفن رجل يغل شاة إلا أتى بها يوم القيامة حاملها على رقبته لها ثغاء فيتبع من ذلك ما شاء أن يتبع» 123

«أنَّ نبيَّ الله عليه السلام نهى عن صوم يوم الفطر ويوم النحر» 150

«أنَّ نبيَّ الله عليه السلام نهى عن نبيذ الجر والحنتم والنقير والمزفت، وقال: «كلّ مسكر حرام» 175

«أنَّ نبيَّ الله ﷺ صلَّى الضحى ذات يوم فأطال فيها فقيل: «يا نبيّ الله، لقد رأيناك تصلِّي صلاة ما رأيناك تصليها» . قال: «إنَّها صلاة رغبة ورهبة، وإني سألت ربي فيها ثلاثا، فأعطاني اثنتين ومنعني واحدة، سألت ربي ألاَّ يسلط على أمَّتي السّنّة فيهلكهم، فأعطانيها، وسألته: ألاَّ يسلط عليهم العدو من غيرهم: فأعطانيها، وسألته: ألاَّ يلبسهم شيعا ويذيق بعضهم بأس بعض فمنعنيها» 93-94

«أنَّ نبيَّ الله ﷺ كان يخطب يوم الجمعة، فجعل يخطب الناس ويعظهم ويذكرهم، وجعلوا يتسللون ويقومون حتَّى بقيت منهم عصابة . قال: «كم أنتم؟»، فعدوا أنفسهم فإذا هم اثنا عشر رجلا وامرأة، ثُمَّ قام يوم الجمعة الثانية فجعل يخطبهم ويعظهم، وجعلوا يتسللون ويقومون حتَّى بقيت منهم عصابة . قال: كم أنتم، فعدوا أنفسهم فإذا هم اثنا عشر رجلا وامرأة، فقال رسول الله ﷺ: «والذي نفسي بيده، لواتبع آخركم أولكم لا لتهب عليكم هذا الوادي نارا» 101

«أنَّ نبيَّ الله ﷺ لم يصلِّهما إلاَّ أن يقدم من سفر فيصلِّي الضحى من قبل أن يدخل إلى أهله» 93

«أنَّ نبيَّ الله ﷺ مرَّ بمسجد قباء ودخل المسجد، فصلَّى الضحى بعد ما أشرقت الشمس . فقال: «إنَّ الأوَّابين كانوا يصلُّونها إذا رمضت الفصال» 93

«أنَّ نبي الله عليه الصلاة والسلام أتاه طعام ذات ليلة فخص به أناسا من أهل الصفة، أتاهم، فقال: «إنه أتانا البارحة طعام فخصصنا به أقواما، ووكلنا أقواما إلى ما في قلوبهم» 125

«أنَّ نبي الله عليه الصلاة والسلام كان إذا قام من الليل قال: «الله أكبر لا إله إلاَّ الله، لا إله إلاَّ الله، الله أكبر الله أكبر كبيرا، أعوذ بالله من الشيطان الرجيم من همزه ونفخه ونفثه»، قيل: «يا رسول الله، ما همزه ونفخه ونفثه؟» قال: «همزه الغيبة، ونفخة الكبر، ونفثه الشعر» 78

«أنَّ نبيَّ الله نهى عن اللعب بالكعبين وقال: «هي ميسر الأعاجم» 172

«إنَّ هذا الشهر قد حضر، وهو شهر مبارك افترض الله صيامه تفتح فيه أبواب الجنَّة، وتغلق فيه أبواب الجحيم ويغل فيه الشياطين، وفيه ليلة القدر خير من ألف شهر، من حرم خيرها فقد حرم» 100

«انظروا فإن جاءت به أجعد الشعر أكحل العينين خدلج الساقين فهو للذي قذفت به» . فولدت جارية كحلاء، قال رسول الله ﷺ: «لولا ما سلف من اليمين لكان لي ولها شأن» 402

«إنَّما نهى رسول الله ﷺ عن لحومها يوم خيبر» 223

«أنه أتى النبي عليه السلام فقال: «يا نبي الله، اكتب لي بأرضي»، فقال له نبي الله: «كيف أكتب بأرض الشام أو بأرض الروم وهي أرض حرب؟»، فقال: «يا نبي الله، والذي بعثك بالحق بشيرا ونذيرا لتملكن ما تحت

أقدامهم» . قال: فأعجب من ذلك النبي ﷺ، فجعل النبي عليه السلام ينظر إليه وأصحابه ينظرون إلى ما يقول أبو ثعلبة، فكتب له رسول الله ﷺ كتابا. فقلت: «يا رسول الله، أنا بأرض صيد فما يحل لنا من ذلك وما يحرم علينا؟»، فقال نبي الله عليه السلام: «إذا أرسلت كلبك المعلم والمكلب وذكرت اسم الله، فأخذ وقتل فكل، وإذا أرسلت كلبك الذي ليس بمعلم، فما أدركت ذكاته فكله، وما لم تدرك فلا تأكله، وما رد عليك سهمك فكل»، قال: فقلت: «يا رسول الله، أنا بأرض أهلها أهل كتاب، وإنا نحتاج إلى قدورهم وآنيتهم»، فقال نبي الله: «لا تقربوها ما وجدتم منها بدا فإذا لم تجدوا بدا فاغسلوها بالماء ثُمَّ اطبخوا واشربوا» 264–265

«أنّه شهد رسول الله ﷺ في يوم مطير فأمر منادٍ ينادي الصلاة في الرحال» 107

«إنّها آية من كتاب الله اختلسها منهم الشيطان، صلَّيت مع النبيّ ﷺ فقرأها حتّى مات، ثُمَّ صلَّيت مع أبي بكر فقرأها حتّى مات، ثُمَّ صلَّيت مع عمر فقرأها حتّى مات، وأنا أقرأها حتّى أموت» 68

«أنّها كانت تغتسل هي ورسول الله ﷺ من إناء واحد» 439

«إنّها مأمورة ومن لعن شيئا لا ينبغي له لعنه رجعت اللعنة على صاحبها» 282

«إني لأعطي الرجل وأمنع الرجل وهو أحبّ إليّ منه ولكن إنَّمَا أعطي هذا التألفه الإسلام وأكمل هذا لما في قلبه» 125

«بينما نحن مع رسول الله ﷺ في بعض أسفاره إذا مال رسول الله ﷺ عن راحلته فدعمته بيدي، ثُمَّ سرنا، فمال رسول الله ﷺ عن راحلته فدعمته فاستيقظ، فقال أبو قتادة: قلت: «نعم، يا رسول الله»، فقال: «حفظك الله كما حفظتنا من ذي الليلة، فإني ما أرانا إلاّ شققنا عليك»، ثُمَّ قال رسول الله ﷺ: «تنح بنا عن الطريق، أو مل بنا عن الطريق»، وأناخ رسول الله ﷺ راحلته، وأنخنا وتوسد كل واحد منا ذراع راحلته، فما استيقظنا حتى أشرقت الشمس» 31

«تزوّج رسول الله عليه السلام ميمونة وهو محرم، وأعرس بها بعد أن حلّ بمكان يقال له سرف» 330–331

«جاءت عير من الشام فخرجوا إليها وتركوا النبي عليه الصلاة والسلام في اثني عشر رجلا وامرأة، فقال هذه المقالة» 101–102

«جلد رسول الله عليه السلام أربعين، وجلد أبو بكر أربعين، فأكملها عمر ثمانين» 249

«حرم الله عز وجل اثنتي عشرة امرأة، وأنا أكره اثنتي عشرة الأمة وأمها والأختان يجمع بينهما والأمة إذا وطئها أبوك والأمة إذا وطئها ابنك والأمة إذا زنت والامة في عدة غيرك والامة لها زوج وأمتك مشركة وعمتك وخالتك من الرضاعة» 412

«خمس من جاء بهنّ يوم القيامة مع إيمان دخل الجنّة: من حافظ على الصلوات المكتوبة ووضوئها ومواقيتها وركوعها وسجودها، وأعطى الزكاة طيبة بها نفسه» 73–74

«خير الصدقة ما أبقت غنى، وابدأ بمن تعول، واليد العليا خير من اليد السفلى» 129

«دخل عليّ رسول الله ﷺ يوم الفتح، فأمر بماء فصب في قصعة، ثمّ أمر بثوب فأخذه بيني وبينه فاغتسل ثم مشى ناحية البيت، فصلى ثماني ركعات، قيامهن وركوعهن وسجودهن وجلوسهن سواء قريب بعضهم من بعض» 94

«رأيت رسول الله ﷺ ينفتل عن يمينه وعن شماله، ورأيته يصلِّي حافيا ومنتعلا، ورأيته يصوم في السفر

ويفطر، ورأيته يشرب قائما وقاعدا» 55
«رأينا بعض الفقهاء يخضب وبعضهم يترك، وبلغنا أن النبي عليه السلام أمر به» 286-287
«رفع القلم عن ثلاث: النائم حتَّى يستيقظ، والمجنون حتَّى يفيق، والصبيّ حتَّى يدرك» 403
«سنّ رسول الله ﷺ فيما سقت السماء والعيون والسايحة والبعل وماكان بعلا العشر كاملا، وما سقي بالرشا (وهي الدوالي) والسواقي نصف العشر» 137
«شرُّ الناس سرقة الذي يسرق من صلاته»، قالوا: «كيف يسرق من صلاته؟» قال: «لا يتمّ ركوعها ولا سجودها» 52
«صلاتك مع الرجل الواحد، أزكى من صلاتك وحدك، وصلاتك مع الرجلين أزكى من صلاتك مع رجل واحد وماكثر فهو أحب إلى الله» 73
«صلى رسول الله ﷺ صلاة الصبح، ثمّ قال: «أشهد فلان؟ أشهد فلان؟» لنفرٍ من المنافقين لم يشهدوا تلك الصلاة، ثمّ قال: «إن هاتين الصلاتين أثقل على المنافقين من سائر الصلوات - صلاة الصبح وصلاة العشاء -، لو يعلمون ما فيهما لأتوهما ولو حبوا» 72-73
«صلَّيت مع رسول الله ﷺ ثمانيا جمعا وسبعا» 440
«صوموا يوم الصبر وثلاثة أيّام من كلّ شهر يذهبن وحر الصدر» 160
«ضحى رسول الله عليه الصلاة والسلام وليس عليكم، وأوتر وليس عليكم، وصلى ركعتين قبل الظهر وليس عليكم، وصلى الضحى وليس عليكم» 87
«عقد في نواصيها الخير والأجر والبركة» 140
«عليكم بالبياض ألبسوه أحياءكم وكفنوا فيه موتاكم، فإنَّه من خير ثيابكم» 112
«عليكم بالصف المقدم فإنَّه على مثل صف الملائكة ولو تعلمون ما فيه لا بتدرتموه» 72-73
«فأتت النبي عليه الصلاة والسلام فقالت: «حين كبر سني، ورق عظمي، واثنى صلبي ظاهر مني زوجي»، فأنزل الله آي الظهار، فدعاه النبي ﷺ فقال: «أتستطيع أن تحرر رقبة؟» فقال: «لا أجد». فقال: «أتستطيع أن تصوم شهرين متتابعين؟». فقال: «إنَّه والله، إنَّه إذا أخطأت الماء في اليوم ثلاث مرَّات لكلّ بصري». فقال: «أتستطيع أن تطعم ستّين مسكينا؟» قال: «لا والله، إلاَّ أن تعينني منك بعون وصلة»، فأعانه رسول الله ﷺ، وجمع الله له أهله والله رؤوف رحيم» 418
«فأتوا النبي عليه الصلاة والسلام فسألوه عن ذلك فنهاهم، فقال: «أليست لكم أسوة فيَّ» 89
«فأتى أسامة إلى رسول الله ﷺ فسأله عن ذلك، فقال النبيّ ﷺ: «يدا بيد» 423
«فإذا سمعتم به بأرض فلا تدخلوها عليه وإذا وقع في أرض وأنتم فيها فلا تخرجوا فرارا منه» 307
«فانتهى إليهم رسول الله عليه الصلاة والسلام من آخر النهار، وقد كادوا يهلكون عطشا، وقالوا: «يا رسول الله قد هلكنا»، فدعا رسول الله ﷺ بالميضة فأبطأها، ثُمَّ دعا بإناء فوق القدح ودون العقب فجعل يصبّ في الإناء، وشربنا حتَّى شرب القوم كلّهم، ثُمَّ نادى منادي رسول الله ﷺ: «هل اكتفيتم؟» فقالوا: «بلى»، ثُمَّ رفع النبيّ ﷺ الميضة وفيها نحو مِمَّا كان فيها، قال فسألناه: «كم كنتم؟» قال: مع أبي بكر وعمر ثمانون، وكنا مع رسول الله ﷺ اثنا عشر» 32-33
«فانطلقت به عائشة إلى رسول الله ﷺ فبال عليها، فدحيته دحية، تقول: ضربته ضربة. فحنكه وسماه

عبد الله، ثم قال لعائشة: «أنت أم عبد الله، وما ولدت ولدا قط» 482

«فجاءت إلى رسول الله ﷺ فقالت له: «أأرجع إلى زوجي الأول؟»، فقال لها رسول الله ﷺ: «هل مسك هذا الآخر منهما»؟ فقالت: «لا»، فقال لها رسول الله ﷺ: «لا يحلّ لك أن تتزوّجيه حتّى يكون قد جامعك الآخر منهما»، فذهبت المرأة ثمّ جاءته فقالت: إنه قد جامعها زوجها الأول، فكذّبها رسول الله ﷺ، ومنعها أن ترجع لزوجها الأول» 368

«فرض رسول الله عليه السلام على أناس من أهل اليمن على كلّ حالم وحالمة دينارا أو قيمته من المعافرية» 139

«فقالت: كنّا نعد لرسول الله ﷺ سواكه وطهوره، فيبعثه الله لما شاء أن يبعثه، فيقوم فيتسوك ويتوضأ ويصلي ثماني ركعات لا يقعد إلا في آخرهن، فيحمد الله ويدعوه ويستغفره، ثم ينهض ولا يسلم ويصلي التاسعة، ثمّ يقعد فيحمد الله ويدعوه ويستغفره ثمّ يسلم تسليما، ثم يصلي ركعتين جالسا، فذلك إحدى عشرة ركعة يا بني. قالت: فلما أسن رسول الله وأخذ اللحم أوتر بسبع ركعات، ثم يصلي ركعتين وهو جالس بعد التسليم، فتلك تسع ركعات يا بني، وكان رسول الله عليه الصلاة والسلام إذا صلى صلاة أحب أن يداوم عليها» 90

«فلاعن رسول الله ﷺ بين هلال بن أمية وامرأته، وأمر أن يفرق بينهما، ثمّ إن المرأة بعد ذلك ولدت غلاما أسود شبيها بالذي رميت به، وأنه أتي به إلى رسول الله ﷺ، فزعموا أن رسول الله ﷺ قال: «لولا الذي كان من أمرها كان لي فيه أمره» 377

«فوجدت رسول الله ﷺ في المسجد مع انتصاف النهار في نفر من أصحابه فسلمت عليه، فرفع رسول الله عليه الصلاة والسلام رأسه، فقال: «سبحان الله يا أبا ذر؟»، قلت: «نعم يا رسول الله، إنما أصابتني جنابة فتيممت أياما، فوقع في نفسي شيء، حتى ظننت أني هالك»، قال: فدعا رسول الله ﷺ لي بماء، فجاءت به أمة سوداء في عس يتخضخض، فاستترت بالراحلة، وأمر رجلا أن يسترني، فاغتسلت، ثم قال رسول الله ﷺ: «يا أبا ذرّ إن الصعيد الطيب طهور صالح ما لم تجد الماء، ولو إلى عشرين سنة، فإذا وجدت الماء فاغتسل به». 492

«في كلّ خمس شاة، وفي عشر شاتان، وفي خمس عشرة ثلاث شياه، وفي عشرين أربع شياه، وفي خمس وعشرين بنت مخاض، فإن لم توجد بنت مخاض فابن لبون ذكر إلى خمس وثلاثين، فإن زادت واحدة؛ ففيها بنت لبون، إلى خمس وأربعين...» 141

«فيم نشرب؟ قال: «في سقاء الأدم التي تلث على أفواهها»، قالوا: «يا نبي الله إن أرضنا كثيرة الجرذان لا يتقى بها». قال النبي عليه السلام: «وإن أكلتها الجرذان» 258

«قال: «يا أم المؤمنين أنبئيني عن قيام رسول الله»، قالت: «أتقرأ هذه السورة ﴿يا أيها المزمل﴾؟» قلت: «نعم»، قالت: «فإن رسول الله افترض القيام في أوّل هذه السورة، فقام رسول الله ﷺ وأصحابه حولا حتّى انتفخت أقدامهم، وأمسك الله خاتمتها اثنا عشر شهرا، في السماء ثمّ أنزل التخفيف في آخر السورة، فكان قيام الليل تطوّعا بعد الفريضة»» 89–90

«قال: يحضر الجمعة ثلاثة رجال، رجل بدعاء وصلاة، فذلك رجل يدعو ربه إن شاء أعطاه وإن شاء منعه، ورجل يحضرها بإنصات وسكون، فذلك حقها،

ورجل يحضرها بلغوفذلك خطأ منه» 105
«قد وجب الله لك أجرك ورد الله إليك أرضك اصنع بها ما شئت» 276
«قرأ رسول الله ﷺ في الصلوات وسكت» 47
«كان أذان رسول الله ﷺ مثنى مثنى، وإقامته مثنى مثنى» 469
«كان رسول الله ﷺ إذا شغله عن صلاة الليل نوم أو وجع صلى ثلاث عشر ركعة من النهار» 90
«كان يكثر الصلاة قائما وقاعدا فإذا صلّى قائما ركع قائما وإذا صلّى قاعدا ركع قاعدا» 65
«كان يمين رسول الله ﷺ لطعامه ولطهوره، وكانت شماله للخلاء وماكان من أذى» 479–480
«كان ينهى أن يصلِّي وهو عاقد شعره من ورائه» 54
«كان ينهى أن يقعيَ الرجل في صلاته» 54
«كذلك فاصنعوا، فأمرنا بهذا الآذان» 469
«كل مسكر حرام» 258
«كنا مع رسول الله ﷺ فحبسنا عن صلاة الظهر والعصر والمغرب والعشاء، فاشتد ذلك عليّ، فقلت: نحن مع رسول الله ﷺ، وفي سبيل الله، فامر رسول الله ﷺ بلالا فأقام فصلى بنا الظهر، ثمّ أقام فصلى العصر، ثم أقام فصلى المغرب، ثمّ أقام فصلى العشاء، ثمّ طاف علينا فقال: «ما على الأرض عصابة يذكرون الله غيركم» . 34
«كنت أنا ورسول الله ﷺ نغتسل من إناء واحد» 487–488
«لا أركب الأرجوان ولا ألبس المعصفر ولا ألبس القميص المكفف بالحرير»، وأهوى الحسن بيده إلى جيب قميصه: «ألا وطيب النساء لون لا ريح فيه ألا وطيب الرجال ريح لا لون فيه» 272
«لا أعافي رجلا قتل بعد أخذ الدية» 237
«لا تحلفوا بآبائكم ولا بالطواغيت، فإنه أحب إلى الله ألا تحلفوا إلا بالله، فإذا حلفتم بالله فاصدقوا» 169
«لا تمنعوا إماء الله أن يخرجن إلى الصلاة» 98
«لا تنكح البكر حتّى تستأمر، ولا الثيب حتّى تستأذن»، قيل: «وما إذنها يا رسول الله؟»، قال: «إذنها أن تسكت» 414
«لا تواصلوا»، فقيل له: «يا نبيّ الله، إنك تواصل؟» قال: «إنّي لست كأحد منكم، إن ربي يطعمني ويسقيني» 148
«لا رقبى، ومن أرقب شيئا فهو لورثة المرقب» 252
«لا شغار في الإسلام» 334
«لا طلاق إلاّ بعد النكاح، ولا عتق إلاّ بعد الملك» 180
«لا عدوى ولا طيرة» 282
«لا مال لك إن كنت صادقا فيما قلت، فبما أصبت من فرجها وإن كنت كاذبا فذلك أبعد لك منها، أمّا أحدكما كاذب وحسابكم على الله» 401–402
«لا وصال في الصوم، ولا رضاع بعد فصال، ولا يُتمَ بعد احتلام أو بلوغ، ولا صمت يوم إلى الليل، ولا طلاق إلاّ بعد نكاح» 180، 391
«لا يأوي الضالّة إلاّ ضال» 279–280
«لا يباشر الرجل الرجل ولا المرأة المرأة، ولا يمشي الرجل بالنعلة الواحدة، ولا يشربن وهو قائم ولا يبولن وهو مستقبل القبلة، وإذا دخل أحدكم الخلاء فيستنجي ثلاث مرّات ولا يستنجي بروثة ولا بعظم، ولا يحدث الرجل بما يخلو به من امرأته ولا تحدث المرأة بما تخلو به من زوجها»، فقالت امرأة: «والله يا رسول الله إنهم ليفعلون ذلك، وإنهن

ليفعلن ذلك»، فقال رسول الله ﷺ: «لا تفعلوا، فإن ذلك مثل الشيطان لقي شيطانة في الطريق فقضى منها حاجته والناس ينظرون» 480–481

«لا يتفل أحدكم عن يمينه وهو يصلّي ولا أمامه فإنّه يناجي ربه، ولكن يتفل عن يساره أو تحت قدمه» 63

«لا يصلّي أحدكم وهو يدافع الأخبثين من الغائط والبول» 43

«لا يقبل الله صدقة من غلول ولا صلاة من غير طهور» 474

«لأعطي الرجل وأمنع الرجل وهو أحبّ إليّ منه ولكني إنّما أعطي هذا لتألفة الإسلام وأكل هذا الما في قلبه» 125

«لأقطعن لسانك، اذهب به يا بلال فاقطع لسانه» قال: فبم يقطع لساني؟ قال: «بالعطية» 125

«لأن يأخذ أحدكم حبلا فيتحامل على عنقه، خير من مسألة الناس أعطوه أو منعوه» 128

«لعلكم تقرؤون في صلاتكم خلف الإمام والإمام يقرأ»، قال لهم ذلك ثلاث مرات، فقال بعضهم: «إنا نفعل ذلك يا رسول الله»، قال: «فلا تفعلوا ولكن ليقرأ أحدكم بفاتحة الكتاب في نفسه» 48

«لعن الله قوما اتخذوا قبور أنبيائهم مساجد» 58

«لقد أمرت بالسواك حتّى خشيت أن يكتب عليّ» 151

«لم تهلكوا ولم تفتكم الصلاة، وإنّما تفوت اليقظان ولا تفوت النائم»، ثُمّ قال رسول الله: «هل من ماء؟» فأتيته بميضة فيها ماء، ثُمّ توضأ رسول الله ﷺ ثُمّ دفعها إليّ وفيها بقية من الماء، ثُمّ قال: «احتفظ بها، فإنّه كائن لها نبأ» فأمر رسول الله ﷺ، بلالاً فأذن، فصلّى رسول الله ركعتين ثُمّ تحول من مكانه فأمره فأقام الصلاة فصلّى صلاة الصبح، ثُمّ قال رسول الله ﷺ: «إن كان الناس قد أطاعوا أبا بكر وعمر فقد رفقوا بأنفسهم، وإن كانوا خالفوهم فقد عنفوا بأنفسهم». 32

«لو يعلم المار بين يدي المصلّي ماذا عليه، لكان أن يقيم حولا أحبّ إليّه من أن يمر بين يديه، ولو يعلم المصلّي بغير سترة ما انتقص صلاته ما صلّى إلاّ بالسترة» 58

«لو يعلم المتخلفون عن صلاة العشاء وصلاة الصبح ما فيهما من الأجر لأتوهما ولو حبوا على أيديهم وأرجلهم» 73

«لَيسَ بَيْنَ الْعَبدِ وَالْكُفرِ إلاَّ تَركُهُ الصَّلاَةَ» 52

«ليس لقاتل خطأ ولا عمدا ميراث» 234

«لينتهينّ عن ذلك أو ليخطفُ الله أبصارَهم» 69

«ما بال أقوام يرفعون أبصارهم إلى السماء في صلاتهم» 69

«ما تجدون في التوراة في شأن الرجم؟» فقالوا: «نفضحهما ويعاقبان». فقال عبد الله بن سلام: «بل كذبوا يا رسول الله، بل في كتابهم الرجم». قال: «فأتوا بالتوراة فاتلوها إن كنتم صادقين»، فجاؤوا بها وجاؤوا بقرائهم، وجعل يقرأ ما قبلها وما بعدها، فقال عبد الله بن سلام: «ارفع يدك»، فباعدها فإذا هو بآية الرجم تلوح، «فأمر رسول الله ﷺ برجمهما» 302

«ما لك أن تسألنيه، وما لي أن أعطيكه، ولو أعطيتكه لم أعطك إلا زماما من نار» 123

«ما من مسلم يأوي إلى فراشه حين يأوي، إلا وعند رأسه ثلاث عقدات، فإن استيقظ فذكر الله انحلت عقدة، وإن توضأ انحلت عقدة، فإن صلى ركعتين انحلت العقدة الثالثة، فولى الشيطان

يركض برجله غضبان فارا، وإن رقد ولم يذكر الله حتى أصبح بال الشيطان في أذنيه ومنخريه» 78
«مباركة، وإذا رأى أحدكم عبده مطلوبا فليعنه» 141
«مطل الغني ظلم، ومن أحيل إلى غنيّ مليء فليحتل» 427
«من أحب لقاء الله أحب الله لقاءه، ومن كره لقاء الله كره الله لقاءه»، فقيل له: «يا رسول الله، كلنا نكره الموت». قال: «إنّما ذلك عند موته إذا بشّر برحمة الله ومغفرته أحبَّ لقاء الله وأحبّ الله لقاءه، وإذا بشر بعذاب الله كره لقاء الله وكره الله لقاءه» 307
«من استعفف أعفه الله، ومن استغنى أغناه الله، ومن سألنا لم ندخر عنه شيئا وجدناه» 128–129
«من أعاذ بالله فأعيذوه ومن سأل لوجه أعطوه» 171
«من أعتق شقصا له في مملوك فعليه خلاصه في ماله إن كان له مال، وإن لم يكن له مال قوم المملوك قيمة عدل ثم يستسعى» 255
«من أكل من هذه الشجرة الخبيثة فلا يصلِّي معنا» 288
«من أنهب فليس منا» 334
«من توضّأ يوم الجمعة فبها ونعمة ومن اغتسل فذلك أفضل؟ قال: نعم» 102
«من حلف بملّة غير ملّة الإسلام كذبا متعمّدا فهو كما قال» 165
«من حلف على يمين كاذبة ليقطع بها مال أخيه لقي الله يوم القيامة وهو غضبان عليه»، وتلا هذه الآية ﴿إِنَّ الَّذِينَ يَشْتَرُونَ بِعَهْدِ اللهِ وَأَيْمَانِهِمْ ثَمَنًا قَلِيلاً أُولَئِكَ لاَ خَلاَقَ لَهُمْ فِي الآخِرَةِ﴾، قال: «فما لمن تركها يا نبي الله؟» قال: «الجنة» 170
«من سأل مسألةً وهو عنها غني كانت شينًا في وجهه إلى يوم القيامةِ» 128
«من قتل قتيلا فإنّه لا يرثه، وإن كان والده أو ولده، وإن لم يكن له وارث غيره» 233
«من كان إمام الناس في الصلاة فليقصد بهم، فإنّه يكون فيهم الكبير والضعيف وذو الحاجة» 67
«من لم يجد إزارا فليلبس سراويل، ومن لم يجد نعلين فليلبس خفين» 440
«نهاني رسول الله ﷺ عن لبس المعصفر وعن القسي وعن خاتم الذهب للرجال وأن أقرأ قرآنا وأنا راكع» 272–273
«نهى أن يصلِّي الرجل وهو مختصر بيديه على حقويه» 54
«نهى رسول الله عليه السلام عن لحوم الحمير الأهلية، وعن كلّ ذي ناب من السباع» 265
«هل سمعت رسول الله نهى أن يختص يوم الجمعة؟ قال: «نعم ورب الكعبة»» 151
«هي لهم في الدنيا وهي لنا في الآخرة» 269
«وأيم الله لا يفعل ذلك إلاَّ مؤمن، وصام شهر رمضان وحجّ البيت إن استطاع إليه سبيلا، وأدّى الأمانة» 74
«وقال فيمن قتل نفسه متعمّدا بشيء عذبه الله به في نار جهنّم» 165
«وقضى ألا يقتل مؤمن بمشرك ولا حر بعبد، وجعل عقل اليهودي والنصراني ثلث عقل المسلم، ثم أمر ألا يستقيد من به جرح من صاحبه حتى يبرأ» 234
«وكان رسول الله ﷺ إذا شغله عن صلاة الليل نوم أو وجع صلَّى ثلاث عشر ركعة من النهار لا نعلم: أنَّ رسول الله ﷺ نام ليلة حتَّى أصبح، ولا قرأ

القرآن كله في ليلة قط، ولا صام شهراكاملا قط إلاَّ رمضان» 90–91
«وكان مما ضرب لهما مثلا: مثل رجلين د فعا إلى مفازة، فقال أحدهما: لا أنام حتى أقطعها، وأنا أقدر عليها، فأصبحا وكل واحد قريب من صاحبه» 88
«يا أهل القرآن أوتروا فإنَّ الله وتر يحب الوتر» 87
«يا أهل قباء إنَّ الله قد أحسن عليكم الثناء في الطهور، فما الذي تصنعون عند الوضوء وعند الغائط؟»، فقالوا: «يا رسول الله، نتبع الغائط الأحجار، ثُمَّ نتبع الأحجار الماء تغسل علينا أثر الغائط والبول»» 479
«يا أيُّها الناس، إنَّ الله قد حرم الخمر فمن كان عنده شيء منها فلا يطعمه ولا يشربه ولا يبعه» 173
«يا رسول الله، المرأة ترى في النوم ما يرى الرجل؟» فقال رسول الله ﷺ: «عليها الغسل إذا أنزلت» . 489
«يا رسول الله، إن بت أجر الجريد البارحة، حتى أصابني برد السحر، فانطلقت إلى أهلي، فإذا أنا برجل مع امرأتي يغشاها» . قال: فأعرض عنه رسول الله عليه الصلاة والسلام، فأكب الصحابة فخافوا على صاحبهم أن يحد، فقال الرجل: «رأت عيني وسمعت أذني ووعى قلبي، وعرفت أنَّ الله لا يظلمني، وإن رسول الله ﷺ لا يجور علي» . قال: فينما هما كذلك إذ نزلت آية التلاعن، فقال رسول الله ﷺ: «إن أحدكما كاذب، فهل منكما تائب؟» فأبيا إلاَّ الإمضاء في التلاعن، ففرق بينهما» 401
«يا نبيّ الله، إنَّه ليس لي ولد إلاَّ ابنة لي أفأتصدق بثلثي مالي؟» قال: «لا» . قال: «فبالشطر» . قال: «لا» . قال: «فالثلث؟» قال: «نعم، والثلث جم» 303
«يحبّ الله الغني الحليم المتعفف، ويبغض الفاحش البذيء السائل الملحف» 127
فوضع نبي الله يده على صدري حتى تصببت عرقا، فكأني أنظر إلى ربي، فوجدت بردها على فؤادي، فقال: «إن جبريل أتاني فقال: يا محمد، اقرأ القرآن على حرف، فقلت: اللهم خفف على أمتي. قال: فأتاني الثانية، فقال لي: يا محمد، اقرأ القرآن على حرف، فقلت: اللهم خفف عن أمتي. فأتاني الثالثة فقال: يا محمد، اقرأ القرآن على سبعة أحرف، ولكل دعوة سؤالها. قال: فقلت: اللهم اغفر لأمتي، اللهم ارحم أمتي، وأخرت دعوتي إلى يوم القيامة، حتى إن إبراهيم يحتاج إلى تلك الدعوة» 76–77

Index of Personal Names فهرس الأعلام

إبراهيم عليه السلام 77

إبراهيم النخعي 40، 59، 76، 80، 84، 87، 95، 108، 132، 147، 163، 165، 182، 211، 314–315، 326، 329–330، 393، 415، 419، 469، 475، 479

إبراهيم بن محمد ﷺ 59

ابن الأزور 61

ابن أم مكتوم (عبد الله) 67

ابن عامر 86، 89

عبد الله بن عبّاس = ابن عبّاس 28، 30، 47–49، 54، 56، 81، 85–86، 88–89، 91، 93–94، 96، 102، 103، 106، 107، 119–120، 122، 147، 150، 152، 158، 169، 171، 179–180، 200، 204، 263، 272، 282، 300، 319، 333، 352، 357، 360، 369–374، 376، 384، 390–391، 399، 415–416، 421، 423، 438–439–440–441–442–443، 448–449، 453–460، 462، 476، 484، 485

ابن عبيد 247

عبد الله بن عمر = ابن عمر 34، 40، 43، 45، 68، 80–81، 83–84–85، 92، 114، 119–120، 132، 136، 168، 171، 173–174، 192، 196، 200، 204، 243–244–245، 268، 270، 273، 288، 301، 302، 328، 360، 370، 416، 445

أبو إسحاق الهمداني = عمرو بن عبد الله السبيعي 72، 82

أبو الجعد 75

أبو الحرّ = علي بن الحصين 30

أبو الدرداء = عويمر بن زيد بن قيس الخزرجي 73، 75، 344

أبو الزبير = محمد بن مسلم 33، 288

أبو العالية الرياحي = رفيع بن مهران 28، 45، 88، 282، 467، 482

أبو القاسم ﷺ 49

أبو المتوكل الناجي = علي بن داؤد 270

أبو المليح = ابن أسامة بن عمير بن عامر بن أقيشر الهذلي 107، 255، 312

أبو النضر (النظر) 29، 36، 51، 164، 271، 272، 480

أبو أيُّوب 76، 421، 468

أبو بكر الصديق 32، 33، 47، 68، 77، 85، 88، 94، 103، 110، 112، 115، 121، 122، 131، 132، 221، 248، 249، 281، 368، 403، 482

أبو ثعلب 264

أبو ثعلبة = الخشني، اختلف في اسمه فقيل: جرهم بن ناشم وقيل: لاشر بن جرشوم 264

أبو حرب بن أبي الأسود 403

أبو حسان = الأعرج 196، 200، 204

أبو حيان الأعرج 301

أبو دجانة الأنصاري 173

أبو ذرّ = الغفاري 44، 491، 492

أبو رافع = الصائغ، نفيع 34، 103

أبو رياح 29، 31

أبو زيد المدني الأنصاري 47، 76

أبو زيد بن عبد الرحمن بن عمر بن مُحَمَّد الزواري 25، 38، 70، 220، 223

أبوسعيد الأنصاري 44
أبوسعيد الخدري 40، 128، 270
أبوسفيان بن حرب 124
أبوسلمة 414
أبوشبرمة = عبد الله بن شبرمة 180
أبوصفوان 94
أبوطلحة العمري 173
مسلم بن أبي كريمة = أبوعبيدة
أبوعبيدة مسلم بن أبي كريمة 30، 33، 42، 46، 61، 64–65، 84، 93، 109، 134–135، 137، 144–145–146، 159–160، 162، 164، 190، 193، 195، 208، 216، 218، 221، 263–264–265–269، 271، 286، 303، 324–325، 328–329، 468، 478–479، 489
أبوعبيدة بن الجراح 77، 301
أبوعثمان النهدي 86،
أبوعيسى المازني 331
أبوقتادة الأنصاري 3
أبوقحافة 281
أبوقلابة = عبد الله بن زيد الجرمي 48، 82، 143، 264، 491–492
أبومضرة 44
أبومعشر = نجيح بن عبد الرحمن السندي 40، 46، 80، 84، 132، 147، 163، 165، 182، 211، 314–315، 326، 329، 393، 415، 469، 475، 479
أبوموسى الأشعري 95، 183، 285، 331، 394، 467
أبونهيك بن إبراهيم 171
أبونوح = صالح الدهان
أبوهريرة 34، 70، 102، 103، 114، 284، 312، 414، 471
أبو يزيد (المدني) 47، 119، 175
أبيّ بن كعب 38، 76–77، 98، 169، 173، 448
الأحنف بن قيس 277
آدم عليه السلام 102، 415
أذينة العبدي 398
أسامة بن زيد 109، 423
أسماء بنت أبي بكر 482
أسماء بنت عميس 221
الأسود بن يزيد 80
الأشجع 257
الأقرع بن حابس 124–125
أم ربيعة المجنونة 66
أم سلمة 415
أم عطيّة الأنصارية 26
أم كلثوم 481
أم هانئ 94
امرأة ابن مسعود = زينب بنت عبد الله بن معاوية بن عتاب الثقفية 132
امرأة أبي بكر = ، أم رومان بنت عامر بن عويمر بن عبد شمس بن عتاب 110
امرأة المغيرة بن شعبة 320
امرأة جابر بن زيد 110، 134
امرأة هلال بن أمية = خولة بنت عاصم 377
امرئ القيس بن عباس 169
آمنة (زوجة جابر بن زيد) 221
أنس بن مالك 33، 47، 55، 63، 66–69، 76، 80، 84، 148، 173
أنس بن معاوية 320
أوس بن الصامت 418
أيُّوب السختياني 34، 43، 48، 81، 84، 92، 94، 107،

143، 174، 192، 261، 264، 272، 274، 276، 301،
328، 402، 415، 492-493
أيوب بن عبد الله بن عمر بن العاص 173
أيوب بن يزيد 46
بديل 65
البر بن شبرمة 180
البراء بن عازب 423
بريرة 355، 406
بشير بن عبد الحميد 308
بشير بن نهيك 255
بكر بن عبد الله المزني (المدني) 308، 494
بلال بن أبي رباح 30، 32، 125، 219
بنات ابن عمر 132
تميمة بنت وهب بن عتيق 368
ثابت بن مُحَمَّد بن زيادة 70
ثوبان مولى رسول الله ﷺ 128
جابر بن حمادة 321
جابر بن زيد (أبو الشعثاء) 27، 35، 38، 54، 56،
60-61، 68، 71، 82، 84، 86-87، 96، 98، 103،
107، 110، 134، 148، 154، 158، 160-162، 166،
178-179، 189-190، 220-221-222-223،
243، 246، 250، 252-253، 255، 263، 296،
304، 321، 328، 333، 339-377، 381-385،
390-391، 396-397، 399، 404، 408-409،
415-416، 419، 423، 431-432، 435، 437-
445، 447-465، 478، 490، 494
جابر بن عبد الله الأنصاري 52، 67، 116، 151، 261،
311-312، 473
الجارود 398
جبريل 77
جبير بن مطعم 33، 180، 391
جعفر بن أبي وحشية = الواسطي 196، 399، 416
حاجب الطائي 44، 109، 130
الحارث بن هشام 124
الحباب (أبو عقيل) 126
حبيب بن أبي حبيب 494
الحجاج 93،
حذيفة بن اليمان 44، 95، 269، 350، 398
الحسن بن علي بن أبي طالب 249
الحسن العدني 182، 393
الحسن بن أبي الحسن البصري 50، 58، 67، 76-78،
84، 93، 98، 102، 105، 107، 114، 130، 134، 135،
143، 148، 158، 169، 183، 211، 220-222، 238،
250، 260، 264، 269، 271-272، 277-278،
287-288، 304، 311، 330، 332، 346-348،
350، 353، 356، 362، 366، 370، 372، 377،
393-394، 399، 403، 411، 419-420، 427،
452، 454، 465، 470-471، 473، 480، 488
حسين 55
حصين بن أبي أساس 249
حفصة بنت عمر 26
حكيم بن أفلح 89،
حليمة بنت عبد الرحمن 335
حماد = بن أبي سليمان، أبو إسماعيل 76، 87، 95،
196، 330
حمزة الأسلمي 149
حمزة بن عبد المطلب 111
حيان الأعرج 399، 419
خالد النضري 128
خالد بن الوليد 139

خالد بن دردير 58
خالد بن ميمون 72، 82
خثيمة بنت عبد الرحمن 335
خلاس = بن عمرو الهجري 254، 263، 271، 410–411
خولة بنت ثعلبة 418
خيثمة بن عبد الرحمن 335
رافع = بن خديج بن رافع بن عدي الأوسي 119
الربيع بن حبيب 30، 49، 55، 57، 61، 64–65، 68، 78، 83، 88، 93، 96، 103، 111، 114، 134، 145، 149، 163، 166، 174، 178، 193، 195، 199، 210–211، 216–217، 219، 262–263، 268، 284، 304، 328، 397، 476، 479، 484، 493
ربيعة بن شهاب 122
رفاعة 368
الزبير بن العوام 35، 40، 169، 274، 286
زرارة بن أبي أوفى 88، 307
الزهري 30، 116، 255، 280، 479
زوج بريرة 406
زياد بن أبي سفيان 440
زياد 308
زيد بن أرقم 93، 423، 481
زيد بن ثابت 235، 328، 415، 443، 469
سالم الغاري 82
سالم بن أبي الجعد 75
سعد بن مالك 86–87، 303
سعيد بن المسيب 30، 44، 52–53، 58، 63، 84، 87، 99، 107، 127، 279–280، 325، 330، 332، 352، 399، 402، 425، 427، 473
سعيد بن جبير 196، 399، 401، 476، 484
سعيد بن عبد العزيز 87
سعيد بن هشام 88–89، 307
سعيد بن يسار 83
سفيان بن سلمة 276
سلام بن تميم 98
سلمة بن المختم 287
سلمة بن جنادة = الهذلي 276
سلمة بن قيس 80
سليمان بن يسار = أبو ايوب 149، 415، 493
سمية بنت وهب بن عتيق 368
سهيل بن عمرو 124
سهيمة بنت عمير 360
سويد بن عبد الله 271، 480
شراحة الهمدانية 251
شريح = القاضي شريح بن الحارث الكندي 182، 245، 247، 393، 410، 428
شريك بن سمحاء 377
شعبة الصنعاني 422
الشعبي = عامر بن شراحيل 247، 251، 261، 271، 406
شهر بن حوشب 284
صالح الدهان 45، 64، 84، 156
صالح بن سالم بن يدر السدريني 120، 183، 255، 385، 494
صفوان بن أمية بن خلف 124
صفية بنت الحارث 66
صفية بنت شيبة 486
الصنعانية 235
صيفي بن سميدة 359
صيفي بن قتيل 359–360

الضحاك بن قيس 470
الضحاك بن مزاحم 180، 391
ضمام بن السائب 61، 140، 157، 221، 315–317، 325، 425، 473، 478
طاووس = بن كيسان 49، 252، 438–439، 441
طلحة بن عبيد الله 35، 286، 398
طلحة بن مصرف 335
طهر بن مبسيل 359
عاصم الأحول 86، 276، 406
عائشة بنت ابي بكر 58، 65، 66، 85، 89، 129، 134، 307، 355، 406، 479، 481–482، 486، 487
عبادة بن الصامت 422–423
العباس السلمي 125
العباس بن أوس العبسي 360
العباس بن طريف القيسي 360
عبد الحميد بن جبير 151
عبد الرحمن بن أبي ليلى 288
عبد الرحمن بن أبي هريرة 268–269
عبد الرحمن بن الزبير = القرظي 368
عبد الرحمن بن القاسم بن محمد 112
عبد الرحمن بن زيد بن الخطاب 143
عبد الرحمن بن عوف 126، 248، 274
عبد الرحمن بن غانم 284
عبد السلام 87
عبد الله بن أبي نضير 72
عبد الله بن الحارث بن نوفل 94، 107
عبد الله بن الزبير 482
عبد الله بن جعفر 249
عبد الله بن دينار 50
عبد الله بن رباح 31
عبد الله بن سلام 302
عبد الله بن شقيق 65
عبد الله بن صفوان 81–82، 244
عبد الله بن عمرو بن العاص 173، 468
عبد الله بن عمرو بن شعيب 277،
عبد الله بن مسعود، أبو عبد الرحمن 33–34، 44، 51، 58–59، 70، 76، 80، 82، 85، 87، 95، 108، 138، 163، 176، 179، 181–182، 314–315، 331، 387، 390، 393–394، 412، 415، 448، 468
عبد الله بن معقل 58
عبد الله بن نجيح 252
عبد الله بن يزيد 58، 150
عبد الملك بن مروان 243
عبد الملك بن يعلى 103
عبيدة بن عمير الليثي 476
عثمان بن حنيف 76، 138
عثمان بن عتّاب 35
عثمان بن عفان 85، 94، 103، 132، 249، 280، 359–360، 415، 471
عدي بن أرطأة 136
عدي بن عدي 169
عروة 87، 182، 269، 393
عطاء الخراساني 406
عطاء بن أبي رباح 86، 116، 175، 180، 387، 391، 438، 440–441، 476
عكرمة 47–48، 93، 96، 158، 179، 307، 347، 351، 352، 363، 376، 390، 402، 421، 448–449، 453، 460، 465
علقمة بن قيس 46، 59، 82، 84، 181، 271، 393
علي بن أبي طالب 38، 85، 109، 116، 149، 180،

238، 249، 251، 254، 263، 271–272، 350،
391، 403–404، 411، 425، 446–448، 470،
488

عليّ بن ثابت 40

علي بن عبد الله البارقي 273

علي بن عبد الله 270

علي بن قرة بن عباد 128

عمار بن ياسر 138، 174

عمر بن الخطاب 28–29، 32–33، 38، 41،
43، 45–48، 50، 58، 66–68، 73، 77، 80،
85، 88، 92، 94، 98، 102، 103، 115–116،
121، 125، 132، 138–139، 143–144، 169،
174–175، 178–179، 182–183، 187–188، 230،
234–235، 238، 244، 247–249، 271، 274،
276–277، 279–280، 285–286، 301، 308،
312، 314–315، 320، 331، 334، 350، 354، 366،
368، 377–378، 387، 390، 393–394، 398،
403–404، 408، 422، 445–447، 467، 473،
481، 493

عمر بن ثعلب 125

عمر بن عامر 481

عمر بن عبد العزيز 104، 136، 296، 309، 378

عمران بن الحصين 271

عمرو بن العاص 173، 274، 468

عمرو بن حزم 378

عمرو بن دينار 49، 81، 246، 401، 415، 416، 422،
437–442

عمرو بن سلمة 479

عمرو بن شعيب 55، 105، 183، 394

عمرو بن هرم 339–378، 381–385، 416، 443–
445، 447–465

عمرو بن يحيى 83

عياض بن هلال 40

عيسى بن أحمد 338

عيينة بن حصين بن حذيفة بن بدر 124–125

غلام أم سلمة 415

فاطمة (بنت النبي ﷺ) 489

فرعون 150

فرقد الشيخ 250

الفضل بن عباس 109

القاسم الشيباني 93، 481

القاسم بن عمرو 51

قبيصة بن ذؤيب 321

قتادة 25، 28–31، 33–34، 38–39، 43–44،
47–48، 50–53، 55–56، 58–63، 66–69،
75–76، 85–86–87–88، 92، 93، 96،
97–109، 114، 116، 120–121، 123–131، 134،
136، 137–140، 142–143، 146–152، 155،
158–162، 164، 168–169، 171–172، 173–175،
182، 187–188، 196، 200، 204، 210–211، 222،
235–237، 242–243، 245–246، 248–249،
251–255، 257، 260–261، 263، 267،
269–271، 273–274، 276–279، 281–284،
287–288، 295–296، 301، 303، 304، 307–
312، 319، 321، 325، 329–334، 337–339،
385–386، 393، 398–399، 401–403، 406،
407، 409–413، 417–418، 420–422، 426–
427، 465، 467–471، 473–475، 479–482،
484–486، 488، 490، 494

قدامة بن مظعون 249

قيس بن سعد 122، 334
كعب 73، 102، 261
لاحق بن حميد 28، 80–81، 138، 174، 244
لوط عليه السلام 250، 298
مجاهد = بن جبر 288
مُحَمَّد بن سيرين 64، 132، 146، 188، 250، 428
محمد بن طلحة 246
محمد بن عباد 151
محمد بن عبد الرحمن الأنصاري 378، 425
مُحَمَّد بن عليّ 51
محمد بن كعب 114
مخلد بن سعيد 247
المسروق بن الأجدع 180، 391
مسلم بن يسار 422، 476
المسور بن مخرمة 30
مطرف = بن عبد الله بن الشخير 394، 419
مسور 114
معاذ بن جبل 76–77، 148، 169
معاوية بن أبي سفيان 86، 95، 122، 470
معدان بن أبي طلحة اليعمري 75
معقل بن مقرن 163
معمر = بن راشد الأزدي 30، 116، 280، 479
المغيرة المصري 48
المغيرة بن شعبة 320–321
المقداد بن الأسود 488
مكحول = بن عبد الله 234
مؤرق العجلي 85
موسى عليه السلام 150
ميمون بن مهران 114
ميمون العناب 285
ميمونة 330، 439
نافع (مولى ابن عمر) 35، 43، 81، 84، 92، 98، 174، 192، 261، 268–269، 272، 328، 370
نافع بن الزبير 40
النجاشي (أصحمة) 116
نجدة = بن عامر 122
النزال بن سبرة 391
النضر بن أنس 255
نوح عليه السلام 151
هرم بن حيان 79
هشام بن عروة 125
هشام بن هبيرة (عبيدة) 410
هلال بن أمية 377، 401
هلال بن حصين 128
هند 480
الوليد بن عقبة بن أبي معيط 95، 249
يحيى بن سعيد 307
يحيى بن أبي كثير 40، 150، 413–414
يحيى 83
يزيد بن أبي سفيان 281
يزيد بن أبي مالك 281، 427
يزيد بن معاوية 122
يعلى بن حكيم 112
يوسف بن عمرو بن شعيب 105
يونس بن عبيدة 45

Index of Places and Locations فهرس الأماكن والبلدان

الأبطح 49

أحد 89

الأحزاب 48

أذربجان 84

البحرين 221

بدر 116، 423

البصرة 197، 221، 360، 441

بيت المقدس 471

بئر زمزم 484

بئر معونة 80

الجابية 271

جامع الصلت 255

جامع الماي 120، 183، 385، 465، 494

الجزيرة 221

الحرم 300، 434

حضرموت 169

خراسان 84، 122، 219، 459

خيبر 30، 83، 124، 223، 287،

دمشق 41

ربيع جدول 493

الروم 89، 264

الزوراء 33

سرف 331

الشام 41، 101، 174، 234، 264–265، 281، 301، 423، 427، 435، 447

الصفا والمروة 432–433، 436

صنعاء 235

قباء 93، 479

قندابيل 359

الكعبة (البيت) 169، 433–434، 471

الكوفة 86، 95، 134، 221، 249

المدينة 88، 131، 144، 173، 221، 378، 492

المربد 435

المزدلفة 432، 437

مصر 48، 221، 402

مكة 81–82، 86، 131، 221، 434–435

منى 85، 149–150، 435

نصيبين 480

نيسابور 84

الهند 360

وادي القرى 423

اليمن 139

Index of Tribes and Sects فهرس القبائل والفرق والكتب المنزلة

آل عمر 328، 378

آل عمرو بن حزم 378

الإنجيل 167، 236، 262

الأنصار 80، 89، 126، 173، 355، 377، 414، 423، 469

أهل البصرة 360

أهل الذمة 301، 382

أهل السواد 277

أهل الشام 447

أهل الصدقة (الصفة) 125

أهل الكتاب 81، 273، 285، 295، 332، 350، 363، 398

أهل بدر 116

أهل جواثا 131

أهل قباء 479

أهل مربد 435

بنو النظير 368

بنو تغلب 139، 262

بنو راشد 35

بنو شيبان 360

بنو عبد القيس 131، 139

بنو عدي 88،

بنو قيس 491

بنو لحيان 80

بنو مرة بن عباد 360

بنو واقف 377

التوراة 73، 167، 236

جهينة 100

ربيعة 257

الصابئون 350

عبد القيس 131، 139، 257، 270، 273

عبدة الأوثان 413

عجلان 401

العجم 445

قريظة 368

قوم لوط 250، 298

كنده 169–170

المجوس 163، 167، 186، 262–263، 267–268، 285، 332، 337، 413–415

مضر 183، 257

المهاجرين 276

نصارى العرب 350

النصارى 150، 163، 167، 170، 209، 224 ، 234، 262، 278، 292–293، 295، 304، 320، 349، 350، 398–399، 402، 407، 413–414، 443

اليهود 54، 150، 163، 166، 170، 209، 224، 234، 262، 278، 292–293، 295، 301، 304، 320، 349، 398–399، 402، 413، 443